tough enough ···to be··· Vikings

Tough Enough
...To Be...
Vikings

Minnesota's Purple Pride From A To Z

BILL BALLEW

OLD NORSE PUBLISHING
Asheville, North Carolina

Old Norse Publishing, Asheville, North Carolina 28806
Copyright © 1999 by Old Norse Publishing
All rights reserved
Published 1999

Printed in the United States of America

Library of Congress Cataloging-Publication Data

Ballew, Bill
　Tough enough to be vikings: minnesota's purple pride from
a to z / Bill Ballew
　　p. cm.
　ISBN 0-9670393-0-4
　1. Minnesota Vikings (Football team)—History.　I. Title

Library Congress Catalog Card Number: 99-70232

Dustjacket designed by Lightbourne
Dustjacket photographs by Rick Kolodziej
Interior photographs used by permission from Minnesota
Vikings and Topps

THIS BOOK IS DEDICATED TO:

Brad and Bryce
the best sons a father could have;

Sam Ballew
the best brother anyone could have;

Kevin Flynn
the best friend a Viking fan could have.

CONTENTS

	Introduction	xi
I.	The Seasons	1
II.	The Players	49
III.	The Head Coaches	355
	The Assistant Coaches	359
	The Numbers	363
	Sources	382

ACKNOWLEDGMENTS

This encyclopedia would not have been completed without the special assistance of Jim Baker and Ryan Monnens, both of whom went out of their way to help make this project the best it could possibly be.

The author also wishes to thank the following people for their contribution and support in making this volume possible: Bill and Shirley Ballew, Robert Barwiler, James Bily, Shannon Bodie, Vivian Bradbury, Brandy, Donna Dorlan, Pete Fierle, Kevin Flynn, Rand Gottlieb, Randy Garrett, Mike Gore, Bret Graff, Barb Gunia, Bob Hagan, Rick Kolodziej, Gaelyn Larrick, Tim Larson, Valerie Long, Sheila, Mary Tucker, Mark and Lin Wahlen and Chris Wills.

No one deserves special thanks more than Hope Ballew, whose coordination, determination and belief in this project is the reason it became a reality.

Introduction

It would be easy to assume that the beginning of professional football in the state of Minnesota centers on the formation of the National Football League's Vikings as an expansion team in 1961. Although that is not the case, the purple-helmeted hosts at Metropolitan Stadium and the Metrodome hold indirect ties to the state's past forays at the game's top level.

Minnesotans were among the first fans to witness the early days of the National Football League. That initial glimpse included contests involving the Minneapolis Marines, between 1921 and 1924. The Marines played at Nicollet Park, a facility that served primarily as a minor-league baseball stadium and was located at Lake Street, Blaisdell Avenue, West 31st Avenue and Nicollet Avenue.

The Marines were a successful semi-pro team that had trouble competing in the NFL. Most of the players were excellent sandlot performers who were outclassed on the professional gridiron. As a result, the team won just one game in each of its first two years, went 2-5-2 in 1923, then lost all six decisions in 1924 before suspending operations. Even though the Marines did not take the field, franchise owners Johnny Dunn and Val Ness continued to pay their league dues for the next four years prior to rejoining the competition as the Minneapolis Red Jackets in 1929. Unfortunately, the resurrected franchise was not unlike its predecessors, winning just two games in two years before folding after the 1930 campaign.

For two seasons—1923 and 1924—Minnesota had a pair of NFL franchises. The Duluth Kelleys were an independent pro team prior to joining the league and playing at Athletic Park in 1923. Co-owners M.C. Gebert and Dewey Scanlon ran the team during the franchise's first season as a member of the league before the players handled the operations for the next two years. Scanlon and Ole Haugsrud acquired the franchise after the 1925 season for $1 and the assumption of debts, and changed the team's name to the Eskimos, who became a touring team for one year. Following a 1-8 showing in 1927, the franchise halted play before being sold to a group from Orange, New Jersey, in 1929.

Nearly three decades passed before professional football returned to the Land of 10,000 Lakes. On October 25, 1959, the Chicago Cards and Philadelphia Eagles battled in a neutral-site game won by the Eagles, 28-24. A solid crowd of 20,112 fans turned out at the three-year-old Metropolitan Stadium, which had yet to be expanded to accommodate major-league sports. Even so, with the American Football League searching for cities in which to begin operations, and the NFL considering expansion to foil the AFL's goals, Minnesota emerged as a desired site on the pro football landscape.

The Twin Cities were slated to become one of the eight charter members of the AFL. Owners Max Winter, E. William Boyer and H.P. Skoglund went so far as to pay a $25,000 deposit to join the fledgling circuit. They even began offering contracts to high NFL draft choices, among them a $7,000 deal to their most coveted target, Dale Hackbart, a quarterback from Wisconsin.

Those moves did not go unnoticed, particularly by Chicago Bears owner George Halas. "Papa Bear" feared that a Twin Cities-based team in a rival league could hurt the Bears' following as well as the popularity of the entire NFL. With his tremendous pull, Halas arranged for Minnesota to join the Dallas Cowboys as NFL expansion franchises.

As with any major purchase, a few kinks had to be worked out in Minnesota. The NFL franchise fee was a little steeper than the AFL's—exactly 40 times more expensive. Therefore, Winter, Boyer and Skoglund needed to find help in order to meet the $1 million entry emolument, consisting of $600,000 up front and $400,000 when the team began play in 1961. The trio found the support in St. Paul newspaper baron Bernard Ridder, Jr., who wound up purchasing 30 percent of the team.

Another obstacle involved Haugsrud, one of the Eskimos' owners in the 1920s. Haugsrud received a major concession from the NFL when he turned the Duluth team over to the league in 1928 before it was sold the following year. If and when the NFL returned to Minnesota, Haugsrud would have the option of purchasing 10 percent of the team. He did just that and became the fifth owner of the league's first franchise to be named for a state.

With the financing arranged, Minnesota withdrew from the AFL on January 27, 1960, and was awarded an NFL franchise the following day at the league owners meetings in Miami. The ownership group hired Joe Thomas, a former scout with the Los Angeles Rams, to scour the country in preparation for the franchise's first drafts. Shortly thereafter, Bert Rose, the Rams' public relations director, was named Minnesota's first general manager. One of Rose's earliest moves was to recommend the nickname "Vikings" for the franchise because it represented both an aggressive person with the will to win and the Nordic tradition in the Upper Midwest that the team represented.

The first Vikings team formed in three quick steps from there. Norm Van Brocklin, who concluded his Hall-of-Fame career as a quarterback by leading Philadelphia to the NFL Championship in 1960, was named the franchise's first head coach. On December 27, 1960, running back Tommy Mason became the league's first overall draft pick as well as the Vikings' first player. Mason joined second-round choice Rip Hawkins, a linebacker, and third-rounder Fran Tarkenton, a quarterback, to form an impressive young nucleus for the purple.

The third step involved the expansion draft. The Vikings were allowed to select three players from the rosters of 12 teams (excluding only first-year Dallas) after the NFL clubs protected 30 of their 38 players. Although Van Brocklin was underwhelmed by the 36 players the process produced, Minnesota acquired a pair of standouts in guard Grady Alderman from Detroit and San Francisco running back Hugh McElhenny, who was in the sunset of his Hall-of-Fame career.

On April 12, 1961, the NFL placed the Vikings in the Western Conference, joining Baltimore, Chicago, Detroit, Green Bay, Los Angeles and San Francisco. Less than four months later, Minnesota took the field for the first time, dropping a 38–13 decision to Dallas in an exhibition game played in front of just 4,954 fans in Sioux Falls, South Dakota.

The franchise's regular-season debut was a bit different, with the Vikings stunning the Bears, 37–13, at Metropolitan Stadium on September 17. Kicker Mike Mercer scored the first points in team history with a field goal, while Bob Schnelker registered the Vikings' first touchdown on a 14-yard pass from Tarkenton. Minnesota won just two more games over the remainder of its inaugural campaign, yet the triumph over Chicago was an appropriate beginning for one of the NFL's premier franchises.

The next defining moment in Viking lore occurred in 1964. Rose resigned as general manager in June and was replaced in September by Jim Finks, who had served as a general manager in the Canadian Football

Introduction

League for seven years. Finks began to accrue an impressive amount of talent over the next few seasons, with his greatest acquisition being the hiring of head coach Bud Grant on March 10, 1967, a month after Van Brocklin resigned from the job. Grant and Finks formed a near-perfect tandem and were the masterminds behind Minnesota's four Super Bowl appearances and emergence as a powerhouse that continues to this day.

Throughout the franchise's first 38 years, the Vikings have thrilled their fans with memorable seasons from many of the game's best and most interesting players, who have posted some of the more impressive numbers in NFL history. Only time will tell if the elusive Super Bowl victory will arrive in 1999 or at some other point in the franchise's future. Yet regardless of what may take place, the Minnesota Vikings already have put together one of the more storied-filled annals professional football has to offer.

one

❖ ❖ ❖

the seasons

1961

3-11, SEVENTH-NFL WESTERN

The Minnesota Vikings did not waste any time proving they were tough enough to compete in the National Football League. After putting some pieces together during the preseason, the purple-helmeted warriors hosted the Chicago Bears on September 17 and became the only expansion team in league history to win its first regular-season game. Behind the efforts of rookie quarterback Fran Tarkenton, who relieved starter George Shaw early in the contest, the Vikings shocked the visitors with a 37–13 triumph in front of 32,236 delirious fans at Metropolitan Stadium.

Tarkenton and the Vikings went on to exceed the expectations of most observers by winning three games during their maiden voyage. Rookie head coach Norm Van Brocklin, who concluded his playing days as a Hall-of-Fame quarterback in 1960, got the most out of a group that he had tabbed "36 stiffs" at the beginning of training camp. Minnesota also garnered a reputation for its toughness as well as a team that no opponent could take lightly.

That point was proven two weeks after beating the Bears. The Vikings traveled to Baltimore and had the powerful Colts on the ropes late in the game. Minnesota kicker Mike Mercer booted a 29-yard field goal with 32 seconds remaining in the contest to give the visitors a 33–31 lead. But quarterback Johnny Unitas rallied the hosts with two pass completions that set up a game-winning, 52-yard field goal by Steve Myrha with one second left.

Preseason		
Aug. 5	Dallas @ Sioux Falls	L 13–38
Aug. 18	@ Baltimore	L 3–13
Aug. 26	San Fran. @ Portland	L 10–14
Sept. 2	Chicago @ Cedar Rapids	L 7–30
Sept. 10	Los Angeles	L 17–21
Regular Season		
Sept. 17	Chicago	W 37–13
Sept. 24	@ Dallas	L 7–21
Oct. 1	@ Baltimore	L 33–34
Oct. 8	Dallas	L 0–28
Oct. 15	San Francisco	L 24–28
Oct. 22	Green Bay	L 7–33
Oct. 29	@ Green Bay (Milwaukee)	L 10–28
Nov. 5	@ Los Angeles	L 17–31
Nov. 12	Baltimore	W 28–20
Nov. 19	Detroit	L 10–37
Nov. 26	@ San Francisco	L 28–38
Dec. 3	Los Angeles	W 42–21
Dec. 10	@ Detroit	L 7–13
Dec. 17	@ Chicago	L 35–52

Although the Vikings lost their next five contests, Minnesota gained some revenge at The Met. Tarkenton outperformed Unitas, whose life was made difficult by an inspired purple defense to help guide the Vikes to a 28–20 victory on November 12. The Rams became Minnesota's third victim three weeks later when Tarkenton put together an aerial show with four touchdown passes and running back Raymond Hayes galloped for 123 yards on the ground to lead the Vikings to a 42–21 triumph.

To be certain, there were holes to be filled, particularly on defense, but the Vikings showed promise in all phases of the game. In addition to

Tough Enough To Be Vikings

Tarkenton, veteran Hugh McElhenny paved the way by rushing for 570 yards, yet rookie Tommy Mason looked to be the long-term answer after gaining 226 yards on 60 carries. Defensively, Jim Marshall displayed his cat-like quickness at defensive end, while rookie linebacker Rip Hawkins led the team in tackles and interceptions.

1962
2-11-1, Sixth-NFL Western

Growing pains were evident during the Vikings' sophomore season in the National Football League. The defense was more porous than in 1961 by allowing 29.3 points per game. The offense, meanwhile, struggled in the early stages by failing to score more than seven points in each of the first four contests. An out-of-step running attack prevented Minnesota from scoring a touchdown on the ground during a six-game stretch and limited the offense's ability to reach paydirt from inside the red zone. As head coach Norm Van Brocklin said, "Most of the time, we had a 'score from 70-yards-out' offense."

The Vikings dropped their first five games of the 1962 slate before taking their frustrations out on the Rams during a trip to Los Angeles. Quarterback Fran Tarkenton threw three touchdown passes to give the visitors a 31–0 halftime lead before cruising to the team's first victory. The winning ways continued a week later when running back Tommy Mason scored three times, including a 74-yard pass reception from Tarkenton, to beat the Eagles, 31–21, at Metropolitan Stadium.

Yet, those two triumphs represented all of the Vikings' winning ways in 1962. The team's spirit

Preseason		
Aug. 11	San Fran. @ Seattle	L 24–30
Aug. 18	Los Angeles @ Portland	L 24–33
Aug. 25	St. Louis	L 21–24
Sept. 2	Baltimore	W 24–13
Sept. 8	Dallas @ Atlanta	W 45–26
Regular Season		
Sept. 16	@ Green Bay	L 7–34
Sept. 23	Baltimore	L 7–34
Sept. 30	@ San Francisco	L 7–21
Oct. 7	Chicago	L 0–13
Oct. 14	Green Bay	L 21–48
Oct. 21	@ Los Angeles	W 38–14
Oct. 28	Philadelphia	W 31–21
Nov. 4	@ Pittsburgh	L 31–39
Nov. 11	@ Chicago	L 30–31
Nov. 18	Detroit	L 6–17
Nov. 25	Los Angeles	T 24–24
Dec. 2	San Francisco	L 12–35
Dec. 9	@ Detroit	L 23–37
Dec. 16	@ Baltimore	L 14–42

appeared to break at Chicago on November 11, when the Bears' Roger LeClerc booted an 18-yard field goal in the waning seconds of the contest to give the hosts a 31–30 win. Two weeks later, the Rams rallied from a 24–10 deficit in the fourth quarter to saddle Minnesota with the franchise's first tie. The Viking defense surrendered 114 points in the final three games, with the lone purple highlights involving Mason's rushing efforts of 138 and 148 yards in the last two contests.

Despite the struggles, the Vikings were building a core of talented players that would serve key roles in the team's future success. Tarkenton, Mason and tackle Grady Alderman improved upon their rookie performances on offense, while Jim Marshall and Rip Hawkins continued their outstanding development as leaders of the defense. Minnesota also added such rookie starters as center Mick Tingelhoff and linebacker Roy Winston to the fold, while cornerback Ed Sharockman made an impressive debut after missing the 1961 campaign with a broken leg. Running back Bill Brown also arrived from Chicago and proved he could be a catalyst for years to come.

1963

5-8-1, Fourth (Tied)-NFL Western

Youth proved to be no deterrent for the Vikings during the franchise's third season. While fielding one of the youngest rosters in the National Football League, Minnesota showed vast improvement in all phases of the game. Talent and depth were found at most positions, and head coach Norm Van Brocklin was able to blend his team's maturing abilities into a more cohesive unit.

The Vikings erased their expansion label by registering five wins and nearly pulling off several upsets. One of the purple's more impressive outings took place at Chicago on December 1. Minnesota built a 17–3 halftime lead before watching the Bears rally for a 17–17 tie on their way to an 11–1–2 record and the NFL Championship. The Vikings also narrowly missed beating Green Bay for the first time, on October 13. Minnesota trailed 30–28 with less than two minutes left when kicker Fred Cox lined up for a 10-yard field goal attempt. Herb Adderley, however, blocked the potential game-winner and Hank Gremminger raced 80 yards with the pigskin for a touchdown in the 37–28 final. Johnny Unitas' 88-yard

Preseason		
Aug. 10	San Fran. @ Portland	W 43–28
Aug. 17	@ Los Angeles	W 27–3
Aug. 25	New York	W 17–16
Aug. 31	Philadelphia @ Hershey	L 27–34
Sept. 6	@ St. Louis	W 35–0
Regular Season		
Sept. 15	@ San Francisco	W 24–20
Sept. 22	Chicago	L 7–28
Sept. 29	San Francisco	W 45–14
Oct. 6	St. Louis	L 14–56
Oct. 13	Green Bay	L 28–37
Oct. 20	@ Los Angeles	L 24–27
Oct. 27	@ Detroit	L 10–28
Nov. 3	Los Angeles	W 21–13
Nov. 10	@ Green Bay	L 7–28
Nov. 17	Baltimore	L 34–37
Nov. 24	Detroit	W 34–31
Dec. 1	@ Chicago	T 17–17
Dec. 8	@ Baltimore	L 10–41
Dec. 15	@ Philadelphia	W 34–13

drive in the last 45 seconds also gave the Colts a 37–34 win over Minnesota on November 17.

Nevertheless, the Vikings had several happy endings. Minnesota beat San Francisco twice, the first coming during the season-opener when Tommy Mason ran a sweep two yards for the game-winning touchdown at Kezar Stadium. Two weeks later at Metropolitan Stadium, Fran Tarkenton, who concluded the campaign as the NFL's sixth-ranked quarterback, threw three touchdown passes and Jim Marshall returned a fumbled handoff to paydirt in the purple's 45–14 triumph. The Vikings also defeated Detroit for the first time in franchise history when Mason plunged into the end zone from two yards out in the fourth quarter for a 34–31 victory at The Met.

Two Vikings were recognized for their efforts. Mason became the first Minnesota player to earn All-Pro honors after he rushed for 763 yards on 166 carries while gaining another 365 yards on 40 receptions. Paul Flatley, a fourth-round draft choice who led the Vikings with 51 catches for 867 yards, was named NFL Rookie of the Year. Cox rejoined the team and significantly upgraded the kicking game, while waiver claim Karl Kassulke added talent and grit to the defensive secondary.

1964
8-5-1, SECOND (TIED)-NFL WESTERN

The Vikings' offense took its efficiency to a higher level in 1964 by fielding one of the most potent attacks in the National Football League. Behind the Pro Bowl performances of quarterback Fran Tarkenton, running backs Tommy Mason and Bill Brown, and offensive linemen Grady Alderman and Mick Tingelhoff, Minnesota recorded the best aerial show in the league and ranked second in rushing with an NFL-high 519 attempts.

The season-opening 34–24 victory over the Colts proved to be a harbinger, with the Vikings gaining 313 yards on the ground behind Mason's 137 yards and another 103 yards from Brown. After two close losses, Minnesota rebounded by defeating the Packers for the first time in franchise annals. Green Bay appeared to have settled the score with a fourth-quarter field goal that gave the Lambeau Field hosts a 23–21 advantage. But with less than a minute to play and no timeouts, Tarkenton hit Gordon Smith with a 44-yard pass on fourth down to set up Fred Cox's game-winning, 27-yard field goal with 18 seconds left.

The Vikings also put together the best stretch of their brief history in the season's final six weeks. Minnesota came within 3:48 of their first shutout while beating the 49ers for the fourth straight time. After a late Johnny Unitas rally gave Baltimore a three-point win on November 15, the Vikings tied the Lions, beat the Rams at home, then traveled to New York and Chicago and emerged with victories over the two teams that had battled in the NFL Championship Game the previous season.

A key to Minnesota's first winning record and a tie with Green Bay

The Seasons

Preseason		
Aug. 8	New York	W 21–7
Aug. 15	St. Louis @ Atlanta	W 24–10
Aug. 22	San Fran. @ Salt Lake	W 24–21
Aug. 29	@ Los Angeles	W 34–23
Sept. 5	Philadelphia @ Hershey	W 21–20
Regular Season		
Sept. 13	Baltimore	W 34–24
Sept. 20	Chicago	L 28–34
Sept. 27	@ Los Angeles	L 13–22
Oct. 4	@ Green Bay	W 24–23
Oct. 11	Detroit	L 20–24
Oct. 18	Pittsburgh	W 30–10
Oct. 25	@ San Francisco	W 27–22
Nov. 1	Green Bay	L 13–42
Nov. 8	San Francisco	W 24–7
Nov. 15	@ Baltimore	L 14–17
Nov. 22	@ Detroit	T 23–23
Nov. 29	Los Angeles	W 34–13
Dec. 6	@ New York	W 30–21
Dec. 13	@ Chicago	W 41–14

for second place centered on the maturation of Tarkenton. When not handing off to his backfield mates, the Scrambler was throwing to them, connecting on 48 occasions with Brown and 23 times with Mason. Tarkenton also galloped for 330 yards on 50 rushes, leading head coach Norm Van Brocklin to concede, "A quarterback is judged on results, not by his style, and I'm willing to judge Francis that way."

The other key to the Vikings' improved performance involved a defense that allowed nearly 100 fewer points than the previous season. Rookie Carl Eller joined the defensive line, while newcomer Bobby Walden helped Minnesota win the game of field position by leading the NFL with an average of 46.4 yards per punt.

1965

7–7, Fifth (Tied)–NFL Western

Minnesota entered the 1965 season possessing great expectations. However, after an 8–5–1 showing the year before that concluded with a three-game winning streak, the Vikings stumbled early and the defense did not continue to make the necessary improvements. Those events, combined with the scrambling style of quarterback Fran Tarkenton, caused head coach Norm Van Brocklin to reach the breaking point and resign in frustration at midseason before returning to the team a day later.

The Vikings did experience some success on their way to a 7–7 record. Minnesota again led the league in rushing, with Bill Brown ranking sixth with 699 yards and Tommy Mason placing 10th with 597 yards. Tarkenton threw for 2,609 yards and 19 touchdowns to help the purple rank fourth in the league with 383 points scored and 4,824 total yards. Kicker Fred Cox also performed well by pacing the NFL with 23 field goals, among them a team-record 53-yard effort against Chicago.

The defense, meanwhile, gave up more points (403), touchdowns (53) and touchdown passes (31) than any team in the league, surrendering 35 or

Tough Enough To Be Vikings

more points in half of its games. Yet, the Minnesota defenders proved they were capable of rising to the occasion. The purple held Jim Brown to a season-low 39 yards on 18 carries during the Vikings' 27–17 victory over Cleveland, the defending NFL champion, on October 31. Linebacker Rip Hawkins' 35-yard interception return for a touchdown with 1:08 left in the game gave the Vikings a 24–17 victory over the Bears on December 19 to end the campaign as well as Hawkins' career on a high note.

Despite the ups and downs, Van Brocklin felt good about the franchise's fifth season in retrospect. "We went 8–5–1 in 1964 then 7–7 in 1965, two more defeats despite adding a year of growth," said the Dutchman. "But we were a better team, we improved. The competition in this league is fantastic. You can be stronger and show a poorer record, or the opposite. Most of the time the difference is very slight."

The biggest addition to the Minnesota fold was 13th-round draft pick Dave Osborn, who played sparingly as a rookie. Center Mick Tingelhoff was named an All-Pro for the second straight year, while he, Tarkenton, Brown and Grady Alderman were voted to the Pro Bowl.

Preseason		
Aug. 14	Pittsburgh @ Atlanta	W 31–21
Aug. 20	Philadelphia	W 35–21
Aug. 28	Washington @ Charlotte	W 20–16
Sept. 3	Dallas @ Birmingham	W 57–17
Sept. 11	New York @ Omaha	W 24–9
Regular Season		
Sept. 19	@ Baltimore	L 16–35
Sept. 26	Detroit	L 29–31
Oct. 3	@ Los Angeles	W 38–35
Oct. 9	New York	W 40–14
Oct. 17	Chicago	L 37–45
Oct. 24	@ San Francisco	W 42–41
Oct. 31	@ Cleveland	W 27–17
Nov. 7	Los Angeles	W 24–13
Nov. 14	Baltimore	L 21–41
Nov. 21	Green Bay	L 13–38
Nov. 28	San Francisco	L 24–45
Dec. 5	@ Green Bay	L 19–24
Dec. 12	@ Detroit	W 29–7
Dec. 19	@ Chicago	W 24–17

1966
4–9–1, Sixth (Tied)–NFL Western

Just as it appeared that the Vikings were about to move into the elite class of teams in the National Football League, Minnesota hit a series of unexpected roadblocks that momentarily derailed its efforts. The defense was not consistent enough for the purple to become a championship-caliber club. Offensively, running back Tommy Mason had difficulty remaining healthy. What's more, the divisiveness between head coach Norm Van Brocklin and quarterback Fran Tarkenton escalated to the point where the two were not on speaking terms, and led to the post-season departures of both men.

The Vikings opened the season with a 20–20 tie at San Francisco and three straight defeats before pounding the Rams, 35–7, behind Tarkenton's 327 passing yards and three touchdown tosses. After a close loss at Baltimore and a convincing victory over the 49ers, Minnesota traveled to Lambeau Field for another battle against the Packers. Running back Bill Brown's one-yard plunge capped a Vikings' rally from a 17–10 deficit and gave Minnesota a 20–17 win. That proved to be Green Bay's only loss at home in 1966 on their way to the first victory in Super Bowl history.

Preseason		
Aug. 6	Detroit @ New Orleans	T 6–6
Aug. 13	Pittsburgh @ Portland	W 35–6
Aug. 20	Los Angeles	W 24–10
Aug. 26	Washington @ Cleveland	W 30–27
Sept. 2	@ Dallas	L 24–28
Regular Season		
Sept. 11	@ San Francisco	T 20–20
Sept. 18	Baltimore	L 23–38
Sept. 25	@ Dallas	L 17–28
Oct. 2	Chicago	L 10–13
Oct. 16	Los Angeles	W 35–7
Oct. 23	@ Baltimore	L 17–20
Oct. 30	San Francisco	W 28–3
Nov. 6	@ Green Bay	W 20–17
Nov. 13	Detroit	L 31–32
Nov. 20	@ Los Angeles	L 16–21
Nov. 27	Green Bay	L 16–28
Dec. 4	Atlanta	L 13–20
Dec. 11	@ Detroit	W 28–16
Dec. 18	@ Chicago	L 28–41

Any momentum from that win vanished a week later after the Lions' Gero Yepremian kicked six field goals in Detroit's 32–31 victory. The Vikings lost their next three outings as well, including a 20–13 decision at Atlanta, a first-year expansion team. It was during that game on December 4 when Van Brocklin benched Tarkenton in front of his hometown friends and family by starting Bob Berry, effectively ending any future the two men had together. Van Brocklin resigned after the campaign, while Tarkenton demanded a trade and was sent to the New York Giants.

While the Vikings ended the 1966 slate with a 41–28 loss at Chicago, the game featured two highlights. Tarkenton concluded his first stint in purple by throwing for three touchdowns and running for a fourth. Running back Dave Osborn also gave the Minnesota faithful something to look forward to by recording his first 100-yard rushing effort with 118 yards.

Three of Minnesota's offensive linemen—Grady Alderman, Mick Tingelhoff and Milt Sunde—earned starting berths in the Pro Bowl, while receiver Paul Flatley, who paced the purple with 50 receptions for 777 yards, was named a reserve. Tingelhoff also received his third straight All-Pro recognition.

Tough Enough To Be Vikings

1967

3-8-3, Fourth-NFL Central

Minnesota general manager Jim Finks made two moves early in 1967 that shaped the Vikings for more than a decade. After Norm Van Brocklin resigned as head coach in February, Finks hired Bud Grant, the head coach of Winnipeg in the Canadian Football League whose mild-mannered, yet disciplined ways provided a stark contrast to those of the Dutchman.

"We need a man for the long haul—a man to get us to the top," Finks said. "Grant's the man; he's a winner."

While the hiring of Grant proved masterful, Finks did nearly as well when he traded quarterback Fran Tarkenton to the New York Giants. In return, the Vikings received two choices in the first two rounds of the 1967 draft who proved to be running back Clint Jones and wide receiver Bob Grim as well as another first-rounder a year later that turned out to be tackle Ron Yary. Add such fellow 1967 draft picks as defensive tackle Alan Page, wide receiver Gene Washington, defensive back Bobby Bryant and tight end John Beasley and Minnesota acquired a significant core of what would eventually lead to four Super Bowl appearances.

Success was not immediate, however. Shaky under center during the early going, the Vikings opened the season with four straight losses. The running game carried the offensive load, with Dave Osborn placing second in the league by rushing for 972 yards. Bill Brown was also effective with 610 yards, including a one-yard touchdown run against Green Bay that gave Minnesota its first win of the season, a 10–7 decision on October 15.

Shortly thereafter, newcomer Joe Kapp, another import from the CFL, started to establish himself

Preseason		
Aug. 12	Philadelphia @ Tulsa	W 34–0
Aug. 18	@ Denver	L 9–14
Aug. 27	New York @ New Haven	L 3–21
Sept. 2	Atlanta @ Cleveland	W 16–3
Sept. 10	Cleveland	L 14–42
Regular Season		
Sept. 17	San Francisco	L 21–27
Sept. 22	@ Los Angeles	L 3–39
Oct. 1	Chicago	L 7–17
Oct. 8	St. Louis	L 24–34
Oct. 15	@ Green Bay (Milwaukee)	W 10–7
Oct. 22	Baltimore	T 20–20
Oct. 29	@ Atlanta	L 20–21
Nov. 5	New York	W 27–24
Nov. 12	Detroit	T 10–10
Nov. 19	@ Cleveland	L 10–14
Nov. 26	@ Pittsburgh	W 41–27
Dec. 3	Green Bay	L 27–30
Dec. 10	@ Chicago	T 10–10
Dec. 17	@ Detroit	L 3–14

at quarterback. Kapp's first strong performance was his 202-yard effort against the powerful Colts during a 20–20 tie on October 22. Two weeks later, Osborn galloped for 115 yards to help the Vikings rally from a 24–7 deficit in the third quarter and beat Tarkenton's Giants, 27–24. Osborn then set a team record by rushing for 155 yards on 21 carries in the rematch with the Packers on December 3.

While the nucleus for better days was forming, three players were recognized for their performances. Center Mick Tingelhoff received All-Pro and Pro Bowl recognition, tackle Grady Alderman earned his fifth straight trip to the Pro Bowl, and Brown was tabbed a Pro Bowl starter.

1968

8–6, NFL Central Champions

The Minnesota Vikings became perennial playoff contenders during their eighth season in the National Football League. In just his second season as head coach, Bud Grant molded a young and talented team into a cohesive unit that succeeded with its dominating defense and a quarterback in Joe Kapp whose performance belied his statistics by making the critical plays whenever necessary.

Preseason		
Aug. 10	Kansas City	L 10–13
Aug. 17	@ Denver	W 39–16
Aug. 24	Philadelphia	W 52–10
Sept. 1	@ St. Louis	L 28–31
Sept. 6	New Orleans @ Shreveport	W 20–17
Regular Season		
Sept. 14	Atlanta	W 47–7
Sept. 22	@ Green Bay (Milwaukee)	W 26–13
Sept. 29	Chicago	L 17–27
Oct. 6	Detroit	W 24–10
Oct. 13	@ New Orleans	L 17–20
Oct. 20	Dallas	L 7–20
Oct. 27	@ Chicago	L 24–26
Nov. 3	Washington	W 27–14
Nov. 10	Green Bay	W 14–10
Nov. 17	@ Detroit	W 13–6
Nov. 24	@ Baltimore	L 9–21
Dec. 1	Los Angeles	L 3–31
Dec. 8	@ San Francisco	W 30–20
Dec. 15	@ Philadelphia	W 24–17
Western Conference Championship		
Dec. 22	@ Baltimore	L 14–24
NFL Playoff Bowl		
Jan. 5	Dallas @ Miami	L 13–17

The Vikings won their first two games in a season for the first time in team annals. Minnesota crushed Atlanta, 47–7, with three touchdowns from running back Bill Brown and three scoring passes from Kapp during his 16-of-20 performance. A week later, the Vikings defeated Green Bay, the defending Super Bowl champion, in a 26–13 win that was culminated by defensive end Jim Marshall's sack of Bart Starr for a safety. In fact, it was during the triumph that the Minnesota front four of Marshall, Carl Eller, Alan Page and Gary Larsen, a.k.a., the Purple People Eaters, firmly established itself as the league's best defensive line. Helping the quartet emerge was the addition of two starters—linebacker Wally Hilgenberg and safety Paul Krause. Hilgenberg solidified the defense with his ability to protect against the run and the pass, while Krause upgraded a secondary that had been prone to long touchdown tosses.

Minnesota slumped after the Green Bay win by losing four of its next five contests before defeating Washington, 27–14, behind Charlie West's NFL-record 98-yard punt return for a touchdown. The Vikings then com-

Tough Enough To Be Vikings

pleted their first season sweeps of the Packers and the Lions. Back-to-back losses to the Colts and Rams evened Minnesota's record at 6–6 before the Vikings won road games at San Francisco and Philadelphia to clinch their first division crown.

While the season ended on a disappointing note with a loss to Super Bowl-bound Baltimore in the playoffs before an uninspired defeat to Dallas in the short-lived Playoff Bowl, the Vikings proved they were an up-and-coming team. Ron Yary was added to the offensive line in the first round of the draft, and was joined by West in the third round and running back Oscar Reed in the seventh. Eller and center Mick Tingelhoff received All-Pro recognition, while they along with Marshall, Page and Brown were selected to play in the Pro Bowl.

1969

12–2, NFL Central Champions

1969 MEDIA GUIDE

Change was rapid in the Upper Midwest in the late 1960s. During the franchise's initial eight seasons in the National Football League, the Vikings' longest winning streak was three games, a feat they accomplished on three occasions. While there had been significant talent on the roster throughout the period, never had Minnesota achieved enough consistency to become league champions.

That scenario changed in 1969. After dropping a season-opening, one-point decision to the Giants in New York, the Vikings reeled off 12 straight triumphs, a string that remains the longest in team history. The streak began in spectacular fashion, with quarterback Joe Kapp throwing an NFL-record seven touchdown passes in

Preseason		
Aug. 2	Miami @ Tampa	W 45–10
Aug. 9	Denver	W 26–6
Aug. 23	St. Louis @ Memphis	W 41–13
Aug. 30	N.Y. Jets @ Winston-Salem	L 21–24
Sept. 6	New York Giants	W 28–27
Sept. 13	Cleveland @ Akron	W 23–16
Regular Season		
Sept. 21	@ New York Giants	L 23–24
Sept. 28	Baltimore	W 52–14
Oct. 5	Green Bay @ U of M	W 19–7
Oct. 12	@ Chicago	W 31–0
Oct. 19	@ St. Louis	W 27–10
Oct. 26	Detroit	W 24–10
Nov. 2	Chicago	W 31–14
Nov. 9	Cleveland	W 51–3
Nov. 16	@ Green Bay	W 9–7
Nov. 23	Pittsburgh	W 52–14
Nov. 27	@ Detroit	W 27–0
Dec. 7	@ Los Angeles	W 20–13
Dec. 14	San Francisco	W 10–7
Dec. 21	@ Atlanta	L 3–10
Western Conference Championship		
Dec. 27	Los Angeles	W 23–20
NFL Championship		
Jan. 4	Cleveland	W 27–7
Super Bowl IV		
Jan. 11	Kansas City @ New Orleans	L 7–23

a 52–14 victory over Baltimore on September 28. The defense proved its worth a week later on the University of Minnesota campus by sacking Green Bay's Bart Starr on eight occasions for 63 yards, then registered the first shutout in Viking lore with a 31–0 whitewashing of the Bears at Chicago.

In fact, so strong was the Minnesota defense that no team would score more than 14 points against the Vikings during the remainder of the regular season, enabling the Purple People Eaters to set an NFL record by allowing just 14 touchdowns during the campaign. The defense constantly put opponents in poor field position and created turnovers. The Kapp-led offense responded to those efforts by leading the league with 379 points. Three times Minnesota scored more than 50 points, including a 51–3 decision over a Cleveland team that would advance to the NFL Championship Game.

The Vikings maintained their dominating ways in the playoffs. Minnesota rallied to beat the Rams, 23–20, at Metropolitan Stadium for the Western Conference Championship. Kapp had the deciding play, a two-yard bootleg around the left side, while defensive end Carl Eller sealed the victory by sacking Roman Gabriel for a safety. A week later, the Vikings used Dave Osborn's 108 rushing yards to trounce the Browns for a second time, 27–7, and become the last champions of the pre-merger NFL.

While Kansas City defeated Minnesota in Super Bowl IV, the loss did not dampen the Vikings' accomplishments. Eller, Alan Page and Mick Tingelhoff were named All-Pro, while Eller, Page, Tingelhoff, Kapp, Paul Krause, Gary Larsen, Jim Marshall and Gene Washington were selected to the Pro Bowl. Bud Grant was named NFL Coach of the Year, while second-round pick Ed White would become a fixture on the offensive line.

1970

12–2, NFC Central Champions

One year after having the best year of his career in the National Football League, Vikings quarterback and inspirational leader Joe Kapp became embroiled in a salary dispute with the Minnesota front office, which led to a deal with Boston. That move left the offense in the hands of Gary Cuozzo, a signalcaller who threw the football better than his predecessor but did not provide the gusto and guidance of Kapp.

The Vikings opened the 1970 campaign with a 27–10 victory over Kansas City, the team that had upset Minnesota in Super Bowl IV. The Purple People Eaters thwarted the Chiefs' so-called "Offense of the '70s" with a spectacular effort. The defense was equally stupendous the next three outings, posting a pair of shutouts while dropping a 13–10 decision to the Packers when Dave Hampton returned a kickoff 101 yards for the deciding points.

Cornerback Ed Sharockman guided the Vikings to a 54–13 whipping of Dallas on October 18 by returning a blocked punt for a touchdown prior to reaching paydirt a second time on an interception return. The defense allowed the Rams just five first downs a week later in a 13–3 triumph. The

minnesota vikings - 1970 media guide

Tough Enough To Be Vikings

Vikings then beat Detroit twice in the next three weeks, with running back Clint Jones scoring three touchdowns in a 24–20 win at Metropolitan Stadium. Dave Osborn ran for 139 yards in the December 5 victory over the Bears before the Vikings closed out the season by defeating Kapp and the Patriots and former Minnesota head coach Norm Van Brocklin's Falcons during the final two weeks.

Despite posting their second straight 12–2 record, the Vikings stumbled in the first round of the playoffs. With temperatures in the single digits, 49ers quarterback John Brodie, the NFL's Most Valuable Player, led the visitors to a 17–14 victory at Metropolitan Stadium. Said Minnesota wide receiver Gene Washington, "The big plays come on third down and we didn't make them. The defense did such a great job today and all year. We let them down."

The defense, which equalled its 1969 performance by allowing an NFL-record 14 touchdowns, placed Alan Page and Carl Eller on the All-Pro team, while center Mick Tingelhoff was an All-Pro for the seventh straight year. Eller, Page, Gary Larsen and Karl Kassulke joined offensive standouts Osborn, Washington and Fred Cox in the Pro Bowl. Tenth-round selection Stu Voigt was the primary addition from the 1970 draft.

Preseason		
Aug. 8	New Orleans @ Canton	L 13–14
Aug. 15	Pittsburgh	L 13–20
Aug. 22	@ Houston	W 14–7
Aug. 30	New York Jets	W 52–21
Sept. 5	@ Cleveland	W 24–21
Sept. 11	@ Chicago	W 31–30
Regular Season		
Sept. 20	Kansas City	W 27–10
Sept. 27	New Orleans	W 26–0
Oct. 4	@ Green Bay (Milwaukee)	L 10–13
Oct. 11	@ Chicago	W 24–0
Oct. 18	Dallas	W 54–13
Oct. 26	Los Angeles	W 13–3
Nov. 1	@ Detroit	W 30–17
Nov. 8	@ Washington	W 19–10
Nov. 15	Detroit	W 24–20
Nov. 22	Green Bay	W 10–3
Nov. 29	@ New York Jets	L 10–20
Dec. 5	Chicago	W 16–13
Dec. 13	@ Boston	W 35–14
Dec. 20	@ Atlanta	W 37–7
NFC Divisional Playoffs		
Dec. 27	San Francisco	L 14–17

1971
11–3, NFC Central Champions

It would be hard to imagine a defensive player having a better all-around season than the one Alan Page put together in 1971. As the leader of the National Football League's best defense, Page halted the running game while putting incredible pressure on quarterbacks from the middle of the line to become the first defender ever to win the league's Most Valuable Player award.

Page, of course, had some help. For the third straight year, the Purple People Eaters thoroughly dominated the competition. The Vikings allowed just 139 points, and posted the only back-to-back regular-season shutouts in team annals by whitewashing Buffalo and Philadelphia in early October. The defense surrendered only two rushing touchdowns during the campaign, and created 44 turnovers with 17 fumble recoveries and 27 interceptions, including seven picks by Charlie West and six each by Paul Krause and Ed Sharockman.

The dominating defensive effort was needed, for the Vikings' offense had trouble putting points on the board. Minnesota scored more than 20 points just once in its first nine games, and did not dent the scoreboard for more than 29 points the entire season. Part of the problem centered on the inconsistency at quarterback. Head coach Bud Grant could not find a steady performer under center, causing him to start Gary Cuozzo on eight occasions, Bob Lee four times and Norm Snead for two games. Another factor that crippled the passing game was injuries to wide receiver Gene Washington and tight end John Beasley, even though Bob Grim, who led the team with 45 catches, and Stu Voigt filled in with outstanding performances.

minnesota vikings - 1971 media guide

Preseason
Aug. 8	New England @ U of Minn.	L 10–17
Aug. 14	@ San Diego	W 34–7
Aug. 21	Chicago	W 34–14
Aug. 28	@ Pittsburgh	W 26–21
Sept. 4	@ Denver	L 7–14
Sept. 11	Miami	W 24–0

Regular Season
Sept. 20	@ Detroit	W 16–13
Sept. 26	Chicago	L 17–20
Oct. 3	Buffalo	W 19–0
Oct. 10	@ Philadelphia	W 13–0
Oct. 17	@ Green Bay	W 24–13
Oct. 25	Baltimore	W 10–3
Oct. 31	@ New York Giants	W 17–10
Nov. 7	San Francisco	L 9–13
Nov. 14	Green Bay	W 3–0
Nov. 21	@ New Orleans	W 23–10
Nov. 28	Atlanta	W 24–7
Dec. 5	@ San Diego	L 14–30
Dec. 11	Detroit	W 29–10
Dec. 19	@ Chicago	W 27–10

NFC Divisional Playoffs
| Dec. 25 | Dallas | L 12–20 |

Nevertheless, the stellar defense guided the Vikings to their fourth straight Central Division title by winning at least 11 games for the third consecutive season. The campaign came to a sudden end, however, for the second year in a row. A Minnesota offense that could not generate enough production in between throwing four interceptions led to a disappointing 20–12 loss to Dallas at Metropolitan Stadium on Christmas Day.

Individually, Page earned All-Pro recognition along with Krause, Carl Eller and offensive tackle Ron Yary. Those four men joined Grim as Pro Bowl performers. Defensive tackle Doug Sutherland and cornerback Nate Wright arrived via trades and contributed, as did defensive back Jeff Wright, a 15th-round draft choice from the University of Minnesota.

Tough Enough To Be Vikings

1972

7-7, Third-NFC Central

minnesota vikings—1972 media guide

The Vikings thought an upgraded offense would enable them to reverse their recent fortunes during the playoffs and return to the Super Bowl. Yet those plans faded after the team suffered a series of physical setbacks and dropped four of their first six games before losing three of their last four to finish the 1972 slate with a .500 record.

The campaign began with mixed emotions. Optimism was high after Minnesota acquired quarterback Fran Tarkenton from the New York Giants and wide receiver John Gilliam from St. Louis. After five seasons in the Big Apple, Tarkenton ranked third in the league in passing while tossing 18 touchdowns and setting a club record with 115 consecutive attempts without an interception. Gilliam earned a spot in the Pro Bowl by leading the purple with 47 receptions for 1,035 yards, the highest total in Viking lore at that point. Tackle Ron Yary earned All-Pro and Pro Bowl recognition, yet those efforts were not enough to offset an injury to receiver Gene Washington and the inability of the Minnesota running backs to rumble for long gains.

Defensively, the Vikings were not as strong as they had been the previous three seasons. Nagging ailments to Alan Page, who joined Paul Krause as the defense's lone Pro Bowl performers, Carl Eller and Gary Larsen limited the effectiveness of the line. Middle linebacker Lonnie Warwick also missed eight games and was replaced by rookie Jeff Siemon, a first-round pick who played well but showed his inexperience at times. As a result, the defense surrendered 113 more points than it did in 1971.

Minnesota also seemed snakebit in the early stages of the season. A blocked punt return for a touchdown by Bill Malinchak proved to be the difference in a season-opening, 24-21 loss to Washington. The Vikings also lost consecutive two-point decisions to Miami and St. Louis, with both teams posting come-from-behind victories. There were big moments, such as Tarkenton's brilliant performance in a 45-41 win over Los Angeles, when the Scrambler threw touchdown passes of 76, 70 and 66 yards.

But such momentum could not be found on a consistent basis. The team remained in playoff contention with two games to play before Green Bay shut down the Minnesota offense and beat the purple, 23-7, on December 10 to end the Vikings' four-year run as Central Division champs.

Preseason		
Aug. 12	San Diego	W 24-13
Aug. 18	@ Buffalo	L 10-21
Aug. 26	@ Cleveland	W 20-17
Sept. 4	Houston	W 26-14
Sept. 10	@ Miami	L 19-21
Regular Season		
Sept. 18	Washington	L 21-24
Sept. 24	@ Detroit	W 34-10
Oct. 1	Miami	L 14-16
Oct. 8	St. Louis	L 17-19
Oct. 15	@ Denver	W 23-20
Oct. 23	@ Chicago	L 10-13
Oct. 29	@ Green Bay	W 27-13
Nov. 5	New Orleans	W 37-6
Nov. 12	Detroit	W 16-14
Nov. 19	@ Los Angeles	W 45-41
Nov. 26	@ Pittsburgh	L 10-23
Dec. 3	Chicago	W 23-10
Dec. 10	Green Bay	L 7-23
Dec. 16	@ San Francisco	L 17-20

1973

12–2, NFC Central Champions

The strength of the Minnesota Vikings during the late 1960s and early 1970s was the team's defense. The offense, meanwhile, was good enough to win on most occasions. Yet that scenario changed in 1973. More comfortable in his second year back under center in Minnesota, Fran Tarkenton had a new weapon. Chuck Foreman arrived as a first-round draft choice and emerged as the quarterback's favorite target, both through the air and on the ground. Combine those options with the deep and consistent help of receiver John Gilliam, and the Vikings fielded their most well-rounded squad to that point in team annals.

Preseason		
Aug. 11	Pittsburgh	W 10–6
Aug. 18	@ Kansas City	W 13–10
Aug. 25	@ Oakland	W 34–10
Aug. 31	Miami	W 20–17
Sept. 8	@ San Diego	W 24–16
Regular Season		
Sept. 16	Oakland	W 24–16
Sept. 23	@ Chicago	W 22–13
Sept. 30	Green Bay	W 11–3
Oct. 7	@ Detroit	W 23–9
Oct. 14	@ San Francisco	W 17–13
Oct. 21	Philadelphia	W 28–21
Oct. 28	Los Angeles	W 10–9
Nov. 4	Cleveland	W 26–3
Nov. 11	Detroit	W 28–7
Nov. 19	@ Atlanta	L 14–20
Nov. 25	Chicago	W 31–13
Dec. 2	@ Cincinnati	L 0–27
Dec. 8	@ Green Bay	W 31–7
Dec. 16	@ N.Y. Giants	W 31–7
NFC Divisional Playoffs		
Dec. 22	Washington	W 27–20
NFC Championship Game		
Dec. 30	@ Dallas	W 27–10
Super Bowl VIII		
Jan. 13	Miami @ Houston	L 7–24

Determined to put the previous season in the past, the Vikings opened the 1973 slate by winning their first nine contests. Foreman's first touchdown was a nine-yard reception for the winning points in the season-opening 24–16 win over Oakland. Fred Cox kicked eight field goals during the next two wins before running back Ed Marinaro helped beat the Lions with a pair of touchdowns. The defense allowed a total of 19 points in Weeks 7–9 before dropping a Monday night contest to Atlanta. Minnesota then clinched its fifth Central Division title in six seasons by scoring 31 points in three of its final four games to finish 12–2.

The Vikings continued to roll in the playoffs. Tarkenton and Gilliam connected for two touchdown tosses during the fourth quarter in the 27–20 win over Washington. A week later, Minnesota put together perhaps the best all-around post-season performance in Viking lore with a 27–10 win over Dallas. While the defense limited the Cowboys to nine first downs, Tarkenton hit Gilliam with a 54-yard touchdown pass and cornerback Bobby Bryant returned an interception 63 yards to paydirt. But that momentum did not carry over into Super Bowl VIII, where Larry Csonka rushed for 145 yards in Miami's 24–7 triumph.

Tarkenton was the second-ranked passer in the NFC, throwing for

Tough Enough To Be Vikings

2,113 yards with 15 touchdowns and just seven interceptions. Bryant ranked third in the league with seven picks, and Alan Page was voted NFC Defensive Player of the Year for the second time in three seasons. Page, Carl Eller, Ron Yary, Tarkenton and Gilliam earned All-Pro recognition, while Page, Yary, Foreman, Gilliam, Eller, Paul Krause and Jeff Siemon were named to the Pro Bowl. Foreman, who earned Rookie-of-the-Year honors, joined Jim Lash, Brent McClanahan and Doug Kingsriter in the draft.

1974

10–4, NFC Central Champions

Few offenses and defenses in the history of the National Football League complemented one another better than the Vikings' two units in 1974. While the defense, led by the unrelenting pressure placed on opposing quarterbacks and ball carriers by Alan Page, Carl Eller, Jim Marshall and Doug Sutherland, shut down opponents with amazing consistency, the Minnesota offense kept the defenders fresh with a ball-control attack that featured running back Chuck Foreman, who led the NFL with 15 touchdowns while placing fourth in the NFC with 777 yards rushing.

Foreman immediately eliminated any thought of a sophomore slump by scoring three touchdowns in the season-opening win over Green Bay before scampering 11 yards to paydirt in a 7–6 victory against Detroit in Week 2. The Vikings improved to 4–0 two weeks later when Fred Cox booted a controversial field goal with two seconds remaining to give Minnesota a 23–21 triumph at Dallas. The winning ways reached five games after quarterback Fran Tarkenton threw three touchdown passes in a 51–10 whipping of the Oilers.

Preseason		
Aug. 10	@ Denver	L 21–27
Aug. 19	@ Miami	L 9–21
Aug. 25	Buffalo	W 32–13
Aug. 31	@ St. Louis	W 14–10
Sept. 7	San Diego	W 42–0
Regular Season		
Sept. 15	@ Green Bay	W 32–17
Sept. 22	@ Detroit	W 7–6
Sept. 29	Chicago	W 11–7
Oct. 6	@ Dallas	W 23–21
Oct. 13	Houston	W 51–10
Oct. 20	Detroit	L 16–20
Oct. 27	New England	L 14–17
Nov. 3	@ Chicago	W 17–0
Nov. 11	@ St. Louis	W 28–24
Nov. 17	Green Bay	L 7–19
Nov. 24	@ Los Angeles	L 17–20
Dec. 1	New Orleans	W 29–9
Dec. 7	Atlanta	W 23–10
Dec. 14	@ Kansas City	W 35–15
NFC Divisional Playoffs		
Dec. 21	St. Louis	W 30–14
NFC Championship Game		
Dec. 29	Los Angeles	W 14–10
Super Bowl IX		
Jan. 12	Pittsburgh @ New Orleans	L 6–16

After two close losses to the Lions and Patriots, the Vikings registered their first shutout in three years with a 17–0 pasting of the Bears. Minnesota outscored St. Louis, 28–24, on *Monday Night Football* before dropping two straight contests, then finished the slate with three straight triumphs to post a 10–4 record.

The Vikings continued to roll in the playoffs by scoring 30 unanswered points in a 30–14 win over St. Louis. A week later, a stubborn defense that refused to allow the Rams more than a single touchdown along with the one-two punch of Foreman and Dave Osborn, who rushed for 80 and 76 yards, respectively, gave Minnesota a 14–10 triumph over Los Angeles. Yet, the Vikings wound up on the wrong end of the scoreboard again in Super Bowl IX by losing a defensive struggle to Pittsburgh, 16–6.

At season's end, All-Pro honors were bestowed upon Page and offensive linemen Ron Yary and Ed White. Page and Yary joined Eller, Foreman, Gilliam, Tarkenton and Paul Krause in the Pro Bowl. The future was made brighter with the additions of linebackers Fred McNeill and Matt Blair, tackle Steve Riley and tight end Steve Craig in the draft along with a trade that brought guard Andy Maurer from New Orleans.

1975

12–2, NFC Central Champions

No season in Viking lore deposited more heartbreak in the memory bank than the 1975 campaign, thanks to an interference penalty that was never called in the waning seconds during the first round of the playoffs.

The purple gang was dominating in all phases of the game, with the offense leading the conference with 377 points while the defense surrendered just 180, good for second on the circuit. Though deemed too old by most observers, the Purple People Eaters featured a near-perfect blend of experience and youth that thrived on opportunistic turnovers, led by Paul Krause's NFC-high 10 interceptions, and goal-line stands. The offense clicked on all cylinders as well. Fran Tarkenton, who moved to the top of the NFL career charts for completions and touchdown passes during the season, was named the National Football League's Most Valuable Player upon pacing all NFC passers with 273 completions, 2,994 yards and 25 touchdowns. Tarkenton completed a conference-best 64.2 percent of his aerials, helping Chuck Foreman top the league with 73 receptions. Running back Ed Marinaro ranked third in the NFC with 54 catches, and John Gilliam was fifth with 50 grabs for a conference-best 777 yards receiving.

Foreman also shined when not catching the ball. Employing his patented spins and other uncanny abilities to make would-be tacklers grab nothing but air, Foreman became the Vikings' first 1,000-yard rusher and placed second in the NFC by running for 1,070 yards, just six behind St. Louis' Jim Otis. The Minnesota running back also led the conference with 132 points on 22 touchdowns. He crossed the goal line three times in the 29–21

Tough Enough To Be Vikings

Preseason		
Aug. 9	N.Y. Jets @ Phoenix	L 15–20
Aug. 17	@ New England	L 10–36
Aug. 23	@ Dallas	W 16–13
Sept. 1	Miami	W 20–7
Sept. 6	St. Louis	L 6–13
Sept. 13	@ San Diego	T 14–14
Regular Season		
Sept. 21	San Francisco	W 27–17
Sept. 28	@ Cleveland	W 42–10
Oct. 5	Chicago	W 28–3
Oct. 12	New York Jets	W 29–21
Oct. 19	Detroit	W 25–19
Oct. 27	@ Chicago	W 13–9
Nov. 2	@ Green Bay	W 28–17
Nov. 9	Atlanta	W 38–0
Nov. 16	@ New Orleans	W 20–7
Nov. 23	San Diego	W 28–13
Nov. 30	@ Washington	L 30–31
Dec. 7	Green Bay	W 24–3
Dec. 14	@ Detroit	L 10–17
Dec. 20	@ Buffalo	W 35–10
NFC Divisional Playoffs		
Dec. 28	Dallas	L 14–17

win over the Jets before reaching paydirt on four occasions in the season finale at Buffalo.

The Vikings won their first 10 games of the season to clinch their seventh Central Division title in eight years and finish with their fourth 12–2 record in seven seasons. But that dominating performance meant little after the Cowboys' Roger Staubach hit Drew Pearson with a 50-yard touchdown pass with 24 seconds left in the divisional playoff game for a controversial 17–14 victory at Metropolitan Stadium.

Six players—Foreman, Tarkenton, Krause, Alan Page, Ed White and Ron Yary—received All-Pro recognition. Those six joined Bobby Bryant, John Gilliam and Jeff Siemon on the NFC Pro Bowl team. The draft produced such contributors as defensive end Mark Mullaney, running back Robert Miller and punter Neil Clabo.

1976

11–2–1, NFC Central Champions

The previous season's playoff loss brought from the woodwork critics who claimed the Vikings were too old to maintain a high level of play. Yet, once again, Minnesota proved the faultfinders wrong by winning its eighth Central Division title in nine years and advancing to the Super Bowl for the fourth time.

The departed John Gilliam and Ed Marinaro were hardly missed due to the arrival of receivers Ahmad Rashad and Sammy White. Their presence enabled Fran Tarkenton to develop one of the most potent passing attacks in league history. Tarkenton led the NFC with 412 pass attempts, 255 completions, 2,961 yards and a completion percentage of 61.9. Running back Chuck Foreman, who paced the Minnesota ground game by ranking fourth in the NFC with 1,155 rushing yards, was second on the loop with 55 catches.

Rashad finished fifth in the conference with 53 grabs, while White pulled in 51 passes with 10 touchdowns on his way to Rookie of the Year accolades.

Tarkenton and White stretched opposing defenses from the start, connecting on a 47-yard touchdown bomb in the season-opening win over New Orleans and a 56-yard touchdown strike a week later during a hard-fought 10–10 tie with the Rams. Following a 10–9 victory over the Lions, the Vikings posted an impressive 17–6 triumph over Pittsburgh, the defending Super Bowl champion, in front a national television audience on Monday night. Foreman led the charge by rushing for 148 yards and two touchdowns against the famed Steel Curtain defense.

The Vikings improved to 6-0-1 prior to a one-point loss to Chicago on October 31. Minnesota rebounded to win three straight and five of its last six to take the Central Division. The playoffs produced similar results. Foreman and White scored two touchdowns apiece against the Redskins before Nate Allen blocked a short Rams' field goal attempt that Bobby Bryant returned 90 yards for a touchdown in the triumph over Los Angeles in the NFC Championship Game. However, Minnesota could not take advantage of Fred McNeill's blocked punt against Oakland, enabling the Raiders to go on to victory in Super Bowl XI.

Foreman received All-Pro honors for the second straight year while Ron Yary earned the recognition for the sixth consecutive time. Foreman and Yary were named to the Pro Bowl, along with White, Tarkenton, Alan Page, Jeff Siemon and Ed White. In addition to Sammy White, James White and Wes Hamilton arrived in the draft.

Preseason		
July 31	@ Miami	L 3–16
Aug. 7	@ Kansas City	W 13–10
Aug. 16	@ Cleveland	L 7–31
Aug. 22	Cincinnati	W 23–17
Aug. 28	Philadelphia	W 20–16
Sept. 5	@ Denver	L 17–30
Regular Season		
Sept. 12	@ New Orleans	W 40–9
Sept. 19	Los Angeles (OT)	T 10–10
Sept. 26	@ Detroit	W 10–9
Oct. 4	Pittsburgh	W 17–6
Oct. 10	Chicago	W 20–19
Oct. 17	New York Giants	W 24–7
Oct. 24	@ Philadelphia	W 31–12
Oct. 31	@ Chicago	L 13–14
Nov. 7	Detroit	W 31–23
Nov. 14	Seattle	W 27–21
Nov. 21	@ Green Bay	W 17–10
Nov. 29	@ San Francisco	L 16–20
Dec. 5	Green Bay	W 20–9
Dec. 11	@ Miami	W 29–7
NFC Divisional Playoffs		
Dec. 18	Washington	W 35–20
NFC Championship Game		
Dec. 26	Los Angeles	W 24–13
Super Bowl XI		
Jan. 9	Oakland @ Pasadena	L 14–32

Media Guide 1976
Minnesota Vikings

1977

9–5, NFC Central Champions

The Vikings received an unexpected glimpse of the future during the 1977 season. Minnesota had won five of its first eight games and was headed toward the sixth victory when Fran Tarkenton suffered the first serious injury of his career. The quarterback broke his leg during a 42–10 triumph over the Bengals on November 13, leaving the team without its leader to navigate the remainder of the voyage.

Backups Bob Lee and rookie Tommy Kramer did as well as could be expected in Tarkenton's absence. Lee gained a split in the Vikings' next two games—a 10–7 loss at Chicago and a 13–6 win at Green Bay—but was replaced by Kramer after watching Minnesota fall behind San Francisco 24–7 in the third quarter on December 4. A legend was born that winter afternoon at Metropolitan Stadium when Kramer threw touchdown passes to Ahmad Rashad and Bob Tucker before hitting Sammy White with a game-winning, 69-yard bomb in the final minute for the 28–27 victory. Kramer, however, looked like a rookie a week later during a loss at Oakland and gave way to Lee, who guided the Vikings to the Central Division title with a 30–21 victory at Detroit.

Lee also was under center in the Vikings' 14–7 upset over the Rams in the first round of the playoffs. Lee engineered an early drive that culminated with Chuck Foreman's five-yard touchdown run. That proved important, for heavy rain made the field muddy and almost unplayable. Lee

Preseason		
Aug. 6	@ Los Angeles	W 22–17
Aug. 13	Cleveland	W 34–33
Aug. 19	@ Baltimore	L 7–29
Aug. 26	Miami	W 33–7
Sept. 3	@ Cincinnati	L 7–26
Sept. 10	@ Buffalo	W 30–6
Regular Season		
Sept. 18	Dallas (OT)	L 10–16
Sept. 24	@ Tampa Bay	W 9–3
Oct. 2	Green Bay	W 19–7
Oct. 9	Detroit	W 14–7
Oct. 16	Chicago (OT)	W 22–16
Oct. 24	@ Los Angeles	L 3–35
Oct. 30	@ Atlanta	W 14–7
Nov. 6	St. Louis	L 7–27
Nov. 13	Cincinnati	W 42–10
Nov. 20	@ Chicago	L 7–10
Nov. 27	@ Green Bay	W 13–6
Dec. 4	San Francisco	W 28–27
Dec. 11	@ Oakland	L 13–35
Dec. 17	@ Detroit	W 30–21
NFC Divisional Playoffs		
Dec. 26	@ Los Angeles	W 14–7
NFC Championship Game		
Jan. 1	@ Dallas	L 6–23

also got the Vikings on the scoreboard again in the fourth quarter, which proved to be enough for the win. Yet that was all the magic Lee could muster, for he and the Vikings struggled a week later against Dallas in the NFC Championship Game.

All three quarterbacks had success due to the presence of Chuck Foreman, who continued to prove he was the most versatile running back in the league. Foreman placed third in the NFC with 1,112 yards rushing while catching 38 passes. Rashad also helped by leading the conference with 51 receptions.

A tiebreaker with Chicago gave the Vikings their fifth straight and ninth Central Division title in 10 seasons. Linebacker Matt Blair earned his first trip to the Pro Bowl and joined teammates Foreman, Jeff Siemon, Ed White, Ron Yary and Sammy White in the post-season all-star game. In addition to Kramer, the draft brought offensive lineman Dennis Swilley, safety Tom Hannon and linebacker Scott Studwell to Minnesota.

1978

8–7–1, NFC Central Champions

Unlike the premature catcalls from recent seasons, the Vikings were an aging team in 1978. Head coach Bud Grant realized that fact and made some adjustments, particularly on defense. Alan Page was traded to Chicago after he and Grant disagreed on the player's weight. Carl Eller and Paul Krause saw their playing time decrease in favor of such youngsters as Mark Mullaney and Tom Hannon. Linebacker Matt Blair, meanwhile, was blossoming into an All-Pro performer. By instilling youth, Grant hoped to avoid a major rebuilding project in the near future.

The offense also featured a different look, one that focused more on the pass than the run. The Vikings had struggled running the ball in 1977 and early 1978. That enabled 38-year-old Fran Tarkenton, who along with center Mick Tingelhoff would retire from football after the season, to post the highest passing totals of his storied career. Newcomer Rickey Young, acquired from San Diego in exchange for Ed White, led the league with 88 receptions. Ahmad Rashad was third in the conference with 66 catches, while Chuck Foreman caught 61 aerials, good for fifth. Tarkenton led the league with 345

Preseason		
Aug. 5	Washington	W 20–13
Aug. 13	@ Kansas City	L 13–17
Aug. 18	@ Miami	L 22–30
Aug. 26	Buffalo	W 30–27
Regular Season		
Sept. 3	@ New Orleans	L 24–31
Sept. 11	Denver (OT)	W 12–9
Sept. 17	Tampa Bay	L 10–16
Sept. 25	@ Chicago	W 24–20
Oct. 1	@ Tampa Bay	W 24–7
Oct. 8	@ Seattle	L 28–29
Oct. 15	Los Angeles	L 17–34
Oct. 22	Green Bay	W 21–7
Oct. 26	@ Dallas	W 21–10
Nov. 5	Detroit	W 17–7
Nov. 12	Chicago	W 17–14
Nov. 19	San Diego	L 7–13
Nov. 26	@ Green Bay (OT)	T 10–10
Dec. 3	Philadelphia	W 28–27
Dec. 9	@ Detroit	L 14–45
Dec. 17	@ Oakland	L 20–27
NFC Divisional Playoffs		
Dec. 31	@ Los Angeles	L 10–34

completions and 3,468 yards while tying for the NFC lead with 25 touchdown tosses.

The alterations led to some uncharacteristic results. The Vikings fell three games out of first place by losing four of their first seven contests. Four straight wins, including a 21–10 victory at Dallas behind Foreman's 101-yard rushing effort during the first Thursday night game in NFL history, put Minnesota back into contention. By the time the purple arrived in Green Bay on November 26, the two teams were tied for first place, then battled to a 10–10 stalemate. Both the Vikings and Packers lost their final two games to finish with identical 8–7–1 records. Minnesota won the Central Division title with a tiebreaker for the second straight season thanks to a 21–7 triumph over Green Bay on October 22.

Yet Minnesota looked past its prime in the playoffs against Los Angeles. The teams battled to a 10–10 draw at halftime before the Rams gained some revenge for the previous four post-season meetings with the Vikings by overpowering the visitors, 34–10.

Blair and Rashad were named Pro Bowl starters in 1978. While Tarkenton, Tingelhoff and Eller played their final games in Minnesota, the Vikings added defensive end Randy Holloway, cornerback John Turner and center Jim Hough via the draft.

1979

7–9, Third-NFC Central

After winning 10 Central Division titles in the previous 11 years, the Vikings discovered how the rest of the division had experienced life since 1968. Minnesota continued to undergo change, this time at the crucial quarterback position. Tommy Kramer replaced the retired Fran Tarkenton and put on an aerial show that was as spectacular at times as any in the National Football League. Yet, Kramer also looked like a first-year starter on occasion, as evidenced by his 24 interceptions. Add the team's inability to develop a consistent rushing attack and a rebuilding defense that lacked the depth and overall talent from earlier versions in the decade and the outcome was the first losing season in the Twin Cities since 1967.

Kramer got off to a great start by completing 21 of 34 passes and throwing four touchdown tosses to Ahmad Rashad in the season opener, a 28–22 win over the 49ers on September 2. After a pair of losses, Kramer found Rashad again for a 50-yard touchdown pass in overtime to guide Minnesota to a 27–21 win over Green Bay. Minnesota rose above the .500 level for the final time that season with a 13–10 win at Detroit on September 30. Five defeats in their next six outings sealed the Vikings' fate, although Kramer made life interesting, including a 308-yard passing effort on 61 attempts and 38 completions during the season finale at New England.

Rashad placed second in the NFL with 80 receptions for 1,156 yards and nine touchdowns. Running back Rickey Young was third in the conference with 72 catches and four scores, while Jimmy Edwards led the circuit with 44 kickoff returns for 1,103 yards, an average of 25.1 yards per attempt. Rashad and linebacker Matt Blair were the Vikings' Pro Bowl representatives.

Kramer under center was not the only sign that the end of an era had arrived. Jim Marshall retired with his consecutive games streak at 282 and took a lap around the Metropolitan Stadium field in the backseat of a convertible during his final home game, on December 9. Paul Krause and Wally Hilgenberg also hung up the cleats, and Chuck Foreman had his last hurrah in purple while giving way to rookie Ted Brown. Three other draft picks made the team—center David Huffman, quarterback Steve Dils and tight end Joe Senser.

Preseason		
Aug. 2	@ Seattle	L 9–12
Aug. 11	@ San Diego	L 0–19
Aug. 18	Miami	L 10–21
Aug. 23	Kansas City	L 0–25
Regular Season		
Sept. 2	San Francisco	W 28–22
Sept. 9	@ Chicago	L 7–26
Sept. 16	Miami	L 12–27
Sept. 23	Green Bay (OT)	W 27–21
Sept. 30	@ Detroit	W 13–10
Oct. 7	Dallas	L 20–36
Oct. 15	@ New York Jets	L 7–14
Oct. 21	Chicago	W 30–27
Oct. 28	Tampa Bay	L 10–12
Nov. 4	@ St. Louis	L 7–37
Nov. 11	@ Green Bay (Milwaukee)	L 7–19
Nov. 18	Detroit	W 14–7
Nov. 25	@ Tampa Bay	W 23–22
Dec. 2	@ Los Angeles (OT)	L 21–27
Dec. 9	Buffalo	W 10–3
Dec. 16	@ New England	L 23–27

1980

9–7, NFC Central Champions

After a one-year hiatus from the playoffs, the Vikings returned to the top of the Central Division due to the most dramatic play in Minnesota annals. Trailing Cleveland 23–22 with five seconds left on December 14, quarterback Tommy Kramer heaved a "Hail Mary" pass from midfield. The ball was tipped before Ahmad Rashad clutched the ball against his hip and stepped across the goal line to give the Vikings the victory and the division title.

That play culminated one of the more impressive second-half improvements ever put together by Minnesota. The Vikings dropped three of their first eight contests, a period that saw Kramer throw 17 interceptions and the team rush for more than 100 yards on just two occasions. The scenario changed drastically in the final eight games, beginning with the 39–14 win at Washington on November 2. Steve Dils threw two touchdown passes while replacing an injured Kramer and the Vikings rolled up 201 yards on

Tough Enough To Be Vikings

Preseason		
Aug. 9	San Diego	W 21–17
Aug. 18	@ Kansas City	L 10–14
Aug. 23	@ Miami	W 17–10
Aug. 30	Cleveland	W 38–16
Regular Season		
Sept. 7	Atlanta	W 24–23
Sept. 14	Philadelphia	L 7–42
Sept. 21	@ Chicago	W 34–14
Sept. 28	@ Detroit	L 7–27
Oct. 5	Pittsburgh	L 17–23
Oct. 12	Chicago	W 13–7
Oct. 19	@ Cincinnati	L 0–14
Oct. 26	@ Green Bay	L 3–16
Nov. 2	@ Washington	W 39–14
Nov. 9	Detroit	W 34–0
Nov. 16	Tampa Bay	W 38–30
Nov. 23	Green Bay	L 13–25
Nov. 30	@ New Orleans	W 23–20
Dec. 7	@ Tampa Bay	W 21–10
Dec. 14	Cleveland	W 28–23
Dec. 21	@ Houston	L 16–20
NFC Divisional Playoffs		
Jan. 3	@ Philadelphia	L 16–31

the ground to produce the victory. A week later, Minnesota posted its first shutout since November 9, 1975, by silencing the first-place Lions, 34–0.

The Vikings moved into a first-place tie with Detroit on November 16 by beating Tampa Bay, 38–30, then owned the top spot after defeating the Buccaneers a second time, 21–10 on December 7. The last-second heroics followed against the Browns a week later before both Minnesota and the Lions lost their season finales, giving both teams a 9–7 record and the Vikings the division title due to the tie-breaker rules.

One of the more impressive facts from the regular season centered on the Vikings losing just three fumbles. Ironically, Minnesota lost that many loose balls in the playoffs against Philadelphia, which, combined with five interceptions, proved to be too much for the purple to overcome in the Eagles' 31–16 victory.

Still, the 1980 season produced several positive results for the Vikings. Led by Kramer, running back Ted Brown and linebacker Scott Studwell, Minnesota fielded a young team that showed signs of improving. Rashad finished fourth in the NFC with 69 receptions, while he and linebacker Matt Blair were named to the Pro Bowl squad. The Vikings also had a productive draft, bringing in defensive tackle Doug Martin, cornerback Willie Teal, guard Brent Boyd and linebacker Dennis Johnson.

1981

7–9, Fourth-NFC Central

The 1981 campaign was a season of streaks for the Vikings during their final year at Metropolitan Stadium. Quarterback Tommy Kramer directed a potent passing attack that was capable of scoring points in a hurry, but an inconsistent defense that did not keep any opponent from registering fewer than 10 points and the offense's late-season slump hurt the team's ability to win games.

The Seasons

Preseason
Aug. 8	Miami	L 6–20
Aug. 14	@ Washington	L 13–27
Aug. 22	Atlanta	W 20–19
Aug. 27	@ Los Angeles	L 31–34

Regular Season
Sept. 5	@ Tampa Bay	L 13–21
Sept. 14	Oakland	L 10–36
Sept. 20	Detroit	W 26–24
Sept. 27	@ Green Bay	W 30–13
Oct. 4	Chicago	W 24–21
Oct. 11	@ San Diego	W 33–31
Oct. 18	Philadelphia	W 35–23
Oct. 25	@ St. Louis	L 17–30
Nov. 2	@ Denver	L 17–19
Nov. 8	Tampa Bay	W 25–10
Nov. 15	New Orleans	W 20–10
Nov. 23	@ Atlanta	L 30–31
Nov. 29	Green Bay	L 23–35
Dec. 6	@ Chicago	L 9–10
Dec. 12	@ Detroit	L 7–45
Dec. 20	Kansas City	L 6–10

There was no denying that Minnesota did not possess the overall talent it had fielded only a couple years earlier. Nevertheless, head coach Bud Grant surprised many knowledgeable observers by guiding the Vikings to a two-game lead in the Central Division after beating New Orleans, 20–10, on November 15. The purple opened the season with two losses, then reeled off five straight wins that included victories on last-second field goals by Rick Danmeier against Detroit and San Diego and a 35–23 whipping of an Eagles team that entered the contest unbeaten in six contests. Back-to-back defeats to the Cardinals and Broncos followed, although two fourth-quarter touchdown runs by Tony Galbreath made the game at Denver interesting in the closing moments. Minnesota's final two triumphs at The Met, against the Buccaneers and Saints, seemed to point toward a second straight division title and a trip to the playoffs.

The post-season train derailed, however, when the Vikings concluded the campaign with five consecutive losses. Minnesota turned the ball over on five occasions during each of the first three defeats before losing possession of the pigskin four times against both the Lions and Chiefs. Even the final contest at Metropolitan Stadium, against Kansas City on December 20, did little to get the offense back on track. Danmeier's two field goals proved to be the only points the purple could muster during that gray afternoon.

Running back Ted Brown was Kramer's favorite target and ranked second in the NFC with 83 receptions. Tight end Joe Senser, who joined receiver Ahmad Rashad and linebacker Matt Blair on the Pro Bowl roster, placed fourth on the loop with 79 grabs for 1,004 yards and eight touchdowns. Eddie Payton had the longest kickoff return in the NFL that year when he raced 99 yards to paydirt against Oakland on September 14. The draft produced tackle Tim Irwin, quarterback Wade Wilson, defensive back John Swain and linebacker Robin Sendlein.

1982

5–4, FOURTH (TIED)–NFC

There were more than a few sad faces when Metropolitan Stadium closed its doors at the end of the 1981 slate. But the Vikings continued their victorious ways in their new home by winning seven of eight contests played at the Metrodome during the strike-marred 1982 campaign.

For the second straight year, the Viking offense threw the ball on nearly 80 percent of their plays. Minnesota tried to bolster its running game in the draft by selecting Darrin Nelson in the first round. Nelson, however, struggled with minor ailments and his consistency with backfield partner Ted Brown. As a result, quarterback Tommy Kramer went to the air, connecting with Brown for a team-high 31 catches. Receiver Sammy White and tight end Joe Senser caught 29 passes apiece, while Ahmad Rashad, who retired after the 1982 campaign, concluded his career with 23 grabs.

The arrival of nose tackle Charlie Johnson and the continued development of defensive end Doug Martin and linebacker Scott Studwell upgraded the defense from the previous season. The defenders rose to the occasion in the first regular-season game at the Metrodome, with Willie Teal intercepting a Doug Williams pass deep in Minnesota territory with 1:10 left to play to seal the 17–10 win. After the Vikings blew a 19–0 lead to lose at Buffalo the following week, the strike hit on September 21, silencing the season until November 21.

The Metrodome continued to be a Viking haven after the strike. Kramer threw five touchdown passes, including three to White, in a 35–7 win over the Bears on November 28. The Vikings won again in the Dome with the help of Rick Danmeier's 40-yard field goal against the Colts on December 12. "Krazy George" then riled the crowd before Kramer hit Rickey Young with a 14-yard touchdown pass late in the fourth quarter in a 31–27 victory over Dallas. Minnesota also beat Atlanta, 30–24, in the first round of the Super Bowl Tournament before traveling to Washington and being eliminated by running back John Riggins.

Martin earned All-Pro recognition after leading the NFL with 11.5 sacks. Linebacker Matt Blair was named a Pro Bowl performer for the sixth and final time of his career. The draft produced two significant offensive pro-

Preseason		
Aug. 7	Baltimore @ Canton	W 30–14
Aug. 14	@ Atlanta	L 17–20
Aug. 21	Seattle	W 7–3
Aug. 28	@ Denver	L 17–27
Sept. 3	New Orleans	W 24–21
Regular Season		
Sept. 12	Tampa Bay	W 17–10
Sept. 16	@ Buffalo	L 22–23
Nov. 21	@ Green Bay (Milwaukee)	L 7–26
Nov. 28	Chicago	W 35–7
Dec. 5	@ Miami	L 14–22
Dec. 12	Baltimore	W 13–10
Dec. 19	@ Detroit	W 34–31
Dec. 26	New York Jets	L 14–42
Jan. 3	Dallas	W 31–27
NFC First-Round Playoffs		
Jan. 9	Atlanta	W 30–24
NFC Second-Round Playoffs		
Jan. 15	@ Washington	L 7–21

ducers for the future—Nelson and tight end Steve Jordan—as well as a pair of promising offensive linemen in tackle Terry Tausch and guard Curtis Rouse.

1983
8–8, FOURTH–NFC CENTRAL

For the second time in as many full seasons, the Vikings crumbled during the second half of the campaign, falling from first place at midseason to fourth place by late December. This time the culprit was injuries, beginning with a severe knee ailment suffered during the preseason that forced tight end Joe Senser to miss the entire slate.

Minnesota started the season on a positive note by intercepting three passes, including a Rufus Bess pick with 40 seconds left, in a 27–21 win over Cleveland. In Week 2, San Francisco handed the Vikings their worst loss in 19 years, a 48–17 decision, before doomsday hit on September 18. Although the purple won the overtime game at Tampa Bay, Minnesota lost quarterback Tommy Kramer and safety Keith Nord for the remainder of the season with injuries. A week later, the defense recorded eight sacks in beating Detroit, 20–17, but defensive end Mark Mullaney was lost for eight weeks with a broken collarbone.

Long touchdown runs by Darrin Nelson and Tony Galbreath enabled Minnesota to beat Chicago, and Ted Brown galloped for 179 yards against the Packers to give the Vikings a 6–2 record and sole possession of first place at the halfway point. Yet, running back Ted Brown succumbed to a separated shoulder on November 6, costing the team its third key offensive player. Minnesota was still in the hunt on December 5, but lost the showdown with the Lions, 13–2. After dropping six of seven decisions, the Vikings managed to win the season finale, a 20–14 victory over Cincinnati in quarterback Wade Wilson's first start in the National Football League.

The Vikings did not

Preseason		
Aug. 6	St. Louis @ London	W 28–10
Aug. 13	Baltimore	L 7–10
Aug. 19	@ Seattle	W 19–17
Aug. 26	Denver	W 34–3
Regular Season		
Sept. 4	@ Cleveland	W 27–21
Sept. 8	San Francisco	L 17–48
Sept. 18	@ Tampa Bay (OT)	W 19–16
Sept. 25	Detroit	W 20–17
Oct. 2	Dallas	L 24–37
Oct. 9	@ Chicago	W 23–14
Oct. 16	Houston	W 34–14
Oct. 23	@ Green Bay (OT)	W 20–17
Oct. 30	@ St. Louis	L 31–41
Nov. 6	Tampa Bay	L 12–17
Nov. 13	Green Bay	L 21–29
Nov. 20	@ Pittsburgh	W 17–14
Nov. 27	@ New Orleans	L 16–17
Dec. 5	@ Detroit	L 2–13
Dec. 11	Chicago	L 13–19
Dec. 17	Cincinnati	W 20–14

Tough Enough To Be Vikings

have a player selected to the Pro Bowl for the first and only time in team history. Nelson paced the NFC in kickoff return average with a 24.7-yard norm on 18 returns. Punter Greg Coleman's 36.5-yard net average was tops in the NFC. Defensive end Doug Martin tied for fifth with 13 quarterback sacks. The draft solidified the Minnesota secondary for the rest of the decade by adding Joey Browner and Carl Lee.

The greatest surprise to the campaign occurred shortly after the final gun when head coach Bud Grant decided to retire to pursue other interests in life after 17 years at the Viking helm. Grant was replaced by Les Steckel, who served as Minnesota's receivers coach in 1983.

1984

3–13, Fifth-NFC Central

After 17 years of winning under the easy-going, yet disciplined direction of Bud Grant, the Vikings turned the top job over to 38-year-old Les Steckel, the youngest head coach in the National Football League.

Steckel left no doubt about what he expected from his team. "I've been asked to characterize a team that I coach," Steckel said during a pre-season interview, "and I like to think it will be a D.I. team. In the Marine Corps, that stands for 'drill instructor.' With the Vikings, it stands for discipline and integrity." Steckel went on to add, "I'm aware that a lot of people think we're going to burn out the players or burn out ourselves. I just can't emphasize enough the word smart."

The head coach lived up to his promise by putting the Vikings through one of the most strenuous training camps in NFL history. Despite Steckel's good intentions, some players had difficulty adjusting to

Preseason		
Aug. 4	Atlanta	W 37–6
Aug. 11	Miami	L 7–29
Aug. 18	Philadelphia	L 10–31
Aug. 24	@ St. Louis	L 0–31
Regular Season		
Sept. 2	San Diego	L 13–42
Sept. 9	@ Philadelphia	L 17–19
Sept. 16	Atlanta	W 27–20
Sept. 23	@ Detroit	W 29–28
Sept. 30	Seattle	L 12–20
Oct. 7	@ Tampa Bay	L 31–35
Oct. 14	@ L.A. Raiders	L 20–23
Oct. 21	Detroit	L 14–16
Oct. 28	@ Chicago	L 7–16
Nov. 4	Tampa Bay	W 27–24
Nov. 11	@ Green Bay (Milwaukee)	L 14–45
Nov. 18	@ Denver	L 21–42
Nov. 25	Chicago	L 3–34
Nov. 29	Washington	L 17–31
Dec. 8	@ San Francisco	L 7–51
Dec. 16	Green Bay	L 14–38

the new regimen. Combine that fact with an overall lack of talented depth, and the results were not positive.

Minnesota started the season in decent fashion. After losing the first two games of the campaign, the Vikings rebounded to beat Atlanta with the help of rookie running back Alfred Anderson's 43-yard touchdown pass to fellow rookie Dwight Collins. A week later, the purple defeated Detroit on five field goals by Jan Stenerud, the Vikings' lone Pro Bowl representative.

Unfortunately, things did not get any better. Minnesota lost its next five games, but none by more than nine points. The Raiders and Lions kicked game-winning field goals in the final minute of play to hand the Vikings back-to-back losses in mid-October. The purple had one go its way when Stenerud's 53-yarder with two seconds remaining lifted Minnesota to a 27–24 triumph over Tampa Bay on November 4.

The wheels came off a week later, when the Packers scored 28 unanswered points in the final quarter-and-a-half. Three first-quarter touchdowns sent the Broncos to a 21–point victory on November 18. From there, Minnesota lost its last four contests, including the most lopsided game in club history, a 51–7 decision to San Francisco on December 8, and dropped 11 of its last 12 games to conclude the campaign with its worst record since 1962.

Within a week of the final game, Grant returned to the Vikings' head coaching helm.

1985

7–9, Third-NFC Central

Minnesota experienced a return to normalcy in 1985. Head coach Bud Grant ended his one-year retirement to get the Viking ship back on course, admitting he did not enjoy the team's fate from the previous year and missed some aspects that coaching offered.

One thing Grant surely missed was performances similar to the one cornerback Rufus Bess had during the season opener. Bess forced three fumbles and intercepted a Joe Montana pass in the end zone late in the fourth quarter to help the Vikings win, 28–21. A week later, Minnesota traveled to Tampa Bay and sealed the victory in the fourth quarter when quarterback Tommy Kramer and running back Ted Brown hooked up for a 54-yard touchdown pass. Anthony Carter, a new arrival from the United States Football League, then caught his first two touchdown passes in the National Football League and helped Kramer throw for 411 yards against the acclaimed Chicago defense in a 33–24 loss to the Bears.

The Vikings returned to their passing ways that typified Grant's offenses late in his previous tenure with the team. Kramer was as capable as any quarterback in the league of putting up impressive numbers. Tight end Steve Jordan was the signalcaller's favorite target, receiving 68 passes for 795 yards. While Mike Jones pulled in 46 tosses and Carter had 43 grabs, running back Darrin Nelson also recorded 43 receptions and rushed for a career-high 893 yards. That attack enabled the Vikings to remain competitive in every game. In fact, four of Minnesota's nine losses were by three or fewer points, including one- and two-point defeats to the Falcons and Eagles, respectively, to conclude the campaign.

Without question, Grant helped the Vikings turn the tide. And the future looked bright. Third-year safety Joey Browner was developing into an All-Pro and earned his first trip to the Pro Bowl. In addition to Carter, Keith Millard, Minnesota's first-round draft pick in 1984, arrived after one year in the USFL and contributed a team-high 11 sacks. The draft was also productive, with such significant contributors as defensive end Chris Doleman, defensive back Issiac Holt and center Kirk Lowdermilk joining the team.

Preseason		
Aug. 10	@ Miami	W 16–13
Aug. 17	Pittsburgh	W 41–34
Aug. 24	Seattle	L 10–27
Aug. 30	@ Denver	W 13–9
Regular Season		
Sept. 8	San Francisco	W 28–21
Sept. 15	@ Tampa Bay	W 31–16
Sept. 19	Chicago	L 24–33
Sept. 29	@ Buffalo	W 27–20
Oct. 6	@ L.A. Rams	L 10–13
Oct. 13	@ Green Bay (Milwaukee)	L 17–20
Oct. 20	San Diego	W 21–17
Oct. 27	@ Chicago	L 9–27
Nov. 3	Detroit	W 16–13
Nov. 10	Green Bay	L 17–27
Nov. 17	@ Detroit	L 21–41
Nov. 24	New Orleans	L 23–30
Dec. 1	@ Philadelphia	W 28–23
Dec. 8	Tampa Bay	W 26–7
Dec. 15	@ Atlanta	L 13–14
Dec. 22	Philadelphia	L 35–37

The positive direction convinced Grant that his work was done. He retired a final time from the coaching ranks at the end of the season and turned the reins over to long-time offensive coordinator Jerry Burns.

1986

9–7, Second–NFC Central

One of the more rapid rebuilding efforts in the National Football League took place in Minnesota during the mid-1980s. Just two years after the team endured a three-win season, the Vikings reemerged as a playoff contender with a solid nucleus of young talent that had little difficulty adjusting to the game's top level.

First-year head coach Jerry Burns knew what kind of talent his youthful team possessed. As Minnesota's long-time offensive coordinator, Burns built the offense around quarterback Tommy Kramer, who responded with the best year of his career. Kramer led the NFC in passing by throwing for 3,000 yards and 24 touchdowns. While Anthony Carter served as the deep threat, resulting in 38 catches for a team-high seven touchdowns, Kramer connected most often with tight end Steve Jordan (58 receptions for 859 yards) and Darrin Nelson (53 catches while rushing for a team-best 793 yards).

The Seasons

A similar renaissance occurred on defense. Safety Joey Browner, who led the team with 139 tackles, received the most attention among an excellent secondary that included Carl Lee and Issiac Holt. Scott Studwell solidified the middle, while Keith Millard became one of the league's fiercest pass rushers from the tackle position.

The Vikings jumped out to a fast start by winning five of their first seven games. Kramer threw three touchdown passes against the Steelers on September 21 before burning the Packers' secondary for six scoring tosses in a 42–7 victory a week later. The quarterback also led the charge against the defending NFL champion Chicago Bears on October 19, with Kramer throwing two long touchdown passes and running for a third score in the 23–7 triumph.

Preseason		
Aug. 9	Miami	W 30–16
Aug. 16	Denver	W 29–27
Aug. 22	@ Seattle	L 17–27
Aug. 30	@ Indianapolis	W 23–20
Regular Season		
Sept. 7	Detroit	L 10–13
Sept. 14	@ Tampa Bay	W 23–10
Sept. 21	Pittsburgh	W 31–7
Sept. 28	Green Bay	W 42–7
Oct. 5	@ Chicago	L 0–23
Oct. 12	@ San Francisco (OT)	W 27–24
Oct. 19	Chicago	W 23–7
Oct. 26	Cleveland	L 20–23
Nov. 2	@ Washington (OT)	L 38–44
Nov. 9	@ Detroit	W 24–10
Nov. 16	New York Giants	L 20–22
Nov. 23	@ Cincinnati	L 20–24
Nov. 30	Tampa Bay	W 45–13
Dec. 7	@ Green Bay	W 32–6
Dec. 14	@ Houston	L 10–23
Dec. 21	New Orleans	W 33–17

Despite the improvement, the fact remained that the Vikings were a young team. That was evident at midseason, when Minnesota lost games to the Browns, Redskins and Giants by surrendering fourth-quarter leads. The team showed its resolve, however, by winning three of its final four contests to finish one game shy of qualifying for the playoffs.

Kramer, Browner and Jordan were rewarded with spots in the Pro Bowl. The acquisitions of former USFL standouts Carter and left tackle Gary Zimmerman cost the Vikings several top draft choices, yet Minnesota still obtained wide receiver Hassan Jones, tight end Carl Hilton and linebacker Jesse Solomon, three players who served as examples of how much stronger the team's depth had become at several key positions.

1987

8–7, Second-NFC Central

Minnesota reached the NFC Championship Game on seven occasions in its first 38 seasons. None was more unexpected than the purple's appearance in the conference's final contest of 1987, a season that is perhaps the most bizarre in the storied history of the National Football League.

Tough Enough To Be Vikings

With Tommy Kramer ailing throughout the season, the Vikings turned to backup quarterback Wade Wilson. The signalcaller overcame three early interceptions to throw three touchdown passes in the season-opening win over Detroit. Wilson also hit Hassan Jones with a 41-yard scoring toss with 30 seconds left a week later versus the Rams to give Minnesota a 2–0 record.

Things turned ugly shortly thereafter. The league's players went on strike, and the owners decided to stage replacement games. The Minnesota management was the final team to hoard new performers, and wound up fielding an awful menagerie that lost all three contests.

The regular players returned in October, and Minnesota resumed its winning ways. Rookie D.J. Dozier helped beat the Broncos by becoming the first Viking to rush for three touchdowns in a game since Chuck Foreman in 1975. The defense then carried the load during November wins over the Raiders and Buccaneers, while Leo Lewis' 72-yard punt return for a touchdown was the key play in the 24–13 win over Atlanta. Yet, after Darrin Nelson's 24-yard scoring run gave Minnesota an overtime win over Dallas, the Vikings ended the regular season by losing thee of their last four.

That did nothing to stall the team's drive in the playoffs. Anthony Carter's 84-yard punt return for a touchdown and Jones' 44-yard touchdown reception at the end of the first half helped the Vikings whip the Saints in the first round. Carter then gained an NFL-record 227 yards on 10 receptions to carry Minnesota to a 36–24 triumph over the 49ers. The Vikings concluded the slate by coming within one play of reaching the Super Bowl before dropping a 17–10 decision to the Redskins in the NFC Championship Game.

The Vikings were well-represented in the post-season honors. Browner, Doleman and left tackle Gary Zimmerman received All-Pro recognition. Those three joined Carter, Steve Jordan and Scott Studwell in the Pro Bowl. The draft added more building blocks in nose tackle Henry Thomas, linebacker Ray Berry, safety Reggie Rutland and running backs Dozier and Rick Fenney.

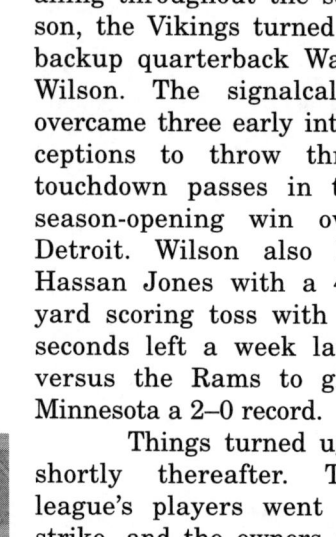

Preseason		
Aug. 15	@ New Orleans	L 17–23
Aug. 22	Indianapolis	W 37–13
Aug. 29	New England	L 27–38
Sept. 3	@ Denver	W 27–17
Regular Season		
Sept. 13	Detroit	W 34–19
Sept. 20	@ L.A. Rams	W 21–16
Oct. 4	Green Bay*	L 16–23
Oct. 11	@ Chicago*	L 7–27
Oct. 18	@ Tampa Bay*	L 10–20
Oct. 26	Denver	W 34–27
Nov. 1	@ Seattle	L 17–28
Nov. 8	L.A. Raiders	W 31–20
Nov. 15	Tampa Bay	W 23–17
Nov. 22	Atlanta	W 24–13
Nov. 26	@ Dallas (OT)	W 44–38
Dec. 6	Chicago	L 24–30
Dec. 13	@ Green Bay (Milwaukee)	L 10–16
Dec. 20	@ Detroit	W 17–14
Dec. 26	Washington (OT)	L 24–27
NFC First-Round Playoffs		
Jan. 3	@ New Orleans	W 44–10
NFC Divisional Playoffs		
Jan. 9	@ San Francisco	W 36–24
NFC Championship Game		
Jan. 17	@ Washington	L 10–17
* replacement games		

1988

11–5, Second–NFC Central

The balance of power in the NFC Central showed signs of changing in 1988. That fact became evident on September 18. The Vikings traveled to Chicago's Soldier Field and, behind three touchdown passes by Tommy Kramer, slaughtered the Bears, 31–7.

Minnesota developed into one of the league's more dominant teams thanks to a defense that featured three players—Joey Browner, Carl Lee and Keith Millard—who garnered All-Pro recognition. The defense scored 46 points on two safeties, five interception returns for touchdowns and two fumble recoveries for touchdowns during the regular season. The unit also grabbed 15 fumbles, picked off 36 passes and sacked opposing quarterbacks 37 times.

The offense, meanwhile, was steady and occasionally spectacular. Quarterback Wade Wilson took over the starting duties from Kramer for the 49–20 win over Tampa Bay on October 23 and wound up leading the NFC for the season in passing with a 91.5 rating and completion percentage of 61.4. Anthony Carter recorded career-highs with 72 receptions and 1,225 yards. Steve Jordan and Hassan Jones scored five touchdowns apiece while pulling in 57 and 40 passes, respectively. The offensive flaw centered on the lack of a running game, with Darrin Nelson leading all Vikings with only 380 rushing yards.

After winning five of their first nine contests, the Vikings rolled to a wild-card berth with a five-game victory string. Beginning with the 43–3 bashing at Dallas on November 13, the Minnesota defense allowed only three field goals during a four-game stretch, including a 24–0 whitewashing of the Lions on Thanksgiving Day for the Vikings' first shutout in more than nine years. Minnesota also capped the regular season by sweeping the first-place Bears with a 28–27 victory at the Metrodome.

Wilson deftly guided the Vikings to a 28–17 win over the Rams in the first round of playoffs by passing for 253 yards, including a game-sealing five-yard touchdown toss to Carl Hilton. But Minnesota's in-

Preseason		
Aug. 7	New Orleans	L 20–23
Aug. 14	Chicago @ Goteborg	W 28–21
Aug. 21	@ Phoenix (OT)	W 19–16
Aug. 26	Miami	W 24–17
Regular Season		
Sept. 4	@ Buffalo	L 10–13
Sept. 11	New England	W 36–6
Sept. 18	@ Chicago	W 31–7
Sept. 25	Philadelphia	W 23–21
Oct. 2	@ Miami	L 7–24
Oct. 9	Tampa Bay	W 14–13
Oct. 16	Green Bay	L 14–34
Oct. 23	@ Tampa Bay	W 49–20
Oct. 30	@ San Francisco	L 21–24
Nov. 6	Detroit	W 44–17
Nov. 13	@ Dallas	W 43–3
Nov. 20	Indianapolis	W 12–3
Nov. 24	@ Detroit	W 23–0
Dec. 4	New Orleans	W 45–3
Dec. 11	@ Green Bay	L 6–18
Dec. 19	Chicago	W 28–27
NFC First-Round Playoffs		
Dec. 26	L.A. Rams	W 28–17
NFC Divisional Playoffs		
Jan. 1	@ San Francisco	L 9–34

Tough Enough To Be Vikings

consistent running game was held to 54 yards a week later in San Francisco's 34–9 triumph.

Tackle Gary Zimmerman joined Browner, Lee and Millard as All-Pro recipients. All four also were named to the Pro Bowl, along with Chris Doleman, Scott Studwell, Carter, Jordan and Wilson. The draft helped solidify the offensive line by acquiring guards Randall McDaniel, Todd Kalis and Brian Habib as well as defensive end Al Noga.

1989
10–6, NFC Central Champions

Never has one trade in the history of the National Football League dominated a team's season more than the deal that brought Herschel Walker from Dallas to Minnesota during the 1989 campaign. The Vikings again fielded one of the best teams on the circuit, and general manager Mike Lynn felt that head coach Jerry Burns' club needed only a dominant running back to make a return trip to the Super Bowl a reality.

The initial returns looked promising. After the Vikings won three of their first five games, Walker arrived in Minnesota just prior to the October 15 matchup with the Packers and proceeded to blister the Green Bay defense for 148 yards on the ground, delighting the 62,075 patrons at the Metrodome. The former Heisman Trophy winner nearly sent the fans into a state of delirium when he galloped 47 yards without one shoe on his first carry from scrimmage. The Vikings won Walker's debut, 26–14, leaving everyone expecting bigger and better things.

That did not prove to be the case, however. While the Vikings went 7–4 after Walker's arrival, the running back did not appear comfortable in the Minnesota backfield and failed to gain 100 yards in any contest for the rest of the season. Rick Fenney even led the ground game on four occasions, and quar-

Preseason		
Aug. 12	Kansas City @ Memphis	W 23–12
Aug. 21	Washington	W 24–13
Aug. 26	@ L.A. Rams	L 14–24
Sept. 1	Cincinnati	W 17–10
Regular Season		
Sept. 10	Houston	W 38–7
Sept. 17	@ Chicago	L 7–38
Sept. 24	@ Pittsburgh	L 14–27
Oct. 1	Tampa Bay	W 17–3
Oct. 8	Detroit	W 24–17
Oct. 15	Green Bay	W 26–14
Oct. 22	@ Detroit	W 20–7
Oct. 30	@ New York Giants	L 14–24
Nov. 5	L.A. Rams	W 23–21
Nov. 12	@ Tampa Bay	W 24–10
Nov. 19	@ Philadelphia	L 9–10
Nov. 26	@ Green Bay (Milwaukee)	L 19–20
Dec. 3	Chicago	W 27–16
Dec. 10	Atlanta	W 43–17
Dec. 17	@ Cleveland (OT)	L 17–23
Dec. 25	Cincinnati	W 29–21
NFC Divisional Playoffs		
Jan. 6	@ San Francisco	L 13–41

terbacks Wade Wilson and Tommy Kramer continued to throw more passes than Lynn had envisioned upon acquiring Walker.

The defense, meanwhile, remained consistent. The line sacked opposing quarterbacks on 71 occasions, just one shy of the NFL record. Chris Doleman led the league by reaching the passer 21 times, while Keith Millard registered 18 sacks and Al Noga had 11.5. The defenders also scored six touchdowns, four on fumble recoveries and two on interception returns.

Despite the firepower on both sides of the ball, the Vikings did not parlay their first division title since 1980 into post-season success. After kicker Rich Karlis, who tied for third in the NFC with 120 points, gave Minnesota a 3–0 lead, Joe Montana threw four first-half touchdown passes in San Francisco's 41–13 playoff victory.

The acquisition of linebacker Mike Merriweather from Pittsburgh cost the Vikings their first-round draft choice. All-Pros Doleman, Millard, safety Joey Browner and guard Randall McDaniel joined cornerback Carl Lee, tight end Steve Jordan and guard Gary Zimmerman in the Pro Bowl.

1990

6–10, Fifth-NFC Central

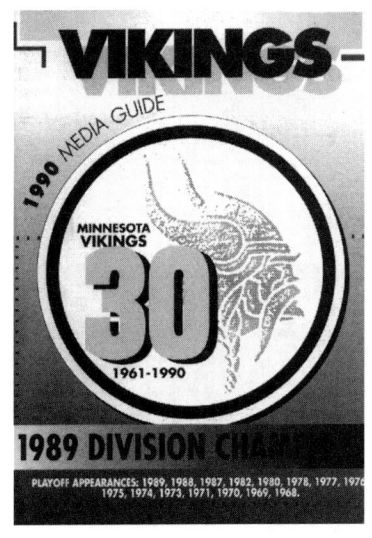

Few things went as expected for Minnesota during the 1990 season. Fresh off three straight successful seasons that included, in order, a trip to the NFC Championship Game, 11 victories, and a Central Division title, the Vikings had visions of the Super Bowl dancing in their heads. Instead, after watching quarterback Wade Wilson and defensive tackle Keith Millard succumb to injuries that adversely affected both the offense and defense, the purple fell to last place with a 6–10 record.

The season began with a thud when the Vikings lost five of their initial six games. Wilson started the first three contests, and threw three touchdown passes on September 16 to lead Minnesota to a 32–3 win over the Saints. But injuries shelved Wilson for 10 games, forcing the Vikings to turn the quarterbacking duties over to the inexperienced Rich Gannon.

After four tough losses, Gannon got the team on the winning track by leading the Vikings to an undefeated November. Minnesota began the string by overcoming a 16–0 deficit to beat the Broncos, 27–22, with the help of a Joey Browner interception return for a touchdown and a 56-yard scoring pass from Gannon to Anthony Carter. Defensive end Al Noga returned a pick 26 yards to paydirt to seal a 17–7 victory over the Lions, kicker Fuad Reveiz booted a 24-yard field goal in a come-from-behind, 24–21 win at Seattle, Gannon threw three touchdown passes in a 41–13 triumph over the Bears, and Noga recovered a fumble in the end zone for the final touchdown in a 23–7 win over the Packers.

Yet, as strong as the Vikings were during that stretch, they could not maintain their momentum during the final four games. Minnesota reverted

Tough Enough To Be Vikings

to its early-season form by dropping all four contests, including four- and three-point defeats to the Raiders and 49ers, respectively, to end the slate.

Despite the disappointing record, several Vikings received recognition for individual performances. Safety Joey Browner, guard Randall McDaniel and defensive end Chris Doleman garnered All-Pro honors. Browner, McDaniel, Doleman, cornerback Carl Lee and tight end Steve Jordan earned trips to the Pro Bowl. The trade for Herschel Walker cost the Vikings their draft choices in the first two rounds, with ninth-rounder Terry Allen the lone pick from 1990 who eventually excelled in purple.

Preseason		
Aug. 11	New Orleans	L 10–13
Aug. 19	@ Cleveland	W 23–20
Aug. 26	Houston	W 22–21
Aug. 31	@ Miami	W 20–17
Regular Season		
Sept. 9	@ Kansas City	L 21–24
Sept. 16	New Orleans	W 32–3
Sept. 23	@ Chicago	L 16–19
Sept. 30	Tampa Bay	L 20–23
Oct. 7	Detroit	L 27–34
Oct. 15	@ Philadelphia	L 24–32
Oct. 28	@ Green Bay (Milwaukee)	L 10–24
Nov. 4	Denver	W 27–22
Nov. 11	@ Detroit	W 17–7
Nov. 18	@ Seattle	W 24–21
Nov. 25	Chicago	W 41–13
Dec. 2	Green Bay	W 23–7
Dec. 9	@ New York Giants	L 15–23
Dec. 16	@ Tampa Bay	L 13–26
Dec. 22	L.A. Raiders	L 24–28
Dec. 30	San Francisco	L 17–20

1991

8–8, Third-NFC Central

For the second consecutive year, the Vikings did not live up to their pre-season expectations. While the defense remained the team's strength, the offense sputtered as often as it purred. The result was an inconsistent showing that led to head coach Jerry Burns' retirement at the end of the campaign.

Quarterback Wade Wilson started the first five games and guided an offense that tried to create a solid balance of running and passing the football. Although there were signs of promise, particularly with Herschel Walker's 125-yard rushing effort in a Week 2 win at Atlanta, the Vikings had trouble putting points on the board. Minnesota did not score more than 20 points in its first five contests, and registered a total of six points in Weeks 4 and 5 during losses to the Saints and Broncos. It was at that point Burns decided to make a change and went with Rich Gannon under center.

Gannon produced a little more offense, with the Vikings averaging 22.9 points in his 11 starts. He passed for more than 200 yards on five occasions, including a season-best 317-yard effort against New England. The signalcaller also led Minnesota to a come-from-behind win at Lambeau Field by throwing a 17-yard touchdown pass to Cris Carter in the third quarter before Walker and Gannon registered five-yard scoring gallops during the fourth quarter of the 35–21 victory.

Despite the 8–8 record, the season provided some solid individual performances. Walker placed fifth in the NFC by rushing for 825 yards and 10 touchdowns. In his first professional season, Terry Allen paced all conference ball carriers by averaging 4.7 yards per rushing attempt. Carter adjusted to the Minnesota attack during his second season with the team and placed fourth in the NFC with 72 receptions for 962 yards and five scores. Harry Newsome topped the loop's punters by averaging 45.5 yards on 68 punts. Guard Randall McDaniel garnered his third straight All-Pro and Pro Bowl honors. He was joined in Hawaii by tight end Steve Jordan and nose tackle Henry Thomas.

The Walker trade cost the Vikings their draft picks in the first two rounds for the second straight year. Nevertheless, Minnesota acquired such future starters as linebacker Carlos Jenkins, wide receiver Jake Reed and safety Todd Scott in the draft.

Preseason		
Aug. 3	@ New Orleans	L 21–24
Aug. 10	Pittsburgh	W 34–24
Aug. 17	@ Cincinnati	L 24–27
Aug. 23	Cleveland	W 31–7
Regular Season		
Sept. 1	@ Chicago	L 6–10
Sept. 8	@ Atlanta	W 20–19
Sept. 15	San Francisco	W 17–14
Sept. 22	@ New Orleans	L 0–26
Sept. 29	Denver	L 6–13
Oct. 6	@ Detroit	L 20–24
Oct. 13	Phoenix	W 34–7
Oct. 20	@ New England	L 23–26
Oct. 27	@ Phoenix	W 28–0
Nov. 3	Tampa Bay	W 28–13
Nov. 11	Chicago	L 17–34
Nov. 17	@ Green Bay	W 35–21
Nov. 24	Detroit	L 14–34
Dec. 8	@ Tampa Bay	W 26–24
Dec. 15	L.A. Rams	W 20–14
Dec. 21	Green Bay	L 7–27

1992

11–5, NFC Central Champions

A new sheriff arrived in the Twin Cities prior to the 1992 season. Following Jerry Burns' retirement, the Vikings hired Dennis Green as the franchise's fifth head coach. A former head coach at Stanford and Northwestern who had served as an assistant with the 49ers, Green made several changes that included the departures of veterans Joey Browner, Keith Millard, Wade Wilson and Herschel Walker. He also instilled a hard-work enthusiasm that produced one of the National Football League's more surprising turnarounds of the 1990s.

Tough Enough To Be Vikings

Preseason		
Aug. 8	Buffalo	W 24–3
Aug. 15	Kansas City	W 30–0
Aug. 24	@ Cleveland	W 56–3
Aug. 29	@ Washington	W 30–0
Regular Season		
Sept. 6	@ Green Bay (OT)	W 23–20
Sept. 13	@ Detroit	L 17–31
Sept. 20	Tampa Bay	W 26–20
Sept. 27	@ Cincinnati	W 42–7
Oct. 4	Chicago	W 21–20
Oct. 15	Detroit	W 31–14
Oct. 25	Washington	L 13–15
Nov. 2	@ Chicago	W 38–10
Nov. 8	@ Tampa Bay	W 35–7
Nov. 15	Houston	L 13–17
Nov. 22	Cleveland	W 17–13
Nov. 29	@ L.A. Rams	W 31–17
Dec. 6	@ Philadelphia	L 17–28
Dec. 13	San Francisco	L 17–20
Dec. 20	@ Pittsburgh	W 6–3
Dec. 27	Green Bay	W 27–7
NFC First-Round Playoffs		
Jan. 2	Washington	L 7–24

The Vikings proved to be a different team from the start. After an impressive preseason that saw the defense allow a total of six points while the offense averaged 35 in four outings, Minnesota opened the regular season at Lambeau Field and beat the Packers in overtime on Fuad Reveiz's 25-yard field goal. Quarterback Rich Gannon threw for 318 yards and four touchdowns in a Week 4 win at Cincinnati. Safety Todd Scott altered the game's momentum a week later by intercepting a Jim Harbaugh pass and returning it 35 yards to paydirt in the Vikings' shocking 21–20 victory over the Bears. Linebacker Jack Del Rio followed suit at Chicago on November 2 by recording the NFC's longest interception return of the season, an 84-yarder for a touchdown in a 38–10 win over the Bears.

After losing three of five games in the second half, the Vikings showed their resiliency by winning a defensive slugfest with the Steelers, 6–3, before trouncing the Packers behind quarterback Sean Salisbury's 292 passing yards. While the season ended on a difficult note, a 24–7 loss to Washington in the first round of the playoffs, the 1992 campaign established the Vikings once again as one of the elite organizations in the NFL.

Running back Terry Allen set a team record and was third in the NFC by rushing for 1,201 yards. Cornerback Audray McMillian tied for the league lead with eight interceptions, including two returns for touchdowns. Harry Newsome topped the conference charts for the second straight season by averaging 45.0 yards on 72 punts. Newsome also recorded the season's longest punt in the NFL, an 84-yarder.

Newsome, McMillian, Scott, Chris Doleman, Randall McDaniel and Gary Zimmerman earned All-Pro recognition. Henry Thomas joined Doleman, McDaniel, McMillian, Scott and Zimmerman in the Pro Bowl. Future Pro Bowler Ed McDaniel headed a productive draft that also included Brad Johnson, Charles Evans, Robert Harris, Roy Barker and Brad Culpepper.

1993

9–7, Second-NFC Central

Dennis Green knew that his head coaching debut in the National Football League resulted in 11 victories despite inconsistent production from the quarterback position. Green and the Minnesota front office tried to remedy the problem with the hope of catching lightning in a bottle. That approach included signing free agent signalcaller Jim McMahon, a proven winner in the NFC Central Division whose primary flaw centered on his inability to stay healthy over the course of a full season.

The Vikings struggled early, splitting their first two games that resulted in Brian Billick's promotion to offensive coordinator following a 10–7 win over the Bears on September 12. Part of the problem centered on McMahon's unfamiliarity with the offense and Minnesota's lack of a running game due to Terry Allen's season-ending injury during training camp and newcomer Barry Word's inability to hang on to the pigskin. Still, the Vikings won four of their first six contests. The most exciting victory came on Fuad Reveiz's game-winning field goal against Green Bay that was set up by Eric Guliford's 45-yard reception with six seconds remaining in the contest.

As many Viking fans feared, McMahon suffered an injury at midseason and missed five starts. While Minnesota lost four of those games, Sean Salisbury did a laudable job in the starter's absence, including a 366-yard performance during a 26–23 come-from-behind win at Denver. Yet, it was not until McMahon's return against Detroit on December 5 and the arrival of a little-known running back named Scottie Graham that the Vikings made a second straight trip to the playoffs a reality. With McMahon making the key passes, Graham bowling over defenders, and the purple defense proving to be one of the league's quickest and most opportunistic, the Vikings won four of their final five games to reach the postseason before dropping a tough decision at New York.

John Randle captured his first All-Pro honors while Randall McDaniel garnered the recognition for the fifth straight season. Randle and McDaniel joined Cris Carter, who tied for fourth in the NFC with 86

Preseason		
Aug. 1	@ Dallas	W 13–7
Aug. 7	Buffalo @ Berlin	W 20–6
Aug. 14	Seattle	W 23–10
Aug. 21	@ Kansas City	L 20–27
Aug. 26	Pittsburgh	W 30–13
Regular Season		
Sept. 5	@ L.A. Raiders	L 7–24
Sept. 12	Chicago	W 10–7
Sept. 26	Green Bay	W 15–13
Oct. 3	@ San Francisco	L 19–38
Oct. 10	Tampa Bay	W 15–0
Oct. 25	@ Chicago	W 19–12
Oct. 31	Detroit	L 27–30
Nov. 7	San Diego	L 17–30
Nov. 14	@ Denver	W 26–23
Nov. 21	@ Tampa Bay	L 10–23
Nov. 28	New Orleans	L 14–17
Dec. 5	@ Detroit	W 13–0
Dec. 12	Dallas	L 20–37
Dec. 19	@ Green Bay (Milwaukee)	W 21–17
Dec. 26	Kansas City	W 30–10
Dec. 31	@ Washington	W 14–9
NFC First-Round Playoff		
Jan. 9	@ New York Giants	L 10–17

Tough Enough To Be Vikings

catches for 1,071 yards and nine touchdowns, and Chris Doleman in the Pro Bowl. Another impressive draft headed by Green produced more building blocks for the future, including running back Robert Smith, wide receiver Qadry Ismail, guard John Gerak and tackle Everett Lindsay.

1994
10–6, NFC Central Champions

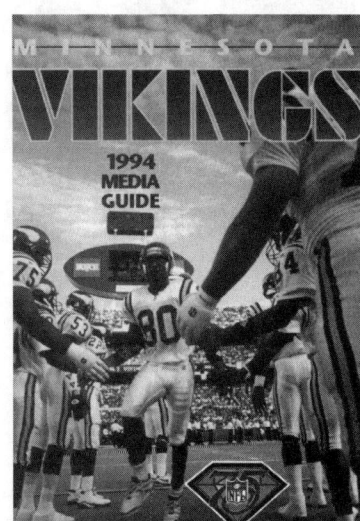

For the second straight season, head coach Dennis Green sought a veteran quarterback who could lead the Vikings deeper in post-season play. Following Jim McMahon's one-year stint in the Twin Cities, Green obtained the services of Warren Moon, who had passed for more yards as a professional than anyone in the history of the game.

Behind Moon's passing ability and Terry Allen's return from his second reconstructive knee surgery, the Vikings got off to a fast start after a season-opening loss at Green Bay. Allen had his best day in purple when he raced 159 yards in a 42–14 win at Chicago. A week later, Moon threw for 326 yards with three touchdown passes to Cris Carter in a win versus Miami. Moon then accumulated at least 271 yards in the air during four of the next five games, including a 420-yard effort against the Saints that featured Qadry Ismail's game-winning 11-yard touchdown catch and run in the game's final seconds.

A mid-season slump began during Week 10, when the Vikings blew a 20–3 halftime lead at New England before losing in overtime. The slide ended on Carter's 65-yard touch-

Preseason		
July 31	@ Dallas	L 9–17
Aug. 7	Kansas City @ Tokyo	W 17–9
Aug. 13	New Orleans	W 21–17
Aug. 20	@ Seattle	L 19–30
Aug. 26	Miami	W 31–16
Regular Season		
Sept. 4	@ Green Bay	L 10–16
Sept. 11	Detroit	W 10–3
Sept. 18	@ Chicago	W 42–14
Sept. 25	Miami	W 38–35
Oct. 2	@ Arizona	L 7–17
Oct. 10	@ New York Giants	W 27–10
Oct. 20	Green Bay (OT)	W 13–10
Oct. 30	@ Tampa Bay	W 36–13
Nov. 6	New Orleans	W 21–20
Nov. 13	@ New England (OT)	L 20–26
Nov. 20	New York Jets	L 21–31
Nov. 27	Tampa Bay (OT)	L 17–20
Dec. 1	Chicago (OT)	W 33–27
Dec. 11	@ Buffalo	W 21–17
Dec. 17	@ Detroit	L 19–41
Dec. 26	San Francisco	W 21–14
NFC First-Round Playoff		
Jan. 1	Chicago	L 18–35

down reception in overtime against the Bears on December 1 and a solid team effort during a 21–17 win at Buffalo on December 11. But while the defense was steady, the offense had trouble scoring in the red zone, a problem that was eased by Fuad Reveiz's conference-high 132 points and league-best 34 field goals. Still, it was not enough to overcome the Bears during the first round of the playoffs.

Moon established the Vikings' single-season record with 371 completions and 4,264 passing yards. Allen provided balance to the Minnesota attack by rushing for 1,031 yards and eight touchdowns. Carter set an NFL record for most catches in a single season by pulling in 122 tosses for 1,256 yards and seven scores. Jake Reed also reached the level Green believed the receiver would by making 85 grabs for 1,175 yards and four touchdowns.

Post-season All-Pro honors were bestowed upon Carter, Reveiz, Randall McDaniel and John Randle. Those four participated in the Pro Bowl along with Moon and middle linebacker Jack Del Rio. For the third straight season, Green orchestrated a strong draft. First-round picks Dewayne Washington and Todd Steussie, who became the first Viking rookies to start 16 games, joined David Palmer, Fernando Smith, Andrew Jordan and Pete Bercich.

1995

8–8, Fourth-NFC Central

The only certainty during the 1995 season was the unusual. The Vikings battled into overtime on four occasions, won one game during regulation on a last-second field goal, beat an AFC power by scoring two defensive touchdowns, and lost a pair of late-season shootouts. In the end, Minnesota missed a fourth straight trip to the playoffs because the football bounced the wrong way on one or two occasions.

The Vikings won their first game of the season in Week 2 when Qadry Ismail caught an 85-yard touchdown pass from Warren Moon that bounced off the head of a Detroit defender. A week later, Minnesota rallied to tie the Cowboys on Cris Carter's eight-yard touchdown grab with 30 seconds remaining in the game before losing on

Preseason		
Aug. 7	@ San Diego	W 23–19
Aug. 12	@ New England	L 14–21
Aug. 18	Oakland	W 20–17
Aug. 26	Kansas City	L 13–17
Regular Season		
Sept. 3	@ Chicago	L 14–31
Sept. 10	Detroit	W 20–10
Sept. 17	Dallas (OT)	L 17–23
Sept. 24	@ Pittsburgh	W 44–24
Oct. 8	Houston (OT)	W 23–17
Oct. 15	@ Tampa Bay (OT)	L 17–20
Oct. 22	@ Green Bay	L 21–38
Oct. 30	Chicago	L 6–14
Nov. 5	Green Bay	W 27–24
Nov. 12	@ Arizona (OT)	W 30–24
Nov. 19	New Orleans	W 43–24
Nov. 23	@ Detroit	L 38–44
Dec. 3	Tampa Bay	W 31–17
Dec. 9	Cleveland	W 27–11
Dec. 18	@ San Francisco	L 30–37
Dec. 24	@ Cincinnati	L 24–27

the first series of overtime. The team rebounded by intercepting six passes and recovering two Steeler fumbles in a 44–24 victory at Pittsburgh. After splitting overtime games in their next two contests prior to dropping back-to-back outings with the Packers and Bears, the Vikings gained revenge against Green Bay when linebacker Jeff Brady made a late interception to set up Fuad Reveiz's game-winning field goal from 39 yards out as time expired.

While the Minnesota defense struggled due to the loss of free agent Henry Thomas and a mid-season injury suffered by Jack Del Rio, the offense flourished behind Moon, who was as effective in the second half of the regular season as any quarterback in Viking lore. Not once did Minnesota score fewer than 24 points during its last eight games. Unfortunately, the purple defense allowed fewer than 24 points on just two occasions down the stretch. The Vikings finished 5–3 to end the slate one game out of the playoffs.

Moon set team records with 377 completions and 33 touchdown passes. Carter tied his franchise mark with 122 receptions and a team-record and league-high 17 touchdowns. Rookie Orlando Thomas paced the league with nine interceptions, including a 45-yard touchdown return against Pittsburgh. David Palmer topped the league charts by averaging 13.2 yards on 26 punt returns, among them a 74-yard touchdown gallop against Detroit on Thanksgiving Day.

Randall McDaniel and John Randle were unanimous All-Pro recipients. McDaniel and Randle played in the Pro Bowl along with Moon and Carter. The draft produced another bounty with Thomas, Derrick Alexander, Korey Stringer, Corey Fuller and Jason Fisk.

1996

9–7, Second–NFC Central

Change, though unexpected, highlighted Minnesota's 1996 season. The quarterbacking baton was passed during the first regular-season game when Warren Moon succumbed to a leg injury that would plague him throughout the campaign. Brad Johnson came off the pines and guided the Vikings back to the playoffs by inserting determination and leadership into the Minnesota offense.

Johnson displayed little rust from his lack of activity during his first four professional seasons by hitting Cris Carter with a game-winning, 31-yard touchdown pass with 1:06 remaining in the season-opening 17–13 victory over Detroit. He then guided the Vikings to a 23–17 win versus Atlanta in his first start. Moon returned in Week 3 and helped improve Minnesota's record to 4–0, topped by a 30–21 triumph over Green Bay. During that game, Robert Smith raced 37 yards to paydirt for the deciding score and John Randle buried Brett Favre on four occasions for sacks.

Moon's success was limited for the rest of the season. Immobile in the pocket and constantly throwing off his back foot due to his lingering injury, Moon experienced inconsistency while the Vikings lost three of their next four games. Johnson started a 21–6 loss to Kansas City before Moon had one of his worst days as a Viking during a 42–23 defeat at Seattle. Johnson started the rest of the way, and was helped by the arrival of Leroy Hoard, beginning with the 16–13 overtime win at Oakland. While Johnson sliced the Raiders' defense for 275 yards, including an 82-yard touchdown pass to Jake Reed, Hoard rushed for 108 yards in place of the injured Smith.

Johnson tossed for at least 195 yards in each of his last six regular-season starts and threw 12 touchdown passes. Hoard also did his part by averaging 70 yards during his six appearances, including two 100-yard efforts as well as two touchdown runs during a 21–10 win over Tampa Bay.

Johnson finished third in the NFC in passing with 195 completions for 2,258 yards and 17 touchdowns. Carter placed fourth in the conference with 96 catches for 1,163 yards and 10 touchdowns. Randle, Carter and Randall McDaniel received All-Pro recognition and represented Minnesota in the Pro Bowl. The Vikings received solid production from Duane Clemons, Moe Williams and Hunter Goodwin in a limited draft.

Preseason		
Aug. 3	San Diego (OT)	W 23–20
Aug. 8	Buffalo	L 12–35
Aug. 19	@ Miami	L 17–24
Aug. 23	@ New Orleans	L 13–16
Regular Season		
Sept. 1	Detroit	W 17–13
Sept. 8	@ Atlanta	W 23–17
Sept. 15	@ Chicago	W 20–14
Sept. 22	Green Bay	W 30–21
Sept. 29	@ New York Giants	L 10–15
Oct. 6	Carolina	W 14–12
Oct. 13	@ Tampa Bay	L 13–24
Oct. 28	Chicago	L 13–15
Nov. 3	Kansas City	L 6–21
Nov. 10	@ Seattle	L 23–42
Nov. 17	@ Oakland (OT)	W 16–13
Nov. 24	Denver	L 17–21
Dec. 1	Arizona	W 41–17
Dec. 8	@ Detroit	W 24–22
Dec. 15	Tampa Bay	W 21–10
Dec. 22	@ Green Bay	L 10–38
NFC First-Round Playoff		
Dec. 28	@ Dallas	L 15–40

1997

9–7, Fourth–NFC Central

The Vikings served notice in 1997 that they should be considered a serious contender to win the Super Bowl. Minnesota jumped out to an 8–2 record behind the continuing emergence of a deep, young core of offensive players that included quarterback Brad Johnson and running back Robert Smith and an opportunistic defense that was much better than the statistics indicated.

Smith rushed for 169 yards in a season-opening 34–13 win at Buffalo before Johnson hit Chris Walsh on a nine-yard game-winning touchdown

Tough Enough To Be Vikings

Preseason		
July 26	Seattle @ Canton	W 28–26
Aug. 2	St. Louis	W 24–6
Aug. 8	@ Buffalo	L 3–19
Aug. 16	@ Cincinnati	L 13–37
Aug. 22	San Diego	W 28–22
Regular Season		
Aug. 31	@ Buffalo	W 34–13
Sept. 7	@ Chicago	W 27–24
Sept. 14	Tampa Bay	L 14–28
Sept. 21	@ Green Bay	L 32–38
Sept 28	Philadelphia	W 28–19
Oct. 5	@ Arizona	W 20–19
Oct. 12	Carolina	W 21–14
Oct. 26	@ Tampa Bay	W 10–6
Nov. 2	New England	W 23–18
Nov. 9	Chicago	W 29–22
Nov. 16	@ Detroit	L 15–38
Nov. 23	@ New York Jets	L 21–23
Dec. 1	Green Bay	L 11–27
Dec. 7	@ San Francisco	L 17–28
Dec. 14	Detroit	L 13–14
Dec. 21	Indianapolis	W 39–28
NFC First-Round Playoffs		
Dec. 27	@ New York Giants	W 23–22
NFC Divisional Playoffs		
Jan. 3	@ San Francisco	L 22–38

pass to beat the Bears, 27–24. After back-to-back losses to the Buccaneers and Packers, the Vikings reeled off six straight wins. Eddie Murray's 38-yard field goal in the final seconds gave Minnesota a 20–19 triumph over Arizona, while Leroy Hoard's one-run touchdown run with 54 seconds left was the difference in a 29–22 win versus Chicago.

But just as a Central Division title appeared imminent, disaster struck over a three-week period. The Lions trounced the Vikings by piling up 477 yards against the Minnesota defense. A week later, center Jeff Christy broke his leg in the waning seconds of a loss to the Jets. Then, against the Packers on Monday night, Johnson was unable to grip the football. He required neck surgery and was lost for the season, replaced by backup Randall Cunningham.

Despite his lack of experience in the offense, Cunningham guided the Vikings to the playoffs with a 39–28 victory over Indianapolis. Minnesota also captured its first playoff win under head coach Dennis Green in dramatic fashion. Trailing 22–13 with less than two minutes to play, Cunningham hit Jake Reed in the back of the end zone with a 30-yard touchdown pass before Murray booted the game-winning field goal from 24 yards out for the triumph. The magic ran out a week later against San Francisco, yet the stage was set for more success in the immediate future.

All-Pro honors were presented to Randall McDaniel, John Randle, Cris Carter, David Palmer and Todd Steussie. Carter, McDaniel, Randle and Steussie were named Pro Bowl starters. The Vikings also benefited from one of the deepest drafts in team annals. Four defensive players—Dwayne Rudd, Torrian Gray, Stalin Colinet and Tony Williams—earned starting assignments by the end of their rookie season. Receivers Matthew Hatchette and Robert Tate also proved to be keepers.

1998

15–1, NFC Central Champions

The NFC's balance of power shifted during the 1998 campaign. After showing signs of dominance the previous year, the Vikings left no doubt throughout the regular season that the road to the Super Bowl went through the Metrodome.

Minnesota established itself early as the leader of the Central Division. In the season opener against Tampa Bay, the Vikings made mince-meat of the lauded Buccaneer defense with a 31–7 win that included a pair of touchdown receptions by first-round draft pick Randy Moss. After quarterback Brad Johnson broke his fibula in Week 2, Randall Cunningham filled in without missing a beat and guided the Vikings to a 4–0 start, setting the stage for a Monday night contest at Green Bay.

Against the Packers, Cunningham and Moss put on an aerial show unlike any ever seen at Lambeau Field. Cunningham burned the Green Bay defense for 442 yards passing, with Moss catching five tosses for 190 yards and two touchdowns. Minnesota then proved this team was unlike most by refusing to experience a letdown in back-to-back victories over the Redskins and Lions.

The Buccaneers recorded what proved to be the lone regular-season loss for the Vikings with a hard-fought win at Tampa Bay. Minnesota again showed its resolve a week later, even when Cunningham was lost with a knee injury. Johnson returned and, despite breaking his thumb early in the second half, guided the Vikings to a 31–24 win over New Orleans. Cunningham was back a week later and led the purple to eight straight wins to finish the regular season at 15–1.

Minnesota continued to play well in the playoffs. Leroy Hoard scored three touchdowns in a 41–21 win over the Cardinals. The Vikings then met the Falcons in the NFC Championship Game and battled in one of the toughest, most competitive games in league history. While Atlanta emerged with the overtime win, Minnesota made its point that the NFL's immediate future included a lot of purple.

Preseason		
Aug. 9	@ New England	W 28–0
Aug. 15	Kansas City	W 34–0
Aug. 22	@ Carolina	W 25–22
Aug. 28	San Diego	W 42–28
Regular Season		
Sept. 6	Tampa Bay	W 31–7
Sept. 13	@ St. Louis	W 38–31
Sept. 20	Detroit	W 29–6
Sept. 27	@ Chicago	W 31–28
Oct. 5	@ Green Bay	W 37–24
Oct. 18	Washington	W 41–7
Oct. 25	@ Detroit	W 34–13
Nov. 1	@ Tampa Bay	L 24–27
Nov. 8	New Orleans	W 31–24
Nov. 15	Cincinnati	W 24–3
Nov. 22	Green Bay	W 28–14
Nov. 26	@ Dallas	W 46–36
Dec. 6	Chicago	W 48–22
Dec. 13	@ Baltimore	W 38–28
Dec. 20	Jacksonville	W 50–10
Dec. 26	@ Tennessee	W 26–16
NFC First-Round Playoffs		
Jan. 10	Arizona	W 41–21
NFC Championship Game		
Jan. 17	Atlanta (OT)	L 27–30

Tough Enough To Be Vikings

Nine Vikings were named All-Pros, including Cunningham, Moss, Randall McDaniel, John Randle, Jeff Christy, Gary Anderson, Robert Griffith, Todd Steussie and Dwayne Rudd. McDaniel, Randle, Christy, Anderson, Cunningham and Steussie were joined in the Pro Bowl by Cris Carter and Ed McDaniel. In addition to Moss, the crop of draft choices again revealed Green's ability to recognize talent, with the Vikings acquiring Kailee Wong, Ramos McDonald, Kivuusama Mays, Matt Birk and Tony Darden.

TWO

◆ ◆ ◆

THE PLAYERS

Bobby Abrams

Seasons: 1993–94   Linebacker   Height: 6'3"
Numbers: 50   Michigan   Weight: 230

While Bobby Abrams earned his keep with Minnesota on special teams, his biggest single contribution occurred on defense, against Green Bay on December 19, 1993.

The Vikings held a 21–17 lead in the game's waning moments, but found themselves backed against the goal line during one final battle with the Packers on the cold afternoon at Milwaukee's County Stadium. Owning a first down at the Minnesota 2-yard line, the hosts placed the football in the hands of running back Darrell Thompson, only to have Abrams slice through the offensive line and cut Thompson down in the backfield for a five-yard loss. Thwarted, Green Bay failed to enter the end zone on the next three plays, leading to a Minnesota victory that helped the Vikings continue a torrid late-season run and reach the playoffs.

Abrams was signed on December 7, 1993, after being released by Dallas, and played the final four games of the season in purple. He then spent the entire 1994 campaign with Minnesota, establishing a team-record 28 hits on special teams. Abrams filled his lane on kick returns with aplomb and possessed a knack for directing his path toward the ballcarrier. He left the Vikings by signing as a free agent with New England for the 1995 season.

Steve Ache

Season: 1987   Linebacker   Height: 6'3"
Number: 53   Southwest Missouri State   Weight: 229

Steve Ache's career in the National Football League consisted of three games with the Vikings as a replacement player in 1987.

Scott Adams

Seasons: 1991–93   Offensive Lineman   Height: 6'5"
Number: 72   Georgia   Weight: 293

Size and hustle enabled Scott Adams to get the most from his ability and piece together a respectable career in the National Football League. A member of the Vikings' practice squad for the first 15 games of the 1991 slate, Adams played in all but one contest in 1992, seeing action with the kickoff return and field goal protection units on special teams while serving as a reserve left tackle.

Moved into the starting lineup at right guard against Chicago in the second game of the 1993 season, Adams handled the first-string duties through Week 10 before giving way to Todd Kalis and resuming a backup role, at left tackle and right guard, for the remainder of the slate. He was released the following year in training camp and later played for the Saints, Bears and Buccaneers.

Tom Adams

Season: 1962 — End — Height: 6'4"
Number: 85 — Minnesota-Duluth — Weight: 215

A huge target who hailed from Keewatin, Minnesota, Tom Adams caught three passes in six games during the 1962 campaign, his only season in the National Football League. Adams averaged 17 yards per reception, with his longest grab covering 32 yards.

Tony Adams

Season: 1987 — Quarterback — Height: 6'
Number: 7 — Utah State — Weight: 198

Nine years after last serving as Kansas City's backup signalcaller and three years since toiling for Toronto in the Canadian Football League, Tony Adams quarterbacked Minnesota during the three replacement contests in 1987. Leading a disoriented menagerie while under constant pressure due to a makeshift line, Adams provided a yeoman's effort by completing 49 of 89 attempts for 607 yards and three touchdowns. He also hurled six interceptions, which helped limit the Vikings to 33 points in the three losses.

John Adickes

Season: 1989 — Center — Height: 6'3"
Number: 68 — Baylor — Weight: 264

A two-year veteran with Chicago, John Adickes signed with the Vikings during the 1989 season and saw action in one game. It proved to be the last appearance of his 23-game NFL career.

Grady Alderman

Seasons: 1961–74 — Tackle — Height: 6'2"
Number: 67 — Detroit — Weight: 245

When Norm Van Brocklin received his first look at the 36 players awarded the Vikings from the 1961 expansion draft, the Minnesota head coach responded in his typical blunt manner. "They gave me 36 stiffs for a football team," said the Dutchman.

Van Brocklin may not have been too far from the truth. One player, however, stood above the crowd. Grady Alderman, an offensive tackle who was pulled from the veterans pool after one season with the Lions, remained with Minnesota for the franchise's first 14 years, the longest tenure of any "original" Viking.

Perhaps the weakest link on the Vikings in the early years was the offensive line. It is for that reason quarterback Fran Tarkenton became a real-life Clark Kent and turned into "The Scrambler," his goal to salvage anything from plays while his linemen felt the brunt of salivating, charging defenders. Alderman's stellar performance gave Tarkenton an extra few moments to make something from nothing, although the tackle admitted Tarkenton had little choice but to run for his life in the backfield, even if it meant eventual exhaustion for everyone involved.

"Blocking for Tarkenton is like trying to stand still in the school hall when somebody rings the recess bell," Alderman once said.

A certified public accountant during the offseason, Alderman moved to tackle with the Vikings after playing guard with Detroit. In fact, the Lions' 10th-round draft pick beat out four veterans to earn a spot on the roster as a rookie in 1960. With Minnesota, he developed into a disciplined, durable starter who played in five Pro Bowls, including starting assignments in 1963

Grady Alderman

and 1966. He also was named the 1965 winner of the Terry Dillon Award, given annually to the Viking player who displays meritorious play and character.

No one received higher blocking grades along the line than Alderman. His top weight of 245 pounds led some opposing linemen to believe they could overpower the tackle. Yet Alderman was so adept at sticking with his man and maintaining his hits that he became a premier blocker, particularly in passing situations. Once a defender would break free from Alderman, he usually discovered it was an instant too late to do any damage.

No player saw the team's transition from an expansion franchise in 1961 to NFL champions eight years later better than Alderman. By 1965, he was the last player selected from the veterans pool remaining on the Viking roster. Through it all, he provided the performance and leadership needed to turn a cast of misfits into perennial powers.

"In the early '60s, when we were just getting started, many of our plays were geared to the personnel," Alderman observed late in the 1969 campaign. "We didn't have much confidence in ourselves. Even if we were ahead by two touchdowns, we went for the bomb because we didn't know if the defense could hold. Now we feel we can win every game. We know the defense will do its job."

Alderman maintained his starting job throughout his days in Minnesota and consistently performed his duties as well as anyone across the offensive front. His efforts were rewarded with respect from his teammates and coaches, who named Alderman the Vikings' offensive captain during his final eight years with the club.

His career came to a close following the 1974 season, but not before he displayed more heart and desire than anyone thought possible. Without any teammate's knowledge, Alderman performed admirably throughout the 1973 slate despite undergoing treatment for a cancerous growth in his lower body. He had the tumor surgically removed after the season, with his closest friends amazed at his resiliency and desire.

Named to the Vikings' Silver Anniversary All-Time Team, Alderman served as a color commentator for Minnesota's radio broadcasts for four years shortly after retiring as a player and worked two years as the club's director of planning and development, a job that included overseeing the construction of the Winter Park office and training complex. He then spent 1981 and 1982 as general manager of the Denver Broncos before opening his own accounting firm in Colorado.

Keith Alex

Season: 1995
Number: 63
Guard
Texas A&M
Height: 6'4"
Weight: 307

A former Falcon who had played for Keith Rowen, Minnesota's offensive line coach from 1994–96, in Atlanta, Keith Alex was active for two games with the Vikings in 1995 but never took the field. Alex was a solid run-blocker who struggled in pass protection, leading to his release during the 1996 training camp.

Derrick Alexander

Seasons: 1995–98
Number: 90
Defensive Lineman
Florida State
Height: 6'4"
Weight: 286

No one needs to remind Derrick Alexander that two primary keys to success in the National Football League are experience and good health. Alexander discovered those axioms during his four years with the Vikings. While he emerged as a steady contributor at right defensive end and occasionally in the middle of the front wall, the first-round pick from the 1995 draft battled a handful of setbacks to attain his stability.

Alexander registered a mediocre rookie campaign that was caused in part by his holdout during training camp. He earned a starting job by Week 5 and held it for the rest of the season, recording 26 solo tackles and two sacks, both of which produced fumbles. Injuries to his knee and hip cost him four games in 1996, yet the right defensive end began to show signs as a big-play performer. He led the front four with seven tackles for a loss while making 59 stops overall. His biggest game came against Chicago on September 15, when Alexander forced two fumbles and blocked his first kick—a field goal attempt that helped salvage the Vikings' 20–14 victory at Soldier Field.

Alexander's production continue to increase in 1997 despite suffering with an ankle injury. In 14 games, he recorded 66 tackles and 4.5 sacks in addition to three forced fumbles, tops on the team. An increase in size and strength for the 1998 campaign led to even more success. Healthy for the first time in purple, Alexander placed second on the team in sacks with a career-high 7.5 while registering 40 tackles.

John Randle created havoc with opposing offensive lines in 1998 by lining up at every one of the four positions across the defensive front. He was able to do that because Alexander could shift inside and stuff the run in addition to sending fear through the hearts of quarterbacks throughout the league from his right end position. That ability and his subsequent production quieted any critics who had wondered if the Florida State product was worthy of being the 11th overall selection in the 1995 draft.

"Derrick plays well inside," said head coach Dennis Green. "He can play left end, under tackle and right end. He's played all three positions during games. That requires, first of all, a player who is really smart, but also one who is real flexible."

Tuineau Alipate

Season: 1995 Linebacker Height: 6'2"
Number: 53 Washington State Weight: 239

An journeyman in the National Football League and former Canadian Football League player, Tuineau Alipate contributed to the Vikings' improved coverage on special teams in 1995. He finished tied for third on the club with 15 special teams tackles, and registered a pair of hits against Pittsburgh and New Orleans in limited opportunities on defense. Alipate was among the final cuts during training camp a year later when rookie free agent Ben Hanks was deemed to have greater upside potential.

Nate Allen

Seasons: 1976–79 Defensive Back Height: 5'11"
Number: 25 Texas Southern Weight: 175

Nate Allen must believe in first impressions.

The defensive back joined the Vikings from the 49ers during the 1976 training camp in exchange for a sixth-round draft choice and immediately contributed to Minnesota's winning ways. With Bobby Bryant out of action due to a broken arm, the energetic and gregarious Allen took over the starting duties at right cornerback and started the first 11 regular-season games before twisting an ankle against Green Bay on November 21. During that period, Allen intercepted three passes, caused two fumbles, returned a blocked punt for a touchdown, and made 66 tackles.

Self-dubbed "The Trashman" for his propensity for picking up loose footballs, Allen also was one of the primary reasons the Vikings became the most adept team in the National Football League at blocking kicks. A superb special teams player who bolted toward kickers from the end of the line, he altered the flight of two field goals and one extra-point attempt in 1976, with both three-point blocks coming against the Rams.

The first blocked field goal salvaged a 10–10 overtime tie in the season's second week, on September 19 at Metropolitan Stadium. Earlier in the game, during the first quarter, Allen had shown his defensive prowess by stacking up John Cappelletti on fourth down at the one to keep the Rams off the scoreboard.

The second Allen swat versus Los Angeles took place in the NFC Championship Game on December 26 and changed the contest's momentum. Rams head coach Chuck Knox so feared the Minnesota defense that he opted to go with the "sure" three points, even though Los Angeles was only inches from the goal line. Allen burst through the protection from the right end of the line and blocked Tom Dempsey's kick. Bryant picked up the pigskin and raced 90 yards to paydirt in the Vikes' 24–13 triumph.

Allen's heroics in the first game against the Rams proved to be the beginning of the best month in the defensive back's career. He deflected Errol Mann's extra-point attempt after holder Joe Reed bobbled the ball to produce a 10–9 Vikings victory on September 26 at Detroit. A week later, on October 4, he had his biggest game in purple during the 17–6 win over the Steelers, with Allen intercepting two passes and recovering a fumble on a punt attempt in front of a national television audience on *Monday Night Football*. He then caught Steve Craig's blocked punt in midair and raced 28 yards for a touchdown in a 24–7 triumph over the Giants on October 17.

Even with Bryant reclaiming his starting job in late November, Allen continued to be a valuable backup cornerback and special teams player for the Vikings in 1977 and 1978. He saw action in every contest during those two years, providing excellent zone coverage in nickel and dime situations while remaining one of the club's best special teams players. His biggest play during those two seasons again came against the Rams. Allen intercepted a Pat Haden pass in the back of the end zone to halt a Los Angeles drive in what proved to be a 14–7 Minnesota victory on December 26.

Allen played the first five contests of the 1979 campaign for Minnesota and intercepted one pass before finishing the season as well as his NFL career with Detroit.

Terry Allen

Seasons: 1990–94   Running Back   Height: 5'10"
Number: 21   Clemson   Weight: 197

Two severe knee injuries created an on-and-off relationship with Terry Allen and the Vikings during the first half of the 1990s. Yet when Allen was on, the Purple Gang had its best all-around running back since Chuck Foreman was in his prime in the 1970s.

The relationship started slowly. Allen missed his rookie season because the ninth-round draft choice in 1990 underwent surgery to repair an injury he suffered in training camp after originally hurting the knee as a senior at Clemson. A strenuous rehabilitation effort enabled Allen to debut on the playing field for 15 games in 1991, gaining 563 yards on 120 carries. He earned the starting nod in six contests and blossomed as the season progressed. Allen was named NFC Offensive Player of the Week after rushing for 127 yards on 14 attempts with two touchdowns, including a 55-yard gallop,

Terry Allen

during a 28–13 victory over Tampa Bay on November 3. He also had the only touchdown reception by a Viking running back that season when he made an over-the-shoulder catch for a nine-yard tally against Green Bay on December 21.

Allen put that experience and his budding talents to greater use under new head coach Dennis Green in 1992 by becoming only the third player in team history to break the 1,000-yard rushing barrier in a single season. He galloped for a Viking single-season record 1,201 yards and tied Foreman's twice-earned mark with 13 rushing touchdowns.

He made Green's debut a successful one with a 51-yard scamper to set up a go-ahead touchdown, then had a 45-yard run in overtime to put the Vikings in position for the game-winning field goal. By the end of the 23–20 win over Green Bay, Allen had gained 140 yards on 12 carries. Three times he reached the end zone during a 42–7 win over Cincinnati on September 27 and a 31–17 triumph against the Rams on November 29. Always a capable receiver out of the backfield, Allen also was second on the team with 49 catches for 478 yards, giving him 1,679 yards of total offense, good for second in the NFC.

But just as it looked as if Allen would climb into the elite class of running backs, disaster struck a second time. Allen attempted to cut upfield during drills in the early stages of the 1993 training camp. Even though there was no contact on the play, he ruptured the anterior cruciate ligament in his left knee, forcing Allen to miss all of the ensuing season. When he returned to the gridiron a year later, Allen was believed to be the first NFL player ever to play after undergoing reconstructive surgery on both knees.

The scars did nothing to slow Allen, however. After gaining a combined 74 yards on 23 carries in his first two games, against Green Bay and Detroit, the running back proved he was good as new with a 159-yard, two-touchdown performance during a 42–14 victory over the Bears on September 18. He went on to eclipse the 100-yard barrier in a 38–35 win against the Dolphins on September 25 as well as during a 36–13 triumph against the Buccaneers on October 30. He concluded the 1994 season with 1,031 yards and eight touchdowns on 255 attempts.

His success notwithstanding, Allen and the Vikings parted ways after the 1994 slate when the realities of the salary cap came into play. With Allen's health history and 1993 first-round draft choice Robert Smith deemed ready to take over the rushing load, Allen was released. He signed with Washington, where he spent four productive seasons.

Allen's departure did not diminish his contributions. Seven times he rushed for at least 100 yards in a game and seven times the Vikings won the contest. His 172 rushing yards against Pittsburgh on December 20, 1992, rank as the third-best total in Minnesota history, while his 33 carries in that contest are tied for first. Allen also averaged 4.4 yards per carry, proving he was one of the more effective runners in team annals.

Alfred Anderson

Seasons: 1984–91
Number: 46
Running Back
Baylor
Height: 6'1"
Weight: 226

It would be difficult to find a more community-minded player than Alfred Anderson. In his eight seasons with the Vikings, the running back worked with such organizations as the Make-A-Wish Foundation and Special Olympics while making numerous appearances with the Vikings' charity basketball team. His efforts typically targeted children, for Anderson believed a professional athlete could make a difference as a role model.

Anderson's abilities on the field also helped the Vikings win games, particularly during the early stages of his professional career. Minnesota's third-round pick and the fourth running back selected overall in the 1984 draft, the Baylor graduate was one of the few bright spots during his rookie season. Anderson led the team as well as all NFC first-year players with 201 carries for 773 yards to earn consensus all-rookie honors. He enjoyed what proved to be his career-best day that year, gaining 120 yards on 19 rushes against Detroit on September 23. Two weeks earlier, against Philadelphia, Anderson threw a 20-yard touchdown pass and galloped for 105 yards on 20 attempts. He wound up throwing seven halfback-option passes in 1984, completing three, with two going for touchdowns. He also found time to return 30 kickoffs for 639 yards, a 21.3-yard norm.

After a handful of injuries limited Anderson to 50 carries and 121 yards in 1985, he placed second to Darrin Nelson on the Vikings in rushing yards the next two years, gaining 347 and 319 yards in 1986 and 1987, respectively. Anderson then showed flashes of filling his rookie role as more of an all-purpose back in 1988, when he led the club with eight touchdowns. In addition to gaining 300 yards on 87 carries for seven scores, he grabbed a career-high 23 tosses for another 242 yards and one tally. Anderson caught 20 more passes for 193 yards and gained 189 yards on 52 carries in 1989, despite missing five games with an injured foot.

A knee injury forced Anderson to miss the first five games in 1990, yet he still managed to gain 207 yards on the ground and another 80 yards on 13 pass receptions. In 1991, he served as a fullback and short-yardage specialist in Jerry Burns' final year as head coach, gaining 118 yards on 26 carries. Anderson also emerged as a key special teams player, tying for third on the team with 17 tackles.

Anderson's career with the Vikings came to end in 1992 when he was among the roster changes made by new head coach Dennis Green. At the time of his release, Anderson ranked among the Vikings' top ten in four career categories, among them rushing touchdowns (sixth with 22), rushing attempts (seventh, 626), rushing yards (eighth, 2,374) and combined attempts (eighth, 782).

Gary Anderson

Season: 1998   Kicker   Height: 5'11"
Number: 1   Syracuse   Weight: 178

Minnesota's most unheralded yet most important move prior to the 1998 slate was the signing of free-agent kicker Gary Anderson. The Vikings had struggled with consistency from their field-goal kickers since Fuad Reveiz was forced to retire with a foot injury prior to the 1996 season. Anderson solved the problem by making every field-goal and extra-point attempt during the regular season, becoming the only kicker in the history of the National Football League to record a perfect campaign.

Anderson signed with the Vikings after spending one year with San Francisco, two in Philadelphia and 13 with Pittsburgh. His desire to wear purple centered on ending his career kicking in a controlled climate like the Metrodome's. Despite never experiencing such comforts on a home-field basis, Anderson put together a Hall of Fame career. During the second game of the 1998 season, he moved past Jan Stenerud and Nick Lowery into first place on the all-time NFL list for field goals and into second place in points. The South Africa native attained his lofty accomplishment with the help of five field goals and a pair of PATs against Detroit in Minnesota's 29–6 victory on Sep-

Gary Anderson

tember 20. He concluded the regular season with 420 field goals and 1,845 points.

The league's oldest non-quarterback in 1998, the 39-year-old Anderson connected on all 35 field-goal attempts to break Reveiz's NFL record with 40 straight field goals. By also succeeding on all 59 extra-point tries, Anderson finished the season with 164 points, tops in the league. He connected on both field-goal attempts in the playoff contest against Arizona as well as his first two tries versus Atlanta before barely missing a 38-yard effort in the fourth quarter in what proved to be his final attempt of the season.

Scott Anderson

Seasons: 1974, 1976 — Center — Height: 6'5"
Number: 56 — Missouri — Weight: 256

Scott Anderson, who lettered at every offensive line position at Missouri before becoming Minnesota's third-round draft pick in 1974, served as a reserve center during his short career in purple. After becoming the Vikings' version of the Maytag Man behind the durable Mick Tingelhoff in 1974, Anderson sat out the 1975 campaign and added 15 pounds of muscle during an extensive weight-lifting program. He returned in 1976 and played in two games before suffering a knee injury that landed him on the injured reserve list in October. He did not play for the Vikings again.

Sam Anno

Seasons: 1987–88 — Linebacker — Height: 6'2"
Number: 53 — Southern Cal — Weight: 230

In 1987, Sam Anno served as the Vikings' long snapper on punts for the final six regular-season games and all three playoff contests after signing as a free agent on November 18. He not only centered the ball to punters Greg Coleman and Bucky Scribner, but hustled downfield to make nine special teams tackles in the regular season, with another two solo hits and one assist in the postseason.

After being released at the end of training camp and re-signed less than three weeks later in 1988, Anno served the same role by registering 14 special teams tackles and causing one fumble in 13 contests. He signed with Tampa Bay as an unrestricted free agent in 1989.

Hasson Arbubakrr

Season: 1984 — Defensive End — Height: 6'4"
Number: 69 — Texas Tech — Weight: 250

Tampa Bay's ninth-round pick in 1983, Hasson Arbubakrr signed with Minnesota on November 23, 1984, with four games remaining on the slate. The part-time kickboxer played defensive end as well as on special teams and recorded 11 tackles. His highlights included a three-yard sack against Washington and two tackles with three assists in the season finale versus Green Bay.

Chuck Arrobio

Season: 1966 — Tackle — Height: 6'4"
Number: 79 — Southern Cal — Weight: 250

Both the National Football League and American Football League decided to pass on Chuck Arrobio in their 1966 drafts after the offensive lineman informed every team that he planned to attend dental school. He changed his mind and signed as a free agent with the Vikings, only to alter his decision again and return home to California during training camp. Yet another decision reversal along with head coach Norm Van Brocklin's acceptance allowed Arrobio to return shortly thereafter and make the Minnesota roster when veteran Archie Sutton succumbed to an injury.

Arrobio saw action in 11 games with the Vikings. The majority of his playing time at tackle occurred late in the 1966 slate, after rookie tackle Doug Davis was sidelined with a knee injury. Having received his taste of the game's top level, Arrobio changed his mind for the final time and left football for good before the 1967 season in order to focus on dentistry.

Walker Lee Ashley

Seasons: 1983–88, 1990 Linebacker Height: 6′
Number: 58 Penn State Weight: 232

The Vikings nabbed Walker Lee Ashley with their third-round selection in the 1983 draft and saw the Penn State product become a solid reserve linebacker and standout special teams player for the remainder of the decade. His greatest moment in purple occurred in the final regular-season game in 1988. Ashley intercepted a Mike Tomczak pass in the fourth quarter and returned the pick 94 yards for a touchdown in Minnesota's 28–27 victory over Chicago on December 19, sealing the 11-win season for the playoff-bound Vikes.

Ashley debuted in purple in 1983, making 28 tackles and causing two fumbles in 15 games. He saw more action at linebacker in 1984, when he stopped the ballcarriers' progress on 78 occasions, including six solo stops and one caused fumble in his only start, versus Green Bay on December 16. After missing all of the 1985 season upon injuring his right Achilles tendon in the second pre-season game, Ashley overcame the ailment and returned to the gridiron in 1986. He made 49 tackles in 16 contests, and was selected by his teammates as the Viking recipient of the Ed Black Memorial Courage Award, which is presented annually to the player who shows the greatest effort in the face of adversity.

However, Ashley's Achilles tendon injury took at least a step of speed from the linebacker, thereby limiting him primarily to special teams work. He provided a workmanlike effort by leading the special teams with 21 tackles 1987 before placing second on the unit in 1988, with 18 stops. Ashley spent the 1989 season with Kansas City, then ended his NFL career by returning for four games with the Vikings in 1990.

Pete Athas

Season: 1975 Cornerback Height: 5′11″
Number: 45 Tennessee Weight: 185

A knee injury that limited Jeff Wright to three contests in 1975 gave Pete Athas an opportunity to wear purple for five games late in the campaign. An ex-Continental League player and former starter for the New York Giants who had been released by Cleveland after six games in 1975, Athas served primarily as a nickel defensive back and intercepted one pass for Minnesota. He also played on special teams, returning one punt for one yard. Athas was released during training camp in 1976.

Obafemi Ayanbadejo

Season: 1998	Fullback	Height: 6'2"
Number: 49	San Diego State	Weight: 237

Obafemi Ayanbadejo had a solid training camp in 1997 but was released by the Vikings due to the depth in the Minnesota backfield. The same situation repeated itself in 1998, although Ayanbadejo was re-signed to the practice squad prior to the season opener. He spent the first 13 weeks of the 1998 campaign on the reserve unit before being activated on December 1, after Robert Smith was lost for three weeks with a sprained knee. Two weeks later, when the Vikings needed depth at wide receiver and signed Tony Bland, Ayanbadejo was released from the active roster and re-signed to the practice squad.

B

Al "Bubba" Baker

Season: 1988	Defensive End	Height: 6'6"
Numbers: 77, 60	Colorado State	Weight: 265

One of the more intense defensive linemen during his first 10 years in the National Football League with Detroit, St. Louis and Cleveland, Bubba Baker showed a few flashes of his younger days during his one-season stint with Minnesota. Signed before the second game of the year, on September 10, after being released by the Browns, Baker recorded 30 tackles, caused one fumble, and was fourth on the team with 5.5 sacks in 1988. His reputation as a grumbler also proved true, with Baker spending September 28–October 6 on the suspended list.

Randy Baldwin

Season: 1991	Running Back	Height: 5'10"
Number: 37	Mississippi	Weight: 216

Randy Baldwin was Minnesota's fourth-round selection and the 11th running back taken overall in the 1991 draft. Inactive for most of his rookie season, Baldwin played in four games on special teams with the Vikings. He touched the ball once, returning a kickoff 14 yards. After being waived a year later by Minnesota, he played a similar role for three years in Cleveland and one year apiece in Carolina and Baltimore.

Jerry Ball

Seasons: 1997–98	Defensive Tackle	Height: 6'1"
Number: 96	Southern Methodist	Weight: 340

Signed as a free agent three games into the 1997 season, Jerry Ball was hired to help clog the middle of the Vikings' defense against the run. Early on, Ball saw action in a handful of series every game, spelling starter Jason Fisk, and did an outstanding job of taking the blocking load off John Randle while making a handful of tackles.

A former Pro Bowl performer with the Lions and Raiders, the 32-year-old Ball, known as "The Governor" to his teammates, contributed with his leadership abilities once he gained the starting job, beginning with the November 16 contest with Detroit. Ball and Fisk split the playing time the rest of season and gave the Vikings an improved presence in the middle. Ball enjoyed a season-high eight tackles against Green Bay on December 1 and registered seven hits, including three for a loss, versus Detroit on December 14. For the season, Ball's five tackles for a loss ranked second among the defensive linemen.

Ball increased his playing load as well as his leadership role in 1998. He started every game and dominated the middle during running situations. Ball tied Ed McDaniel for the team lead with 15 tackles for a loss, registered 30 total hits, and recovered one fumble.

Gary Ballman

Season: 1973	Tight End	Height: 6'1"
Number: 85	Michigan State	Weight: 215

Gary Ballman concluded his 12–year career in the National Football League with the Vikings, playing in three games during the 1973 season after opening the campaign with the New York Giants. Ballman even gained some revenge against his former employer by making both of his catches in purple against the Giants during Minnesota's 31–7 victory in the final regular-season game, on December 16.

Antonio Banks

Seasons: 1997, 1998	Cornerback	Height: 5'10"
Number: 30	Virginia Tech	Weight: 195

Minnesota's fourth-round draft pick in 1997, Antonio Banks suffered a foot injury on the third day of training camp in his rookie season and spent the entire slate on injured reserve. He was released the following year in training camp, signed with Winnipeg in the Canadian Football League, then rejoined the Vikings' practice squad in November after former college teammate Torrian Gray was lost for the season with a knee injury. Banks contributed on special teams as well as in a reserve capacity for four games in the secondary by recording 10 tackles.

Roy Barker

Seasons: 1992–95	Defensive Lineman	Height: 6'4"
Number: 92	North Carolina	Weight: 280

Minnesota's fourth-round draft pick in 1992, Roy Barker underwent an impressive metamorphosis, developing from a raw but talented lineman to an effective run stopper and occasional pressure rusher during his four seasons with the Vikings.

The rap on Barker during his college days involved his tendency to let up at times. He was also viewed as a player who did not push himself to stay in tip-top shape. Some of that proved true in Minnesota, with Barker experiencing occasional inconsistency on the field.

Even so, when experience was added to Barker's lithe body and good strength, a solid player emerged. After being shifted to the offensive line briefly during his early days with the Vikings, Barker played sparingly in nine games as a rookie. His role increased significantly in 1993, with Barker starting all 16 games, recording 40 solo tackles, six sacks, and tying for the team lead with three forced fumbles. He earned defensive player-of-the-week honors from *The Sporting News* after posting a sack and forcing and recovering a game-sealing fumble during a 14–9 victory over the Redskins on December 31.

In 1994, Barker stepped in for the departed Chris Doleman at left end and, despite struggling to generate the type of pass rush needed at the position, performed well with 42 solo tackles, 3.5 sacks and 4.5 tackles for a loss. He took his game a notch higher in 1995, when he registered 40 primary hits, six sacks and three tackles for a loss.

But just as the Vikings were reaping the rewards of developing a solid defensive end, Barker signed a lucrative free-agent contract with San Francisco after the 1995 season, a deal Minnesota's coaching staff hated to see, but could not match.

Bill Barnes

Seasons: 1965–66 Running Back Height: 6'1"
Number: 33 Wake Forest Weight: 198

    Bill Barnes was a teammate of head coach Norm Van Brocklin on the Eagles' 1960 championship team, which led to Barnes' acquisition from Philadelphia for a 20th-round draft choice in September of 1965. Barnes provided the Vikings with the same kind of hard-nosed running he displayed in his initial seven years in the National Football League. When giving starter Tommy Mason's weary knees a break, Barnes galloped 148 yards on 48 carries and grabbed three passes out of the backfield for 15 yards.

    A year later, in 1966, Barnes' role centered more on special teams. He caught one toss for 20 yards and toted the pigskin just five times for 16 yards. Barnes scored his lone touchdown for Minnesota on a three-yard run in the fourth quarter of a 32–21 loss to Detroit on November 13, 1966.

Tomur Barnes

Season: 1996 Cornerback Height: 5'10"
Number: 23 North Texas State Weight: 188

    A week after being released by Houston, Tomur Barnes was signed in October of 1996 to replace Rod Smith and provide depth in the defensive backfield and on special teams. He saw limited action against Chicago and Kansas City before being released after three weeks in purple to make room on the roster for running back Leroy Hoard.

Harlon Barnett

Seasons: 1995–96 Safety Height: 5'11"
Number: 42 Michigan State Weight: 203

    A five-year veteran of the National Football League who was signed as a free agent before the 1995 season, Harlon Barnett arrived in Minnesota with a reputation for being an enforcer in the secondary. His nickname, given to him by his father, was "Da Bang Stick," in recognition of his bone-crunching hits against the run on defense and special teams.

    An ankle injury hindered Barnett during most of his first year with the Vikes. Although he started 12 games and missed only one contest, his effectiveness was limited, particularly in pass coverage. He finished the season with 29 tackles, two passes defensed and 10 special teams stops.

    The emergence of Robert Griffith landed Barnett in a nickel-back and reserve role in 1996, yet his production increased substantially due to his improved health. Barnett was credited with 64 tackles, one sack, 2.5 tackles for loss, and six passes defensed. He also contributed on special teams again, with eight solo hits and one assisted tackle.

    Despite his upgraded performance in 1996, Barnett found himself looking for employment when the Vikings allowed him to become a free agent prior to drafting defensive backs Torrian Gray and Antonio Banks in April of 1997.

Anthony Bass

Season: 1998 Defensive Back Height: 6'1"
Number: 38 Bethune-Cookman Weight: 203

    Signed as a college free agent before being released during the final cuts of training camp in 1998, Anthony Bass was re-signed to the Vikings' practice squad on September 17 following a brief stint with Green Bay and joined Minnesota's 53–man roster on November 10, when Torrian Gray was lost for the season with a knee injury.

Injuries to a couple starters forced Bass to see some reserve activity at both cornerback and safety during the last two games of the regular season and the playoff victory over Arizona. He concluded the regular season with one tackle.

Jim Battle

Season: 1963   Guard   Height: 6'
Number: 63   Southern Illinois   Weight: 240

Jim Battle went from toiling as a First Class Seaman with the Navy for three-plus years in the French theater to starting a handful of games and playing in all 14 regular-season contests at guard for the Vikings in 1963. A tight end and defensive end in college, Battle moved to guard and saw considerable playing time due to the constant building of the expansion team's offensive line. While the 25-year-old's rookie performance was laudable, it did not lead to any more playing time in the National Football League.

David Bavaro

Season: 1992   Linebacker   Height: 6'
Number: 52   Syracuse   Weight: 228

Among the final cuts during training camp in 1992, David Bavaro rejoined the team later that season, on November 24, when Greg Manusky suffered a kidney injury against Houston. The brother of former Giants All-Pro tight end Mark Bavaro and the son of Anthony Bavaro, who played for the 49ers, David employed his blue-collar style on special teams in the final five games of 1992 and finished the year with six tackles, including two solo hits.

Rick Bayless

Season: 1989   Running Back   Height: 6'
Number: 32   Iowa   Weight: 202

A local product from Hugo, Minnesota, Rick Bayless suited up for one game with the Vikings in 1989 and did not touch the football. That proved to be his lone appearance in the National Football League.

Tim Baylor

Seasons: 1979–80   Safety   Height: 6'5"
Number: 47   Morgan State   Weight: 199

Tim Baylor's only active year with the Vikings came in 1979, when he served as a fifth defensive back and started at free safety against St. Louis on November 4 after being acquired during training camp off waivers from Baltimore. He was productive nearly every time he walked on the field, recording 23 unassisted tackles, including 10 hits on special teams, and forcing one fumble. Baylor also used his extraordinary height for a defensive back to block one field goal attempt.

Baylor spent all of the 1980 season on the injured list and did not return to the gridiron with the Vikings again.

Autry Beamon

Seasons: 1975–76   Safety   Height: 6'1"
Number: 27   East Texas State   Weight: 190

The biggest day as a Viking for Autry Beamon came against Los Angeles on September 19, 1976. Although the season's second game ended in a 10–10 tie, Beamon played a large role in keeping a notch out of the loss column. The versatile defensive back who saw most of his playing time on special teams recovered a Rams' fumble in the end zone to stop one drive. He later intercepted a pass at the Minnesota 3-yard line in the final 10 seconds of regulation and returned the ball 41 yards to send the game into the extra period.

Playing in every game in 1975 and 1976, Beamon's other contributions came as a punt returner in head coach Bud Grant's three-deep formation. He carried back eight punts in his two years with the Vikes, including seven for 19 yards in 1976.

Minnesota's 12th-round draft pick in 1975, Beamon was traded along with Amos Martin to Seattle before the 1977 season in exchange for an eighth-round selection.

John Beasley

Seasons: 1967–73 Tight End Height: 6'3"
Number: 87 California Weight: 230

The Vikings were recruiting size and strength at the tight end position to upgrade their running game when they took John Beasley eighth in the 1967 draft. They instead acquired one of the league's first tight ends who combined good speed with great hands and a tough mentality, making him equally effective when blocking or running pass routes.

Beasley, a former linebacker and an All-American rugby player at the University of California, caught passes in traffic and punished tacklers after making the grab. He made a positive first impression by pulling in a touchdown pass in his first game, a four-yarder from Ron VanderKelen during a 27–21 loss to San Francisco on September 17, 1967. He went on to score three more touchdowns to lead all Minnesota receivers in his rookie season despite serving a reserve role behind starter Marlin McKeever, Beasley's childhood hero.

When McKeever was traded to Washington for safety Paul Krause prior to the 1968 season, Beasley earned the starting role and caught 23 passes for 289 yards, including six grabs against Baltimore during a 21–9 loss on November 24. He also earned the reputation for having the ability to make the tough reception, particularly in traffic, and was most effective while running pass patterns up the middle and through the heart of the defense. Said head coach Bud Grant, "John has great strength, the best hands on our team and a knack for the big catch."

In 1969, Beasley's role increased even more with an improved aerial game. A favorite target of Joe Kapp, he often beat linebackers downfield by catching passes over his right shoulder before turning upfield and unleashing all the wrath his 230 pounds could produce onto outmanned defensive backs. Beasley pulled in 33 passes for 361 yards and four touchdowns for the National Football League champions, with his first points of the season representing the sixth Viking score on September 28, when Kapp tied the NFL record with seven touchdown tosses. He also added a 60-yard gallop on a fumble recovery of a kickoff return for a touchdown during a 52–14 win over Pittsburgh, on November 23, 1969, an effort that proved just how well the ball bounced for Minnesota that season.

His production fell to 17 receptions for 237 yards and two scores in 1970 before Beasley missed the entire 1971 campaign after suffering a knee injury against Miami in the final pre-season game, on September 11. He returned to action in 1972 by placing third on the team with 28 catches for 232 yards and one touchdown.

Beasley also experienced a little national attention in 1972 when a man with the same surname, claiming to be a long-lost relative, called the tight end and offered him a job in the silver-mining business. The football player wound up spending his offseasons working with the caller.

By 1973, Beasley had lost a step, caused in part by his knee injury two years earlier. He opened the season in purple, seeing action in five games and making just one catch, a three-yard touchdown during a 22–13 triumph over Chicago on September 23. But the emergence of Stu Voigt and rookie Doug Kingsriter made Beasley expendable and, by mid-October, he was toiling for New Orleans, where he spent the last year-and-a-half of his NFL career.

Nick Bebout

Season: 1980　　　　　Tackle　　　　　　　Height: 6'5"
Number: 63　　　　　　Wyoming　　　　　　Weight: 261

Nick Bebout played the 97th and final game of his career in the National Football League in 1980. The tackle took the field for the Vikings for one contest before being waived on September 17 to make room on the roster for John Vella.

Hal Bedsole

Seasons: 1964–66　　　Flanker-Tight End　　Height: 6'4"
Number: 86　　　　　　Southern Cal　　　　Weight: 235

Minnesota envisioned Hal Bedsole becoming the franchise's long-term solution at tight end when the Vikings drafted him in the second round in 1964. He had all the tools—great size, speed, strength and all-around athleticism. In fact, a more gifted athlete may not have lined up for the Metropolitan Stadium hosts in the mid-1960s.

Head coach Norm Van Brocklin loved Bedsole's potential. Dutch referred to Bedsole as "the next (Mike) Ditka" and was determined to make the Southern Cal product an All-Pro. Though occasionally temperamental, Bedsole showed promise as a rookie. In his second game in the National Football League, the flanker made sensational touchdowns grabs of 34 and 26 yards against the Bears on September 20. Yet, after dropping three passes a week later, Bedsole was on the bench until midseason and was moved to tight end. He finished the year catching 18 passes for 295 yards and five touchdowns in 14 outings.

Various injuries, among them a "trick" knee, slowed the former All-American's progress in 1965, the year he caught just eight aerials for 123 yards and three touchdowns in nine games. Leg ailments continued to hamper Bedsole in 1966, limiting his contributions to one game without a catch.

In addition to his injuries, Bedsole never reached his potential in Minnesota partly because he refused to dedicate himself to the game. Deemed anti-establishment and a loner, his departure prior to the 1967 season, when Bedsole, Tommy Mason and a second-round draft pick were sent to Los Angeles for Marlin McKeever and a first-round selection, did not dampen the eyes of many of his teammates.

Rick Bell

Season: 1983　　　　　Running Back　　　　Height: 6'
Number: 33　　　　　　St. John's (Minn.)　　Weight: 217

Rick Bell rebounded from being among the final cuts of the Vikings' training camp to emerge as one of the more productive members of Minnesota's special teams in 1983. Re-signed after the second game of the season, the St. Cloud native saw action in the final 14 contests. His most notable contribution was a blocked punt against Chicago in a 19–13 loss on December 11.

Bell also returned a kickoff 14 yards versus Detroit on December 5. He was again among the final cuts in 1984 but did not resurface in the National Football League.

Barry Bennett

Season: 1988   Concordia   Height: 6'4"
Number: 78   Defensive End   Weight: 257

A nine-year veteran of the National Football League and a native of St. Paul, Barry Bennett was signed to bolster the Vikings' depleted defensive line on December 17, 1988. Ironically, he initially signed with Minnesota in 1982 but was released in training camp. History repeated itself in 1988 before the Vikings summoned Bennett a third time toward the end of the campaign. Bennett took the field for three plays against Chicago on December 19 in his only appearance with Minnesota. He went on the injured reserve list a day later and did not suit up for the Vikings again.

Pete Bercich

Seasons: 1995–98   Linebacker   Height: 6'1"
Number: 56   Notre Dame   Weight: 238

Pete Bercich grabs his lunch pail on the way to work every day before employing his all-out fury on opponents, particularly on special teams. No one works harder than Bercich, who grew up in a football household. His father, Bob, played safety for the Cowboys in 1960–61.

The first player to be drafted by the Vikings out of Notre Dame since Dave Huffman in 1979, the seventh-round pick spent all of the 1994 season on the practice squad. Bercich saw action in nine games in 1995, including the last eight, and tied for sixth on the club with 13 special teams tackles, including three against Cleveland on December 9. Bercich was second on the team in that category in each of the next two years by racking up 15 hits in 1996 and 21 stops, including a career-high four against Green Bay on September 21, in 1998.

"Pete is a very heady guy, an overachiever, which he has to be," said Gary Zauner, Minnesota's special teams coach since 1994. "He has really come to the top as the cream rises because he just keeps making plays and he's smart."

Though primarily a reserve with the Vikings, Bercich has been productive when given a chance at linebacker. His first start came against Detroit on December 8, 1996, when Bercich made five tackles while filling in for the injured Dixon Edwards. He was back in the lineup two weeks later and recovered his first fumble while making a personal-best seven hits. He also filled in well for Dwayne Rudd in 1998, playing most of the Vikings' 37–24 win over Green Bay on October 5 and all of the 41–7 victory over Washington on October 18, when he made five sticks.

"I know what I have to do to stick around," said Bercich, who made 21 tackles during the 1998 campaign. "I know I have to do the little things. But the great thing about football is you can't just be an athlete. There's being durable, being strong, being smart. And if you can just find out what your strong points are and then work on those, that's what's going to keep you around."

Mitch Berger

Seasons: 1996–98 Punter Height: 6'4"
Number: 17 Colorado Weight: 220

He may be a punter by trade, but Mitch Berger earned a spot with the Vikings for his ability to sail kickoffs into the end zone while kicking in a domed stadium. Minnesota's special teams had become notorious for allowing lengthy runbacks in the mid-1990s, so head coach Dennis Green figured the best way to solve the problem was to prevent runbacks from occurring in the first place.

Three years later, Berger was one of the most effective players on the Vikings. He set a team record with five touchbacks during a 41–7 victory over Washington on October 18, a feat he would equal on three other occasions during the season. He also showed how much he had improved his open-field punting by booming back-to-back 66-yard efforts against Cincinnati on November 15 to set a Minnesota single-game record for punting average at 55.8 yards and net punting average at 48.2 yards and earn NFC Player of the Week honors for special teams. He was a repeat winner a week later against Green Bay, and was named NFC Special Teams Player of the Month for November. For the season, Berger led the National Football League in touchbacks on kickoffs with 40 while averaging 44.7 yards on 55 punts, including 17 that were downed inside the 20-yard line.

"We're a dome team, so Mitch is part of what we've put together here—a guy who can kick off and make a team have to drive the ball 80 yards for a touchdown, which doesn't happen very often," Green said.

Berger performed his role with aplomb during his first year in purple, tying for fourth in the NFL with 17 touchbacks in 1996. He also did an admirable job while replacing the popular Mike Saxon at punter. Berger averaged 41.1 yards on 88 punts, led the NFL with 28 fair-caught punts, and tied for fourth in the league with 26 punts inside the 20-yard line. He also showed a little toughness during the regular season by making 10 hits during runbacks.

A hip injury suffered during the preseason shelved Berger for the first two games of the 1997 campaign. He returned in Week 3 and punted as well as he ever had, but was limited to just one kickoff until early November. His performance for the season—a 42.9-yard average—proved the Vikings had found their punter for the immediate future.

Mitch Berger

Bob Berry

Seasons: 1965–67, 1973–76 Quarterback Height: 5'11"
Number: 17 Oregon Weight: 185

Bob Berry sandwiched a five-year stint as Atlanta's starting quarterback between two tours of duty as the Vikings' backup signalcaller, with Berry never throwing more than 48 passes in a single year for the Metropolitan Stadium hosts.

One of the best quarterbacks in the University of Oregon's history, Berry struggled to overcome his lack of size in the NFL. He was acquired from Philadelphia with Ted Dean in exchange for Terry Kosens, Chuck Lamson, Ray Poage and Don Hultz in 1964 and spent the 1965–67 seasons with Minnesota, completing 16 of 46 passes for 258 yards. The majority of his playing time occurred on December 4, 1966, during a controversial start against the Falcons. Berry received his first of two starts in purple when head coach Norm Van Brocklin said he wanted to give the youngster some experience. The real reason centered on a lingering feud between Dutch and Fran Tarkenton, with the head coach proving a point to Sir Francis by benching him in the first game against the expansion team that hailed from Tarkenton's hometown. Berry did not fare well, succeeding on just 11 of 33 attempts with one touchdown and five interceptions in the Falcons' 20–13 victory.

Sold via waivers to Atlanta just prior to the season opener in 1968, Berry was traded back to Minnesota along with a first-round draft pick in exchange for Bob Lee and Lonnie Warwick in 1973. Serving primarily as insurance behind Tarkenton, he completed 47 of 78 passes in his final four seasons with the Vikings, with most of his playing time coming late in the 1974 campaign.

Berry performed best while relieving Tarkenton and his ailing arm prior to the playoffs, completing 14 of 22 attempts for 114 yards and one touchdown in Minnesota's 23–10 win over Atlanta on December 7, 1974. He also saw significant action against Kansas City a week later in the season finale, a 35–15 win. Berry completed 11 of his 12 attempts, his only misfire coming on a swing pass that was tipped by linebacker Bobby Bell.

A broken ankle during the preseason in 1975 sidelined Berry for all but one game that season, yet Grant considered him one of the game's best reserves of the mid-1970s.

"If you are a contending team, it's important that you have depth and quality at that position," Grant said. "It's been proven. When (Roger) Staubach went down, (Craig) Morton came in. When (Bob) Griese went down, (Earl) Morrall was around. (Billy) Kilmer and (Sonny) Jurgensen picked each other up. Bob has the qualities that could lead us to a title."

Still hobbled by the ankle that required surgery after the 1975 season, Berry did not throw a pass in 1976 before receiving his release from Minnesota during training camp the following year.

Ray Berry

Seasons: 1987–92 Linebacker Height: 6'2"
Number: 50 Baylor Weight: 230

Ray Berry endured the difficult experience of replacing a legend. After playing beside Scott Studwell for nearly four years, the Baylor University product stepped in for the retired icon at middle linebacker in 1991. Berry responded to the challenge with some bone-crushing intensity, registering 159 tackles (91 solos) to place second on the team. He recorded at least 10 tackles in 10 of the 16 games, including a career-high 18 hits (11 solos) and a forced fumble against New Orleans on September 22.

Prior to that season, Berry had emerged as one of the more versatile linebackers in Vikings history, displaying his ability to play equally well inside or out. Drafted in the second round in 1987, he was fourth on the club in special teams tackles as a rookie and third in the same category a year later. His first significant defensive action took place in the 28–17 wild-card playoff win over Los Angeles on December 26, 1988, with Berry rising to the occasion by leading the team with 10 stops.

Berry joined the starting lineup for the sixth game of the 1989 season and proved to be particularly adept at stopping the run. He wound up third on the team in tackles with 113 (78 solos), recorded double digits in hits in eight of the last nine contests, and posted his first safety during Minnesota's 26–14 win over Green Bay on October 15. In 1990, Berry was again third on the team with 118 tackles while seeing time at all three linebacker positions.

But after Berry's first year as the Vikes' starting middle linebacker, changes took place that directly affected the versatile player. Minnesota hired Dennis Green as the new head coach, and Jack Del Rio was signed as a Plan B free agent. Those moves left Berry in a reserve role for most of 1992 before he suffered a deep thigh bruise against the Bears on November 2 and was placed on the injured reserve list. By the time he returned the following year in training camp, the outspoken Berry had fallen out of favor with Green and was released while ranking ninth on the Vikings' all-time list for games played by a linebacker with 82.

Rufus Bess

Seasons: 1982–87 Defensive Back Height: 5'9"
Number: 21 South Carolina State Weight: 189

The September 9, 1985 contest was a significant game for the Vikings. In the season's first outing after the most difficult year in team history, Minnesota was looking for respectability while head coach Bud Grant returned to the sidelines for one more year.

The Vikings regained some pride by beating the 49ers, 28–21, thanks in large part to Rufus Bess. The left cornerback earned *Sports Illustrated*'s Defensive Player-of-the-Week honors after forcing a club-record three fumbles, making 10 tackles, recovering one loose ball and intercepting a pass in the end zone to thwart San Francisco and Joe Montana's final drive. A week later, in a 31–16 win at Tampa Bay, Bess deserved an encore for recovering another fumble, blocking a punt and registering 10 more tackles. Without question, those were the two best games of Bess' career.

Acquired off waivers from Buffalo just prior to the 1982 season, Bess debuted in purple by making 17 tackles and returning two punts for 17 yards while playing in the final eight regular-season games as well as the playoffs. His best performance came in the 30–24 victory over Atlanta, when Bess set a team post-season mark by returning five punts for 65 yards.

He moved into the starting lineup for six of his 14 appearances in 1983 while serving as the team's primary punt returner. Bess intercepted three passes on defense and galloped an average of 7.5 yards on 21 punt returns. In 1984, he paced the defense with three pickoffs and ranked third with 104 total tackles. After his terrific start in 1985, he wound up making 59 tackles in the campaign's first 11 games before suffering a shoulder separation against Detroit on November 11, 1985, and spending the last five weeks on injured reserve.

Bess was back in 1986 and played primarily in passing situations and on special teams, returning 23 punts for a 7.0-yard average and 31 kickoffs for a 22.7-yard norm. After registering a 16.9-yard average on 10 kickoffs early in the 1987 season, Bess was released, only to return and become the starting cornerback on the Minnesota replacement team. He later played arena football in Chicago before breaking an ankle and calling it a career on the gridiron.

Ryan Bethea

Season: 1988 Wide Receiver Height: 6'3"
Number: 85 South Carolina Weight: 206

Talk about a whole lot of moves for nothing. The Vikings selected Ryan Bethea in the fifth round of the 1988 supplemental draft after the wide receiver was deemed ineligible for his senior season of college. Having missed the campaign's first seven games upon signing with Minnesota on October 17, Bethea spent his first two contests on the exempt list, was on the inactive list a week later against Detroit, then resided on injured reserve with an ailing hamstring for the final six games. He wound up never playing in a game in the National Football League.

Matt Birk

Season: 1998	Offensive Lineman	Height: 6'4"
Number: 75	Harvard	Weight: 308

No one in the National Football League's 1998 draft could have been happier than Matt Birk. After three solid seasons at Harvard, Birk was drafted in the sixth round by his childhood favorite team. Birk attended Cretin-Derham Hall High School in St. Paul and wanted nothing more than to wear the purple before beginning a career as an investment banker.

Though inactive during the early stages of his rookie season, the quick and aggressive Birk proved to the Vikings' coaching staff that he has a future on the Minnesota offensive line. After playing well at guard, tackle and center during the preseason, he backed up Korey Stringer at right tackle, took three snaps at right guard when David Dixon suffered a stinger at Tampa Bay on November 1, saying "That was the most exciting time in my life," and played well at guard during a 24–3 win against Cincinnati. He also finished with a bang, seeing action for 31 snaps in the season finale against Tennessee.

Bill Bishop

Season: 1961	Defensive Tackle	Height: 6'4"
Number: 73	North Texas State	Weight: 250

Bill Bishop was an aging yet still-productive player upon joining the Vikings for their maiden voyage. A regular defensive right tackle for the Bears and a 1954 Pro Bowl honoree, Bishop fostered no lost love for George Halas, particularly after the Bears' head coach exposed him in the expansion pool. Bishop considered hanging up the cleats instead of suiting up for Minnesota, yet wound up playing one season in purple, proving he could still hit opponents as hard as anyone in the league.

The Vikings' defensive captain, Bishop played 10 games in 1961. The rugged, vinegary lineman also threatened to give head coach Norm Van Brocklin a lick or two on the flight home after the season's final contest before better judgment and some teammates who did not want to be named as accessories convinced Bishop to vent his frustrations in other ways. Given that scenario, it is little wonder why Bishop's tenure in purple lasted just one season.

Keith Bishop

Season: 1987	Quarterback	Height: 6'4"
Number 12	Wheaton College	Weight: 190

Keith Bishop was on the Vikings' roster as a replacement player in 1987 but did not take the field. A high school math teacher in 1987, he was not working when Minnesota called to play football because the Chicago teachers union was on strike.

Joe Blahak

Seasons: 1974–75, 1977	Defensive Back	Height: 5'10"
Number: 21	Nebraska	Weight: 188

Joe Blahak was a valuable member of the Vikings' special teams in between jumping around the NFL. Houston's eighth-round draft pick in 1973, he joined Minnesota a year later off the waiver wire and saw action in seven games. The two-time All-Big Eight honoree played in nine contests in 1975, intercepting his lone pass for the Vikes and recording a safety upon blocking a punt through the end zone during a 29–21 win over the Jets on October 12.

After moving to Tampa Bay in the expansion draft and later going to the Patriots, Blahak rejoined the Vikings in 1977 via waivers and played in the final 12 games of his career, mostly on special teams.

Matt Blair

Seasons: 1974–85
Number: 59
Linebacker
Iowa State
Height: 6'5"
Weight: 230

Matt Blair

Beginning in the mid-1970s and continuing for the next dozen years, the Vikings rarely worried when a big play was needed. They knew that, one way or the other, Matt Blair would get the job done.

Regardless of whether the big play was needed on defense or on special teams, the high-flying Blair produced when the game was on the line. Twenty times in his 12-season career he altered the flight of an opponent's kick. That number ranks second in the history of the National Football League. As a starting outside linebacker, a role he assumed in the latter part of his rookie campaign by unseating injured veteran Roy Winston, Blair made 1,452 tackles, a total that puts him second on the Viking hits list, behind Scott Studwell. With those gaudy stats, it is little wonder why Blair earned all-rookie honors and saw action in six consecutive Pro Bowls.

Those achievements only begin to tell the Blair tale. A perennial All-NFC choice and a seven-year team captain, Blair was not lauded by the national media, although coaches and personnel managers throughout the league marveled at his consistency. The second-round draft pick in 1974 started as a youngster on the aging Minnesota defense in the mid-1970s and emerged as the unit's heart and soul in the early 1980s. His performance was so outstanding that he was named the NFC's Most Valuable Linebacker in 1980. As great a person as he was a player, Blair was selected by the Jaycees as one of the 10 Outstanding Young Men in America in 1983.

The Minnesota coaching staff was initially enamored with Blair's 4.7 speed in the 40, even though he suffered a serious knee injury during his junior season at Iowa State. So great was Blair's speed that head coach Bud Grant's staff even toyed with the idea of placing him at strong safety. Those thoughts soon vanished upon watching Blair during his six rookie starts in place of Winston. He also showed his big-play ability early in his career by blocking a punt that Terry Brown recovered for Minnesota's only touchdown in Super Bowl IX against Pittsburgh.

Shifted from left linebacker to the right side in 1975, Blair saw regular action as a sophomore in the NFL, mainly in passing situations. He gained a permanent starting job back on the left side in 1976 and responded with two interceptions, five recovered fumbles, two blocked conversions and one blocked punt.

More of the same followed in 1977, the year Blair garnered his first Pro Bowl recognition. In addition to tying for the team lead with 109 primary tackles and picking off another pass, Blair rose from the middle of the line to knock down two field goals and a conversion. He also swatted back a punt and ran the football 10 yards for a touchdown in a 10–7 loss to the Bears on November 20.

Blair found the end zone again a year later against Chicago when he recovered a fumble and raced 49 yards in a 24–20 win over the Bears on September 25, 1978. He ranked second on the team with 136 solo tackles, and had four quarterback sacks, two fumble recoveries, one blocked conversion and three interceptions. A third straight trip to the Pro Bowl followed his 1979 performance, when Blair blocked five conversions, had four sacks, two fumble recoveries and a team-high 132 unassisted hits.

Blair became the 11th Viking to receive All-Pro recognition, an honor he earned in 1980. Despite missing two games with a shoulder injury, he still managed to make 114 primary stops. In 1981, he blocked four extra points to surpass Alan Page as the Minnesota record holder for blocked kicks. He also had 146 solo tackles, good for second on the team, paced the defense with six sacks, caused four fumbles and recovered two, and intercepted a pass. An example of how dominating he could be was seen during Minnesota's 35–23 win over Philadelphia on October 18. Blair blocked a conversion, picked off a pass, recovered a fumble and made 14 primary tackles with five assists.

The strike-marred 1982 season saw Blair earn his sixth straight trip to the Pro Bowl after registering 45 solo tackles, two sacks, two forced fumbles and two blocked conversions. He had 191 total tackles in 1983 and intercepted one pass to become the Vikings' career leader in picks for a linebacker. A knee injury limited Blair to 11 games in 1984, although he still surpassed Jeff Siemon as Minnesota's all-time leading tackler. Knee problems further hampered Blair in 1985, when he played in just six games.

The ailing knee and age robbed Blair of his speed and led to the end of his football career in July of 1986. Nevertheless, he remains one of the most dominating linebackers in Vikings history, and was named to Minnesota's Silver Anniversary All-Time team in 1985.

Paul Blair

Season: 1990
Number: 68
Tackle
Oklahoma State
Height: 6'4"
Weight: 280

Paul Blair's career had difficulty getting off the ground with the Vikings. He initially signed with the club on November 1, 1989, but was released three days later without having played in a game. Re-signed the following offseason, Blair saw action as a backup tackle for two games during the 1990 campaign.

Tony Bland

Seasons: 1996–97, 1998
Numbers: 18, 84
Wide Receiver
Florida A&M
Height: 6'3"
Weight: 213

Having seen what big, physical receivers like Jake Reed and Cris Carter can do for an offense, the Vikings envisioned Tony Bland developing into a similar-style pass catcher.

Signed as an undrafted college free agent, Bland spent the first 15 weeks of the 1996 campaign on the practice squad before moving to the roster and being de-activated for the season finale. He returned to the practice squad in 1997 for the first 12 contests prior to being activated but playing little in Weeks 14 and 15, against San Francisco and Detroit, respectively. Bland continued to show promise the following year in training camp and blocked a punt in the preseason against Carolina that led to a come-from-behind victory, only to be released in the final cutdowns. He was re-signed once again during the last week of the 1998 season after injuries struck the Vikings' receiver corps and made a tackle on special teams against Tennessee on December 26.

Orlando Bobo

Seasons: 1997–98
Number: 74
Guard
Northeast Louisiana
Height: 6'3"
Weight: 299

A physical lineman with some quickness, Orlando Bobo spent the entire 1996 season on the Vikings' practice squad. He was back on the unit to open the 1997 campaign before joining the 53-man roster on September 12 when guard David Dixon went down for four weeks. Bobo averaged about one offensive series per game during Dixon's absence, and saw the majority of his playing time on the field goal protection unit and on kickoff returns.

Bobo again played most of the 1998 season on special teams before fracturing his right fibula during a kickoff return against Detroit on October 25, forcing him to miss the remainder of the slate. He was acquired by the Cleveland Browns in the expansion draft prior to the 1999 campaign.

Bookie Bolin

Seasons: 1968–69   Guard   Height: 6'2"
Number: 66   Mississippi   Weight: 245

Treva Gene Bolin was an All-American at Ole Miss and a starter for most of his six years with the Giants, yet served primarily as a reserve behind Milt Sunde and Jim Vellone in Minnesota. "Bookie" was on the Vikes' reserve squad for the first half of 1968 before being activated and taking the gridiron in six games after Larry Bowie was injured in early November. He toiled mostly on the pines the next year, playing in six games once again while giving the winners of the last NFL Championship Game solid veteran depth upfront. His days in Minnesota ended prior to the 1970 season when he was traded to Miami for cornerback Dick Westmoreland.

Steve Bono

Seasons: 1985–86   Quarterback   Height: 6'3"
Number: 13   UCLA   Weight: 216

Steve Bono, drafted by Minnesota with the Vikings' first sixth-round choice in 1985, spent his first two years in the National Football League wearing purple as a third-string quarterback. Though active for all 16 games as a rookie, his lone appearance came in the third quarter against Philadelphia on December 1, when he completed just one of 10 passes for five yards before giving way to starter Wade Wilson. The only other pass Bono threw as a Viking came nearly a year later, on November 30, 1986, when he succeeded on his lone attempt for three yards in a 45–13 victory over Tampa Bay.

Bono later proved he was better than he had shown while with the Vikes. He saw some reserve action with San Francisco before emerging as Kansas City's starting quarterback in 1995.

David Boone

Season: 1974   Defensive End   Height: 6'3"
Number: 71   Eastern Michigan   Weight: 245

Natural talent may have enabled David Boone to overcome being out of shape in college, but it did nothing to help him in the National Football League. After the 11th-round draft pick had a dismal showing during Minnesota's rookie camp in 1974, Boone displayed physical progress in training camp, particularly with his quickness. He wound up spending the year as a reserve on the defensive line, seeing limited action in five games.

Todd Bouman

Seasons: 1997–98   Quarterback   Height: 6'2"
Number: 8   St. Cloud State   Weight: 195

A practice squad player for the first 15 weeks of the 1997 season, Todd Bouman was activated as the third-string quarterback after starter Brad Johnson was lost for the year with a herniated disk in his neck. Bouman did not see any action, but impressed the Vikings' brass after a successful two-sport career at St. Cloud State and solid showings in training camp and on the scout team.

"He has a lot of great qualities about him," said Ray Sherman, Minnesota's quarterbacks coach from 1995–97. "He's got something about him. He has a lot of self-confidence. It doesn't seem like anything rattles him."

Bouman beat out Jay Fiedler for the third-string quarterback role in 1998. He remained on the roster throughout the campaign but did not take a snap during a regular-season game.

Larry Bowie

Seasons: 1962–68   Guard   Height: 6'3"
Number: 61   Purdue   Weight: 255

The Vikings' offensive line was in shambles during the team's inaugural season, caused in large part by a limited amount of talent. With Fran Tarkenton running for his life out of necessity instead of by design, the Minnesota front office was looking for solid players as well as help along the offensive front in its second college draft. The brass achieved both goals when it plucked Larry Bowie in the sixth round in 1962.

Bowie paid immediate dividends by seeing action in several places as a rookie. He then stepped into the starting lineup at guard during his second training camp and remained there for the next half-dozen years.

The battling strongman possessed great lateral movement and an intense desire to be the best player he could be. In 1962, he played defensive end and a handful of spots across the offensive line before settling as a reserve defensive right tackle for the campaign's duration. Head coach Norm Van Brocklin was impressed, saying, "No matter where we put him, he winds up being our best football player there."

The same could be said when the position nomad landed at right guard in 1963. Quiet though well-liked among his teammates, Bowie was never shy about putting a well-placed pop or two on charging defensive linemen. He joined Mick Tingelhoff and Grady Alderman as fixtures on the Vikings' front wall, then combined with Milt Sunde in 1965 to give Minnesota one of the best sets of guards in the league. He was also dependable, answering the bell for every game during his first six years.

Yet, in what was a surprise to many Vikings observers, Bowie retired after playing in eight games during the 1968 season. A good example of what Bowie meant to Minnesota was seen in the comments made by the typically reserved Bud Grant before the 1969 campaign. "We have suffered several major personnel setbacks," said the head coach. "Larry Bowie, a regular guard, has retired. Larry had seven years of experience . . . he was just beginning to gain the rewards of that experience. We'll miss him."

After establishing himself as one of the better all-around guards in Minnesota annals, Bowie continued to contribute to the Vikings' cause after retiring as a player by serving as a part-time scout.

Brent Boyd

Seasons: 1980–86   Guard   Height: 6'3"
Number: 62   UCLA   Weight: 275

After an impressive first season that saw him earn a spot on the UPI All-Rookie team, Brent Boyd endured a frustrating final six years in the National Football League, with injuries spoiling what could have become a more-accomplished professional career.

Minnesota's third-round draft pick in 1980, Boyd impressed the Viking coaching staff as a member of the North squad in the Senior Bowl. He then established himself in the league as a rookie by being ready when injuries afflicted others. Boyd played in every game and started nine contests, including six at left guard in place of Jim Hough and three at right guard for Wes Hamilton.

He took over the starting duties at left guard for the first three games of the 1981 season before injuring a knee and landing on injured reserve. The ailment caused Boyd to spend the first two-and-a-half months of the 1982 campaign on the physically unable to perform list prior to being activated in mid-November and seeing action in four contests.

Boyd filled a reserve role at guard and center in 1983 and played in every game before starting the season finale against Cincinnati at right guard. But just as he appeared to be rounding back into shape, Boyd succumbed to a broken left fibula during the 1984 training camp and missed the entire regular season. Upon recovering, he moved back into the starting lineup in 1985 and started 14 games at left guard, missing only the Detroit game on November 3 due to a sprained ankle. His efforts earned him the 1985 Terry Dillon Award, which is presented to the Viking player who exemplifies dedication as a player and as a man.

Unfortunately, Boyd's career took one final wrong turn. He played in five games in 1986 before returning to the injured reserve list on October 30, which proved to be the final transaction of his career.

Malik Boyd

Season: 1994 Safety Height: 5'10"
Number: 36 Southern Weight: 185

The lone rookie free agent to play in all 16 games for the Vikings in 1994, Malik Boyd led the team's non-starters with 30 tackles, even though most of his playing time came as a fifth or sixth defensive back. His only start came against New England on November 13, with Boyd recording 13 hits while filling in for the injured Anthony Parker at cornerback. He also defensed four passes during the season and intercepted a pass against the New York Giants on October 10, which Boyd returned 22 yards.

Despite such a steady performance by a young player, Boyd ran into a numbers game the following year in training camp after Corey Fuller and Orlando Thomas were drafted and was released prior to the season opener.

Jim Boylan

Season: 1963 End Height: 6'1"
Number: 80 Washington State Weight: 185

Jim Boylan's claim to fame occurred in an otherwise-dismal Viking showing on December 8, 1963. The wide receiver, who saw action in three games late in the franchise's third campaign, caught an 18-yard touchdown pass from Fran Tarkenton in the second quarter of what turned out to be a 42–10 loss to Baltimore. Boylan pulled in five other passes during the 1963 season, averaging 13 yards per reception.

Jeff Brady

Seasons: 1995–97 Linebacker Height: 6'1"
Number: 50 Kentucky Weight: 243

A journeyman who wore six different uniforms in his first five years in the National Football League, Jeff Brady proved in 1995 that all he needed to become a starter was a chance.

Having signed with the Vikings for his ability on special teams, Brady landed in the limelight during the second half of a 14–6 loss to

Chicago on October 30, 1995. Replacing the injured Jack Del Rio at middle linebacker, Brady took over the starting job the following week against Green Bay and earned NFC Defensive Player of the Week honors in his initial start. The former Kentucky standout was a madman against the Packers in Minnesota's 27–24 triumph, registering six tackles, his first career sack, a forced fumble, a tackle for a loss and an interception late in the game that led to Fuad Reveiz's game-winning field goal. He went on to record 12 hits against Arizona on November 12, and finished the year third on the team with 67 stops, even though he started less than half the season.

With Del Rio departing the following offseason, Brady held on to the starting middle linebacker duties for most of the next two years. His debut in 1996 earned him his second NFC Defensive Player of the Week recognition. On September 1 against the Lions, Brady helped guide the Vikes to a 17–13 win by intercepting two Scott Mitchell passes—the first he lateralled to Dewayne Washington for Minnesota's first touchdown of the season and the second stopped Detroit's last-minute drive deep in Viking territory. From there Brady led the team with three fumble recoveries and 146 tackles, including seven contests with at least 10 hits. His three pickoffs tied for the NFC lead among linebackers.

In 1997, Brady got off to a slow start until he responded with solid performances in wins against Arizona and Carolina in early October. He maintained his starting job through Week 14, then an injury forced him to miss the Detroit game before another ailment, suffered during a kickoff, landed Brady on injured reserve. With Ed McDaniel playing well at middle linebacker in his absence, Brady was released and joined the Carolina Panthers in 1998.

Don Bramlett

Season: 1987 Defensive Tackle Height: 6'2"
Number: 61 Carson-Newman Weight: 270

One of the first cuts of training camp in 1987 after signing as an undrafted college free agent, Don Bramlett returned to the Vikings as the starting right tackle for the three replacement games. His father, John, played seven years in the National Football League.

David Braxton

Seasons: 1989–90 Linebacker Height: 6'1"
Number: 53 Wake Forest Weight: 232

David Braxton serves as the poster boy for the Vikings' most disappointing draft in team history. Having lost its first-round pick due to the acquisition of Mike Merriweather, Minnesota used its second-round selection on the linebacker from Wake Forest. The undermotivated Braxton played in only three games as a reserve during his rookie year, recording one solo tackle while missing time with a groin injury and a thigh contusion. He then played in just one game in purple in 1990 before receiving his release. Braxton joined Phoenix later that season and played three more years with the Cardinals before spending his last year in the league—1994—with Cincinnati.

Bob Breitenstein

Season: 1967	Tackle	Height: 6'3"
Number: 75	Tulsa	Weight: 272

Having spent most of 1966 and the first two games of 1967 as a starter for the American Football League's Denver Broncos, Bob Breitenstein joined the Vikings after Minnesota officials acquired his draft rights from Washington for a fifth-round draft choice.

At 272 pounds, the enthusiastic Breitenstein had excellent size and strength for the tackle position. He contributed in 11 games as a reserve during his one season in the Upper Midwest, backing up starters Grady Alderman and Doug Davis. Released the following year by the Vikings, Breitenstein resurfaced with Atlanta in 1969 and 1970.

Greg Briggs

Season: 1997, 1998	Linebacker-Safety	Height: 6'3"
Numbers: 54, 43	Texas Southern	Weight: 220

After spending the previous two seasons as a special teams performer with Dallas and Chicago, Greg Briggs signed with the Vikings for the 1997 campaign to serve in a similar capacity. He emerged as one of Minnesota's more consistent tacklers on kickoff and punt coverage by beating double-team blocking on the outside. He recorded 11 hits on special teams, and blocked a field goal attempt in the 28–17 loss to San Francisco on December 7. A linebacker throughout his career, Briggs received his first taste at the safety position during some October practices after the Vikings suffered a handful of injuries at the position.

Briggs was released during training camp the following season before being re-signed to play on the special teams coverage units during the playoffs after Kailee Wong was placed on injured reserve.

James Brim

Season: 1987	Wide Receiver	Height: 6'3"
Number: 84	Wake Forest	Weight: 187

James Brim was initially acquired off waivers from St. Louis in August of 1987 before receiving his release prior to the regular season. He then re-inked with the club for the replacement games and emerged as the Vikings' leader in rushing average, receiving and scoring. In the three contests, he averaged 18 yards on two carries, gained 282 yards on 18 catches, and scored three touchdowns. He spent the rest of the season on injured reserve with a knee ailment and was waived the following August during training camp.

Michael Brim

Seasons: 1989–90	Cornerback	Height: 6'
Number: 44	Virginia Union	Weight: 188

Signed on November 8, 1989, Michael Brim served as a reserve defensive back for the season's final seven games. He finished the slate with seven total tackles, three passes defended, and blocked an extra-point attempt in Minnesota's 27–16 victory over Chicago on December 3.

Brim continued to play a reserve role in 1990, participating in all 16 games and making two interceptions for 11 return yards. He then signed with the Jets and played two years in New York prior to spending three seasons with Cincinnati.

Charley Britt

Season: 1964
Number: 17
Defensive Back
Georgia
Height: 6'2"
Weight: 180

In four years with the Rams, Charley Britt earned a reputation as a ballhawk, a decent emergency quarterback despite playing defensive back, and one of the league's best golfers. None of those traits was that evident in 1964, when Britt played the final five games of his National Football League career with the Vikings, all in the defensive secondary and on special teams.

Bill Brown

Seasons: 1962–74
Number: 30
Running Back
Illinois
Height: 5'11"
Weight: 228

George Halas made few personnel mistakes during his days as Chicago's owner and head coach. His worst move, however, greatly benefited the Vikings, the team that proved to be a constant thorn in Papa Bear's paw. With a surplus of fullbacks such as Rick Casares and Joe Marconi in 1962, Halas decided to unload a brash, bow-legged rookie named Bill Brown on the fledgling expansion team in exchange for a fourth-round draft pick. It was a deal Halas regretted for the next 14 seasons.

Minnesota general manager Bert Rose always pointed to Brown as one of the best deals he ever made for the Vikings. That's because Brown was nothing less than one of the best all-purpose backs in the game during his 13 years with Minnesota. Though occasionally as prickly as his crewcut, Brown feared no one or any situation. He was enthusiastic in every practice and every game and excessively competitive, a throwback player who excelled in blasting into the line by lowering his head and gaining the necessary short yardage. As his nickname "Boom Boom" suggests, rarely did Brown lose a physical confrontation, regardless of whether he was hitting defenders, goal posts or walls.

Bill Brown

Described accurately by head coach Bud Grant as "the epitome of the Vikings," Brown, with his rough-house style of running, doled out more punishment on defensive players than they ever considered handing back. Teaming for most of his career with Dave Osborn in the Minnesota backfield, Brown bowled over would-be tacklers while donning short sleeves in even the coldest of weather. A banger of a ballcarrier, he was also an excellent receiver with great running balance. He led with his actions as well as with his words. And when his efforts were not deemed the best option possible at running back, Brown gladly took over as captain of the special teams.

An All-Big Ten fullback at Illinois, Brown gained 103 yards on 34 carries while alternating with Doug Mayberry and Mel Triplett at fullback in his first season with the Vikings. He became a more vital part of Minnesota's attack in 1963, earning a starting job and ranking second on the team with 445 yards and five touchdowns on the ground and fourth with 17 catches for two more scores. Always a standout on special teams, he also ran back the first touchdown on a kickoff return in Vikings' annals, a 78-yarder, on October 20, 1963, against the Rams.

By 1964, Brown was one of the game's best fullbacks. He ranked fourth in the NFL with 866 yards rushing and 11th in receiving with 48 catches, all of which took much of the defensive pressure off halfback Tommy Mason. Brown also scored 16 touchdowns—nine in the air and seven on the ground. Those efforts led to the Viking Fan Club's choice as the team's Best Offensive Player as well as his first Pro Bowl appearance, where he scored twice more for the winning West squad.

A pre-season shoulder ailment slowed "Boom Boom" somewhat in

1965, yet he still earned another Pro Bowl invitation after leading the Vikings in rushing with 699 yards while catching 41 passes for another 503 yards. He also posted the best game of his career that year, gaining 138 rushing yards during a 27–17 win at Cleveland on October 31. Brown was again among the NFL elite a year later, placing fourth in the league with 829 yards and six touchdowns on 251 carries while ranking second on the team with 37 receptions for 359 three-footers. His one-yard plunge proved to be the deciding tally in Minnesota's 20–17 win over Green Bay on November 6, giving the Vikings the distinction of being the only team to beat the Packers at Lambeau Field in 1966.

In 1967, Brown and Osborn formed one of football's best backfields. While "Ozzie" gained 972 yards, thanks in large part to the deft lead blocking of Brown, "Boom Boom" registered another 610 yards on 185 carries with six scores while pulling in 22 aerials for 263 yards. He earned Pro Bowl recognition for the fourth time in 1968 after scoring a career-high 14 touchdowns for the Central Division champs, gaining 805 yards on the ground and another 329 yards on 31 grabs. After that slate, Grant said of Brown, "He is the complete player. He is the best fullback in the league because he does everything well and he always gives maximum effort."

Injuries limited Brown again in 1969, although he still rushed for 430 yards and caught 21 passes 183 yards to help the Vikings make their first Super Bowl appearance. Ailments slowed him as well in 1970, when he gained 324 yards on the ground and 149 on 15 pass receptions. Brown served in a reserve capacity in 1971, rushing for 136 yards on 46 carries while catching 10 tosses. While his responsibilities on offense may have decreased, his efforts on special teams continued, with "Boom Boom" putting the hurt on Detroit's Lem Barney on a kickoff return that produced a fumble and led to the Vikings' game-winning field goal in Minnesota's 16–13 triumph on September 20.

By the end of 1972, Brown was among the top 10 ground gainers in NFL history and had been atop the Vikings' charts for the previous six years. He again placed second in rushing yardage (263) and scoring (36 points) while placing fifth on the team in receptions (22). The captain of the Vikings' special teams was the NFL's oldest running back in 1973, the year he gained 206 rushing yards, including a 101-yard effort against the Lions on November 11 to improve the team's record to 9–0. Brown closed out his career with 41 yards on the ground and five catches in 1974.

Brown's accomplishments, which earned him a spot on the Vikings' Silver Anniversary All-Time Team in 1985, are not relegated to his aggressive approach. His numbers are as impressive as those of any other NFL ball carrier. He is the only running back in league history to have played in 200 games, checking in with 205. His nine touchdown receptions from 1964 represents the league mark for a running back. He reached paydirt on pass receptions 23 times in his career, a record equalled only by Chuck Foreman and one that serves as the Minnesota standard for a running back. He also ranks second to Cris Carter with 76 touchdowns, second to Darrin Nelson with 9,237 combined yards and third with eight 100-yard rushing games in Vikings annals.

Given those numbers, it's little wonder why Halas never forgave himself for giving the Vikings Bill Brown.

Ivory Lee Brown

Season: 1993	Running Back	Height: 6'2"
Number: 22	Arkansas-Pine Bluff	Weight: 245

Ivory Lee Brown was signed in late October during the 1993 season after Charles Evans was lost for the campaign's duration with a broken hand. Brown did not take the field while wearing purple after playing in seven games for Arizona a year earlier.

Larry Brown

Season: 1987	Wide Receiver	Height: 5'11"
Number: 80	Mankato State	Weight: 180

A four-year letterman at Mankato State, Larry Brown played in one replacement game with the Vikings and did not catch a pass.

Richard Brown

Seasons: 1994–96	Linebacker	Height: 6'3"
Number: 52	San Diego State	Weight: 240

The Vikings were looking for coverage help on special teams late in the 1994 season after Brent Novoselsky, one of the unit's best players, suffered a career-ending neck injury. The team found its man in Richard Brown, a former special teams standout with Cleveland who had played for Minnesota special teams coach Gary Zauner at San Diego State.

Signed on December 5, 1994, Brown averaged three special teams tackles in his three appearances that season. He filled the same role for the next two years while seeing a handful of plays at middle linebacker. Brown was third on the club with 15 special teams stops in 1995, with his best game taking place when he had three solo hits during a 44–24 win at Pittsburgh on September 24. He added nine tackles on special teams and six on defense in 1996 before Minnesota opted to go with lower-priced young players instead of the 32-year-old Brown in 1997.

Robert Brown

Season: 1971	Tight End	Height: 6'3"
Number: 89	Alcorn State	Weight: 225

After missing the early stages of the 1971 season with an ankle injury, Robert Brown filled in admirably for the hurt John Beasley during the last eight games of the campaign. Acquired with Nate Wright in a trade with St. Louis that sent Dale Hackbart and Mike McGill to the Cardinals, Brown shared playing time with a young Stu Voigt and caught six passes for 141 yards, including one reception that covered 48 yards. His time in Minnesota proved to be short, for he was traded to the Saints in 1972 for a sixth-round draft pick in 1973 and a fourth-rounder in 1974.

Ted Brown

Seasons: 1979–86	Running Back	Height: 5'10"
Number: 23	North Carolina State	Weight: 198

Many observers felt the Vikings had wasted a first-round pick when Minnesota drafted Ted Brown in 1979. The four-time All-Atlantic Coast Conference standout was labelled too small without breakaway speed. When the fourth-leading rusher in NCAA history struggled as a rookie while running on just one good leg, there were many I-told-you-so's heard. But that talk soon grew silent when Brown and his stop-and-go running style emerged as one the top backs in Minnesota history, despite playing in a pass-oriented offense.

Most of Brown's achievements as a rookie came on special teams. Still, he found enough opportunity to carry the ball 130 times for 551 yards while catching 31 passes for 197 yards. His biggest play came in overtime against Green Bay on September 23, 1979. Brown took the kickoff past midfield, setting up a Tommy Kramer-to-Ahmad Rashad touchdown pass minutes later in the 27–21 victory.

Brown became an integral part of the offense in 1980. Serving as Kramer's primary option in the backfield, he ranked seventh in the NFC with 912 yards rushing and eighth in the conference with 62 receptions for 623 yards. Brown averaged 5.5 yards every time he touched the ball, scored nine touchdowns, and lost just one fumble during the 281 times the pigskin was in his possession. He also played a major role in the incredible 28–23 comeback win over Cleveland on December 14 that earned Minnesota a playoff berth. Brown caught the lateral from Joe Senser in the final seconds of play and got the Vikings within striking distance for the Hail Mary pass by getting out of bounds to stop the clock.

He continued to excel in 1981 by becoming only the second Viking to rush for more than 1,000 yards in a season when he gained 1,063 on 274 carries. He also ranked third in the National Football League with 83 pass receptions for another 694 yards. Brown's combined production of 1,757 yards fell just four yards shy of Chuck Foreman's team record, set in 1975. The strike-shortened 1982 season was similar, with Brown leading the team in rushing yards (515) for the third consecutive year and in receptions (31) for the second straight season.

A sprained ankle and a separated shoulder cost Brown about half the 1983 season, when he led the team with 11 touchdowns, was second in rushing with 476 yards, and placed third in receiving with 41 catches. The arrival of another first-round pick, Darrin Nelson, cut into the former All-American's time for the rest of his career, although Brown still managed to remain productive in a reserve role. He led the club with 13 total touchdowns and was second in rushing in 1984 and 1985 before ranking third on the Vikings with his 251 yards on the ground in 1986.

Waived just prior to the season opener in 1987, Brown concluded his NFL career by ranking third in Vikings history in rushing yards (4,546), receptions (339) and touchdowns scored (53) and eighth in reception yards (2,850). Those numbers alone reveal that Ted Brown was anything but a wasted first-round draft pick.

Terry Brown

Seasons: 1972–75 Safety Height: 6'2"
Number: 24 Oklahoma State Weight: 205

Terry Brown's nose for the football enabled him to make things happen when he took the field for the Vikings. A classic case occurred during Super Bowl IX. Brown scored Minnesota's only points in the 16–6 loss to Pittsburgh when he recovered a blocked punt in the fourth quarter and trotted the pigskin to paydirt.

Brown was purchased off waivers as a three-year NFL veteran with St. Louis in 1972 to help fill the void at safety created by the career-ending motorcycle accident suffered by Karl Kassulke. The versatile Brown served as a backup strong safety and fifth defensive back, and played on most of the special teams units.

His first big play with the Vikings occurred in the New York snow during the season finale on December 16, 1973. Brown intercepted a Randy Johnson pass, broke two tackles and returned the ball 63 yards for a touchdown in Minnesota's 31–7 win over the Giants. He picked off two passes in reserve duty in 1974, and had two more interceptions in 1975.

The 1975 season proved to be his most productive campaign in purple, with Brown starting 12 games after Jeff Wright went down with a knee injury and finishing the year as Minnesota's second-leading tackler. He also visited the end zone for the third and final time as a Viking by returning a fumble 26 yards for six points during Minnesota's season-opening 27–17 triumph over San Francisco on September 21.

After reporting to training camp with the Vikings in 1976, Brown concluded his NFL career by spending the regular season with Cleveland.

Joey Browner

Seasons: 1983–91 Safety Height: 6'2"
Number: 47 Southern Cal Weight: 231

Joey Browner was Jerry Burns' type of player. The Vikings' head coach described the team's impact defenders as his "big knockers." Browner may have headed Burnsie's list, for few defensive backs in the history of the National Football League have added more punch to their hits and done so with more frequency than the Minnesota safety.

So special were Browner's abilities that not only could he see the whites in the eyes of opposing receivers, he could decipher the fear. He excelled in stopping the run and created terror while preventing receivers from going over the middle. A karate expert, he also possessed the speed and the instincts to stay with the league's fastest pass catchers. The combination begot six Pro Bowl invitations and team leadership in interceptions on three occasions.

Browner joined the Vikings as the first defensive back ever taken by the team in the first round, selected with the 19th overall selection in the 1983 draft. The former USC Trojan contributed in his rookie season by leading the special teams with 21 tackles and ranking ninth on the defense with 53 primary hits. His third-down sack in overtime against Green Bay on October 23 forced the Packers to punt and resulted in Minnesota's winning drive that culminated with a 32-yard field goal by Benny Ricardo in the 20–17 triumph at Lambeau Field.

In 1984, Browner started half of the team's 16 games, including the season opener against San Diego, when he took a fumble recovery 63 yards for a touchdown. He was seventh on the club with 76 total tackles and third with 12 solo hits on special teams.

Browner became a full-time starter at strong safety in 1985 and earned a spot in the Pro Bowl because of his abilities on special teams. He placed second on the club with 188 total tackles and led the Vikings with five fumble recoveries, including an NFL record three against San Francisco on September 8. He also reached paydirt by returning his first of two interceptions 15 yards for a touchdown during a 31–16 win over Tampa Bay on September 15. His second Pro Bowl appearance came in 1986, when he was named the starting strong safety for the NFC after leading the Viking defense with 107 tackles, tying for the team lead with three forced fumbles and four recovered loose balls, and placing second with four interceptions. He again found the end zone by racing 39 yards on a pickoff against Detroit in a 24–10 victory on November 9.

Browner took his game to the next level in 1987 when he became the first Viking to be named an All-Pro since Matt Blair achieved the feat in

Joey Browner

1980. The safety emerged as the heart of the defense, pacing the unit for the second straight year with 131 total tackles while picking off six passes. All-Pro recognition followed again in 1988, with Browner making 125 total hits and intercepting five tosses. He also came through with two aerial steals during a 28–17 victory over the Rams in the playoffs before victimizing the 49ers once a week later.

Such efforts were producing victories in Minnesota on a consistent basis, and Browner felt he deserved his reward, particularly after quarterbacks Wade Wilson and Tommy Kramer were given large contracts. Browner even threatened to boycott his role on special teams and became embroiled in a bitter feud with team president Mike Lynn until Burns threw his support behind the safety and helped work out matters. Browner responded to the security by earning Pro Bowl honors for a fifth straight time in 1989, thanks to his fifth straight year with more than 100 tackles while leading the Vikings again with five interceptions. He also was named to the second-team All-NFL squad of the 1980s.

The 1990s began in a similar manner. Browner was a consensus All-Pro and Pro Bowl selection after tying for the league lead with seven pass interceptions. He also earned NFC Defensive Player of the Month honors in November after recording 23 solo tackles, one sack and four picks, including a 26-yard touchdown return during a 27–22 triumph over Denver on November 4.

Injuries forced Browner to miss two games in 1991, yet he still led the Viking defense with five interceptions and finished third on the team with 102 total tackles. His performance, however, did show signs of slipping. Combine that with the safety's outspokenness during the time Dennis Green was named head coach in 1992, and Browner found himself on the outside looking in during training camp. Green's decision not to keep Browner proved to be the right one, for he played only seven more games with Tampa Bay before his NFL career concluded.

Nevertheless, Browner left the team with nine top 10 rankings in the Vikings' record book. He was first with three interceptions returned for touchdowns, third with 76 passes defensed, fourth with 37 interceptions, 465 interception return yards and 18 forced fumbles, fifth with 17 recovered fumbles and 1,098 total tackles, and sixth with 743 solo tackles and 355 assisted tackles. Without question, those big knocks led to many big notches in the Minnesota win column during Browner's nine seasons with the Vikings.

Bob Bruer

Seasons: 1980–84　　　Tight End　　　Height: 6'5"
Number: 82　　　Mankato State　　　Weight: 240

A two-year veteran of the Canadian Football League following three unsuccessful tries with the National Football League, Bob Bruer joined the Vikings in September of 1980 after being waived by San Francisco. He proceeded to make numerous important catches over the next two years prior to putting together one of the better seasons by a Minnesota tight end.

After failing to catch a pass while playing on special teams and in blocking situations for 12 games in 1980, Bruer was used mostly in two-tight end and goal-line formations the next two years. He responded by scoring three touchdowns on seven catches in 1981 and two scores on eight receptions in 1982. Both of his six-pointers in 1982 came in the second quarter of a 23–22 loss at Buffalo on September 16.

Bruer blossomed into an offensive threat in 1983, when he ranked fourth on the team with 31 catches for 315 yards and two touchdowns. His best day as a Viking took place during a 19–13 loss to the Bears on December 11, with Bruer pulling in a team-high six tosses for 97 yards. His scoring catches came on a three-yard pass from Steve Dils during a 20–17 win over Detroit on September 25 and a two-yard reception from Dils during a 21-point, fourth-quarter rally in a 41–31 loss to St. Louis on October 30.

A left knee injury landed Bruer on injured reserve for all of the 1984 season. His NFL career came to a close the following summer when he was released during training camp.

Larry Brune

Season: 1980 Safety Height: 6'2"
Number: 24 Rice Weight: 202

Larry Brune's career with the Vikings began four years later than he originally hoped. Drafted in the seventh round in 1976 by Minnesota before being released during his first training camp, the former college teammate of Tommy Kramer headed north and spent three seasons in the Canadian Football League before re-signing with the Vikings in 1980.

In his only season wearing purple, Brune played in all 16 games and was a stellar special teams performer, ranking third on the club with 17 unassisted tackles. He also saw action as a fifth and sixth defensive back. Brune intercepted two Joe Theismann passes on November 2, returning one pick 52 yards, in Minnesota's 39–14 win at Washington.

David Bruno

Season: 1987 Punter Height: 6'1"
Number: 13 Moraine Valley Community College Weight: 235

A former first-team Junior College All-American, David Bruno punted in two of the Vikings' three replacement games in 1987. He was busy, kicking 13 times for an average of 35.7 yards per pooch.

Bobby Bryant

Seasons: 1967–80 Cornerback Height: 6'
Number: 20 South Carolina Weight: 175

No player in Minnesota history had a greater penchant for making a big play in pressure situations than Bobby Bryant. A case in point occurred in the 1976 NFC Championship Game against Los Angeles. With the Rams leading 7–0, head coach Chuck Knox opted to go for the "sure" three points after his team was kept out of the end zone during a tremendous goal-line stand by the Viking defense. On Tom Dempsey's field-goal attempt, Nate Allen blocked the kick and Bryant scooped the pigskin and ran 90 yards to paydirt in Minnesota's eventual 24–13 win.

Big-play performances were nothing new to for the rail-thin Bryant. In 1972, he ran 24 yards with a fumble recovery for a touchdown in a 23–10 win over the Bears on December 3. In the 1973 playoff contest with Dallas, Bryant returned an interception 63 yards for six points to ice the 27–10 victory. He also salvaged a regular-season win over Detroit on November 12, 1972, when he blocked a short field goal on the game's final play for a 16–14 triumph over the Lions.

The fact that the fragile-looking Bryant was even on the gridiron surprised many observers. Despite his skinny frame, the cornerback was an excellent tackler and a solid coverman, leading to 51 interceptions in his career, including eight in 1969. Four times he led the team in picks.

A seventh-round draft pick in 1967 who as a left-handed pitcher set the University of South Carolina record for strikeouts, Bryant spent his

Bobby Bryant

rookie season on the Vikings' taxi squad after a knee injury slowed his progress during training camp. He contributed in 1968, serving as a reserve cornerback, where his interception return of 51 yards for a touchdown against New Orleans on October 13, 1968, proved to be a harbinger. He also toiled as a kick returner and galloped 81 yards to the end zone in the Playoff Bowl against Dallas.

Bryant used his outstanding quickness and reaction ability to earn starting honors at right cornerback in 1969. He set the team's single-season record with eight interceptions and earned three game balls in the first nine contests before missing the last third of the campaign with a knee injury. One of his biggest plays that season occurred in the final seconds of a 9–7 triumph over Green Bay on November 16, when Bryant thwarted the Packers' drive by intercepting a pass at the Minnesota 8-yard line to seal the victory. Ailments again slowed him in 1970, when he picked off three tosses in 11 games, including a 39-yarder for a touchdown in a 30–17 win at Detroit on November 1. Bryant again showed the talent to be one of the league's best defensive backs in 1971, yet shoulder problems cost him some playing time and limited him to three picks.

Finally healthy for most of 1972, Bryant continued to make things happen by intercepting four passes. He resumed his spot among the league's elite corners in 1973. The former Gamecock paced the NFC with seven interceptions, among them a 46-yard return for a touchdown in a 31–7 win at Green Bay on December 8. Bryant also paced the team with 25 punt returns for a 5.6-yard norm.

Bryant missed all but one game with a broken arm in 1974, yet returned to start every game in 1975, when he intercepted six more passes. Another broken arm suffered during training camp in 1976 caused Bryant to lose his starting job to Nate Allen until his replacement hurt an ankle against Green Bay in late November. Bryant proved he was up to the task by starting the last three regular-season games and all three post-season matchups. His best single-game performance took place against the Rams in the NFC Championship Game. In addition to his 90-yard gallop for six points on the blocked field goal, Bryant also intercepted two Pat Haden passes to seal the 24–13 triumph on December 26.

Back as a starter in 1977, Bryant led the Vikings for the third time in his career with four interceptions, his biggest pick coming in the end zone on the last play of the game in the snow to save a 13–6 win on November 26 at Green Bay. Bryant then tied Ed Sharockman with his fourth season leading the team in interceptions by picking off six aerials in 1978. He started 14 games in 1979 with two more steals before retiring after the 1980 slate, when Bryant intercepted the final three tosses of his career over a 14-game span.

Bryant ranks second all-time on the Vikings' interceptions list with 51 pickoffs, just two behind Paul Krause. At the time of his retirement, he was one of five Minnesota players to have three interceptions in one game and the only player to accomplish the feat twice, against Cleveland on November 9, 1969, and Green Bay on December 8, 1973. Bryant played in four Super Bowls and the 1975 Pro Bowl, and was named to the Vikings' Silver Anniversary All-Time Team in 1985.

Tim Bryant

Season: 1987
Number: 94
Linebacker
Southern Mississippi
Height: 6'1"
Weight: 217

A one-year veteran of the Canadian Football League, Tim Bryant's days with Minnesota were limited to one game as a replacement player during the 1987 season.

Bart Buetow

Season: 1976
Number: 74
Tackle
Minnesota
Height: 6'5"
Weight: 250

A native of Mounds View, Minnesota, who played football and hockey for the Golden Gophers, Bart Buetow was drafted in the third round by the Vikings in 1973 but did not make the team during his first training camp. After hooking on with the New York Giants, playing two years in the Canadian Football League, and beginning the 1976 campaign with Denver, Buetow was signed by the Vikes midway through the 1976 slate after Scott Anderson was placed on the injured reserve list.

Buetow was active for 10 games as well as the postseason and saw some action in three contests. He was released for a second time by the Vikings during training camp in 1977.

Mike Bundra

Season: 1964
Number: 75
Defensive Tackle
Southern Cal
Height: 6'3"
Weight: 255

Mike Bundra passed through Metropolitan Stadium briefly while playing for four teams in four years in the National Football League. After spending his first two seasons with Detroit, Bundra joined the Vikings early in the 1964 campaign when he was acquired from the Lions with Larry Vargo in exchange for a sixth- and seventh-round draft pick. He played four games in purple before being traded to Cleveland prior to Week 6 for a fourth-round draft choice. His final professional season consisted of an eight-game stint with the Giants in 1965.

Derek Burton

Season: 1987
Number: 71
Tackle
Oklahoma State
Height: 6'2"
Weight: 270

A former New Jersey General in the United States Football League, Derek Burton's claim to fame as far as the Vikings are concerned consists of starting three games at right tackle with the Minnesota replacement team in 1987.

Billy Butler

Seasons: 1962–64
Number: 22
Defensive Back-Running Back
Tennessee-Chattanooga
Height: 5'10"
Weight: 200

One of the few two-way players in Vikings history, Billy Butler also held two jobs, one as a six-year veteran in the National Football League and another as a deputy sheriff in Berlin, Wisconsin.

Butler, who was acquired from Pittsburgh in 1962 for a sixth-round draft pick, had short legs but decent speed and a tough-as-nails determination. He also possessed a nose for the ball on defense, as evidenced by his interception and 39-yard gallop to paydirt in a 38–14 win over the Rams on October 21, 1962. That pick marked the first interception return for a touchdown in Minnesota history. Earlier in that same game, Butler recovered a fumble to set up the Vikings' first touchdown. He had five interceptions in 1962 and two in 1964, the year he earned a $500 bonus from head coach Norm Van Brocklin after a spectacular showing during a 24–23 win over Green Bay on October 4.

As far as carrying the football is concerned, Butler's efforts in 1962 centered on returning kicks. He brought back 12 punts for a 14.1-yard norm and 26 kickoffs for a 22.6-yard average. In 1963, while catching four passes for 39 yards and rushing 17 times for 48 yards, he was fourth in the NFL in punt returns with 21 attempts for 220 yards, 60 of those coming on a touchdown gallop in Minnesota's 45–14 win over the 49ers on September 29, marking only the second time the feat had been achieved in Viking annals. He also led the league with 33 kickoff returns that year, averaging 21.6 yards per attempt. In 1964, he averaged 7.1 yards on 22 punt returns and 23.0 yards on 26 kickoffs returns. Butler also gained 11 yards on five carries and caught a 58-yard pass before focusing all of his efforts on law enforcement.

Duane Butler

Seasons: 1997–98　　　　　Safety　　　　　　　　Height: 6'1"
Number: 31　　　　　　　Illinois State　　　　　　Weight: 203

Excuse Duane Butler if he seemed confused about his place with the Vikings.

Take the 1997 season, for example. Released as a college free agent during training camp, Butler was re-signed to the Minnesota practice squad prior to the season opener and joined the 53–man roster for four weeks before being released in November. Re-signed to the practice squad a few days later, Butler rejoined the active roster for the final four games and saw action on special teams by making seven total tackles.

Butler resumed his special teams duties with aplomb in 1998 before severely injuring an ankle against Cincinnati on November 15. Although the ankle was initially feared to be broken, he returned to action three weeks later and finished the season with 11 total tackles in 14 contests. His confusion in Minnesota ended in February of 1999 when he was selected in the expansion draft by the Cleveland Browns.

Ken Byers

Seasons: 1964–66　　　　　Guard　　　　　　　　Height: 6'1"
Number: 66　　　　　　　Cincinnati　　　　　　　Weight: 245

The Vikings tried to get Ken Byers as part of the deal that sent Hugh McElhenny to the Giants in 1963. The Giants refused, only to release the lineman during the following season. Minnesota put in the waiver claim immediately on November 4 to acquire the versatile guard.

Byers' first start for Minnesota came against his former employer. After seeing action only on special teams due to a knee injury during his first month in purple, Byers did a solid job on the line in the Vikings' 30–21 win at Yankee Stadium on December 6, 1964. He then served as a swing man in 1965, playing in all 14 games while backing up Larry Bowie and Milt Sunde at the two guard positions. Byers was in training camp with the Vikings in 1966 but did not see any action in the regular season.

The Players

Ivan Caesar

Season: 1991	Linebacker	Height: 6'1"
Number: 53	Boston College	Weight: 237

Ivan Caesar played in 14 games and started two during his lone season in the National Football League. The Vikings' 11th-round draft pick in 1991, Caesar spent the first two games on the practice squad before experiencing a steady increase in playing time.

In addition to seeing action at defensive end, inside linebacker and on special teams, the Virgin Islands native started at outside linebacker in Minnesota's 28–0 win at Phoenix on October 27, recording five tackles and recovering a fumble. In his other start, a 28–13 triumph against Tampa Bay on November 3, he posted five tackles and fell on another loose ball. Caesar also ranked fifth on special teams with 15 hits.

Jamie Caleb

Season: 1961	Running Back	Height: 6'1"
Number: 23	Grambling	Weight: 210

One of six players acquired from Cleveland in the Jim Marshall trade just prior to the 1961 season, Jamie Caleb served as the Vikings' primary kickoff returner and as a reserve running back in his only season in purple. Caleb ran back 22 kicks for 504 yards, a 22.9-yard average. He also returned one punt for eight yards, ran three times from scrimmage for 11 yards, lost eight yards on two receptions, and threw an incompletion on his lone pass attempt.

Lee Calland

Seasons: 1963–65	Defensive Back	Height: 6'
Number: 23	Louisville	Weight: 190

The Vikings were stunned to see Lee Calland available as a college free agent when the 1963 draft concluded. Minnesota's coaching staff considered the former Louisville standout an excellent athlete, and watched him make the team by joining Don Hultz and Terry Dillon as undrafted free agents who became first-team players as rookies.

Using his excellent speed and range and outstanding open-field tackling ability at left cornerback, Calland played in all 14 games during his first season. He recovered a fumble and returned two kicks, among them a 31-yard punt return during Minnesota's 34–13 win at Philadelphia on December 15.

Calland broke his arm in the season-opener against Baltimore in 1964 and missed the remainder of the campaign. He saw action in five games with the Vikings in 1965 before Atlanta nabbed the defensive back from the expansion pool the following offseason.

John Campbell

Seasons: 1963–64	Linebacker	Height: 6'3"
Number: 55	Minnesota	Weight: 215

John Campbell holds the distinction of being the first Golden Gopher drafted and signed by the Vikings. A reliable receiver at the University of Minnesota in the early 1960s, Campbell was told by head coach Norm Van Brocklin, "You have terrible hands. You're going to be a linebacker." Consequently, he was moved to outside linebacker during his tenure in the National Football League, which included two years with Minnesota, four with Pittsburgh and two seasons with Baltimore.

The Vikings' 11th-round draft pick in 1963, the Wadena, Minnesota, native had 6.0 speed in the 50 while dressed in full uniform. Campbell played in all 14 games in both 1963 and 1964 for Minnesota, with most of his contributions coming on special teams. He was traded with a sixth-round draft choice to the Colts in 1965 for the rights to guard Larry Kramer.

Bill Cappleman

Season: 1970	Quarterback	Height: 6'3"
Number: 17	Florida State	Weight: 210

Tabbed the top pro prospect in Florida after setting 13 passing records at Florida State, Bill Cappleman joined the Vikings as a second-round draft choice in 1970 and played one regular-season game in purple. After starting the "all-rookie" preseason opener against New Orleans, the third-string quarterback completed four of seven passes for 49 yards in relief of Bob Lee late in the Vikings' 35–14 victory at Boston on December 13. He was traded the following season to Philadelphia for a fourth-round draft pick.

Preston Carpenter

Season: 1966	Tight End	Height: 6'1"
Number: 40	Arkansas	Weight: 210

Preston Carpenter arrived in Minnesota from Washington in September of 1966 in exchange for a sixth-round draft choice and became one of the Vikings' more consistent receivers, pulling in 27 passes for 487 yards to rank fourth on the team.

A 10–year veteran of the National Football League prior to becoming a Viking, the brother of Minnesota assistant coach Lew Carpenter caught a touchdown pass in each of the season's final three games and had four for the year. His most exciting plays included a 40-yard strike from Fran Tarkenton in Minnesota's 28-3 win over San Francisco on October 30 and a 52-yard score from Bob Berry in a 20–13 loss to the Falcons on December 4. He also grabbed an 11-yard touchdown pass from Tarkenton in a 28–16 win at Detroit on December 11 and a six-yard scoring toss from Tarkenton during a 41–28 defeat at Chicago on December 18.

Carpenter's final professional season came a year later with Miami after reporting to training camp with the Vikings.

Ron Carpenter

Season: 1993	Defensive Back	Height: 6'1"
Number: 36	Miami (Ohio)	Weight: 189

Minnesota signed Ron Carpenter during the 1993 season and sent the rookie into battle as a member of the special teams for seven games. He made four solo tackles on kick coverages prior to being waived in November and joining the Bengals for the final six contests of the campaign.

Jay Carroll

| Season: 1985 | Tight End | Height: 6'4" |
| Number: 84 | Minnesota | Weight: 232 |

Jay Carroll returned home to the Land of 10,000 Lakes just prior to the 1985 season-opener after being released by Tampa Bay. The Minnesota alum and Winona native played in all 16 games for the Vikings in 1985 as a third-team tight end and a member of the special teams. His lone pass reception was an eight-yard catch during a 27–20 win at Buffalo on September 29. He also tied for second on the team with 10 solo tackles on kick coverages.

Malcolm Carson

| Season: 1984 | Guard | Height: 6'2" |
| Number: 97 | Tennessee-Chattanooga | Weight: 260 |

Malcolm Carter's career in the National Football League consisted of one game during the 1984 season. Carson made the roster as a free agent out of training camp and took the field briefly in the season opener against San Diego on September 2 before being waived two days later.

Anthony Carter

| Seasons: 1985–93 | Wide Receiver | Height: 5'11" |
| Number: 81 | Michigan | Weight: 181 |

If Mary Tyler Moore could turn the world on with her smile, Anthony Carter's constant grin could send Vikings fans into a state of euphoria. Few players in the history of the National Football League have enjoyed playing the game more than Carter. And when he and the Minnesota offense were clicking on all cylinders, a more exciting, dominating brand of football was nearly impossible to find.

A three-year veteran of the defunct United States Football League, Carter's rights were acquired by Minnesota from the Dolphins prior to the 1985 season in exchange for linebacker Robin Sendlein and a second-round draft pick. That deal is one of the best in Vikings history, for Carter immediately emerged as one of the premier offensive forces in football.

Having thrashed the Golden Gophers in college with regularity, the former Michigan All-American needed no introduction to football followers in the Twin Cities. He wasted no time getting on the fans' good side by leading the Vikings with eight touchdown receptions and 821 receiving yards and tying for third on the club with 43 catches in 1985. He tied John Gilliam's franchise record with five games of more than 100 yards receiving and caught two touchdown passes in three different games, the most exciting pair coming against Philadelphia that capped a Vikings' rally from a 23–0 deficit in Minnesota's 28–23 triumph on December 1.

Despite missing the first four games in 1986 after undergoing arthroscopic knee surgery at the end of training camp, Carter still led the Vikings with seven touchdown receptions while ranking second with 686 receiving yards. His first Pro Bowl invitation came a year later, when A.C. again paced the team with 38 receptions, 922 receiving yards and seven touchdowns. Yet the greatest example of Carter's abilities to dominate on the gridiron took place at the end of that campaign, during the Vikings' drive to the 1987 NFC Championship Game.

After leading the Vikings to a 44–10 upset over New Orleans in the first round by pulling in six passes for 143 yards and scurrying 84 yards on a punt return for a touchdown on January 3, 1988, Carter shattered NFL playoff marks with 10 catches for 227 yards in the 36–24 thrashing of San Francisco a week later. Two of his receptions went for 63 and 40 yards. Nine grabs

Anthony Carter

produced first downs, and all 10 receptions occurred during scoring drives. He also added a 30-yard gallop on a reverse, and returned two punts for 21 yards to post one of the most dominating individual performances in Minnesota annals.

Carter broke the century mark in receiving yardage three times in 1988, the year he garnered his first starting Pro Bowl assignment after setting a Minnesota single-season record with 1,225 yards receiving on a team-high 72 grabs. His best day of the season came against Detroit on November 6, when his 186 receiving yards represented the highest total by any wide receiver in the NFC that year.

In 1989, despite being disgruntled with his contract situation, he joined Ahmad Rashad as the only Vikings receivers to have back-to-back 1,000-yard seasons by leading the team with 1,066 yards on 65 catches. More team records fell in 1990, with Carter becoming the first Minnesota pass catcher to have three straight 1,000-yard receiving campaigns while establishing a new mark with 80 straight games with at least one grab. That streak extended to 95 games by the end of the 1991 slate, when for the seventh straight year he tied for the club lead in receiving touchdowns with five.

The 1991 season, however, signified the first time Carter started to show signs of slowing down. He still possessed the remarkable ability to tie up defenders by changing directions two or three times on a single route, enabling him to pull in 51 passes in 1991 and 41 a year later. Yet the breakaway speed could no longer discover that final gear, and such teammates as Cris Carter were becoming the go-to guys. He also saw his consecutive games streak conclude at 105 upon failing to catch a pass against Cleveland on November 22, 1992. Still, Carter sacrificed his body when necessary and remained a threat to score anytime the pigskin was cradled in his arm due to his ability to elude defenders after making the catch.

Despite his smile, Carter was not shy about voicing his opinions when he felt footballs were not flying in his direction often enough. His complaints did not please head coach Dennis Green, although A.C. returned to the Vikings in 1993 when many considered him history. He remained a productive player, placing second to Cris Carter with 60 receptions for 775 yards and five touchdowns. Even so, Carter was not tendered a contract prior to the 1994 season, when the Vikings decided to go with an unproven Jake Reed, and spent his last year-and-a-half in the league with Detroit.

At the time of his departure, A.C. held the Vikings' record with 7,636 receiving yards and 52 touchdown catches. He was second in receptions (478), third in average-per-reception (16.0) and fifth in total touchdowns and combined net yards. His 290 yards rushing also rated as the most ever by a Minnesota receiver. It's certain those numbers produced a reflection of Carter's smile on the faces of the Vikings' faithful.

Cris Carter

Seasons: 1990–98   Wide Receiver   Height: 6'3"
Number: 80   Ohio State   Weight: 216

"All he does is catch touchdown passes."

Those words were uttered by Buddy Ryan in 1990, when the Philadelphia Eagles' head coach placed Cris Carter on waivers. The best claim in the history of the National Football League, the Vikings plunked down the $100 waiver fee and came away with a player who emerged as a certain Hall-of-Famer and the best all-around wide receiver in Minnesota annals.

Carter, however, admits that he is not the same player with the Vikings that he was for the Eagles. "I was a bad boy on the field and off the field at Philadelphia," said Carter, who revealed in 1997 that Ryan protected him and that problems with drugs and alcohol led to his departure from the Eagles. "I was released and deserved to be released. I started a new life when I got to Minnesota. Roger Craig talked to me a lot about why Jerry Rice had become a great receiver. Craig taught me how important it was to work hard."

Other forces also played a role in Carter's emergence in Minnesota. He committed his life to God during his early days with the Vikings, a belief that led to his becoming an ordained minister. He patterned his life in order to be a stellar role model, earning the Athletes in Action Bart Starr Award in 1995 for outstanding character and leadership on and off the field. He was also given the Midwest Sports Channel Citizen Athlete Award.

But his good works off the field did not diminish his toughness on the gridiron. His fire remained most evident in the locker room, where Carter served as the team's unquestioned leader. He never backed down from voicing his opinions when things were not going as he saw fit, worked with young players, including heralded rookie Randy Moss, and passed along his incredible knowledge and insight to offensive coordinator Brian Billick to make the Vikings' attack one of the league's most potent.

Cris Carter

The returns from his hard work have been staggering. After catching 27 passes for 413 yards and three touchdowns as Minnesota's third receiver in 1990, Carter emerged as the go-to guy in 1991, a role he maintained for the next seven years. Employing the game's best hands along with amazing leaping ability and body control that made throwing the alley-oop pass in the corner of the end zone nearly impossible to defend, Carter's intelligence makes up for his lack of blazing speed. Highlight reel catches have become the norm for the former Buckeye, regardless of whether the receptions take place in the end zone, over the middle or near the sidelines.

"Talk to any defensive coordinator who plays us," Billick said. "They'll say their number one priority is to stop Cris Carter. There's only a handful of players who truly can command that type of attention."

The attention is centered on the fact that Carter is the best inside receiver in the game. He gains position against defenders, not unlike a basketball player, and employs his incredible hands to create awe-inspiring catches. He excels with his quickness, not his speed, which has enabled him to remain among the game's elite pass catchers throughout the 1990s.

His numbers are simply amazing. After a 72–reception season in 1991, Carter's production fell to 53 grabs due to a four-game absence with a broken collarbone in 1992. He returned to catch 86 passes a year later before setting the NFL record with 122 grabs in 1994. He equalled that performance the following season while pulling in a career-high 17 touchdown tosses, then caught 96 passes for 10 six-pointers in 1996.

To list Carter's best catches is a near-impossible feat due to the quality and quantity. Some highlights would have to include the 65-yard touchdown pass from Warren Moon on December 1, 1994, a reception Carter turned into the game-winning score in the 33–27 win over the Bears. His acrobatic, game-clinching grab off the helmet of a Buccaneer defender on December 15, 1996, in a 21–10 win was another one for the highlight reel. Carter, meanwhile, says his one-handed grab inside the 10-yard line against Atlanta on September 8, 1991, ranks at the top of his book.

With 89 catches for 1,069 yards and 13 scores in 1997 and 78 grabs for 1,011 yards and 12 touchdowns in 1998, Carter's career numbers rank among the best in NFL history. He concluded the 1998 campaign ranked second all-time with 101 touchdown receptions and fourth with 834 catches. Carter also combined with Randy Moss to break the NFL single-season mark for receiving touchdowns by a tandem with 29. Based on his comments in the latter part of the slate, he has set his sights on the 1,000–catch mark.

"In this system, where I know I'm going to get a lot of chances, I believe 1,000 is realistic," said Carter, who earned his sixth straight trip to the Pro Bowl in 1998. "Times have changed, and receivers are catching so many more balls."

As far as team records are concerned, Carter tied the Minnesota mark by scoring his 76th touchdown, against Detroit on October 25, 1998. He broke the record he shared briefly with Bill Brown by pulling in a 14-yard touchdown reception from Brad Johnson against New Orleans on November 8, and concluded the campaign with 82 touchdowns as a Viking. An early-game injury suffered against the Bears on December 6 ended his consecutive game streak with at least one pass reception at a team-record 106. He also holds team records with 8,997 receiving yards and 28 100-yard receiving contests.

Dave Casper

Season: 1983 — Tight End — Height: 6'4"
Number: 44 — Notre Dame — Weight: 240

Acquired from Houston on September 21, 1983, along with Archie Manning in exchange for second- and fourth-round draft picks, Dave Casper was in the twilight of his National Football League career while with the Vikings. One of the game's best tight ends during his six-and-a-half years with the Raiders, Casper moved into the Minnesota starting lineup in his third game and finished the year with 13 receptions for 172 yards.

After a hamstring injury cost him the final three contests in 1983, Casper was moved to guard during training camp in 1984 but was released prior to the regular season. He concluded his career that year with an encore in Oakland.

John Charles

Season: 1970 — Defensive Back — Height: 6'
Number: 25 — Purdue — Weight: 205

The Patriots' first-round draft choice in 1967, John Charles was acquired along with Boston's first-round selection in 1972 in exchange for Joe Kapp. He played in eight games as a reserve defensive back and special teams performer with the Vikings during the 1970 season and intercepted one pass, returning the ball 25 yards.

Jim Christopherson

Season: 1962 — Linebacker-Kicker — Height: 6'
Number: 36 — Concordia — Weight: 218

A local boy from Henning, Minnesota, and Concordia College, Jim Christopherson was a rookie linebacker who had never kicked in the league when he was told to replace the released Mike Mercer. Considering the circumstances, Christopherson performed admirably, making all 28 extra points. He was less accurate on field-goal attempts, however, putting just 11 of 20 through the uprights.

In addition to his kicking duties, Christopherson saw limited duty on defense. Released during training camp in the franchise's first season before a successful stint a year later, he contributed to the Vikings' cause by intercepting one pass and returning it 32 yards. Considered on the small side for a linebacker, his services were not deemed necessary in 1963, when Fred Cox took over the kicking chores.

Jeff Christy

Seasons: 1993–98   Center   Height: 6'3"
Number: 62   Pittsburgh   Weight: 282

One of the Vikings' more impressive developmental projects has been the emergence of Jeff Christy into one of the most consistent and best all-around centers in the National Football League. Acquired off waivers from Arizona in 1993, Christy took over the starting job a year later and has done nothing but improve every time he has snapped the ball, so much so that he is now a Pro Bowl performer.

A member of the Cardinals' practice squad in 1992 after joining the team that year as a fourth-round draft pick, Christy served as a backup to Adam Schreiber while playing in nine games on special teams for Minnesota in 1993. The Vikings released Schreiber the following offseason and signed Cowboys free agent Frank Cornish to be the starter, only to watch Christy earn first-team honors during training camp.

Known as "Krusty" to his teammates, Christy helped anchor an offensive line in 1994 that enabled the Minnesota offense to establish a team record for total yards while surrendering a sack for every 22.7 passes thrown, the second-best ratio in team annals. He was the lone offensive lineman who did not miss any time due to injuries in 1995, then further established himself in 1996 while the Vikings initiated quarterback Brad Johnson into the starting lineup.

Jeff Christy

The Minnesota coaching staff raves about Christy's sound fundamentals. The unquestioned leader of the line is excellent at picking up stunts and blitzes, and is considered to be the Vikings' best all-around blocker. He is a tremendous athlete, as evidenced when he pulls on outside running plays. Unheralded in part because of the presence of All-Pro Randall McDaniel to his left, Christy has surpassed the high expectations head coach Dennis Green and his staff had upon signing the young center.

Christy was headed for a Pro Bowl invitation in 1997 when he broke two bones in his left ankle in the final seconds of the 23–21 loss to the New York Jets on November 23. At the time he had started 60 straight games, the team's third-longest active streak and the second-longest in team history for centers, behind only Mick Tingelhoff.

"I think Jeff Christy was playing as good as any center in the National Football Conference when he got injured," said Mike Tice, Minnesota's current offensive line coach. "There aren't many centers with the athletic ability and quickness to pull like Jeff Christy. Jeff was having an outstanding season."

Christy rehabilitated the ankle much faster than doctors expected and was back at full strength during mini-camp the following May. He then picked up where he left off in 1997, starting all 16 regular-season games and dominating most of the time in the middle of the line to earn a starting berth in the Pro Bowl and second-team All-Pro honors. One reason the Vikings' frequent quarterback changes between Johnson and Randall Cunningham went so smooth was Christy's ability to adjust at a moment's notice. He concluded the 1998 season ranking fourth on the club's all-time list for starts by a center with 78.

Neil Clabo

Seasons: 1975–77
Number: 12
Punter
Tennessee
Height: 6'
Weight: 200

After growing frustrated with the inconsistency of Mike Eischied in 1974, the Vikings drafted All-Southeastern Conference punter Neil Clabo in the 10th round the following spring and watched the team's overall punting performance improve for most of the next three years.

Clabo averaged 41.1 yards on 73 kicks as a rookie to rank fourth in the NFC. His strength was placing the ball inside the opponents' 10-yard line, a feat he accomplished on nine occasions that year, tying him for the lead in the National Football League. He continued to punt well early in 1976 before a mid-season slump dropped his average to 38.8 yards per kick. His worst day occurred on Halloween, when the winds at Soldier Field played tricks on the punter, limiting him to a 28.3-yard average on seven attempts. Clabo also entered the Vikings' record book when he became the team's first punter not called upon in a game during Minnesota's 31–23 victory over Detroit on November 7. His best game came against Washington in the playoffs, when he punted six times for a 46-yard norm during the Vikes' 35–20 triumph over the Redskins on December 18.

In 1977, Clabo did not have a punt blocked for the second straight season while averaging 39.8 yards on 83 efforts. In what proved to be his final year in the league, Clabo had a career-long 69-yard punt against Chicago, and dropped 19 kicks inside the opponents' 20-yard line, a total that more than tripled his output from 1976.

Jessie Clark

Seasons: 1989–90
Number: 33
Running Back
Arkansas
Height: 6'1"
Weight: 232

Jessie Clark played on Minnesota's special teams and sparingly at running back during the final month of 1989 and the early stages of 1990. Signed on December 6, 1989, after being released by the Cardinals, Clark participated in the final three regular-season games. Most of his playing time as a Viking occurred four days after signing, in a 43–17 win against Atlanta. He carried the ball 10 times from scrimmage for 57 yards, which represented his season total in purple. He added two special teams tackles versus the Falcons and one more a week later against Cleveland.

Clark played a similar role in 1990, gaining 49 yards on 16 carries in five games before receiving his release.

Ken Clarke

Seasons: 1989–91
Number: 71
Defensive Tackle
Syracuse
Height: 6'2"
Weight: 280

Just as Ken Clarke's career as a Viking appeared over, he proved to be a vital part of the purple defense. Released prior to the start of the 1990 season and re-signed on October 2, Clarke started 10 of the last 11 games at defensive tackle in place of the injured Keith Millard and finished eighth on the club with 79 solo hits. A strong inside pass rusher who excelled in collapsing the pocket, he added seven sacks, good for third on the team. His best showing took place on December 30, when Clarke registered a season-high 11 tackles with three sacks in a 20–17 loss to the 49ers.

A six-year starter with Philadelphia during the late 1970s and 1980s, Clarke joined the Vikings as a free agent one game deep into the 1989 slate after being waived by Seattle. He played in 11 games that season, registering 11 tackles and two sacks. Following his strong showing in 1990, Clarke was back in purple a year later, when he played in all 16 games, forced a fumble, and piled up 87 stops, good for seventh on the team. He was not re-signed after the 1991 campaign, bringing an end to his 14-year career in the National Football League.

Leon Clarke

Season: 1963   End   Height: 6'4"
Number: 81   Southern Cal   Weight: 232

Leon Clarke spent his eighth and final season in the National Football League with Minnesota. Acquired in a trade from Cleveland prior to the 1963 slate for running back Mel Triplett, Clarke reported late to training camp and was out of shape, featuring a plump torso on his stick-thin legs. His poor physical condition landed him on the bench and in head coach Norm Van Brocklin's doghouse during the first half of the season. He played in three games down the stretch and caught three passes for 34 yards, but was otherwise a non-factor in the Upper Midwest.

Duane Clemons

Seasons: 1996–98   Linebacker-Defensive End   Height: 6'5"
Number: 92   California   Weight: 285

Minnesota's first-round pick in 1996, Duane Clemons did not progress as quickly during his rookie season as the Vikings hoped upon drafting him. Moved from linebacker in college to defensive end in the National Football League, Clemons saw brief playing time in 13 games as a reserve in his first year, but watched most of the action go to veteran Martin Harrison in pass-rush situations.

"A lot of people automatically call you a bust just because you didn't come out as a rookie and have a phenomenal year," said Clemons, who recovered his first fumble and registered a tackle for a loss against Seattle on November 10, 1996. "Some people don't realize that it didn't have to do with just me, but the team situation."

With Harrison out of the picture in 1997 in order to give the first-rounder more opportunity, Clemons began to contribute in his second season. He shared reserve time with rookie Stalin Colinet in the campaign's first half, then saw significant action beginning at midseason. Clemons recorded the first two sacks of his career against the Patriots in a 23–18 win on November 2, 1997. He continued to improve with every opportunity, recording four tackles, two sacks and two forced fumbles in his first start, a 23–21 loss to the Jets on November 23. Clemons went on to register seven quarterback dumps in his final seven games of the 1997 slate.

Clemons started to become more of a complete player in 1998. His defense against the run improved and he made more big plays as a defensive end in pass-rushing situations. The lineman wound up starting two games and concluded the campaign with 25 tackles and 2.5 sacks.

Bob Cobb

Seasons: 1984   Defensive End   Height: 6'4"
Number: 75   Arizona   Weight: 260

Bob Cobb, a former third-round pick of the Rams, played in the first two games of the 1984 season and recorded a sack before going on the exempt list one day prior to the Atlanta contest, on September 16. He remained out of action for the remainder of the campaign before receiving his release prior to training camp in 1985.

Marvin Cobb

Season: 1980	Defensive Back	Height: 6'
Number: 26	Southern Cal	Weight: 188

A former Brown and Steeler who could play all four positions in the defensive secondary, Marvin Cobb was active for seven games and played in two for Minnesota in 1980 after being claimed on waivers in October. He received his release from the Vikings the following year in training camp, thereby ending his six-year career in the National Football League.

Paul Coffman

Season: 1988	Tight End	Height: 6'3"
Number: 89	Kansas State	Weight: 222

A 10–year veteran of the National Football League, Paul Coffman was signed at the end of training camp in 1988 and spent two months with the Vikings before being waived on October 25. The former Packer played in eight games with Minnesota, mostly on special teams and in blocking assignments, and did not have a reception.

Al Coleman

Season: 1967	Cornerback	Height: 6'2"
Number: 37	Tennessee State	Weight: 190

Featuring great size, speed and quickness, Al Coleman impressed the Minnesota coaching staff with his athleticism during his first training camp after being drafted in the fourth round in 1967. He opened the season on the taxi squad before taking the field briefly for two games late in the campaign. Released by Minnesota prior to the 1968 season, Coleman spent five more seasons in the National Football League, including stints as a kick returner with the Bengals and Eagles.

Dan Coleman

Season: 1987	Defensive End	Height: 6'4"
Number: 91	Murray State	Weight: 225

Dan Coleman reminded few Vikings fans of Chris Doleman during the three replacement games in 1987. Coleman did give his best imitation of the All-Pro defensive end by leading the team with a pair of sacks.

Greg Coleman

Seasons: 1978–87	Punter	Height: 6'
Number: 8	Florida A&M	Weight: 178

The gridiron has served as a springboard to acting careers for a handful of Vikings. Ed Marinaro and Joe Kapp are two that immediately come to mind. But when it came to great stage performances on the field, no one did it better than Greg Coleman.

He could have been a stellar professional wrestler, albeit a skinny one, for Coleman's theatrics began rolling any time a defender got within shouting distance of his right leg. Coleman appeared at times to be a battlefield cadaver, never to arise again. But such award-winning performances resulted in penalties that led to Minnesota victories on at least five occasions.

After watching rookie Mike Wood fail to establish any consistency with his punting in 1978, head coach Bud Grant did the unusual by making a kicking change during the regular season. Seven games deep in the slate, the

Vikings signed Coleman, a noted bad weather punter who had recorded some success with the Browns in 1977. The cousin of baseball's Vince Coleman and a high hurdler in college, Coleman responded by averaging 39 yards with his line-drive style, including an outstanding effort on the first Thursday night television broadcast in National Football League history. In his second outing with Minnesota, Coleman had seven punts for a 48-yard average, and kicked five inside the 10 during a 21–10 win over the Cowboys at Dallas on October 26. That performance marked the beginning of the longest punting tenure in team history.

Coleman averaged 39.5 yards on a single-season team record 91 punts in 1979, including 23 that came to rest inside the 20-yard line. He placed third in the NFC with 20 pooches inside the 20 in 1980, then had a career-long 73-yard effort during the 26–24 win versus Detroit on September 20, 1981.

In 1982, Coleman established team records with 12 punts in the 26–7 loss to Green Bay on November 21 and by averaging 53.2 yards on five efforts in the 13–10 win over Baltimore on December 12. He led the conference in net punting in 1983 while his 28 punts inside the 20 ranked third. Coleman again paced the NFC in net punting in 1984, and placed second with a 42.4-yard norm on 82 boots. His 42.8-yard average in 1985 represented his career-high before concluding with averages of 41.4 and 39.7 yards in 1986 and 1987, respectively.

A torn muscle in his kicking leg late in the 1987 season led to a dismal performance in the second half of a 30–24 loss to Chicago on December 6. His erratic play forced Coleman to give way to Bucky Scribner for the campaign's final three games as well as throughout the playoffs. Coleman lost his job to Scribner a year later during training camp, which brought to a close one of the more unexpected careers in Vikings annals.

Coleman was named to the Vikings' Silver Anniversary All-Time Team in 1985 and still heads the team record books with 721 punts and 154 boots inside the 20. His 40.8 gross-yard average ranks second and his 34.7 net-yard average places third in Minnesota annals. He's also first among punters for penalties drawn, even if a few may have brought less pain than others, regardless of how they appeared.

Greg Coleman

Stalin Colinet

Seasons: 1997–98 Defensive End Height: 6'6"
Number: 99 Boston College Weight: 274

The Vikings' third-round draft choice in 1997, Stalin Colinet served as a pass rush specialist on third downs before taking over a starting job during the final month of his rookie year. The former All-Big East performer shared reserve time early in the season with Duane Clemons, who made some significant strides with his extra year of experience. Colinet, meanwhile, contributed 14 solo tackles and three hits for loss yardage. He also blocked a field goal against San Francisco on December 7, and established a career-high with seven stops in the 23–22 playoff victory over the New York Giants on December 27.

So impressive was Colinet's rookie performance, the Vikings felt secure enough to release starter Fernando Smith, who was beset with constant nagging injuries, low production and a large salary, just prior to training camp in 1998. Injuries, however, slowed Colinet's progress for much of his second season, with the defensive end missing time early in the campaign before a sprained ankle suffered in practice cost him three games in November. He finished the year with 11 tackles and a sack.

Dwight Collins

Season: 1984	Wide Receiver	Height: 6'1"
Number: 84	Pittsburgh	Weight: 209

Minnesota's sixth-round draft pick in 1984, Dwight Collins played in all 16 games as a rookie. The reserve receiver caught 11 passes for 143 yards, including a 43-yard touchdown pass on the halfback option by Alfred Anderson during a 27–20 win over Atlanta on September 16. Collins also had four catches during the 42–21 loss to Denver on November 18 and three grabs in his only start, a 38–14 loss to Green Bay on December 16.

Fabray Collins

Season: 1987	Linebacker	Height: 6'2"
Number: 59	Southern Illinois	Weight: 215

A replacement player for the Vikings in 1987, Fabray Collins' best showing among his three contests was his seven-tackle performance against Tampa Bay on October 18.

Jeff Colter

Season: 1984	Defensive Back	Height: 5'10"
Number: 43	Kansas	Weight: 171

Jeff Colter made the Vikings' roster in 1984 as an undrafted free agent. He led Minnesota with 13 solo stops on special teams, tied for second with 17 total tackles, and added 16 more hits as a reserve cornerback. Released the following summer in training camp, Colter reemerged in the National Football League for one game with Kansas City in 1987.

Kerry Cooks

Season: 1998	Strong Safety	Height: 5'11"
Number: 20	Iowa	Weight: 204

The Vikings' fifth-round draft pick in 1998, Kerry Cooks opened his rookie season on the Minnesota roster and was inactive for the first two games. He was placed on waivers when the team had to sign quarterback Jay Fielder to replace an injured Brad Johnson and was acquired by Green Bay before Minnesota could place Cooks on the practice squad.

Adrian Cooper

Seasons: 1994–95	Tight End	Height: 6'5"
Number: 87	Oklahoma	Weight: 268

Head coach Dennis Green was looking for a big tight end who could block and catch a slew of passes when he pushed for the trade for Adrian Cooper from Pittsburgh in exchange for third- and sixth-round draft picks before the 1994 season. What the Vikings got was an under-motivated player who failed to live up to the potential he showed with the Steelers.

The tight end started the first 12 games of the 1994 season and caught 32 passes before missing the last five contests due to a torn rotator cuff. His most notable showing took place during a 31–21 loss to the Jets on November 20. Cooper had 101 yards receiving, the most for a Minnesota tight end since Steve Jordan's 179 yards against Washington in 1986, and combined with Cris Carter and Jake Reed to become the second receiving trio in Vikings history to reach the century mark in the same game.

In 1995, a healthy Cooper lost more playing time to second-year tight end Andrew Jordan. As a result, Cooper's numbers fell to 18 catches for 207 yards in 13 outings. With his production dropping and his disruptive attitude becoming more apparent, Cooper was set free during the following offseason and signed with San Francisco.

Frank Cornish

Season: 1994 Offensive Lineman Height: 6'4"
Number: 63 UCLA Weight: 292

The Vikings released Adam Schreiber as their starting center and signed Frank Cornish as the replacement just prior to training camp in 1994. The former Cowboy did not perform as hoped and lost his starting job to Jeff Christy before the regular season opened. Cornish played on special teams in seven games before receiving his release midway through the campaign after getting into a fight with John Randle during practice. Cornish was released in favor of waiver-wire acquisition Mike Ruether.

Fred Cox

Seasons: 1963–77 Kicker Height: 5'11"
Number: 14 Pittsburgh Weight: 200

Persistence paid off for Fred Cox.

Acquired from Cleveland in a preseason trade in 1962, Cox was released by head coach Norm Van Brocklin after the kicker had an outstanding debut in purple during the 45–26 exhibition win over Dallas on September 8. Incumbent Mike Mercer was kept because he was an experienced kicker and punter, thereby occupying just one roster spot. Van Brocklin did not feel the expansion roster could merit two kicking specialists, so Cox returned to his native Pennsylvania and taught school.

"I was discouraged because I had kicked as well as I'd ever kicked," said Cox, who later showed his loyalty to the Vikings by painting his house and barn in Delano, Minnesota, purple and white. "I went back and taught school for a year. I really had decided I wasn't going to play anymore. I felt that I hadn't made it so let's go do something else."

Fred Cox

Van Brocklin invited Cox back for training camp in 1963 following Mercer's release during the 1962 campaign. Cox earned the job, and after succeeding on 12 of 24 field goal attempts and all 39 extra-point tries while punting 70 times for a 38.7 yard average in 1963, he proceeded to hold the Vikings' place-kicking duties for the next 15 seasons, including appearances in 210 straight games, the third-longest streak in team history.

With that length of tenure, it should come as no surprise that Cox owns most of the Vikings' kicking records. He holds the franchise's all-time scoring mark with 1,365 points. He booted 519 point-after-touchdown attempts, including a team-record 199 straight, and made 282 field goal tries. He also ranks near the top in several league categories, including 10th in PATs, tied for 12th in field goals, and 13th in points.

One of the game's last straight-ahead kickers, Cox did not possess the league's strongest leg but was usually a cinch inside 40 yards on field goal attempts. He was affected more than most when the goal posts were moved to the back of the end zone beginning with the 1974 season, even to the extent of missing nine PATs that year. Even so, head coach Bud Grant felt comfortable with Cox as his kicker. When questioned about Cox's range, Grant would always point to his consistency, such as a 9–for–9 performance inside the 40 in 1975.

Early in his career, Cox was nothing short of a godsend for Minnesota. So miserable had the Vikings' place-kicking efforts been that Cox's 11-of-21 performance in 1963 was considered a vast improvement. Cox got better as well, and was considered one of the National Football League's best young legs after leading all kickers with 23 field goals and in scoring with 113 points in 1965. In a 24–19 loss at Green Bay on December 5, Cox became the first Viking to kick four field goals in one game, with one of his three-pointers in that contest going for a career-long and team-record 53 yards.

Cox led the Vikings in scoring every year from 1963–73 as well as in 1976. He paced the NFL in scoring in 1969 with 121 points, the most ever at that point by a kicker. He led the NFC in scoring with 125 points in 1970, the same year he had his NFL-record streak of 31 consecutive games with at least one field goal snapped. Cox also established the league standard by scoring in 151 straight games, a streak that was broken when the Bengals shut out the Vikings, 27–0, on December 2, 1973.

"The one word for Fred is consistency," Grant said. "We all have seen a lot of kickers come and go, with some hot years, but short careers. Fred is consistent year after year."

Among the more memorable plays involving Cox occurred on October 12, 1969. With Minnesota leading 7–0 in the third quarter, Cox had a 47-yard field goal attempt blocked by the Bears' Garry Lyle. The pigskin ricochetted into Cox's hands. Instead of panicking, Cox reverted to his college days as a fullback and galloped 11 yards for a first down. The Vikings went on to score a touchdown and win the game 31–0 on their way to the NFL Championship.

The most controversial field goal of Cox's career was one even his teammates admitted could have been judged either way. Cox was credited with a 27-yarder with one second left on the clock that gave the Vikings a 23–21 victory at Dallas on October 6, 1974. "I've found it helps if you signal yourself that it's good," Cox said sheepishly after the game.

One aspect that the records do not reveal is the less-than-ideal conditions Cox kicked in during his career. The Minnesota autumn and early winter did little for his range, and the poor conditions late in the season throughout the league were a far cry from the pristine fields of today. To help offset the cold, which could reduce a kick by upwards of 10 yards, Vikings equipment manager Dennis Ryan kept a bag of warm footballs ready for Cox's use.

Cox also had an advantage due to the consistency of his other partners on field goals and PAT attempts. He never had to worry about the snap or the hold, for center Mick Tingelhoff and holder Paul Krause were among the game's best in those responsibilities. Cox simply had to focus on the task at hand, a skill he possessed better than most.

"The key is definitely concentration," Cox said during his career. "That encompasses the fact that you're going to keep your head down. If you're concentrating, you shouldn't be overwhelmed by pressures that come on you and you shouldn't see the other players or hear the crowd."

Kicking a football was not the only part of Cox's life. In addition to teaching early in his career, Cox opened a chiropractic office in 1974. He also invented the Nerf football, a foam rubber football that remains a steady seller more than a quarter-century after its invention.

When Cox retired after the 1977 season, he left the game as one of just three players to score 1,300 points in NFL history. He made 282 field goals on 455 attempts and converted 519 of 538 PATs. The kicker also earned Pro Bowl honors in 1970, and was named to the Vikings' Silver Anniversary All-Time Team in 1985. Yes, it is safe to say that persistence paid off for Fred Cox.

Roger Craig

Seasons: 1992–93　　　　Running Back　　　　Height: 6′
Number: 33　　　　　　　Nebraska　　　　　　Weight: 219

The final two seasons of Roger Craig's Hall of Fame-caliber career took place in Minnesota, serving as a co-starter at running back with Terry Allen in 1992 and as a third-down back a year later.

A perennial high-stepping Pro Bowl performer and one of the best receivers out of the backfield in league history while with the 49ers, Craig instilled the Vikings with leadership and a burning desire to excel after signing as a Plan B free agent in 1992. Those traits as well as his incredible physical condition were seen when he underwent knee surgery during the campaign, yet missed only one game. He rushed for 416 yards, placing second on the team, and was tied for fifth with 22 receptions. Craig also reached paydirt on four occasions, including two touchdowns against Tampa Bay in Minnesota's 35–7 win on November 7 and the game-deciding, one-yard plunge to cap the Vikes' incredible 21–20 come-from-behind victory over the Bears on October 4.

Even though Allen missed all of 1993 with a knee injury, Craig's contributions decreased due to the acquisitions of Barry Word and Scottie Graham. He carried the ball a career-low 38 times for 119 yards and one touchdown. Craig added 169 yards and another score on 19 receptions, with many of those coming in crucial third-down situations.

When the Vikings decided against re-signing Craig for the 1994 season, he came to terms with the 49ers and retired the same day so he could officially end his career with San Francisco.

Steve Craig

Seasons: 1974–78　　　　Tight End　　　　Height: 6′3″
Number: 84　　　　　　　Northwestern　　　Weight: 230

With the likes of Stu Voigt and Bob Tucker handling the tight end chores for the Vikings during the 1970s, Steve Craig found the playing time limited to special teams and goal-line situations during his five years in purple.

Even so, Craig discovered ways to contribute to the Vikings' cause. A high school, college and professional teammate of Minnesota receiver Jim Lash, Craig was most proficient in blocking punts. Against the Giants in a 24–7 win on October 17, 1976, the tight end blocked a punt that Nate Allen grabbed in mid-air and took 28 yards for a touchdown. He blocked another punt against Cleveland during the 1977 preseason, and knocked down a third against Tampa Bay that Fred McNeill turned into a 16-yard scoring run in Minnesota's 24–7 win on October 1, 1978.

Minnesota's first third-round draft pick in 1974, Craig also contributed as a receiver and played in all 72 regular-season games during his five years with the Vikes. He caught four passes as a rookie, including a 10-yard touchdown toss in a 51–10 win over Houston on October 13. He pulled in six more passes for 68 yards in 1975 and grabbed three aerials for 33 yards in 1976. His production fell to one 14-yard catch in 1977 and four receptions for 31 yards in 1978. His time in purple ended the following year in training camp when Craig lost his roster spot to rookie Joe Senser.

Brad Culpepper

Seasons: 1992–93	Defensive Tackle	Height: 6'1"
Number: 77	Florida	Weight: 260

He may not have been drafted until the 10th round in 1992, but Brad Culpepper played like a first-rounder during his initial training camp. The right defensive tackle piled up four-and-a-half sacks during the preseason to earn the starting nod in the lidlifter against Green Bay. In doing so, Culpepper became the first Viking defensive rookie to start in a season opener since Al Noga in 1988, and was the lowest selection in the 1992 draft to start on opening weekend.

A week later, a player named John Randle took over the starting duties. Culpepper, meanwhile, started one more game and saw action in 11 contests during the campaign before suffering a dislocated toe and missing the remaining five games of the season. He concluded the year with 10 total tackles on defense and another three hits on special teams.

The intense Culpepper, called "Caveman" by his teammates, played mostly on special teams during 1993 before Henry Thomas was felled in the final three games. Culpepper and Esera Tuaolo shared the nose tackle job, with Culpepper registering three tackles against both Dallas on December 12 and Washington on December 31.

Culpepper looked to have made the Vikings' roster again in 1994 when he was not among the final cuts of training camp, only to receive his release just prior to the season opener. He joined Tampa Bay shortly thereafter and emerged as a starter in the middle of the Bucs' defensive front.

Ed Culpepper

Season: 1961	Defensive Tackle	Height: 6'1"
Number: 71	Alabama	Weight: 255

Possessing the heart but not the talent to star in the National Football League, Ed Culpepper amazed his teammates during his only training camp with the Vikings by downing huge amounts of goober peanuts without gulping.

Nicknamed "Penguin" while with Minnesota because of his pear-shaped body and baggy football pants, Culpepper arrived on the northern prairie as an expansion pool draftee from St. Louis. He took the field in all 14 games for the Vikings in 1961 and helped make the defense respectable by plugging the middle of line and limiting the opponents' rushing attack. With the Vikings looking for more youth in their second year, Culpepper moved on to Houston for the 1962 and 1963 campaigns, playing in every contest with the Oilers before calling it a career.

Doug Cunningham

Season: 1979	Wide Receiver	Height: 6'2"
Number: 89	Rice	Weight: 195

A college teammate of Tommy Kramer, Doug Cunningham beat long odds by earning a spot on the Vikings' roster as a undrafted free agent in 1979. He saw action in five early-season games and made five catches for 50 yards. His best showing came in the second contest of the year, with Cunningham reliving old times by pulling in two passes from Kramer for 15 yards against Chicago on September 9. The clock struck midnight shortly thereafter for the Cinderella receiver, who was waived on October 24.

Randall Cunningham

Season: 1997–98
Number: 7
Quarterback-Punter
Nevada-Las Vegas
Height: 6'4"
Weight: 205

Once among the premier quarterbacks and a two-time Most Valuable Player in the National Football League, Randall Cunningham decided during his one-year retirement from the game that he had the rest of his life to install marble in homes. At the behest of head coach Dennis Green, Cunningham decided to return to professional football, a move that turned out to be one of the most important transactions for Minnesota over the next two years.

Known as "Cash" to his teammates, Cunningham served as the Vikings' backup signalcaller in 1997. Though many observers feared the once-moody Cunningham could become a disruptive element while playing behind the inexperienced Brad Johnson, the veteran proved to be a humble cheerleader while watching Johnson emerge as one of the premier quarterbacks in the NFC.

Cunningham served as Minnesota's punter for the first two games of the 1997 season due to the hip injury to Mitch Berger and averaged 34.3 yards on eight kicks, including a 63-yarder from the Minnesota end zone against the Bills in a 34–13 Vikings win on August 31. He did not see action again until he took over the quarterbacking duties late in the 27–11 loss to Green Bay on December 1, and remained under center for the remainder of the campaign while Johnson was out with a herniated disk in his neck. Rusty due to his long absence from game competition, Cunningham completed 44 of 88 attempts for 501 yards and rushed for another 127. His best outing came during a 39–28 victory over Indianapolis in the season finale. Cunningham threw four touchdown passes, including three to former Eagles teammate Cris Carter.

Signed to a new two-year deal prior to the 1998 season, Cunningham parlayed an outstanding showing during the preseason into the starting assignment when Johnson went down with a broken fibula in Week Two. Unlike the previous campaign, Cunningham made Minnesota a better team and guided the Vikings to 13 victories in the regular season. He stayed in the pocket longer than in the past, enabling him to discover his second or third receivers. He also meshed well with rookie Randy Moss as well as Carter, Jake Reed and Andrew Glover to form a spectacular aerial show.

His best performance came against Green Bay on October 5 on *Monday Night Football*. The quarterback blistered the Packers for 442 passing yards, a total that represents the fifth-highest total in Minnesota history and the most ever surrendered by the Pack at Lambeau Field. He threw two touchdown passes longer than 50 yards, and tied a Viking record with his second straight four-touchdown game. He wound up being named the conference's top player for October, and became the first player ever to earn back-to-back NFC Offensive Player of the Week honors, taking home the award for his efforts on September 27 and October 5.

"He's a talented player who's totally at peace with himself," Green said during the 1998 season. "He brings athletic ability, a good deep ball. He can scramble. He knows our offense much better than he did last year, and the team has a lot of confidence in him."

Cunningham continued to insist throughout the 1998 season that the starting nod would go to Johnson once he returned from his injury. That scenario appeared to unfold on November 8, when Cunningham went down with an injured knee early in the contest and Johnson returned to lead the Vikings to a 31–24 win over New Orleans. But Johnson broke his thumb during the

Randall Cunningham

contest and Cunningham, after undergoing arthroscopic knee surgery the following day, returned a week later to guide a 24–3 triumph over Cincinnati.

By the end of the season, Cunningham was named a first-team All-Pro by the Associated Press and voted a backup for the Pro Bowl. He led the league in passer rating at 106.0, set a team record with 34 touchdown tosses, and threw four touchdown passes on four occasions during the season to establish another Viking mark. His 162 passes without an interception also represents the second-longest streak in Minnesota annals. Cunningham was rewarded for those efforts at the end of the season with a five-year contract extension.

Rick Cunningham

Season: 1995 Tackle Height: 6'6"
Number: 67 Texas A&M Weight: 307

Rick Cunningham was signed as a free agent to be Minnesota's starting right tackle for the 1995 season while serving as a mentor to rookie Korey Stringer. That plan fell apart when Cunningham succumbed to a severe sprain to the medial collateral ligament in his left knee in the season-opener with Chicago. While Stringer never relinquished the starting job, Cunningham returned to see action in 10 games on special teams and did a commendable job of teaching Stringer the finer points of offensive line play at the game's top level. He was not re-signed after the 1995 campaign.

Gary Cuozzo

Seasons: 1968–71 Quarterback Height: 6'1"
Number: 15 Virginia Weight: 195

Minnesota acquired Gary Cuozzo's services from New Orleans in exchange for first-round draft picks in 1968 and 1969. While the scholarly passer would graduate first in his class from the University of Tennessee's dental school as a member of the Vikings, he also did an outstanding job of backing up Joe Kapp before getting his opportunity to start in 1970.

Long the backup to Johnny Unitas in Baltimore, Cuozzo was a steady, winning, precision-throwing quarterback who guided the Vikings to a 16–5 record as a starter during his four years with the team. Intelligent yet prone to injuries, he held the job full-time in 1970 and shared the role with Norm Snead and Bob Lee as part of the signalcaller shuffle in 1971.

A left shoulder injury cost Cuozzo five pre-season and six regular-season games in 1968. He still managed to post an incredible completion percentage of 72.2, succeeding on 24 of 33 pass attempts. His most valiant effort came in relief on October 6. Facing Detroit, Kapp was woozy on the sidelines after sustaining a mild concussion in the first half. Cuozzo took over, only to suffer a separated shoulder. Since the Vikings had dressed only two quarterbacks, Cuozzo stayed on and led Minnesota to the stay-ahead touchdown by completing five of seven aerials. Kapp returned in the second half while Cuozzo made his way to the hospital before the team's 24–10 victory had been recorded.

Cuozzo started the season-opening loss to the Giants in 1969 before giving way to Kapp. Even so, he had two critical saves during the team's NFL Championship run, when he completed 49 of 98 passes for 693 yards and four touchdowns. One of his more impressive outings as a Viking occurred on November 23. Cuozzo stepped in for Kapp and connected on 12 of 19 tosses for two touchdowns in Minnesota's 52–14 victory over Pittsburgh.

In 1970, Cuozzo took over the starting job and had his best year in the National Football League. Despite missing two games and part of a third with an ankle injury, the quarterback registered 1,720 yards through the air on 128 completions in 257 attempts for seven touchdowns. Cuozzo was effective against Dallas in a 54–13 win on October 18 and threw a pair of scoring tosses two weeks later against the Lions in a 30–17 triumph.

Ailments hindered his production again in 1971. Cuozzo opened the season as the starter but lost the job to Snead in the early going and to Lee down the stretch. He wound up starting eight games and completed 75 of 168 passes for six scores and eight interceptions. After the season, he was sent to St. Louis for John Gilliam along with a second- and fourth-round draft pick. That deal proved to be one of the better trades in Vikings history.

It could be argued that Cuozzo's biggest page in the Vikings' history book came as a member of the Baltimore Colts. Replacing the ailing Unitas in 1965, Cuozzo made his first start and tossed five touchdown passes against his future employer to lead the Colts to a 41–21 pasting on November 14. The defeat was so bad that Minnesota head coach Norm Van Brocklin announced his resignation for the first time a day later.

Travis Curtis

Season: 1989 Safety Height: 5'10"
Number: 49 West Virginia Weight: 180

Travis Curtis served as the third safety in every game for the Vikings in 1989. He was credited with knocking 77 ballcarriers off their pins, and added six tackles in the playoff loss to San Francisco. Curtis also made six stops on special teams and returned one kickoff for 18 yards. After one year in Minnesota, the former Redskin spent his final full season in the National Football League with the Jets.

Bernard Dafney

Seasons: 1992–94	Guard-Tackle	Height: 6'5"
Numbers.: 71, 75	Tennessee	Weight: 317

Even though his starting experience as an offensive lineman consisted of a half-season at the University of Tennessee, Bernard Dafney made a rapid rise with the Vikings. Drafted by Houston in the ninth round in 1992 prior to being released, Dafney joined the Minnesota practice squad after the season opener before moving to the active roster when Hassan Jones was placed on the injured reserve list midway through the season.

Having played in two games in 1992, Dafney used his quick feet to spell veteran Tim Irwin at right tackle for the first half of the following year. He then moved to the other side of the line, to left tackle, when rookie Everett Lindsay succumbed to a season-ending shoulder injury, and started the final four games of the 1993 campaign as well as the playoff contest against the Giants.

Dafney was on the move again in 1994. He opened training camp at left tackle before switching to right guard, a shift that allowed veteran Chris Hinton to become the right tackle in place of the departed Irwin. Dafney started all 16 games, helping quarterback Warren Moon establish a team record for passing yardage in a season and running back Terry Allen rush for 1,000 yards for the second time in his career.

Ironically, Dafney's fall was as rapid as his rise. His minimal progress as a starter along with the continued improvement of David Dixon and the return of Hinton to guard led to his release with an injury settlement during training camp in 1995.

Carroll Dale

Season: 1973	Wide Receiver	Height: 6'2"
Number: 84	Virginia Tech	Weight: 200

A 13-year veteran of the National Football League and a three-time Pro Bowler, Carroll Dale spent his 14th and final campaign with Minnesota. Serving as quarterback Fran Tarkenton's possession receiver, the former Ram and Packer caught 14 passes for 192 yards during the 1973 slate. He pulled in two tosses during three regular-season games and another pair for 31 yards in Minnesota's 27–20 win over Washington in the divisional playoffs on December 22. His longest reception was a 40-yarder in the Vikings' 22–13 triumph over the Bears on September 23.

Dale hung up his cleats for good after the 1973 slate and had his role filled by Jim Lash.

LeShun Daniels

Season: 1997	Offensive Lineman	Height: 6'1"
Number: 69	Ohio State	Weight: 304

A high school and college teammate of fellow lineman Korey Stringer, LeShun Daniels made the Vikings' practice squad as a rookie free agent and was promoted to the 53–man roster in mid-November of 1997 after starting center Jeff Christy was lost for the year. Inactive for four games, Daniels served as the backup center in the final three contests when Christy's replacement, Scott Dill, was injured, and played during the 39–28 victory over the Colts on December 21. He was released the following year in training camp, but re-signed to the practice squad during the final weeks of the 1998 slate.

Rick Danmeier

Seasons: 1977–83	Kicker	Height: 6'
Number: 7	Sioux Falls	Weight: 194

Rick Danmeier was one of the final two football dinosaurs. As a straight-ahead kicker, Danmeier was outlasted only by Washington's Mark Moseley before every pigskin poocher in the National Football League as well as the college ranks employed the side-winding, soccer-style approach.

Danmeier was a rare breed when he replaced another dinosaur—Fred Cox—and earned the Vikings' starting job in 1978. He had been cut by Minnesota in 1975 before signing with the team in October 1977 and going on injured reserve after being active for one game. Bud Grant favored straight-ahead kickers, and both Danmeier and Cox provided the head coach with consistency if not exceptional range.

A defensive nose guard in college, Danmeier proved Grant right in the early days of his career. In his first home game at Metropolitan Stadium in 1978, Danmeier put four field goal attempts through the uprights, including a 44-yarder in overtime, to provide all the Vikings' tallies in the 12–9 victory over Denver on September 11. When he failed, such as the missed attempt in overtime against Green Bay on November 26, 1978, the critics emerged from the woodwork and wondered why Grant did not opt to "modernize" his kicking game.

Nevertheless, Danmeier remained the Vikings' kicker through the 1982 season. During that time, he succeeded on nearly two-thirds of his field goal tries (70 of 106) and almost 93 percent of his extra points, including all 23 PATs in 1982. One of his most memorable boots came on October 11, 1981, when Minnesota recovered Danmeier's onsides kick while trailing the Chargers, 31–30, in the final seconds. Shortly thereafter, on the final play of the game, he split the goal posts from 38 yards out for a 33–31 win. Danmeier also has the distinction of scoring the last points at the Met by connecting on a 33-yarder in the third quarter of the Vikings' 10–6 loss to Kansas City on December 20, 1981.

Sidelined for all of 1983 with an ailing back, Danmeier's tenure with the Vikings came to an official end when new head coach Les Steckel opted to go with Jan Stenerud and released the dinosaur, all but bringing the days of straight-ahead kickers to extinction.

Tony Darden

| Season: 1998 | Defensive Back | Height: 5'11" |
| Numbers: 32, 25 | Texas Tech | Weight: 187 |

The Vikings' compensatory seventh-round draft choice in 1998, Tony Darden made the 53–man roster out of training camp but was not active for the first seven games of his rookie season. He was placed on injured reserve just prior to Week Nine due to a heel ailment, forcing him to miss the remainder of the campaign.

Ron Daugherty

| Season: 1987 | Wide Receiver | Height: 6'3" |
| Number: 82 | Northeastern | Weight: 185 |

Ron Daugherty was an advertising copywriter in Chicago when he signed with the Vikings as a replacement player. He caught two passes for 21 yards during the three replacement games in 1987.

Brian Davis

| Season: 1994 | Cornerback | Height: 6'2" |
| Number: 34 | Nebraska | Weight: 190 |

Signed just prior to the 1994 campaign to add veteran depth and speed to the secondary, Brian Davis made 11 solo tackles and one assisted hit in nine games as a reserve cornerback. His most important play came late in the Vikings' 38–35 win over Miami on September 25. Davis swatted away a Dan Marino pass in the end zone, saving what looked to be a certain touchdown. His days in purple ended when the Vikings did not re-sign Davis the following offseason.

Doug Davis

| Seasons: 1966–72 | Tackle | Height: 6'4" |
| Number: 71 | Kentucky | Weight: 255 |

Doug Davis became a fixture at right tackle shortly after being selected by the Vikings in the fifth round of the 1966 draft. Taking over the blocking duties held by Errol Linden, who had been traded to Atlanta, Davis played on the opening offensive snap in the first pre-season game and became the only rookie to earn a spot in the starting lineup. He did not relinquish his position that year until a knee injury suffered against Green Bay on November 27 sidelined Davis for one game.

The hard-working strongman who excelled in pass protection overcame some bothersome injuries in 1967 to maintain his starting job during his 11 appearances. He continued to hold first-team honors until a knee injury forced him to miss four games late in the 1969 slate. While Ron Yary emerged as the starter at right tackle in his absence, Davis became a swingman at the two tackle positions upon his return from the ailment in 1970 prior to splitting duties at left tackle with Grady Alderman in 1971. His playing time decreased to five games in 1972, which proved to be Davis' final season in the National Football League.

The highlight of Davis' career may have come on September 28, 1969. Thanks to his stellar blocking performance against the Colts' aggressive defense, Davis received one of the three game balls handed out by the Vikings' staff after Minnesota handed Baltimore a 52–14 thrashing. Joe Kapp, who hurled seven touchdown tosses in the game, received another pigskin, while politician and team supporter Hubert Humphrey took home a third.

Greg Davis

Season: 1997   Kicker   Height: 6'
Number: 5   The Citadel   Weight: 205

An 11-year veteran of the National Football League, Greg Davis beat out incumbent Scott Sisson for the Vikings' kicking chores to open the 1997 season. His tenure in Minnesota lasted only four regular-season games, with Davis succeeding on seven of 10 field goal attempts. His undoing occurred when he missed a 22-yarder against Green Bay on September 21, thereby killing the Vikings' momentum in a 38–32 loss. Davis was released the following week in favor of veteran Eddie Murray.

Isaac Davis

Season: 1998   Guard   Height: 6'2
Number: 63   Arkansas   Weight: 320

The Vikings picked up Isaac Davis off waivers on October 28, 1998, after backup guard Orlando Bobo broke his fibula while playing on special teams. A former starter with San Diego and New Orleans, Davis suffered a bout of dehydration shortly after joining the team. He did not take the field for Minnesota prior to being released on December 1, when the Vikings activated running back Obafemi Ayanbadejo.

Dale Dawson

Season: 1987   Kicker   Height: 6'
Number: 4   Eastern Kentucky   Weight: 213

One of the Vikings' final cuts prior to the 1987 regular season after booming numerous field goals over 50 yards long during training camp, Dale Dawson returned to serve as Minnesota's kicker for the three replacement games. His performance mirrored that of the entire squad, with Dawson making just one of five field goal tries and all four of his extra points.

Rhett Dawson

Season: 1973   Wide Receiver   Height: 6'1"
Number: 86   Florida State   Weight: 182

A possession receiver who earned All-America honors in college, Rhett Dawson was picked up off waivers by the Vikings in 1973. He played in two games and caught both of his passes, totalling 24 yards, against Atlanta in the Falcons' 20–14 win on November 19.

Ted Dean

Season: 1964   Running Back   Height: 6'2"
Number: 24   Wichita   Weight: 213

After spending his first four professional seasons with the Eagles, Ted Dean suited up for the Vikings for two games in 1964 before disaster struck. The running back drove his car into a tree on a rain-soaked road in south Minneapolis. The wreck ruined his hip, thereby preventing him from playing again.

Prior to the accident, Dean was traded to the Vikings along with the rights to Bob Berry in exchange for Chuck Lamson, Terry Kosens, Ray Poage and Don Hultz. He faced Baltimore and Chicago while with Minnesota and had five carries for 30 yards, one pass reception for 23 yards and three kickoff returns for 50 yards.

Jack Del Rio

Seasons: 1992–95	Linebacker	Height: 6'4"
Number: 55	Southern Cal	Weight: 246

Shortly after Jack Del Rio signed with the Vikings in 1992, he approached former Minnesota middle linebacker Scott Studwell and asked to wear Studwell's old uniform number, 55.

Studwell's answer was brief and stern. "Just don't embarrass the number," he said.

On September 6, 1992, Minnesota beat the Packers, 23–20, in overtime. It was Del Rio's first game as a Viking, and the linebacker had his worst performance in purple. Afterwards, he told Studwell, "I'll never do that to your number again."

He didn't.

Jack Del Rio

The best Viking acquisition during the Plan B free agent years, Del Rio was the heart and soul of an aggressive, opportunistic defense that helped carry the team to the playoffs in his first three years as Minnesota's starting middle linebacker. He made up for his lack of speed with his natural instincts and his ability to stuff plays between the tackles. His presence was the major reason the Vikings were nearly impossible to rush the football against in the early 1990s and ranked atop the National Football League against the run in 1994.

After his less-than-stellar debut in 1992, Del Rio quickly established himself thereafter. He paced the Vikings in tackles with 153, including a team-high 113 solo hits. Never was he better than in Minnesota's 38–10 win over Chicago on November 2. Del Rio earned NFC Defensive Player of the Week honors after forcing a fumble, making nine tackles and picking off two passes, the second of which he returned 84 yards for the first touchdown of his career.

In 1993, his team-leading 169 tackles (108 solos) played a significant role in the Vikings' ranking as the NFL's top defense. After opening the campaign with 15 hits against the Raiders on September 5, Del Rio tied the franchise record with three interceptions in a game during a 13–0 win at Detroit on December 5. He also picked off a pass on the goal line late in a 19–13 victory over the Bears on October 25 to preserve the triumph.

Pro Bowl recognition came Del Rio's way for the only time in his career in 1994. He opened his third season in purple by winning NFC Defensive Player of the Month accolades in September, an honor that was earned in part by his two interceptions against Miami in Minnesota's 38–35 win on September 25. He garnered his second NFC Defensive Player of the Week award after intercepting a pass, defensing three others and registering a sack in a 21–17 win at Buffalo on December 11. Ten days earlier, he had a career-high 19 tackles against Chicago, and finished the season with a team-best 185 hits, including 118 solo shots.

Del Rio looked to be a fixture in the middle of the Viking defense after signing a contract extension during the 1995 season. He had a strong first half of the campaign and ranked as Minnesota's fourth-leading tackler with 70, even though he missed the last eight games upon suffering a knee injury against Chicago on October 30.

That knee injury, however, spelled the end of Del Rio's career. At age 32, Del Rio's knee and contract could not be handled in the era of salary caps. Released by the Vikings, he signed with Miami, only to be let go by new head coach Jimmy Johnson during training camp. Amazingly, in the wink of an eye, Del Rio's career had come to a close, but not before he maintained Minnesota's legacy for superior middle linebackers.

Jarrod Delaney

Season: 1989   Wide Receiver   Height: 6'1"
Number: 89   Texas Christian   Weight: 205

An undrafted college free agent, Jarrod Delaney was on the Viking roster briefly in 1989 but did not participate in any games.

Greg DeLong

Seasons: 1995–98   Tight End-Fullback   Height: 6'4"
Number: 85   North Carolina   Weight: 251

Talk about rapid rises. In 1995, after being acquired off waivers as a rookie from Cleveland and signed to the Vikings' practice squad, Greg DeLong joined the active roster in mid-November when John Gerak shifted from tight end to guard. A shortage of tight ends arose in early December after Adrian Cooper succumbed to a rotator cuff injury. DeLong stepped in and caught two passes in his first start, a 27–11 victory against the Browns on December 9, before grabbing four passes versus San Francisco on December 18.

DeLong started half the Vikings' games in 1996 and caught eight passes for 34 yards. A steady blocker with good hands, he was part of the tight ends' emergence in the passing game in 1997 while teaming with Andrew Glover and Hunter Goodwin at the position. He caught eight passes for 75 yards, including a career-long 23-yarder during a 10–6 win at Tampa Bay on October 26.

The addition of Randy Moss in 1998 led Minnesota to go with more three wide receiver sets instead of two tight ends. As a result, DeLong became more of an H-back, oftentimes lining up at fullback with Robert Smith in the backfield when not in motion as a lead blocker. He also grabbed eight passes for 58 yards, making him one of the quiet contributors to the Vikings' explosive offense.

"I know my role on this football team, and it's to be a blocker," DeLong said. "If I can get a pass here and there, it's great. It keeps your hopes up and keeps you working. I know what I'm here for, and I'm happy doing it."

DeLong's days as a Viking concluded when he followed Minnesota offensive coordinator Brian Billick to Baltimore by signing as a free agent with the Ravens prior to the 1999 season.

Calvin Demery

Season: 1972   Wide Receiver   Height: 6'1"
Number: 27   Arizona State   Weight: 190

Minnesota's eighth-round draft pick in 1972, Calvin Demery played on special teams and in a few three-receiver formations for five games late in his rookie season. He did not catch a pass that year, which proved to be his lone appearance in the National Football League.

Earl Denny

Seasons: 1967–68   Running Back   Height: 6'1"
Number: 28   Missouri   Weight: 205

Earl Denny looked to be one of the next great running backs in the National Football League before a severe knee injury suffered at Missouri limited his production. The Big Eight Conference's long jump champion as a junior and the Vikings' third-round draft choice in 1967, Denny spent two seasons in purple as a hard-hitting member of the special teams and a backup running back.

As a rookie, he played in 13 games, recovered two fumbles and returned a kickoff 18 yards. He saw action in all 14 games in 1968, running back three kickoffs for 19 yards and rushing the ball twice for nine yards.

Al Denson

Season: 1971　　　　　Wide Receiver　　　　　Height: 6'2"
Number: 86　　　　　　Florida A&M　　　　　　Weight: 208

The Vikings acquired Al Denson, a seven-year veteran with the Broncos, from Denver in exchange for a fourth-round draft choice and John Charles before the 1971 season. Denson played seven games in purple, posting 10 receptions for 125 yards. All of his grabs occurred in a three-game stretch, during the final three weekends of October. His best performance with Minnesota was a five-catch effort for 47 yards in the Vikes' 17–10 win over the Giants on Halloween.

Bob Denton

Seasons: 1961–64　　　Offensive Lineman-Defensive End　　Height: 6'3"
Number: 62　　　　　　Pacific　　　　　　　　Weight: 244

Bob Denton served a variety of needs in the trenches for the Vikings. Acquired from Cleveland in 1961 for a 10th-round draft choice, Denton was a reserve guard and defensive end in his first year in Minnesota. He went on to play some tackle on the offensive line, and was considered the second-string center, behind starter Mick Tingelhoff, during his final year with the team.

A reserve throughout his days in purple, Denton never missed a game in four seasons with the Vikings, taking the field for all 56 games, mostly as a member of the special teams during field goals and extra points.

Dean Derby

Seasons: 1961–62　　　Defensive Back　　　　Height: 6'
Number: 25　　　　　　Washington　　　　　　Weight: 185

Acquired midway through the 1961 season from Pittsburgh in a trade for Bob Schnelker, Dean Derby helped shore up the Vikings' Swiss cheese secondary for the final eight games of the inaugural season and during 11 contests in 1962.

Derby, who tied for the National Football League lead with seven picks as a member of the Steelers in 1959, intercepted three passes for Minnesota in his first tour of duty and had four aerial steals a year later.

Jim Dick

Season: 1987　　　　　Linebacker　　　　　　Height: 6'1"
Number: 52　　　　　　North Dakota State　　　Weight: 230

Jim Dick's professional football career consisted of three replacement games with the Vikings in 1987. His best showing came against the Bears on October 11, when he recorded seven tackles.

Paul Dickson

Seasons: 1961–70　　　Defensive Tackle　　　　Height: 6'5"
Number: 76　　　　　　Baylor　　　　　　　　　Weight: 225

Los Angeles' first-round draft pick in 1959, Paul Dickson bounced around from the Rams to Dallas to Cleveland in his first two professional seasons before finding a home in Minnesota just prior to the Vikings' inaugural voyage. He also had experienced trouble finding a position before joining the purple-clad team, but that movement ceased as well when Dickson landed at defensive tackle and stayed there for 10 seasons.

A mild-mannered sort who read poetry away from the gridiron, Dickson was known as "The Growler" for his disagreeable disposition on the field. He arrived in the Upper Midwest along with Jim Prestel, Jamie Caleb, Jim Marshall, Dick Grecni and Billy Gault from the Browns in exchange for second- and 11th-round draft picks in 1962. He warmed the bench his first year with Minnesota before earning a starting job a year later and becoming one of the franchise's first outstanding defensive performers. Though tough against the run, Dickson excelled at rushing the quarterback from the tackle position. He credited his All-America experience in college as an offensive right tackle for his ability to excel when lined up on the other side of the ball.

Dickson maintained his starting job through the 1967 season despite overcoming several ailments, including a bad back in 1966. He actually experienced a surge in 1967, when the Vikings tabbed defensive tackle Alan Page in the first round. "Fear of losing your job is a very powerful incentive," said Dickson. He moved into a reserve role behind Page and Gary Larsen for the final three years of his Minnesota career. When many of his teammates corrected those who called the Vikings' defensive line the "Front Four" instead of the "Front Five," they were adding Dickson to the mix.

Few players during the 1960s were better leaders among the Vikings than Dickson. Never afraid to speak his mind in the right situation, the defensive tackle gave Norm Van Brocklin an earful when the head coach resigned for the first time before returning to the team a day later. After the Dutchman made a brief speech to the team announcing his return, Dickson stood up and said, "I don't want you to come back." He called Van Brocklin a quitter, a term the Minnesota players had been labeled constantly over the years by their head coach. Many of his teammates harbored similar feelings, yet only Dickson was secure enough to say it.

Dickson addressed others more eloquently as an active member of the Twin Cities community. The tall Texan earned praise throughout the region for his inspirational speeches, particularly to children's groups. The same can be said for his efforts on the professional gridiron, which came to an end when he retired after spending the 1971 season with St. Louis.

Scott Dill

Seasons: 1996–97　　　　　　Tackle　　　　　　　　Height: 6'5"
Number: 76　　　　　　　　　Memphis　　　　　　　Weight: 294

Scott Dill was the Vikings' unsung hero during the 1997 season. He stepped in for the injured David Dixon and made three starts at right guard early in the campaign with absolutely no dropoff in production. Just as Dixon was deemed ready to return, right tackle Korey Stringer went on the shelf for a couple games. Dill simply moved over a spot on the line and picked up the slack, again without any noticeable difference in performance.

He went on to spell Dixon and Stringer throughout the remainder of the campaign before replacing the injured Jeff Christy at center. Yet, in his first start in the middle of the line, Dill suffered a lower back injury against Green Bay on December 1 and missed the last three games of the campaign. The back ailment was so severe that Dill was forced to retire from football.

Signed as an eight-year NFL veteran during training camp in 1996, Dill was active but did not play in the first seven games that season. He moved to the line protection units on field goal and extra point attempts during the final nine games while seeing some action for three contests at right tackle for the ailing Stringer.

One of the most versatile offensive lineman ever to wear purple, Dill played all five line positions due to his solid blocking skills and above-average athletic ability. While his contributions may have gone unnoticed by most fans, without Dill's performance, the Vikings would not have reached the playoffs in 1997.

Terry Dillon

Season: 1963 Defensive Back Height: 6'
Number: 25 Montana Weight: 193

Terry Dillon surprised everyone in 1963. Considered a long shot to make the roster during training camp, the free-agent defensive back earned a spot on the taxi squad prior to being activated at midseason and playing well for a rookie in seven games.

Unfortunately, Dillon's career—and life—ended more surprisingly than his 1963 performance. He fell from a bridge and was killed on May 28, 1964, while working construction on the Clark's Fork of Yellowstone River in Montana.

Head coach Norm Van Brocklin said that Dillon reminded him of Detroit's great defensive back, Yale Lary. The Vikings later named an annual award after Dillon to recognize a team player who overcomes adversity, does not receive much recognition, and lets his actions speak for themselves.

Steve Dils

Seasons: 1979–83 Quarterback Height: 6'1"
Number: 12 Stanford Weight: 191

Selected in the fourth round of the 1979 draft, Steve Dils served as Tommy Kramer's relief man throughout his five seasons in purple. The possessor of great intellect but only an average arm, he nonetheless took the field with guns firing and walked away on one occasion having hit the bull's-eye on two Vikings records.

After playing in every game as the holder on kicks as a rookie, Dils served in the same capacity in 1980 while receiving his first start in the National Football League. On November 2, Dils completed 18 of 29 attempts for 200 yards and a pair of touchdown tosses in the Vikings' 39–14 victory over Washington.

He also started the first two games of the 1981 campaign, including a shootout against Tampa Bay in the season opener. Dils completed 37 of 62 passes for 361 yards in the Bucs' 21–13 win on September 5. His pass attempts in the game established the Vikings' single-game record and tied for second-most in NFL history while his completions were one shy of the Minnesota mark and ranked third in league annals. However, Dils did not have a chance to build on that performance after separating a shoulder in the season's second game, which forced him to miss the rest of the slate.

In 1982, Dils resumed his job as the holder while completing 11 of 26 passes during the season. He then received the most playing time of his career in 1983 by starting 12 straight games in place of the injured Kramer. He began the string in relief and guided Minnesota to a 19–16 overtime win against Tampa Bay on September 18. His best performance of the year came against St. Louis, when Dils succeeded on 27 passes for 314 yards on October 30. By the end of the campaign, Dils' 2,840 passing yards and 239 completions ranked seventh for one season in Vikings history.

With fellow backup Wade Wilson ready to play in 1984, Dils' days with the Vikings ended during training camp when he was traded to the Rams in exchange for a fourth-round draft choice.

David Dixon

Seasons: 1994–98	Guard	Height: 6'5"
Number: 71	Arizona State	Weight: 348

The heaviest Viking before the arrival of teammate Korey Stringer and the only player in franchise history to hail from New Zealand, David Dixon possessed virtually no football savvy when he was signed to Minnesota's practice squad in 1992. After all, he came to the United States as a rugby player at Ricks Junior College in Rexburg, Idaho. He later played two years as a nose tackle for the Arizona State University football team before being drafted in the ninth round by New England in 1992. After receiving his release during training camp, Dixon worked as a boilermaker in Houston prior to impressing the Vikings with his size, strength and 5.16 speed in the 40.

Dixon was re-signed then released by Minnesota the following preseason and wound up spending all of 1993 as a defensive lineman with Dallas. He returned to the Vikings in 1994 and was active as a reserve right guard and right tackle for the entire season, playing in one game on goal-line situations. In 1995, he played on the field-goal protection units for 15 games and started five times at right guard. He then moved into the starting lineup for the final six contests in 1996 and was one of the major reasons the Vikings' running game, behind the ballcarrying efforts of Leroy Hoard, was potent once again.

Better in running situations than in pass protection due to his enormous size, Dixon continued to start in 1997, although a knee injury kept him out of action for three games early in the year. Even so, Dixon began to bury defenders on running plays, thereby keeping defenders from foiling the Vikings' scheme.

Re-signed to a lucrative free-agent deal in 1998, Dixon's best game as a Viking occurred in the 31–7 win against Tampa Bay on September 6. The New Zealander received the game ball for his dominating performance against the Bucs' Pro Bowl tackle Warren Sapp. He overcame some stingers in his shoulder at midseason and continued to improve as the year progressed, serving as a significant cog in an offensive line that proved to be a major reason for the team's NFC Central Division championship. His campaign ended on a down note, however, during the NFC Championship Game against Atlanta when Dixon suffered a torn anterior cruciate ligament that required reconstructive surgery on his left knee.

Chris Doleman

Seasons: 1985–93	Linebacker-Defensive End	Height: 6'5"
Number: 56	Pittsburgh	Weight: 275

Experiments undertaken with individual players succeed less than half the time in the National Football League. There's little question on which side of the ledger Chris Doleman's name would appear after making the move from outside linebacker to defensive end after his second season in the league.

The Vikings' first-round draft pick in 1985, Doleman moved into the starting lineup for 13 games at strong-side linebacker during his rookie season after veteran Matt Blair succumbed to an ankle injury. Doleman never quit terrorizing quarterbacks nor kept them from seeing life in a purple haze for the next nine years. His production was impressive from the start, including 113 tackles and a sack, even though his performance raised some questions due to his occasional tentativeness and difficulties in pass coverage.

The situation grew worse under defensive coordinator Floyd Peters in

Chris Doleman

1986. Doleman appeared lost on many plays, so much so that his uneven showings resulted in his being benched in favor of Chris Martin. Granted, he intercepted a pass and returned it 59 yards for a touchdown in a 23–10 victory against Tampa Bay on September 14, and caused a fumble against the Bucs that resulted in a recovery for a touchdown in a 45–13 triumph on November 30. Yet, at the end of his three-sack, 49-tackle campaign, Doleman was moved to defensive end in hopes of reversing a disturbing pattern.

Minnesota got its wish, for Doleman emerged as the prototype end in the 4–3 defense during the 1987 season. Reborn due to the change of scenery, he proved to be the total package, possessing strength, size, speed and instincts. While few players have ever had more success in reaching the quarterback, Doleman was effective against the run as well. He blossomed into a dominating force, earning various All-Pro honors for leading the Vikings with 11 sacks and six forced fumbles, with four coming in four straight games, a Minnesota record. His emergence also played a huge role in Minnesota's late-season run to the NFC Championship Game.

A second straight trip to the Pro Bowl came after tying for the club lead with eight sacks in 1988. A year later, Doleman, who lost a court bout with team president Mike Lynn over an option year in his contract, established the Vikings' record with 21 sacks (one shy of the NFL record), good for 196 yards in lost yardage, including a team record-tying four in the do-or-die, 29–21 win over Cincinnati in the season finale on December 25. His efforts enabled the Vikings to finish the campaign with 71 quarterback dumps, one short of the NFL single-season record. Doleman also earned consensus All-Pro recognition, and was considered the league's most dominating pass rusher.

More production continued in 1990. Doleman again led the team with 11 sacks and four forced fumbles, recorded his first solo safety, against New York on December 9, and took home unanimous All-Pro honors for a second straight year. His 1991 efforts, which included seven sacks and 56 solo hits, were highlighted by his NFC Defensive Player of the Week award for making seven hits, two sacks and his lone forced fumble of the season during a 34–7 win over Phoenix on October 13.

Doleman showed he could still dominate in 1992. He got the season off to a strong start by earning NFC Defensive Player of the Week honors in the first game with seven tackles, two sacks, three forced fumbles and one fumble recovery in a 23–20 overtime win against Green Bay on September 6. He also earned Player of the Month honors in September after making seven sacks and 20 solo hits. He concluded the campaign with 49 tackles and 14.5 sacks.

Grumpy as always due to his contract demands, Doleman overcame his moodiness to register 12.5 sacks in 1993. Yet, by the end of the season, his constant complaining had become tiresome around the Winter Park offices. Like Gary Zimmerman the year before, Doleman's wishes were granted when he was traded to Atlanta in exchange for second- and first-round draft picks, which the Vikings used to obtain Derrick Alexander and David Palmer.

Doleman recorded 88.5 sacks during his nine seasons with Minnesota, led the team in the category on six occasions, and earned trips to six Pro Bowls. No one has ever wondered if those numbers are worthy of deeming his shift to defensive end a success.

Oscar Donahue

Season: 1962   End   Height: 6'3"
Number: 84   San Jose State   Weight: 195

Oscar Donahue averaged 17.8 yards on 16 receptions while playing in 13 games for Minnesota in 1962. Green Bay's sixth-round draft pick earlier that year, Donahue's biggest moment in purple came in the fourth quarter on November 25. The receiver hooked up with Fran Tarkenton on a 45-yard touchdown pass in a game that resulted in a 24–24 tie between the Vikings and Rams.

D.J. Dozier

Seasons: 1987–90   Running Back   Height: 6'
Number: 42   Penn State   Weight: 200

There are times when too much talent, if improperly channelled, can be more harmful to one's career than a lack of natural ability. If ever that statement applied to a Viking, D.J. Dozier would be the player.

Minnesota's first-round draft pick in 1987, the multi-talented athlete put his fledgling minor league baseball career with the New York Mets ahead of his football responsibilities. The results included large helpings of promising yet marginal statistics and countless statements that began, "If only . . .".

Dozier's most productive season in the National Football League was his first. With Darrin Nelson out with an injury, Dozier became the first offensive rookie since Nelson in 1982 to start a season opener. He responded with 57 yards on 12 carries and two touchdowns to help lead Minnesota to a 34–19 win over Detroit on September 13, 1987. He went on to rank fourth on the team with 257 yards on the ground and scored seven touchdowns, including a franchise record-tying performance with three rushing scores in the 34–27 victory against Denver on October 26.

A hip injury suffered in the preseason contest with Chicago in Sweden cost Dozier the first seven games of 1988 and limited him to 167 yards on 42 carries for the year. In 1989, he averaged 21.5 yards on 12 kickoff returns, was third on the team with 207 rushing yards and seventh with 14 catches for 148 yards. His best game came against Atlanta on December 10, when he rushed for a season-high 54 yards, including a career-long 38-yard dash, and threw a 19-yard touchdown pass to Anthony Carter in Minnesota's 43–17 win.

Even with his limited contributions, Dozier's efforts really began to suffer in 1990 because of his interest in baseball. Despite playing only at the Double-A level in the Mets' farm system, Dozier did not report to the Vikings until November. He wound up carrying the ball just six times for 12 yards while gaining another 12 yards on one pass reception. Frustrated, the Vikings released Dozier, who spent his final NFL season, 1991, returning kickoffs for the Lions. Meanwhile, his major league baseball career consisted of 25 games with the Mets in 1992.

Bill Dugan

Season: 1984   Guard   Height: 6'4"
Number: 56   Penn State   Weight: 275

Bill Dugan signed with Minnesota on September 10, 1984, and was waived 15 days later after seeing limited action in one game.

Doug Dumler

Seasons: 1976–77
Number: 57
Center
Nebraska
Height: 6'3"
Weight: 242

The Vikings reduced Mick Tingelhoff's responsibilities late in his career by acquiring Doug Dumler from New England in 1976 in a trade for sixth- and eighth-round draft picks. Dumler handled all the long snapping for punts and kicks in 1976 and 1977 while serving as Tingelhoff's little-used backup at center.

Mark Dusbabek

Seasons: 1989–92
Number: 59
Linebacker
Minnesota
Height: 6'3"
Weight: 236

A four-year starter for the Golden Gophers and winner of the University of Minnesota's Carl Eller Award as the top defensive player, Mark Dusbabek returned to the Upper Midwest in 1989 as a Plan B free agent after toiling for two seasons with Houston. He paced the Vikings with 23 special teams tackles during his first year with the club before emerging as the starting strong-side linebacker in 1990. Dusbabek registered 55 stops on defense and another 12 hits on special teams. He also recorded the only points of his career when he nailed New Orleans' Dalton Hilliard in the end zone for a safety in Minnesota's 32–3 win over the Saints on September 16.

Back in the starting lineup to open the 1991 season, Dusbabek suffered a torn anterior cruciate ligament in his left knee during the first game against Chicago, on September 1, and missed the remaining 15 contests of the campaign. He also spent the first half of the 1992 season on injured reserve before receiving his release.

Brad Edwards

Seasons: 1988–89 Safety Height: 6'2"
Number: 27 South Carolina Weight: 196

The Vikings were hoping Brad Edwards, the team's second-round draft choice in 1988, would be the long-term answer at free safety. His career in purple began positively enough, with Edwards stepping in for the injured John Harris and starting six games as a rookie. He responded with 43 total tackles and two interceptions, including one he turned into a 37-yard touchdown return in Minnesota's 14–13 win over Tampa Bay on October 9.

Edwards' role decreased in 1989, when he saw action in just nine games and recorded an interception, 21 total tackles and a blocked field goal attempt. With his performance failing to live up to the team's expectations, Edwards' career in purple came to a close. He signed with Washington for the 1990 campaign and divided the next eight seasons between the Redskins and Falcons.

Dixon Edwards

Seasons: 1996–98 Linebacker Height: 6'1"
Number: 59 Michigan State Weight: 228

Dixon Edwards was Minnesota's lone significant acquisition prior to the 1996 season. After winning a Super Bowl ring with Dallas, the speedy free-agent defender moved north to fill the strong-side linebacker slot vacant by the release of Broderick Thomas.

His role changed, however, on the second day of training camp. Weak-side linebacker Ed McDaniel succumbed to a season-ending knee injury in July, forcing Edwards to move to the other side of the defense to fill McDaniel's void. He responded to the challenge by leading the Vikings with 10 tackles for a loss, ranking second on the club with a career-high 122 total stops, and registering 3.5 sacks despite missing nearly two games with a hamstring injury. Edwards' best outing was his career-high 16-tackle performance in a 15–10 win over the Giants on September 29.

The return of McDaniel in 1997 enabled Edwards to move back to his more natural strong-side linebacker position. Despite the familiar surroundings, he struggled for the next two seasons. Edwards had 72 hits and tied for the team lead with two forced fumbles in 1997 before recording 45 stops a year later.

Jimmy Edwards

Season: 1979   Running Back   Height: 5'9"
Number: 32   Northeast Louisiana   Weight: 185

Before wearing purple for one season in the National Football League, Jimmy Edwards began his professional career with a two-year stint in the upstart World Football League. He moved north to the Canadian Football League when the WFL folded and earned the CFL's Most Valuable Player award after gaining 1,581 yards with Hamilton.

Signed by Kansas City and cut at the end of training camp in 1979, Edwards joined the Vikings shortly thereafter and served as the team's primary kick returner. Despite losing the handle on 10 occasions, Edwards led the NFC and ranked second in the league in kickoff return average with a 25.1 norm on 44 attempts. He was also Minnesota's most active punt returner, taking back 33 boots for a team-best 5.6-yard average.

Edwards returned to the Vikings for training camp in 1980, but his inability to maintain possession of the pill caused him to lose his job to Eddie Payton.

Pat Eilers

Seasons: 1990–91   Safety   Height: 5'11"
Number: 24   Notre Dame   Weight: 195

After earning degrees in mechanical engineering and biology at Notre Dame, Pat Eilers joined the Vikings' practice squad on October 1, 1990, more than a month after the college free agent was released by Minnesota in the final roster cutdowns. Activated on November 9, the St. Paul native played in the final eight games of the season and ranked sixth on special teams with 11 tackles.

He spent all of 1991 in purple, playing in 16 contests and leading the Vikings' special teams with 14 solo hits and 22 total tackles. The all-out Eilers also recovered two fumbles on kick coverage, averaged 19.8 yards on five kickoff returns, and made a total of 10 stops in limited defensive opportunities. Despite his solid performance, Eilers was not re-signed for the 1992 campaign, and spent the next two years with Washington.

Mike Eischied

Seasons: 1972–74   Punter   Height: 6'
Number: 11   Upper Iowa   Weight: 190

Mike Eischied was property of the Vikings nine years before he ever punted the pigskin in purple during a regular-season game. Signed as a free agent in 1963, the former NAIA All-America safety was a member of the Minnesota taxi squad before holding the same job with the Bears and becoming the Raiders' punter in 1966. After five-and-a-half years in Oakland and a half-season in Kansas City, he rejoined the Vikings in exchange for a fourth-round draft choice before the 1972 campaign.

The short and squat punter's best year with the Vikings was his first. In 1972, Eischied averaged 42.8 yards on 62 punts, the highest average for a Minnesota punter since 1964. He also established a dubious first in Vikings history. After 681 successful punts in Minnesota annals, Eischied's effort in the season opener versus Washington was blocked by Bill Malinchak, who carried the football 16 yards for a touchdown.

Eischied watched his norm drop to 39.8 yards on 66 efforts a year later, although his statistics do not reveal how effective he was directing the ball to the sidelines and in the coffin corners. With the approval of head coach

Bud Grant, Eischied opted to punt the ball out of bounds instead of pooching it high and short.

"It's thrilling to punt the ball out of bounds down in the corner," Eischied said. "It helps your team, makes you feel like you're more a part of the team. And working on placing the ball eases the monotony of practice, too."

His practice time with the Vikings did not last long, however. When Eischied ranked next-to-last in the NFC with a 36.1-yard average in 1974, he lost his job to rookie Neil Clabo the following year during training camp.

Clifton Eley

Season: 1987　　　　　　Tight End　　　　　　Height: 6'5"
Number: 87　　　　　　Mississippi State　　　　Weight: 230

Clifton Eley took the field for two replacement games during the 1987 strike.

Carl Eller

Seasons: 1964–78　　　　Defensive End　　　　Height: 6'6"
Number: 81　　　　　　Minnesota　　　　　　Weight: 245

Alan Page may have received more awards and recognition, and Jim Marshall may have been lauded more for his incredible consecutive games streak. But the spiritual leader of the Purple People Eaters was Carl Eller, the swift, graceful and powerful defensive end who improved with age and developed into one of the best all-around defensive linemen the National Football League has ever seen.

A 1964 first-round pick of the Vikings as well as the American Football League's Buffalo Bills, Eller remained in Minneapolis when the All-American Golden Gopher joined the NFL team fresh off the University of Minnesota campus. He immediately impressed the Vikings' coaching staff with his tenacious ability to pursue the passer and his 4.5 speed in the 40 that made him fast enough to catch running backs from behind. That talent earned Eller a starting job in his first year as well as the team's outstanding rookie award, as selected by the Viking Fan Club. He displayed just how fleet afoot he was on October 25 by scooping up a George Mira fumble at San Francisco and outracing everyone for 45 yards to score a touchdown and give the visitors a 27–22 victory.

Carl Eller

Regardless of how effective Eller was as a rookie, he took time to mature and develop into a consistent performer. In 1965, Eller experienced the sophomore slump, with his safety of New York quarterback Earl Morrall serving as one of his lone highlights in an otherwise disappointing season. He bounced back in 1966 to lead a rejuvenated Minnesota defense, and continued to emerge as one of the league's best and most-feared defensive linemen while overcoming pre-season knee surgery in 1967. "Moose" then blossomed by earning unanimous All-Pro recognition in 1968.

"Carl has just now reached his potential," said head coach Bud Grant after the 1968 campaign. "He should go on to be one of the superstars of this league for years to come."

Eller did not disappoint Grant or any other follower of the Vikings. With his outstanding quickness and mobility for a man his size, he earned All-Pro recognition again in 1969, 1970 and 1971. Eller also was named winner of the George Halas Award in 1971, an honor voted on by the players and presented to the league's best defender.

"Moose" was able to take his game to the next level late in the decade because of his determination to improve and his ability to adapt. A straight bull-rusher during his early days in the NFL, he became more versatile as the Purple People Eaters began to emerge as perennial Super Bowl contenders. Eller garnered some finesse to go with his natural strength, which allowed him to be equally effective on the inside against the run and outside rushing the quarterback.

Few players studied the game more than Eller, who also seemed to possess a sixth sense regarding where the next play was going. He used his height and long arms to his greatest advantage by consistently batting passes down when he did not reach the quarterback. In essence, "Moose" was the quintessential linemen in an era that produced many of the best defenders the game has ever known.

"Carl is the prototype of what a defensive end should be—extremely strong, fine mobility and one of the fiercest pass rushers in the game," Grant said. Fran Tarkenton agreed with that assessment, particularly after facing his former teammate while quarterbacking the New York Giants. "It's not that he's so big or so fast or so devastating," Tarkenton said. "It's the fact that he's all of these things simultaneously. The first thing he does that bothers you is that he shuts out the sun. One time I actually considered throwing under him."

An injured right knee suffered during training camp that became more serious in Week Three against Miami limited Eller's mobility and cut his production in 1972, yet he still earned spots on two all-conference teams. He resumed his All-Pro recognition in 1973, the same year he blocked two field goals and recovered a fumble.

Eller also displayed his leadership in the first round of the playoffs in 1973. Though known as a quiet leader, Eller took the vocal responsibility on his shoulders during halftime against Washington on December 22. The Vikings struggled to remain close during the first half, and many of the players grumbled about their frustrations upon entering the locker room. Prior to the coaches' arrival from the field, the off-season actor destroyed a blackboard and gave an Academy Award performance, saying, "We've come too damn far to play like this. We're so tight that we're embarrassing ourselves. Let's relax and start playing our game." The talk worked, for the Vikings went out and defeated Washington, 27–20, on their way to Super Bowl VIII.

A year later, he jarred six footballs loose and earned his sixth trip to the Pro Bowl before recovering two more fumbles and knocking three others out of opponents' clutches in 1975. Eller also registered 13 sacks that year and picked off the first pass of his career, victimizing Atlanta's Kim McQuilken at the Falcons' 8-yard line in the second quarter to set up a touchdown in Minnesota's 38–0 victory on November 9.

In 1976, "Moose" recorded 15 sacks, caused three fumbles and blocked a field goal against Pittsburgh. One of his best performances came against the Rams in the NFC Championship Game, when Eller sacked Pat Haden twice and made eight unassisted tackles to help guide the Vikings to a 24–13 triumph on December 26. He returned with a team-high 16 sacks in 1977, the same season he blocked a field goal and an extra-point attempt, and dumped Randy Hedberg in the end zone for a safety in Minnesota's 9–3 win over Tampa Bay on September 24.

Despite being reunited with his college coach, Murray Warmath, who took over as the Vikings' defensive line coach in 1978, Eller started to show some signs of slowing down. His pre-season holdout and a thumb injury limited Eller to seven starts. He still managed to lead the linemen with 56 unassisted tackles and ranked second on the team with five sacks. Yet, his production dropped, with alcohol and drug problems contributing to his downfall. His Viking career came to an end in 1979, when Minnesota sent the defensive end and an eighth-round draft choice to Seattle for defensive tackle Steve Niehaus. He retired after one season with the Seahawks.

Now a fixture among the Vikings' alumni, Eller's numbers are more than worthy of a place in the Pro Football Hall of Fame. He recovered 23 opponents' fumbles, which was third-best in NFL history at the time of his retirement. He also registered 133.5 sacks (all but three in purple), a total that currently ranks in the top 10 in league annals and first in Minnesota history. Eller played in four Super Bowls, was named All-Pro five times (1968–71 and 1973), and was selected for six Pro Bowls (1968–71, 1973–74). He had 766 solo tackles and 202 assists for 968 total hits, and was named to the Vikings' Silver Anniversary All-Time Team in 1985.

As his numbers reveal and his former teammates testify, Eller was the man who had as much to do with making Minnesota the land of the Purple People Eaters than anyone else.

Neil Elshire

Seasons: 1981–86   Defensive Tackle   Height: 6'6"
Numbers: 65, 73   Oregon   Weight: 270

When the Redskins tried to activate Neil Elshire from injured reserve by sliding him through waivers midway through the 1981 season, the Vikings stepped forward and acquired the steady defensive lineman. Elshire went on to see significant starting time in between a couple of injuries over the next five years.

After taking the field for four games with Minnesota in 1981, Elshire played in the first five contests of 1982 before injuring a knee and missing the rest of the season. In 1983, he moved into the starting lineup in the seventh game and proved to Bud Grant that the head coach had made the proper decision in acquiring his services. On October 16, in one of the best games ever by a Viking defensive tackle, Elshire paced the defense in Minnesota's 34–14 win over Houston with six solo shots, nine assisted tackles, three sacks, a deflected pass, a fumble recovery, and a forced fumble that resulted in a 50-yard touchdown return. He concluded the year ranked second on the team with 9.5 sacks while leading the club by picking up three loose balls.

Another knee surgery in 1984 limited Elshire to 12 games, including 10 starts, with 62 total tackles and two sacks. He played in all 16 contests in 1985 and started three, placing second on the team with five sacks. Elshire then played sparingly for 10 games in 1986 before receiving his release on November 28.

Charles Emanuel

Season: 1997   Safety   Height: 6'
Number: 47   West Virginia   Weight: 196

The only college free agent to make the Vikings' opening day roster in 1997, Charles Emanuel was active for the first two games of the season before being placed on waivers prior to the third contest. The team had hoped to slip Emanuel onto the practice squad, but the safety was claimed by Philadelphia and signed to a one-year deal.

Charles Evans

Seasons: 1992–98	Running Back	Height: 6'1"
Number: 29	Clark College	Weight: 244

Offensive coordinator Brian Billick's scheme typically called for a one-back set. Yet, on those occasional plays when a fullback was employed, Charles Evans was the player called upon nearly every time.

An 11th-round draft pick in 1992, Evans possessed most of the qualities needed to succeed at fullback. Aggressive with good size for blocking and excellent hands and speed to catch passes out of the backfield, Evans was a role player who quietly and effectively went about his business, making others around him as well as his team that much better.

A member of the Vikings' practice squad in 1992 and on injured reserve for most of 1993 with a broken right wrist, Evans started to contribute in 1994 by finishing fourth on the Vikings with 16 special teams tackles. His fullback duties began in earnest in 1995, when he caught 18 passes for 119 yards, including his first career touchdown on a one-yard reception from Warren Moon in Minnesota's 27–11 win over Cleveland on December 9.

In 1996, "Diesel" caught passes in 15 of the Vikings' 17 games, totalling 22 receptions for a career-high 135 yards. Billick then gave Evans the football more often early in 1997 to surprise opposing defenses, with the fullback responding with 157 rushing yards and two touchdowns on 43 carries. He also caught 21 tosses for 152 yards to become a legitimate offensive weapon.

With the Vikings employing more three-wide receiver sets in 1998, Evans' role as a yardage producer slipped, although he remained a steady blocker in the backfield. He gained 67 yards on 23 rushes and 84 yards on 12 receptions, and scored a touchdown on a one-yard run during the 50–10 win over Jacksonville on December 20. He left Minnesota prior to the 1999 season by signing as a free agent with the Baltimore Ravens.

David Evans

Seasons: 1986–87	Cornerback	Height: 6'
Number: 26	Central Arkansas	Weight: 178

A special teams performer who started once at cornerback in 1986 in place of Issiac Holt, David Evans finished fourth on the Vikings with eight solo tackles and four assisted hits on kick coverage. A three-year veteran of the Birmingham Stallions in the United States Football League, Evans was released just prior to the season opener in 1987, but returned to play in Minnesota's three replacement games later that year.

Eric Everett

Season: 1992	Cornerback	Height: 5'11"
Number: 31	Texas Tech	Weight: 170

Eric Everett spent his fifth and final season in the National Football League with the Vikings. A backup cornerback who saw most of his action as a dime defensive back, the former Eagle, Buccaneer and Chief played in all 16 games in 1992 and recorded 11 total tackles on defense and three more hits on special teams.

Hap Farber

Season: 1970
Number: 51
Linebacker
Mississippi
Height: 6'1"
Weight: 225

Minnesota's seventh-round draft pick in 1970, Hap Farber played in three games on special teams as a rookie for the Vikings prior to seeing action in five contests with New Orleans to comprise his only season in the National Football League.

Paul Faust

Season: 1967
Number: 54
Linebacker
Minnesota
Height: 6'1"
Weight: 225

A Minneapolis native who was raised in a football-playing family, Paul Faust spent most of the 1967 season on the Vikings' taxi squad after making the team as a college free agent. An All-Big Ten honoree while playing for the Golden Gophers, he was activated for the season finale against Detroit on December 17 prior to being released the following year in training camp.

Faust's father, George, also starred at the University of Minnesota before playing professionally with the Chicago Cardinals.

Willie Fears

Season: 1990
Number: 91
Defensive Tackle
Northwestern State
Height: 6'3"
Weight: 278

Willie Fears, whose previous experience in the National Football League consisted of three games with the Bengals in 1987, was with the Vikings for the first six contests of the 1990 season. He took the gridiron briefly against Chicago and Detroit before receiving his release.

Grant Feasel

Seasons: 1984–86
Number: 64
Center-Tackle
Abilene Christian
Height: 6'8"
Weight: 280

One of the tallest players ever to wear purple, Grant Feasel was signed on October 21, 1984, to fill the void at center created by Jim Hough's injury. Feasel played in the season's final nine games and started three along the offensive line while recording seven total tackles on special teams.

Torn knee ligaments suffered during training camp landed Feasel on injured reserve for the entire 1985 season. He spent the first three months of the 1986 campaign on injured reserve before being activated on November 20. Waived eight days later, Feasel was picked up by Seattle, where he spent the next six seasons.

Tough Enough To Be Vikings

Rick Fenney

| Seasons: 1987–91 | Running Back | Height: 6'1" |
| Number: 31 | Washington | Weight: 240 |

An unheralded eighth-round draft pick in 1987, Rick Fenney became one of the more popular players among the Vikings' faithful for the way he sacrificed his body for the team, regardless of whether it was banging ahead for a tough yard, blocking for one of his backfield teammates, or making a key hit on special teams.

Fenney's best season unfolded throughout the 1989 campaign. He established personal highs that year with 151 carries for 588 yards and four touchdowns while pulling in 30 passes for 254 yards and two more scores. Even with the likes of running backs Herschel Walker and D.J. Dozier on the Minnesota roster, Fenney paced the team in rushing for five games during the season and scored two touchdowns on two occasions—the 38–7 win against Houston on September 10 and the 26–14 triumph versus Green Bay on October 15.

Considered a long shot to make the Vikings' roster as a rookie, Fenney contributed 174 yards on 42 carries and 27 yards on seven catches in 1987. A year later, his average of 4.9 yards per carry (271 yards on 55 attempts) topped the NFC and was fourth in the league. Fenney also stuck his hat in on numerous special teams plays, with his hit against Chicago on September 18, 1988, causing a fumble that was recovered for a Viking touchdown in Minnesota's 31–7 triumph.

Fenney built on his best season with another strong showing in 1990. Despite missing four games with a variety of ailments, he ranked second on the team with 87 rushing attempts for 376 yards, and was sixth with 17 receptions for 112 yards. In 1991, Fenney was sidelined for four more contests with a hamstring injury before gaining 99 yards on 23 carries and 11 more yards on two catches.

Unfortunately for Fenney, his last two seasons in the league proved to be a harbinger. The hard-nosed running back was banged up again during training camp and was cut on August 25, 1992. A hip injury that may have been caused by a congenital condition contributed to the end of his days on the gridiron.

Rick Fenney

Bob Ferguson

| Season: 1963 | Running Back | Height: 5'11" |
| Number: 35 | Ohio State | Weight: 220 |

An All-American fullback at Ohio State under head coach Woody Hayes, Bob Ferguson came to Minnesota five games into the 1963 season via Pittsburgh, where he had struggled as a first-round draft pick. Head coach Norm Van Brocklin liked what he saw in Ferguson and was convinced he could resurrect the former Buckeye's career and lead him to greater heights.

Acquired from the Steelers for a third-round draft pick, Ferguson possessed a determined attitude but hurt his knee in his second week with the Vikings and participated in only a handful of plays during two games in 1963. The following year in training camp, both the head coach and player entered the process with high hopes before the situation quickly deteriorated. The two engaged in a brief argument in the hotel room of writer Jim Klobuchar, with Van Brocklin telling the player to "do me a favor and stop at the equipment room to turn in your gear." Ferguson said, "Coach, it would be a pleasure," and never played in purple nor the National Football League again.

Charley Ferguson

Season: 1962   End   Height: 6'5"
Number: 88   Tennessee State   Weight: 217

Known as "High Pockets" and "Skyhooks" during his six seasons in the National Football League, Charley Ferguson spent his second professional campaign pulling in passes for the Vikings. He was acquired from Cleveland along with Fred Cox, Tom Franckhauser and Errol Linden prior to the 1962 season for a sixth-round draft pick and wound up catching 14 passes for 364 yards, an outstanding 26-yard average, and six touchdowns.

Ferguson had one of the best days ever by a Vikings receiver. On November 11, 1962, he became the second Minnesota pass catcher to pull in three touchdown passes in a game. He hooked up with Fran Tarkenton against the Bears at Wrigley Field, catching a 23-yard score in the first quarter, an 89-yarder late in the second stanza, and an 18-yarder early in the third. While the 89-yarder still represents the longest pass completion in Vikings' annals, Ferguson is best remembered for eliminating some of the Chicago pep band that was stationed behind a short wall after catching a shorter scoring toss. Despite his heroics, the Bears won the game, 31–30.

Jay Fiedler

Season: 1998   Quarterback   Height: 6'1"
Number: 11   Dartmouth   Weight: 215

Released after a solid showing during the 1998 training camp, Jay Fiedler was re-signed by the Vikings when Brad Johnson succumbed to a broken fibula during the season's second game. A former backup with Philadelphia, Fiedler took over the second-string role, behind starter Randall Cunningham, during Johnson's absence. He saw mop-up action in two games, completing three of seven passes for 41 yards.

Steve Finch

Season: 1987   Wide Receiver   Height: 6'
Number: 85   Elmhurst   Weight: 200

Steve Finch's career in the National Football League consisted of the Vikings' first replacement game in 1987, when he caught three passes for 54 yards.

Jason Fisk

Seasons: 1995–98   Defensive Tackle   Height: 6'3"
Number: 72   Stanford   Weight: 291

Head coach Dennis Green was certain he had found a starter at nose tackle during the 1995 draft. Yet the player he expected to fill the hole was second-round selection James Manley, not Jason Fisk, the Vikings' second seventh-round pick.

Though far from the game's most talented player, Fisk emerged as a starter during the latter part of the 1996 season due to his tremendous desire and constant hustle. Fundamentally sound with a nonstop motor, Fisk outperformed Manley, incumbent Esera Tuaolo and veteran Robert Goff to start the final six games of the year as well as the playoff game with Dallas, when he paced the defense with nine tackles. For the regular season, he had 44 total tackles, a sack and an interception.

Fisk, who played in eight games on special teams and goal-line situations as a rookie in 1995, maintained his starting assignment during the first half of 1997. He continued to play about half the defensive snaps after Minnesota signed former Pro Bowler Jerry Ball to anchor the middle of the line, and finished the year with 37 total tackles, three sacks and the second interception of his career.

The former Stanford Cardinal continued to rotate with Ball in 1998, seeing most of his action in the nickel package. Fisk recorded 16 tackles with 1.5 sacks and a fumble recovery during the regular season, then had his best performance during the NFC Championship Game against Atlanta by sacking quarterback Chris Chandler twice. That proved to be his swan song in purple, for Fisk signed a free agent deal with the Tennessee Titans prior to the 1999 campaign.

Jamie Fitzgerald

Season: 1987　　　　　　　　Safety　　　　　　　　Height: 6'1"
Number: 29　　　　　　　　Idaho State　　　　　　　Weight: 187

After playing in two games for the Vikings' replacement team in 1987, Jamie Fitzgerald was re-signed by Minnesota the following March. Despite a solid showing in training camp, he was among the team's final cuts.

Mike Fitzgerald

Seasons: 1966–67　　　　　　Defensive Back　　　　　Height: 5'10"
Number: 37　　　　　　　　Iowa State　　　　　　　Weight: 180

Mike Fitzgerald joined the Vikings during training camp in 1966 by way of the Continental League. A member of the Minnesota taxi squad for the season's first month, Fitzgerald saw action in nine games after being activated on October 21. His above-average speed led to his returning 14 kickoffs for an average of 21.5 yards. He also intercepted a pass while filling in at cornerback and returned the pick 18 yards.

Fitzgerald saw limited action in six games with the Vikings in 1967 before playing two games each with the Giants and Falcons to finish the season.

Paul Flatley

Seasons: 1963–67　　　　　　End　　　　　　　　　Height: 6'1"
Number: 85　　　　　　　　Northwestern　　　　　　Weight: 187

Paul Flatley, Minnesota's fourth-round draft choice in 1963, earned a reputation for his expert moves on and off the field with the Vikings. In five seasons, the savvy receiver used his choppy stride to create holes in opposing defenses. Three times he caught at least 50 passes in a season, and led the team in receptions in 1963, 1965 and 1966.

The Vikings were surprised Flatley was still available with their fourth pick in 1963, for the Minnesota scouting department rated the receiver one of the top 10 seniors in the draft. He proved those rankings were accurate by earning a starting job on the second day of training camp before garnering Rookie of the Year honors in the National Football League.

Nicknamed "Peerless" by head coach Norm Van Brocklin, Flatley set a Viking record by catching 51 passes for 867 yards in his first season, numbers that were most impressive in the run-oriented 1960s. His best catch may have been his spectacular tightrope act down the sidelines, inside the Packers' 10-yard line. He was particularly tough against Green Bay, pulling in touchdown tosses in both Packer games in 1963 after catching long passes in both series prior to scoring. He quickly became a favorite target of Fran Tarkenton by using his ability to get open before waving his arm to attract the scrambling quarterback's attention.

A shoulder separation forced Flatley to miss four games in 1964. Nevertheless, he caught 28 passes for 450 yards and three touchdowns, including a six-catch, 99-yard effort in zero-degree weather against the Rams in a 34–13 win on November 29. Flatley moved to the top of the franchise's career pass receptions-related charts with his 50-catch, 896-yard, seven-touchdown performance in 1965, the same year he served as the cover boy for the Vikings' first-ever yearbook. He then earned Pro Bowl recognition in 1966 after making 50 grabs for 777 yards and three scores.

Despite his success, complete dedication to his sport was not one of Flatley's strengths. He endured a hot-and-cold relationship with Van Brocklin, who would refer to the receiver as "the man caught from behind more times than any player in the history of the NFL" when the relationship went south. Flatley's approach also clashed with the discipline-oriented Bud Grant in 1967. The new head coach insisted on a team dinner and meeting on evenings prior to games, but Flatley opted instead to listen to the call of the wild. The situation became so strained that Flatley told Grant he wanted to be traded after the 1967 campaign, a season in which the receiver's production fell to 23 receptions for 232 yards. Grant refused to surrender to the player's demands. As a result, Flatley reported in good shape to training camp in 1968, only to receive his walking papers shortly thereafter. Undaunted, Flatley reemerged in the NFL with Atlanta under Van Brocklin.

Flatley's name is still prominent in the Vikings' record book. His 51 receptions are tied for second with Sammy White for a Minnesota rookie, while his 867 yards rank third for a first-year player. Flatley also is second for most receiving yards in a game, gaining 202 yards during a 42–41 win over San Francisco on October 24, 1965. His three consecutive games in 1963 with at least 100 yards receiving is tied with Anthony Carter for the second-longest streak in team annals.

Chris Foote

Seasons: 1987–91 Center Height: 6'4"
Number: 62 Southern Cal Weight: 266

Chris Foote was the Mike Morris of the late 1980s for the Vikings. Obtained from the Giants in exchange for a 12th-round draft pick, Foote played in the final six regular-season games and all three playoff contests in 1987 as the long snapper on field goal and extra-point situations. He served the same role for the next three years, playing in all 48 regular-season games and the three post-season matchups.

Foote also backed up Kirk Lowdermilk at center. He was called upon to start five games in 1988 in place of the injured starter as well as the first three contests of 1990 for the same reason.

Chuck Foreman

Seasons: 1973–79 Running Back Height: 6'2"
Number: 44 Miami (Fla.) Weight: 210

Bud Grant's affinity for veterans was legendary. But even with the most disciplined of head coaches, exceptions can be made. Chuck Foreman was one of those rare, yet very special exceptions.

With veteran Dave Osborn's best days behind him, Foreman arrived in Minnesota as the Vikings' first-round draft choice in 1973. The Twin Cities' media was more than a little skeptical, for Foreman did not pile up overwhelming stats in the college ranks. That's because Foreman played a variety of positions at the University of Miami. Recruited as a defensive tackle, he toiled at running back as a freshman and junior, cornerback as a sophomore, and split end and flanker as a senior.

What's more, the Minnesota front office was not united in the selection. While most favored Foreman, particularly after watching him rush for more than 100 yards in the Senior Bowl, others wondered if he fumbled too much. Instead, the naysayers wanted to trade the draft choice in exchange for a proven veteran running back. General manager Jim Finks finally stepped in, supported Grant, and made the final decision on Foreman.

Foreman's Viking career got off to a dubious start. The running back dined on cold chicken just prior to his first practice during minicamp, only to regurgitate it upon taking the field. Yet any doubts quickly evaporated when the back earned a starting job in training camp. He was immediately accepted by his veteran teammates because of his professional approach and immense talent. He also wasted little time proving his worth by registering his first points in the National Football League when he pulled in a nine-yard pass from Fran Tarkenton to score the go-ahead touchdown in the 24–16 season-opening victory against the Raiders on September 16. From there, no running back in Viking annals has been more productive or more exciting than Foreman.

Chuck Foreman

With his elusive stride, sudden burst of power and the ability to turn the corner, a threat the Vikings rarely possessed in the franchise's first dozen years, Foreman overcame any doubts by being named NFL Rookie of the Year by *Pro Football Weekly* and NFL Offensive Rookie of the Year by the Associated Press in 1973. Despite missing two games with a knee injury, he led the Vikings with 801 rushing yards, including 116-yard and 114-yard efforts against the Bears and Lions, respectively, and was second on the team with 37 receptions. He also scored six touchdowns while tying the club record with three 100-yard rushing games in a season. He capped the campaign by playing in the Pro Bowl.

"He is unbelievable, a phenomenal talent," Tarkenton said after the 1973 season. "He gives our offense a whole new concept. He has Gale Sayers' moves and he weighs 215."

Foreman built on those accomplishments in 1974, when the slashing running back led the NFL with 15 touchdowns and topped all non-kickers with 90 points. He quashed any thought of a sophomore slump by opening the season with three touchdowns in a 32–17 win over Green Bay on September 15, then galloped 11 yards for the winning touchdown in a 7–6 win over Detroit a week later. A unanimous All-NFC performer, Foreman ranked fourth in the league with 777 rushing yards and sixth with a club-record 53 receptions, good for another 586 yards. He sealed the season by helping the Vikings reach their second straight Super Bowl by rushing for 114 yards and catching five passes in the 30–14 triumph over St. Louis on December 21. For his efforts, Foreman was named the NFC Player of the Year by *The Sporting News*.

Said Grant, "If there is one thing that distinguishes him from ordinary runners, it's the ability to turn it on when he sees or senses the opening. The great ones have that. Simpson, Sayers, Jimmy Brown, McElhenny. A few yards, then woosh."

More success followed in 1975, when Foreman spent most of the season at fullback, became the first player in NFL history to win rushing and receiving titles in the same year, and just missed becoming the first in league annals to win a conference's "offensive triple crown." He set a franchise mark with 73 catches (the highest total ever for an NFL running back at that point) and scored 132 points. He reached paydirt three times against the Jets in a 29–21 victory on October 12 and on four occasions versus Buffalo in a 35–13 win on December 20. His 85-yard effort against the Bills made Foreman the Vikings' first 1,000-yard rusher, spinning and dashing for 1,070 yards to rank second in the NFC, just six yards shy of the Cardinals' Jim Otis. He also set single-season club records for the most rushes (280), touchdowns (22) and 100-yard rushing games in a season (five).

Foreman gained more than 1,000 yards rushing for the second straight year in 1976. With Tarkenton out with bruised ribs, Foreman carried the Minnesota offense against two-time world champion Pittsburgh, toting the pigskin 27 times for 148 yards and two touchdowns in the 17–6 win on October 4. Three weeks later, he left observers shaking their heads with his amazing ability.

On October 24, 1976, Foreman set Minnesota's single-game rushing record with 200 yards against Philadelphia, gaining 116 yards and scoring twice in the final 13 minutes of the 31–12 win over the Eagles. Touchdown runs of 32 and two yards highlighted his afternoon, and he added another 65 yards on six catches. By the end of the contest, most observers were certain they had just seen the game's best running back of the mid-1970s.

Foreman concluded the campaign by ranking first in the NFC with 14 touchdowns, placed second with 55 receptions, and was fourth in rushing, breaking his club record by gaining 1,155 yards.

He continued to be one of the league's best running backs in 1977, gaining 1,112 yards on the ground and catching 38 passes for another 308 yards while scoring nine touchdowns. A knee injury suffered in the fourth game against the Bears in 1978 caused Foreman to miss two contests and hampered his performance for the rest of the slate. He still gained 749 yards on the ground and caught 61 passes for 396 yards while crossing the goal line on seven occasions. In the process, he set the Viking standard for career receptions and tied Bill Brown for the most touchdowns. Foreman also raced for more than 100 yards for the 17th time in his career, gaining 101 versus Dallas in a 21–10 victory on October 26.

Another knee injury slowed him in 1979, when Foreman rushed for 215 yards and caught just 19 passes for 147 yards. With rookie Ted Brown and Rickey Young seeing most of the playing time, Foreman failed to rush for more than 40 yards in a game during his last year in purple.

In his prime, Foreman displayed the perfect blend of speed, finesse and power to become, as Grant said on many occasions, "the best all-purpose back in the league." His speed was far from world-class, relying instead on his uncanny instincts and body control to pile up yardage. Every move he made was so graceful, whether it was avoiding would-be tacklers with his patented spin, tearing through a hole created by his line, or rising above the pile to pick up a crucial yard on third down. His head fakes could buckle the knees of any defender, while his change of direction could cause the feet to go out from under would-be tacklers. And when his moves resulted in a touchdown, he acted like the achievement was commonplace. Never did he follow the feat with celebrations, just a simple flip of the football to the official.

Those abilities enabled Foreman to set the Viking career standards with 52 rushing touchdowns and 5,879 rushing yards. Seventeen times he galloped for 100 yards or more in a single game, three times he gained at least 1,000 yards during a season, and five times he was a Pro Bowl selection.

But carrying the ball was only part of Foreman's repertoire. With Tarkenton quarterbacking the team, Foreman became one of the game's most prolific receivers out of the backfield, and even lined up at wide receiver on occasion. In fact, with Foreman's help, the Vikings employed the so-called "West Coast Offense" long before San Francisco head coach Bill Walsh was credited with the concept in the 1980s. The lack of attention notwithstanding, Foreman caught 336 passes for 3,057 yards and 23 touchdowns as a Viking.

He was also a money player in crunch time. Take the Vikings' 24–13 victory over Los Angeles in the NFC Championship Game on December 26, 1976, for example. Having been held to 32 yards on six first-half carries, Foreman dashed 62 yards to the Rams' 2-yard line on the second play after halftime to set up his one-yard touchdown run. By the time the final gun sounded, Foreman had 118 rushing yards on 15 carries and five catches for 81 yards.

Ironically, despite all his achievements, Foreman's accomplishments rarely stood the test of the time. Not in the mid-1970s, not now. One reason might center on the running back's once-reticent nature. Never one to promote himself as a player, Foreman preferred to simply do his job on the field. That approach led some members of the media to mistake Foreman as arrogant and self-centered.

"I'm a pretty happy, well-adjusted guy," Foreman said during his career. "I'm quieter than some of the big money guys. I'm not sure I've found the real Chuck Foreman or the best Chuck Foreman and maybe that's just what I'm looking for. Not frantically, just looking."

Despite his talent, Foreman's ability eroded due to the constant use, and contract problems led to his departure in 1980, when he was traded to New England for a third-round draft choice in 1981. Nearly 20 years after his final performance in purple, he continues to reside among the franchise's all-time leading rushers. Foreman is the only Viking to rush for more than 1,000 yards in three straight seasons (1975–77), and still holds most of the team's other rushing marks, including yards in a game and touchdowns in a career (52). He concluded his career in Minnesota having played in three Super Bowls, while being named All-Pro in 1975 and 1976, and selected to the Vikings' Silver Anniversary All-Time Team in 1985. For those reasons and more, it's little wonder why Grant made Foreman one of his few exceptions to the rule.

Dennis Fowlkes

Seasons: 1983–85 Linebacker Height: 6'2"
Number: 50 West Virginia Weight: 236

Dennis Fowlkes saved his best for last, and that took place only because he got a second chance.

After two years with the Vikings, Fowlkes was waived during the final roster cuts in 1985, only to be re-signed on September 11. He took the field for the team's final 15 games, and became a starter for the first time in his career during the campaign's last eight contests, replacing the released Dennis Johnson at linebacker.

Fowlkes responded to the opportunity by leading the Vikings with eight solo tackles, eight assisted hits and one sack in his first start, a 16–13 win over Detroit on November 3, 1985. A week later, in a 27–17 loss to Green Bay, Fowlkes tied a single-game team record by forcing three fumbles. By the end of the season, he led the team by creating five loose balls and was third with 114 total tackles.

Prior to 1985, Fowlkes was a solid contributor on the Vikings' special teams after signing with Minnesota on October 6, 1983. He recovered two fumbles in 11 games his first year in purple, then led the special teams with 12 primary hits and nine assists in 1984.

Tom Franckhauser

Seasons: 1962–63   Defensive Back   Height: 6'
Number: 40   Purdue   Weight: 195

A reserve defensive back who was acquired from the Browns as part of a deal that included Fred Cox prior to the 1962 season, Tom Franckhauser's career came to a sudden halt when he nearly died on a Bemidji State College practice field during training camp in 1964. Franckhauser collided with fullback Darrell Lester and linebacker John Campbell. Although he said he felt fine at the time, three plays later Franckhauser had to be helped off the field due to the hemorrhaging. A blood clot formed on Franckhauser's brain, requiring the immediate help of trainer Fred Zamberletti and subsequent emergency surgery. While he eventually recovered from the accident, Franckhauser never took the field again.

Franckhauser began his career with the Rams and was an original Dallas Cowboy. He was also one of the better defensive backs during the Vikings' early days. Franckhauser saw action in 14 games as a reserve cornerback in his first season in purple and intercepted four passes for 27 return yards. He picked off two more tosses in 14 games in 1963 while playing mostly at safety. He also returned four kickoffs for 94 yards.

Donald Frank

Season: 1995   Cornerback   Height: 6'
Number: 37   Winston-Salem State   Weight: 192

Donald Frank struggled as a starter during the early stages of the 1995 season before a sprained toe landed the cornerback on the bench shortly thereafter in favor of rookie Corey Fuller. He then played sparingly until the final month of the season, when he intercepted two passes, including a 42-yard return against San Francisco on December 18 that he nearly turned into a touchdown. He finished fourth on the team with nine passes defensed and made 33 tackles in his only season with the Vikings.

Steve Freeman

Season: 1987   Safety   Height: 5'11"
Number: 22   Mississippi   Weight: 185

A 12-year veteran with Buffalo in which he established several Bills records, Steve Freeman played his final season in the National Football League with the Vikings after he was traded to Minnesota for "past considerations."

Freeman played in 12 games in 1987 as a defensive back in nickel and dime packages while covering on kickoffs and punt returns. He tied for second on special teams with 17 total tackles and was third with 11 solo hits. Upon reporting to training camp the following July, Freeman decided his playing days had come to an end and retired.

David Frisch

Season: 1996   Tight End   Height: 6'7"
Number: 83   Colorado State   Weight: 260

Head coach Dennis Green likes his tight ends to be blockers first and receivers second. David Frisch fit the mold in 1996, with the huge target seeing action as the Vikings' blocking tight end while sharing playing time with Hunter Goodwin, Greg DeLong and Andrew Jordan.

Frisch's first catch as a Viking was a three-yard touchdown toss from Brad Johnson during a 23–17 triumph at Atlanta on September 8. He pulled in two other passes during the season, including a 21-yarder against Denver on November 24.

Frisch suffered a severe ankle injury and reached an injury settlement with Minnesota before receiving his release toward the end of training camp in 1997.

Phil Frye

Season: 1987 Running Back Height: 5'11"
Number: 37 California Lutheran Weight: 180

Phil Frye saw action in one replacement game in 1987, gaining four yards on four carries and 25 yards on three pass receptions.

Corey Fuller

Seasons: 1995–98 Cornerback Height: 5'10"
Number: 27 Florida State Weight: 205

An intense cornerback who was a second-round draft choice in 1995, Corey Fuller developed into a leader in the Vikings' secondary while his improvements during the 1998 slate served as a major reason teams had minimal success throwing against the purple defense.

Fuller stepped into the Viking lineup in the third game of his rookie season, replacing veteran Donald Frank. After forcing Dallas' Emmitt Smith to fumble in Fuller's first start, the cornerback returned a loose ball 12 yards for a touchdown and intercepted his first pass on the following series during Minnesota's 44–24 rout of Pittsburgh on September 24, 1995. By the end of the campaign, he led the team's secondary with 67 tackles and was fifth with eight passes defensed.

In 1996, Fuller overcame a lingering knee injury to intercept three passes, knock down 15 other tosses, and force two fumbles. In the regular season finale against Green Bay, the cornerback delivered one of the most devastating tackles in team history when Fuller knocked Packer wide receiver Antonio Freeman upside-down on a hit to the shoulder pads. He was also fined in that game for poking Frank Winters in the eye after the Green Bay center hit Fuller late on a play before getting in the defensive back's face. Fuller was docked $30,000, believed to be the largest fine ever levied against a Minnesota player.

Further establishing himself in the defensive backfield in 1997, Fuller led the team with 18 passes defensed, the sixth-highest total in Viking history. He was also fourth on the squad with a career-high 95 tackles, forced two fumbles, and picked off two passes. The 1998 campaign was similar, with the former Seminole upgrading his man-to-man coverage while ranking fourth on the team with 80 tackles, recording one sack, and intercepting four tosses. By the end of the season, Fuller had started 42 straight games, including the playoffs, before signing a lucrative free agent contract with the expansion Cleveland Browns prior to the 1999 slate.

Darrell Fullington

Seasons: 1988–90 Safety Height: 6'1"
Number: 29 Miami Weight: 195

Minnesota's fifth-round draft choice in 1988, Darrell Fullington battled a handful of off-field problems during his days in purple that seemed to hinder his career in the National Football League.

Fullington served as an extra defensive back and a member of the special teams in his first two seasons with Minnesota. He recorded three interceptions and 19 total tackles as a rookie, with two of his picks coming in a

43–3 win over Dallas on November 13, 1988. In 1989, Fullington had another interception and ranked fourth on special teams with 12 solo stops.

A starting job at free safety came Fullington's way for 11 games in 1990. He responded by recording 103 total tackles, good for sixth on the team, with one interception and the first sack of his career. He also ranked eighth on special teams with eight tackles and a fumble recovery.

Despite his production, Fullington was released by Minnesota in training camp and signed with New England. After a half-season with the Patriots, he concluded his professional football career in 1992 with Tampa Bay.

Tony Galbreath

Seasons: 1981–83	Running Back	Height: 6'
Number: 32	Missouri	Weight: 228

One of the game's best receivers out of the backfield during his days with the Saints, Tony Galbreath arrived in Minnesota from New Orleans just prior to the 1981 season in exchange for a third-round draft choice. Galbreath served primarily as a third-down running back for three years with the Vikings and took some heat off quarterback Tommy Kramer with his ability to get open in the flats.

In his first season with Minnesota, Galbreath gained 198 yards on the ground and 144 more on 18 receptions. His highlight included two one-yard touchdown plunges during Minnesota's fourth-quarter comeback that fell short in a 19–17 loss to Denver on November 2. The 1982 campaign was practically a carbon copy, with Galbreath rushing for 116 yards and catching 17 passes for 153 yards.

His greatest contributions in purple took place in 1983. Galbreath helped pick up some slack while running back Ted Brown was out with an injury and finished third on the team with 474 rushing yards and second with 45 receptions for 348 yards. His biggest day as a Viking came when he gained 104 yards and scored on a 52-yard gallop in Minnesota's 23–14 win at Chicago on October 9. Then, in a case of deja vu in the season finale, Galbreath scored two fourth-quarter touchdowns with one-yard runs, only this time the comeback was successful—a 20–14 win over Cincinnati on December 17.

Galbreath's days with Minnesota came to an end when he was traded to the Giants for linebacker Brad Van Pelt on July 12, 1984. While Galbreath played four more years with New York, Van Pelt refused to join the Vikings. As a result, he was dealt to the Raiders for a sixth-round pick in 1985 and a second-round selection in 1986.

Frank Gallagher

Season: 1973	Guard	Height: 6'2"
Number: 66	North Carolina	Weight: 245

A six-year starter with the Lions from 1967–72, Frank Gallagher joined the Vikings in October 1973 after being waived by Atlanta. He played in four games with Minnesota before starting at guard in Super Bowl IX against Pittsburgh in place of the injured Milt Sunde. He was released the following year in training camp.

Jim Gallery

Season: 1990
Number: 6
Kicker
Minnesota
Height: 6'1"
Weight: 200

A former All-Big Ten performer with the Golden Gophers, Jim Gallery was with the Vikings for games at Philadelphia and Green Bay in 1990 but did not attempt a field goal.

John Galvin

Season: 1989
Number: 90
Linebacker
Boston College
Height: 6'3"
Weight: 230

John Galvin signed with Minnesota as a Plan B free agent and saw action on the Vikings' special teams units in 11 of the 16 games during the 1989 season. He registered seven tackles on kick and punt coverage, and spent four weeks on injured reserve during the campaign with an ailing neck.

Rich Gannon

Seasons: 1987–92
Number: 16
Quarterback
Delaware
Height: 6'3"
Weight: 197

Rich Gannon

Vikings fans had flashbacks during the 1987 preseason. Many of the purple faithful felt they were watching the second coming of Fran Tarkenton when rookie quarterback Rich Gannon led the team in rushing with 142 yards on 18 carries. While that showing proved he was one of the league's fastest signalcallers, Gannon had to serve as Minnesota's quarterback-of-the-future for several years before earning a chance to play.

New England's fourth-round pick in 1987, Gannon was acquired by the Vikings just prior to training camp in exchange for fourth- and 11th-round draft choices. With Tommy Kramer and Wade Wilson holding starting honors under center, Gannon served as the third-string quarterback and played mainly in mop-up situations during his first three years in Minnesota.

He received his first significant opportunity in 1990 while Wilson struggled with a thumb injury. For the next two years, the debate raged regarding which quarterback should start. The situation split the team into two camps—one preferring Wilson's veteran leadership, the other desiring Gannon's scrambling, wide-open style.

Gannon made his first start in the 23–20 overtime loss to Tampa Bay on September 30, 1990, completing 19 of his 37 passes for 253 yards and two touchdowns. He followed that performance by throwing for more than 200 yards in his next three games. His best showing was a 23-for-35 outing for 227 yards and two touchdowns, including a 78-yard scoring toss to Cris Carter, in the 32–24 loss at Philadelphia on October 15. For the year he succeeded on 52.1 percent of his attempts for 16 touchdowns and 16 interceptions.

Gannon again took over the starting duties during the 1991 season in place of Wilson and led the team in pass attempts (354), completions (211), yards (2,166) and touchdowns (12). He set a National Football League record by throwing 63 aerials without an interception in the 26–23 loss at New England on October 20, and went on to establish a Viking mark with 156 consecutive passes without having one picked off. His best game of the season came in the 34–7 win over Phoenix on October 13, when Gannon completed 23 passes for 254 yards and two touchdowns while rushing five times for 34 yards and another score.

Wilson was released prior to the 1992 season and Gannon took over the quarterback duties, starting the first 10 games. The most outstanding showings of his career occurred during the first half of the campaign. His 25-

for-32 performance for 318 yards and two touchdowns during a 42–7 win over Cincinnati on September 27 earned him NFC Player of the Week honors. A week later, Gannon was 20 for 25 with one touchdown in the come-from-behind 21–20 victory over Chicago on October 4. Yet, various ailments and some poor decisions in November forced head coach Dennis Green to go with Sean Salisbury for four of the final five regular-season games as well as the playoff loss to Washington. Gannon finished the year completing 57 percent of his passes for 12 touchdowns and 13 interceptions.

Disgruntled with his playing time and the signing of free agent quarterback Jim McMahon, Gannon was traded during the 1993 training camp to Washington in exchange for a fifth-round draft pick. He later enjoyed success as a reliever with Kansas City from 1995-98.

Teddy Garcia

Season: 1989   Kicker   Height: 5'10"
Number: 2   Northeastern Louisiana   Weight: 187

Teddy Garcia served as the Vikings' placekicker during the first three games of the 1989 season. Although he made all eight of his extra-point attempts, Garcia made just one of five field goal tries, with his lone success a 35-yarder against Houston in Minnesota's 38–7 season-opening win on September 10. His time in purple came to an end when Rich Karlis joined the team for the fourth game.

David Garnett

Seasons: 1993–94, 1996   Linebacker   Height: 6'2"
Number: 54   Stanford   Weight: 219

Dave Garnett, who played for head coach Dennis Green at Stanford, was the only rookie to see action in every game with the Vikings in 1993. Playing mostly on special teams, he placed second on the kick-coverage squad with 20 tackles. He also responded with a career-high seven tackles while playing in a special four-linebacker alignment due to the absence of injured nose tackle Henry Thomas during a 30–10 win over Kansas City on December 26.

A knee injury forced Garnett to miss seven games in 1994. He still managed to record 11 tackles on defense and seven more on special teams. Garnett also recovered a fumble that led to a touchdown in a 42–14 win over Chicago on September 18 and pounced on an onsides kick that resulted in a field goal in a 38–35 victory against Miami on September 25.

Selected by Carolina in the expansion draft before the 1995 season, Garnett returned to the Vikings after a one-year hiatus. In 12 appearances in 1996, he posted 19 defensive tackles, six special teams stops and one fumble recovery.

Billy Gault

Season: 1961   Cornerback   Height: 6'1"
Number: 44   Texas Christian   Weight: 185

Part of the six-player deal with Cleveland that brought Jim Marshall to Minnesota just prior to the Vikings' maiden voyage, Billy Gault played on special teams in four games in 1961, his only campaign in the National Football League. Gault's most notable statistical contribution involved returning two kickoffs for 41 yards.

William Gay

Season: 1988
Number: 78

Defensive End
Southern Cal

Height: 6'5"
Weight: 260

William Gay, a 10-year veteran with Detroit, experienced nearly as many roster moves as he did plays with the Vikings. Placed on injured reserve after the season's third game, he was activated just prior to the Monday night contest against the Giants on October 30 and released nine days later, on November 8. He wound up playing in five games for Minnesota, all in a reserve role.

Ron George

Season: 1997
Number: 55

Linebacker
Stanford

Height: 6'2"
Weight: 236

A starter during his four years with Atlanta, Ron George signed as a free agent with Minnesota before the 1997 season even though the three first-string linebacker positions were filled. His presence gave the Vikings their deepest talent in the heart of the defense since Dennis Green was named head coach in 1992.

George played in all 16 games for the Vikings in 1997. Seeing regular time behind Dixon Edwards on the strong side throughout the campaign, he made eight solo tackles, including two for lost yardage. He also improved the special teams on kick coverage, posting 13 additional hits. Released by Minnesota after the season, George spent the 1998 season with Kansas City.

John Gerak

Seasons: 1993–96
Numbers: 66, 46

Guard-Tight End
Penn State

Height: 6'3"
Weight: 295

The first overall pick in the third round of the 1993 draft, John Gerak was a versatile blocker who was always willing to change positions whenever a need arose.

After playing sparingly for four games at left guard when Randall McDaniel moved into the backfield in 1993, Gerak took the field at four different positions and wore two uniform numbers in 1994. Through the first 12 contests of the campaign, he shared the right guard position with Bernard Dafney while lining up as a fullback once. When Adrian Cooper and Brent Novoselsky suffered season-ending injuries, Gerak became a starter as the Vikings' blocking tight end. Regardless of where he played, he gained a reputation for using every trick in the book, tactics that upset Green Bay's Reggie White, among others.

In 1995, Gerak toiled the first 10 games at tight end before taking over the starting duties at right guard for the final six contests. He held that position for the first 10 games of 1996 before losing the starting assignment to David Dixon, who was inserted for his run-blocking abilities. Gerak saw some action at guard down the stretch, primarily in passing situations.

Frustrated with his situation in Minnesota, Gerak signed as a free agent with the Rams in the offseason and spent the 1997 season with St. Louis. He declined an invitation to rejoin the Vikings during the 1998 campaign.

Carl Gersbach

Seasons: 1971–72   Linebacker   Height: 6'1"
Number: 56   West Chester   Weight: 230

Nicknamed "Otto" by Neill Armstrong because the Vikings' defensive coach said, "There are too many Carls on the defensive team", Carl Gersbach served as a backup linebacker for two seasons after being released by Philadelphia.

The former Little All-American at West Chester started 10 games in 1971 in place of injured middle linebacker Lonnie Warwick. His most memorable performance came against his former employer. Gersbach was awarded the game ball in the Vikings' 13–0 victory over Philadelphia on October 10 after serving as a key to the team's triumph.

Gersbach saw action in all 14 games a year later. He started the finale for the ailing Roy Winston at outside linebacker and emerged as the team's leading tackler for the contest. He also was a finalist to participate on a fall television program on WCCO, a role that that eventually went to "Benchwarmer Bob" Lurtsema. Gersbach's tenure in purple ended after the 1972 season when he and Clint Jones were traded to San Diego for second- and third-round draft choices.

Willie Gillespie

Season: 1987   Wide Receiver   Height: 5'9"
Number: 86   Tennessee-Chattanooga   Weight: 170

Willie Gillespie caught two passes for 28 yards in the third and final game for the Vikings' replacement team in 1987.

John Gilliam

Seasons: 1972–75   Wide Receiver   Height: 6'1"
Number: 42   South Carolina State   Weight: 195

With Gene Washington suffering from a foot ailment and the offense needing more speed, the Vikings acquired John Gilliam along with a second- and fourth-round draft pick from St. Louis in exchange for quarterback Gary Cuozzo on April 26, 1972. Gilliam became one of the league's premier wide receivers while in purple, a perpetual deep threat who teamed with quarterback Fran Tarkenton to help lead Minnesota to its second and third Super Bowl appearances.

Gilliam was a fleet receiver with 9.4 speed who ran precise patterns. In his first year with the Vikings, Gilliam became Tarkenton's favorite target. He set a team record with 1,035 receiving yards on 47 passes, led the National Football League with a 22.0 yards-per-catch average, and was one of just two NFC receivers to top the 1,000-yard mark in 1972. He caught touchdown tosses in his first three games with Minnesota, including 40- and 56-yard bombs. Gilliam later had scoring receptions of 44 and 66 yards, giving the Vikings a receiver who could stretch defenses and open up the running and short passing games underneath. He also established a team mark by averaging 26.4 yards on 14 kickoff returns.

Known as one of the league's most stylish dressers, Gilliam led the Vikings in receiving for a second straight season in 1973, catching 42 passes for 907 yards and eight touchdowns while averaging 17.4 yards on 10 kickoff returns. He also ran the end around reverse five times that season, averaging 14.2 yards per rushing attempt, including a 44-yard touchdown gallop in a 28–21 win over the Eagles on October 21. He saved his best for last, catching two touchdown tosses in the fourth quarter of the 27–20 playoff win over

Washington on December 22 and another 54-yard score versus Dallas in Minnesota's 27–10 triumph during the NFC Championship Game a week later.

"I'll tell you the guy who reads me. It's Francis," Gilliam said. "The man knows what I'm going to do before I do. He knows what John Gilliam wants."

With opponents focusing on shutting down the receiver by double-teaming him on nearly every play, Gilliam's production fell to 26 receptions for 528 yards and five touchdowns in 1974. He remained a big-play performer, catching an 80-yard bomb in a 51–10 trouncing of Houston on October 13 before grabbing two touchdown passes from Tarkenton in the 30–14 playoff victory over St. Louis on December 21.

Despite his success with the Vikings, Gilly looked for greener pastures. He decided to play out his option and signed with the World Football League in 1975. He was back in Minnesota, however, four days prior to the season opener when the Chicago Winds folded. His presence was welcomed, for the Vikings' passing game struggled during the preseason without Gilliam. He wound up catching 50 passes for 777 yards and seven scores in what proved to be his final season in purple. Gilliam signed as a free agent with Atlanta in 1976 before splitting the 1977 campaign between New Orleans and Chicago.

Vencie Glenn

Seasons: 1992–94 Safety Height: 6'
Number: 25 Indiana State Weight: 201

Free safeties are required to make things happen in the secondary. Vencie Glenn had a knack for doing just that, regardless of whether it involved making a key interception or punishing a ball carrier who managed to break through the Vikings' first wave of defenders.

Glenn, a six-year veteran signed as a Plan B free agent, was a reserve for the first part of 1992, his first season with Minnesota, before taking over the starting duties at free safety for an injured Felix Wright in Week 13. Four games later, Glenn earned his first NFC Defensive Player of the Week award after tying the Viking record by picking off three passes in a 27–7 triumph over Green Bay on December 27.

That type of performance enabled the hard-hitting Glenn to remain Minnesota's starting free safety for the next two seasons. In 1993, he led the club with five interceptions, placed second with 10 passes defensed, and was fifth with 76 tackles. A determined, gutsy player, Glenn proved how valuable his effort could be against the Packers on December 19. After leaving the field following the game's first play, he returned in the second half to salvage the 21–17 Minnesota win. Glenn deflected a sure touchdown toss in the end zone on fourth-and-goal to stop one Green Bay drive, then intercepted a pass on the Packers' last series to settle the outcome.

Glenn continued to lead the Vikings' secondary in 1994, tying Anthony Parker for the team lead with four interceptions and ranking third with 86 tackles. Yet, with Glenn turning 30 during the regular season, Minnesota traded the safety to the Giants on draft day in 1995 for a sixth-round draft choice.

Andrew Glover

Seasons: 1997–98	Tight End	Height: 6'6"
Number: 82	Grambling	Weight: 253

Unwanted by the Raiders after six seasons in the National Football League, Andrew Glover became a Viking when college teammate Jake Reed put in a good word for the tight end to the Minnesota coaching staff. Reed's endorsement led to Glover's signing shortly after training camp opened in 1997 and gave the Vikings yet another weapon in their potent offensive attack.

A knee injury forced Glover to miss the season's first three games. He gained some rhythm with quarterback Brad Johnson shortly thereafter, with Glover making a 28-yard catch over the middle in his first appearance, against Green Bay. Two weeks later, Glover pulled in one of the season's most important grabs when he caught a 43-yard toss over the middle in the final minute of play to set up Eddie Murray's game-winning field goal a few seconds later in the 20–19 victory at Arizona on October 5. Despite battling with inconsistency in catching the ball during the season, Glover finished the year with 32 grabs for 378 yards and three touchdowns.

"We were very fortunate to get Glover, who was just out there looking for the right combination," said head coach Dennis Green. "He is really a good, big target. You can get the ball to him in a lot of different ways. And he's been a solid blocker."

In 1998, Glover returned to the starting lineup and made several key plays while hooking up with Johnson and Randall Cunningham. He had the best game of his career when he caught nine passes for 93 yards in the Vikings' 31–24 win over New Orleans on November 8. By the end of the year, he was third on the team with 35 catches for 522 yards and five touchdowns. Glover also registered six points on a 15-yard reception in the 41–21 playoff victory over Arizona on January 10, 1999.

Robert Goff

Season: 1996	Defensive Lineman	Height: 6'3"
Number: 94	Auburn	Weight: 280

Signed as a veteran free agent prior to the 1996 season, Robert "Pig" Goff was expected to provide some bulk and experience in the middle of the Vikings' defensive line. Although the former Saint remained on the roster for the entire season, his contributions were minimal. Goff saw brief action in five games at right end and inside on goal line situations while failing to register a tackle.

Bob Goodridge

Season: 1968	End	Height: 6'2"
Number: 82	Vanderbilt	Weight: 190

Minnesota tabbed Bob Goodridge with its sixth-round draft choice in 1968 after the receiver led the collegiate ranks with 79 catches for 1,114 yards the previous fall at Vanderbilt. Goodridge found the playing time harder to come by in the National Football League. Stuck behind Gene Washington at left end, Goodridge caught just one pass for five yards while seeing action in 11 games on special teams.

Charles Goodrum

Seasons: 1972–78	Guard	Height: 6'3"
Number: 68	Florida A&M	Weight: 256

Charles "Goody" Goodrum was a fixture on the great Minnesota offensive lines of the 1970s. A ninth-round draft pick in 1972, the college All-American moved from tackle to become a starter at left guard in 1976 and did not miss a start for the next three seasons.

Goodrum preferred the running game but did well in pass protection, a necessity with Fran Tarkenton playing quarterback. He served on the Vikings' taxi squad in 1972, leading head coach Bud Grant to say, "He surprised us. In the first week of training camp we didn't think he had a chance. But he's progressed and we feel has a shot at it this year." Shifted from guard to tackle in 1973, Goodrum saw action in 10 games on short-yardage and goal-line plays. He moved into the starting lineup at left tackle in 1974, then shared first-string honors with Steve Riley in 1975.

Moved back to guard a year later, Goodrum and Riley teamed to give the Vikings steady production on the left side of the line for the next three seasons. Goodrum was released in training camp in 1979 when Minnesota decided to go with younger players, including rookie Jim Hough.

Hunter Goodwin

Seasons: 1996–98	Tight End	Height: 6'5"
Number: 87	Texas A&M	Weight: 274

Minnesota's fourth-round draft choice in 1996, Hunter Goodwin made the move from a college tackle to a professional tight end so well that he joined the starting lineup for the final six games of his rookie campaign. The only Viking first-year player to start that season, the high-intensity Goodwin proved he can be a dominating run blocker and was a major reason for the team's improved rushing attack in the final month-and-a-half of the year.

Goodwin started during the early stages of 1997 before veteran Andrew Glover received the nod. Goodwin, however, remained the primary tight end in running situations, and continued to do an excellent job in pass protection. He also played a bigger role as a receiver, catching seven passes for 61 yards after making just one grab for 24 yards as a rookie.

Goodwin continued to serve as a dominating blocker while catching three passes for 16 yards in 1998. He also became a contributor on the special teams' coverage units, recording four tackles.

Scottie Graham

Seasons: 1993–96	Running Back	Height: 5'9"
Number: 31	Ohio State	Weight: 215

The Vikings found lightning in a bottle or, more accurately, a player with lightning in his legs who was biding his time filling prescription bottles in a Columbus, Ohio, pharmacy until Minnesota came calling for the running back in 1993.

Prior to the Detroit game on December 5, 1993, Graham had not carried the ball once for the Vikings after being activated a month earlier following a six-week stint on the practice squad. By the end of the month, the powerful back with tree trunks for legs was the team's leading rusher for the season, having gained 488 yards on 118 carries.

Graham got his chance to play when his Ohio State teammate, Robert Smith, suffered a knee injury against the Lions. Two weeks later, the former Buckeye registered his first 100-yard rushing day by gaining 139 yards on 30 carries in a 21–17 win over Green Bay. The next game, on December 26, Gra-

Scottie Graham

ham recorded the fourth-highest single-game rushing effort in team history, piling up 166 yards on 33 attempts in the 30–10 triumph over Kansas City. His 305 yards in those two games are the most ever by a Viking running back over a two-game stretch.

While Graham never again reached those lofty heights during the next three years with the Vikings, he was a vital reserve and solid special teams performer. In 1994, he gained 207 yards on 64 carries and made nine tackles on kick coverages. Graham re-emerged in December of 1995, when he led the team in rushing in four of the last five games, including a season-high 115 yards in the 27–24 loss to Cincinnati on December 24. He finished that year with 406 yards on 110 carries and nine tackles, then gained 138 yards on 57 attempts while playing behind Smith and Leroy Hoard in 1996.

Graham left the Vikings after signing a free-agent contract with Cincinnati for the 1997 season. He returned to Minnesota for training camp in 1998 and was among the final cuts. Even so, "Mr. December" holds the Minnesota regular-season record for most chances without a fumble in his career with 368 attempts (349 rushes, 19 receptions).

Rory Graves

Season: 1993   Tackle   Height: 6'6"
Number: 73   Ohio State   Weight: 288

Signed in October 1993, Rory Graves, a four-year veteran of the National Football League and former starter with the Raiders, added experienced depth to the offensive line but did not see any game action during his brief stint on the Vikings' roster.

Torrian Gray

Seasons: 1997–98   Safety   Height: 6'
Number: 23   Virginia Tech   Weight: 198

A second-round draft pick, Torrian Gray emerged as one of two Minnesota rookies to see action in every game during the 1997 season. His production was impressive enough for Gray to earn the starting job at free safety for the final two regular-season games and the two playoff contests after Orlando Thomas was shelved with a recurring hamstring problem. He concluded his first professional campaign with 25 total tackles, one pass defensed, and 10 special teams tackles.

Displaying excellent instincts for the game, Gray again played in nickel coverages and on special teams during the first nine games of the 1998 season before suffering a dislocated knee cap and a torn anterior cruciate ligament on a kickoff return against New Orleans on November 8. The injury cost Gray the remainder of the season, with the safety posting 26 tackles, three passes defensed, a sack, an interception and a fumble recovery.

Dick Grecni

| Season: 1961 | Linebacker | Height: 6'1" |
| Number: 50 | Ohio | Weight: 230 |

Dick Grecni was another of the six players obtained in the Jim Marshall trade with Cleveland before the 1961 season. A small college All-American at Ohio, Grecni backed up starter Rip Hawkins at middle linebacker and played in 12 games with the Vikings during his only year in the National Football League. He intercepted one pass and returned the ball 16 yards.

Robert Green

| Season: 1997 | Running Back | Height: 5'8" |
| Number: 32 | William & Mary | Weight: 210 |

A three-year veteran with the Bears, Robert Green signed with the Vikings just prior to training camp in 1997 to add veteran depth to the offensive backfield. While Green played in just three games, he stepped to the forefront in Week 9 against New England in place of the injured Robert Smith and Leroy Hoard. Green responded by rushing five times for 19 yards and recovered an offensive fumble at the Patriot goal line that led to a touchdown in Minnesota's 23–18 win on November 2.

Marcellus Greene

| Season: 1984 | Defensive Back | Height: 6' |
| Number: 25 | Arizona | Weight: 184 |

A three-year veteran of the Canadian Football League, Marcellus Greene signed with the Vikings at the start of the 1984 season and played on special teams in Minnesota's final 14 games. Greene contributed six unassisted tackles and four assists on kick coverage before receiving his release the following year in training camp.

Robert Griffith

| Seasons: 1994–98 | Defensive Back | Height: 5'11" |
| Number: 24 | San Diego State | Weight: 189 |

A wiry, reckless strong safety who has earned a reputation for being one of the game's most physical players and hardest hitters in the open field, Robert Griffith solidifies the secondary by excelling against the run. He was a big factor in the Vikings' improved defense in 1998 with his bone-crunching stops and his solid pass coverage at strong safety. He also became one of the league's best aerial pirates, picking off two passes against both St. Louis and Green Bay in regular-season play before repeating the performance in the 41–21 playoff victory over Arizona.

Undrafted out of San Diego State, the late-blooming Griffith earned a roster spot with his strong play on special teams and as a nickel back during his first two seasons in Minnesota after one year in the Canadian Football League. He was third on the team with 25 stops on special teams in 1994 (a total that ranks fifth in Vikings history), then set the franchise record with 29 special teams tackles a year later. He also saw more playing time on defense in 1995, and led all non-starters with 39 hits.

In 1996, Griffith moved into the starting lineup and registered 103 tackles, becoming the first Viking defensive back to top the century mark for stops since Joey Browner and Felix Wright accomplished the feat in 1991. He also placed second on the team with four interceptions, all of which came in Minnesota wins, and paced the team with 67 return yards.

Robert Griffith

Griffith continued to excel in 1997, leading the team with 103 solo tackles while becoming the first Viking defensive back since Browner to have back-to-back seasons with 100 or more hits. He took his game to a higher level in 1998 by ranking third on the team with 88 stops while placing second with five interceptions to earn second-team All-Pro recognition from the Associated Press. Without question, Griffith became the glue of the improved defensive backfield, thereby making the signing of this free agent one of head coach Dennis Green's most unsung moves.

"Robert really works hard on developing his game," Green said. "He's very smart, a heavy-duty hitter. I think he has been one of our most improved players in the program."

Bob Grim

Seasons: 1967–71, 1976–77   Wide Receiver   Height: 6'
Numbers: 27, 26   Oregon State   Weight: 188

One of the most versatile players ever to play for the Vikings, Bob Grim earned his keep during two stints with the team by doing anything asked of him by head coach Bud Grant.

For example, as a rookie in 1967, Grim's primary responsibility came in catching six passes for 108 yards as a reserve flanker. Yet Minnesota's second-round draft pick was also employed as a defensive back, kick returner and running back. He averaged 22.4 yards on 22 kickoff takebacks and four yards on 25 punt returns, and gained 20 yards on his lone carry from scrimmage. His 81-yard punt return against the Giants led to a critical touchdown in the Vikings' 27–24 win on November 5.

A knee injury suffered on the first day of training camp cost Grim all but one game in 1968. He returned to catch 10 passes for 155 yards in 1969, with his lone score coming in the second quarter of quarterback Joe Kapp's record-setting seven touchdown tosses in a 52–14 win over the Colts on September 28. Grim also saw regular action on special teams, a role in which he took pride.

"The ballplayers believe in the slogan '40 for 60 minutes,'" Grim said. "It puts equal emphasis on the special teams, because they are involved in about 20 to 25 percent of the game."

A part-time starter at flanker in 1970, Grim caught 23 passes for 287 yards and teamed with John Henderson to give the Vikings their best production at the position since Grant took the head coaching helm. Grim parlayed that opportunity into becoming Minnesota's top receiver in 1971, when he led the squad with 45 catches, 691 yards and seven touchdowns. He pulled in two scoring passes from quarterback Gary Cuozzo in a 20–17 loss to Chicago on September 26. His season-long 55-yard reception from Norm Snead broke a fourth-quarter tie to give the Vikings a 17–10 win over the Giants on October 31. Grim also had a two-touchdown game against Chicago on December 19, when the Vikings gained revenge for the earlier defeat with a 27–10 triumph.

Grim's great season made him one of the primary parts of the trade with New York that brought quarterback Fran Tarkenton back to the Twin Cities. After three seasons with the Giants and one with the Bears, Grim returned as well, signing with the Vikings as a free agent when Jim Lash was traded to San Francisco. He caught nine passes for 108 yards in 1976 and three tosses for 65 yards in 1977. Grim also returned 11 punts for 69 yards in his final season after a five-year hiatus from the chore.

Ron Groce

Season: 1976
Number: 47
Running Back
Macalester
Height: 6'2"
Weight: 211

Drafted in the 15th round by Minnesota in 1976, Ron Groce was released at the end of training camp prior to re-signing with the team in October after Mark Kellar broke an ankle in the season's third game. Groce played in six contests, with all three of his rushing attempts and 18 yards coming in the Vikings' 29–7 win over Miami on December 11.

Neal Guggemos

Seasons: 1986–87
Number: 41
Defensive Back
St. Thomas
Height: 6'
Weight: 190

His career statistics do not show it, but Neal Guggemos scored on his first play in the National Football League. The event took place in a pre-season game against Miami on August 9, 1986. The college free agent intercepted a pass and returned the ball 20 yards for a touchdown in what proved to be a 30–16 win over the Dolphins.

Unfortunately for Guggemos, he broke his thumb during that contest and spent the first 12 weeks of the 1986 season on injured reserve. He recovered in time to play in the last four games of the year as a reserve free safety and on special teams and finished his rookie campaign with six unassisted tackles.

The Winsted, Minnesota, native played a greater role in 1987. Guggemos led the team and finished fifth in the NFC by averaging 22.4 yards on 36 kickoff returns. He also recorded 36 total tackles as a nickel and dime back and posted his first official interception during the season-opener against Detroit on September 13, a 34–19 Minnesota victory. The former St. Thomas College standout was waived the following year during training camp.

Eric Guliford

Seasons: 1993–94
Number: 84
Wide Receiver
Arizona State
Height: 5'8"
Weight: 165

Eric Guliford's lone reception as a Viking was a big one. With Minnesota trailing Green Bay by one point in the September 26, 1993, contest, quarterback Jim McMahon found Guliford uncovered deep in Packer territory. On the first play from scrimmage in his career, Guliford got behind an out-of-position Terrell Buckley, caught the ball for a 45-yard completion with six seconds left and stepped out of bounds to set up a Fuad Reveiz field goal on the next play to give the Vikes a 15–13 triumph.

Otherwise, Guliford's contributions came on special teams. Though neither big nor fast, he used his quickness to average 7.3 yards on 29 punt returns in 1993 and 2.8 yards on five attempts in 1994. Guliford also recorded three tackles on coverage units before being selected in the expansion draft by Carolina after the 1994 season.

Jim Gustafson

Seasons: 1985–90
Number: 80
Wide Receiver
St. Thomas
Height: 6'1"
Weight: 185

A Minneapolis native who earned All-American and academic All-American honors at nearby St. Thomas College, Jim Gustafson was the classic possession receiver who provided solid depth to the Vikings' pass-catching corps.

Cut by the Vikings in training camp in 1984, Gustafson returned a year later and made the team, although he spent all of the 1985 slate on injured reserve after separating a shoulder in a pre-season game against Pittsburgh on August 17. In 1986, he played in 14 games and caught five passes, with his first two receptions going for touchdowns. He victimized Detroit on September 7 on a five-yarder for the Vikings' only touchdown in a 13–10 loss. Two weeks later, in a 31–7 win over Pittsburgh, Gustafson pulled in a nine-yard pass for six points.

Gustafson continued to produce in limited opportunities in 1987, catching four passes for 55 yards, with three coming against Chicago during a 30–24 loss on December 6. He became the Vikings' third receiver in 1988 and responded with his best season—15 receptions for 231 yards and one touchdown. In 1989, Gustafson caught 14 passes, eight of which came on third-down situations. He spent all of the 1990 slate on injured reserve before receiving an injury settlement from the team.

Brian Habib

Seasons: 1988–92	Guard-Defensive Tackle	Height: 6'7"
Numbers: 91, 74	Washington	Weight: 299

A common practice among college coaches is to move struggling defensive linemen to the other side of the ball. The Vikings did that with Brian Habib, investing three years in turning their 11th-round draft choice in 1988 from a reserve defensive tackle into a starting right guard for the 1991 and 1992 campaigns.

Habib, who took over the starting duties at right guard from Todd Kalis midway through the 1991 campaign, excelled in run blocking. He made up for his lack of foot speed in the pass rush with his aggressiveness at the point of impact. He also became more consistent as he gained experience and emerged as a solid component to one of the best lines in Vikings annals.

After making 23 starts with Minnesota, Habib signed a free-agent contract with Denver. The Broncos surprised the league by making Habib the highest-paid offensive lineman when they signed him to a three-year deal worth $4.2 million, beginning with the 1993 season.

Dale Hackbart

Seasons: 1966–70	Defensive Back	Height: 6'3"
Number: 49	Wisconsin	Weight: 210

Dale Hackbart was courted by professional football interests in Minnesota before a team officially existed.

Prior to the founding of the National Football League's Vikings in 1960, owners E. William Boyer and H.P. Skoglund had a brief romance with the American Football League. Boyer and Skoglund even got to the point of offering contracts to high NFL draft choices, among them a $7,000 deal to their most coveted target, Hackbart, a quarterback from Wisconsin. That turned out to be one deal Hackbart did not sign, although he was at one point under contract with the Green Bay Packers, the Canadian Football League's Winnipeg Blue Bombers and baseball's Pittsburgh Pirates.

Five years after his initial courtship with the Vikings, Hackbart arrived in the Twin Cities as a defensive back following mediocre showings with Green Bay and Washington. He was released by Minnesota during training camp in 1965 after engaging Jerry Reichow and Hal Bedsole in fisticuffs. Re-signed to the taxi squad for the 1965 slate after a fling in the CFL, Hackbart earned a spot on the Vikings' roster in 1966 before gaining notoriety as one of the game's premier "enforcers" and devastating hitters in 1967 and 1968.

Head coach Bud Grant appreciated "The Hacker's" aggressive approach. Hackbart showed great determination and a desire to play, and was labelled an "unnecessarily rough player" by many observers. At the same time, Grant detested the penalty yardage that oftentimes came with such aggressiveness, including Hackbart's more than 100 yards of setbacks in 1967. But for every mental error came a handful of intimidating hits, none better than the bone-crushing tackle Hackbart made against the Rams' Ron Smith on a kickoff return in the Vikings' 23–20 triumph over Los Angeles in the Western Conference Championship Game on December 27, 1969.

"Hackie" also had a nose for the ball. In his first active year with the Vikings, he picked off five passes for 73 yards, including a 41-yard scamper for a touchdown against Detroit on November 13, 1966. The defensive back intercepted two more tosses in 1967 and reached paydirt again when he returned a pick 21 yards versus St. Louis on October 8.

Toward the end of his career, Hackbart had to prove annually that rumors about the end of his NFL career were greatly exaggerated. Even though he was in his early 30s, he thrilled in traveling the game's most treacherous tracks by punishing opponents on kick and punt coverages. "When I was younger, I wasn't too keen on special teams," Hackbart admitted in 1970. "But I enjoy it now."

His time in purple concluded after the 1970 season when he, Mike McGill and a fourth-round draft choice were sent to St. Louis for Nate Wright and Bob Brown. Hackbart spent two years with the Cardinals and part of the 1973 campaign as a Bronco.

John Haines

Season: 1984 Defensive Tackle Height: 6'6"
Number: 90 Texas Weight: 266

Minnesota's first seventh-round selection in the 1984 draft, John Haines spent the first half of his rookie season on the physically unable to perform list before seeing action in the campaign's final eight games. His best showings came in back-to-back contests, with Haines recovering a fumble versus Tampa Bay on November 4 and registering a tackle, two assists and an eight-yard sack against Green Bay a week later.

Dick Haley

Season: 1961 Defensive Back-Flanker Height: 5'10"
Number: 28 Pittsburgh Weight: 195

Dick Haley's tenure with the Vikings was one of the shortest among those who played with the expansion team in its first year. Selected from Washington in the veterans pool, the two-way player took the field with the Vikings for four games and recovered a fumble before being traded to Pittsburgh for the final eight contests of the 1961 season in exchange for a sixth-round draft pick in 1962.

Steven Hall

Season: 1996 Cornerback Height: 6'
Number: 23 Kentucky Weight: 205

Steven Hall came and went during the 1996 season. Signed to the Vikings' practice squad on November 6, Hall was activated and saw action in one regular-season game. When Minnesota placed him on waivers in hopes of returning Hall to the practice squad toward the end of the campaign, he was claimed by Indianapolis.

Tom Hall

Seasons: 1964–66, 1968–69 Wide Receiver Height: 6'1"
Numbers: 86, 28 Minnesota Weight: 195

A defensive back during his first two seasons in the National Football League with the Lions, Tom Hall decided his future would be better served on the other side of the line and became an aggressive flanker during his first stint with the Vikings.

Never afraid to use an elbow to free himself from a defender, Hall emerged as a gutty receiver who usually came down with passes thrown in a crowd. Acquired from Detroit with safety Bruce Zellmer for a fifth-round draft choice, he caught 23 passes in 1964, his first year in purple, and was a primary reason the Vikings were able to beat Green Bay for the first time in franchise history on October 4, 1964. Hall caught six passes for 97 yards and a touchdown during Minnesota's 24–23 triumph over the Pack.

The Vikings' fastest receiver during his first tour of duty in Minnesota, Hall pulled in 15 passes while sharing time with Jim Phillips at flanker in 1965. He took over starting duties in 1966 and responded with 23 catches for 271 yards and a pair of touchdowns before being plucked by the Saints in the expansion draft. After one year in New Orleans, the Golden Gopher returned home for two more seasons with the Vikes and caught 19 passes for 268 yards in 1968 and one toss in three games in 1969.

In addition to being a steady receiver and good downfield blocker, Hall also earned a reputation in Minnesota for making training camp a little more difficult for rookies. He always seemed to have a hearing problem when the young newcomers would sing their school fight songs at the top of their lungs during meal times and would ask the rookies to repeat their rendition. Yet, after the initiation period, Hall would provide any help he could to the green peas, thereby making the Vikings a better team.

Windlan Hall

Seasons: 1976–77 Defensive Back Height: 5'11"
Number: 40 Arizona State Weight: 175

Acquired from the 49ers for guard Steve Lawson during training camp in 1976, Windlan Hall became the Vikings' captain of the kicking team, the first player to hold the honor since Bill Brown retired in 1974. Versatile enough to start or back up at any of the four positions in the secondary, Hall served at safety and left cornerback, and filled in admirably when Nate Wright sprained an ankle during the 1976 season.

Hall played in all 14 games his first year with Minnesota, then took the field for five games in purple in 1977 before spending the last eight contests of the season with the Redskins.

Wes Hamilton

Seasons: 1976–85 Guard Height: 6'3"
Number: 61 Tulsa Weight: 270

Minnesota's third-round draft pick in 1976, Wes Hamilton impressed the Vikings' scouts with his strength and explosiveness off the line of scrimmage. Those traits earned Hamilton starting honors at right guard for seven seasons before injuries brought his career to a premature end.

Hamilton saw most of his action in short-yardage situations and on the special teams units in 1976. The former Chicago high school wrestling champion started six games at right guard a year later, beginning with the Vikings' 28–27 victory over San Francisco on December 4 when Ed White was injured during the game. Hamilton took over the full-time duties in 1978, even though he was bothered by a hyperextended knee early in the campaign. Always willing to play through injuries, Hamilton did not miss a game in his first three years as a starter before a sore knee kept him out of three contests in 1980.

He was back full-time along the front wall for the next three seasons until a right knee injury led to arthroscopic surgery in 1984. He played in only four games that year, then spent all of 1985 on injured reserve with a back ailment that occurred during the preseason. The pain and frustration caused by the injuries along with no guarantee from head coach Jerry Burns that a job awaited in the Vikings' youth movement led Hamilton to announce his retirement just prior to the beginning of the 1986 training camp.

Shelly Hammonds

Season: 1995 Cornerback Height: 5'10"
Number: 23 Penn State Weight: 189

Drafted in the fifth round by the Vikings in 1994, Shelly Hammonds spent all of 1994 and most of 1995 on the Minnesota practice squad. Moved to the active roster for three games in 1995, his lone appearance came in the Vikings' 44–24 win over Pittsburgh on September 24. Cut the following August in training camp, Hammonds' football handicap was his inability to sustain speed and play single coverage against receivers in the National Football League.

Alonzo Hampton

Season: 1990 Cornerback Height: 5'10"
Number: 25 Pittsburgh Weight: 197

Alonzo Hampton was one of the four players to make the Vikings' roster from the 1990 draft. In his only season in purple, Hampton played in 11 games as a sixth defensive back, contributing five total tackles and one pass breakup in limited activity.

Ben Hanks

Season: 1996 Linebacker Height: 6'2"
Number: 51 Florida Weight: 222

The only college free agent to make the Minnesota roster out of training camp in 1996, Ben Hanks was among the Vikings' best special teams players during his one season with the club. Though undersized for a linebacker in the National Football League, Hanks used his outstanding speed and toughness to tie for fourth on the squad with 10 special teams tackles in 12 outings. After going on injured reserve late in the campaign with a sprained ankle, Hanks was the Vikings' final cut prior to the 1997 season.

Tom Hannon

Seasons: 1977–84 Safety Height: 5'11"
Number: 45 Michigan State Weight: 184

Hard-hitting Tom Hannon served as one of the primary defensive links from the dominating Viking teams of the late 1970s to the roller coaster rides of the early 1980s.

After playing primarily on special teams as a rookie and recovering a crucial onsides kick in the 28–27 win over San Francisco on December 4, 1977, the third-round draft choice took over at free safety in the third game of the 1978 campaign. He ranked fourth on the team with 114 hits while intercepting his first two passes that year. The two-time All-Big Ten performer then placed second on the Vikings with 121 solo stops in 1979 and paced the team with three fumble recoveries and four picks. He made 122 unassisted hits in 1980 and reached paydirt for the first time by returning one of his four interceptions 41 yards in the 34–14 win over Chicago on September 21.

Hannon again led the team with four interceptions while registering

105 solo stops in 1981. He also recorded a safety when he dropped punter Bob Parsons in the end zone during a 10–9 loss to the Bears on December 6. Hannon failed to intercept a pass during the strike-interrupted 1982 season, but made 75 total tackles. A 165-hit season followed in 1983, a year that included his October 9 performance in which Hannon forced one fumble and recovered two others in the 23–14 win over Chicago. He started every game for the sixth straight year in 1984 and ranked second on the team with 153 hits.

Considered a step slow by 1985, Hannon was waived during training camp. At the time of his release, he ranked sixth on the Vikings' career list with 728 solo tackles and 1,096 total hits and ninth with 15 interceptions.

Don Hansen

Seasons: 1966–67 Linebacker Height: 6'3"
Number: 55 Illinois Weight: 228

The Vikings' third-round draft pick in 1966, Don Hansen struggled with injuries during his two years in purple. His playing time limited due to ailments early in his rookie campaign, Hansen came on strong to see regular action at all three linebacking slots down the stretch in 1966 and emerged as one of the team's best defensive prospects. Injuries again cost Hansen much of the following training camp and forced him to split time at right linebacker with John Kirby during the regular season.

One of Hansen's more notable contributions occurred during the early days of training camp in 1967. Head coach Bud Grant was implementing his discipline-oriented approach, which included standing at attention during the national anthem. As a member of the National Guard, Hansen was appointed the drill instructor, with orders to teach his teammates how to stand at a 45-degree angle to the flag. Though successful in that role, Hansen's remaining nine years in the National Football League were spent elsewhere, with seven seasons coming in Atlanta.

Mark Hanson

Season: 1987 Guard Height: 6'2"
Number: 64 Mankato State Weight: 260

Mark Hanson interrupted his stint as offensive line coach at Mankato State in 1987 to play one game with the Vikings' replacement team.

Jim Hargrove

Seasons: 1967–70 Linebacker Height: 6'3"
Number: 50 Howard Payne Weight: 223

The presence of Jim Hargrove made Lonnie Warwick a better player. Hargrove, the Vikings' 14th-round draft pick in 1967, debuted with a strong training camp as a rookie and served as Warwick's backup at middle linebacker. Noticing Hargrove's toughness, desire and ability, Warwick worked hard to improve his game, particularly in defending the pass. As a result, Warwick maintained the starting job until giving way to Jeff Siemon in 1972.

Hargrove, meanwhile, saw most of his action as a reserve and on special teams during his rookie season prior to departing for military service. The highlight of his first campaign in purple involved blocking the team's only kick of the year, a punt against Pittsburgh in a 41–27 Minnesota victory on November 26 that Hargrove recovered in the end zone for a touchdown. He then played mainly on special teams for the next three seasons before being traded to St. Louis for guard Mike LaHood in 1971.

Sam Harrell

| Seasons: 1980–82, 1987 | Running Back | Height: 6'2" |
| Number: 36 | East Carolina | Weight: 230 |

Sam Harrell was on the Vikings' roster during four different campaigns, but saw action in just six regular-season games. A hip ailment forced him to spend all of 1980 on injured reserve. He played in four contests in 1981 and gained seven yards on one rush and 23 yards on two catches. Active for all but one game in 1982, Harrell took the field just once, returning two kickoffs for 21 yards. His swan song came as a replacement player in 1987, five years after his last appearance in the National Football League, when he gained eight yards on five carries in the 20–10 loss to the Buccaneers on October 18.

Bill Harris

| Seasons: 1969–70 | Running Back | Height: 6'2" |
| Number: 35 | Colorado | Weight: 204 |

Acquired from the Falcons prior to training camp, Bill Harris served as a special teams performer for 13 games with the Vikings in 1969. He also took the field for a few plays at running back, rushing for 13 yards on six carries and gaining 13 yards on a pair of pass receptions. A knee injury landed Harris on injured reserve for the entire 1970 slate before he was traded to New Orleans for Doug Sutherland in 1971.

Darryl Harris

| Season: 1988 | Running Back | Height: 5'10" |
| Number: 32 | Arizona State | Weight: 173 |

Darryl Harris earned a spot on the Vikings' roster in 1988 as a rookie free agent and became the team's primary kickoff returner. In 14 games, Harris averaged 21.4 yards on 39 returns, with his longest effort covering 30 yards. He also caught six passes for 30 yards and had 34 rushes for 151 more. His biggest moment occurred in the season's second game, on September 11 in a 36–6 whipping of New England, when Harris scored a touchdown from two yards out to conclude the game's scoring.

James Harris

| Seasons: 1993–95 | Defensive End | Height: 6'6" |
| Number: 99 | Temple | Weight: 255 |

After developing with the Vikings for two years, James Harris, a former rookie free agent, blossomed in 1994. He earned the starting job at right defensive end during training camp and, in his first start, scooped up a fumble and returned the football 13 yards for the Vikings' only touchdown against Green Bay on September 4. He recorded his first sack a week later, versus Detroit, then batted down three aerials, tying for the second-best single-game performance in Minnesota history, against the Packers on October 20. By the end of the year, he led the defensive line with six passes defensed and three fumble recoveries and registered three sacks.

The Vikings had been waiting for such a performance from Harris for a couple of years. Signed to the practice squad on September 10, 1992, Harris missed most of the remaining season with a broken foot. He spent the majority of 1993 on special teams before emerging at defensive end a year later.

Harris' breakthrough season did not lead to prosperity in purple, however. Foot surgery caused Harris to get off to a slow start in 1995. He wound up recording just one sack and eight tackles and lost his starting job to Derrick Alexander during the campaign. His lack of production combined with an off-the-field incident that included domestic violence spelled the end of Harris' Viking career. He later toiled in the National Football League with Oakland.

Joe Harris

Season: 1979 Linebacker Height: 6'1"
Number: 52 Georgia Tech Weight: 225

A solid special teams performer, Joe Harris signed with the Vikings during training camp in 1979 and played the first two games of the season in purple. He was waived on September 15 when Phil Wise was restored to the roster from the exempt list and played the rest of the season with the Rams.

John Harris

Seasons: 1986–88 Safety Height: 6'2"
Number: 44 Arizona State Weight: 198

The Vikings added veteran experience to the secondary prior to the 1986 season when they acquired John Harris from Seattle in exchange for a seventh-round draft choice. He gave the team what it was looking for during his first start by intercepting a pass and returning it 27 yards in the 23–10 win over Tampa Bay on September 14. Harris started the rest of the season and finished the year as the fourth-leading tackler on the club with 56 solo hits while picking off three passes.

In 1987, Harris added 41 total tackles and three steals, including a fourth pick that set up the Vikings' final touchdown of the first half in the 44–10 playoff win over New Orleans on January 3, 1988. He had 23 solo tackles while recording his third straight three-interception season with the Vikings in 1988.

Minnesota decided to allow the 12-year pro test the market as an unrestricted free agent after that season, but Harris did not play in the league again.

Paul Harris

Season: 1978 Linebacker Height: 6'3"
Number: 57 Southern Cal Weight: 220

Paul Harris sandwiched one game with the Vikings between two stints with Tampa Bay. After seeing action in 14 games with the Buccaneers in 1977, Harris took the field in purple on special teams for the season opener at New Orleans before toiling five games later in the campaign with Tampa Bay.

Robert Harris

Seasons: 1992–94 Defensive End Height: 6'4"
Number: 90 Southern Weight: 290

Free agency kept the Vikings from receiving maximum benefits from Robert Harris, who arrived in Minnesota as a raw, second-round draft choice and developed into a semi-productive, yet oft-injured defensive end in his final season with the team.

Harris' only serious contributions to the team came in 1994. His playing time was limited as a rookie, partly because of a knee injury he suffered in his professional debut. He played in all 16 games and the playoff contest the following year, rotating at left end with Roy Barker while struggling with some nagging ailments. Harris registered a sack in the 15–0 win over Tampa

Bay on October 10, 1993, and saw some action on the field goal and extra-point block teams.

In 1994, Harris replaced the departed Chris Doleman and shared playing time with James Harris. He showed progress in rushing the passer by registering two sacks, and made 14 total tackles. Despite starting only a handful of games and making a few plays, Harris showed enough improvement that the New York Giants offered him a lucrative free agent contract. Head coach Dennis Green wanted to keep Harris, but admitted the Giants' deal was beyond what the Vikings felt Harris was worth.

Steve Harris

Season: 1987 Running Back Height: 5'11"
Number: 32 Northern Iowa Weight: 194

In two replacement games in 1987, Steve Harris rushed for three yards on four carries and gained 17 yards on two catches.

Martin Harrison

Seasons: 1994–96 Defensive End Height: 6'5"
Number: 91 Washington Weight: 251

The Vikings turned back the clock on a few occasions in the mid-1990s. After employing a five-man defensive line with Bob Lurtsema on pass-rush situations some two decades earlier, Minnesota used the same concept in 1994 and 1995 after adding Martin Harrison to the fold as a free agent on September 12, 1994.

Harrison was signed by the Vikings after being released by San Francisco on the final roster cutdowns. It was during his time with the 49ers he had one of his best games in the National Football League, against Minnesota. Harrison had five tackles and 2.5 sacks in a 38–19 Vikings' loss on October 3, 1993.

For three seasons in purple, Harrison was a productive player who was never fully appreciated. After making 11 special teams tackles in 1994, he overcame an early-season broken thumb a year later and blossomed in passing situations, registering 4.5 sacks (good for third on the team), 13 defensive tackles and 13 more hits on special teams. Harrison was superb down the stretch, when he had at least a half-sack in four straight games, beginning with the 43–24 win over New Orleans on November 19 and including two sacks against Tampa Bay in the 31–17 win on December 3.

Saying there was "less than a one percent chance" he would return after seeing virtually no activity against Cincinnati in the season finale in 1995, Harrison was back with the Vikings a year later. He played in all 16 games and started four times in place of the injured Derrick Alexander. Harrison finished the year third on the team with seven sacks and 41 total tackles. Despite his strong showing, Harrison was allowed to sign as a free agent with Seattle while Minnesota opted to go with 1996 first-round draft choice Duane Clemons.

Todd Harrison

Season: 1993 Tight End Height: 6'4"
Number: 48 North Carolina State Weight: 260

With the Vikings suffering injury problems at tight end late in the 1993 season, Todd Harrison was signed with two games remaining on the slate but did not take the field in purple. A solid in-line blocker, he returned to Minnesota for training camp in 1994 but did not make the team.

Mike Hartenstine

Season: 1987   Defensive Tackle   Height: 6'3"
Number: 78   Penn State   Weight: 251

Mike Hartenstine created havoc against the Vikings as a 12-year member of the Bears. After he was released by Chicago, the defensive tackle changed allegiances in 1987, his final season in the National Football League. Hartenstine was signed on Halloween and played in five games for Minnesota before receiving his release on December 15.

Clint Haslerig

Season: 1975   Wide Receiver   Height: 6'
Number: 87   Michigan   Weight: 189

Having suited up for the 49ers, Bears and Bills as a rookie in 1974, Clint Haslerig came to the Vikings from Buffalo during the 1975 campaign and played mostly on special teams. Activated in late November when Doug Kingsriter was placed on injured reserve, Haslerig recorded the only two receptions of his professional career and gained 28 yards while in Minnesota before moving on to the Jets in 1976.

Don Hasselbeck

Season: 1984   Tight End   Height: 6'7"
Number: 88   Colorado   Weight: 245

A seven-year veteran of the National Football League, Don Hasselbeck joined the Vikings just prior to the 1984 season and played in all 16 games on special teams and as a third tight end, behind Steve Jordan and Mike Mularkey. Hasselbeck caught one pass during the season, a 10-yarder during a 31–17 Washington win on November 29.

Matthew Hatchette

Seasons: 1997–98   Wide Receiver   Height: 6'2"
Number: 89   Langston   Weight: 195

Matthew Hatchette proved during the last five weeks of the 1998 regular season that he is another big-play receiver with the potential to be a fleet, huge and physical target in the mode of Jake Reed, Cris Carter and Randy Moss. A seventh-round draft choice in 1997, Hatchette replaced an injured Reed in the starting lineup in late November and responded with 15 receptions for 216 yards.

Prior to his late-season performance, Hatchette showed considerable potential in three- and four-receiver sets. He caught three passes for 54 yards as a rookie, with his first catch coming at a critical moment. Hatchette's 38-yard reception versus Carolina on October 12 set up the game-winning touchdown. He later scored his first professional points on a 13-yard toss from quarterback Randall Cunningham in the playoffs against San Francisco on January 3, 1998.

Hatchette was inactive for the season's first 11 games in 1998 before replacing Reed in the lineup. His best game came during the 38–28 victory over Baltimore on December 13, when Hatchette caught a career-high six passes for a team-leading 95 yards. He also reached paydirt during the playoffs by pulling in a five-yard toss from Cunningham against Atlanta in the NFC Championship Game.

Tough Enough To Be Vikings

Rip Hawkins

Rip Hawkins

Seasons: 1961–65   Linebacker   Height: 6'3"
Number: 58   North Carolina   Weight: 235

One of the major reasons the Vikings were respectable as an expansion team in 1961 had to do with their savvy college draft. Sandwiched between first pick Tommy Mason and third selection Fran Tarkenton was middle linebacker Rip Hawkins, who served as the heart of the Minnesota defense during the franchise's first five years.

Born Ross Cooper Hawkins but nicknamed Rip as a small child by his father who was amazed at the youngster's penchant for sleep, a la Rip Van Winkle, Hawkins began the Vikings' long tradition of employing outstanding middle linebackers. After a slow start due to a knee injury suffered in practice for the College All-Star Game, the two-time All-Atlantic Coast Conference honoree led Minnesota with 134 tackles and five interceptions during the team's maiden voyage. Aggressive and occasionally mean as he was smart, Hawkins contributed to the Vikings' reputation for being one of the league's most punishing defenses. He also did his job well, making 17 solo hits during the Vikings' 28–20 win over Baltimore on November 12.

Hawkins was again the Vikings' top defensive player in 1962 and 1963, and was designated a co-captain while emerging as one of the league's most consistent linebackers. He set the Minnesota standard for tackles in a game on two occasions in 1962, recording 18 solo hits against both the Lions on November 18 and versus the 49ers on December 2. Those performances still represent the Vikings' team record.

In 1964, he intercepted two passes and returned both for touchdowns, a 56-yarder in the 30–10 win over Pittsburgh on October 18 and a 29-yarder in the season-ending 41–14 victory at Chicago on December 13. He picked off three more tosses in 1965, including a 35-yard interception with 1:08 left in the game for the deciding score in the Vikings' 24–17 win over the Bears on December 19.

That game-winning interception came in what proved to be Hawkins' swan song in the National Football League. Oddly, he left the game before his body or talent expired. Hawkins retired after the 1965 season, holding the Minnesota record with three defensive touchdowns. Years later, he said of concluding his playing days prematurely, "It had nothing to do with any injury or really anything else. I just thought it was time to do something else."

Leo Hayden

Season: 1971   Running Back   Height: 6'
Number: 44   Ohio State   Weight: 212

The Vikings' depth in the early 1970s kept a few poor draft decisions from causing excessive harm. Leo Hayden is a good example. Minnesota's first-round pick in 1971, Hayden played just seven games in purple, with all of his appearances coming on special teams as a rookie.

A year later, just prior to training camp, head coach Bud Grant said, "Leo has had a year to learn our system. We know he has ability, now he'll have an opportunity to display it." That opportunity came with the Cardinals, for whom Hayden played a total of six games during the 1972 and 1973 seasons.

Raymond Hayes

Season: 1961
Number: 32
Running Back
Central Oklahoma
Height: 6'3"
Weight: 235

Teaming with Hugh McElhenny, Tommy Mason and Mel Triplett in the Vikings' backfield during the 1961 season, Raymond Hayes was a capable, yet corpulent fullback who was a decent blocker with good hands. Minnesota's 13th-round pick in its first draft, the 26-year-old Hayes came to the Upper Midwest after three-and-a-half years in the Air Force. He arrived weighing 251 pounds and was told to get down to 225 by the end of training camp. He achieved the feat by eating an orange in the morning and soup at lunch. The diet took its toll, however, with Hayes passing out one evening while going through the cafeteria line.

Even though his meal portions increased after fainting, Hayes made his weight as well as the Vikings' roster—for one season. In his only campaign in the National Football League, he caught 16 passes for 121 yards and gained 319 yards on 73 rushes. He owns the distinction of being the first Viking to ramble for 100 yards in a game, gaining 123 yards on 18 carries against the Rams on December 3. For the year, Hayes scored two touchdowns on the ground, but also fumbled on five occasions, thereby limiting his long-term contributions to the team.

John Henderson

Seasons: 1968–72
Number: 80
Wide Receiver
Michigan
Height: 6'3"
Weight: 200

When John Henderson arrived in Minnesota for the 1968 season after three years with Detroit, he wasted little time proving that his reputation for not wanting to catch passes in a crowd was unfounded.

Henderson's days in purple started slowly, not unlike his beginnings to most seasons. The former All-Big Ten recipient shared time with Tom Hall and caught four passes for 42 yards in 1968. He began to show signs of breaking out in the two playoff games that year, when he hauled in six tosses for 74 yards.

In 1969, he emerged as one of quarterback Joe Kapp's key receivers during the drive to the NFL Championship, pulling in 34 catches for 553 yards and five touchdowns as the starting flanker. He scored twice in two games—the 27–10 win over St. Louis on October 19 and the 52–14 triumph over the Steelers on November 23. Henderson also was one of the few bright spots in the Super Bowl against Kansas City, with the receiver posting his only 100-yard game in purple, catching seven passes for 111 yards.

Henderson produced a carbon copy in 1970, when he caught 32 passes for 527 yards and two touchdowns. Reminiscent of 1969, he was at his best late in the season after a slow start. His two scores came in the regular season's final three games, and he excelled in the playoff loss to San Francisco, pulling in five passes for 80 yards. A shoulder injury cost Henderson most of the 1971 season, limiting him to two receptions for 18 yards in seven appearances. Nagging ailments again affected his performance in 1972, although he did catch 10 passes, including a career-long 70-yard bomb from Fran Tarkenton in Minnesota's 45–41 win over Los Angeles on November 19.

Keith Henderson

Season: 1992	Running Back	Height: 6'1"
Number: 30	Georgia	Weight: 220

Head coach Dennis Green envisioned Keith Henderson as a versatile running back who could add more power to the ground game and catch passes out of the backfield. After all, while with the 49ers in 1991, Henderson led the team in rushing and had 30 receptions.

Yet, within a couple months of acquiring Henderson for an eighth-round draft choice on September 16, 1992, Green realized the troubled back had little long-term worth. His lone highlight as a Viking came against the Rams on November 29. In that 31–17 Minnesota win, Henderson rushed for an eight-yard touchdown and threw a 36-yard scoring pass to Terry Allen. That showing, however, was merely a flash in the pan, for Henderson succumbed to a knee injury late in the season after gaining 113 yards on 34 carries, and was not re-signed for the 1993 campaign.

Wymon Henderson

Seasons: 1987–88	Defensive Back	Height: 5'10"
Number: 24	Nevada-Las Vegas	Weight: 186

A three-year veteran of the United States Football League, Wymon Henderson spent the first two of his eight seasons in the National Football League with the Vikings. He started eight of the 12 regular-season games in 1987 and finished second on the team with four interceptions and fifth with 53 solo tackles and 17 assists. A standout on kick coverage, Henderson added 12 solo stops and 17 total hits on special teams.

In 1988, Henderson was primarily a fifth or sixth defensive back, registering 25 total tackles and picking off one pass. Once again his greatest contributions came on special teams, where he led the Vikings with 18 solo hits and 23 total tackles while causing one fumble. He departed Minnesota the following offseason, signing as a Plan B free agent with Denver, where he played the next four years.

Matt Hernandez

Season: 1984	Tackle	Height: 6'6"
Number: 60	Purdue	Weight: 262

The Vikings signed Matt Hernandez two games into the 1984 season and sent him on the field for 13 contests. Hernandez saw action on most of the special teams units and as a reserve offensive lineman, playing occasionally in relief of starting tackles Tim Irwin and Steve Riley.

Wally Hilgenberg

Seasons: 1968–79	Linebacker	Height: 6'3"
Number: 58	Iowa	Weight: 225

Minnesota's defensive line of the late 1960s and 1970s, commonly known as "The Purple People Eaters," received much of the media attention during the team's four trips to the Super Bowl. But an equally important unit was the Vikings' leathery linebacking corps. And no one among that group possessed a better combination of talent and tenacity than Wally Hilgenberg.

An All-American and co-captain with Paul Krause at the University of Iowa, Hilgenberg was tougher than a pine knot. He wrestled a 550–pound bear to a draw during one offseason, and battered opposing offenses with his amazing instincts and love for hitting.

"Wally has all the ingredients needed to be a linebacker," said head coach Bud Grant. "He's a great athlete; quick and equally good against the run or pass."

Hilgenberg stepped into the lineup at right outside linebacker midway through the 1968 season and immediately upgraded the Minnesota defense. He blanketed the right side, displaying excellent speed and range on pass coverage and stuffing the run with his aggressive and occasionally violent tackles. No sweep or screen pass was considered safe to Hilgenberg's side. He emerged as the unit's key man in 1969, and for the next seven years Hilgenberg served as a catalyst on the attacking Viking defense.

Hilgenberg was stolen off waivers from Pittsburgh on September 7, 1968. The Steelers had acquired him from Detroit prior to training camp that year after the Lions' coaching staff deemed the linebacker too wild off the field to develop into a productive player. Ironically, when brought into Minnesota's discipline-oriented environment employed by Grant, Hilgenberg thrived.

Wally Hilgenberg

One of the reasons Hilgenberg succeed involved his uncanny nose for the football. He intercepted the first two tosses of his career in 1970 before having one of his best all-around campaigns a year later. In 1972, he set the franchise record with 13 assisted tackles against Chicago on October 23, then a week later picked off a pass for a 14-yard touchdown return during a 27–13 victory at Green Bay. Another stellar campaign followed in 1973, when he intercepted the sixth pass of his career, and carried a fumble two yards for six points in a 28–7 win over Detroit on November 11.

Hilgenberg caused two fumbles and intercepted a pass during the 1974 regular season before making the most important steal of his career in the NFC Championship Game against Los Angeles. After safety Jeff Wright had made a touchdown-saving tackle by stopping Rams wide receiver Harold Jackson just short of the goal line, Hilgenberg intercepted a James Harris toss in the end zone on second down. The Vikings went on to win the game 14–10, an outcome that may not have occurred without Hilgenberg's heroics.

Hilgenberg forced two fumbles, intercepted two passes and picked up two loose balls, one of which he lateralled to Krause to complete an 86-yard touchdown play against the Lions on December 14, during the 1975 campaign. He started every game again in 1976, registering 83 solo hits, two sacks, one caused fumble and a fumble recovery.

Always a big-game performer, Hilgenberg rose to the task once again to send the Vikings to yet another Super Bowl at the end of the 1976 slate. He dumped Pat Haden on a blitz in the fourth quarter of the NFC Championship Game to push the Rams out of field-goal position, resulting in a punt. Earlier in the contest, Hilgenberg stuffed Haden on a quarterback sneak on third down to keep the Rams out of the end zone. One play later, Nate Allen blocked Tom Dempsey's field-goal attempt, and Bobby Bryant picked up the football and raced 90 yards to paydirt.

Hilgenberg moved into a backup role in 1977 and played in four-linebacker sets and on special teams for the next three years. While he never earned Pro Bowl recognition, the underrated Hilgenberg is one of the top linebackers in Minnesota annals, and his veteran leadership was missed upon his retirement after the 1979 slate.

Gary Hill

Season: 1965	Defensive Back	Height: 6'
Number: 43	Southern Cal	Weight: 200

Signed during the 1965 season, Gary Hill played in eight games for the Vikings as a reserve defensive back and a member of the special teams. He was released the following year in training camp.

King Hill

Season: 1968	Punter-Quarterback	Height: 6'3"
Number: 10	Purdue	Weight: 215

King Hill had 10 seasons of experience in the National Football League as a quarterback and punter with the Cardinals and Eagles when he was traded to Minnesota from Philadelphia during the 1968 campaign for a third-round draft pick. Hill played in eight games and took over the Vikings' punting chores, with the former All-American signalcaller averaging 41 yards on 33 punts. He did not see any time at quarterback in the Twin Cities.

Ira Hillary

Season: 1990	Wide Receiver	Height: 5'10"
Number: 89	South Carolina	Weight: 190

A Plan B free agent from Cincinnati, Ira Hillary played in three games with the Vikings in 1990. He averaged 5.6 yards on eight punt returns and carried back one kickoff for six yards during his brief time in purple.

Carl Hilton

Seasons: 1986–89	Tight End	Height: 6'3"
Number: 82	Houston	Weight: 230

Talk about clutch receivers. Carl Hilton caught five passes during his four campaigns with the Vikings, including three in the regular season and two during the playoffs. All five went for touchdowns, thereby creating one of the most amazing statistics in team annals.

An All-American at the University of Houston and the first tight end in Southwest Conference history to catch 100 passes in a career, Hilton joined the Vikings as a seventh-round draft choice in 1986. He ranked third with 13 unassisted tackles on special teams as a rookie, then was the only Minnesota player to block a kick in 1987, when he knocked down a punt that led to a touchdown in the 24–13 win over Atlanta on November 22. He also victimized the Falcons with an eight-yard scoring reception from Wade Wilson, his second career catch, after pulling in another eight-yarder from Wilson in the 21–16 triumph over the Rams on September 20.

Hilton added a seven-yard reception from Wilson in the 36–24 playoff win over San Francisco on January 9, 1988. He then missed the first eight weeks of the 1988 season with a broken wrist, but returned to catch a one-yard touchdown toss in the 45–3 pasting of New Orleans on December 4. Three weeks later, in the wild-card playoff game on December 26, Hilton struck against the Rams, catching a five-yard scoring pass in Minnesota's 28–17 victory.

Despite his touchdown-catching ability and his contributions as a blocker and on special teams, Hilton suffered several injuries late in his professional football career. He wound up playing in just one game in 1989 before his days with the Vikings came to an end.

John Hilton

| Season: 1970 | Tight End | Height: 6'5" |
| Number: 85 | Richmond | Weight: 225 |

    John Hilton came to Minnesota during the 1970 season after playing five years with Pittsburgh and one in Green Bay. He wore purple on the gridiron for seven games, playing mostly on special teams while serving as a blocking tight end on a handful of occasions.

George Hinkle

| Season: 1992 | Defensive Tackle | Height: 6'5" |
| Number: 98 | Arizona | Weight: 269 |

    A former starter with San Diego, George Hinkle provided bulk and experience while backing up Henry Thomas at defensive tackle and Chris Doleman at defensive end in 1992. Acquired with Joe Johnson from Washington in exchange for a sixth-round draft pick, Hinkle once described himself thusly: "I think I'm a mediocre player who can do some things well. I can't do a lot of things great." Having spent the latter part of the season on injured reserve with pneumonia, he ended his lone campaign with Minnesota by playing in nine games and recording one solo tackle.

Chris Hinton

| Seasons: 1994–95 | Tackle-Guard | Height: 6'4" |
| Numbers: 75, 78 | Northwestern | Weight: 300 |

    There was a time in his National Football League career when Chris Hinton was one of the game's best offensive linemen. For that, Hinton can thank Dennis Green. As Northwestern's head coach, Green moved Hinton from outside linebacker to tight end as a junior and to left tackle prior to the player's senior season and watched him become a first-round draft choice who was the key figure in the John Elway trade between Denver and Indianapolis.

    After 11 years in the NFL and seven Pro Bowl appearances, Hinton was reunited with Green in Minnesota when the lineman signed a three-year free agent deal with the Vikings. Though still productive, Hinton quickly showed signs that the constant warfare in the trenches had taken its toll on his 33-year-old body. Playing right tackle in 1994, Hinton helped Minnesota set a single-season team record with 5,848 total yards, but he was no longer among the game's elite. Younger, stronger and quicker defensive linemen held their own against Hinton in both the running and passing game.

    A move inside to the more-familiar right guard slot did not increase his productivity significantly in 1995, when Hinton played in just four games before succumbing to an ankle injury and arthroscopic knee surgery. Hinton did not return for the final year of his contract due to salary cap reasons.

Jimmy Hitchcock

| Season: 1998 | Cornerback | Height: 5'10" |
| Number: 37 | North Carolina | Weight: 195 |

    The Vikings went from fielding one of the National Football League's worst pass defenses in 1997 to the most improved in 1998. They accomplished the feat by replacing just one of their 11 starters. Yes, cornerback Jimmy Hitchcock made that much difference.

    Minnesota upgraded its defense at cornerback by allowing Dewayne Washington to sign with Pittsburgh as a free agent and acquiring Hitchcock on draft day from New England in exchange for a third-round draft choice. A

Jimmy Hitchcock

part-time starter for the Patriots during three seasons, Hitchcock was Minnesota's third choice to replace Washington, yet proved to be nothing less than the perfect addition. Targeted by opposing passers early in the 1998 slate, he persevered in those games to record game-clinching interceptions in victories over Tampa Bay and St. Louis. Hitchcock established himself for good in the 34–13 win over Detroit on October 25, when the cornerback silenced Herman Moore all afternoon and sealed the triumph by returning an interception of a Charlie Batch aerial 79 yards to paydirt. He then took his game to a Pro Bowl level by returning a Brett Farve toss 58 yards for a touchdown in Minnesota's 28–14 triumph over Green Bay on November 22.

Hitchcock also showed he is among the toughest customers on the gridiron. He severed the ring finger on his right hand during the game against the Rams but refused to leave. He received stitches in the digit at halftime and wore padded protection the following week, yet never left the lineup.

"I think Jimmy has always had courage, and this just showed the world that this guy can play," said defensive coordinator Foge Fazio. "He never said a word about it and just kept playing."

By the end of the campaign, Hitchcock had put together as fine a season as any cornerback in the league. He concluded his first year in purple by setting single-season team records with three interception returns for touchdowns, 242 interception return yards, and 30 passes defensed. He also tied for second in the NFL with seven picks, and recorded 67 tackles.

Leroy Hoard

Seasons: 1996–98 Running Back Height: 5'11"
Number: 44 Michigan Weight: 225

When Robert Smith was lost for the year with a knee injury midway through the 1996 campaign, the Vikings went looking for emergency help at running back. They found their man in Leroy Hoard, a former Pro Bowl back with Cleveland who had been released by Baltimore and Carolina earlier in the regular season.

Signed by Minnesota on November 5, 1996, Hoard made his debut two weeks later and gained 108 yards rushing in the 16–13 overtime win at Oakland on November 17. In the process, he joined Herschel Walker as the only Vikings to break the century mark on the ground in their first game with the team. He added a 37-yard catch, the longest by a Vikings running back since Rick Fenney in 1988, and two touchdowns in the 41–17 victory over Arizona on December 1. Two weeks later, Hoard trampled Tampa Bay for 101 yards in a 21–10 triumph.

By the end of the season, Hoard had gained 420 yards rushing in six games to place second on the team. The Vikings, meanwhile, went 4–2 in games he started and 3–0 during contests he carried the ball at least 20 times.

Smith returned in 1997, but the Vikings re-signed Hoard to give the team a power runner between the tackles. Despite struggling with some nagging injuries, including broken ribs at midseason, Hoard served as a solid backup to Smith. He gained 235 yards and four touchdowns on 80 carries, with his one-yard touchdown run in the final minute against the Bears on November 9 sealing Minnesota's 29–22 victory.

Hoard's role increased in 1998, when he proved to be the perfect change of pace to the speed-oriented Smith before taking over for his injured backfield mate for three games in December. Quick between the tackles with explosive power, Hoard took the field when the Vikings wanted to go with a punishing, ball-controlled offense or in short-yardage and goal-line situations. He scored nine touchdowns on the ground, including gallops of 12 and 50 yards during a 46–36 victory over Dallas on Thanksgiving Day. After finishing the regular season with 479 yards on 115 carries and another 198 yards and a score on 22 receptions, Hoard capped his best season in purple by becoming the first Minnesota player to score three touchdowns in a playoff game as well as the first Viking to have a rushing and receiving touchdown in the same playoff contest, accomplishing the feat during the 41–21 triumph over Arizona on January 9, 1999.

"I just try to be physical," Hoard said. "I'm not a guy who is going to run away from people. I know that. So, why try? You have to play to your strengths. My strengths are straight ahead."

Leroy Hoard

John Holland

Season: 1974 Wide Receiver Height: 6'
Number: 85 Tennessee State Weight: 190

A standout baseball player who was drafted by the Philadelphia Phillies, John Holland opted instead to sign with the Vikings as a second-round draft choice in 1974. Holland possessed excellent speed and quickness, but did not have natural football instincts. As a result, he played just one season in the Twin Cities, catching five passes for 84 yards, with three grabs coming in Minnesota's 23–21 victory over Dallas on October 6. He spent three more years in the National Football League, all with Buffalo.

Randy Holloway

Seasons: 1978–84 Defensive Tackle Height: 6'5"
Number: 75 Pittsburgh Weight: 255

Minnesota took Randy Holloway in the first round of the 1978 draft and, after two years of grooming and patience, watched the former Pitt All-American take over the left end spot on the Viking defensive line in 1980.

Always possessing the size, speed and strength to succeed in the National Football League, Holloway struggled with the work ethic necessary to gain the consistency at the game's top level. In between giving veteran Jim Marshall an occasional breather in 1978 and 1979, his major contributions during his first two years came in blocking six kicks in the middle of the Minnesota line.

When Marshall retired after the 1979 campaign, Holloway stepped in and recorded four sacks, a safety and 39 unassisted tackles in what proved to be his lone season as a full-time starter. He lost his job to Doug Martin in the final game of the 1980 slate, then regained his position with the first team midway through 1981, finishing the year with 5.5 sacks, 40 solo hits, and a 45-yard fumble recovery for a touchdown in the 30–13 win over Green Bay on September 27.

Martin reclaimed the left defensive end job in 1982, relegating Holloway to passing situations. Even so, Holloway ranked second among the linemen with 29 solo stops, had four sacks, and intercepted a pass against Detroit. He played in every game for the sixth straight season in 1983, starting two while posting 36 hits and a career-high 7.5 sacks as a reserve. Holloway toiled in more eight games in 1984 and had the biggest day of his career. The defensive end registered a team-record five sacks against Atlanta during a 27–20 win on September 16.

That moment proved to be the final highlight of Holloway's inconsistent career in Minnesota. The disgruntled player was waived by head coach Les Steckel on October 23. He finished the regular season with St. Louis.

Bruce Holmes

Season: 1993 Linebacker Height: 6'2"
Number: 54 Minnesota Weight: 235

A former Golden Gopher, Bruce Holmes played in one game on the Vikings' special teams in 1993. He sprained an ankle and was placed on injured reserve before receiving his release. That was Holmes' first experience in the National Football League since his three-game stint with the Chiefs in 1987.

Issiac Holt

Seasons: 1985–89 Cornerback Height: 6'1"
Number: 30 Alcorn State Weight: 199

The Vikings acquired a ballhawk when they selected Issiac Holt in the second round of the 1985 draft. In college, he had established the NCAA Division I-AA record for most career interceptions, then continued that trend in the National Football League by picking off 14 passes in four-and-a-half years with Minnesota.

Holt stole his first aerial as a rookie in a 21–17 win over San Diego on October 20, 1985. He moved into the starting lineup in 1986 and tied for fourth in the NFC while leading the Vikings with eight interceptions, including picks in four consecutive games. An outstanding special teams player, Holt also paced the team with two blocked punts that year, victimizing Green Bay in each of the two victories over the Packers. He also recovered a blocked punt in the end zone for a touchdown in the 27–24 overtime win at San Francisco on October 12.

A knee injury hampered Holt in 1987, when he intercepted two passes in the regular season. The biggest pick of his Viking career came in the first quarter of the 44–10 playoff win over New Orleans, on January 3, 1988. That interception helped turn the game's momentum and enabled Minnesota to destroy the heavily favored Saints.

In 1988, Holt started nine games before a thigh contusion forced him out of the lineup for three contests. He had two more interceptions prior to the injury, including one that sealed a 23–21 win over Philadelphia on September 25. He also registered his first career safety by tackling New England punter Jeff Feagles in the end zone in Minnesota's 36–6 win over the Patriots on September 11.

Holt played with Minnesota for the first five games of the 1989 season. He picked off an Eric Hipple pass and returned the pigskin 90 yards to paydirt in Minnesota's 24–17 win over the Lions on October 8. The eighth-longest play in team history, that proved to be Holt's swan song with the Vikes. The following week he was part of the trade that brought Herschel Walker to the northern plains from Dallas.

Jim Hough

Seasons: 1978–86 Offensive Lineman Height: 6'2"
Number: 51 Utah State Weight: 275

The Vikings' great defensive line began to change faces late in the 1970s. The same thing happened on the other side of the ball, leaving the Minnesota management to develop young prospects for the future. One of those who panned out was Jim Hough, the Vikes' fourth-round draft choice in 1978.

A reserve right guard and center as well as the deep snapper on punts during his rookie season, Hough took over the left guard duties as well as all the long-snapping chores during the latter half of the 1979 campaign.

He started 10 games in 1980 in between stints on the injured reserve list that cost him six contests. Hough reclaimed his starting job from Brent Boyd four games in the 1981 season and started every game through the 1983 slate.

In 1984, Hough moved back to center due to the one-year retirement of Dennis Swilley, but injuries to his calf and knee that required post-season surgery limited him to three starts. A torn tricep muscle allowed Hough to play in just four games in 1985. He recovered and returned to his starting role at left guard in 1986, yet his leg continued to give him problems and led his retirement from football just prior to the start of the 1987 training camp.

Hough also enjoyed competing off the field. The ardent weightlifter teamed with Scott Studwell in the National Football League's arm-wrestling championships for three years in the early 1980s, with the duo winning the title in 1981.

Bobby Houston

Season: 1998 Linebacker Height: 6'2"
Number: 55 North Carolina State Weight: 238

A former starter with the Jets under defensive coordinator Foge Fazio, Bobby Houston arrived in Minnesota as a free agent in 1998 and provided special teams help as well as relief support at outside linebacker. Houston started the season finale against Tennessee, and for the year recorded 20 tackles and a fumble recovery.

Bryan Howard

Season: 1982 Safety Height: 6'
Number: 24 Tennessee State Weight: 200

Minnesota's ninth-round draft choice in 1982, Bryan Howard was released at the end of training camp and re-signed two weeks later when Mardye McDole was placed on injured reserve. Active for seven games during his only season in the National Football League, Howard played in two contests as well as the playoff matchup with Atlanta and recorded three solo tackles on special teams.

David Howard

Seasons: 1985–89 Linebacker Height: 6'2"
Numbers: 51, 99 Long Beach State Weight: 232

Along with Anthony Carter, Keith Millard and Gary Zimmerman, David Howard joined the Vikings from the defunct United States Football League and played a significant role in the team's fortunes during the latter half of the 1980s.

Selected in the third round of the 1984 supplemental draft after two seasons with the Los Angeles Express, Howard spent the first half of the 1985 campaign as a special teams performer before earning a starting job on defense. In his first start in purple, the linebacker led the team with 12 solo tackles, seven assists, one forced fumble and two hits for loss in the 28–23 win over Philadelphia on December 1. He finished the campaign with 80 total tackles, with all but seven stops coming in the final eight games.

In 1986, Howard ranked sixth on the defense with 88 hits and paced the unit with three forced fumbles despite missing four games with an elbow injury. Various ailments cost him four games in the strike-shortened 1987 campaign, when Howard had 33 tackles and his first career interception. His production increased to 46 total tackles and three pickoffs in 1988. His strongest performance of the season came during the 43–3 win over Dallas on

November 13, when Howard had a nine-yard sack, forced a fumble and recovered another loose ball.

Howard played with the Vikings for the first five games of the 1989 season before becoming part of the Herschel Walker trade with the Cowboys on October 13. He remained in the NFL for three more years, with his last two campaigns coming with New England.

David Huffman

Seasons: 1979–83, 1985–90   Offensive Lineman   Height: 6'6"
Numbers: 56, 72   Notre Dame   Weight: 285

David Huffman has the distinction of being the only Viking player to leave the team and play in the United States Football League, only to return to continue his career in purple.

Minnesota's second-round draft choice in 1979, Huffman was part of the team's master plan to rebuild the aging offensive line. Although he never became a fixture at any one position, the consensus All-American center from Notre Dame filled in admirably at all five slots along the front wall as well as occasionally at tight end on short-yardage situations.

Strong and intelligent with excellent athleticism for a massive player, Huffman played in 13 games on special teams and as a reserve center during his rookie season. He backed up at guard and tackle and started two games at right tackle for Ron Yary in 1980, then saw action in 13 games at guard in 1981, nine games at center in 1982, and 15 games across the line in 1983. The highlight of his career came when Huffman recovered a blocked punt for a touchdown against Detroit in a 20–17 Vikings victory on September 25, 1983.

At what proved to be the halfway point of his Minnesota tenure, Huffman left the Vikings for the USFL, spending one season each with the Arizona Wranglers and Memphis Showboats. He returned to the Upper Midwest after the first game of the 1985 campaign and played in 15 contests, starting the final three at left tackle. Huffman again saw action in all 16 games in 1986 and started once at left guard.

Huffman finally earned a starting job in 1987, when he stepped in for the retired Jim Hough at left guard. A back injury limited him to two games in 1988. He returned to play in all 16 games in 1989, although Randall McDaniel had secured the starting honors at left guard during his absence. Huffman played in one more game in 1990 before calling it a career on the field and moving to the Vikings' broadcast booth as a frank color analyst. One of the more popular former players in franchise history, Huffman died in an automobile accident while traveling to a Notre Dame football game on November 21, 1998.

Don Hultz

Season: 1963   Defensive End   Height: 6'3"
Number: 83   Southern Mississippi   Weight: 235

Don Hultz arrived in training camp in 1963 as a rookie free agent with little chance of sticking with the Vikings come September. Instead, he not only made the team but became the starter at defensive end. By the end of the season, he had established a record in the National Football League with nine fumble recoveries in a single campaign.

Strong and quick, Hultz emerged as the Vikings' best defensive end during the early days of the franchise. He possessed a great motor and a knack for being at the right place at the right time. In addition to his nine fumble recoveries, Hultz tied Jim Marshall for the team lead with 10.5 sacks.

He also intercepted a Sonny Jurgensen pass in the fourth quarter and returned the ball 35 yards to paydirt to help seal a 34–13 Minnesota victory over Philadelphia in the season finale, on December 15, 1963.

Hultz's tenure in Minnesota lasted only one season. After the Vikings drafted Carl Eller, who took over the starting job at left end in 1964, Hultz was one of four players traded to Philadelphia in exchange for Ted Dean and the rights to Bob Berry. He played 11 more seasons in the NFL, all but one with the Eagles.

Gerry Huth

Seasons: 1961–63   Guard   Height: 5'11"
Number: 65   Wake Forest   Weight: 228

Life changed considerably for Gerry Huth during his football career. The offensive lineman sandwiched a two-year stint in the army between two National Football League championships, beginning with the Giants in 1956 and concluding with the Eagles in 1960.

Head coach Norm Van Brocklin appreciated the way Huth blocked when they were teammates in Philadelphia and nabbed the guard when he was made available to the Vikings in the veterans pool. Huth was an undersized lineman who succeeded with quickness and explosiveness. He served as Minnesota's starting left guard during the franchise's first three seasons and played in every game before missing one during the 1963 campaign. Huth retired during training camp in 1964.

Donald Igwebuike

Season: 1990	Kicker	Height: 5'9"
Number: 4	Clemson	Weight: 184

The Vikings were left without a kicker when Rich Karlis refused to play for the team in 1990. As a result, Minnesota signed Donald Igwebuike off waivers from Tampa Bay on September 5.

Igwebuike played in the first eight games of the 1990 campaign and led the team in scoring by connecting on 14 of 16 field goal attempts and all 19 extra points. His best outing included his trio of three-pointers and PATs in Minnesota's 32–3 win over New Orleans on September 16.

The former Clemson kicker missed the second half of the season due to his arrest regarding illegal drug activity. The Vikings signed Fuad Reveiz in Iggy's absence, then parted company with Igwebuike for good the following year in training camp.

Darryl Ingram

Season: 1989	Tight End	Height: 6'2"
Number: 86	California	Weight: 230

One of only two picks from the Vikings' 1989 draft class to make the team, Darryl Ingram's best day in purple came early in his rookie season. With tight ends Steve Jordan and Carl Hinton injured during the opener with Houston on September 10, the fourth-round draft choice stepped in and caught four passes for 45 yards in the 38–7 Minnesota victory. He pulled in just one more pass the rest of the year, a two-yard touchdown grab in the 43–17 victory over Atlanta on December 10. Ingram's other contributions consisted of three solo tackles and five assists on special teams before being waived the following year in training camp.

Tim Irwin

Seasons: 1981–93	Tackle	Height: 6'7"
Number: 76	Tennessee	Weight: 297

Tim Irwin filled some big shoes during the early days of his career in the National Football League. With Ron Yary having been traded to the Rams for his final professional season, Irwin stepped in behind the perennial Pro Bowl honoree and faltered nary a bit for the next dozen seasons, a streak that included 191 appearances.

"He's one of the fiercest competitors I've ever coached," said John Michels, Minnesota's offensive line coach from 1967–93. "He loves people until they have a different color uniform on."

Drafted in the third round in 1981 after earning academic All-American honors at Tennessee, Irwin saw reserve action at right and left tackle in seven games as a rookie. He replaced Yary by starting every game at right tackle in 1982 and 1983, and made a positive early impression on head coach Bud Grant.

"Tim Irwin at tackle was a question mark going into last season and he came out as one of our most improved players," Grant said prior to the 1983 season. "He stepped in when Ron Yary was traded and played and got better all year, so I think he's going to be a dominant player for us. He's a big, strong, intelligent young man who is a fierce competitor, not unlike Yary. Ron was named All-Pro many times and I think Tim has the capacity to approach that level of play."

Irwin did just that. He moved to left tackle for five games in 1984 so that Steve Riley, who had his left hand in a cast, could switch sides. He returned to right tackle in 1984 and started every game at the position for the next nine seasons. At 6-foot-7 and nearly 300 pounds, Irwin blocked out the sun while anchoring the offensive line. He cleared the way for Minnesota's running backs and beat back charging linemen to protect the quarterback with incredible consistency and tenacity. He was one of the primary reasons the Vikings led the league in rushing yardage in 1991 and was a key contributor to Terry Allen's 1,201 yards in 1992.

In addition to his contributions at right tackle, Irwin was an efficient kick blocker for the Vikings. Powering his way from the middle of the line, Irwin's massive paws were able to alter the path of 10 kicks, a total that is tied for third in Minnesota history. He also tied a Viking record by knocking back two field goal attempts against Atlanta on December 15, 1985.

Making Irwin's efforts all the more impressive was the fact that he underwent off-season surgery on nine occasions. Yet despite having his knees and other parts of his anatomy sliced more often than a watermelon, Irwin always answered the bell when training camp opened in July and did not miss a start after earning the right tackle duties in 1982. He missed only the three replacement games in 1987, and concluded his career in purple with 181 consecutive starts to rank third in Minnesota history.

Irwin's career came to a close in Minnesota when the coaching staff decided to go with Bernard Dafney in 1994, leaving Irwin to spend his final NFL season with Tampa Bay and Miami before deciding to put his law degree to work full-time in Tennessee. Unlike Irwin, who replaced Yary, Dafney did not follow the trend and was replaced by rookie Korey Stringer in 1995.

Tim Irwin

Qadry Ismail

Seasons: 1993–96   Wide Receiver   Height: 6′
Number: 82   Syracuse   Weight: 196

The rap on Qadry Ismail upon entering the National Football League as Minnesota's second-round draft pick in 1993 centered on his preference to catch the ball against his body instead of with his hands. He also was known as being more of a track star than a pure football player. Those criticisms proved to have merit during his four seasons with Minnesota, but "The Missile's" explosiveness and penchant for making the big play oftentimes overcame any negatives.

Ismail, the brother of fellow receiver Raghib Ismail, was one of the fastest straight-ahead runners ever to don purple. He caught 19 passes for 212 yards as a rookie, with his greatest contribution in 1993 coming on November 28. Ismail caught a season-long 37-yard pass in the final minute to set up a game-tying field goal in what turned out to be a 17–14 overtime loss to the Saints.

A year later, on November 6, Ismail enabled the Vikings to gain revenge against New Orleans. With 11 seconds remaining and Minnesota without any timeouts, Ismail caught a Warren Moon pass on the 5-yard line. Instead of going out of bounds, he faked and juked his way to the end zone for a 21–20 win. He wound up catching touchdown passes in four straight games that season, and finished the year with 45 receptions for 696 yards.

More quirkiness occurred in 1995. In the season's second game, Ismail caught a fourth-quarter, 85-yard touchdown pass that bounced off the helmet of a Detroit defender in Minnesota's 20–10 win over Detroit on September 10. Counting kickoff returns, he had four plays of 50 or more yards in 1995, the third-highest single-season total in team history. For the year he had 32 receptions for 597 yards.

Ismail also earned his keep by returning kickoffs. In 1995, he became only the fourth Viking to gain more than 1,000 yards on kickoff returns by placing second in the NFC with an average of 24.7 yards per effort, including a career-long 71-yarder. That showing followed averages of 21.5 yards and 23.1 yards in 1993 and 1994, respectively.

Yet, as exciting as Ismail could be, he was equally exasperating at times. Those moments seemed to increase in 1996, when Ismail's already-shaky route-running became more erratic while his hands produced more drops. He lost his job as the third receiver to Chris Walsh by season's end, and finished the year with 22 catches for 351 yards and three touchdowns. His kickoff returns fell off considerably as well, to a career-low 18.8-yard average on 28 returns.

With Ismail failing to show any significant progress, he was not re-signed in 1997. He instead agreed on a free-agent deal with Green Bay prior to being traded to Miami before the season opener.

Alfred Jackson

Seasons: 1995–96	Cornerback	Height: 6'
Number: 25	San Diego State	Weight: 183

A former Ram, Brown and standout in the Canadian Football League, Alfred Jackson spent two seasons as a reserve in the Vikings' secondary. Jackson excelled in man-to-man coverage, and received most of his playing time in nickel packages.

In 1995, Jackson filled in for injured cornerback Dewayne Washington and intercepted a pass in the 44–24 win over Pittsburgh on September 24. His other start that year came in the season finale, against Cincinnati. Jackson stepped in front of a Jeff Blake aerial and returned the pick 37 yards for his first touchdown in the National Football League. For the year he defensed six passes despite playing in only half of the team's games.

Jackson also was productive in 1996. He played in 14 contests and intercepted two more passes while recording 24 solo tackles. Despite his success as a Viking reserve, Jackson returned to his old stomping grounds in Canada and resumed his career as a wide receiver with the British Columbia Lions.

Harold Jackson

Season: 1982	Wide Receiver	Height: 5'10"
Number: 89	Colorado	Weight: 175

After a stellar 14-year career with the Rams, Eagles and Patriots, Harold Jackson was signed by the Vikings on December 30, 1982, when tight end Bob Bruer was placed on injured reserve. Jackson played in Minnesota's 31–27 win over Dallas during the season finale on January 3, 1993, and did not catch a pass in limited action.

Joe Jackson

Season: 1977	Defensive Tackle	Height: 6'4"
Number: 76	New Mexico State	Weight: 262

Joe Jackson, a two-year veteran of the World Football League, played briefly in three games with the Vikings in 1977 while spending most of the campaign on the inactive list.

Dick James

Season: 1965	Running Back	Height: 5'9"
Number: 47	Oregon	Weight: 185

Acquired from the Giants for a seventh-round draft choice just prior to the 1965 season, Dick James did not have the opportunity to show Minnesota fans why he is considered one of the more versatile backs in Washington Redskins history. Playing in just four games for the Vikings, James returned 11 kickoffs for a 19.3-yard average and one punt for five yards in his 11th and final campaign in the National Football League.

Noel Jenke

Season: 1971   Linebacker   Height: 6'1"
Number: 52   Minnesota   Weight: 218

The captain of the Golden Gophers' football team in 1968 and one of the last three-sport stars at the University of Minnesota, Noel Jenke opted for professional baseball out of college and spent two seasons in the Boston Red Sox's farm system as an outfielder, reaching as high as the Triple-A level. The Vikings' 12th-round draft pick in 1969, Jenke gave football a shot in 1971 and played on special teams and as a reserve linebacker in 14 games with Minnesota. He then spent one season with Atlanta and two with Green Bay before changing careers again.

Carlos Jenkins

Seasons: 1991–94   Linebacker   Height: 6'3"
Number: 51   Michigan State   Weight: 219

Though undersized compared to most strong-side linebackers, Carlos Jenkins brought speed and range to the position in 1992, the season Minnesota fielded a new-and-improved defense that led the Vikings to the playoffs under first-year head coach Dennis Green.

Jenkins, who was dubbed "Mr. Excitement" by Green, played as big a role as anyone in 1992. Coming off a disastrous rookie season that saw him play just three games on special teams while missing most of the campaign following an ankle injury suffered playing basketball, Jenkins blanketed opposing tight ends and more than held his own against the run. He tied for fourth on the team with 69 total tackles and led the linebackers with four sacks.

A big-play performer early in his career, Jenkins also tied for second in the Vikings' record book with two defensive touchdowns in a season. He posted his first career score on a 19-yard interception return in a 38–10 win over Chicago on November 2. The following week versus Tampa Bay, Jenkins became the first Viking to record defensive touchdowns in consecutive games by racing 25 yards to paydirt on a fumble recovery in the 35–7 triumph. He was even part of another score on November 18, when Anthony Parker picked up Jenkins' forced fumble and scampered 58 yards for a touchdown against Houston.

Jenkins was steady once again in 1993. He placed third on the team with 88 tackles, led the linebackers with 2.5 sacks, intercepted two passes and forced a team-high three fumbles. In fact, Jenkins' hard hit on Glyn Milburn caused the pigskin to come loose inside the Vikings' 30-yard line in the closing minutes of the game and helped seal a 26–23 victory over Denver on November 14.

Yet, not unlike teammate Todd Scott, for some unexplained reason Jenkins' performance dropped considerably in 1994. Despite placing fourth on the team with 84 total tackles, his pass defense was not as tight as it had been and he was overpowered regularly on running plays. The Vikings decided to add bulk to the position by signing free agent Broderick Thomas for 1995 while Jenkins signed with the St. Louis Rams.

Izel Jenkins

Season: 1993
Number: 28
Cornerback
North Carolina State
Height: 5'10"
Weight: 190

Izel Jenkins earned the nickname "Krazy Kat" for his all-out effort in the defensive secondary and on special teams while with the Eagles. Signed by Minnesota as an unrestricted free agent prior to the 1993 season, Jenkins did not have much opportunity to live up to the moniker with the Vikings. Playing mostly on special teams, he recorded two solo tackles and an assist on kick coverages in four games. He was released in October when the team signed veteran Rory Graves to add depth to the offensive line.

Bill Jobko

Seasons: 1963–65
Number: 57
Linebacker
Ohio State
Height: 6'1"
Weight: 230

Acquired from Los Angeles for a sixth-round draft pick just prior to the 1963 season, Bill Jobko had a reputation for being a good open-field tackler who was capable of dishing out some punishment. He stepped into the starting outside linebacker slot and immediately upgraded the position from the team's first two years. Jobko maintained the first-team job in 1964 and was having his best year in the National Football League before breaking his arm against San Francisco on November 8, costing him the rest of the season.

Known as "The Red Owl" for his round, glowing face, Jobko returned to his starting position in 1965 prior to joining the Falcons in the expansion draft in 1966.

Brad Johnson

Seasons: 1992–98
Number: 14
Quarterback
Florida State
Height: 6'5"
Weight: 224

The first trade Dennis Green made as the Vikings' head coach sent linebacker Jimmy Williams to Tampa Bay for a ninth-round draft pick in 1992. That choice turned out to be Brad Johnson, the 227th overall selection who had seen minimal action in college but showed developmental potential upon working out with Minnesota offensive coordinator Jack Burns.

Expectations were minimal. Fifteen quarterbacks, among them Rich Gannon, Sean Salisbury, Jim McMahon, Warren Moon, Gino Torretta and Chad May, came and went during Johnson's tenure as a little-used reserve. Although he excelled nearly every August during the exhibition games, Johnson was not active for a single contest during his first two seasons, and did not take a snap until seeing spot duty in 1994, completing 22 of 37 passes for 150 yards. His progress was steady, yet not spectacular until he toiled in the World League in the spring of 1995 and emerged as one of the game's more promising quarterbacks. He followed that effort the next fall by completing 25 of 36 passes for 272 yards in five relief appearances of Moon.

Through it all, Green knew that Johnson had the arm strength, the intelligence and the desire to succeed in the National Football League. It is for that reason the head coach incorporated the classic example of how to develop a professional quarterback by keeping Johnson on the roster for his first few seasons instead of releasing him without considering the future.

"I learned for four years totally without pressure," Johnson said. "I worked and waited my turn. I got better and was confident and ready when my turn came. I knew it might be my only chance. But once I got out there, everything worked."

Possessing a healthy dose of self-confidence, the signalcaller from Black Mountain, North Carolina, proved he had not been whistling *Dixie* on

Brad Johnson

the sidelines when opportunity knocked during the season opener against the Lions on September 1, 1996. Johnson's scrambling 31-yard touchdown pass to Cris Carter in the final two minutes gave the Vikings a 17–13 win over Detroit. His first start came the following week at Atlanta, with Johnson earning NFC Offensive Player of the Week honors after passing for 275 yards and two touchdowns in the 23–17 victory over the Falcons.

Johnson wound up starting eight games, posted a 4–1 mark in the final five games to lead the Vikings to the playoffs, and completed 62.7 percent of his passes for 2,258 yards and 17 touchdowns. His quarterback rating of 89.4 was third in the NFL, behind only Steve Young and Brett Favre. That performance earned Johnson the full-time job and a four-year, $15.5 million contract.

The signalcaller quickly proved the Vikings had not wasted their money. In a Pro Bowl-type performance, Johnson guided Minnesota to the brink of the playoffs by tying for third in the NFC with 20 touchdown passes and fourth with 3,036 passing yards in 1997. He was at his best late in games, leading the NFL with 11 fourth-quarter touchdown passes and guiding the team to come-from-behind victories against Arizona, Carolina and Chicago twice.

One of the more bizarre plays in league annals occurred in the Vikings' 21–14 win over the Panthers on October 12. With the Vikings threatening on the 3-yard line, Johnson had a pass batted backwards by a Panther defender at the line of scrimmage. Johnson caught the rejection, side-stepped a linebacker, then used a Scott Dill block to reach the end zone. In the process, Johnson became the first NFL quarterback to complete a touchdown pass to himself.

The miraculous finishes ended, however, when Johnson injured his neck prior to the game against Green Bay on December 1. He started the Monday night contest before losing his ability to grip the football, caused by the loss of strength in his hand. He was placed on injured reserve a few days later and missed the rest of the campaign.

"I don't know if you'd consider this a setback or a challenge, but usually I win in the end," Johnson said upon undergoing surgery.

His words proved prophetic, for the quarterback made an impressive recovery before suffering another setback in the second game of the 1998 season. Johnson fractured his right fibula in the fourth quarter of a 38–31 win over St. Louis on September 13 and missed the next six games. He recovered in time to relieve an injured Randall Cunningham against New Orleans on November 8, only to suffer a broken thumb on the first play of the second half. He remained in the game and completed 11 of his second-half 14 tosses to finish with 316 yards passing, the third 300-yard passing effort of his career.

Other than a second-half relief appearance against Jacksonville on December 20, Johnson did not see any significant action after the New Orleans game. He finished the 1998 season having played in just four contests, completing 65 passes for 747 yards and seven touchdowns. In Johnson's absence, the Vikings signed Cunningham to a lucrative contract, and Green was determined to unload Johnson. In one of the riskier moves in Minnesota annals, Johnson was traded to the Washington Redskins prior to the 1999 season in exchange for three high-round draft picks.

Charlie Johnson

Seasons: 1982–84 Nose Tackle Height: 6'3"
Number: 65 Colorado Weight: 282

Acquired from Philadelphia during training camp in 1982 for a second-round draft pick, former All-Pro Charlie Johnson served as a valuable cog on a line that was continuing to struggle with the departures and retirements of the Purple People Eaters from the late 1970s.

Serving as the nose tackle in the 3–4 defense, Johnson moved into the starting lineup for the final six games and the playoffs of the strike-marred 1982 season and recorded 22 solo tackles and 19 assists. He also came up with a big play, returning a fumble 44 yards for a touchdown in Minnesota's 34–31 win over Detroit on December 19. His presence in the lineup turned out to be the primary difference in the improved play of the defensive line.

"Charlie is not a holler guy; he's not out there clapping his hands or jumping up and down," said head coach Bud Grant. "But he has great work habits and a great reputation as an All-Pro and a Pro-Bowler. The stature he had, the kind of person he is, his work habits in practice, his preparation, his enthusiasm, his all-out play were good examples for everyone."

In 1983, Johnson continued to be a leader and found the end zone for the second time in as many seasons with Minnesota. He picked up a fumble caused by Neil Elshire and rumbled 50 yards to paydirt in the 34–14 win over Houston on October 16. He ranked second on the line with 46 solo tackles for the season and intercepted one pass. Johnson then added 113 total tackles, good for fifth on the defense, and paced the Vikings with five sacks in 1984.

When Grant returned to the team in 1985, the Vikings started employing the 4–3 defense more often. That change combined with Johnson's age (33) led to his release in training camp.

Chris Johnson

Season: 1996 Safety Height: 6'
Number: 35 San Diego State Weight: 199

After failing to stick with the Vikings during training camp in 1995, Chris Johnson earned a spot on the practice squad a year later before being activated on November 15, 1996. Johnson played in five of the season's last six games as well as the playoff contest, recording four defensive tackles and three solo hits on special teams. His best performance came against Green Bay on December 22, when Johnson had four tackles and caused a fumble on a punt return. He was released again in 1997 during training camp.

Dennis Johnson

Seasons: 1980–85 Linebacker Height: 6'3"
Number: 52 Southern Cal Weight: 235

Dennis Johnson, Minnesota's fourth-round draft choice in 1980, had no problem stepping in behind legends during his first two seasons with the Vikings. As a rookie, the former college All-American started twice at outside linebacker in place of the ailing Matt Blair and finished the slate with 26 solo tackles. A year later, he moved inside and started the season finale, filling in for the injured Jeff Siemon. Johnson concluded the 1981 campaign with 21 hits.

Johnson became a starter in 1982 and played inside linebacker alongside Scott Studwell in the Vikings' 3–4 defense. He ranked third on the team with 47 solo stops, eight of which came in the 31–27 victory over Dallas on January 3, 1983. Johnson maintained his starting job for the next two years, recording 118 total tackles in 1983 while blocking a field goal attempt in the

20–17 overtime win over Green Bay on October 23. He added 98 total hits in 1984 while leading the team in tackles on three occasions.

Despite being a three-year starter, Johnson's attitude began to affect his play during head coach Bud Grant's encore in 1985. After eight games that season, Johnson was released before signing with Tampa Bay.

Gene Johnson

Season: 1961   Defensive Back   Height: 6'
Number: 41   Cincinnati   Weight: 195

Gene Johnson was acquired in the veterans pool from Philadelphia in 1961. He played in four games for the expansion Vikings at left safety before he was shipped to the Giants midway through the campaign for a ninth-round draft pick.

Henry Johnson

Seasons: 1980–82   Linebacker   Height: 6'2"
Number: 53   Georgia Tech   Weight: 235

The Vikings' seventh-round draft pick in 1980, Henry Johnson spent three years serving almost exclusively on kick coverage for Minnesota's special teams. As a rookie, Johnson ranked second on the squad with 19 primary hits. He was fourth on the team with 14 stops in 1981, followed by a nine-tackle showing in 1982, which tied for third among the Vikes' special teams performers.

Joe Johnson

Season: 1992   Wide Receiver   Height: 5'8"
Number: 89   Notre Dame   Weight: 170

Acquired along with George Hinkle from the Redskins for a sixth-round draft choice, Joe Johnson played behind Anthony Carter and Cris Carter at wide receiver early in the 1992 campaign before seeing his playing time increase when Hassan Jones went down with a back injury.

Dubbed by many Viking followers as a Leo Lewis clone, the quick and sure-handed Johnson was seventh on the team with 21 catches and sixth with 211 receiving yards. He scored a touchdown on a three-yard catch during a 17–13 win over Cleveland on November 22, rushed four times for 26 yards, and returned five kickoffs for 79 yards. Although he attended minicamp prior to the 1993 season, Johnson was deemed expendable after Minnesota drafted Qadry Ismail.

Ken Johnson

Seasons: 1989–90   Safety   Height: 6'2"
Number: 22   Florida A&M   Weight: 203

Ken Johnson bounced on and off several lists after signing with Minnesota as a college free agent in 1989. Waived twice by the Vikings during the season only to be re-signed, Johnson spent 12 games on the practice squad and was on the active roster for two contests, playing in one on special teams. He then took the field in purple for four games on special teams in 1990 before being released by the Vikings for the final time during the campaign.

Sammy Johnson

Seasons: 1976–78 Running Back Height: 6'1"
Number: 48 North Carolina Weight: 226

With Chuck Foreman in his prime during the late 1970s, opportunities were limited for Sammy Johnson after he arrived from San Francisco during the 1976 season. A fourth-round draft pick in 1974, Johnson was acquired from the 49ers in exchange for wide receiver Jim Lash. The Vikings needed backup help when Mark Kellar went down, and were impressed with Johnson's ability to run tough between the tackles and catch passes out of the backfield.

Johnson's greatest contributions came during his first year in purple. He played in eight regular-season contests and three playoff games and started one, a 20–9 win over Green Bay on December 5, 1976. Johnson rushed six times for 43 yards and gained 22 more yards on two receptions versus the Packers. His single greatest contribution took place in the 24–13 win over the Rams in the NFC Championship Game on December 26, when Johnson sealed the victory by barrelling up the middle and over defenders for a 12-yard touchdown run in the fourth quarter.

The remainder of Johnson's career in the Upper Midwest came while giving Foreman a breather. He scored two touchdowns and was third on the team with 217 yards on 55 carries in 1977. A year later, Johnson was placed on the non-football injury list after suffering a broken ankle while playing basketball in the offseason. Added to the roster in October, he gained just 41 yards on 11 carries in three appearances during the 1978 campaign to end his days with the Vikings.

Clint Jones

Seasons: 1967–72 Running Back Height: 6'
Number: 26 Michigan State Weight: 205

A darting, daring halfback who earned All-American recognition at Michigan State, Clint Jones was the Vikings' initial first-round draft pick of head coach Bud Grant's era. Although he never attained superstar status, Jones was a valuable running back and an excellent kick returner during his six seasons with Minnesota.

As an understudy to Dave Osborn during his rookie season, the snake-loving Jones contributed mostly by carrying back 25 kicks for 597 yards, including a 96-yard touchdown dash in Minnesota's 27–24 win over the Giants on November 5, 1967. He helped pick up the slack while Osborn missed most of the 1968 campaign with a knee injury by placing second on the team with 536 rushing yards. His best day took place during the season opener. Jones sliced through the Falcons' defense for 101 yards on 17 carries in the Vikings' 47–7 victory on September 14.

Jones' opportunities were more limited due to the return of Osborn in 1969. He made the most of one chance, however, racing for a team-record 80 yards (the longest run in the National Football League in five years) to paydirt on a carry against Chicago in a 31–14 win on November 2. He wound up gaining 241 yards on the ground with three touchdowns while averaging 26.1 yards on 17 kickoffs, then re-emerged as the Vikings' second-leading rusher with 369 yards and a team-high nine touchdowns in 1970. Three of those tallying efforts occurred on November 15, when Jones registered scoring runs of three, one and five yards in the 24–20 triumph over Detroit.

His best season as a pro followed in 1971, with Jones piling up a team-high 675 yards and four touchdowns. He shined late in the season, gaining more than 400 yards in the campaign's last four games. Jones tied

Osborn's team record by rushing for a career-high 155 yards in the 24–7 win over Atlanta on November 28. Among his carries that afternoon was a 73-yard touchdown jaunt.

Free agency was more than two decades away in 1972, so Jones teamed with Gene Washington and Charlie West in hopes of gaining better leverage in contract negotiations with the Vikings. The tough stand did nothing to help their cause. Jones missed eight games after breaking a bone in his right elbow against Chicago, yet still managed to gain 162 yards and score two touchdowns for the year. He also got the campaign off to a good start by returning the opening kickoff of the preseason's first game 100 yards for a touchdown against San Diego.

Jones' days in purple came to an end after the 1972 season, when he and linebacker Carl Gersbach were traded to San Diego for second- and third-round draft picks.

Hassan Jones

Seasons: 1986–92 Wide Receiver Height: 6'
Number: 84 Florida State Weight: 202

He was far from the fastest wide receiver on the team, but no player during his seven-year tenure with the Vikings had softer, more dependable hands than Hassan Jones.

Minnesota's fifth-round draft choice in 1986, Jones wasted no time making a good first impression. He began his professional career by leading the Vikings in yards-per-catch average during his initial five seasons. A starter in place of the injured Anthony Carter for the first six contests of 1986, Jones had two 100-yard receiving games and finished sixth on the team with 28 receptions while averaging 20.4 yards per grab. He also became the second rookie in Minnesota annals to score two touchdowns in one game, victimizing the Steelers on September 21 in a 31–7 Vikings victory.

The players strike and a healthy Carter limited Jones to seven catches for a 27-yard norm during the 1987 regular season. His biggest play of the campaign came on September 20, when he worked his way open and caught a Wade Wilson toss at the goal line in a last-minute 21–16 victory over the Rams. Jones also pulled in two touchdowns in the playoffs, including a 44-yard reception in the 44–10 win over New Orleans and a five-yarder during the 36–24 whipping of San Francisco.

In 1988, Jones caught 40 passes for 778 yards and five touchdowns and teamed with Carter and Steve Jordan to pull in more tosses for more yards than any other starting trio in the league. He ranked second among the Minnesota receivers over the next two years, making 42 grabs for 694 yards in 1989 and a career-high 51 catches for 810 yards and seven scores in 1990.

Knee surgery prior to training camp in 1991 led to a disappointing campaign, one that saw Jones catch 32 tosses for 384 yards and one touchdown. He rebounded early in 1992 by grabbing five passes, including two for touchdowns, in a 23–20 overtime victory against Green Bay on September 6. He pulled in 18 aerials during the season's first six games prior to suffering two broken bones in his lower back while running a reverse during the October 15, 1992, meeting with Detroit. He returned late in the season before sitting out the last two contests due to back pain, and finished the year with 22 catches for 308 yards and four scores.

A free agent following the 1992 season, Jones opted to sign with Cleveland. He departed at the top of the Vikings' career charts by averaging 16.8 yards on his 222 receptions.

Mike Anthony Jones

Seasons: 1983–85	Wide Receiver	Height: 5'11"
Number: 89	Tennessee State	Weight: 183

With Tommy Kramer under center in the early- and mid-1980s, the Vikings passed the pigskin as much as anyone in the National Football League. One of the benefactors of that philosophy was Mike Jones, Minnesota's sixth-round draft pick in 1983.

Jones blossomed in 1984 after playing all 16 games as a rookie on special teams and catching six passes for 95 yards. His production increased with a starting role in his second season, with Jones hauling in 38 tosses for 591 yards. Among his receptions was his first touchdown grab, a 70-yard aerial from Kramer against the Raiders on October 14. That proved to be the longest play from scrimmage for the Vikings during the 1984 campaign.

A year later, Jones ranked second on the team with 46 catches and four touchdown receptions and was third with 641 receiving yards. He paced the Vikings in both games against the Packers, including a six-catch, one-touchdown effort on October 13.

After reporting to training camp with Minnesota in 1986, Jones' days in purple came to an end when he was traded to New Orleans in exchange for running back Wayne Wilson.

Mike Alonzo Jones

Seasons: 1990–91	Tight End	Height: 6'3"
Number: 89	Texas A&M	Weight: 265

The Vikings' first of two third-round draft picks in 1990, Mike Jones' role consisted of playing on special teams and serving as an extra tight end on short-yardage situations.

After playing in 11 games as a rookie and registering three tackles on special teams, Jones made the most of his opportunities a year later. In addition to his 10 special-teams hits, he caught the only two passes of his Viking career and scored touchdowns on both receptions. His first catch was a three-yard pass in a 35–21 win at Green Bay on November 17, 1990, followed by a five-yard scoring toss during a 26–24 triumph at Tampa Bay three weeks later.

Richard Jones

Season: 1993	Kicker	Height: 6'3"
Number: 3	Arizona State	Weight: 200

Richard Jones was signed as insurance on kickoffs for the 1993 playoffs. The left-footed Jones, released by the Vikings earlier in the season during training camp, was signed in case Fuad Reveiz's sore ankle became worse and prevented him from kicking off.

Shawn Jones

Season: 1993	Defensive Back	Height: 6'
Number: 32	Georgia Tech	Weight: 200

The all-time leading passer in Georgia Tech history who guided the Yellow Jackets to a share of the national championship in 1990, Shawn Jones did not have enough arm strength to play quarterback in the National Football League. He did have the athleticism to earn a job on Minnesota's practice squad as a safety before being activated for the final two games of the 1993 season. After seeing limited action in dime packages, Jones pursued his dream to be a professional signalcaller and signed with the Canadian Football League's Baltimore franchise in 1994.

Wayne Jones

Season: 1987   Guard   Height: 6'4"
Number: 69   Utah   Weight: 270

Wayne Jones saw his only action in the National Football League five years after he was drafted by the Dolphins in the 10th round in 1982. The offensive lineman who provided depth at guard and center signed as a free agent with the Vikings on September 10, 1987. He played on the protection unit for field goal attempts during six games before being waived on November 17.

Andrew Jordan

Seasons: 1994–97   Tight End   Height: 6'4"
Numbers: 83, 89   Western Carolina   Weight: 254

There were times during his rookie season when Andrew Jordan had to pinch himself to make sure he was not dreaming. Minnesota's sixth-round choice, Jordan emerged as one of the 1994 draft's best late-round selections with his consistent production. To top it off, he had the opportunity to play with his childhood idol, Steve Jordan, who was pulled out of retirement and signed in early December after a rash of injuries struck the team.

Jordan, at times, attracted favorable comparisons to his hero. He outplayed veteran Adrian Cooper by leading the Vikings' tight ends with 35 catches for 336 yards, the most receptions by a Minnesota rookie since Sammy White had 51 in 1976. That performance earned Jordan consensus all-rookie recognition.

More success followed for Jordan in 1995. He continued to outshine Cooper by pulling in 27 catches, tops again among the team's tight ends, and was a consistent if not overpowering blocker. Jordan also caught his first two touchdown tosses, one in the season opener against Chicago on September 3 and the second versus Green Bay in the Vikings' 27–24 win on November 5. A late-season ankle injury that caused him to miss the final four games served as the lone negative in Jordan's output.

Jordan's situation, however, changed in 1996. While he again paced the tight ends with 19 catches and 128 receiving yards, his performance dropped considerably upon signing a contract extension. Things got worse when Jordan suffered a mild shoulder injury and began to sulk at midseason after Hunter Goodwin was awarded the starting job at tight end in order to give the Vikings a greater blocking presence. His attitude became so poor that Jordan was deactivated for three of the final five games.

Little improvement was seen from Jordan in 1997. He slipped to third on the depth chart, behind Goodwin and Greg DeLong, and failed to catch a pass in the team's first four games. When newcomer Andrew Glover was deemed healthy enough to contribute, Jordan was released in late September.

Jeff Jordan

Seasons: 1965–67   Defensive Back   Height: 6'3"
Number: 22   Tulsa   Weight: 190

A psychology major at Tulsa who narrowly missed a Rhodes Scholarship in 1965, Jeff Jordan was a primary reason for the secondary's improvement during the latter half of the 1965 season. Employing tight coverage and an uncanny intelligence for the game, the reserve intercepted four passes in the final three contests while serving as a sure tackler in the defense's third wave.

The Vikings' eighth-round draft pick in 1965, Jordan had his world turn upside-down a year later. A foot injury and the death of his wife, Cheryl, in an airline crash caused him to miss most of the 1966 preseason. One of the team's best competitors, he returned to play in all 14 regular-season games as a reserve at free safety. Jordan handled the same role behind starter Dale Hackbart for 11 games in 1967, which proved to be his final season in the National Football League.

Steve Jordan

Seasons: 1982–94　　　Tight End　　　Height: 6'3"
Number: 83　　　Brown　　　Weight: 240

Steve Jordan was one of the Vikings' best offensive weapons for nearly a decade. The silky-smooth tight end earned Pro Bowl recognition on six occasions by running excellent routes and finding seams in defenses for long gains down the middle of the field. By the time he retired from the National Football League after the 1994 season, Jordan topped the Minnesota record book with 498 receptions.

The Vikings' seventh-round draft pick in 1982, Jordan played sparingly behind Joe Senser and Bob Bruer during his first two years in the league. Seeing action mostly in two-tight end formations and on special teams, he scored his first touchdown during a 34–14 win against Houston on October 16, 1983, on a 23-yard pass from Steve Dils. He grabbed another scoring toss, a two-yarder from Wade Wilson on December 17, 1983, during a 20–14 triumph over Cincinnati. In all, he caught 18 passes in his initial two campaigns.

The scenario changed drastically for Jordan during the 1984 preseason, when Senser suffered a foot injury and Bruer underwent knee surgery. Thrust into the starting job, the civil engineer tackled the opportunity and designed a football career with his impressive athleticism and dependable hands that made him a consistent threat in Minnesota's pass-oriented offense.

Steve Jordan

In his first year as a starter, Jordan tied Mike Jones for third on the team with 38 catches and scored two touchdowns, one on a four-yard sweep around left end against Tampa Bay during a 27–24 win on November 4. He became one of the league's elite tight ends in 1985 when he paced the NFC at his position with 68 catches. His first Pro Bowl recognition came in 1986, with Jordan again leading the Vikings with 58 catches and 859 yards. His best game that season came on November 2 against Washington. Jordan pulled in six passes for 179 yards, including a career-long 68-yard touchdown reception. That marked the best game by a Minnesota receiver in 10 years and represented the most yards ever accumulated by a tight end in team history. He also had six catches for 112 yards and two touchdowns during a 42–7 win over Green Bay on September 28 and seven receptions for 97 yards and one score in a 45–13 victory versus Tampa Bay on November 30.

Jordan further established himself in 1987. His top performance of the strike-marred season took place in the playoffs when he pulled in five passes, including a five-yard touchdown grab, against New Orleans. Pro Bowl invitations came the next three years as well, with Jordan catching at least one pass in 52 straight games (excluding the three replacement contests in 1987) before having his streak snapped versus Denver on November 4, 1990.

In 1991, Jordan received Pro Bowl honors for the final time in his career while placing second on the team with 57 catches for 638 yards. He also became the Vikings' all-time leading pass receiver when he caught three tosses against Detroit on November 24, 1991. Jordan continued to come up with the big catches, particularly on third down, in 1992, when he had the second-longest touchdown catch of his career, a 60-yarder in Minnesota's 38–10 win at Chicago on November 2.

Jordan caught at least one pass in the 14 games he started in 1993 and finished third on the team with 56 receptions for 542 yards and a touchdown. Eligible for free agency, and with the Vikings drafting Andrew Jordan and acquiring Adrian Cooper, Jordan was content to pursue his construction interests before head coach Dennis Green called the tight end late in the 1994 campaign. Injuries to Brent Novoselsky and Cooper left the Vikings shorthanded. Jordan made a comeback and provided some veteran leadership to help Minnesota reach the playoffs for the third straight year under Green. He also caught three passes for 23 yards, including two more in the playoffs against Chicago.

Always philosophical in his approach to the game, Jordan is one of the few people who could draw parallels between his two careers. "Construction can produce the same kind of intensity as playing football," Jordan said. "In a sense, everyone is expected to perform in a certain way. If there's a mistake, it could cost thousands of dollars." Rarely was Jordan involved in such missteps, regardless of which kind of hard-hat he was wearing. No matter the field, he was one of the best.

Don Joyce

Season: 1961　　　　　　　Defensive End　　　　　　　Height: 6'3"
Number: 83　　　　　　　　Tulane　　　　　　　　　　Weight: 225

Don Joyce arrived in Minnesota with a well-earned reputation as a headhunter for the Colts during their championship days in the 1950s. By the time he was deemed expendable by Baltimore and obtained by the Vikings from the veterans pool, Joyce still possessed a mean streak, even if his movement, both laterally and straight-ahead, had decreased by his 11th season in the National Football League. Even so, the rotund Joyce emerged as a starter on Minnesota's first defensive line and played in all 14 games before spending his last professional season with Denver.

K

Todd Kalis

Seasons: 1988–93 Guard Height: 6'5"
Number: 69 Arizona State Weight: 280

For three years, the Vikings fielded two former Arizona State teammates at the starting guard positions. Randall McDaniel and Todd Kalis, selected by Minnesota in the first and fourth rounds, respectively, in the 1988 draft, provided the Twin Cities with a Sun Devils' look by making up 40 percent of the offensive line between 1989 and 1991.

While McDaniel has carved out a Hall of Fame-type career, Kalis gave the purple solid guard play, particularly as a one-on-one drive blocker, on the right side for a half-dozen seasons. After playing in 14 games as a reserve guard and tackle during his rookie year, Kalis replaced the departed Terry Tausch in 1989 and emerged as one of four Vikings offensive linemen to start every game. Tabbed to *Inside Sports'* All-Underrated team, Kalis added 14 starts in 1990, missing two games with a bruised sternum, then started the first half of the 1991 campaign before losing his first-string status to Brian Habib.

A knee injury suffered in the final pre-season game shelved Kalis for the entire 1992 slate. He returned to form in 1993, seeing action in all 16 contests prior to signing a lucrative free-agent deal with Pittsburgh.

Joe Kapp

Seasons: 1967–69 Quarterback Height: 6'3"
Number: 11 California Weight: 215

When Fran Tarkenton decided his first stint with Minnesota had run its course and demanded a trade after the 1966 season, Vikings general manager Jim Finks used his connections from earlier days spent in the Canadian Football League to find a replacement. Joe Kapp, an eight-year veteran of the CFL who had won league Most Valuable Player honors in 1963 and guided Vancouver to the Grey Cup, was acquired by Minnesota in 1967. Kapp's contract situation had become messy, including an agreement to play with Houston in the American Football League. But thanks to Finks, the Vikings emerged the victors after some lengthy negotiations.

Kapp was acquired when head coach Bud Grant determined that Ron VanderKelen, the heir apparent to Tarkenton's job after four years of waiting and watching, was not cut out for starting duties. Kapp, meanwhile, showed some of his predecessor's ability to improvise, only not as gracefully as the Scrambler. Never afraid to leave the pocket, Kapp succeeded with his ability to throw accurate, albeit ugly, passes while rolling out. Other times he would keep the ball and run while lowering his shoulder and doling out punishment to any would-be tackler.

"I'm paid to win," Kapp said. "I'm only going out there and doing my job with the tools that I have. I may not run with much speed, but I make up

Joe Kapp

for it with a lot of desperation. And if people don't think it's pretty, that suits me just fine as long as we win."

He jumped when throwing the ball as often as he remained on his feet. Though his passes wobbled, his athleticism unorthodox and his performances a bit inartistic, the self-confident Kapp became an unquestioned leader in Minnesota with his fun-loving, charismatic personality. An example of just how sanguine Kapp was came just prior to the 1967 season when the quarterback told Dale Hackbart, "I'm going to make it big in the NFL."

Upon taking over for VanderKelen in Minnesota's second game of the campaign, Kapp displayed his fearless machismo and salty language by shouting "F— you, Rams" to the Fearsome Foursome. Three weeks later, Kapp engineered a shocking 10–7 triumph over unbeaten Green Bay, the defending champions of the National Football League, on October 15.

He could be as bad as he was good on the gridiron, but Kapp always gave his full effort. He looked lost at times, particularly during the 1967 season, yet never grew frustrated. His cause was helped immeasurably by VanderKelen, who sacrificed playing time for the good of the team by teaching Kapp the minute details of the Minnesota offense. Through it all, Kapp completed 102 of 214 passes for 1,386 yards, including eight touchdowns and 17 interceptions during his first year in purple. His best game came against the mighty Colts, against whom Kapp completed 15 of 25 attempts for 202 yards and one touchdown in the 20–20 tie on October 22.

His efforts improved in 1968, leading the Vikings to their first Central Division title by succeeding on 129 of 248 pass attempts for 10 touchdowns and another 17 interceptions. Kapp started the campaign ablaze by setting a team completion percentage mark with a 16-of-20 performance in the 47–7 win over Atlanta on September 14. Against Detroit on October 6, Kapp showed how tough and resilient he was on the field. Knocked virtually unconscious while succumbing to a Detroit blitz in the first half, Kapp returned in the third quarter after his lone backup, Gary Cuozzo, fractured his shoulder. Kapp mixed his passes with several scrambles to set up two Bill Brown touchdown plunges to guide the Vikings to a 24–10 victory. He also ended the slate on an impressive note, with his 26-of-44 effort against Baltimore in the Western Conference Championship Game on December 22 establishing club records for most attempts and completions in a single contest.

But as good as 1968 may have been for Kapp, the 1969 season unfolded as one of the most outstanding campaigns in Vikings annals. Included during the year was one of the best individual performances in NFL history. On September 28, the Pro Bowl signalcaller pelted the Colts with seven touchdown tosses, joining Sid Luckman, Y.A. Tittle and Adrian Burke as the only quarterbacks in league annals to throw that many scoring passes in a single game. Grant had removed Kapp from the contest after his sixth touchdown, but returned to the field after Cuozzo went down with an injury.

Kapp led the Vikings to their first Super Bowl appearance by completing 120 of 237 passes for 1,726 yards, 19 touchdowns and 13 interceptions. At a December banquet held by the Vikings Fan Club, he became noted in Minnesota history for turning down team Most Valuable Player honors. In his "unacceptance" speech, Kapp said, "I know for a fact that there is no most valuable Viking. There are only 40 most valuable Vikings. Forty for 60, put it that way. I just can't accept this. Thank you."

He was indeed the most valuable Viking a couple weeks later, for never was Kapp better than in the comeback victory over Los Angeles in the Western Conference Championship Game on December 27. The game was a defensive struggle, but the quarterback knew he was on the verge of cracking the Rams. As the Purple People Eaters returned to the field in the fourth quarter, Kapp hollered continuously, "Get me that pill back!" Both Minnesota units lived up to their roles, with Kapp registering the death blow on his goal-line bootleg in which he reached the end zone untouched.

Ironically, the end of Kapp's reign in Minnesota came as fast and pronounced as his arrival. When he was carted off the field with an injured shoulder with eight minutes remaining in Super Bowl IV on January 11, 1970, Kapp had made his final appearance with the Vikings. The quarterback became embroiled in a salary impasse and bitter holdout with Finks during the next training camp, leading to a trade to New England for safety John Charles and a first-round draft pick three games into the regular season. Kapp spent one year with the Patriots before another contract battle led to the premature end of his NFL career.

Rich Karlis

Season: 1989　　　　　　　　Kicker　　　　　　　　Height: 6′
Number: 3　　　　　　　　　Cincinnati　　　　　　　Weight: 180

The Vikings' kicking situation looked desperate in the early days of the 1989 season. Teddy Garcia would have had trouble kicking his dog, not to mention booting a football through a pair of vertical yellow posts. Five times Garcia attempted field goals in the first three games of the campaign, and four times he missed, including relative chip shots from 33, 34 and 37 yards away.

With a vein on the verge of exploding in the middle of his forehead, head coach Jerry Burns sought help. He found it in Rich Karlis, who had been released after failing to come to terms on a contract with Denver. After a shaky start that featured four misses in six attempts, the former Bronco succeeded on 28 of his next 31 tries. He went on to establish a club record with 31 three-pointers in a season and led the Vikes with 120 points, the fourth-highest single-season total at the time in franchise annals.

Karlis established a league record on November 5, 1989. In Minnesota's 23–21 overtime win against the Rams, the kicker converted all seven of his field goal attempts. He also had two five-field goal performances, coming during a 43–17 win over Atlanta on December 10 and a 29–21 beating of the Bengals on December 25.

The brother-in-law of center Kirk Lowdermilk, Karlis wound up playing just one season in Minnesota when another contract dispute forced the Vikings to part company with the kicker.

Karl Kassulke

Seasons: 1963–72　　　　　　Defensive Back　　　　　Height: 6′
Number: 29　　　　　　　　　Drake　　　　　　　　　Weight: 195

The Vikings' world came to a momentary stop in the summer of 1973. One day prior to the start of training camp, Karl Kassulke was involved in a motorcycle accident that not only ended his playing career, but left him permanently paralyzed from the waist down.

Prior to the accident, Kassulke played the game the way he lived his life—with reckless abandon. Acquired off waivers from Detroit in 1963, the safety's aggressive style was physical enough that post-play altercations with opponents became common. He was tough, always playing through injuries until he could no longer perform, and was one of the most fierce hitters in the National Football League, past or present. No defensive back in Minnesota history doled out more punishment, including 498 total tackles. Kassulke also had an uncanny knack for blocking punts and contributed regularly on special teams. Anything asked of him, Kassulke did it with all-out exuberance.

Kassulke achieved his feats thanks to his outstanding athleticism. As a senior at Drake, he led the team in rushing, caught 21 passes and scored 10 touchdowns, two coming on interception returns. He joined Detroit as an 11th-round draft pick in 1963 before being cut by the Lions and purchased off waivers by the Vikings. "Hunkie" immediately joined the Minnesota secondary as a starter and upgraded a unit that had been miserable for most of its first two years. His toughness against the run and his outstanding tackling ability in the open field led to Kassulke's move to strong safety in 1964. He was head coach Norm Van Brocklin's type of player, with Dutch saying, "I don't have a player who plays with more fervor than Kassulke."

After picking off three passes in 1964, Kassulke had two interceptions in each of the next three years. He also continued to improve his play and was named winner of the Terry Dillon Award for the 1967 season. He blocked two punts in 1968, and intercepted two more passes in 1969. Three more picks and more stellar special teams play followed in 1970, with Ed Sharockman returning two of Kassulke's blocked punts for touchdowns during the slate. Those efforts resulted in the lone Pro Bowl appearance of his career.

A knee injury forced Kassulke to miss nearly half of the 1971 season, while a broken leg forced the safety to sit out six games a year later. Even so, he picked off two passes in both seasons to give him 19 for his career.

Kassulke's motorcycle accident affected Minnesota off the field as well as on the gridiron. He was the Vikings' most popular player, always needling his teammates and creating the most laughter. It was for that reason and many more that the safety was honored with Karl Kassulke Day during the final regular-season home game of the 1973 season, on November 25. Following the 31–13 victory over the Bears, receiver John Gilliam presented Kassulke with the game ball. Twelve years later, he was named to the Vikings' Silver Anniversary All-Time Team.

Mark Kellar

Seasons: 1976–78　　　Running Back　　　Height: 6'
Number: 39　　　Northern Illinois　　　Weight: 225

Mark Kellar looked another direction when the Vikings drafted him in the sixth round in 1974. Instead of donning purple, the running back opted to play for two years with the Chicago entry in the World Football League before the fledgling circuit crashed and burned.

When he arrived in Minnesota two years late, Kellar served on special teams, gained 25 yards on the ground, and caught a pair of passes in three outings in 1976 before landing on injured reserve with a cracked bone in his ankle. He returned to play in all 14 games in 1977, gaining 15 yards on seven carries while seeing most of his action on special teams. His role was identical in his 16 appearances in 1978, his last year in the National Football League, with Kellar tallying 34 yards on 11 carries while pulling in three tosses.

Brady Keys

Season: 1967　　　Defensive Back　　　Height: 6'
Number: 43　　　Colorado State　　　Weight: 185

A Pro Bowl performer during his six years with the Steelers, Brady Keys was acquired by the Vikings during the 1967 season from Pittsburgh for a third-round draft choice. He played in eight games as a reserve cornerback and part-time punt returner. While he gained just two yards on five punt runbacks, Keys scooted 30 yards on his lone interception with Minnesota and recovered one fumble. He was traded a year later along with a seventh-round draft pick to St. Louis in exchange for another seventh-round selection.

Keith Kidd

Seasons: 1984–85, 1987   Wide Receiver   Height: 6'1"
Number: 44   Arkansas   Weight: 195

Keith Kidd has one game to show for his three different seasons on the Vikings' roster. Drafted in the ninth round in 1984, he spent his rookie season on injured reserve due to a knee injury he suffered in his senior year at Arkansas. After a similar fate in 1985, Kidd returned to the Twin Cities and played in one of the replacement games in 1987.

Phil King

Seasons: 1965–66   Running Back   Height: 6'4"
Number: 24   Vanderbilt   Weight: 225

A Cherokee Indian known as "Chief" who came to the Vikings after seven years with the Giants and one season in Pittsburgh, Phil King provided solid backup services at running back for Minnesota in 1965. Acquired from the Steelers for a sixth-round draft pick, King filled in for the ailing Tommy Mason and Bill Brown and averaged 4.9 yards per carry by gaining 356 yards on 72 rushes. He also provided solid blocking and caught a dozen passes for 96 yards, including a two-yard touchdown toss from Fran Tarkenton in Minnesota's 29–7 win at Detroit on December 19.

King, who as a collegian set the Vanderbilt rushing record, played a reduced role while taking the field for all 14 games in 1966. He completed the only pass attempt of his career, gained 40 yards on 17 carries, and caught two passes for 24 yards, one a six-yarder for a touchdown against the Colts on October 23.

Doug Kingsriter

Seasons: 1973–75   Tight End   Height: 6'2"
Number: 89   Minnesota   Weight: 225

Doug Kingsriter's success on the Twin Cities' gridirons occurred more often as a collegian with the Golden Gophers than in the National Football League. A native of Little Falls, Minnesota, an All-American in 1971 and an Academic All-American in 1971 and 1972, Kingsriter served as a reserve tight end and lined up occasionally at wide receiver for the Vikings. The sixth-round draft pick in 1973 possessed good hands and blocking skills, with his unexpected success in his first training camp leading to the release of veteran John Beasley.

Kingsriter caught two passes as a rookie while playing mostly in multiple-tight end formations. He then pulled in five tosses for 89 yards in 1974 before a knee injury limited him to three games in 1975, his final season in the NFL.

John Kirby

Seasons: 1964–69   Linebacker   Height: 6'3"
Number: 36   Nebraska   Weight: 228

Minnesota's fifth-round draft pick in 1964, John Kirby emerged late in the 1965 season after seeing limited opportunities as a rookie. He became a starter at right outside linebacker in 1966, replacing Lonnie Warwick, who had moved inside to fill in for the retired Rip Hawkins. Though slender for his height at linebacker, Kirby employed his vicious tackling ability along with good speed and range to hold his job with the first unit for nearly three years.

An All-Big Eight linebacker who was also drafted by San Diego in the American Football League, Kirby was a solid defender against both the pass and the run. Although primarily an outside linebacker, he moved inside during the 1966 and 1967 seasons for a handful of games when Warwick sat out with a back injury. When he lost his starting job in 1968, Kirby served as a swingman, seeing significant time at both positions. He then played in two games with the Vikings in 1969 before ending the season with the Giants.

William Kirksey

Season: 1990	Linebacker	Height: 6'2"
Number: 52	Southern Mississippi	Weight: 221

Signed as a free agent in 1990, William Kirksey made the Vikings' roster and contributed six tackles while playing in nine of the team's first 10 games. His best performances included a three-tackle outing on special teams against Chicago on September 23 and two assisted hits at linebacker versus Philadelphia on October 15.

Waived by Minnesota on November 19 before spending the last six weeks of the season on Atlanta's practice squad, Kirksey rejoined the Vikings for training camp in 1991 but did not make the team.

Kurt Knoff

Seasons: 1979–82	Safety	Height: 6'2"
Number: 25	Kansas	Weight: 190

When Houston placed Kurt Knoff on waivers with the purpose of activating him from injured reserve during the 1979 season, the Vikings put in the claim with the hope of filling a void that would be left by the impending retirement of Paul Krause. The move paid immediate dividends for the purple when Knoff picked off a pass against Chicago on his first play as a starter. He went on start seven games for the Vikings in 1979, posting 47 solo tackles and two interceptions.

The former Minnesota High School Athlete of the Year and native of East Grand Forks started every game in 1980 and 1981. He ranked second on the team with 138 unassisted tackles, forced one fumble and intercepted three passes in 1980. His highlight included a pick he returned 67 yards for a touchdown in a 34–0 win over Detroit on November 9. Knoff added 94 solo hits in 1981, good for fourth on the team, along with three steals, two forced fumbles and the recovery of one loose ball.

Knoff's playing time decreased in 1982, when he started four of nine games and ranked 10th on the team with 30 solo stops while posting one sack and an interception. During the early days of the 1983 training camp, after four solid years in purple, the 29-year-old Knoff decided to retire from the game.

Greg Koch

Season: 1987	Guard	Height: 6'4"
Number: 68	Arkansas	Weight: 270

Having spent nine years with the Packers and one season with Miami before arriving in Minnesota during the 1987 season, Greg Koch earned a spot in the heart of Vikings fans everywhere when he said of his former employer, "In Green Bay, a nice wardrobe means you have 10 bowling shirts hanging in your closet."

Acquired from the Dolphins for a sixth-round draft pick on October

20, 1987, Koch started the final six regular-season games and all three playoff contests at right guard in place of Terry Tausch, who had been placed on injured reserve with a bad ankle. The veteran's steady performance played a significant role in the Vikings' run to the NFC Championship Game. Koch's services were not needed, however, when Tausch returned to action the following year in training camp.

Terry Kosens

Season: 1963　　　　　Defensive Back　　　　Height: 6'3"
Number: 26　　　　　　Hofstra　　　　　　　　Weight: 195

Terry Kosens, Minnesota's 10th-round draft pick in 1963, saw action in eight games as a rookie, mostly on special teams. A two-way player at Hofstra who was considered the finest receiver in school history, Kosens was a good tackler but lacked the necessary quickness to succeed as a defensive back in the National Football League. His days in Minnesota ended in 1964 when he, Chuck Lamson, Ray Poage and Don Hultz were traded to Philadelphia for Ted Dean and the rights to Bob Berry.

Kent Kramer

Seasons: 1969–70　　　Tight End　　　　　　Height: 6'4"
Number: 89　　　　　　Minnesota　　　　　　Weight: 235

Acquired from the Saints for a fourth-round draft choice prior to the 1969 slate, Kent Kramer backed up starting tight end John Beasley for two seasons with the Vikings.

Kramer, who had been a two-year starter for the Golden Gophers, was an excellent blocker who pulled in two passes in his first season in purple. One of his receptions was a 13-yard touchdown toss from Joe Kapp in a 52–14 triumph over Baltimore on September 28, the fourth TD thrown by the quarterback in his record-setting performance of seven scoring aerials. Kramer played in 11 games for Minnesota in 1970 and caught one pass for 10 yards before spending his last four years in the National Football League with Philadelphia.

Tommy Kramer

Seasons: 1977–89　　　Quarterback　　　　　Height: 6'2"
Number: 9　　　　　　 Rice　　　　　　　　　Weight: 205

Perhaps the most unenviable task in professional sports comes in having to follow a legend. As far as the Vikings are concerned, no one experienced greater scrutiny than Tommy Kramer, who filled the shoes of Fran Tarkenton as well as anyone could have hoped. In fact, Kramer's brash and feisty leadership and never-say-die attitude enabled the underrated quarterback to emerge as one of the league's best signalcallers through most of the 1980s.

The Vikings began preparing for the day Tarkenton would retire when they made Kramer the franchise's first quarterback taken in the first round of the draft, in 1977. He showed significant promise during the preseason before receiving his opportunity sooner than expected. Kramer threw three touchdown passes against Cincinnati after Tarkenton broke his leg during Minnesota's 42–10 win on November 13. Three weeks later, after Bob Lee had been ineffective against San Francisco, Kramer endeared himself to the Metropolitan Stadium faithful with one of the greatest comebacks in team history.

With Minnesota trailing the 49ers 24–7 on December 4, Kramer took over in the fourth quarter and guided the Vikings to a touchdown in five

Tommy Kramer

plays, capped with an eight-yard scoring pass to Ahmad Rashad. After Minnesota recovered an onsides kick, Kramer repeated the process by hitting Bob Tucker with a nine-yard touchdown strike. San Francisco responded with a field goal, leaving Kramer with 1:37 remaining and the ball on his own 31, trailing by six. One play later, a 69-yard pass to Sammy White in the middle of the field for a touchdown enabled Kramer to accomplish the unbelievable.

"I'm not being cocky, but I knew I could put some points on the board if I was given the chance," Kramer said after the game.

That's not to say it was easy in the early going for the former standout from Rice University. Though Kramer was considered the Vikings' quarterback-of-the-future, his predecessor made comments to suggest otherwise. And, at times, Tarkenton appeared correct. After a credible showing in 1979 that saw him complete 60 percent of his attempts despite having virtually no running game, Kramer got off to a slow start in 1980. If not for the patience of head coach Bud Grant, Kramer would have never received the chance to lead the Vikings to an unexpected playoff berth with 19 touchdown passes and virtually no mistakes down the stretch.

Kramer also earned the reputation as "Two-Minute Tommy." One of his first noteworthy games of his career came in 1979, when he engineered a great second half and hit Rashad with four touchdown passes to open the regular season with a 28–22 win over San Francisco on September 2. He then solidified his place as one of the league's best in the waning minutes of the season finale against the Browns in 1980. With 23 seconds remaining and no timeouts, Kramer completed a hook-and-ladder play with Joe Senser and Ted Brown to place the football at the Cleveland 46 with four ticks of the clock left. He then lofted a bomb toward the front right corner of the end zone. The ball bounced off the leaping group of players and into the outstretched left hand of Rashad to give the Vikings the win and the Central Division title. Forgotten in the miracle is Kramer's performance for the game, including single-game team records of 38 completions and 456 passing yards along with four touchdown passes.

Despite such heroics, Kramer's career followed the same path as most young quarterbacks by getting off to a slow start. He had the two spectacular moments in his three rookie relief appearances in 1977. Tarkenton's return and a concussion in 1978 limited Kramer to just 16 pass attempts, seven of which came in overtime after Tark had injured his thumb against Denver. Kramer guided the Vikings down the field, resulting in Rick Danmeier's game-winning, 44-yard field goal in the 12–9 victory over the Broncos on September 11.

With Tarkenton out of the picture in 1979, Kramer overcame his doubters to become the only quarterback to throw every pass for the Vikings in a season. He started with four touchdown tosses against San Francisco and finished with 23 scoring aerials, just two shy of Tarkenton's team record at the time. Kramer continued to direct the pass-oriented offense in 1980 and set a club record with 3,582 yards in the air.

Kramer overcame a sore knee that kept him from playing the first two games in 1981 to lead the NFC with 593 passing attempts, 322 completions and 3,912 yards, topping his team mark he had set the year before. He also broke Tarkenton's single-season touchdown mark by throwing for 26 scores. The highlight of his 1982 performance was his five touchdown passes, including three to Sammy White, against Chicago in a 35–7 win at the Metrodome on November 28.

After playing with several nagging injuries early in his career, Kramer missed his first significant stretch as a starter in 1983. He had completed all eight passes for 78 yards and a touchdown against the Bucs at

Tampa Stadium on September 18 when he tore a ligament in his right knee and missed the last 13 games. He overcame the ailment to start the first eight contests of the 1984 slate, completing 113 of 217 attempts for 1,556 yards and eight touchdowns, before he was hit from behind and suffered a separated right shoulder against Detroit on October 21. Kramer returned four weeks later versus Denver but reinjured the shoulder again and missed the remainder of the campaign.

Healthy in 1985, Kramer started every game but one and had five outings with more than 300 yards passing, including three touchdowns and 436 yards against the eventual Super Bowl champion Bears on September 19. His best season followed in 1986. Although he missed three games due to injury, Kramer finished as the NFL's top-rated quarterback and was named the NFC's starting Pro Bowl signalcaller and a second-team All-Pro. He set a Viking single-season record against Washington on November 2 by throwing for 490 yards in a 44–38 overtime loss, making him the first quarterback to have two 450-yard passing contests in NFL history. He earned NFC Player of the Week honors for throwing a personal-best six touchdown passes in a 42–7 win over Green Bay on September 28. Kramer also paced the league with his 24 touchdown passes.

Nerve damage to his neck suffered during an August exhibition game against New England cost Kramer most of the 1987 season. He did not make his first start until November 8, against the Raiders, then failed to complete any of his six starts, including the playoff game against New Orleans. He wound up completing 40 of 81 passes for 452 yards and four touchdowns before giving way to Wade Wilson against the 49ers in the second round of the postseason.

Six more starts followed while he shared time with Wilson in 1988. Kramer lived up to his reputation against Philadelphia by leading the team on a nine-play, 54-yard drive with less than two minutes left in the game to set up the winning field goal in Minnesota's 23–21 victory over the Eagles on September 25. Yet that effort proved to be one of the last heroic moments on the gridiron for Kramer. His string of ailments over the previous three years had taken its toll on the quarterback's productivity, forcing his retirement from the game at the end of the season.

From a career standpoint, Kramer ranks second to Tarkenton in most Minnesota team categories, including 3,648 passes, 2,011 completions, 24,775 yards, 159 touchdowns, 157 interceptions and lowest percentage of passes intercepted at 4.3. He holds numerous season and game marks in Viking annals, among them 38 completions in a game (two occasions), 16 consecutive passes completed (versus Green Bay on November 11, 1979), 490 yards passing (versus Washington, November 2, 1986), most games with 300 or more yards passing (19), most games with four or more touchdowns passes (nine), and most games with four or more touchdowns in a season (three).

Paul Krause

Seasons: 1968–79 Safety Height: 6'3"
Number: 22 Iowa Weight: 205

Justice was finally served on January 24, 1998. Nearly two decades after he last performed in purple and became the National Football League's all-time leader with 81 interceptions during his 16-year career, Paul Krause was elected to the Pro Football Hall of Fame.

A better free safety has never played the game. In fact, Krause defined how the position should be handled. Using great peripheral vision and uncanny instincts to determine what the opposing quarterback would do, the

Paul Krause

defensive back patrolled the middle of the field by foiling pass attempts and making consistent tackles to solidify the famed defense known as The Purple People Eaters.

"Paul personified the term free safety," said head coach Bud Grant. "For 12 years for us he was, in a sense, free to play down and distance, the tendencies, the quarterback's eyes, double the key receivers, play a hunch, use his intelligence and great athletic ability to be the greatest free safety of all time."

Ironically, Krause may have never toiled in the NFL if not for an injury he suffered in college. After an outstanding sophomore year for the University of Iowa baseball team, Krause had no fewer than 12 major-league clubs interested in signing the outfielder. He watched the bidding increase to $50,000, a princely sum in those days prior to baseball's amateur draft. Yet the baseball offers disappeared when he hurt his shoulder on a pass pattern versus Michigan on November 17, 1962, effectively ending his days on the diamond.

He instead became the Washington Redskins' second-round pick in 1964 and, after leading the loop with 12 interceptions, emerged as the league's first rookie to earn All-Pro recognition. Krause picked off two Frank Ryan passes in his first game, against Cleveland, and went on to garner All-Pro honors in his first two NFL seasons. Despite his success, Washington defensive backs coach Ed Hughes wanted Krause to make more tackles and play more like a strong safety rather than a free safety. When Krause failed to meet those standards, he was labelled a timid finesse player and was traded to Minnesota in exchange for tight end Marlin McKeever and a seventh-round draft pick on July 4, 1968.

The truth be told, the Vikings had no idea what an impact Krause would have on their team. While his addition in 1968 was not as heralded as that of Alan Page the year before, the former Redskin served as the final key to the dominating Minnesota defense. Krause shored up the backfield as much as Page contributed to the inside pass rush. Rarely did opponents pull off long gains on the ground or through the air, for Krause was always in the proper place in the secondary.

"We knew that if a ball hung up in the air too long, he wouldn't be too far away from it," said defensive end Jim Marshall. "We knew Paul would get there."

In first year with Vikings, Krause set a team record with seven interceptions, including picks in six straight games, another franchise mark. He stole five more passes in 1969, while another six interceptions followed in 1970. Krause finally overcame the undeserving labels and won All-Pro honors as well as his first of five straight Pro Bowl appearances in 1971. He later broke his own mark by reestablishing the Vikings' record for most interceptions in a season with an NFC-best 10 in 1975, the same year he was named All-Pro for the second time in purple.

"Paul can get the ball in a crowd very well," said defensive coordinator Bob Hollway. "He's a good, disciplined athlete who prevents opponents from throwing down the middle."

Krause also had a nose for the end zone. His first score as a Viking came on November 23, 1969, when the safety returned an interception 77 yards in a 52–14 win over Pittsburgh. Three years later, he scooped up a fumble and galloped 32 yards to paydirt in a 27–13 triumph over Green Bay on October 29, 1972, before racing 30 yards to score in a 45–41 victory at Los Angeles on November 19, 1972. He added another interception return for six points against Detroit on December 14, 1975, when he dashed 70 yards for the Vikings' only touchdown of the game.

"I believe I was an offensive kind of defensive back," said Krause, who missed just two games in 16 seasons. "When the ball went up, I thought it was just as much mine as it was the receiver's. The way I look at it is, I gave my offense the ball 81 times and stopped 81 defensive drives. That's pretty significant to me."

While his primary duties centered on playing safety for the Vikings, Krause also performed the unheralded task of holding for field-goal and extra-point attempts. Krause was near-perfect with his duties, executing 331 consecutive holds before mishandling two versus Pittsburgh on November 26, 1972. He even came through with a surprise. In overtime against the Bears on October 16, 1977, Krause took the long snap from center on a fake field-goal try and tossed a game-winning, 11-yard touchdown pass to Stu Voigt. As a result, he is the only defensive back in Minnesota history to complete a pass for a touchdown.

Still, Krause is best-known for his ability to thwart passing attempts by opposing quarterbacks. Two of his better performances took place against the 49ers. The first one occurred in the divisional playoff loss to San Francisco on December 27, 1970, when Krause returned one fumble for the game's first touchdown and ran another one deep into opposing territory. Three seasons later, on October 14, 1973, he picked off two Steve Spurrier passes in the fourth quarter at San Francisco to halt potential scoring drives in the Vikings' 17–13 victory.

Krause remained an effective performer through his final year in the league. A leg injury in 1978 cost him his starting job to Tommy Hannon, but Krause still played in every game. He then set the NFL record he shared with Emlen Tunnell by picking off the Rams' Vince Ferragamo on December 2, 1979, for his 80th career interception. He added the final one of his career later in the game by victimizing former teammate Bob Lee.

In addition to the league mark for interceptions, Krause holds numerous other standards in Viking history. His 53 career interceptions for Minnesota represent the team record, as do his 852 interception return yards in a career. Other franchise marks include most games played by a safety (171), most seasons with five or more interceptions (six), and most opponent fumble return yards in a career (143). He also played in four Super Bowls in purple and was named to the Vikings' Silver Anniversary All-Time Team in 1985.

"Winning 10 division titles is what really stands out in my mind," Krause said when he was elected to the Hall of Fame. "We were very close as a team. My biggest disappointment is that we didn't win a Super Bowl, even though we were there four times. That is really the only down thing in my career."

Todd Krueger

Season: 1987
Number: 5

Quarterback
Northern Michigan

Height: 6'5"
Weight: 210

Todd Krueger was a reserve quarterback for one Viking replacement game in 1987 but did not see any action.

L

Bob Lacey

Season: 1964   Center   Height: 6'3"
Number: 59   North Carolina   Weight: 205

Minnesota's sixth-round draft pick in 1964, Bob Lacey's career in the National Football League consisted of two games, one with the Vikings as a rookie and a second one with the New York Giants a year later, in 1965.

Chuck Lamson

Seasons: 1962–63   Safety   Height: 6'
Number: 21   Wyoming   Weight: 190

Chuck Lamson was the Vikings' fourth choice in their first draft, taken by general manager Bert Rose as a "future," meaning his services were not required until the 1962 season. That strategy brought to the Upper Midwest a former college quarterback who emerged as a hard-hitting strong safety and a sure tackler in the open field.

Lamson turned down higher offers from Oakland in the American Football League and Toronto in the Canadian Football League to sign with the Vikings. He saw action in 14 games as a rookie and 12 contests in 1963, and intercepted a pass in each of his two seasons in purple. He was traded with Terry Kosens, Ray Poage and Don Hultz to the Eagles in exchange for halfback Ted Dean and the rights to Bob Berry prior to the 1964 campaign before spending three years with the Los Angeles Rams.

Jim Langer

Seasons: 1980–81   Center   Height: 6'2"
Number: 58   South Dakota State   Weight: 253

The greatest center in Dolphins history, Jim Langer played the final two seasons of his 12-year, Hall-of-Fame career with the Vikings after he asked to be traded to Minnesota in order to be closer to his Royalton home. Miami officials complied by sending the center to the Twin Cities in September of 1980 for fifth- and sixth-round draft choices.

Quick and powerful with a non-stop motor, Langer eased the retirement of Mick Tingelhoff by tutoring the team's center-of-the-future, Dennis Swilley, and helping the entire offense that was in transition with young quarterback Tommy Kramer. Langer also led by example with his consistent play, taking the field in 13 regular-season games in 1980 and nine more in 1981 before calling it a career.

Bill Lapham

Season: 1961	Center	Height: 6'3"
Number: 52	Iowa	Weight: 238

Selected from Philadelphia in the expansion draft, Bill Lapham's claim to fame involved a hunting accident in which he was hit in the head with a bullet, yet suffered no ill effects. He also has the distinction of taking plenty of shots while serving as the Vikings' first center.

A journeyman who had toiled in 12 contests with the Eagles, Lapham started all 14 games in 1961 for Minnesota. He gave a solid effort but was part of a woeful offensive line that made life difficult for quarterback Fran Tarkenton and the Vikings' running backs. He lost his job to free agent Mick Tingelhoff the following summer and was released early in training camp.

Gary Larsen

Seasons: 1965–74	Defensive Tackle	Height: 6'5"
Number: 77	Concordia (Minn.)	Weight: 260

After serving one year as the top reserve of the Rams' "Fearsome Foursome," Gary Larsen joined Minnesota in 1965 and emerged as one of the key links of the "Purple People Eaters" by helping guide the Vikings to their first three Super Bowl appearances.

Larsen proved to be the perfect addition to the front wall that included Jim Marshall and Carl Eller upon his arrival from Los Angeles. He even looked the part, the quintessential Viking in that he was big, strong, blond and fearless. Acquired by Minnesota along with Jim Phillips in exchange for unsigned top pick Jack Snow, the ex-Marine and all-conference basketball player and Little All-American tackle at nearby Concordia College replaced veteran Jim Prestel as the starting defensive tackle midway through the 1965 season and immediately displayed his love of hitting opponents. He maintained that job throughout the 1966 slate, then split time at left tackle with rookie Alan Page in 1967.

Gary Larsen

The Vikings' coaching staff found starting jobs for both Larsen and Page in 1968. Considered one of the strongest men ever to wear the purple uniform, the durable Larsen worked on his balance and pass rush, enabling the entire Minnesota defense to improve. His aggressive approach helped him thwart the run in the middle of the defense, resulting in Pro Bowl appearances after the 1969 and 1970 season. He remained a dominating force in 1971, then suffered a broken arm that sidelined Larsen for the first half of the 1972 campaign before he rebounded to his stellar form during the season's latter half.

Larsen was back as the defense's anchorman in 1973. His season started by wearing uniform number 140. Actually, Larsen served as a walking billboard on the first day of training camp for head coach Bud Grant. After Minnesota endured a disappointing 7–7 season in 1972, Grant wanted his team to shoot for an undefeated campaign, and knew the determined Larsen would have no trouble getting across the message.

Throughout his career, Larsen could be found talking to himself on the bench prior to the opening kickoff. Using tactics he learned in the Marines, Larsen worked himself into a fury, becoming more hostile by the second. By the time he took the field, opposing offensive linemen found themselves embroiled in an all-out battle. Larsen, in fact, considered the opponent his enemy, people who were capable of taking food off his family's table, and compared life in the trenches to war. Larsen usually emerged the victor by stuffing the run and thwarting screens, draws and traps.

While Page, Marshall and Eller received the headlines by "meeting at the quarterback," Larsen provided the blue collar-effort by staying home and helping the Vikings win the war in the trenches. Yet, his most outstanding accomplishment came as a pass rusher. In a 24–10 win over Detroit on October 6, 1968, Larsen sacked Lions quarterback Bill Munson on three consecutive plays, making Larsen the only player in Minnesota annals to accomplish the feat. Another one of Larsen's most dominating performances took place in the 27–10 bashing of the Cowboys in the NFC Championship Game on December 30, 1973, with the defensive lineman recovering two fumbles in the game to help decide the outcome.

The 1974 slate proved to be Larsen's 11th and final season in the National Football League. He split time with Doug Sutherland, his heir apparent in the middle of the line, and helped lead the Vikings back to the Super Bowl. Always a philosopher in good times and bad, Larsen said after the loss to Pittsburgh, "Tomorrow, 800 million Chinamen are going to get up and not give a damn about who won or lost the Super Bowl." That proved to be his last appearance as a player. Larsen left the game as one of the most consistent, overpowering defensive linemen in Vikings' history, and was honored on Minnesota's Silver Anniversary All-Time Team in 1985.

Jim Lash

Seasons: 1973–76　　　Wide Receiver　　　Height: 6'1"
Number: 82　　　　　　Northwestern　　　　Weight: 192

Jim Lash, who set the Big Ten record with 226 receiving yards against Michigan State in 1972, brought his 4.55 speed in the 40 and the ability to catch passes in traffic to Minnesota when the Vikings drafted him in the third round in 1973. His speed was needed, for Gene Washington had been forced into retirement a year earlier.

As with any rookie, Lash needed time to adapt to the professional ranks. He started his first game in the National Football League, only to be replaced by veteran Carroll Dale during the second week of the 1973 campaign. Lash wound up catching just two regular-season passes as a rookie, but emerged in the postseason with a reception in each of the three games.

That post-season performance proved to be a harbinger. Lash lived up to his larger role in 1974 by ranking second on the team with 32 catches for 631 yards. His longest reception was a 57-yarder against New Orleans that set up a touchdown and enabled the Vikings to clinch the NFC Central with a 29–9 victory on December 1. He reached the end zone just once that season, but it was an important touchdown. Lash put the first points of the game on the board by scoring on a 29-yard toss from Fran Tarkenton in the second quarter of Minnesota's 14–10 victory over Los Angeles in the NFC Championship Game on December 29.

With John Gilliam signing to play in the World Football League, Lash looked to be the Vikings' go-to receiver in 1975, only to watch Gilliam return just as the regular season opened. Nevertheless, Lash pulled in 37 passes for 535 yards and four scores. Never did he display his speed any better than when he broke free from all Chicago defenders for a 45-yard touchdown reception to give Minnesota a 13–9 win on October 27. Another touchdown came on a fumble recovery in the end zone during a 35–13 win at Buffalo on December 20.

Although Gilliam was gone for good in 1976, the addition of Ahmad Rashad and rookie Sammy White limited Lash's contributions. He caught four passes for 52 yards in five games with the Vikings that season before being traded in October to the receiver-poor 49ers for running back Sammy Johnson.

Steve Lawson

Seasons: 1973–75   Guard   Height: 6'3"
Number: 65   Kansas   Weight: 265

    A starter for the Bengals in 1971 before injuries slowed his progress a year later, Steve Lawson joined the Vikings in 1973 and spent three seasons as a reserve guard on both the right and left side.

    Lawson, an All-American at Kansas who was acquired by the Vikings from Cincinnati for a third-round draft choice, was active for four games in his first year in purple. He started six times at left guard in 1974 before Andy Maurer was acquired from New Orleans. Lawson returned to reserve duty and saw action in 11 games in 1975.

    The following year in training camp, the 49ers lost three offensive linemen to injuries. With the Vikings set across the front wall, Minnesota sent Lawson to San Francisco for safety Windlan Hall just prior to the 1976 season.

Terry LeCount

Seasons: 1979–84, 1987   Wide Receiver   Height: 5'10"
Number: 80   Florida   Weight: 172

    Terry LeCount joined the Vikings off waivers from San Francisco prior to the fourth game of the 1979 season. Nicknamed "Ice Tea," LeCount gained single coverage in three-receiver formations due to the presence of Sammy White and Ahmad Rashad, helping the newcomer find his niche immediately. He led the team with a 19.8 yards-per-catch average on six receptions, two of which went for touchdowns, and contributed on special teams by downing punts deep in enemy territory for his best friend, Greg Coleman.

    LeCount continued to produce as the Vikings' third receiver in 1980, catching 13 passes for 178 yards while making 13 hits on special teams. The former Florida quarterback then put together the best season of his career in 1981. He caught 24 tosses for 425 yards and two touchdowns, and paced Minnesota with an average of 17.7 yards per reception. His best game in the National Football League also took place that season, in the 33–31 win over San Diego on October 11. Against the Chargers, LeCount grabbed six passes for 120 yards and two scores, rushed once for 17 yards, and recovered the onsides kick late in the contest that set up Rick Danmeier's game-winning field goal.

    An injury to White landed LeCount in the starting lineup for the final three games of 1982, the season he had 14 catches for 179 yards. The retirement of Ahmad Rashad gave LeCount a starting role for the first eight games of the 1983 campaign, when he added 21 receptions to his career total, yet lost his job with the first team while out with a sprained knee. Waived on September 11, 1984, after making one catch in two games, LeCount returned to play for the Vikings' replacement team for one outing in 1987.

Amp Lee

Seasons: 1994–96   Running Back   Height: 5'11"
Number: 32   Florida State   Weight: 197

    Minnesota's third-down back for three seasons, Amp Lee introduced himself to Vikings fans two years before wearing purple for the first time. As a member of the 49ers, Lee had a career-best day by rushing for 134 yards and a touchdown during San Francisco's 20–17 win over Minnesota on December 13, 1992.

    Released by the 49ers in 1994, Lee joined the Vikes and tied for third on the club with 45 receptions while rushing for 104 yards on 29 carries. His most productive game came in the 35–18 playoff loss to Chicago on January

1, 1995. Lee set a Minnesota post-season record by catching 11 passes, while his 159 yards represent the second-most by a Viking in a single playoff contest.

Lee was third on the team with 371 yards rushing and 71 catches in 1995. More quick than fast, he showed some breakaway ability in the 31–17 victory over Tampa Bay on December 3. Lee rushed for 90 yards on eight carries, among them a career-high 66-yard touchdown jaunt, which represented the eighth longest run in team annals at that time.

"When I am called on to go in on third down, I feel I have to convert," Lee said of his role. "From a team standpoint, you realize it can be a play that provides more chances to score during a drive instead of having to punt. It is a big down and you have to make a play."

His production was similar again in 1996, placing third on the club with 161 yards on the ground and 54 catches for two touchdowns. He also did an admirable job of returning punts for the injured David Palmer, averaging 8.4 yards on 11 returns and 10 fair catches. Yet, Lee's inability to fill the rushing shoes of the injured Robert Smith led to the Vikings' decision to sign Leroy Hoard during the season before re-signing Hoard prior to the 1997 campaign. With Smith returning as well, Lee was the odd-man out and wound up joining the Rams.

Bob Lee

Seasons: 1968–72, 1975–78 Quarterback-Punter Height: 6'2"
Number: 19 Pacific Weight: 195

Insurance in professional football is usually found on the bench. For eight seasons in the late 1960s and much of the 1970s, Bob Lee kept the Vikings' reserve quarterback role in good hands, always moving the offense in relief while stepping in and serving as the team's punter for two years. In fact, Lee owns the highest winning percentage of any Viking quarterback with at least 10 starts, going 9–2 (.818) in his 11 starting opportunities for Minnesota.

Lee overcame long odds by making the Vikings' reserve squad in 1968 as a 17th-round draft pick following a strong showing in training camp. He joined the active roster a year later as a third-string quarterback and regular punter, averaging 40 yards on 67 kicks. He had little difficulty overcoming inclement weather, and helped win two games for the Vikings during the championship season due to his outstanding punting in poor conditions.

He also performed well in poor weather while under center. In 1970, Lee started and won two games when Gary Cuozzo was injured, completing 47 of his 90 passes with five touchdowns in muddy wins over Boston (35–14 on December 13) and Atlanta (37–7 on December 20). He returned to punting after a one-year hiatus in 1971, averaging 39.5 yards on 89 punts, and guided the offense for four games down the stretch. He threw for 271 yards and two touchdowns in the season finale, a 27–10 victory at Chicago, enabling him to nearly match his 1970 output with 45 completions in 90 attempts for 598 yards and two scores. Lee also got the starting nod over Snead and Cuozzo for the playoff contest against San Francisco, yet was relieved after tossing two interceptions.

After seeing action in just two games in 1972, Lee played out his option and wound up being traded along with Lonnie Warwick to the Falcons for Bob Berry and a first-round draft pick. A starter in Atlanta who garnered the nickname "General Lee," he returned to Minnesota in 1975 as a free agent after Berry succumbed to a broken ankle, and threw two touchdown passes in his 14 mop-up attempts. He played in five games in 1976, keying a

17–6 win over Pittsburgh with a late touchdown pass to Ahmad Rashad on *Monday Night Football* on October 4. Lee also was one of the lone shining points for the Vikings in the 32–14 Super Bowl XI loss to Oakland by completing seven of nine tosses for 81 yards and a touchdown late in the contest.

Lee's biggest moments as a Viking occurred in 1977. With Fran Tarkenton out with a broken leg, Lee stepped in and guided Minnesota to three important victories. He completed 42 of 72 passes for four touchdowns, and was instrumental in the 14–7 playoff triumph over Los Angeles on December 26 in what many Vikings fans refer to as the "mud bowl game."

Tarkenton's return and the emergence of first-round pick Tommy Kramer limited Lee to four passes in 1978. Lee lost the reserve role to Steve Dils in 1979 and spent his last two seasons in the league with the Rams.

Carl Lee

Seasons: 1983–93 Cornerback Height: 5'11"
Number: 39 Marshall Weight: 188

His name might not be the first mentioned, but Carl Lee was one of the most consistent defensive backs ever to wear purple. He emerged as a starter in 1986, intercepted eight passes in 1988, and earned three consecutive trips to the Pro Bowl, from 1988–90.

Ironically, Lee nearly had his consistent seasons with Pittsburgh. After placing second on the Vikings with 17 special teams tackles as a rookie and playing out of position at free safety under head coach Les Steckel in 1984, Lee was released by returning head coach Bud Grant during training camp in 1985, only to be re-signed after veteran John Swain put in an unspectacular, nonchalant effort in the final pre-season game against Denver. Defensive backs coach Pete Carroll convinced Grant to bring back Lee, who was on the verge of coming to terms with the Steelers.

Minnesota's seventh-round draft pick in 1983, Lee was a track star in addition to an All-Southern Conference performer at Marshall. He used his exceptional speed to play in all 16 games as a rookie and perform admirably on special teams before emerging as the starting left cornerback for the last three games. Lee became the starting free safety in 1984 and responded with 100 total tackles, good for fourth on the club, prior to receiving his release the following year in training camp.

Back at cornerback upon his return, Lee started five games in 1985, tied Willie Teal for second on the club with three interceptions, and paced the team with 68 return yards. He was also eighth on the team with 87 tackles, and led the special teams with 21 solo hits.

Lee took over as a starter at cornerback in 1986, had three interceptions, and ranked third on the team with 64 solo tackles. He excelled in slowing down receivers at the line of scrimmage with his physical bump-and-run tactics. His best game came in the season finale against New Orleans, on December 21, when Lee led the defense with 10 unassisted hits and picked off two passes in Minnesota's 33–17 victory.

He then elevated the Minnesota defense to playoff contention in 1987 before blossoming into one of the game's better cornerbacks a year later. His dedication and work ethic made Lee the leader of the defensive secondary and helped earn him All-Pro recognition from the Associated Press and his first Pro Bowl job. He led the Vikings with eight interceptions in 1988, tying him for second in the NFC and ranking as the third-highest total for a single season in Vikings history. Lee returned a pick 48 yards for a touchdown

Carl Lee

against Miami on October 2. Two months later, on December 4 against New Orleans, he was named NFC co-Defensive Player of the Week after returning an aerial 58 yards for another six points while posting four defensed passes and three solo tackles in Minnesota's 45–3 win.

A second trip to the Pro Bowl came in 1989 after Lee intercepted two passes and made 57 solo tackles. He earned a third consecutive visit to Hawaii following the 1990 campaign, when Lee defensed 19 passes. He added 14 more passes defensed in 1991 before missing the final two games of the season with a wrist injury. Lee started all 16 contests in 1992 and pulled down two interceptions. In 1993, he was fourth on the team with 62 tackles and 77 solo stops and third on the club with three picks.

Despite his strong play, Lee's age and salary requirements caused the Vikings to release the cornerback after the 1993 season. He left Minnesota ranked first in passes defensed (128) and sixth in interceptions (29) and interception yardage (296). He also leads the Vikings with most starts by a cornerback with 144.

Jim Leo

Seasons: 1961–62 Defensive End Height: 6'2"
Number: 59 Cincinnati Weight: 225

Jim Leo registered the only two points of his National Football League career on December 9, 1962. The defensive end beat a block and dropped a Detroit ball carrier in the Lions' end zone for a safety in the Vikings' 37–23 loss at Tiger Stadium.

Although that safety proved to be one of Leo's highlights, he was a steady if unspectacular performer in purple during the franchise's first two seasons. Acquired from the Giants during the 1961 training camp for a seventh-round draft choice, Leo moved from linebacker to defensive end in Minnesota and joined the Vikings' starting lineup. He played in all 14 games in both 1961 and 1962, and led the team with eight tackles for lost yardage during his second campaign. His tenure with the Vikings proved short, however, when he lost his job in 1963 to rookie Don Hultz.

Darrell Lester

Season: 1964 Running Back Height: 6'2"
Number: 31 McNeese State Weight: 228

Darrell Lester may have been a running back who hailed from Lake Charles, Louisiana, the same hometown as halfback Tommy Mason, but that's where the similarities end. While Mason earned All-Pro honors with the Vikings, Lester was limited to six games on special teams and brief backup duty in 1964. Minnesota's ninth-round draft pick earlier in the year, he gained 18 yards on four carries as a rookie before moving on to Denver for the next two seasons.

Dave Lewis

Season: 1987 Running Back Height: 5'11"
Number: 49 Northern Iowa Weight: 200

Dave Lewis was on the Vikings' replacement team roster in 1987 but did not take the field.

Leo Lewis

Seasons: 1981–91
Number: 87
Wide Receiver
Missouri
Height: 5'8"
Weight: 170

"Little" Leo Lewis used his speed and quickness to not only survive among the National Football League's behemoths, but excel.

A former member of the Calgary Stampeders in the Canadian Football League, Lewis received a tryout invitation from head coach Bud Grant, who had played and coached the player's father. After a successful training camp in 1981, Lewis wound up playing 11 seasons in Minnesota to become the Vikings' all-time leader with 194 punt returns and 1,812 return yards. He also carried back one punt for a touchdown, a 78-yarder against Atlanta on November 22, 1987, marking only the fourth time in Minnesota history (and the first time in 19 years) a Viking returned a punt to paydirt.

Lewis was active for the last six games of the 1981 season and caught two passes for 58 yards. He played a bigger role in 1982, seeing action in every contest and catching eight passes for 150 yards with three touchdowns to tie for third on the team in scoring. He had a 31-yard reception against Chicago on November 28, and two scoring grabs against the Lions, a five-yarder and a 39-yard Hail Mary at the end of the half in a 34–31 victory on December 19 in the Silverdome.

After making 12 catches in 14 games in 1983, Lewis put together his best year in 1984 by leading the club with 47 receptions for 830 yards (good for seventh in the NFC) and four touchdowns, two of which came from Archie Manning in the second half against Washington on November 29. A sprained right arch limited Lewis to 29 catches for 442 yards and three scores in 1985, including the most timely reception of his career. In the waning moments of the October 20, 1985 matchup with San Diego in the Metrodome, Lewis caught a Tommy Kramer aerial in the end zone with 17 seconds left to give the Vikes a 21–17 victory.

He continued to show his big-play capability a year later, when Lewis ranked fourth on the team with 32 catches. He set a Viking single-game record by averaging 53 yards per reception versus Washington on November 2. He caught three tosses for 159 yards, including touchdown grabs of 68 and 76 yards. That record stood until Randy Moss eclipsed it against Dallas on November 26, 1998.

Lewis caught 24 passes with two touchdowns in 1987. In 1988, while his receiving role diminished to 11 receptions, he passed Charlie West and became the Vikings' all-time leader in career punt return yards and established single-season records with 58 punt returns and 550 yards. Lewis' 12 grabs in 1989 enabled him to move into the top 10 among Vikings' all-time receivers, while his punt return efforts earned Lewis a spot in the NFL record book. No one in league annals raised his hand more often when standing under punts than Lewis did during the 1989 season. Twenty-seven times he called for a fair catch. He also returned 44 punts and averaged an outstanding 10.1 yards per effort, with a season-long of 65 yards.

Released by the Vikings prior to the 1990 season, Lewis spent four games with Cleveland before returning to Minnesota and leading the team with 25 punt returns for 180 yards. After catching four passes in 1991 and returning 30 punts for 225 yards, Lewis' unlikely playing career in the NFL came to an end.

"I was always considered too small to play," Lewis said. "I made the best out of the situation. When I was called upon to get the job done, I did it. So overcoming those odds was the story of my entire career."

Since retiring as a player after the 1991 slate, Lewis has remained

Leo Lewis

Tough Enough To Be Vikings

Errol Linden

Seasons: 1962–65   Tackle   Height: 6'5"
Number: 73   Houston   Weight: 260

Acquired from Cleveland in the Fred Cox trade just prior to the 1962 season, Errol Linden was a useful offensive tackle for the Vikings. "Moose" saw limited during his first year-and-a-half with Minnesota until he took over the starting right tackle job midway through the 1963 campaign. He maintained the position in 1964 and 1965, helping Fran Tarkenton emerge as one of the league's elite passers while enabling the Vikings to pace the National Football League in rushing attempts in 1965.

After four years in purple, Linden had the opportunity to experience another expansion process when he was drafted by Atlanta from the veterans pool in 1966. He spent three years with the Falcons and two more with the fledgling Saints.

Everett Lindsay

Seasons: 1993–98   Offensive Lineman   Height: 6'4"
Number: 61   Mississippi   Weight: 302

Everett Lindsay was all but a savior in Minnesota during his rookie season. After Gary Zimmerman refused to play for the Vikings, the team had a tremendous hole at the all-important left tackle slot. Lindsay, a fifth-round draft choice, stepped in and started the first 12 games of the 1993 campaign before a shoulder injury ended his year. In the process, Lindsay became the first Minnesota rookie to start on the offensive line on opening day, and earned all-rookie recognition from *Football News*.

Unfortunately, following his quick start, Lindsay's career hit a series of road bumps. Moved to right guard in training camp in 1994 due to the drafting of left tackle Todd Steussie, Lindsay missed the regular season after blowing out his shoulder again. He served as a reserve guard while playing on the line on field goal attempts in 1995, then sat out all of 1996 upon injuring a knee while playing basketball in the offseason. After a stellar showing in the World League in 1997, Lindsay regained his confidence and returned to his reserve role before emerging as the starting center for the final three regular-season games as well as the playoffs following season-ending injuries to starter Jeff Christy and Scott Dill.

Lindsay continued to prove his value to the Vikings in 1998. Capable of playing all five line positions, he started at both tackle slots when Steussie and Korey Stringer missed time with injuries. He also stepped in for David Dixon at right guard on occasion. Regardless of where he lined up, Lindsay proved to be an aggressive run blocker and a capable performer in pass protection whose strength came from his tenacious approach. While he was not a full-time starter after his rookie year, Lindsay gave the Vikings a versatile sixth man, providing the type of superior depth all championship teams must have.

"We like Lindsay because he works hard and he's versatile," said head coach Dennis Green. "He can play tackle, guard or center. He's like a sixth starter for us."

Jim Lindsey

| Seasons: 1966–72 | Running Back | Height: 6'2" |
| Number: 21 | Arkansas | Weight: 205 |

With Dave Osborn and Bill Brown handling most of the running back chores, Jim Lindsey contributed to the Vikings' cause as a third-down back and captain of the special teams in the late 1960s and early 1970s.

Possessing loping speed and dependable hands, Lindsey helped the Vikings as a rookie after joining the team as a second-round draft choice in 1966. He scored three touchdowns during his first campaign in addition to rushing for 146 yards, catching 20 passes for 250 yards, and returning four kickoffs for a 19.7-yard norm. An Academic All-American in college, Lindsey served primarily as a blocker on offense in 1967, but earned the nickname "Captain Crunch" for his punishing hits on special teams.

Always ready when called upon by head coach Bud Grant, Lindsey helped the Vikings win their first Central Division title in 1968. He had several key runs while gaining 48 yards on 10 carries in the 14–10 victory over Green Bay on November 10, then scored the winning touchdown on a two-yard run in the 13–6 win at Detroit a week later. His efforts on the kick coverage units also led to Minnesota's first Super Bowl appearance in 1969, with Grant saying, "Special teams can turn a game around, and Jim Lindsey's leadership and example have done this."

Lindsey continued to serve in the special teams capacity for three more years, and added tight end to his job description in 1970. His 49-yard catch on a pass from his best friend, Gary Cuozzo, helped set up the winning touchdown in Minnesota's 24–20 win over Detroit on November 15. His most productive season on the ground occurred in 1971, when he rushed for 182 yards on 46 carries. He victimized the Lions again by recovering a fumble in the end zone for a touchdown on December 11, 1971. Lindsey then concluded his career in the National Football League on special teams in 1972, playing in 13 games for the Vikings.

Bob Lingenfelter

| Season: 1978 | Tackle | Height: 6'7" |
| Number: 76 | Nebraska | Weight: 277 |

The Vikings tried to arrange a trade for Bob Lingenfelter in the months leading up to the 1978 season but were rebuffed by the bearded offensive lineman's employer, the Cleveland Browns. Released by the Browns during the final cuts before working on his father's farm for a month, Lingenfelter signed with Minnesota in October of 1978 as a free agent and participated in five games. He returned to his father's farm a year later upon being waived by the Vikings in training camp.

Cliff Livingston

| Season: 1962 | Linebacker | Height: 6'3" |
| Number: 55 | UCLA | Weight: 215 |

At 215 pounds, Livingston may have been light for a linebacker, but many of his tackles felt like being struck by a Mack truck to opposing ball carriers. He spent the 1962 season with the Vikings, the ninth campaign of his 12-year career in the National Football League, and gave the young defense a hard-hitting presence. Just ask Green Bay's Paul Hornung, who was limited to nine games that year after being leveled by Livingston at Metropolitan Stadium on October 14.

After playing in 12 games with the Vikings in 1962, Livingston was traded with Clancy Osborne to the Rams for a sixth-round draft choice.

Mike Livingston

Season: 1980	Quarterback	Height: 6'4"
Number: 13	Southern Methodist	Weight: 210

An 11-year veteran with Kansas City, including five seasons as the Chiefs' starting quarterback, Mike Livingston spent most of the 1980 campaign with the Vikings. Serving as the third-stringer behind Tommy Kramer and Steve Dils, Livingston did not play in any games in purple prior to being waived on December 18.

Chris Liwienski

Season: 1998	Offensive Lineman	Height: 6'5"
Number: 76	Indiana	Weight: 308

Detroit's seventh-round draft pick in 1998, Chris Liwienski was released by the Lions in training camp and signed to the Vikings' practice squad in September. He joined the 53-man roster prior to Week 11 when fellow lineman Bob Sapp was suspended for violating the National Football League's policy on anabolic steroids. Liwienski showed potential as a right guard with his tough, hard-working approach while serving a reserve role for the final six games of the 1998 campaign.

Fletcher Louallen

Season: 1987	Safety	Height: 6'
Number: 38	Livingston	Weight: 191

Fletcher Louallen, who played one season with Birmingham in the United States Football League, started at free safety in the Vikings' three replacement games in 1987. He intercepted one pass and returned it 16 yards.

Terry Love

Season: 1987	Safety	Height: 6'2"
Number: 23	Murray State	Weight: 205

A three-year veteran of the United States Football League, Terry Love played one game with the Vikings' replacement team in 1987.

Kirk Lowdermilk

Seasons: 1985–92	Center	Height: 6'3"
Number: 63	Ohio State	Weight: 280

Few positions require more schooling than center. The job is so varied, ranging from calling the signals for the offensive line to forming a relationship with every quarterback on the team to handling all of his responsibilities in run- and pass-blocking against oncoming defensive linemen.

Kirk Lowdermilk was no different than most in that he required a couple seasons in the National Football League before emerging as a top-flight center. By the time he reached the lofty level of play, he had developed into a tough, scrappy, intense leader who was not afraid of the aggressive aspects of the job.

"Lowdermilk is a combination of (Mick) Tingelhoff and Jim Langer, a throwback to those type of guys," said John Michels, Minnesota's offensive line coach from 1967–93. "I can't give him a greater compliment than that. He's smart, he's aggressive and he challenges everybody, opposing linemen as well as his teammates.

"As an athlete, he has great pride. He has unbelievable balance, which he gets from his wrestling background as a varsity member of the Ohio

State wrestling team. And he's utterly fearless. I don't think he'd back down from the devil himself."

An example of Lowdermilk's toughness was seen against Tampa Bay on November 15, 1987. Lowdermilk left the game with a sprained knee, only to return three plays later after Dennis Swilley succumbed to a broken leg. He played the rest of the contest as well as the remainder of the season without missing a beat.

Lowdermilk also was well-versed in the tricks of the trade. He was adept at drawing offsides penalties from defensive linemen with his slight of hand and other nearly undetectable gyrations as the quarterback barked his signals. And while he often gave away pounds and inches to opposing defensive linemen, Lowdermilk more than held his own, slaying several giants with his combination of skill, positioning and sly tactics in the trenches.

He became the 59th player selected overall in the 1985 draft when the Vikings used their first third-round pick to take the Ohio State All-American. Lowdermilk's rookie season was limited to two late-season starts in addition to serving as the Vikings' long snapper and a blocker on the kickoff return team. He again saw action on special teams in the last 11 games of 1986 after an injured knee forced him to miss the first five contests.

Lowdermilk overtook Swilley at center in 1987 and started all 12 games and the three playoff contests. At 24, he was the youngest starting center in the league that season. His efforts escalated to honorable mention All-Pro recognition and a member of the All-Madden team in 1988 despite missing four games with a broken right thumb that prevented him from snapping the ball. He started every game in 1989, the same year his brother-in-law, kicker Rich Karlis, played for the Vikings. Lowdermilk then missed the opening game of the 1990 slate due to contract negotiations, forcing him out of the starting lineup for the first three contests.

In 1991, he overcame numerous nagging injuries to start all 16 games and anchor the line that helped Minnesota lead the league in rushing yardage. Lowdermilk started all 16 games again in 1992 and was nothing less than the heart-and-soul of a front wall that emerged as one of the league's best.

Despite being such a valuable contributor on the offensive line, Lowdermilk's value became too steep for the Vikings on the free-agent market. Admitting the offer was too good to turn down, he signed a three-year, $6 million deal with Indianapolis after the 1992 season.

Kirk Lowdermilk

Derrel Luce

Seasons: 1979–80 Linebacker Height: 6'3"
Number: 57 Baylor Weight: 227

Derrel Luce was acquired by the Vikings off waivers from Baltimore prior to the 1979 season and proceeded to play in all 16 games that year, starting two. He recovered a pair of fumbles, created one loose ball, and made 26 tackles, including seven on special teams. After completing his law degree in the offseason, Luce saw action in four contests in 1980 before being waived by Minnesota on September 30 and joining the Lions for the remainder of the campaign.

Bob Lurtsema

Seasons: 1971–76	Defensive End	Height: 6'6"
Number: 75	Western Michigan	Weight: 250

"Benchwarmer Bob" Lurtsema turned his reserve role on the defensive line into a lucrative business career, including appearing in advertisements for Twin City Federal and later owning a pair of restaurants and publishing *Viking Update*.

Lurtsema's entrepreneurial acumen, however, should take nothing away from his abilities on the gridiron. He broke into the National Football League in 1966 with the New York Giants and immediately took Don Davis' starting position at defensive end. Lurts held the job until he was released 10 games into the 1971 campaign, when, as the team's player rep, he gave owner Wellington Mara an honest answer regarding the owner's popularity (or lack thereof) among the troops.

The Vikings picked up Lurtsema three days after the Giants let him go, and he spent the next four full seasons giving the Purple People Eaters an occasional breather. Though versatile enough to play tackle or defensive end, he was most productive as a fifth lineman in passing situations, registering four sacks in both 1974 and 1975 and pouncing on two fumbles in the latter campaign. He was particularly effective in confusing the offense with head coach Bud Grant's last-second substitutions, a ploy NFL commissioner Pete Rozelle later ruled illegal.

It was also during that time Lurtsema began starring as "Benchwarmer Bob," the loveable loser in print and television advertisements, a gig that would last 13 years.

"I loved doing those commercials," Lurtsema said. "We'd have spots where there would be Carl Eller Day at The Met and show people scalping tickets to get in. Then they would have Bob Lurtsema Day and the place would be empty. At the end of the commercial I would say, 'At least my wife and kids could've shown up.' Those commercials have made me pretty well-known."

After playing in 44 games with the Vikings, Lurtsema spent the first contest of the 1976 season in Minnesota before being dealt to Seattle in the trade for Ahmad Rashad. He received a hero's welcome with special ceremonies upon his return to The Met on November 14, when Minnesota beat the Seahawks 27–21. Lurtsema retired from the game after two years with Seattle and returned to the Twin Cities, where his off-beat popularity continues to this day.

Mike Lush

Season: 1986	Safety	Height: 6'2"
Number: 27	East Stroudsburg	Weight: 195

The Vikings picked up Mike Lush on October 15, 1986, after the rookie from East Stroudsburg was let go by the Lions. A former player in the United States Football League, Lush took the field for six games with Minnesota and registered one tackle on special teams before landing on injured reserve on November 26.

Mark MacDonald

Seasons: 1985–88 Guard Height: 6'4"
Number: 71 Boston College Weight: 265

    Mark MacDonald was a reserve guard and special teams contributor during his three-plus seasons with the Vikings. A fifth-round draft pick in 1985, he started a career-high three games as a rookie in place of the injured Jim Hough. A left knee injury limited MacDonald to 10 relief appearances in 1986. A year later, he started against Tampa Bay on November 15 for the ailing Terry Tausch and served in a backup capacity during the other 11 games. Waived at the end of training camp in 1988, MacDonald returned to the Vikings on September 28 before receiving his final release in Minnesota on October 31, 1988.

Earsell Mackbee

Seasons: 1965–69 Defensive Back Height: 6'1"
Number: 46 Utah State Weight: 195

    The Vikings' scouts noticed Earsell Mackbee while watching film on Utah State tackle Jim Harris, Minnesota's fourth-round draft pick in 1965 who never joined the team. Mackbee, meanwhile, was a wide receiver and an excellent basketball player who signed as an undrafted free agent after a stint in Europe with the armed services. He impressed the Minnesota coaching staff with his speed, was moved to the secondary, and despite having never played defense, emerged as a tough, consistent performer in the defensive backfield for five seasons.

    Mackbee proved mature and confident from the start of his professional career. His time in the armed services meant Mackbee was older than most first-year players, and he refused to take the hazing all rookies experience. He was a full-blooded fighter, a warrior who took his job seriously. It was not long before Mackbee became one of the team's most respected players.

    The gritty, hard-hitting defender quickly developed a style that included bumping receivers all the way down the field. He also was not afraid to further the Vikings' reputation for punishing opponents. After watching Baltimore receiver Jimmy Orr burn the Vikings during a previous engagement, head coach Norm Van Brocklin told Mackbee to hit the Colt in the mouth on the first play of the game. Mackbee followed orders without blinking to start one of the grander in-game brawls in Minnesota annals.

    Mackbee opened the 1965 season on the taxi squad before joining the roster when cornerback Lee Calland succumbed to an injury. He took over the starting duties at left cornerback in the regular-season opener against San Francisco in 1966 and picked off two passes during the campaign. Mackbee further established himself in 1967 with five interceptions, among them a 32-yard dash to paydirt against Pittsburgh on November 26, and a 55-yard gallop for a touchdown on a fumble recovery during a 10–10 tie with the Lions on November 12. During the season, head coach Bud Grant described Mackbee as "one of the best corners in the league."

He continued to start in 1968 and intercepted two passes, including one against Green Bay on November 10 that clinched the Vikings' 14–10 win, their first victory ever over the Pack at The Met. Mackbee followed that performance with a career-high six interceptions in 1969. Three pickoffs came during a 24–10 win versus Detroit on October 26, tying the team record for the most picks in a game.

An example of how tough the left cornerback was could be seen in the last two games of his career in the National Football League. Mackbee injured his shoulder in the playoffs against the Rams, but returned in time to participate in the Super Bowl. He hurt the shoulder again versus the Chiefs, had it taped tighter, only to go down upon his return to the field. That ailment proved to be the beginning of the end for Mackbee, who reported to training camp with the Vikings in 1970 but did not play another regular-season game.

James Manley

Seasons: 1996–97 Defensive Tackle Height: 6'2"
Number: 75 Vanderbilt Weight: 305

Critics smirked when the Vikings took James Manley in the second round with the 45th overall pick in the 1996 draft. While Minnesota officials envisioned Manley as a run-stuffing tackle in the middle of the defensive line, others argued that Manley was a fringe professional player with little desire.

Those same critics said "I told you so" on September 22, 1997, the day the Vikings admitted their mistake by releasing Manley four weeks into the campaign. Inactive for 18 of his 20 regular-season games with Minnesota, Manley's only appearance came during mop-up time in the playoff loss to Dallas when he made three tackles.

Archie Manning

Seasons: 1983–84 Quarterback Height: 6'3"
Number: 4 Mississippi Weight: 211

After being physically battered as the Saints' lone bright spot throughout the 1970s, Archie Manning experienced little relief upon joining the Vikings via Houston on September 21, 1983. Manning arrived in Minnesota along with Dave Casper from the Oilers in exchange for second- and fourth-round draft picks.

The 34-year-old Manning missed most of the 1983 season with the Vikings due to a thyroid condition. In 1984, he relived the past in his first start. The former Pro Bowl performer completed 14 of 24 passes for 138 yards in a loss at Chicago on October 28 before suffering a mild concussion while being sacked for the 11th time in the contest. He later suffered a bruised tailbone in his second and final start in purple, a 51–7 loss on December 8 versus San Francisco. His best showing was a relief appearance against Washington on November 29, when he completed half of his 22 tosses for 164 yards and two touchdowns to lead a 17-point second half.

For the season, Manning was successful on 52 of 94 passes for two touchdowns and three interceptions. His tenure with the Vikes, as well as his career in the National Football League, came to an end during training camp in 1985.

Greg Manusky

Seasons: 1991–93   Linebacker   Height: 6'1"
Number: 91   Colgate   Weight: 233

Due to the presence of Ray Berry and Jack Del Rio at middle linebacker, Greg Manusky never became a starter in Minnesota as he had been with the Redskins. Nevertheless, Manusky contributed with his all-out hustle and inspirational leadership on special teams. His efforts were so impressive that he was named the special teams player on the All-Madden team in 1991.

Manusky placed second on the team with 22 stops on special teams in his first year with Minnesota. He ranked third in 1992 with 17 hits, even though he missed five games with a bruised kidney, and paced the club with 26 tackles on the kick coverage units in 1993.

Cut unexpectedly during training camp in 1994, Manusky signed with Kansas City and played the next five seasons at linebacker and on special teams with the Chiefs.

Ed Marinaro

Seasons: 1972–75   Running Back   Height: 6'2"
Number: 49   Cornell   Weight: 212

Long before Ed Marinaro became a well-known television actor on *Hill Street Blues*, he spent six seasons in the National Football League, the first four coming with Minnesota. The Vikings' second-round draft pick in 1972, the sure-handed Cornell product, who established several NCAA rushing records and was runner-up in balloting for the Heisman Trophy as a senior, gained 223 yards on the ground and 218 yards on 28 catches as a rookie, leading head coach Bud Grant to say, "We were not disappointed in what we saw, but we want to see some more."

With the arrival of Chuck Foreman and Brent McClanahan in 1973, Marinaro never equalled his college accomplishments in the professional ranks. Still, he was a dependable receiver out of the backfield who joined Foreman as a starter during the latter part of the 1975 season. Though not blessed with great speed, his evasiveness and strong repertoire of moves in the open field made life difficult for linebackers and defensive backs.

Despite the arrival of Foreman, Marinaro was the Vikes' third-leading rusher and pass receiver in 1973, gaining 302 yards on 95 carries and 196 yards on 26 receptions. One of his best days as a Viking came during his second pro season, on October 7 at Tiger Stadium. Marinaro hauled in nearly identical swing passes of 12 and eight yards for touchdowns in the first quarter to lead Minnesota to a 23–9 triumph over Detroit. His production slipped in 1974 to 124 rushing yards and 132 yards on 17 catches.

By 1975, Marinaro's role came primarily as a receiver and a blocker for Foreman. While he rushed for only 101 yards, he excelled in quarterback Fran Tarkenton's short passing game. Marinaro pulled in a career-high 54 receptions for 462 yards, reaching paydirt on three occasions. During a 28–13 win over San Diego on November 23, he caught a team-record 11 passes, among them Tarkenton's record-setting 2,931st career completion. With Foreman also catching more than 50 tosses, the two became the NFL's first running back tandem to accomplish the feat.

Marinaro's days in purple came to an end the following year when he played out his option and signed with the New York Jets just prior to the 1976 season.

Jim Marshall

| Seasons: 1961–79 | Defensive End | Height: 6'4" |
| Number: 70 | Ohio State | Weight: 240 |

Jim Marshall

In the late 1950s and early 1960s, Paul Brown had a problem every owner and coach in the National Football League would love to possess. The head man of the Cleveland Browns had so much talent that he had to constantly unload players. But instead of simply releasing players, Brown would package them to teams he considered minimal threats in exchange for draft picks.

Such was the case in 1961, when Brown and Minnesota general manager Bert Rose came to terms on a trade that brought Marshall, Paul Dickson, Jim Prestel, Jamie Caleb, Dick Grecni and Billy Gault to the Vikings in exchange for second- and 11th-round picks. While it was not one of Brown's better deals, it is without question the best trade in purple annals and a major reason the franchise reached respectability as quickly as it did.

Marshall went on to play the next 18 seasons with the Vikings. No lineman ever got off the ball faster than Marshall, who used his outstanding power, acceleration, agility and range to foil countless plays. He possessed as much speed as many receivers and backs. He also succeeded by giving every ounce of energy he possessed on every play, even outhustling rookies during training camp, enabling him to lead the Vikings in sacks during the team's first six seasons and record more than 950 tackles during his career.

Drafted sixth by the Browns in 1960 after passing up his senior year at Ohio State to play the 1959 season with Saskatchewan in the Canadian Football League, Marshall saw action in 12 games with Cleveland before being stricken with encephalitis while stationed at an army training camp in the spring of 1961. The lineman lost 40 pounds and was told he would not play football again. He instead fought the ailment and reported to the Browns' training camp. Still in the recovery phase, Marshall was deemed expendable by the contending Cleveland club. Traded to Minnesota, he joined the starting lineup after two days in Bemidji and immediately contributed to the expansion team's cause.

Head coach Norm Van Brocklin admired the youngster from the start, saying Marshall was the quickest defensive lineman he had ever seen. Marshall reciprocated the compliment, crediting the Dutchman's confidence for his early success in Minnesota.

"Norm gave me an opportunity to play when I wasn't completely healthy," Marshall said. "I think the type of pressure he put on me—by handing me a job—helped me develop. I had to play regardless of how I felt. I had to push myself to the limits and it helped me. Then I got stronger and my health improved."

Marshall's durability and consistency proved strong enough that the lineman put together one of the more amazing statistics in pro football annals. By the time his career came to an end after the 1979 season, Marshall had started an NFL-record 282 straight games, including the first 270 contests in Minnesota history.

"I never even thought about taking a day off," Marshall said. "People brought it up once in a while, but I wanted to play. I loved the game and I loved being out there. I didn't ever want to miss a game."

"Jim Marshall is one of those rare people who has the durability to play this game," head coach Bud Grant said during Marshall's career. "There is no question he does get hurt from time to time, but it does not affect the caliber of his play. He is one of the great football players.

"Durability breeds greatness, and Jim is a durable guy who loves to play football. He's a marvel to all of us who are close to him. He has such resiliency week after week. After we play a game on an artificial field, others will be stiff and sore; Jim comes out like a colt."

Making that string more incredible was Marshall's various ailments. He suffered through a sleeping sickness for much of his career. A gun enthusiast, he accidently shot himself below the rib cage shortly after joining the Vikings. Another time he was hospitalized for nearly a week when a grape became lodged in his windpipe. Marshall also tempted fate with his numerous interests, among them parachuting from as high as 32,900 feet, skiing and scuba diving.

"I guess I've always felt there are so many things in this world to do," Marshall said. "I owe it to myself as an individual to try as many as I can. But I feel I have a great rapport with my body. With my mind and body working together, I can accomplish much more than I would trying to work strictly on the physical or mental planes. I think it is this harmony within me that enables me to continue playing even under very adverse conditions."

Adding to Marshall's off-beat career was one of the game's all-time bloopers. On October 25, 1964, at Kezar Stadium, the lineman ran the length of the field with a fumble, only to give the 49ers a safety. Minnesota led San Francisco 27–17 in the fourth quarter when the 49ers' Billy Kilmer fumbled after catching a pass from George Mira. Marshall scooped the pigskin into his palms and took off for the end zone. When he crossed the goal line some 66 yards later, Marshall heaved the ball in the air, only to be patted on the head by San Francisco center Bruce Bosley, who informed the defensive end about what he had done.

Marshall took in stride the ribbing from his teammates, particularly when they kidded him about wanting the defensive end to pilot the plane home in hopes of landing in Hawaii. However, he was crushed by the subsequent laughter that arose in the press. The play wound up having no effect on the score, with the Vikings coming out on top, 27–22. In fact, Marshall had been a hero just a few plays before the safety. He had crushed Mira and caused a fumble that Carl Eller picked up and ran 45 yards for what proved to be the Vikings' deciding touchdown.

Despite the blooper, Marshall was one of the game's best defensive players in league history. Superb against the run, he dominated while rushing the quarterback. He attacked like a coiled snake, the quickest striking force in football. He was credited with telling other members of the Purple People Eaters, "Let's meet at the quarterback." By the time he took an encore ride around The Met in the back of a convertible after his final game, Marshall was among the NFL's all-time leaders with 127 sacks, a total that ranks second in Viking history, just three behind Eller.

While Marshall was the most consistent performer in the Minnesota defense during the franchise's first two decades, he made constant improvements to his game, many of which led the Vikings to the NFL Championship in 1969. "My style has changed," Marshall said in 1969, three years after becoming the team's defensive captain. "The same is true of the entire unit. It used to be more of an individual pass rush. Now each member of the defensive unit is more dependent on every other member."

Bob Hollway, Minnesota's defensive coordinator from 1967–70 and 1978–86, was more succinct, saying, "Jim's one of the finest athletes I've seen who gets better every year." Grant described Marshall as one of the key components in the head coach's disciplined approach after taking over the team in 1967, adding, "We couldn't have made it without Jim."

Rewarded for his efforts with Pro Bowl honors in 1968 and 1969, Marshall registered his first safety by dumping Packers quarterback Bart

Starr for two points in Milwaukee during a 26–13 victory on September 22, 1968. He has said on several occasions that while the 1970s represented the team's greatest string of success, the 1969 campaign holds a special place in his memory bank.

"One period in particular stands out as memorable," Marshall said. "Against the Rams in the '69 playoffs, we had periods in that game when we were bending, but the fans' enthusiasm was so infectious, it kept us from breaking. We came back to win that game and beat Cleveland a week later. That may have been the most memorable two games of my career."

Marshall established records on a regular basis during the final few years of his amazing career. He set the NFL mark with his 26th fumble recovery during a 38–0 win over Atlanta in 1975. A year later, he climbed to the top of two more NFL charts—most consecutive games played (236) and most games played with one team (224).

The defensive end continues to hold numerous team marks, most of which will not be broken, including most years of service (19), most games played (270), most consecutive games played (270), most games started (270), most consecutive games started (270), most opponents' fumble recoveries (29), and is tied for first with most times leading the team in sacks (six, from 1961–66). He registered 701 solo tackles and 258 assists, played in four Super Bowls, served as defensive captain during his final 14 seasons, and was named to the Vikings' Silver Anniversary All-Time Team in 1985. Simply put, his omission from the Pro Football Hall of Fame is a travesty.

Larry Marshall

Season: 1974 Defensive Back Height: 5'10"
Number: 48 Maryland Weight: 195

Larry Marshall saw action in five games with Minnesota during the first half of the 1974 season. The former Chief returned five punts for 46 yards (9.2 average) and four kickoffs for a mediocre 56 yards and one fumble. Having failed to impress the Vikings' brass, Marshall finished the year with Philadelphia before spending four more seasons in the league.

Amos Martin

Seasons: 1972–76 Linebacker Height: 6'3"
Number: 55 Louisville Weight: 228

Amos Martin's most important game with the Vikings came during one of his last appearances in purple. Martin started at middle linebacker for the injured Jeff Siemon in the NFC Championship Game against Los Angeles on December 26, 1976, and his steady performance helped Minnesota reach its fourth Super Bowl by defeating the Rams, 24–13.

Otherwise, Martin's greatest contributions in five years with the Vikes came as a reserve linebacker at all three positions and on special teams. An offensive guard in college and the Vikings' sixth-round draft pick in 1972, Martin moved across the line and beat out a couple of veterans to win a roster spot as a rookie. After playing in five games his first year, Martin started three times in 1973, replacing an injured Wally Hilgenberg at right linebacker twice and Roy Winston on the left side once. His playing time increased in 1974, resulting in a 15-yard fumble recovery return for a touchdown in the season-opening 32–17 win over Green Bay on September 15 and three interceptions on the season. A knee injury limited Martin to five games in 1975 before seeing action in every contest a year later.

Martin's time with the Vikings ended just prior to the 1977 season, when he and Autry Beamon were traded to Seattle for an eighth-round draft pick.

Billy Martin

Season: 1968   Tight End   Height: 6'4"
Number: 89   Georgia Tech   Weight: 235

Acquired from Atlanta in 1968 in exchange for defensive tackle Jerry Shay, Billy Martin's lone season with the Vikings and his last year in the National Football League involved sharing time at tight end with John Beasley and splitting the punting chores with King Hill.

The former All-American at Georgia Tech pulled in 10 passes for 101 yards, and scored the first playoff points in Viking lore with a one-yard touchdown pass from Joe Kapp against Baltimore on December 22. Martin also punted the pigskin 28 times for a 37.4-yard average during the regular season.

Chris Martin

Seasons: 1984–88   Linebacker   Height: 6'2"
Numbers: 56, 94, 98, 57   Auburn   Weight: 231

Chris Martin put together a solid career with the Vikings by serving on special teams and as a part-time starting linebacker. Acquired off the waiver wire just prior to the first game of the 1984 season, Martin received most of his playing time during the final 10 contests of the 1986 campaign, when he was the starting strong-side linebacker. He finished that year ranked ninth on the team with 65 tackles, while recovering a loose ball against Chicago on October 5 and forcing a fumble against Cleveland on October 26.

Martin's biggest play in purple occurred during his first year with the Vikings. Playing all 16 games and starting against the Redskins in 1984, Martin picked up a fumbled punt and returned it eight yards for a touchdown against Detroit on September 23, giving the Vikings a 23–14 lead in their 29–28 win. In 1985, he saw action in 12 contests and made 95 tackles while battling a knee injury. After a solid 1986 showing, he played in 12 games in 1987, starting four, with his best performance being his five tackles against the Raiders on November 8 and his three solo hits in the 36–24 playoff victory over San Francisco on January 9, 1988.

Martin contributed in nine games during the 1988 season, scoring his second career touchdown when he recovered a fumble in the end zone in Minnesota's 31–7 win over the Bears on September 18. Waived by the Vikings on November 1, he was picked up by Kansas City and played with the Chiefs for three years before spending two seasons with the Rams.

Doug Martin

Seasons: 1980–89   Defensive End   Height: 6'3"
Number: 79   Washington   Weight: 258

For the fourth time in six years, the Vikings used their first-round draft choice on a defensive lineman in 1980. Minnesota plucked Doug Martin with the ninth overall selection, adding him to a stable that included fellow top picks Mark Mullaney (1975), James White (1976) and Randy Holloway (1978). Of the four, Martin had perhaps the most productive career.

Martin's early days with the Vikings were far from smooth. He reported late in 1980 after holding out due to a contract dispute and did not get in good playing shape until midseason, yet still finished second on the team with 4.5 sacks. He started the first eight games of the 1981 season at right end before being replaced by Holloway, thanks to Martin's reluctance to go all-out on every play. Nevertheless, he tied for second on the team with 5.5 sacks.

It was during his third season in the National Football League that Martin emerged as one of the loop's best defensive linemen. He blossomed upon moving to the left side in 1982 by flip-flopping positions with Mullaney. Martin earned All-Pro recognition from *Pro Football Weekly* for leading the league with 10.5 sacks, causing three fumbles and making 32 tackles. On many occasions, he spent more time in the opponents' backfield than the ball carriers. That type of performance is what Bud Grant had been expecting, and allowed Martin to escape from the head coach's doghouse.

Also helping Martin emerge was the strong play of nose guard Charlie Johnson, who was acquired from Philadelphia before the 1982 season. "The defense as a whole got better as a result of Doug's play," Grant said in 1982, "and he got better as a result of other people's play, too." Martin dominated against Detroit by intercepting a pass, causing a fumble that Johnson returned 44 yards to paydirt, and adding three sacks, three solo tackles and one assist in Minnesota's 34–31 win at the Silverdome on December 19, 1982.

Martin had 12 sacks to lead the team for the third straight year in 1983 while playing left end in the 3–4 defense and left tackle in the 4–3 alignment. His best performance of the season came against Green Bay on October 23, when he had eight tackles, three assists and four sacks for 32 yards.

A sprained ankle and other ailments limited Martin to six starts and one sack in 1984. He returned to the starting lineup for most of the 1985 slate and recorded four sacks. He got the year off to a good start by recovering a fumble and returning the loose ball to the 49er 1-yard line to set up the tying score in Minnesota's 28–21 win over San Francisco on September 8, 1985. In 1986, Martin was named NFC Defensive Player of the Month for September after registering eight unassisted tackles, six assists, three sacks, two forced fumbles and one fumble recovery in the season's first four games. He finished the year leading the team with three forced fumbles, and was second with nine sacks.

Another nine-sack season followed in 1987 before a contract squabble cost Martin the first three weeks of the 1988 season and a knee injury forced the lineman out of the final two games as well as the playoffs. He played in just seven games in 1989 before his 10-year NFL career came to a close. He retired with 50.5 sacks in 126 games.

Tommy Mason

Seasons: 1961–66 Running Back Height: 6'1"
Number: 20 Tulane Weight: 196

Tommy Mason was the first player ever drafted by the Vikings, selected with the first overall pick in November 1960. That choice proved to be one of the primary reasons Minnesota never slipped to the ranks of the pathetic during the team's infancy. Although Mason never established milestones worthy of his tremendous talent and unmatched effort due to the compilation of numerous ailments that professional football offers its participants, the picture-book halfback still was among the National Football League's premier runners during his six seasons in purple.

Mason possessed a slashing style that continually improved due to his willingness to learn from his coaches and veteran teammate Hugh McElhenny. He shook off a pinched nerve in his neck suffered during the preseason to rush for 226 yards on 60 carries as a rookie. He also returned a team-high 14 punts for 146 yards, and led the Vikings with 1,097 total yards.

The guitar-playing Tulane graduate took over the starting duties at halfback four games into the 1962 season and used his 9.8 speed in the 100-yard dash and his plethora of moves to finish with 740 yards and two touchdowns on the ground. He also became one of quarterback Fran Tarkenton's favorite targets. By perfecting the swing-and-up toss with the quarterback by always getting open when matched one-on-one with a linebacker, Mason pulled in 36 receptions for 603 yards and four more scores. He finished the year leading the Vikings with 1,696 combined yards.

His best game that year came against Philadelphia, when Mason scored three touchdowns, one of which was a 74-yard pass reception from Tarkenton, in a 31–21 victory on October 28. Another stellar performance came on December 9, when Mason warmed up the 21-degree day at Tiger Stadium with a combined 235 yards against Detroit. He set a team record with 138 yards rushing on 16 carries, caught three passes for 55 yards, and returned two kickoffs for 37 yards. Included in his rushing total was a 71-yard scamper to the Lions' 1-yard line in the third quarter. A week later, he increased the team mark by galloping for 143 yards on 20 carries against the Colts to finish 10th among the NFL's leading rushers.

Mason became the Vikings' first consensus All-Pro a year later after placing fourth in the league in rushing with 763 yards on 166 attempts for a 4.6-yard average. He also caught 40 passes for 365 yards and two touchdowns during the campaign. Mason got the 1963 season off on the right note when his two-yard plunge gave the Vikings a 24–20 victory over the 49ers on September 15. Among his feats was a 70-yard touchdown run against Baltimore on his way to 146 yards on November 17. The following week, Mason ran for two touchdowns, including the game-winner, to help Minnesota beat the Lions for the first time ever, 34–31.

Mason's production declined in 1964 after he suffered a hyperextended elbow in the season's second game, against the Bears, that limited his output during the first half of the season. He still managed to be the NFL's eighth-leading rusher that year with 691 yards, with 51 coming on an audible up the middle versus Chicago that set the tone in the Vikings' 41–14 victory on December 13. He also made mince-meat of the Colts' defense yet again, gaining 137 yards on 20 carries at The Met on September 13. Bill Brown also gained 103 yards in that contest, making them the first duo to post 100-yard games in the same contest in Vikings history.

More injuries cost Mason four full games in 1965, when he gained 597 yards on 141 carries. Even so, head coach Norm Van Brocklin praised his halfback, saying, "We know that when Mason's healthy, he's the best running back in the National Football League." He underwent knee surgery after the 1965 season and was banged up again during an early-season loss to Dallas in 1966. "Torrid Tommy's" ailing knees wound up limiting him to 235 rushing yards on 58 carries, with more than a fifth of his output coming on a 52-yard touchdown run against Baltimore on September 18.

With his production in decline and his knees in constant pain, Mason was packaged with Hal Bedsole and a second-round draft pick to Los Angeles in exchange for Marlin McKeever and a first-round pick, which turned out to be Alan Page. Upon his departure, Mason ranked as the leader in most Viking offensive categories. He rushed for more than 100 yards on six occasions during his days in purple. His name remains prominent in the Minnesota record book, including most consecutive games with a touchdown (six, tied for second), career average gain per carry (4.27, second), average per carry in one game (12.2 against Baltimore on November 17, 1963, first), most touchdowns in a game (three, against San Francisco on October 24, 1965, tied

Tommy Mason

for first), most consecutive games rushing for a touchdown (five, second) and punt return average for a rookie (10.4 yards, first).

Andy Maurer

Seasons: 1974–75   Guard   Height: 6'3"
Number: 66   Oregon   Weight: 265

The acquisition of Andy Maurer from New Orleans for a third-round draft pick during the 1974 season allowed Ed White to shift back to his natural right guard position, where he went on to have a Hall of Fame-caliber career. Maurer, meanwhile, played eight games that year with the Vikings and joined the starting lineup at left guard during the ninth contest.

After performing well in his first season with Minnesota, Maurer began the 1975 campaign as the first-string left guard, lost the job to John Ward, then regained it. Maurer wound up starting seven games as well as the playoff meeting with Dallas while playing in all 15 contests. Released the following summer in training camp, he played with San Francisco and Denver in 1976 and 1977, respectively.

Chad May

Season: 1995   Quarterback   Height: 6'1"
Number: 5   Kansas State   Weight: 219

Chad May did nothing to ingratiate himself with the Vikings during his brief tenure with the team. He sulked about falling to the fourth round of the 1995 draft after hoping to be a first-round selection. His cocksure attitude did not impress his teammates, and his failure to pick up the Minnesota system irritated the coaching staff. As a result, he saw no action as a rookie in 1995 and, instead of becoming the Vikings' quarterback-of-the-future, lost the third-string job to unheralded Jay Walker during the 1996 training camp.

Marc May

Season: 1987   Tight End   Height: 6'6"
Number: 88   Purdue   Weight: 295

Marc May's most outstanding attribute was his size as the Vikings' tight end on the 1987 replacement team. In his three starts, he caught one pass and carried the pigskin 22 yards before fumbling.

Doug Mayberry

Seasons: 1961–62   Running Back   Height: 6'1"
Number: 35   Utah State   Weight: 220

The Vikings' 10th-round selection in their first draft, Doug Mayberry possessed one of the most impressive physiques on a team that had a whole city's worth of beer bellies in 1961.

Primarily a special teams performer, "The Horse" carried the football 13 times for 40 yards as a rookie prior to having difficulty holding onto the pigskin a year later. Although he gained 274 yards on 74 carries, he lost the ball five times in 1962, the most crucial coming late in the game at Chicago in what turned out to be a 31–30 Bears' victory on November 11. On a more positive note, both of Mayberry's scores came in the same game. He tallied a touchdown on a 13-yard pass from Fran Tarkenton in the first quarter and galloped five yards up the middle to paydirt in the second quarter of the Vikings' 38–14 win over the Rams on October 21.

His inability to hang on to the football forced Mayberry to conclude his professional career with the Raiders in 1963.

Mike Mayes

Season: 1991 Cornerback Height: 5'10"
Number: 23 Louisiana State Weight: 187

The Vikings picked up Mike Mayes on October 16, 1991, and fielded the former New York Jet in nine contests over the remainder of the season. In his first game as a Viking, Mayes blocked an extra-point attempt against New England on October 20. Playing on special teams and as a reserve defensive back, Mayes made six tackles, and registered a sack against Green Bay on December 21. He was released the following season in training camp.

Kivuusama Mays

Season: 1998 Linebacker Height: 6'3"
Number: 53 North Carolina Weight: 244

Drafted in the fourth round in 1998, Kivuusama Mays spent most of his first year playing on special teams and as a backup middle linebacker. He emerged as the leader of the special teams by bursting through wedges to pace the kick coverage unit with 20 tackles. His best play came during the 38–28 win over Baltimore on December 13. The rookie turned the game's momentum with a devastating hit on Corey Harris to force a fumble that Mays recovered. Said special teams coach Gary Zauner, "He puts an exclamation point on what we call setting the tempo."

Stafford Mays

Seasons: 1987–88 Defensive Tackle Height: 6'2"
Number: 73 Washington Weight: 264

Though productive while with the Vikings, Stafford Mays probably grew leery of reading the transactions in the newspaper. Signed and released by Minnesota during training camp in 1987, Mays rejoined the Vikings for the final two replacement games, registering three sacks. He remained with the club when the parody ended and started four games in place of the injured Keith Millard. Mays finished the slate ranked third on the defense with seven sacks and tied for the team lead with two fumble recoveries. His best game came against the Bears on December 6, when he had two sacks, one forced fumble and a fumble recovery.

Waived at the end of training camp in 1988 and re-signed four days later, Mays was released for the final time by the Vikings after the first regular-season game, in which he made three tackles.

Brent McClanahan

Seasons: 1973–80 Running Back Height: 5'10"
Number: 33 Arizona State Weight: 202

Brent McClanahan was drafted four picks after first-rounder Chuck Foreman in 1973, and for a couple of seasons in the mid-1970s, the two formed the Vikings' starting backfield behind quarterback Fran Tarkenton.

McClanahan possessed 4.7 speed in the 40, making him a valuable man when carrying the ball and on special teams. As a rookie, he ranked fifth in the NFC by averaging 25.6 yards on 16 kickoff returns. His production fell to a 23.9-yard norm in 1974 before becoming a greater part of the offense a year later.

He started the first two games in 1975 while Foreman was sidelined with a bruised knee. McClanahan began the year with 61 yards rushing along with six receptions for 73 yards in a season-opening 27–17 victory over San Francisco on September 21. His highlight that season came in the playoff game against Dallas on December 28, when McClanahan scored the go-ahead touchdown in the fourth quarter before disaster struck in the 17–14 loss. By the end of the campaign, he had emerged as the team's third-leading rusher with 336 yards on 92 carries while averaging 21.2 yards on 17 returns.

A starting job, alternating between halfback and fullback with Foreman, followed in 1976 and 1977. McClanahan excelled in Tarkenton's short-yardage passing game, ranking third among NFC running backs with 40 receptions for 252 yards and a touchdown. He also rushed for 382 yards and three scores, with his biggest day coming when he gained 101 yards on 20 attempts in the 35–20 playoff win over Washington on December 18. He established the tone of the game by racing 41 yards on the first play from scrimmage to set up the Vikings' first touchdown. In fact, Foreman gained 105 yards in the contest, making them the first pair of Viking running backs to gain more than 100 yards in the same game since Bill Brown and Tommy Mason accomplished the feat in 1964. Yet, three weeks later in Super Bowl XI, McClanahan saw the other side of success when he fumbled at the goal line following a first-quarter blocked punt against Oakland.

McClanahan returned in 1977 to rank second on the team with 324 yards on 95 carries while catching 34 passes for 276 yards. His best game was a 53-yard effort on the ground and eight catches for 87 yards and two touchdowns in the 42–10 win over Cincinnati on November 13. He wound up starting all 14 games before knee surgery sidelined him for the playoffs.

Rickey Young's arrival in 1978 relegated McClanahan to special teams and an occasional third-down play on offense during his final three years in purple. He caught a combined 12 passes in 1978 and 1979 before being waived on October 30, 1980.

Skip McClendon

Season: 1992　　　　Defensive Tackle　　　　Height: 6'7"
Number: 96　　　　Arizona State　　　　Weight: 302

Skip McClendon's time in purple was brief. After making the roster out of training camp in 1992, the reserve defensive tackle was released four games into the slate to make room for rookies Tripp Welborne and Roy Barker, both of whom were activated from the injured reserve list.

John McCormick

Season: 1962　　　　Quarterback-Punter　　　　Height: 6'1"
Number: 15　　　　Massachusetts　　　　Weight: 208

A strong-armed reserve quarterback, John McCormick took over the punting duties from Mike Mercer midway through the 1962 campaign. The rookie did the unthinkable in the eyes of many observers by performing worse than his predecessor. McCormick averaged 39 yards on 46 punts while completing seven of 18 passes for 104 yards with five interceptions. After one season in Minnesota, he spent four more years in the American Football League with Denver and punted once.

Sam McCullum

Seasons: 1974–75, 1982–83　　　　Wide Receiver　　　　Height: 6'2"
Numbers: 84, 80　　　　Montana State　　　　Weight: 190

Sam McCullum sandwiched an outstanding six-year stint as a Seahawk with two tours of duty with Minnesota.

The Vikings' ninth-round draft pick in 1974, the quick receiver known as "Sudden Sam" made the most of his rookie-year opportunities by scoring three touchdowns on his seven catches. His first reception in the National Football League resulted in six points, a 20-yard pass from Bob Berry late in the Vikings' 51–10 win over Houston on October 13. The other six catches and two touchdowns came in Minnesota's 35–15 triumph at Kansas City on December 14. He also returned 12 punts for 85 yards and 12 kickoffs for a 25-yard norm during the campaign.

After catching two passes and averaging 24.6 yards on nine kickoff returns in 1975, McCullum was acquired by Seattle in the expansion draft. Claimed off waivers by Minnesota on September 15, 1982, McCullum played in six games and started the last four, catching 12 passes for 131 yards. He then concluded his NFL career in 1983 with 21 receptions for 314 yards, including touchdown catches against St. Louis on October 30 and Pittsburgh on November 20.

Mike McCurry

Season: 1987 Guard Height: 6'3"
Number: 74 Indiana Weight: 258

An Arena Football League player, Mike McCurry started at right guard for Minnesota during the three replacement games in 1987.

Ed McDaniel

Seasons: 1992–98 Linebacker Height: 5'11"
Number: 58 Clemson Weight: 230

No run-stuffing Minnesota linebacker has ever been better at getting into an opponent's backfield than Ed McDaniel. Using a combination of intuition, anticipation and quickness, the undersized defensive force has been among the National Football League's leaders in tackles for lost yardage for most of the past five years, including an NFL-best 19.5 hits in 1995, a total that no one came within six of equalling.

That type of ability makes it hard to believe McDaniel was considered too small for the professional ranks during his days at Clemson. Drafted in the fifth round by the Vikings in 1992, he hung up when Minnesota officials telephoned to inform McDaniel of their selection, for the linebacker believed it was college teammate Chester McGlockton pulling a practical joke. It wasn't, and McDaniel began his career on the practice squad before being activated midway through his rookie season and playing on special teams.

Ed McDaniel

Torn tendons in his right shoulder forced McDaniel to miss nine weeks of the 1993 slate, when he split time with Fred Strickland and registered 21 total tackles. With Strickland out of the picture in 1994, McDaniel emerged as one of the league's best outside linebackers. He finished second on the squad with 171 tackles, including 13 hits behind the line of scrimmage to tie for the league lead. McDaniel also paced the team with three forced fumbles, and led the Vikings' linebackers with 2.5 sacks. His best game came in the season opener against Green Bay on September 4, when McDaniel had a career-high 21 tackles, the second-highest single game tally in team annals.

McDaniel became even more of a force in 1995. In addition to leading the loop in tackles for loss, his 136 primary hits topped the Vikings, while his five forced fumbles were the most by a Minnesota player since Chris Doleman had six in 1992. He also defensed eight passes and recorded 4.5 sacks to round out one of the best all-around seasons ever enjoyed by a linebacker wearing purple.

"He's the most instinctive player I've ever coached," Tony Dungy, Minnesota's defensive coordinator from 1992–95, said during the 1995 season.

"He is absolutely the most productive player in the National Football League."

McDaniel's early success could be attributed in part to John Randle. Though listed as a weakside linebacker, McDaniel usually lined up inside, behind Randle, who was constantly double-teamed. The situation created an open lane, which McDaniel filled better than anyone to nail ball carriers behind the line of scrimmage.

"If you need two to block (Randle), I'm gonna sneak past you, and you're not gonna get past me," McDaniel said. "I'm always telling John, 'If you look good, I look good.'"

But just as it looked like McDaniel would join the All-Pro ranks, a torn left anterior cruciate ligament suffered on the first day of training camp in 1996 cost him the entire season. He rebounded in 1997, overcoming some early rust to register 135 hits, including five for losses. He moved inside in place of an injured Jeff Brady for the final couple games of the slate and performed so well he became the starter at middle linebacker in 1998.

The Vikings featured the game's most improved defense in 1998 and McDaniel was a primary reason for the upgrade. Not unlike his days at outside linebacker, McDaniel worked his way into opposing backfields faster than a speeding bullet. His penetration thwarted numerous third down-and-short situations throughout the season, resulting in 15 tackles for lost yardage, tying Jerry Ball for the team lead. He also added a team-high 155 tackles, set a team record for sacks in a season by a linebacker with seven, and received his first invitation to play in the Pro Bowl. Unfortunately, his season ended on a sour note during the NFC Championship Game against Atlanta, when McDaniel suffered another torn anterior cruciate ligament, this time involving his right knee.

Randall McDaniel

Seasons: 1988–98　　　　　Guard　　　　　　　Height: 6'3"
Number: 64　　　　　　　Arizona State　　　　　Weight: 279

The best left guard in Vikings history, Randall McDaniel is a throwback to players from a previous generation. Despite weighing much less than most of the defenders he goes up against and possessing one of the ugliest stances in the game, McDaniel rarely loses the battle and always wins the war. His outstanding quickness, strength and athletic ability along with his great hands enable him to stop larger players in their tracks. He also has a powerful upper body, one that set the collegiate deadlift record in 1986 by hoisting 620 pounds, thereby making him equally effective when blocking for the run or the pass.

"I look at the way he works and his attitude," said left tackle Todd Steussie. "He's my role model. He does things that nobody else can do because of his physical ability. But I think everyone on the offensive line models themselves after his attitude."

Minnesota's first-round draft choice in 1988, McDaniel was available with the 19th overall selection because of his perceived inability to maintain enough bulk to dominate in the National Football League. That reputation quickly proved to be a farce, for McDaniel took over the starting chores during his second regular-season game after David Huffman succumbed to an injury. He went on to start the final 15 games that year as well as both playoff contests to establish a team single-season record for starts by a rookie guard, surpassing the old mark of 14, set by Larry Bowie in 1962.

Since then, McDaniel has spent the last decade as the lone constant on the Minnesota front wall. Countless honors have come his way during that

Randall McDaniel

time, including Pro Bowl recognition in his second NFL campaign and All-Pro honors during his third. Through the 1998 season, he has been named a Pro Bowl starter an NFL-record 10 straight occasions. He has also put together 10 All-Pro seasons, a mark that tops the Minnesota record book.

Those honors have followed McDaniel because he does so many things well. No lineman gets ahead of the running back on screens and blocks in the open field better than McDaniel. Noticing those abilities, head coach Dennis Green has employed McDaniel as a fullback in the offensive backfield on occasion in order to get a better surge for the running back in short-yardage situations. So athletic is McDaniel, his number has been called on two occasions on running plays. He even caught a touchdown pass in the Pro Bowl after the 1996 season.

McDaniel also has the uncanny ability to coerce an oncoming lineman into going where he wants, thereby opening holes for the likes of Robert Smith, and before him, Terry Allen. It is no coincidence that McDaniel was a member of the line when the Vikings led the league in rushing in 1991 or when Smith set the team's single-season rushing record with 1,266 yards in 1997, the same year the Vikings got a first down on 18 of 19 carries on third or fourth down with less than three yards to go, with the majority coming on the left side.

His forte may be his pass-blocking ability. McDaniel rarely gets beat one-on-one while possessing the wherewithal to foil blitzing linebackers and safeties. Even with his left leg sticking back and out as if it were a broken chicken leg, McDaniel dominates opponents during most games. Again, McDaniel anchored the line that helped Minnesota set league records for points and total net yards in 1998, and held opponents to a sack every 22.7 attempts in 1994, the second-best ratio in team history.

McDaniel's ability and leadership also help make his fellow linemen better players. When McDaniel broke in, he teamed with left tackle Gary Zimmerman for the first five years to form the best left side in football. The same has held true with Steussie and McDaniel for the last five campaigns, particularly the last two, when Steussie has joined his teammate by wearing flowered shirts in Hawaii during early February. McDaniel has had the same tenures with centers Kirk Lowdermilk and Jeff Christy, with Christy earning his first Pro Bowl trip for his efforts in 1998.

Despite being the smallest member of Minnesota's offensive line, McDaniel has been among the most durable Vikings, missing only two games in his career, both coming due to a sprained knee early in the 1989 slate. He concluded the 1998 season with 160 consecutive starts during regular-season and post-season play, most for a guard in team history, and has started 172 games in all, which ranks among the top 10 in Minnesota annals. That consistency combined with his stellar performances should be more than enough to earn McDaniel a spot in the Pro Football Hall of Fame once he decides his body has given the game all it can take.

Mardye McDole

Seasons: 1981–83 Wide Receiver Height: 5'11"
Number: 88 Mississippi State Weight: 198

A former All-American at Mississippi State, Mardye McDole was the Vikings' first pick as a second-round selection in the 1981 draft. He played in nine games as a rookie and returned 11 kickoffs for a dismal 15.5-yard average before succumbing to a sprained ankle. A thigh injury cost him all but two games in 1982, when he returned one kickoff for 26 yards. After he made three catches for 29 yards in 15 games in 1983, the Vikings tried McDole at safety during training camp in 1984 but did not see enough potential to keep him on the roster.

Ramos McDonald

Season: 1998 Defensive Back Height: 5'11"
Number: 34 New Mexico Weight: 202

The Vikings' third-round pick in the 1998 draft, Ramos McDonald saw most of his action on special teams during the early stages of his rookie season before assuming the nickel role in passing situations for the last six games after Anthony Phillips went down with an injury. McDonald displayed excellent ability in man-to-man coverage, and finished the regular season making 11 total tackles while breaking up four passes.

Hugh McElhenny

Seasons: 1961–62 Running Back Height: 6'1"
Number: 39 Washington Weight: 195

Nearly every player made available to the Vikings in the expansion pool was an outcast, a veteran rating somewhere between a has-been and a never-was in the minds of league executives and head coaches. Hugh McElhenny, conversely, still possessed the traits that had made him one of the National Football League's best halfbacks during the 1950s. The problem centered on his former employer, 49ers head coach Red Hickey, who preferred to run the shotgun offense and deemed McElhenny's talents useless.

Although McElhenny may not have been the dominating runner he was during his first nine years in the league, the Californian did nothing in his two seasons in Minnesota to tarnish his abilities or harm his chances for enshrinement in the Pro Football Hall of Fame. The Vikings' first offensive captain, McElhenny proved he was a great open-field runner. Despite not having a talented line to create holes, "The King" led Minnesota and ranked 15th in the league by galloping for 570 yards and three touchdowns on 120 carries in 1961. He also gained 283 yards and scored thrice more on 37 receptions, good for second on the squad, and carried back eight punts for 155 yards, including an 81-yard lightning-like touchdown jaunt against the Bears on December 17 for the franchise's first punt return for a touchdown. Not surprisingly, he earned the team's most valuable player award while becoming the second running back in league history to gain 10,000 total yards in a career.

An example of how his performance bordered on ballet was seen in his first matchup against his former teammates. Having scored earlier in the game on a Statue of Liberty play, McElhenny took the ball from quarterback Fran Tarkenton and deftly dodged every would-be tackler while displaying his best Houdini imitation by breaking free from seven hits. By the time he crossed the goal line some 32 yards later, the 49ers were strewn throughout the field, wondering why the team ever let him get away.

McElhenny's presence was felt for several years after he left the Vikings. He constantly provided rookie Tommy Mason with advice and suggestions, which enabled Mason to take McElhenny's job by the fourth game of the 1962 season. Even so, "The King" was fourth on the team with 200 yards on 50 carries and tied for third with 16 receptions for 191 yards. With Mason holding down the starting halfback duties, McElhenny was sent to the New York Giants for the 1963 campaign in exchange for a fourth-round draft pick in 1964 and a second-round choice in 1965.

Reggie McElroy

Season: 1994 — Tackle — Height: 6'6"
Number: 60 — West Texas State — Weight: 290

The Vikings were looking for a veteran reserve along the offensive line when they picked up Reggie McElroy late in the 1994 season. Yet, with the steady play of rookie Todd Steussie and a healthy Randall McDaniel on the left side, McElroy's services were rarely needed. He saw action in 10 games, mostly on special teams.

Mike McGill

Seasons: 1968–70 — Linebacker — Height: 6'2"
Number: 55 — Notre Dame — Weight: 235

Mike McGill excelled on special teams and as a reserve linebacker for three seasons after being drafted by the Vikings in the third round in 1968. An All-American at Notre Dame, McGill played exclusively on special teams in 14 games as a rookie. His special teams and backup roles increased in 1969, despite spending some time on the reserve list. In 1970, his efforts were rewarded when he scooped up a fumble and scampered five yards to paydirt in Minnesota's 26–0 shutout of New Orleans on September 27. His days in purple ended in 1971 when McGill was traded to St. Louis with Dale Hackbart and a fourth-round draft pick in exchange for Nate Wright and Bob Brown.

Lamar McGriggs

Seasons: 1993–94 — Safety — Height: 6'3"
Number: 37 — Western Illinois — Weight: 210

Signed as a free agent on November 3, 1993, Lamar McGriggs produced huge results for the Vikings a month later. Starting for the injured Todd Scott at free safety, the former New York Giant intercepted his first career pass and raced 63 yards for a touchdown in Minnesota's 13–0 victory over Detroit on December 5. A week later, he made a career-high 13 tackles and forced a fumble against the Cowboys, and concluded the year with 30 defensive hits and three more stops on special teams.

McGriggs' role centered on special teams for most of 1994 while playing behind Scott and Vencie Glenn. He intercepted one pass and placed second on the squad with 26 special teams tackles, 21 of them solo shots. With the signing of free agent Charles Mincy, McGriggs was not offered a contract for the 1995 campaign and wound up playing outside linebacker in the Canadian Football League.

Marlin McKeever

Season: 1967 — Tight End — Height: 6'1"
Number: 86 — Southern Cal — Weight: 235

Prior to the 1967 season, the Vikings acquired Marlin McKeever along with a number one draft pick that proved to be Hall of Famer Alan Page from Los Angeles in exchange for Tommy Mason, Hal Bedsole and a second-round draft choice. A six-year veteran of the National Football League who also played some linebacker with the Rams, McKeever saw action in all 14 games for Minnesota in his only campaign in purple, pulling in 14 passes for 184 yards.

McKeever spent six more seasons in the league after his one year in Minnesota. The Vikings surrendered his services along with a seventh-round draft pick to Washington in exchange for Paul Krause in 1968. As a result, despite his marginal performance on the field, McKeever was part of two of the best trades in team history.

Jim McMahon

Season: 1993 — Quarterback — Height: 6'1"
Number: 9 — Brigham Young — Weight: 195

After watching quarterbacks Rich Gannon and Sean Salisbury post inconsistent performances during his first year as head coach, Dennis Green led the charge to sign Jim McMahon in 1993 to a two-year contract worth $3.2 million.

"Jim brings us tremendous on-field productivity and leadership," Green said upon signing McMahon. "He's a guy who's been in a lot of wars and battles and carries a certain kind of national respect as a quarterback. I won't say he's going to be everything to us. That wouldn't be fair to our team. But our approach in free agency is to get players who we expect to play a major role for us."

The media and fans responded with a barrage of questions, most of which centered on the thought process behind signing a 33-year-old who had not played a full season since his rookie year, in 1982. McMahon also had been a reserve the last few years, most recently with Philadelphia, and his arm strength caused his passes to be timed with a sun dial instead of a radar gun.

Green and the front office appeared to be right through the first half of the 1993 campaign. McMahon's competitiveness and leadership contributed significantly to Minnesota's 4–2 start. Injuries then forced McMahon to miss the next five games before he heroically returned with a 13–0 win at Detroit on December 5. The Vikings went 3–1 the rest of the way to clinch a playoff berth, with McMahon tossing three touchdown passes in a 21–17 triumph at Green Bay on December 19 and two more a week later in Minnesota's 30–10 triumph over the Chiefs.

But after a 76.2 quarterback rating that included completing 60.4 percent of his passes, throwing nine touchdowns and eight interceptions, and winning eight of his 11 starts, McMahon was released the following offseason. He continued his journeyman ways with Arizona and Green Bay while the Vikes opted for another aging signalcaller, Warren Moon.

Jim McMahon

Audray McMillian

Seasons: 1989–93 — Cornerback — Height: 6'
Number: 26 — Houston — Weight: 190

Audray McMillian feared the worst when the new coaching staff took over in Minnesota prior to the 1992 season. Numerous personnel changes were made, and McMillian feared he might be on the way out. Instead, he emerged under head coach Dennis Green and assumed the starting right cornerback job after Reggie Rutland went down with a back injury. His efforts contributed greatly to the team's improved defensive play that enabled the Vikings to reach the playoffs in 1992 and 1993.

McMillian succeeded at the game's top level with his natural instincts and insatiable desire to win. He was the team's nickel back during his first three seasons with the Vikings after signing as a Plan B free agent in 1989. He placed second on the club with 18 special teams tackles in his first year in Minnesota before pacing the unit with 20 hits a year later. In 1991, McMillian picked off four passes to equal the combined production of starters Rutland and Carl Lee, thereby setting the stage for 1992.

In his first full year as a starter, McMillian opened the campaign by intercepting four passes in the Vikings' first four games. He later put together the best day of his career on November 22 against Cleveland. The cornerback became the 10th player in Minnesota annals to intercept three aerials in one game, the last pickoff coming in the fourth quarter when McMillian galloped 25 yards to paydirt to give the Vikings a 17–13 win. He repeated the feat against San Francisco on December 13 by returning a Steve Young toss 51 yards for a touchdown.

Green, naturally, was impressed, saying, "Audray's smart, he's alert, he reads coverages properly, he's extremely coachable and he's a great warrior. That adds up to a pretty good football player."

By season's end, McMillian tied for the league lead with eight interceptions and earned Pro Bowl recognition. His performance in 1993 was similar, with the cornerback intercepting four passes, including a 22-yard pickoff for a touchdown in a 19–12 victory over the Bears on October 25. He also defensed 10 other passes, tying for second on the team, and had 64 tackles.

Yet, for all his contributions, McMillian was not re-signed after the 1993 season, with the Vikings looking for more youth and speed. McMillian went out on top, for he did not play in another regular-season game in the National Football League.

Tom McNeil

Season: 1970   Punter   Height: 6'1"
Number: 12   Stephen F. Austin   Weight: 195

Tom McNeil sandwiched a year with the Vikings between three-season stints with the Saints and Eagles. Acquired off waivers by Minnesota during the 1969 season before spending the rest of the campaign on the reserve squad, McNeil beat out Bob Lee for the punting duties in 1970. He averaged 37.9 yards on 61 punts, the only season of his career that he did not post at least a 41-yard norm.

Fred McNeill

Seasons: 1974–85   Linebacker   Height: 6'2"
Number: 54   UCLA   Weight: 230

Head coach Bud Grant believed that Fred McNeill had the ability to start as a rookie upon selecting the UCLA product with the 17th overall pick in the first round of the 1974 draft. A defensive end in college, McNeill possessed 4.65 speed in the 40, enabling him to cover receivers as well as he rushed the passer. Those traits, in Grant's esteemed estimation, made McNeill an ideal outside linebacker in the Minnesota defensive scheme.

True to form, Grant did not overestimate McNeill's abilities. While he did not emerge as a full-time starter until his fourth campaign, McNeill displayed an extraordinary knack for making things happen when he took the field, resulting in one of the more productive defensive careers in Vikings lore.

Although he played primarily on special teams as a rookie while learning the system behind starter Wally Hilgenberg, McNeill debuted in the National Football League by causing a Green Bay fumble on a punt return that resulted in a Minnesota touchdown during a 32–17 win at Lambeau Field on September 15, 1974. After playing in all 14 games in his first professional season, McNeill moved into the starting lineup in Week 11 in place of the injured Roy Winston and wound up starting five games in 1975. He also recovered a muffed punt in the playoffs to set up Minnesota's first touchdown against Dallas on December 28.

McNeill, whose brother, Rod, played three years in the NFL, opened the 1976 slate as a starting outside linebacker before a succession of injuries caused him to lose starting honors to Matt Blair in 1976. He continued to shine on special teams, with his biggest play coming in Super Bowl XI. McNeill blocked and recovered a Ray Guy punt deep in Oakland territory in the first quarter versus the Raiders, but the Vikings were not able to capitalize on the linebacker's stellar performance.

He took over starting duties at right linebacker in 1977 and began a string of consistent campaigns in which the linebacker lived up to Grant's lofty projections. McNeill paced Minnesota with 136 total tackles in 1977, then led the Vikings with six recovered fumbles while blocking a field goal and intercepting two passes a year later. He also returned a blocked punt 16 yards for a touchdown in the 24–7 victory at Tampa Bay on October 1.

McNeill had three sacks in 1979, and was fifth on team with 105 solo tackles in 1980. He picked off two passes during the 1981 slate, continued to excel in 1982, and increased his consecutive starts streak to 102 games before having his string broken in the final regular-season contest of 1983. He returned to the lineup in 1984 and started the first 13 games before succumbing to a rib injury. McNeill then played in 10 games for Minnesota in 1985 before deciding his playing days had come to an end.

McNeill currently ranks third in Minnesota history with 386 assisted tackles. He played in 167 games and recorded seven interceptions for 27 return yards.

Dan McQuaid

Season: 1988 Tackle Height: 6'7"
Number: 60 Nevada-Las Vegas Weight: 278

Dan McQuaid, who spent his first three years in the National Football League with Washington, saw action on special teams for three games with the Vikings in 1988 before being waived on September 20. He went on to play one game with Indianapolis later that season, which proved to be the end of his NFL career.

Bill McWatters

Season: 1964 Running Back Height: 6'
Number: 32 North Texas State Weight: 225

Minnesota's eighth-round draft choice in 1964, Bill McWatters impressed the Vikings' brass during his first and only preseason with the team. His enthusiasm and powerful, straight-ahead running style earned him a reserve fullback job behind starter Bill Brown. One coach even went so far as to call McWatters "a big Jim Taylor."

McWatters, however, spent only one year in the National Football League. In 1964, the native Texan who enjoyed snake hunting in his free time carried the ball 14 times for 60 yards and one touchdown over the course of 11 games for the Vikings.

Tim Meamber

Season: 1985 Linebacker Height: 6'3"
Number: 53 Washington Weight: 233

Injuries limited Tim Meamber's career to four games. After playing in the season opener against San Francisco as a rookie, Minnesota's second third-round draft pick in 1985 underwent hernia surgery and was placed on the injured reserve list for the next seven weeks. He returned to play three contests in November before going back on the shelf with a knee injury. Released the following year in training camp, his career stats include one solo hit and two assisted tackles.

Mike Mercer

Seasons: 1961–62 Kicker Height: 6′
Number: 18 Arizona State Weight: 220

Mike Mercer, Minnesota's 15th-round pick in the franchise's first draft, provided the Vikings with a strong leg for both punting and kicking chores but the inconsistency that typifies an expansion team. He holds the distinction of recording the first points in team annals, connecting on a short field goal in the first quarter of Minnesota's shocking 37–13 triumph over Chicago on September 17, 1961.

The burly and moody kicker's most noteworthy performance occurred in the team's third game, on October 1, 1961, at Baltimore. "Moko" appeared to be the hero after booting four field goals against the Colts before Steve Myhra blasted a 52-yarder through the uprights in the hosts' 34–33 triumph.

Otherwise, Mercer's appearance for field goal attempts caused opposing fans to stand and cheer. While doing a respectable job on punts, averaging 39 yards on 63 efforts in 1961, Mercer connected on just nine of 21 three-point tries, with four successes coming in the one game against the Colts. He also had a bad performance against Detroit during a 37–10 loss, leading head coach Norm Van Brocklin to scold the kicker by saying, "Mercer, you couldn't kick a sick whore off a potty."

A year later, while averaging 43.5 yards on 19 punts, Mercer found himself unemployed after missing his first five field goal tries in the Vikings' opening four games. Fortunately for Mercer, he rebounded and spent nine more years in professional football, including kicking the first field goal in Super Bowl history, a 31-yard effort for the Chiefs on January 15, 1967.

Mike Merriweather

Seasons: 1989–92 Linebacker Height: 6′2″
Number: 57 Pacific Weight: 226

The arrival of free agency in the National Football League during the early 1990s did nothing to help Mike Merriweather. One of the league's most consistent and dominating linebackers who earned Pro Bowl recognition in three of his six seasons with the Steelers in the 1980s, Merriweather forced a change of scenery by sitting out the 1988 campaign after he and Pittsburgh could not come to terms on a contract. He wound up being traded to Minnesota in a draft-day deal, costing the Vikings their first-round pick in 1989. Merriweather proved to be worth the price by putting together four outstanding seasons in purple.

Playing as if he had something to prove, Merriweather was a terror in his first year with the team. He displayed excellent speed and an aggressive, attacking style to pace the defense with six forced fumbles. The linebacker also returned an interception 15 yards for a touchdown in a 24–17 win over the Lions on October 8. He earned NFC Defensive Player of the Week accolades after dominating Detroit on October 22 with six hits, two sacks, an 11-yard interception, a forced fumble and a recovered fumble, helping lead the Vikes to a 20–7 triumph.

Merriweather also entered the NFL record books in 1989. When he blocked a Dale Hatcher punt out of the end zone in Minnesota's 23–21 win over the Rams on November 5, it marked the only overtime game in league annals to end with a safety.

His performance improved the next two years. In 1990, Merriweather received All-Pro consideration after leading the Vikings with 155 tackles and four recovered fumbles. He earned NFC Defensive Player of the Week honors again by registering one of the biggest days ever by a Minnesota linebacker—13 tackles, 1.5 sacks, two forced fumbles and a 33-yard fumble recovery for a touchdown in a 41–13 thrashing of the Bears on November 25. A year later, Merriweather again paced the team with a career-high 189 tackles and had 10 or more hits in 13 of his 16 outings. He also found paydirt for the fifth time in his career on a 22-yard interception return against Tampa Bay in Minnesota's 28–13 win on November 3.

Merriweather continued to produce in 1992, registering 104 tackles, good for second on the team, with three sacks. But, as was the case with many other veterans in the 1990s, the 32-year-old Merriweather was not offered a contract for the 1993 season. The Vikings wanted to add youth, speed and size to the defense, resulting in Merriweather's ouster. He wound up spending the campaign, his last in the league, with the Jets.

Wayne Meylan

Season: 1970 — Linebacker — Height: 6'
Number: 56 — Nebraska — Weight: 235

Acquired off waivers from the New York Giants, Wayne Meylan played on special teams for two games with the Vikings in 1970. He was released the following year in training camp.

Phil Micech

Season: 1987 — Defensive End — Height: 6'5"
Number: 56 — Wisconsin-Platteville — Weight: 265

Phil Micech saw playing time in all three replacement games for the Vikings in 1987.

Tom Michel

Season: 1964 — Running Back — Height: 5'11"
Number: 21 — East Carolina — Weight: 215

The Vikings drafted Tom Michel as a future with their 14th pick in 1964 and later discovered the East Carolina product was eligible to play that same season. A 245-pound fullback in college who lost 30 pounds to play tailback with Minnesota, Michel saw limited playing time behind Tommy Mason in his only season in the National Football League. He carried the ball from scrimmage 39 times for 129 yards but fumbled on three occasions. Michel also caught a 14-yard pass and returned eight kickoffs for a 24-yard average.

Dave Middleton

Season: 1961 — End — Height: 6'1"
Number: 84 — Auburn — Weight: 190

Not unlike most players in the National Football League during the 1950s and 1960s, Dave Middleton pursued another career when not earning a living on the field. Few, however, practiced medicine, as did Middleton, a gynecologist and obstetrician.

Acquired by Minnesota from Detroit in the expansion pool, "Doc" had a minor tie with the Vikings prior to joining the team. He delivered the first grandchild of team owner Bernie Ridder while Middleton was completing his residency in Ann Arbor, Michigan. He was equally successful in football, ranking third on the Vikings with 30 receptions for 444 yards. He had been considered one of the league's top receivers during his seven-year tenure with the Lions, and showed flashes of that form while wearing purple.

A sprinter at Auburn University, Middleton caught two touchdown passes in 1961. His first came in the franchise's first game, the fourth of four Fran Tarkenton scoring aerials to hammer the nails into the Bears' coffin during Minnesota's 37–13 victory on September 17. Middleton then grabbed a 57-yard pass from Tarkenton for the winning touchdown to break the team's seven-game losing streak in the 28–20 triumph over Baltimore on November 12.

Unfortunately for Vikings fans, Middleton decided against delivering on the gridiron after 1961. Twenty-eight years old and ready to begin his private practice, Middleton focused on his medical career on a full-time basis.

Keith Millard

Seasons: 1985–91 Defensive Tackle Height: 6'5"
Number: 75 Washington State Weight: 264

Keith Millard

The 1984 season proved to be a case of deja vu for the Vikings. After losing several draft choices to the rival American Football League in the early- and mid-1960s, Minnesota failed to sign its first-round pick some two decades later when Keith Millard opted to sign with the Jacksonville Bulls of the United States Football League instead of donning purple.

The 13th overall selection in the National Football League's 1984 draft, Millard joined Minnesota during training camp in 1985 and worked his way into the Vikings' defensive lineup as a rookie, starting five games when the team employed a 4–3 defense. He made a quick impression by leading the squad with 11 sacks and in sack yardage, numbers that enabled Millard to become a starter in 1986 and emerge as one of the game's most feared quarterback rushers.

Employing his mayhem from the middle of the line, Millard received some All-Pro consideration during the 1986 campaign. His 10 sacks led the team for the second straight year. For those who had failed to notice his efforts, Millard left little doubt about his effectiveness while facing the Browns on October 26. Millard posted six unassisted tackles, including three sacks for 27 yards, versus Cleveland. He also displayed his athleticism with his first career interception during a 31–7 win over Pittsburgh on September 21.

A torn calf muscle in 1987 caused Millard to miss most of four games, and limited him to 3.5 sacks for the season. He did recover two fumbles that resulted in 10 Vikings points in a 23–17 win over Tampa Bay on November 15, and returned in time to be a force in the playoffs, including five solo tackles, one assist, a sack and a fumble recovery in the 44–10 rout at New Orleans on January 3, 1988.

Millard took his game to a higher level in 1988. A prime example was his effort against Philadelphia on September 25. The tackle recorded four sacks to go with eight solo hits in the 23–21 victory, good for the second-best individual sack effort in team history. Millard had eight quarterback dumps and two recovered fumbles for the season, and was rewarded with his first All-Pro selection and his first trip and starting assignment in the Pro Bowl.

That outstanding performance set the stage for 1989. Millard was named the NFL's Defensive Player of the Year and voted to the second-team All-NFL squad of the 1980s after finishing third in the league with 18 sacks, tying for the second-highest total in Minnesota history. He also earned his second straight All-Pro and Pro Bowl honors. Millard had three games with at least three sacks, including four versus Green Bay on October 15, when he victimized the Packers' Don Majkowski, three sacks and a 48-yard interception against Detroit on October 8, and three sacks against Houston on September 23. He also returned a fumble 31 yards for a touchdown against Atlanta on December 10.

But just as it appeared that Millard was at his peak and headed for a shot in the Hall of Fame, an injury cost him most of the 1990 season and led to the team's disappointing 6–10 record. He started the first four games and recorded two sacks before succumbing to a knee injury against Tampa Bay on September 30 and undergoing surgery two days later. He also missed all of the 1991 slate, thereby robbing Millard of his skills.

Millard was among the veterans who departed Minnesota around the time Dennis Green was hired as head coach in 1992. The defensive tackle was traded to Seattle for a second-round and third-round draft choice, but never played at a competitive level again.

Kevin Miller

Seasons: 1978–80 Wide Receiver Height: 5'10"
Number: 87 Louisville Weight: 180

Kevin Miller made the most of his lone reception in the National Football League. During the third quarter at Detroit on December 9, 1978, Miller pulled in a 35-yard reception from Fran Tarkenton for a touchdown. His other contributions that year came on special teams, with the free agent acquisition averaging 21.4 yards on 40 kickoff returns and five yards on 48 punt returns.

A shoulder injury suffered in the preseason forced Miller to miss all but three games in 1979, when he returned 18 punts for 85 yards. Waived after the first three games in 1980 and re-signed for the finale, Miller saw practically no activity in what proved to be his final NFL season.

Larry Miller

Season: 1987 Quarterback Height: 6'4"
Number: 5 Northern Iowa Weight: 220

Larry Miller relieved the injured Tony Adams in the second replacement game in 1987. On his first pass attempt, Miller threw an interception that was returned 23 yards for a touchdown in Chicago's 27–7 victory. He wound up completing just one of six tosses to a Viking receiver.

Robert Miller

Seasons: 1975–80 Running Back Height: 5'11"
Number: 35 Kansas Weight: 204

In his six seasons with the Vikings, Robert Miller was a steady reserve running back and solid special teams player who failed to answer the bell just once during his career in the National Football League.

The fifth-round draft choice was one of only four rookies to make the Minnesota roster in 1975, when he rushed for 93 yards on 30 carries, gained 35 yards on four receptions, and averaged 18.6 yards on five kickoff returns. His first professional touchdown came on a one-yard plunge immediately after Miller turned a short swing pass into a 32-yard gain to the goal line in a 42–10 win over Cleveland on September 28.

Miller's best season was his second year in purple. He ranked third on the team with 286 yards rushing and caught 23 passes for 181 yards. Nine of those receptions came against Green Bay during a 17–10 win on November 21, 1976. Two weeks later, in a 20–9 pounding of the Pack at The Met, Miller had his best rushing day, gaining 95 yards on the ground and another 37 yards on five receptions.

In 1977, Miller had a career-high 27 catches for 246 yards while gaining 152 yards on 46 carries. He added 213 rushing yards and 22 receptions for 230 yards in 1978. His role centered primarily on special teams during his last two years with the team, with Miller concluding his days in Minnesota with career totals of 951 rushing yards and 95 catches.

Ted Million

Season: 1987　　　　　　　　Guard　　　　　　　　　Height: 6'4"
Number: 64　　　　　　　　Washington　　　　　　　Weight: 255

Ted Million played in one game with the Vikings' replacement team in 1987.

Charles Mincy

Season: 1995　　　　　　　　Safety　　　　　　　　　Height: 5'11"
Number: 21　　　　　　　　Washington　　　　　　　Weight: 197

In his lone season with the Vikings, Charles Mincy proved to have a nose for the football while serving as a part-time starter. The former Chief recovered one fumble and tied for second on the team with three intercepted passes, victimizing the Steelers, Packers and Browns, all during Minnesota victories. Mincy finished the year with 62 tackles, including 48 hits, and returned four punts for a 5.5-yard norm.

Despite his contributions, Mincy could not beat out rookie Orlando Thomas at free safety. He was allowed to join defensive coordinator Tony Dungy in Tampa Bay, where Mincy emerged as a starter.

Mel Mitchell

Season: 1980　　　　　　　　Guard　　　　　　　　　Height: 6'3"
Number: 68　　　　　　　　Tennessee State　　　　　Weight: 260

A former Lion and Dolphin who had earned Black All-American honors as a tackle in college, Mel Mitchell saw most of his action on special teams during six games with the Vikings in 1980.

Fred Molden

Season: 1987　　　　　　　　Defensive Tackle　　　　Height: 6'2"
Number: 90　　　　　　　　Jackson State　　　　　　Weight: 272

Fred Molden played in two replacement games for the Vikings in 1987 and recorded one sack. His performance was impressive enough for the team to invite him to training camp the following summer, but he failed to make the cut.

Warren Moon

Seasons: 1994–96　　　　　　Quarterback　　　　　　Height: 6'3"
Number: 1　　　　　　　　 Washington　　　　　　　Weight: 219

The Vikings hoped Warren Moon had some sunshine left in his career when Minnesota acquired the quarterback from Houston for third- and fourth-round draft choices on April 14, 1994. While Moon beamed on occasion, his effort was blemished by a lack of leadership and even less mobility.

Moon shined brightest during the second half of the 1995 season, when the former Oiler and Canadian Football League star showed how he became the first professional quarterback to throw for 60,000 yards in his career. Moon completed 188 of 304 passes for 2,358 yards with 23 touchdowns and just five interceptions while leading the Viking offense to an average of 31.3 points in the final eight games. He was named the NFC Offensive Player

Warren Moon

of the Month for November and earned his eighth straight trip to the Pro Bowl.

For the year, Moon established the Minnesota record with 33 touchdown passes in a season and helped the team set the franchise standard for most points (412) and total yards (5,938) in a campaign. He also broke Rich Gannon's record with 193 consecutive pass attempts without an interception. His 152.9 rating, based on completing 25 of 32 tosses in the 43–24 triumph over New Orleans on November 19, 1995, represented the highest one-game rating for a Viking signalcaller in team annals. Yet, for all his accomplishments, Minnesota went 5–3 down the stretch to finish the year 8–8, missing the playoffs for the only time under head coach Dennis Green.

Moon's performance in 1994 was similarly effective. He had his high moments, including NFL Offensive Player of the Week accolades for his 326 yards and three touchdowns in the 38–35 win over Miami on September 25. He also topped the NFC with 4,264 passing yards and 371 completions, and earned a job in the Pro Bowl. At the same time, he threw 19 interceptions to his 18 touchdown tosses, and was just 8–8 in his starts over 15 regular-season games and one playoff contest.

Hobbled with an ankle injury in 1996, Moon slipped considerably in his third season with the Vikings. He completed 134 of 247 passes and threw seven touchdown tosses and nine interceptions. He continued to throw off his back leg and was little more than a tackling dummy when pressured in the pocket. While Green initially refused to bench Moon, the head coach was given little choice after the veteran had a 14-of-30 performance with two interceptions in a 42–23 loss to Seattle on November 10. That proved to be Moon's final showing in purple.

Even with two seasons remaining on his contract, the 40-year-old Moon was not brought back in 1997 after he refused to accept the job as a backup to Brad Johnson. He signed with Seattle and showed a little magic with the Seahawks in 1997 and 1998.

Leonard Moore

Season: 1987 Running Back Height: 6'
Number: 45 Jackson State Weight: 222

After reporting to training camp with the Vikings and being waived in August of 1987, Leonard Moore returned to the team for one replacement game. He carried the ball four times for 11 yards and caught a pass for a gain of eight.

Manfred Moore

Season: 1977 Running Back Height: 6'
Number: 36 Southern Cal Weight: 200

Football is a man's game, and Manfred Moore rarely took the safe way out while wearing purple. Signed early in the 1977 season by Minnesota after being released by the Raiders, Moore emerged as the Vikings' regular punt returner, taking back 47 boots for a 5.9-yard average. Only twice did he deem it necessary to call for a fair catch, but he fumbled on three occasions. Moore also returned 24 kickoffs for a 21.8-yard norm. Despite his bravery, he lost his job the following summer to Kevin Miller.

Kyle Morrell

Seasons: 1985–86   Safety   Height: 6'1"
Number: 35   Brigham Young   Weight: 190

A first-team All-American in college, Kyle Morrell got off to a bad start in the professional ranks. The Vikings' second fourth-round draft choice in 1985 wrecked his knee in his first pre-season game, against Miami on August 10, and underwent surgery the following morning. He wound up spending the entire season on the injured reserve list before returning to action in 1986. In what proved to be his only experience in the National Football League, Morrell played in five games on special teams before receiving his walking papers on October 7.

Jack Morris

Season: 1961   Defensive Back   Height: 6'
Number: 40   Oregon   Weight: 190

A former Ram who was selected from Pittsburgh in the expansion draft, Jack Morris started at cornerback for the Vikings in 1961. Considered one of the team's fastest players, the bald-headed defensive back played in all 14 games during the inaugural season and intercepted two passes, returning them a total of 90 yards. His second pick of the season took place in the finale, when he scampered 65 yards to the Chicago 16-yard line to set up a Viking touchdown on December 17.

Mike Morris

Seasons: 1991–98   Center   Height: 6'5"
Number: 68   Northeast Missouri State   Weight: 276

Every team in the National Football League has a long snapper, yet the job is not deemed worthy of Pro Bowl status. If it were, Mike Morris would have several all-expenses-paid vacations to Hawaii under his belt.

Considered by head coach Dennis Green, his kickers and contemporaries as the best long snapper in football, Morris has made the chore of centering the ball to punters and field goal holders an art. He can accurately get the ball to the punter in seven-tenths of a second (eight-tenths and under is considered excellent). For that reason it is little wonder the likes of Harry Newsome, Mike Saxon, Fuad Reveiz and Gary Anderson had the best seasons of their careers while wearing purple.

"He might be in for eight snaps a game, but he has to throw a strike every time," said Green, noting the importance of Morris' job.

Morris joined the Vikings during the 1991 preseason and turned the game's most anonymous role into one of the most visible in Minnesota. In addition to doing his job better than anyone in the league, his off-beat, outgoing personality earned him more promotional work and appearances on radio talk shows and commercials than any of his teammates. In 1994, *Pro Football Weekly* tabbed him one of the three craziest players in the league for his off-the-field antics, while in 1996 he starred in one of Fox Television's promotional spots, featuring Morris centering a fake cat.

"I play with people sometimes," Morris said. "I have fun with the media and with that kind of stuff."

His on-field activities are even more noteworthy. In addition to playing in 136 straight games since joining the Vikings, Morris' talents are revealed in the fact that he has taken part in the two longest field goal and point-after-touchdown streaks in NFL history. He was the snapper for all of Reveiz's 30 straight field goals, with the record-breaker occurring on September 10, 1995. Morris centered the standard-setter for Eddie Murray, who established the mark for consecutive PATs when he booted number 235 through the uprights against Carolina on October 12, 1997. Morris also handled every attempt for Anderson, who did not miss a field goal or PAT in 1998 while setting an NFL record for points by a kicker in a season with 164 and breaking Reveiz's NFL record for consecutive field goals by connecting on 40 straight attempts.

A former journeyman in both the United States Football League and the NFL, Morris had one string come to an end during the 1998 season. For the first time in his career, the long snapper's name appeared on the weekly injured report. Morris said, tongue in cheek, that he didn't want his consecutive games streak "to become a distraction for the team." With his performances, Vikings fans can rest assured that has never been the case.

Harold Morrow

Seasons: 1996–98   Running Back   Height: 5'11"
Number: 33   Auburn   Weight: 210

A weak spot for the Vikings in the mid-1990s was their coverage units on special teams. The loss of such standouts as Greg Manusky and Brent Novoselsky left Minnesota vulnerable to long kick returns, thereby putting the defense in an unenviable position.

The Vikings acquired Harold Morrow off waivers from Dallas after the final cuts had been made in the 1996 preseason with the sole purpose of improving the special teams. The Minnesota coaching staff had rated Morrow the top special teams player coming out of college that year. Even though he took the roster spot of popular punter Mike Saxon, Morrow responded with 14 tackles, good for third on the team, despite playing in only eight games.

Morrow continued to excel in the role in 1997, and added kickoff return duties to his responsibilities when Robert Tate succumbed to an ankle injury in the season's fifth game. After averaging 19.5 yards on six returns as a rookie, Morrow responded by producing at a 19.8-yard clip on five returns in 1997. He also set the Vikings' single-season special teams record with 32 tackles. Early-season injuries caused Morrow to miss five games in 1998, yet he still managed to record 16 tackles on special teams, just three behind team leader Kivuusama Mays.

Eric Moss

Seasons: 1997–98   Tackle   Height: 6'4"
Number: 79   Ohio State   Weight: 325

Signed to the practice squad on November 26, 1997, after starting center Jeff Christy went down with a broken leg, Eric Moss was activated two weeks later when Scott Dill was placed on injured reserve with an ailing back. Though he played little in late December, Moss was expected to be on the Vikings' active roster in 1998, only to have a high ankle sprain suffered during the preseason cost him the entire campaign.

Unbelievably, Moss had not played football in three years prior to signing with the Vikings. The half-brother of wide receiver Randy Moss, he displayed outstanding athletic ability for a big man, with head coach Dennis Green describing Moss as "a sleeper."

Randy Moss

Season: 1998
Number: 84
Wide Receiver
Marshall
Height: 6'4"
Weight: 211

Paybacks are hell.

Just ask the 19 teams (including Cincinnati on two occasions) that passed on Randy Moss in the first round of the 1998 draft. While Moss was without question one of the top three prospects available, teams refused the wide receiver's immense talents because of a shaky past that included an assault on a fellow high school student and possession of marijuana. It was not until Vikings head coach Dennis Green decided to give Moss the benefit of the doubt and draft him with the 21st overall pick was his future sealed at the game's highest level.

Moss wasted no time letting his actions speak for themselves while proving he is the most physically gifted receiver in the game. He caught two touchdown passes from quarterback Brad Johnson in his first game in the National Football League, against Tampa Bay on September 6, to guide the Vikings to a 31–7 victory. In the process, Moss became the first Minnesota rookie to score two touchdowns in his first game and only the fourth Viking to score at all in his first game. And that was just the start.

The green pea's coming-out party took place four weeks later, at Green Bay on *Monday Night Football*. With Randall Cunningham under center, Moss caught five passes for 190 yards (the third-highest total in team history) and two touchdowns, and had a third score, a 75-yard bomb early in the contest, called back due to a holding penalty. If anyone had questioned his potential impact in the league, the receiver silenced any lingering critics during the Vikings' 37–24 thrashing of the Pack on October 5.

Randy Moss

"I think if I had something to say about it, I would have been the first pick," Moss said. "But I don't feel any animosity toward anyone. I'm happy where I'm at. I'm going going to make the best of it."

As if opposing defensive backs did not have enough to worry about when facing Moss, Johnson revealed midway through the receiver's rookie season that Moss was only running three different patterns. "Just wait until he starts using more of the offense," Johnson said.

Much to the league's chagrin, Moss did increase his repertoire when Jake Reed was sidelined for the season's final five contests. He moved into the starting lineup against Dallas on November 26 and responded with three touchdown receptions, all for more than 50 yards. He became the first Viking receiver to catch three touchdowns of more than 50 yards in one game, while his average of 54.3-yards per reception also established the team's single-game mark.

By the end of the season, Moss had established every Minnesota record for a rookie receiver and then some. He set the Vikings' mark for first-year players with 69 receptions, 1,313 yards and 17 touchdowns. The Marshall product also established the team standard for consecutive games with a touchdown reception with seven, pulling in a scoring toss in every contest between the November 15 meeting with Cincinnati through the end of the slate, against Tennessee on December 26. Moss also became the first Viking to catch three touchdown tosses in consecutive contests, victimizing the Bears thrice in a 48–22 victory on December 6 after dominating Dallas 10 days earlier.

Moss then capped the season with a two-yard touchdown catch in the first round of the playoffs against Arizona before pulling in a 31-yard touchdown toss from Cunningham in the NFC Championship Game against Atlanta.

Those performances, including leading the NFL with 17 touchdown receptions and an average of 19 yards per catch, earned Moss a slew of post-season awards. He became the fourth Viking to win NFL Rookie of the Year honors, following in the footsteps of Paul Flatley (1963), Chuck Foreman (1973) and Sammy White (1976). Moss also was named a first-team All-Pro and voted a starter in the Pro Bowl.

Rich Mostardi

Season: 1961   Defensive Back   Height: 5'11"
Number: 24   Kent State   Weight: 188

While head coach Norm Van Brocklin was constantly on the verge of popping a vein, the Vikings needed some levity to counterbalance the Dutchman's tirades. Much of that was provided by Rich Mostardi, who emerged as the team comic in the expansion team's first year.

Unfortunately, few things were funny about some of Mostardi's performances. Acquired from Cleveland in the veterans pool, the left safety had some highlights, picking off two passes, good for 22 return yards. His most obvious error, meanwhile, came on October 22, 1961. Mostardi got beat by more than 30 yards on a routine pass to Boyd Dowler on the Packers' first play from scrimmage, setting the tone for Green Bay's 33–7 victory at The Met.

Due to an error at the Kent State registrars office, Mostardi's name throughout college and during his first year in the National Football League was spelled "Mostardo." Although that mistake is still seen in reference books, it took the Vikings to get the spelling right in 1961.

Mark Mullaney

Seasons: 1975–87   Defensive End   Height: 6'6"
Number: 77   Colorado State   Weight: 242

Mark Mullaney, the Vikings' first-round draft choice in 1975, never filled the massive shoes of Carl Eller or Jim Marshall. That being said, Mullaney put together an unheralded career in Minnesota that included playing in a Super Bowl and for three of the five head coaches in franchise history.

The 25th overall selection in the 1975 draft, Mullaney possessed 4.9 speed in the 40. It was that speed as well as his agility that impressed the Vikings' scouts to the point where they believed the offensive tackle during his final two seasons at Colorado State could excel as a defensive end in the National Football League.

As a rookie, Mullaney played primarily in short-yardage situations and on special teams, where he blocked an extra-point attempt. A sprained ankle kept him from replacing Eller for more than the first game of the 1976 season, yet Mullaney still managed to record three sacks, recover two fumbles, cause another loose ball, and block a conversion in limited opportunities. One of Mullaney's greatest accomplishments came at the end of the campaign, during the 1976 NFC Championship Game on December 26. With the Rams threatening deep in Minnesota territory, Mullaney stuffed Ron Jessie during a goal-line stand to help the Vikings pull out the 24–13 win and advance to Super Bowl XI.

Mullaney batted down a field goal try and registered another sack in 1977 while continuing to serve as a backup defensive end. He then began to show his long-held promise in 1978 by starting nine games at left end and responding with a team-high nine sacks while recovering a fumble and blocking a field goal attempt. He took over the starting duties in 1979 and led the team again with eight sacks while knocking down six passes. Mullaney paced the team for the third straight year with six sacks in 1980 before recording three quarterback dumps and placing second on the line with 70 solo tackles in 1981.

Moved to right defensive end in 1982, Mullaney caused a fumble in the end zone against Buffalo on September 16 that resulted in a safety, and had 4.5 sacks for the season. A broken left collarbone in 1983 cost him more than half the slate, while injuries to his hamstring, eye and neck limited Mullaney to seven games in 1984. He returned to the starting lineup in 1985 and intercepted the lone pass of his career, against San Francisco on September 8, and returned it for a touchdown, only to have the return nullified by a clipping penalty. He concluded the season with two sacks in 15 outings.

Injuries hampered Mullaney again in 1986, when he played in 11 games and started nine while battling a recurring knee injury. He spent all of the 1987 season on injured reserve after hurting his neck during the preseason. Waived early in training camp in 1988, Mullaney concluded his career in purple by playing in 151 games and recording 13.5 sacks.

Mike Mularkey

Seasons: 1983–88   Tight End   Height: 6'4"
Number: 86   Florida   Weight: 236

Mike Mularkey was one of the Vikings' most consistent special teams performers and a steady reserve tight end in the 1980s. Acquired off waivers from San Francisco shortly before the start of the 1983 season, Mularkey saw action on special teams for the first three games that year prior to spraining a foot and spending the rest of the campaign on the injured reserve list.

In 1984, Mularkey caught touchdown passes against Tampa Bay on October 7 and versus the Raiders a week later. For the season he had 14 receptions, including seven in his first career start, against Green Bay on December 16. Mularkey was in the starting lineup five times in 1985, when he caught 13 passes for 196 yards, among them a career-long 51-yard touchdown grab in a 21–17 win over San Diego on October 20.

Mularkey had two more touchdown catches in 1986 among his 11 receptions. He pulled in three passes, including a seven-yard score, in a 42–7 demolition of Green Bay on September 28. Two weeks earlier, Mularkey and Tommy Kramer connected on a 10-yard scoring pass in the 23–10 triumph over Tampa Bay. A knee injury limited Mularkey to nine games and one catch in 1987. His role continued to fade in 1988, when he caught three passes for 39 yards while making nine hits on special teams. A free agent after the 1988 season, Mularkey concluded his playing days by spending three years in Pittsburgh.

Nelson Munsey

Season: 1978   Cornerback   Height: 6'1"
Number: 31   Wyoming   Weight: 198

Nelson Munsey was signed by the Vikings just prior to the 1978 playoffs after Nate Wright suffered a broken arm. Though on the active roster, he did not take the field for Minnesota and was released the following year in training camp.

Fred Murphy

Season: 1961   End   Height: 6'3"
Number: 88   Georgia Tech   Weight: 205

Fred Murphy joined Rich Mostardi by arriving in Minnesota from Cleveland in the veterans pool. And like Mostardi, Murphy spent only the 1961 season in purple. He played in 13 games at left end and on special teams. Murphy did not catch a pass after pulling in two with the Browns as a rookie in 1960.

Eddie Murray

Season: 1997   Kicker   Height: 5'10"
Number: 3   Tulane   Weight: 177

A constant Minnesota nemesis with his accurate leg while with Detroit, Eddie Murray was pulled from the brink of retirement by the Vikings four weeks into the 1997 season. Greg Davis had been inconsistent in his first year on the job, leading head coach Dennis Green to call the 41-year-old veteran out of the broadcast booth and off the golf course and back onto the field.

Murray, who had not played during the 1996 season, contributed significantly in his second week of employment by booting a 38-yarder with 10 seconds remaining to cap the Vikings' incredible 20–19 comeback victory at Arizona on October 5. A week later, against Carolina, Murray connected on his 235th consecutive extra point, a streak that covered nearly 10 years and broke the NFL record previously held by San Francisco's Tommy Davis.

Those feats proved to be the highlights of Murray's short tenure in Minnesota. He succeeded on 12 of 17 field-goal attempts, but connected on just five of 10 tries from 30 yards and beyond. That performance led to the Vikings' signing of Gary Anderson prior to the 1998 season.

Frank Myers

Seasons: 1978–80   Tackle   Height: 6'5"
Number: 74   Texas A&M   Weight: 255

The Vikings had no choice but to provide Frank Myers with experience early in his career. After acquiring the aggressive rookie tackle at the end of training camp in 1978 from Baltimore in exchange for an eighth-round draft pick, head coach Bud Grant was forced to put Myers in the fire when starter Steve Riley went down in the fifth game. Myers went on to start the final 11 contests of the campaign and did a laudable job considering the circumstances.

Myers did not take off from there, however. He played in 12 games as a reserve in 1979 and was on the roster for the first three games in 1980 prior to receiving his release on September 23.

Pete Najarian

Season: 1987　　　　　　　Linebacker　　　　　　　Height: 6'2"
Numbers: 51, 59　　　　　　Minnesota　　　　　　　 Weight: 233

Pete Najarian was waived by the Vikings on September 7, 1987, just prior to the season opener, but returned to play in the three replacement games a few weeks later. Far and away the best player on Minnesota's dismal squad, Najarian led the team in tackles every game, making 12 hits in each of the first two outings and eight solo shots in the third contest.

That performance earned him a job later in the campaign, when he was signed on November 5. Najarian played in two games before being released on November 25. He re-signed on December 2 and was let go six days later.

Chuck Nelson

Seasons: 1986–88　　　　　　Kicker　　　　　　　　Height: 5'11"
Number: 1　　　　　　　　　Washington　　　　　　　Weight: 172

After failing to earn a roster spot in the National Football League during the 1985 campaign, Chuck Nelson reported to the Vikings' training camp in 1986 and beat out five other kickers who were vying to replace the retired Jan Stenerud. Nelson proceeded to set several team standards over the next three seasons, and held the Minnesota marks for most extra points (48) and most extra-point attempts (49) in a single season before Gary Anderson shattered those records in 1998.

In his first season with the Vikings, Nelson finished fourth in the NFL with 110 points, the most by a Minnesota kicker since Fred Cox had 125 in 1970. He was second in the NFC by converting 79 percent of his field goal attempts, including the game-winning boot in the Vikings' 27–24 overtime win against San Francisco on October 12.

After leading the team with 75 points during the 1987 regular season, a period in which Nelson struggled by connecting on just 13 of 24 field goal attempts, he set an NFL single-game playoff record with five three-pointers in the 36–24 triumph over the 49ers on January 9, 1988. He also established numerous Minnesota team playoff marks for a single game, among them points (18), field goals attempted and made (five), and field goal accuracy (100 percent).

Ironically, Nelson's best season was his last in Minnesota. He was named second-team All-NFC in 1988 upon finishing fourth in the conference with 108 points. Nelson produced all of the Vikings' points with four field goals in the 12–3 win over Indianapolis on November 20. He also contributed the game-winning tallies with a 32-yard field goal with 15 seconds remaining in the 23–21 win over Philadelphia on September 25.

Darrin Nelson

Seasons: 1982–89, 1991–92 Running Back Height: 5′9″
Number: 20 Stanford Weight: 185

The Vikings took a beating for several years in the national press for selecting Darrin Nelson instead of Marcus Allen with the seventh overall pick in the 1982 draft. But while Allen went on to have a Hall-of-Fame career, Nelson also was a productive player in the National Football League, particularly during his two stints with the Vikings.

Nelson's running style—a stop-and-go, poor man's version of Barry Sanders—enabled him to lead the Vikings in both rushing and receiving in 1983. His stats were limited in part to his diminutive size. Not that his stature prevented him from doing the job; the Minnesota coaching staff feared his body would not withstand the constant pounding, thereby preventing Nelson from becoming a full-time force.

The Minnesota scouting department was enthralled with Nelson's multiple offensive abilities that enabled him to become the NCAA's all-time all-purpose yardage leader during his four years at Stanford. He battled a tender ankle as an NFL rookie yet still managed to contribute, placing second on the Vikings with 136 rushing yards while catching nine passes for 100 yards. He also became the first Minnesota rookie running back to start his first game, achieving the feat against Tampa Bay on September 12, 1982. Yet those numbers did nothing to silence any critics after the season, and left head coach Bud Grant defending his young player.

"A lot of people have expressed disappointment in what Darrin Nelson did last year, but we didn't feel that way," Grant said prior to the 1983 slate. "We think he does some things exceptionally well, his attitude is excellent, and he will only get better. He was nicked a couple of times and he just kept aggravating his ankle. So we just kept him out, particularly because the others (running backs) were doing such a good job."

His role increased substantially in 1983, with Nelson leading Minnesota in rushing with 642 yards on 154 carries as well in pass receptions and kickoff return average. He paced the NFC in kickoff returns with a 24.7-yard norm on 18 attempts, and ranked 18th in the conference with 51 catches for 618 yards.

The running back's best performance came against Green Bay on November 13, when Nelson reached the century mark on the ground for the first time in his career. He also set a club record for all-purpose yardage in a game with 278, gaining 119 rushing, 137 receiving and 22 on returns. Nelson's 137 yards on seven catches was the highest total for a Viking receiver during the 1983 season. He also had the team's longest run from scrimmage during the campaign with a 56-yard touchdown gallop during a 23–14 win at Chicago on October 9.

Nelson shared the starting halfback duties with Ted Brown in 1984 and contributed more with his all-around abilities than strictly as a running back. He ranked third in the NFC with a 22.8-yard average on kickoff returns while placing third on the team with 406 yards rushing. He also caught 27 passes for 162 yards.

In 1985, Nelson hit his stride and led the Vikings with 893 rushing yards. He posted his biggest days in back-to-back games, beginning with 122 yards in a 16–13 victory over Detroit on November 3, followed by a career-high 146 yards versus Green Bay on November 10. He also tied for third on the team with 43 receptions, including a team-best 12 receptions for 67 yards during a 21–17 triumph over San Diego on October 20. What's more, Nelson led the Vikings in punt returns, taking back 16 boots for 133 yards.

Darrin Nelson

Nelson paced the team in rushing for a second straight season in 1986 by gaining 793 yards on 191 carries, and was second on the club with a career-high 53 catches. In 1987, his 4.9-yard average on the ground topped the NFL, with Nelson gaining 642 yards on 131 carries while catching 26 passes for 129 yards. He also recorded a career-long 72-yard run in the 34–27 win over Denver on October 26, marking the longest carry from scrimmage in the NFC that year.

Despite his contributions, one event from Nelson's career still haunts Viking fans. In the waning moments of the 1987 NFC Championship Game against Washington, Nelson dropped a Wade Wilson pass at the goal line. Had Nelson caught the ball, Minnesota would have tied the score and, with all the momentum, likely sent the game into overtime. Instead, the Vikings turned the ball over on downs and watched the Redskins go to the Super Bowl and become NFL champions.

After leading the team in rushing for a fourth straight year by gaining 380 yards on 112 carries in 1988 before accumulating 124 yards on 31 attempts during the first five games in 1989, Nelson departed Minnesota on October 12 as part of the Herschel Walker trade with Dallas.

He resurfaced with the Vikings two years later after announcing his retirement following his release by San Diego. A third-down specialist and kick returner in 1991, Nelson paced Minnesota with 682 yards on 31 kickoff returns, ranked as the team's fourth-leading rusher with 210 yards on 28 attempts, and was the sixth-leading receiver with 19 catches for 142 yards. He also completed the only pass of his career that season, a 25-yard effort to Anthony Carter for a touchdown against Detroit on November 24.

Serving primarily as a kickoff returner in 1992, Nelson helped set the tone for at least two Minnesota triumphs with excellent runbacks to open games, and finished his career by leading Minnesota with 626 yards on 29 kickoff returns. He currently ranks among the Vikings' top 10 in several career categories, including first in kickoff returns (159), kickoff return yards (3,619) and combined net yards (10,365).

Richard Newbill

Season: 1990　　　　　　Linebacker　　　　　　Height: 6'1"
Number: 53　　　　　　　Miami (Fla.)　　　　　　Weight: 240

Houston's fifth-round draft choice in 1990, Richard Newbill was signed by the Vikings after he was released by the Oilers in training camp. Waived after playing in two games on special teams with Minnesota, he was picked up by Seattle, where he played sparingly in 1991 and 1992.

Pat Newman

Season: 1990　　　　　　Wide Receiver　　　　　Height: 5'11"
Number: 86　　　　　　　Utah State　　　　　　　Weight: 189

The Vikings' first 10th-round draft pick in 1990, Pat Newman was on the active roster briefly the following fall but did not take the field for a regular-season game.

Harry Newsome

Seasons: 1990–93　　　　Punter　　　　　　　　Height: 6'
Number: 18　　　　　　　Wake Forest　　　　　　Weight: 185

Harry Newsome virtually rewrote the Vikings' record book during his four seasons in the Twin Cities. On the Minnesota career charts, his average gross yards of 43.8 per punt tops second-place Greg Coleman by three full yards. His 45.5-yard average in 1991 and 45.0-yard norm in 1992, both of which paced the National Football Conference in their respective seasons, rank second and third all-time in Viking annals. Meanwhile, his 84-yard punt against Pittsburgh on December 20, 1992, is the longest ever by a Viking punter.

Signed as a Plan B free agent in 1990 after five seasons with the Steelers, Newsome was fifth in the NFC with a 42.3-yard average in his first season in the Upper Midwest. After pacing the conference the next two years, the steady kicker averaged 42.9 yards on 90 boots, 25 of which landed inside the 20-yard line, in 1993. Despite his consistency, the Vikings allowed Newsome to sign elsewhere after the campaign. Minnesota went with unproductive Bryan Barker out of training camp before signing Mike Saxon just prior to the start of the 1994 regular season.

Tim Newton

Seasons: 1985–89 Defensive Tackle Height: 6'
Number: 96 Florida Weight: 277

Minnesota needed a boost in several areas in 1985 after the worst overall season in team history and received a major one where the Vikings least expected it. Tim Newton, the team's second sixth-round draft choice, stepped into the middle of the defensive line as a rookie and solidified a unit that helped the purple rebound with a 7–9 record.

Newton earned a spot on the Pro Football Writers' All-Rookie team after recording 106 total tackles in 16 games, including 14 starts. He also became the first Minnesota defensive lineman to intercept two passes in one season. His first pick came in the 27–20 win over Buffalo on September 29, when Newton returned the interception 63 yards to set up a touchdown. On December 8, in the 26–7 victory over Tampa Bay, the tackle got his second steal on a deflection to set up a Vikings' field goal.

He built on his rookie year with a solid showing in 1986, leading the line with 92 total tackles. Newton earned Defensive Player of the Week honors from *Sports Illustrated* after recording 11 solo stops in the 27–24 win over San Francisco on October 12. The rest of campaign consisted of hills and valleys, with Newton getting the starting nod in nine of 15 games while missing two contests with a toe injury.

Newton's production decreased significantly beginning in 1987, when newcomer Henry Thomas took over the first-team role. He made 13 tackles in nine games that year, then played in 14 contests in 1988. His best performance came in his lone start, a seven-tackle showing in the 12–3 win over Indianapolis on November 20. Newton was once again a reserve in 1989, when he played in nine games. His final year in purple produced one big play of note, with Newton recovering a fumble and rumbling five yards to paydirt in Minnesota's 43–17 win over Atlanta on December 11.

Steve Niehaus

Season: 1979 Defensive Tackle Height: 6'4"
Number: 71 Notre Dame Weight: 255

Steve Niehaus joined the history books by becoming the first draft pick in Seattle Seahawks annals, the second player taken overall in the 1976 draft. Three years later he was traded to the Vikings during the preseason in exchange for Carl Eller and an eighth-round draft choice. Knee problems landed Niehaus on the injured reserve list for the first 11 weeks of the 1979 season before he was activated for the final five games, seeing limited action in three. He was waived during Minnesota's first training camp cuts in 1980.

Roosevelt Nix

Season: 1994   Defensive Tackle   Height: 6'6"
Number: 79   Central State (Ohio)   Weight: 292

Head coach Dennis Green envisioned Roosevelt Nix developing into a run-stuffing tackle in the middle of the Minnesota defensive line. The former Bengal's development was slow, however, resulting in his taking the field just twice in 1994 without making a play. He signed as a free agent with Green Bay after the campaign, but did not discover success in the National Football League.

Al Noga

Seasons: 1988–92   Defensive End   Height: 6'1"
Number: 99   Hawaii   Weight: 269

One of the quickest defensive ends off the snap in Vikings history, Al Noga was a pass-rushing specialist who often seemed to be on the brink of greatness. While he never attained that level of respect, he and Chris Doleman formed a terrific pair of bookends at the defensive end positions in the late 1980s and early 1990s.

A third-round draft pick in 1988, Noga blossomed in his second season with the Vikings after missing nearly half of his rookie year with a viral infection. The native of Samoa emerged as a starter and responded with 11.5 sacks in 1989. He was particularly effective in Minnesota's two triumphs over the Lions, posting a season-high nine hits, 2.5 sacks and a forced fumble during the 24–17 win on October 8 and two sacks and a fumble recovery in the 20–7 victory on October 22.

In 1990, a six-sack season for the defensive end, Noga recorded his first pass interception against the Lions and returned it 26 yards for a touchdown during the Vikings' 17–7 triumph on November 11. He also earned NFC Defensive Player of the Week honors for his showing in the 23–7 win over Green Bay on December 2. In that game, Noga had three solo tackles, a sack and a forced fumble he recovered in the end zone for a touchdown.

After a subpar showing in 1991, when he had just three sacks, Noga's best all-around season turned out to be his last in Minnesota. He reported to training camp 15 pounds lighter and dumped opposing signalcallers on nine occasions, forced two fumbles, and had 41 solo tackles. Although he had as many offsides penalties as some teams accumulate in a year, Noga was defended by the Vikings' coaching staff, who said the defensive end had garnered a bad rap. He came off the ball as well as anyone, and had excellent speed around the corner to reach the quarterback in the pocket. Though never that effective against the run, the undersized Noga had the legs to compensate for mistakes and make plays downfield.

Despite their praise, the Minnesota coaches grew weary of Noga's mental mistakes and allowed him to sign with Washington after the 1992 season.

Keith Nord

Seasons: 1979–85   Safety   Height: 6'
Number: 49   St. Cloud State   Weight: 188

Six years of perseverance as a role player led to a starting job for Keith Nord. The Minneapolis native made the Vikings' roster as a rookie free agent out of St. Cloud State in 1979 and worked as hard as anyone in purple to become a member of the first team in 1985.

Nord started the first 13 games of the 1985 season at free safety and produced 105 total tackles, good for sixth on the club. He was at his best against New Orleans on November 24, when Nord had nine solo hits and two assists. He added eight total stops and caused a fumble in the 31–16 win at Tampa Bay on September 15, and posted six primary tackles and four assists in the 28–21 victory over San Francisco on September 8, the first start of his career in the National Football League.

The fact that Nord started in 1985 is more remarkable when his past is considered. Captain of the kicking teams, a unit he led in tackles during each of his first four seasons with the Vikings, Nord ruptured the Achilles tendon in his right leg during the third game of the 1983 season. He missed the rest of that campaign as well as all of 1984 before recovering and emerging as a starter.

Nord became captain of the special teams squad with his all-out hustle. A quarterback in college, he impressed head coach Bud Grant as a rookie with his willingness to sacrifice his body on all plays, leading to 19 special teams tackles, a forced fumble and a quarterback sack during his first season. Nord added 21 unassisted tackles in 1980, yet his highlight of the campaign came at Washington on November 2. The safety picked up a kickoff and returned the football 70 yards for a touchdown in Minnesota's 39–14 thrashing of the Redskins.

In 1981, Nord again led the team in kick coverage tackles. He saw extensive time on defense against Chicago and registered 12 unassisted hits in the 24–21 victory on October 4. He overcame a concussion during the 1982 season to lead the special teams in tackles. His first career interception came in the 27–21 win over the Browns on September 4, 1983, before suffering his Achilles injury two games later.

After starting in 1985 before losing his job for the last three games of the season, Nord was released in training camp just prior to the 1986 campaign. Aside from his outstanding hustle on special teams during his seven years in purple, Nord was one of the most visible Vikings in the community. He was nominated for the NFL Man-of-the-Year Award in 1984, and was particularly active in the March of Dimes and the Muscular Dystrophy Association.

Tony Norman

Seasons: 1979, 1987　　　Defensive End　　　Height: 6'5"
Number: 97　　　Iowa State　　　Weight: 270

Tony Norman spent the 1979 season on injured reserve with the Vikings prior to receiving his release during training camp the following year. After a six-year stint in the Canadian Football League, Norman played in two replacement games for the Vikings in 1987.

Brent Novoselsky

Seasons: 1989–94　　　Tight End　　　Height: 6'2"
Number: 85　　　Pennsylvania　　　Weight: 237

Originally signed as a free agent on September 13, 1989, after being released by Green Bay, Brent Novoselsky emerged as an exemplary special teams player and backup tight end during his six seasons with Minnesota. No one stuck his neck out more often on kick coverage than Novoselsky, who rarely had difficulty finding the action, resulting in 91 special teams tackles during his days in purple.

While he earned his reputation on special teams, Novoselsky ranks third in Vikings history for most consecutive games at tight end, with 66. He served mostly as a blocker at the position, but often found a seam and made a big catch when the opportunity arose. His most noted accomplishment occurred when he made a diving, over-the-shoulder grab just inside the end zone on fourth down in the 1989 season finale against Cincinnati. That grab led the Vikings to a 29–21 victory and a trip to the playoffs. Two of his four catches went for touchdowns in 1989, with Novoselsky also pulling in four passes in each of his next two seasons with the team.

Ironically, Novoselsky's propensity for making plays eventually cost him his career in the National Football League. He suffered a neck injury that resulted in a herniated disk against the Bears on December 1, 1994, and was lost for the remainder of the campaign. Upon further review in the off-season, doctors advised Novoselsky from playing again.

"Brent was our number one special teams player the last three years," head coach Dennis Green said after Novoselsky went down. "I think not having him affected us. We missed him because he was a good player."

O

Dave O'Brien

| Seasons: 1963–64 | Guard | Height: 6'3" |
| Number: 74 | Boston College | Weight: 247 |

The Vikings outbid Boston of the American Football League for Dave O'Brien's services after head coach Norm Van Brocklin saw the All-Yankee Conference performer during the Crusade Bowl in Baltimore. Minnesota's 13th pick in the 1963 draft, O'Brien impressed the Vikings with his toughness and agility, and was employed as a backup guard and special teams performer for all 14 games in both 1963 and 1964. His tenure in the Upper Midwest concluded when he was traded to the Giants in 1965 for defensive end Bob Taylor.

Frank Ori

| Season: 1987 | Guard | Height: 6'5" |
| Number: 69 | Northern Iowa | Weight: 255 |

Frank Ori started at left guard on the Vikings' offensive line during the three replacement games in 1987.

Dave Osborn

| Seasons: 1965–75 | Running Back | Height: 6' |
| Number: 41 | North Dakota | Weight: 208 |

It did not take long for Dave Osborn to prove just how tough a running back he was.

Head coach Norm Van Brocklin took pride in fielding tough players, and had just his type of performer in training camp in 1965. Dale Hackbart had joined the Vikings after establishing himself as one of the league's most physical secondary performers. In July, Hackbart was trying to prove himself to his new teammates while earning a roster spot, and figured he could make an example out of a rookie running back during one-on-one drills.

The exercise calls for a ball carrier to start at his 5-yard line while the defensive player begins in the end zone. The defensive player cannot cross the goal line until the ball carrier moves past the five. The winner is determined when either the ball carrier scores or the defensive player makes the tackle. Without question, it is one of the toughest, most physical drills in camp.

Hackbart was pitted against Osborn, a rookie 13th-round draft choice whom few of his teammates knew. The running back took the ball, headed straight toward Hackbart, and buried the defender on his way to the end zone. The veteran demanded a rematch, only to experience the same result. A third confrontation saw Osborn score a third time, again with the safety wondering what had hit him. When Hackbart rose to his feet, he said, "Rookie, I don't know who you are, but you should make this team."

The rest is history. The Vikings have had their fair share of standout running backs during their first 38 seasons, but no one was tougher or more

Dave Osborn

intense than Osborn. Reserved and serious about every aspect of life, Osborn was not shy about becoming a human battering ram on the gridiron. He was not the fastest runner and his moves were neither graceful nor impressive. Yet regardless of the task, the fearless Osborne ran over would-be tacklers from both the fullback and halfback positions and brought defenders to their knees when blocking.

"No one can match him for concentration and enthusiasm, with a good measure of ability, too," said Jerry Burns, Minnesota's offensive coordinator from 1968–85.

Head coach Bud Grant marveled about an Osborn trait that he said he had never seen another player possess. Though never the most fleet afoot, Osborn could elevate his speed when necessary. He could find an extra gear no one knew he had and out-run even the league's fastest defenders.

"Ozzie and Bill Brown epitomize the Vikings," Grant said late in Osborn's career. "Desire and hustle guys. They love football, the games, the practices, and will do anything to help the team win. Dave is in a secondary role now, but he could get us a hundred yards any week."

The Vikings drafted Osborn based on scouting reports that said he was a hard-nosed runner with good outside speed and a willingness to block who needed to improve his pass receiving ability. He wound up gaining 106 yards with two touchdowns on 20 carries while returning 18 kickoffs for 422 yards in his rookie campaign. He continued to improve during the 1966 season, including his 118-yard effort on 19 carries against the Bears on December 18. That performance enabled Osborn to finish as the team's second-leading rusher for the year with 344 yards and a touchdown. He also upgraded his receiving skills by catching 16 tosses for 147 yards and two scores.

With his unmatched determination and vast array of second-effort moves, Osborn stepped into the starting lineup in 1967 and became the offense's top performer. He led Minnesota in rushing and pass receiving by ranking second in the National Football League with 972 yards on the ground (at the time a Viking record), while catching 34 passes for 272 yards. He also set the team mark for most rushing yards in a single game with 155 against Green Bay on December 3, and registered the longest run from scrimmage when he galloped 73 yards versus San Francisco on September 17.

A knee injury caused Osborn to miss most of the 1968 season, limiting him to 140 yards on 42 carries. He rebounded to lead the Vikings to the NFL Championship in 1969. Osborn paced the team with 643 yards rushing and seven touchdowns on 186 carries while catching 22 passes for 326 yards and another score. He added two touchdowns in Minnesota's 23–20 victory over Los Angeles in the Western Conference Championship Game on December 27, and rushed for 108 yards and one touchdown in the 27–7 triumph against Cleveland in the NFL Championship Game on January 4. A week later Osborn capped the campaign by scoring the first Minnesota touchdown in Super Bowl history, a four-yard gallop against the Chiefs.

With the help of a 139-yard effort in the 16–13 win over the Bears on December 5, Osborn again steered the Vikings in rushing with 681 yards during the 1970 season to earn his lone Pro Bowl invitation. A knee injury hampered him throughout the second half of the 1971 slate, yet he still accumulated 349 yards and five touchdowns on the ground while catching 25 passes for 195 yards. Lingering knee problems hampered Ozzie again in 1972 and held him to 261 yards on 82 carries and another 166 yards on 20 receptions. All three of his touchdowns that year came in the season's second game, a 34–10 triumph at Detroit on September 24.

Osborn relieved rookie Chuck Foreman in 1973 but still ran well when called upon, gaining 216 yards on 48 carries for a 4.5-yard norm. In fact, the acquisition of Foreman was the last of several occasions during his 11-year career that the Vikings thought Ozzie needed to be replaced. The most notable period came in 1967, when Minnesota acquired Clint Jones, a former All-American with the kind of athletic talent most players only dream about. Osborn, however, refused to relinquish his job without a fight, sacrificing every ounce of energy to ensure success.

A classic example of how his hard work paid dividends was seen in 1974, when Osborn regained his starting job and formed a solid one-two punch with Foreman. While Foreman was the feature back on his way to Rookie of the Year honors, Osborn rushed for more than 90 yards in four games to finish with 514 yards on 130 carries for the season. His best performance came in Minnesota's 14–10 victory in the NFC Championship Game against the Rams, with Ozzie gaining 76 yards on the ground and scoring the winning points on a one-yard plunge.

Osborn backed up Ed Marinaro and carried the pigskin just 32 times for 94 yards in 1975 while serving primarily on special teams. Even though his number was not called often on offense, Osborn contributed with his leadership and the example he provided with his hard work. Those traits were missed when he retired prior to the 1976 season with 4,320 yards rushing (currently fourth in Minnesota history) and 29 touchdowns. He also caught 173 passes for 1,412 yards and seven scores.

Clancy Osborne

Seasons: 1961–62　　　　　Linebacker　　　　　Height: 6'3"
Number: 31　　　　　　　　Arizona State　　　　Weight: 217

Clancy Osborne, who failed to make the Rams' roster in 1958 because he was too skinny, joined the Vikings from the veterans pool after gaining 20 pounds and starting for two years in San Francisco.

Osborne started most of the 1961 season with Minnesota. He led the Vikings with eight tackles for lost yardage and was second on the team with four interceptions. Two of his picks led to touchdowns. He victimized Johnny Unitas and the Colts by returning an interception to the Baltimore 16-yard line on October 1. Another key steal took place late in the game on December 3, setting up a Raymond Hayes' scoring gallop in the Vikings' 42–21 win over Los Angeles.

Osborne played in all 14 games in 1962 but gave way to the team's younger linebackers over the course of the campaign. After Minnesota posted a disappointing 2–11–1 record, Osborne was among the veterans sent packing when he and Cliff Livingston were traded to the Rams in 1963 for a sixth-round draft choice.

P

Alan Page

Seasons: 1967–78	Defensive Tackle	Height: 6'5"
Number: 88	Notre Dame	Weight: 255

A more successful, albeit unusual, resume may not exist. Key member of a national championship team in college. First-round draft pick in the National Football League. First NFL defensive player to earn Most Valuable Player honors. Inductee into the Pro Football Hall of Fame. Minnesota Supreme Court Justice.

In fact, if Alan Page had his way, most people would be awed only slightly by his on-field accomplishments. Then again, Page is unlike most people ever to wear shoulder pads. The determined, driven defensive tackle always did things his way, for he believed—correctly—that no one knew his abilities and limitations better than he.

While Page never made much of his accomplishments on the gridiron, the results are a primary reason the Vikings were Super Bowl contenders in each of his dozen seasons with the team. Although he almost always missed the first few weeks of training camp in order to complete summer semesters at the University of Minnesota's law school, Page proved to be the final link to a dominating defensive line that already featured Carl Eller, Jim Marshall and Gary Larsen. He became a starter during the fourth game of his rookie season, then played a pivotal role in Minnesota's 10–7 victory over Green Bay a week later. For the next decade, no one in NFL history played the defensive tackle position better than Page.

His performance always under control, Page dominated with his amazing footwork. Said head coach Bud Grant, never one to exaggerate a player's ability, Page "was the best defensive player I've ever seen." The lineman had an uncanny ability to react at the snap of the ball and excellent speed and range to go with his cat-like quickness. He also seemed to possess a sixth sense that placed him around the football, particularly on key fumble recoveries and the occasional pass interception.

But it was his ability to remain on his feet regardless of what opposing linemen were trying to do that allowed Page to run down ball carriers and reach quarterbacks more rapidly and efficiently than anyone thought possible. He was also one of the most competitive players ever to wear purple. Whether it was refusing to quit when knocked off-stride or trying to improve his game with new methods, Page made the majority of his plays because he simply refused to quit, never wanting the offensive opponent to have the satisfaction of saying he got the upper hand on Page.

The former member of the Fightin' Irish was acquired with a first-round choice the Vikings obtained from the Rams in the trade that sent Tommy Mason and Hal Bedsole to Los Angeles in exchange for Marlin McKeever and the pick. He emerged as the only rookie to start in Grant's first season at the Viking helm. While he would disagree with Grant on occasion, Page became the first and one of the few rookies to earn a starting job under

Alan Page

the head coach. Ironically, he played at 278 pounds in his first year but lost 20 pounds prior to the next season in order to improve his quickness. The alteration worked, for Page earned his first Pro Bowl invitation during the 1968 campaign.

Page blossomed into a perennial All-Pro performer in 1969. His interception of a Roman Gabriel pass sealed Minnesota's 23–20 win over Los Angeles in the Western Conference Championship on December 27. Earlier in the campaign, he deflected a pass that was intercepted by Marshall, who lateraled the ball to Page, who rumbled 15 yards for a touchdown during the 27–0 victory against the Lions in snowy, muddy Detroit on November 27. He posted another score on a 65-yard fumble recovery a year later against Chicago, a 24–0 triumph on October 11. That year Page also was Defensive Player of the Year in the NFC and received All-Pro recognition for the third straight season.

An All-Pro again in 1971, the year he became the first defensive player to be named MVP in the NFL, Page continued to dominate on the field and in the award balloting. He earned his fifth straight Pro Bowl invite in 1972 despite suffering a deep pull in his right calf muscle in the second preseason game before aggravating it early in the campaign during practice. He played the year in pain, which hampered his speed and power. Back to health in 1973, Page was named NFL Lineman of the Year by *Pro Football Weekly* before registering 14 sacks in 1974.

Page put more pressure on the quarterback with 14 sacks while causing seven fumbles in 1975. He dumped the signalcaller on a career-high 20 occasions during the regular season and postseason in 1976. The lineman then tied for the club lead with 107 solo tackles and registered a dozen sacks in 1977.

Page also was proficient at blocking field goals and extra point attempts. Never were he and his teammates better at keeping footballs from reaching the uprights than in 1976, when he batted down two field goal tries and three conversions. Page blocked a PAT and a field goal against Pittsburgh on October 4 during a 17–6 Minnesota win on *Monday Night Football*. He also led the tremendous defensive charge to gain some belated revenge from Super Bowl IX.

Despite his effectiveness, Page's career with Minnesota came to an end in 1978, the same year he earned his law degree from the University. He had shed more than 50 pounds from his 6-foot-5 frame since his rookie year and more than 30 pounds over the previous two seasons, down to 225. Grant firmly believed that a defensive tackle could not survive, not to mention succeed, at that weight in the NFL, a point Page disagreed with wholeheartedly. The two icons butted heads, resulting in Page's being waived midway through the season. He joined defensive coordinator Buddy Ryan in Chicago and had another couple of productive campaigns before pursuing his other interests on a full-time basis.

His departure from the Vikings notwithstanding, Page's accomplishments are still awe-inspiring. In addition to earning league MVP honors, he went to eight straight Pro Bowls, earned All-Pro recognition on six occasions, played in four Super Bowls, and was inducted into the Pro Football Hall of Fame in 1988. Although sacks were not an official stat until 1982, Page retired ranking second all-time in league history in quarterback dumps with 148.5 (113 coming with the Vikings). He also excelled on special teams, and ranks second in Minnesota annals with 16 blocked kicks. Dressed in purple, he had 868 solo tackles and 1,120 total stops, and was named to the Vikings' Silver Anniversary All-Time Team in 1985.

David Palmer

Seasons: 1994–98
Number: 22
Wide Receiver
Alabama
Height: 5'8"
Weight: 169

David Palmer

When David Palmer arrived in Minnesota as a second-round draft pick in 1994, the former Alabama quarterback-running back-wide receiver said he could make the first defender miss him every time on punt returns. For the past five years, Palmer has lived up to his claims while becoming the most proficient punt returner in Vikings history.

Through the 1998 season, Palmer ranked as the club's all-time leader in punts returned for a touchdown with two. His first victim was Detroit on Thanksgiving Day in 1995, when Palmer weaved through traffic before hitting the right side and dashing 74 yards to paydirt. The following season, on September 29 at New York, he scurried 69 yards to the end zone. He also had a scoring punt return called back due to a penalty during a Thanksgiving Day contest against Dallas in 1998.

Additionally, Palmer is the franchise leader in punt return average (10.6) and ranks second to Leo Lewis in punt return yardage (1,484) and punt returns (140). He was at the top of his game in 1995, when he led the National Football League in punt return average with a team-record 13.2 yards per attempt. The 1997 season was similar, with Palmer placing first in the NFC with a punt return norm of 13.1 yards, while in 1998 he returned the Vikings' first kickoff for a touchdown since 1989 when he raced 88 yards to paydirt during the 38–28 victory at Baltimore on December 13.

As proficient as Palmer has been returning kicks, the Vikings longed for more contributions from the multi-talented athlete early in his career. The fourth wide receiver during his first three years in Minnesota, Palmer caught just 24 passes during that time, with his 12 receptions for 100 yards in 1995 serving as the high-water mark. Quarterback Warren Moon complained that he could not find the diminutive Palmer in traffic, while the Minnesota coaches said that Palmer needed to improve his route running.

Regardless of the reason for his minimal production, Palmer moved to running back in 1997, replacing Amp Lee as the third-down back. Early on the situation remained unchanged, leaving Palmer disappointed.

"It's been an ongoing story for three years now," Palmer said midway through the 1997 slate. "But you know, I'm still around here, so they must like something about my game. Of course, I've been very frustrated, but I have to keep my cool and stay calm. I'm just waiting for my chance . . . There's still time for me. I will put up some big numbers. My time will come."

Palmer may have a future in soothsaying, for his role increased significantly in the second half of 1997. He enjoyed the biggest day of his career in a 29–22 victory over Chicago on November 9. Against the Bears, Palmer ran untouched for eight yards on a pitch-out for the team's first touchdown, then displayed Cris Carter-like abilities by dragging his toes inbounds for a seven-yard TD catch. Later in the campaign, he added a career-high 249 all-purpose yards against Green Bay on December 1, giving everyone associated with the Vikes hope that Palmer could become a significant cog in the Minnesota engine.

He did just that in 1998. With his exceptional quickness and ability to change direction, Palmer showed how tough he could be by excelling in third-down situations. He caught 18 tosses for 185 yards and even lined up at quarterback to run the single-wing formation on a couple of occasions. Combine that performance with his 289 yards on punt returns and 1,176 yards on kickoff returns and Palmer was a key, yet unheralded component in the Vikings' Central Division championship season.

Anthony Parker

| Seasons: 1992–94 | Cornerback | Height: 5'10" |
| Number: 27 | Arizona State | Weight: 181 |

Anthony Parker went from a journeyman reserve to a starting cornerback during his three seasons with the Vikings. A standout in the World League in 1991 who bounced between with Chiefs, Jets and Colts early in his career, Parker found a temporary home in the northern plains and responded by epitomizing defensive coordinator Tony Dungy's opportunistic defense with numerous big-play performances.

Parker intercepted three passes as a nickel back during his first season in purple. He had an outstanding month in November, picking off the first aerial of his professional career in the 35–7 win at Tampa Bay on November 8, and returning a fumble 58 yards to paydirt against the Oilers a week later. A career-best 42-yard punt return followed on November 22 to set up a touchdown in the 17–13 win versus Cleveland. Parker then intercepted two passes versus the Rams on November 29, one of which led to a touchdown in Minnesota's 31–17 triumph.

Leg and ankle injuries limited Parker's playing time and production to one interception in 1993. He rebounded to earn a starting job in 1994, when Parker was fifth on the team with 78 total tackles and paced the club with four interceptions. Once again he had a career month, setting a league record by scoring defensive touchdowns in three consecutive games. He returned a Dave Brown toss 44 yards for six points in Minnesota's 27–10 win over the Giants on October 10. Ten days later, he scooped up a fumble and raced 23 yards to the goal line in the Vikes' 13–10 overtime victory against the Packers. The following week, during a 36–13 triumph at Tampa Bay on October 30, Parker scampered 41 yards to score on a first-quarter interception. Those efforts earned him NFC Defensive Player of the Month honors for October.

Parker also provided the Vikings with their first legitimate punt returner since Leo Lewis retired in 1991. He possessed the quickness, vision and instincts to catch the ball and head upfield. As a result, he finished fourth in the NFC with a 10.2-yard average in 1992. Ailments limited him to nine returns in 1993, while the arrival of David Palmer placed Parker's responsibilities solely on defense in 1994, his final year in purple before signing as a free agent with the Rams.

Rickey Parks

| Season: 1987 | Wide Receiver | Height: 6'1" |
| Number: 81 | Arkansas-Pine Bluff | Weight: 179 |

In two replacement games with Minnesota in 1987, Rickey Parks caught three passes for 46 yards.

Doug Paschal

| Seasons: 1980–81 | Running Back | Height: 6'2" |
| Number: 40 | North Carolina | Weight: 200 |

Doug Paschal received praise from Bud Grant after the running back's rookie season when the head coach said he should have used Paschal more often during the 1980 campaign. Seeing action in all 16 games as a reserve running back and special teams performer, Paschal carried the ball 15 times for 53 yards, and scored a touchdown on a 10-yard run during Minnesota's 23–20 win over New Orleans on November 30. He also caught two passes for 18 yards and returned four kickoffs for 66 yards.

Paschal looked to play a bigger role in 1981 until his hopes were dashed when he injured his right knee while returning a kickoff in the final pre-season game, against Los Angeles. He underwent surgery and spent all of 1981 on injured reserve. Paschal was forced to retire on August 9, 1982, after the knee failed him during training camp.

Jerry Patton

Season: 1971   Defensive Tackle   Height: 6'3"
Number: 79   Nebraska   Weight: 265

After playing with Omaha in the Continental League in 1969, Jerry Patton spent all of the 1970 season and most of 1971 on the Vikings' taxi squad before seeing limited action in three games. He went on to play two full years in Buffalo and another with Philadelphia.

Eddie Payton

Seasons: 1980–82   Kick Returner   Height: 5'6"
Number: 31   Jackson State   Weight: 179

Eddie Payton, known as "The Human Pinball," never reached the lofty accomplishments of his brother, Walter Payton, yet did an impressive job as a return man for the Vikings during the early 1980s. With the Metropolitan Stadium crowd chanting "Ed-die, Ed-die" as he stood near the goal line awaiting kickoffs, Payton emerged as the most exciting returner in Minnesota annals during his short tenure with the team.

Signed as a free agent after one year in the Canadian Football League, the former Lion made an impression on head coach Bud Grant when he returned a kickoff and a punt for touchdowns against Minnesota in a 30–21 Vikings' victory over Detroit on December 17, 1977. Grant remembered that performance and acquired the returner in 1980, when Payton amassed the most punt returns (34), kickoff returns (53) and kickoff return yardage (1,184) in the National Football League during his first season in purple. In spite of those numbers, he was deemed the tilter of the playoff game with Philadelphia upon fumbling a punt after taking his eye off the ball, allowing the Eagles to recover and take control of the 31–16 decision on January 3, 1981.

Payton recorded the longest kickoff return for a touchdown in the league in 1981 and the second-longest play in Minnesota history, dashing 99 yards to paydirt against the Raiders on September 14. Payton also averaged 23 yards on kickoffs and eight yards on punts, then posted norms of 8.1 yards on punts and 22.6 yards on kickoffs in 1982, his final year in the league.

After being released by the Vikings, Payton became the first player to sign a contract with the upstart United States Football League by catching on with Memphis in 1983.

Jayice Pearson

Season: 1993   Safety   Height: 5'11"
Number: 24   Washington   Weight: 187

Jayice Pearson signed with Minnesota for $550,000, about $150,000 less than his employer for the previous seven years, the Kansas City Chiefs, were offering in 1993. His reasoning centered on Pearson's desire to be reunited with defensive coordinator Tony Dungy.

After he was slowed by a knee injury during much of training camp, Pearson played in 13 games with the Vikings, recording 20 total tackles and intercepting one pass. He served as Minnesota's dime back and saw some action in nickel coverage, particularly when Vencie Glenn was injured. He was released by the Vikings after his first and only campaign in purple.

John Pentecost

Season: 1967   Guard   Height: 6'2"
Number: 66   UCLA   Weight: 250

A two-year veteran of the Canadian Football League, John Pentecost spent most of the 1967 season on the Vikings' taxi squad. Activated when starter Milt Sunde went down with a knee injury, Pentecost stepped on the gridiron for four games in a reserve role during the latter part of the campaign.

Pete Perreault

Season: 1971   Guard   Height: 6'3"
Number: 68   Long Beach State   Weight: 248

Signed during the regular season, Pete Perreault played in 10 games as a member of the special teams with the Vikings in 1971, which proved to be the final 10 contests of his 86-game career in the National Football League.

Dick Pesonen

Season: 1961   Defensive Back   Height: 6'
Number: 22   Minnesota-Duluth   Weight: 190

A native of Grand Rapids, Minnesota, Dick Pesonen joined the Vikings from the veterans pool after spending his rookie season with Green Bay. He took the field in purple for 11 games in 1961 and intercepted one pass. Pesonen also placed fourth on the team with six kickoff returns for 136 yards, his longest a 60-yard gallop in the fourth quarter of the Vikings' 52–35 loss to Chicago on December 17.

Ken Peterson

Season: 1961   Center   Height: 6'2"
Number: 66   Utah   Weight: 235

Minnesota's 14th-round selection in its first amateur draft, Ken Patterson played in 12 games at guard and center as part of the Vikings' porous offensive line in 1961. His duties were reduced to backup center, behind Mick Tingelhoff, the following year during training camp, but his performance did not merit a spot on the roster to see any additional game action.

Anthony Phillips

Season: 1998   Cornerback   Height: 6'2"
Number: 28   Texas A&M-Kingsville   Weight: 209

Signed as a free agent after spending three years with the Atlanta Falcons, Anthony Phillips spent the first seven weeks of the 1998 season on the reserve-physically unable to perform list due to a knee injury he suffered during mini-camp. He was activated prior to the Tampa Bay game on November 1 and saw his first action in the defensive secondary a week later, when Torrian Gray suffered a major knee injury against New Orleans on November 8. After serving as the Vikings' nickel back for two weeks, Phillips returned to the injured list and missed the last six contests.

Bobby Phillips

Season: 1995
Number: 30

Running Back
Virginia Union

Height: 5'9"
Weight: 187

After leading the team in scoring with 18 points during the preseason, Bobby Phillips became the only undrafted rookie to spend the entire 1995 campaign with the Vikings. A special teams performer and reserve running back, Phillips gained 26 yards on 14 carries and was fourth on the team with four kickoff returns for a 15-yard average.

An all-out type of player, Phillips never rested, even during the bye week. He instead got married at the Mall of America before being waived during training camp in 1996.

Jim Phillips

Seasons: 1965–67
Number: 82

End
Auburn

Height: 6'1"
Weight: 195

More beautiful, precise routes have never been run by a Viking than those of Jim "Red" Phillips. His craftsmanship as well as his determined, aggressive approach to the game served as primary reasons the red-head enjoyed near-unprecedented success in his six years with the Rams. By the time the Vikings acquired his services along with those of Gary Larsen in exchange for the rights to unsigned wide receiver Jack Snow in 1965, Phillips ranked among the top 10 receivers in the history of the National Football League.

The move to Minnesota did little to halt Phillips' accomplishments. Despite suffering from a hand infection, he caught 15 passes for 185 yards and a touchdown in 12 games during the 1965 season. He shifted to tight end in 1966 due to Hal Bedsole's injury and still ranked second on the team with 554 yards receiving and three touchdowns while placing third with 32 catches. His most satisfying grab had to be the longest pass play of the season for the Vikings. Phillips hauled in a 68-yard bomb from quarterback Fran Tarkenton in the second quarter on his way to a six-reception performance in Minnesota's 35–7 win over Los Angeles on October 16.

Phillips credited his pass-catching ability to his childhood job in Alexander City, Alabama. He had 190 customers on his 10-mile paper route that required rising at 3:30 a.m., when he would roll every newspaper. "When you fold papers, you use your hands in a full range of motion," Phillips said. "I think that maybe I got strong hands, which you need as an end, accidently, folding newspapers for five years."

Phillips' swan song took place in 1967. He bowed out with 21 catches in 13 games with the Vikings, including three touchdown grabs, two of which came in the final three contests of his NFL career.

Joe Phillips

Season: 1986
Number: 91

Defensive Tackle
Southern Methodist

Height: 6'4"
Weight: 278

Joe Phillips, the Vikings' fourth-round draft choice in 1986, was caught in a numbers game during the final cutdowns of his second season. After serving sufficiently in a reserve role as a rookie, Phillips was waived on September 7, 1987, while Minnesota opted to keep four other defensive tackles, among them Stafford Mays and Tim Newton. Ten years later, Phillips was entering his sixth straight season as a starter on the Kansas City line following a five-year stint with the Chargers.

While wearing purple, Phillips played in 16 games and started one, against Cincinnati on November 23 in place of the injured Keith Millard.

Phillips recorded five tackles during the campaign and recovered a fumble versus Detroit on November 9.

Kurt Ploeger

Season: 1987   Defensive Tackle   Height: 6'5"
Number: 63   Gustavus Adolphus   Weight: 259

Kurt Ploeger, who attended LeSueur High School in Minnesota, saw the game played similar to the prep level during his one appearance for the Vikings' replacement team in 1987.

Ray Poage

Season: 1963   End   Height: 6'3"
Number: 86   Texas   Weight: 200

Deals involving the Vikings' first two picks left third-rounder Ray Poage as Minnesota's highest-drafted player in 1963. A fullback at Texas, the former Longhorn was moved to end after suffering a separated shoulder during his first training camp. He wound up playing seven games in purple, catching 15 passes for 354 yards.

Both of his touchdowns were long-range strikes, and both came against the 49ers in Minnesota's 45–14 triumph over San Francisco on September 29. Poage caught a 57-yard scoring toss from quarterback Fran Tarkenton to tie the game at 7–7 in the second quarter, then tied the game at 14–14 on the Vikes' next possession when he hauled in a 67-yard touchdown pass.

With Hal Bedsole on board in 1964, Poage was traded to Philadelphia along with Chuck Lamson, Terry Kosens and Don Hultz in exchange for Ted Dean and the rights to Bob Berry.

Randy Poltl

Season: 1974   Safety   Height: 6'3"
Number: 29   Stanford   Weight: 190

Randy Poltl sipped from the expensive crystal containing the finest wine during his brief time with the Vikings. Minnesota's 12th-round pick in 1974 played in just five regular-season games as an extra defensive back in dime coverages. He then participated in the postseason and intercepted a James Harris pass against the Rams in the NFC Championship Game on December 29 before recovering a fumble against Pittsburgh in Super Bowl IX. He moved on to Denver in 1975 and played in another Super Bowl during his three seasons as a Bronco.

Ron Porter

Season: 1973   Linebacker   Height: 6'3"
Number: 52   Idaho   Weight: 232

Acquired from Philadelphia during training camp in exchange for a fifth-round draft choice, Ron Porter was a six-year veteran of the National Football League who served on the Vikings' special teams for 13 games in 1973, his final season at the game's top level.

Art Powell

Season: 1968
Number: 24
Wide Receiver
San Jose State
Height: 6'3"
Weight: 211

The finale of Art Powell's 10-year career in professional football was a one-game appearance with the Vikings in 1968. Powell caught a 31-yard pass in the season opener, a 47–7 triumph over Atlanta at Metropolitan Stadium on September 14.

John Powers

Season: 1966
Number: 83
Tight End
Notre Dame
Height: 6'2"
Weight: 215

After four years with Pittsburgh, John Powers slid through Viking Land for five games as a blocker during the 1966 season. His presence was deemed unneeded after Minnesota traded for veteran Marlin McKeever and drafted John Beasley the following offseason.

Jim Prestel

Seasons: 1961–65
Number: 79
Defensive Tackle
Idaho
Height: 6'5"
Weight: 275

Jim Prestel arrived in Minnesota from Cleveland as one of six players acquired in the Jim Marshall deal just prior to the start of the 1961 season. The Browns' sixth-round draft pick in 1959, Prestel earned a starting job on the Vikings' defensive line and remained there for the franchise's first five years.

Prestel was without question the Vikings' top lineman during the team's first season. Although nothing about his play was flashy or overwhelming, the off-season school teacher was a steady performer who received plaudits throughout the National Football League as one of the better performers in the middle of the line. He also was dependable, making every start in the first four seasons and playing in all but one contest in his final campaign in purple.

The Indianapolis native had a couple of big plays for the Vikings. He led the team with two blocked kicks in 1961 before adding one in each of the next two seasons. Prestel lived every lineman's dream when he intercepted a pass and returned the ball 26 yards for a touchdown during a 23–23 tie with Detroit on November 22, 1964. A year later, he registered one of three Vikings safeties on the season while making life as difficult as possible for opponents in the center of the defense.

After five seasons with the Vikes, Prestel's career in purple ended when Minnesota went with a youth movement in 1966. Prestel and Larry Vargo were traded to the Giants in exchange for Bill Briggs and a sixth-round draft choice.

Anthony Prior

Seasons: 1996–97
Number: 40
Cornerback
Washington State
Height: 5'11"
Weight: 186

Anthony Prior was signed on December 4, 1996, to provide depth on the Vikings' punt and kickoff coverage units. He played in the final three games as well as the playoff contest against Dallas, registering two special teams tackles against Green Bay.

Re-signed for 1997, Prior made 12 hits, including four solo shots, on special teams before landing on injured reserve in early December. He was released by the Vikings after the season and signed with Kansas City.

Ted Provost

Season: 1970	Defensive Back	Height: 6'3"
Number: 28	Ohio State	Weight: 195

Ted Provost came to the Vikings in his rookie year after being drafted in the seventh round by the Rams. Acquired from Los Angeles for a fifth-round draft pick, Provost showed some ability as a cornerback and safety during his seven-game stint in purple in 1970. His potential, however, was not considered strong enough for Minnesota to employ his services beyond training camp the following year.

Palmer Pyle

Season: 1964	Guard	Height: 6'3"
Number: 69	Michigan State	Weight: 247

Palmer Pyle may not have been a relative of the fictitious television Marine private Gomer Pyle, but the football player always seemed to be involved in unusual circumstances. Topping the charts was an event at New York against the Giants on December 6, 1964. While residing on the sidelines, Pyle, who missed half of the 1963 season with a head injury, built a bonfire, only to become a human torch. He also was involved in some fisticuffs and related extracurricular events, with head coach Norm Van Brocklin and Pyle's wife, Marie, the daughter of a Chicago Mafia leader, serving as his primary opposition.

The guard, who was acquired from the Colts in exchange for Steve Stonebreaker, played in 10 games as a reserve offensive lineman for the Vikings in 1964. While his Minnesota tenure lasted just one season, his six-year career in the National Football League concluded with the Raiders two seasons after the Vikings traded him to the Bears in 1965 for a fifth-round draft choice.

Kelly Quinn

Season: 1987	Linebacker	Height: 6'1"
Number: 92	Michigan State	Weight: 220

    Kelly Quinn took the field for all three of Minnesota's replacement contests in 1987 after toiling for two years in the Canadian Football League.

Mike Rabold

Seasons: 1961–62
Number: 64
Guard
Indiana
Height: 6'2"
Weight: 239

"Most of the time, we had a 'score from 70-yards out' offense," head coach Norm Van Brocklin said after the 1962 season. One reason for that approach centered on the Vikings' inability to run the ball effectively, with Minnesota enduring one six-game stretch in 1962 in which the team failed to score a rushing touchdown.

One of the early scapegoats was Mike Rabold. Selected from St. Louis in the veterans pool, Rabold started the franchise's first 28 games at right guard. While his effort was never questioned, the former All-Big Ten lineman did not possess the talent necessary to help take the Vikings to the next level. As a result, Rabold was replaced by Larry Bowie, a former defensive player, for the 1963 campaign. Rabold played four more years with Chicago before dying tragically in a highway accident shortly after retiring from the game.

John Randle

Seasons: 1990–98
Number: 93
Defensive Lineman
Texas A&I
Height: 6'1"
Weight: 285

The Tasmanian Devil is alive and well in Minnesota. But instead of appearing as a cartoon character, he takes the field every autumn Sunday afternoon, employing his nonstop motor to create havoc for opposing offenses every time the pigskin is snapped.

This incredible defender is none other than John Randle, simply the best defensive lineman in the National Football League. Possessing outstanding short-area quickness, strong, active hands and a brand of psychological warfare that can unnerve the best offensive linemen, Randle has earned six straight trips to the Pro Bowl, and has recorded 95 sacks since 1991, the most of any player during that period.

The accolades and compliments mount with every game. As head coach Bill Parcells said after the Vikings played his Jets team in 1997, "I think (Minnesota has) the best defensive player in the league in John Randle."

Despite being considered small for the middle of the trenches, Randle's explosiveness and strength require at least two and sometimes three blockers to keep him under control. While such tactics may hurt Randle's stats, they free other Vikings for the slaughter in those rare instances the tackle finds himself detained.

What makes Randle's place as the league's best defensive tackle a jaw-dropping success story is his background. Dirt poor as a child in Texas, he considered becoming a garbage man while in college because they got off work at noon. Yet before he pursued a career in sanitation, the undersized Randle, who carried 240 pounds on his 6-foot-1 frame, gathered an invitation to the Vikings' training camp in 1990 after receiving no interest in the draft following his 26 sacks as a senior in college. His impressive quickness amazed the Minnesota coaching staff and earned him a job, resulting in lim-

John Randle

ited action as a reserve behind Chris Doleman, including 21 tackles, one sack and a forced fumble as a rookie.

His playing time increased in 1991, with Randle starting eight games at left end and posting 58 tackles with 9.5 sacks. He began to blossom in 1992, a move that coincided with the arrival of head coach Dennis Green and defensive coordinator Tony Dungy as well as a shift inside, to the "under" tackle position. Teaming with Henry Thomas as the unit's interior linemen, Randle had added 35 pounds of muscle without sacrificing any quickness. He registered 56 hits and 11 sacks that year and 59 tackles and 12.5 sacks in 1993, the season he earned his first of six straight Pro Bowl invitations.

"People are always doubting you right off the bat and you have to make them notice you and respect you," Randle said. "A big part of making myself noticeable was going out and getting sacks. Not many tackles do that."

The sacks continued in 1994, the year Randle tied for the NFC lead with 13.5 quarterback dumps while making 47 hits. He followed that showing with a team-best 10.5 sacks in 1995 and 11.5 sacks in 1996. Not only did he earn All-Pro honors both seasons, he also made the nation take note during an impressive 30–21 victory against Green Bay. He received NFC Defensive Player of the Week honors on September 22, 1996, by thoroughly rattling Packer quarterback Brett Farve, sacking the signalcaller on 3.5 occasions and forcing two fumbles. Since that game, Farve has admitted that Randle is the only defensive player in the game who scares him.

It was also during the 1996 season Randle started employing a tactic that rattles opposing players into submission. He began reading anything he could get his hands on about upcoming opponents in order to use a little psychology on the gridiron.

"You take any edge you can get, and sometimes you can get players off their game" Randle said. "You just need to take their concentration away for a split second."

With all his weapons in tow, Randle was all but unstoppable in 1997. He led the NFL with 15.5 sacks, the fourth-highest single-season total in Minnesota annals, and became the first Viking player to pace the league in that category since Chris Doleman in 1989. He also led the defensive line with 67 tackles, four passes defensed, 7.5 tackles for loss and two fumble recoveries. He had three sacks during a 21–14 victory over Carolina on October 12 and versus Detroit on December 14, and established a career-high with 10 hits against San Francisco on December 7.

Randle was rewarded by Minnesota after the 1997 season with the richest contract ever given to a defensive player in NFL history. He then added a new twist to his game in 1998. After playing a couple of contests at defensive end in 1996 and 1997, Randle spent the entire campaign moving among the four line positions. The movement kept opponents guessing, preventing them from developing game plans aimed at double- and triple-teaming Randle. While he still rarely faced just one blocker on any play, he created ulcers among all five offensive linemen, not just the guards and center.

The strategy helped Randle earn All-Pro recognition for the sixth straight season while he led Minnesota with 10.5 sacks and 80 quarterback hurries. He currently ranks fourth on the Vikings' career list with 96.5 sacks, having paced or tied for the team lead in that category for six consecutive years and seven of the last eight. He has never missed a game due to injury, and has played in 144 straight contests, second only to Alan Page's 163 among Viking defensive tackles.

Al Randolph

Season: 1973   Defensive Back   Height: 6'2"
Number: 34   Iowa   Weight: 205

Signed as a free agent prior to the 1973 season after stints with the 49ers, Packers and Lions, Al Randolph toiled for 11 games on the kick coverage units and saw brief duty at strong safety while wearing purple. Released by Minnesota during training camp in 1974, the stockbroker played one more season in the National Football League, splitting his time with San Francisco and Buffalo.

Ahmad Rashad

Seasons: 1976–82   Wide Receiver   Height: 6'2"
Number: 28   Oregon   Weight: 200

Ahmad Rashad

Mention the term "Hail Mary" around Viking fans, and the first name mentioned will be Ahmad Rashad. Even though for seven years he established himself as one of the great receivers in Minnesota annals, Rashad's grab on December 14, 1980, against Cleveland will be recalled forever.

The play was a classic. Trailing 23–21 with four seconds remaining, quarterback Tommy Kramer sent three receivers wide and deep on the right side. After taking the snap, Kramer drifted back, pumped once, then lofted a high-arcing bomb near the goal line. The ball was tipped at least once; Rashad did not leap for the ball. He instead drifted in front of the pack, cradled the deflection with his left, outstretched hand and backpedaled into the end zone. The reception not only gave the Vikings a 28–23 victory, it provided the team with the Central Division title.

Though no single play compares to that catch, Rashad served an integral role for the Vikings, beginning in 1976. The departure of John Gilliam left Minnesota worried about its depth at wide receiver. Former Viking coach Jack Patera had a similar problem as Seattle's head coach, only his shortcomings involved the defensive line. After a couple weeks of discussion, Patera and Minnesota's Bud Grant made a deal, with Rashad going to the Vikings for "Benchwarmer Bob" Lurtsema and a fourth-round draft pick.

While Lurtsema did a solid job with the fledgling Seahawks, Rashad teamed with rookie Sammy White to form one of the great wide receiver tandems in team history. Rashad did most of his damage on sideline patterns, while White burned secondaries as a deep threat.

Amazingly, Rashad, who was originally known as Bobby Moore, had been released earlier in his career by St. Louis and Buffalo and deemed a trouble-maker for wanting to change his name due to his religious beliefs. "You wonder why teams lose?" quarterback Fran Tarkenton said after Minnesota acquired the receiver. "That's a perfect example, if they can't recognize a talent like (Rashad)."

His reputation proved to be a farce, for Rashad became the most popular player among his teammates. He emerged as a starter for the fourth game of the 1976 season and wound up catching 53 passes, at the time a club record for wide receivers. His biggest performance came against his former Seattle teammates, when Rashad grabbed nine tosses for 93 yards in Minnesota's 27–21 win on November 14.

Rashad led the Vikings as well as the NFC with 51 catches in 1977. Once again, he proved to be a big-game player, catching eight passes for 139 yards to help Minnesota clinch the division title with a 30–21 win at Detroit on December 17. With 104 catches in his first two years in purple, he had pulled in more passes than he had in his first four seasons in the National Football League.

After setting another Viking record for wide receivers with 66 receptions, eight of which resulted in touchdowns, to earn his first Pro Bowl invitation in 1978, Rashad made the quarterback transition from Tarkenton to Tommy Kramer smoother due to his ability to continue making plays with the young signalcaller under center. In 1979, Kramer's first year as a starter, Rashad paced the NFC with 80 catches and added nine touchdown grabs. He also set a single-season record with 1,156 receiving yards and moved atop the Vikings' career chart with 3,317 yards. To top it off, Rashad set a club mark with four touchdown catches against San Francisco, guiding Minnesota to a 28–22 victory over the 49ers on September 2.

In 1980, Rashad ranked second in the NFC with 1,095 receiving yards and fourth in the NFL with 69 receptions. Included that season was a career-high 11-catch, 160-yard performance in the 24–23 win over Atlanta on September 7. His 58 grabs in 1981 enabled Rashad to surpass Chuck Foreman's Minnesota career reception mark of 336. The receiver also had his third-best season in reception yards with 884.

Rashad's production fell off in 1982, his last year with the Vikings, when he caught 23 passes for 233 yards. His consecutive games streak with at least one reception ended at 78, the third-longest string in team history. Hurt late in the year, Rashad went on the injured reserve list on December 24, and decided to retire to the broadcast booth.

Named to the Vikings' Silver Anniversary All-Time Team in 1985, at the time of retirement Rashad was the 12th leading receiver in NFL history with 495 receptions, catching 400 with Vikings for 5,489 yards and 34 touchdowns. His six seasons with 50 or more receptions rank second to Cris Carter in Minnesota annals. He also played in four straight Pro Bowls, between 1978–81, and earned Most Valuable Player honors in his first Pro Bowl appearance.

Randy Rasmussen

Seasons: 1987–89 Guard Height: 6'2"
Number: 52 Minnesota Weight: 254

Randy Rasmussen added depth to the Vikings' offensive line after signing with Minnesota on November 16, 1987. The former Golden Gopher and Pittsburgh Steeler played in five games as a backup guard during his first season in purple. Waived and re-signed in the early stages of 1988, Rasmussen saw action in nine contests, including the two playoff games, on special teams and short-yardage situations. He was active briefly in 1989 but did not take the field before receiving his release.

John Reaves

Season: 1979 Quarterback Height: 6'3"
Number: 11 Florida Weight: 210

A starter as a rookie with the Eagles in 1972, John Reaves was acquired by the Vikings off waivers from Cincinnati prior to the 1979 season. Reaves did not see any action with the Vikings as a third-string quarterback while watching Tommy Kramer take every snap during the campaign.

Jarvis Redwine

Seasons: 1981–83 Running Back Height: 5'10"
Number: 22 Nebraska Weight: 201

After a consensus All-American career as a running back at Nebraska, Jarvis Redwine tasted success during two of his three years with the Vikings as the primary kickoff returner.

Redwine played in just three games as a rookie in 1981 before contributing in his second campaign. The speedster ranked fifth in the National Football League by leading Minnesota with a 23.8-yard average on 12 returns in 1982. His longest run was a 76-yard dash during a 34–31 win at Detroit on December 19.

Most of his contributions came in his final season with the team. Redwine carried back 38 kicks for a 22.1-yard average, with a long of 41 yards. Released the following year in training camp, he left Minnesota ranking fifth in the franchise record book with 50 returns and sixth with 1,124 return yards.

Bobby Reed

Seasons: 1962–63   Running Back   Height: 5'11"
Number: 27   Pacific   Weight: 190

Scouting on Norm Van Brocklin's part added some incredible speed to the Vikings' roster for two seasons. During a trip to California, the head coach noticed Pacific's Bobby Reed during spring practice and was impressed with the youngster's strong legs and outstanding balance. When Reed announced after the school year that he did not intend to return for his senior season, Van Brocklin signed the running back as a college free agent.

Reed immediately impressed his new teammates during training camp by tying sprint star Charlie Tidwell in a 50-yard dash, clocking in at 5.6 seconds in full football gear. Considered one of the team's more stylish dressers, the rookie went on to average 25.9 yards on 13 kickoff returns, 9.1 yards on nine punt returns, and 9.3 yards on four receptions (including a touchdown) before missing the last eight games due to a chest injury suffered against Los Angeles.

A year later, Reed galloped 98 and 99 yards to paydirt on kickoffs during pre-season games against the 49ers and Giants, respectively. He wound up playing in 10 regular-season contests, posting norms of 28.2 yards on 13 kickoff returns, 10.1 yards on nine punt returns, 10.5 yards on 13 catches, and 4.2 yards on 22 carries.

Jake Reed

Seasons: 1991–98   Wide Receiver   Height: 6'3"
Number: 86   Grambling   Weight: 219

For most of the 1990s, when observers point to the Vikings' standout receivers, Cris Carter is usually mentioned first. But while Carter is without question Hall-of-Fame material, Jake Reed emerged as one of the league's top pass catchers as well.

The 1997 season served as a prime example of his value. Reed caught 68 passes and led the team with 1,138 receiving yards. He established a Viking record with four straight games of 100-plus yards and tied the team mark with five 100-yard outings in a season. He also finished second in the NFC in yards per catch with a 16.7 norm and was named NFC Offensive Player of the Month for September after pulling in 34 tosses for 521 yards, including a career-high 12 catches during a 27–24 victory at Chicago on September 7.

Acquired with a third-round draft pick in 1991 obtained in the Herschel Walker trade, Reed's recent production makes it easy to forget how much work it took for him to become one of the best receivers in the National Football League. After spending his rookie year either as an inactive player or on injured reserve, Reed discovered he had a problem with his eyesight. Although his vision was 20/20, he had difficulty following the tracking of the

Jake Reed

ball. As a result, Reed went through daily drills for up to eight hours at a time under the supervision of eye disorder specialists.

"I can now look the ball all the way into my hands better than before," Reed said prior to the 1993 season. "Before, I didn't get that sharp a look, especially when it came from my left side. The doctors said it was because my right eye was much stronger and my eye-hand coordination was not good. But now I see the ball a lot better from either side. All the work we put in everyday was worth it."

His eye-hand coordination improved, and Reed eventually filled the departed Hassan Jones' role as the Vikings' third receiver. He caught six passes in 1992, and had five catches in 1993 after recovering from a fractured left fibula. Although he dropped some passes early in the 1994 season, much to the dismay of head coach Dennis Green and quarterback Warren Moon, Reed soon found consistency. By the end of the campaign, he had put together a breakthrough year, resulting in 85 grabs for 1,175 yards and four touchdowns while combining with Carter to set an NFL record for receptions by a receiving duo with 207. He continued to shine with back-to-back 72-catch seasons in 1995 and 1996 before pulling in 68 passes in 1997.

Back surgery that cost him the last five regular-season games as well as the arrival of rookie Randy Moss limited Reed's production to 34 receptions for 474 yards and four touchdowns in 1998. Nevertheless, he remained one of the team's primary weapons, and contributed even when he was not catching the ball. One of Reed's most overlooked talents is his ability to block downfield. Said offensive line coach Mike Tice, "When we spring those long cutback runs with Robert Smith, Jake usually has a big block on those plays. Nobody ever mentions it, but Jake is definitely our best downfield blocker."

Reed concluded the 1998 campaign ranking second in team history with 11 50-plus yard plays, third with 16 100-yard games, fifth with 30 touchdown catches, and sixth with 5,481 receiving yards and 342 receptions.

Oscar Reed

Seasons: 1968–74   Running Back   Height: 6'
Number: 32   Colorado State   Weight: 222

When the Vikings made their championship marches in 1969 and 1973, Oscar Reed played a significant role in the supporting cast. One of the quickest players ever to wear purple, Reed gave the team a lift every time he entered the game. His explosiveness in head coach Bud Grant's steady offense proved to be a combination that helped lead to some of the bigger wins in franchise history.

Nicknamed "Golden Shoes" in high school and "Big O" in college, Reed arrived in Minnesota as a seventh-round draft choice in 1968 after setting most of the rushing records at Colorado State. He played sparingly in seven games as a rookie, then emerged as a key running back during the 1969 title drive. Reed gained 393 yards on 83 carries, caught seven passes for 59 yards, and found the end zone three times. A low-rider who coach Bus Mertes said was "like trying to catch a pumpkin seed," Reed proved to be the perfect change-of-pace complement to Dave Osborn and Bill Brown in the Viking backfield.

Fame, however, proved to be fleeting for Reed, who gained only 132 yards in 1970 while struggling with an ankle injury and 182 yards a year later in a reserve role. Yet, just as it appeared Reed had seen his best days and his reputation as a fumbler continued to hold him back, he became an offensive catalyst in 1972. In quarterback Fran Tarkenton's first year back with Minnesota, Reed paced the Vikings with 639 rushing yards on 151 carries and was second on the team with 30 receptions for 205 yards.

Reed continued to play a major role even with the arrival of Chuck Foreman in 1973. He took the job of the injured Osborn and finished second on the team with 401 yards on the ground and scored three touchdowns. Reed saved his best game for when it meant the most. He set up two scores in the first half of a 31–13 win over the Bears on November 25, with 91 of his 97 rushing yards coming in the first two periods of play. On December 22, in the divisional playoffs against Washington, Reed guided the Vikings to a 27–20 victory by rushing for 95 yards and gaining 76 yards on five catches, with his 46-yard gallop and 50-yard pass reception setting up scores. His season concluded on a down note, however, when he fumbled in Super Bowl VIII against Miami after taking a hard hit from linebacker Nick Buoniconti.

The roller coaster ride went down again in 1974 for Reed. Injuries hampered the runner, limiting him to 215 yards on 62 attempts in seven games. With Foreman clearly the starter and the likes of Ed Marinaro and Brent McClanahan in the fold, Reed was traded to Atlanta in 1975 for a fifth-round draft choice.

Jerry Reichow

Seasons: 1961–64　　　Halfback-End-Tight End　　　Height: 6'3"
Number: 89　　　　　　Iowa　　　　　　　　　　　　Weight: 220

Before Jerry Reichow moved to the Vikings' front office to head the scouting staff, the former Iowa signalcaller toiled four seasons in purple, giving the expansion franchise one of the toughest and most athletic players ever to wear the Minnesota uniform. A steady receiver, Reichow emerged as one of quarterback Fran Tarkenton's favorite targets and the most dependable pass catcher during the team's fledgling years. Though not particularly graceful, he succeeded by lowering his head and making the best of a situation instead of finessing an opponent.

Acquired from the Eagles in 1961 in exchange for a seventh-round draft choice, Reichow had a stellar first season with the Vikings. The All-Big Ten honoree and Minnesota's third-string quarterback caught 50 passes for 859 yards and 11 touchdowns and led the team in scoring to join Hugh McElhenny as the franchise's first two Pro Bowl selections. His 11 scoring grabs ranked fourth in the National Football League and remained the Vikings' single-season record until Cris Carter topped it in 1995. One of his scoring catches came in the season-opening 37–13 win over the Bears on September 17. Three months later, Reichow pulled in three more touchdowns in a loss at Chicago, thereby becoming the first Viking to register the hat trick.

In 1962, Reichow again paced the team with 39 catches for 561 yards and three touchdowns despite missing two games with a shoulder separation. His numbers remained steady upon moving to tight end in 1963, when Reichow caught 35 tosses for 479 yards with three more scores. "Old Reliable" added 20 more receptions for 284 yards and two touchdowns in 1965, his final season as a player.

With the Vikings stockpiling a core of young receivers, Reichow was released in what trainer Fred Zamberletti has described as "the hardest cut the team has made in my career." Reichow moved to the Minnesota front office in the fall of 1965 and became the Vikings' chief scout, replacing Joe Thomas, who joined the Miami Dolphins. The present-day dean of the Vikings' braintrust was promoted to director of player personnel in 1966, to director of football operations in 1975, and to his current position, assistant general manager for national scouting, in 1997.

Mike Reilly

Season: 1969   Linebacker   Height: 6'3"
Number: 56   Iowa   Weight: 250

A college teammate of Paul Krause and Wally Hilgenberg at Iowa, Mike Reilly was acquired from Chicago via Dallas in 1969. He played in 10 games for Minnesota as a reserve linebacker and member of the special teams on the Vikings' first Super Bowl squad.

Reilly's greatest moment as a Viking occurred in the 31–0 victory at Chicago on October 12. Reilly burst through the middle of the line in the first quarter and blocked Bobby Joe Green's punt. The linebacker continued his pursuit of the pigskin and slid on top of the ball in the end zone for Minnesota's first touchdown of the game. Although his other achievements were not as noteworthy, Reilly helped make the Vikings' special teams a solid part of the last champions of the pre-merger National Football League.

Gilbert Renfroe

Season: 1990   Quarterback   Height: 6'1"
Number: 14   Tennessee State   Weight: 195

Signed as a rookie free agent during the 1990 season, Gilbert Renfroe was with the Vikings for seven mid-season games but did not see any action.

Lance Rentzel

Seasons: 1965–66   End   Height: 6'2"
Number: 19   Oklahoma   Weight: 215

Norm Van Brocklin was nothing if not stubborn. In the latter days of his tenure as Minnesota's head coach, Dutch was determined to shift Lance Rentzel from halfback, his college position, to wide end, in place of Paul Flatley. The results in Minnesota were hardly successful, with Rentzel catching just two passes for 10 yards in his two years with the team.

The Vikings' second-round draft choice in 1965, Rentzel served mostly as a kickoff returner with Minnesota. He led the team by averaging 26.2 yards on 23 returns in 1965, including a 101-yard dash to paydirt on November 14 against the Colts. The second kickoff return for a touchdown in Viking lore, it remains the longest in team annals. Yet even that performance did not please Van Brocklin. The head coach stayed on Rentzel throughout the player's rookie season. In fact, after a Rentzel fumble led to an opposing touchdown, Dutch sent the rookie back on the field and said, "See if you can screw up another one."

Rentzel was sidelined early in his second year with Minnesota due to a sprained ankle before being charged with an exposure complaint that was dismissed in court. Employing Midwestern virtues, the Vikings traded Rentzel to Dallas for a third-round draft choice. As a Cowboy and later with the Rams, he reached Van Brocklin's expectations by becoming one of the top receivers in the National Football League.

Fuad Reveiz

Seasons: 1990–95   Kicker   Height: 5'11"
Number: 7   Tennessee   Weight: 225

The Vikings landed one of their most consistent kickers in team history almost by accident. Donald Igwebuike started the 1990 season as Minnesota's placekicker before running into off-the-field problems midway through the campaign. Desperate for someone capable of putting the pigskin through the uprights, the Vikes called upon Fuad Reveiz, who had been released four games earlier in the season by San Diego.

Reveiz responded to the challenge by succeeding on 11 of 12 field goal tries during the campaign's final eight contests, including a game-winning 24-yard effort against Seattle on November 18. He proceeded to beat out Igwebuike and the rest of his training camp competition the next summer to begin a six-season run as one of the steadiest kickers in league annals.

Though he appeared to grimace prior to every field goal attempt, Reveiz never let his emotions enter into his preparations. "When I go out there, I'm going out there full-blast," said the kicker. "I'm not going out there to be timid. You have enough pressure out there as it is without getting all wrapped up in the game and the consequences." Reveiz also was not afraid to stick his head in on tackles during runbacks. On more than one occasion the former high school linebacker reverted to his old ways with a jarring, touchdown-saving hit.

In 1991, the native of Bogota, Colombia, set the Viking record with 19 consecutive field goals and 21 touchbacks. He also led the team in scoring with 85 points, connecting on 17 of 24 attempts, including two 50-yard boots. He improved his record with 26 touchbacks in 1992 while making 19 of 25 field goal tries. Reveiz booted game-winners in the season-opening 23–20 overtime triumph over Green Bay and during the 6–3 victory over Pittsburgh on December 20 to clinch the Central Division title.

Fuad Reveiz

Reveiz was steady again in 1993, making 26 of 35 field-goal tries. His top performance came against Green Bay, when Reveiz booted five field goals, among them the game-winner with four seconds left on September 26, an effort that earned him *Pro Football Weekly's* Golden Toe Award. He also set the team record for the longest field goal in Viking playoff history with a 52-yarder against New York on January 9.

The Vikings' inability to score consistently in the red zone in 1994 led to Reveiz's Pro Bowl recognition. The kicker's three extra points against the 49ers in the season finale enabled him to tie Chuck Foreman's 1975 team record for most points in a season with 132, achieved by succeeding on 34 of 39 field goal attempts and all 30 PATs.

His consistency reaped its greatest reward early in the 1995 season. With his first three-pointer of the year, a 32-yarder against Detroit on September 10, Reveiz tied the National Football League record by making 29 straight field goal attempts. He broke the mark in the third quarter of the same game with a 27-yarder, and extended it to 31 before missing a 48-yarder against Dallas on September 17. By the end of the season, he connected on 26 of 36 tries as well as all 44 extra-point attempts for 122 points.

But just as it looked as if Reveiz would continue to be the answer to Minnesota's kicking chores, ailments to his plant foot cost the kicker his abilities. He initially underwent surgery in 1994. A repeat procedure took place two years later, this time without the desired results.

With his left foot slow to heal, Reveiz retired from the game during the 1996 training camp. While many of his marks were broken by Gary Anderson in 1998, Reveiz hung up the spikes holding the NFL record with 31 consecutive field goals as well as 39 straight three-pointers on attempts from 45 yards or less. His Viking team records included percentage of field goals made in a career (77.8 percent on 133 of 177) and during a season (91.6 percent in 1990, going 11 for 12) and field goals made in a season (34 in 1994). He continues to hold two marks—most 50-yard field goals in a career (eight) and in a game (two, versus Tampa Bay on December 8, 1991). Reveiz also made the final 95 extra-point attempts of his career.

Buster Rhymes

Seasons: 1985–87	Wide Receiver	Height: 6'1"
Number: 88	Oklahoma	Weight: 218

For one full season, George "Buster" Rhymes provided Vikings fans with as much excitement on kickoff returns as the Metrodome has ever witnessed. The fourth-round draft choice in 1985 had a knack for finding the right crease and getting upfield. The subsequent good field position played a role in the Vikings' reversal of fortunes from the 1984 season's 3–13 disappointment.

Rhymes was at his best as a rookie. In 1985, he set the National Football League's single-season record with 1,345 yards gained on 53 kickoff returns. His yardage remains the Viking standard, while his number of returns equals the top mark set by Eddie Payton in 1981. His best day as a returner took place on September 19, when he set a team record by gaining 182 yards on six returns against Chicago. His 88-yard return versus Philadelphia on December 22 is tied for the sixth-longest in Viking lore.

The 1985 campaign, however, proved to be Rhymes' lone season in the spotlight. A broken left wrist suffered on October 5 against Chicago limited him to five games and nine kickoff returns for a 23.7-yard average in 1986. A year later, Rhymes was placed on injured reserve on September 1, activated on October 20, and waived on November 3.

Benny Ricardo

Season: 1983	Kicker	Height: 5'10"
Number: 1	San Diego State	Weight: 170

When Rick Danmeier was unable to answer the bell due to an injury in 1983, the Vikings signed Benny Ricardo to serve as the team's placekicker for one year. While his range was minimal, Ricardo was consistent from short yardage, even succeeding on a then-club record 15 straight field goal attempts during the early stages of the campaign.

For the season, Ricardo made 25 of his 33 three-point tries and missed only one of his 34 extra-point attempts. His longest field goal was 44 yards, a feat he accomplished twice. He also booted two game-winners in overtime, a 42-yarder in a 19–16 win over Tampa Bay on September 18 and a 32-yarder in a 20–17 triumph against Green Bay on October 23.

Ricardo, who saw some action on the pro racquetball circuit, ended up having a short tenure in Minnesota. He was released by Les Steckel shortly after Ricardo openly questioned the military approach to the new head coach's training camp regimen.

Allen Rice

Seasons: 1984–90	Running Back	Height: 5'10"
Number: 36	Baylor	Weight: 206

Jerry Burns was considered an innovative offensive mind who often had a trick or two hidden up his sleeve. One of those football frolics took place in the first round of the 1987 playoffs. With the Vikings leading New Orleans 17–7 in the second quarter, Burns and his staff called on Allen Rice for the dirty deed. Rice took the handoff from quarterback Wade Wilson, only to pass the pigskin 10 yards to Anthony Carter for six more points, breaking the spirit of the heavily favored Saints. In the process, Rice became the only player other than a quarterback in Minnesota annals to throw a touchdown toss in the playoffs.

While Rice's other career pass attempt fell incomplete during his second season in the National Football League, the Vikings' fifth-round draft choice from 1984 was one of the team's unheralded role players as a reserve running back and special teams standout. For example, in his first regular-season game, on September 2, 1984, Rice rushed four times for 29 yards, caught two passes for 33 yards, and returned two kickoffs for 21 yards. Although he played primarily on special teams for the rest of the year, he scored two touchdowns, one on a three-yard run against the Raiders on October 14 and a second on a 15-yard reception at Denver on November 18.

His role increased on the offense in 1985, when he scored four touchdowns. Rice rotated with college teammate Alfred Anderson as the starting fullback in 1986, establishing career-highs with 30 catches for 391 yards and three touchdowns. He then caught a team-high eight passes against Seattle on November 1, 1987, while making 19 grabs for the season.

Rice's greatest contributions to the offense came in 1988. Filling in for an injured Darrin Nelson for four games, Rice finished the season ranked second on the team with 110 attempts, 322 yards and six touchdowns on the ground while placing second with 30 catches for 279 yards. An injured knee limited Rice to the first four games of 1989. His activity centered on special teams for most of 1990, his last year with the Vikings, when Rice returned a career-high 12 kickoffs for a 14.7-yard average.

Greg Richardson

Seasons: 1987–88 Wide Receiver Height: 5'7"
Number: 89 Alabama Weight: 172

Minnesota's sixth-round draft pick in 1987, Greg Richardson did little to stand out in the first two games of his rookie season. He averaged just 19 yards on four kickoff returns and 4.8 yards on four punt returns, numbers that landed him on the inactive list for the final 10 games after the strike. He also did not receive any playing time in the early part of the 1988 campaign prior to being waived on October 22.

Steve Riley

Seasons: 1974–84 Tackle Height: 6'6"
Number: 78 Southern Cal Weight: 260

The Vikings had big hopes for Steve Riley when they selected the USC offensive lineman with the 25th overall pick in the 1974 draft.

"He could well be another Ron Yary, a big man who can play in this league for 10 or 12 years. He's a fine prospect now and is only going to get better. But he might be two or three years away," said head coach Bud Grant, shortly after acquiring Riley.

Grant knew what he was talking about. Riley saw action in just two games as a rookie in 1974 before receiving a greater opportunity when Grady Alderman retired. Riley beat out Charles Goodrum, who was moved to left guard, and became the first-team left tackle midway through the 1975 season, starting seven games as well as the playoff contest against Dallas. He maintained the job throughout the next two years before a recurring pinched nerve in his neck took its toll on the lineman in 1978, causing him to miss the last 11 games of the campaign.

He resumed his starting job in 1979, then was traded to New Orleans for third- and fifth-round draft picks in 1980. However, Riley never suited up for the Saints because he could not pass the team's physical. Undaunted, Riley returned to Minnesota and resumed his starting duties at left tackle in 1980 and joined Dennis Swilley as the only two offensive linemen to start every game that season. The same scenario held true for the next two years, with Riley becoming the team's elder statesman across the front in 1982 when Yary was traded. He started every game again in 1983 except for the season finale.

In 1984, in what proved to be his last year in the National Football League, Riley played with his left hand in a cast due to a broken thumb. He started the first six games at his left tackle slot, moved to right tackle for the next five contests, then concluded the campaign at left tackle.

Upon retiring from the professional ranks, Riley played in 138 games for the Vikings during his career, including 121 starts.

Gerald Robinson

Seasons: 1986–87　　　　Defensive End　　　　Height: 6'3"
Number: 95　　　　　　　Auburn　　　　　　　Weight: 261

Gerald Robinson is not remembered as one of the more successful first-round draft choices in Minnesota history.

The Vikings' first draft pick in 1986, the Auburn product got off to a slow start in his initial training camp due to a toe injury. He recovered to earn a starting job by the fifth game, then experienced the highlight of his Minnesota career during a 23–7 win over the Bears on October 19. Robinson was named the NFC Defensive Player of the Week after registering five solo tackles, one assist and 2.5 sacks. His other big game took place a week earlier, during a 27–24 overtime win against San Francisco, when Robinson had six tackles and blocked a punt that was recovered in the end zone for a touchdown.

Otherwise, the Vikings have little to show for selecting Robinson. A sprained knee suffered at midseason halted his production for the remainder of his rookie year. In 1987, Robinson was placed on injured reserve on September 23 and recalled to the roster on November 25. He wound up recording one solo tackle in five games.

Moved from defensive end to linebacker during the 1988 training camp, Robinson's poor work habits led to the Vikings' decision to waive the defensive player on August 30.

Mark Rodenhauser

Season: 1989　　　　　　Center　　　　　　　Height: 6'5"
Number: 60　　　　　　　Illinois State　　　　Weight: 262

Mark Rodenhauser played in all 16 regular-season games on special teams for the Vikings in 1989. Although his stay in Minnesota consisted of just one year, he became a solid long snapper during the 1990s, including a three-year stint with the Carolina Panthers.

Dave Roller

Seasons: 1979–80　　　　Defensive Tackle　　　Height: 6'2"
Number: 76　　　　　　　Kentucky　　　　　　Weight: 270

Dave Roller was "every man," a reason the macho game of football is America's most beloved sport. The gregarious defensive lineman looked like Joe Sixpack, a heavy-set brawler who was living the American dream.

Roller made an immediate impression upon signing with the Vikings in 1979. Waived by the Packers just prior to the campaign's first game, Roller jumped in his car and drove all night without stopping in order to make practice after Minnesota called and expressed interest in obtaining Roller's services.

The results were equally impressive. The six-year veteran who had toiled in the National Football League, Canadian Football League and World Football League played in 15 games for the Vikes in 1979. He took some playing time from veteran Doug Sutherland by starting the last six games at left defensive tackle. He concluded the campaign with 34 solo tackles and another 14 assists to rank third among the defensive linemen.

Roller maintained his starting job for the first two games of the 1980 slate before losing the position due to a variety of injuries. He still managed to play in every contest but one, and finished the season with 13 tackles, with most of those coming on short-yardage situations.

George Rose

Seasons: 1964–66	Defensive Back	Height: 5'11"
Number: 44	Auburn	Weight: 190

Minnesota's third-round draft choice in 1964, George Rose made the shift from wide receiver in college to starting defensive halfback as a rookie in the National Football League. He obviously retained some of his previous skills, intercepting a team-high six passes for 48 return yards, including one pick he returned 32 yards for six points during the Vikings' 34–13 win over the Rams on November 29.

That's not to say Rose didn't encounter some challenges. He gained the starting assignment after Lee Calland went down with a broken arm in the slate's first game. Chicago quarterback Billy Wade noticed the change and did his share of picking on the rookie by completing 10 passes to Johnny Morris in the second contest of the 1964 campaign, a 34–28 Bears victory on September 20. Yet, when the two teams met again on December 13 for the season finale, an experienced Rose held Morris to just one catch for five yards.

Rose, who had above-average speed and great agility, saw action at both safety and cornerback in 1965 and intercepted one pass in 10 games. He played in 10 more contests for Minnesota in 1966 and picked off the eighth pass of his career before New Orleans nabbed him in the 1967 expansion draft.

Ted Rosnagle

Seasons: 1985, 1987	Safety	Height: 6'3"
Number: 28	Portland State	Weight: 207

After playing briefly in the Canadian Football League in 1984, Ted Rosnagle was the only free agent to make the Vikings' roster in 1985. He saw action in the season opener, but suffered a knee injury during the contest and spent the next 10 weeks on injured reserve. Rosnagle returned to play in the season's final five games and recorded two solo tackles and five assisted hits.

Released prior to the 1986 season, Rosnagle returned to the Vikings in 1987, when he served as the starting strong safety for Minnesota's replacement team.

Curtis Rouse

Seasons: 1982–86	Guard-Tackle	Height: 6'3"
Number: 68	Tennessee-Chattanooga	Weight: 335

Curtis Rouse, nicknamed "Boo-Boo" due to his resemblance to a bear cub, was in and out of the lineup while constantly battling his weight during five seasons with the Vikings. Minnesota's 11th-round draft pick in 1982, he saw reserve action in the last five regular-season games and two playoff contests as a rookie. Rouse then played on special teams and as a reserve tackle in all 16 games in 1983, and started at left tackle in the team's 20–14 win over Cincinnati on December 17.

In 1984, Rouse earned a starting job at left guard for the season's first

15 games, then moved one spot to the important left tackle position in 1985 to replace the retired Steve Riley. Rouse was plagued with inconsistency while protecting the quarterback's blind side and started the first 13 games before losing the job to veteran David Huffman.

Rouse possessed good quickness for a big man, but his performance was impaired by his excess weight. That fact led to his being waived at the end of training camp in 1986 prior to re-signing on November 11. He played a reserve role in five of the last six games of the campaign before receiving his final release from the Vikings on September 7, 1987.

Ray Rowe

Season: 1994 Tight End Height: 6'2"
Number: 89 San Diego State Weight: 256

Signed at the end of training camp in 1994, Ray Rowe was thought to have the ability to serve as the Vikings' blocking tight end. Although listed as a starter for the first two games of the season, the former Redskin's only action came when he appeared in the 1994 team photo. He was released prior to the third contest after Minnesota signed Martin Harrison.

Justin Rowland

Season: 1961 Defensive Back Height: 6'2"
Number: 47 Texas Christian Weight: 188

Picked up by the Vikings during the 1961 season, Justin Rowland served primarily as a member of the special teams for five games, returning eight kickoffs for a 21.9-yard average. He also recorded the only interception of his 21-game career in the National Football League and returned the ball four yards.

Karl Rubke

Season: 1961 Linebacker Height: 6'4"
Number: 54 Southern Cal Weight: 239

Selected by Minnesota from San Francisco in the veterans pool, Karl Rubke became somewhat of a team legend while displaying his love for malted beverages during training camp. His performance at linebacker, however, was much more sobering. Rubke played in 13 of the 14 games during the Vikings' maiden voyage and intercepted one pass, returning the ball to the Colts' 7-yard line to set up a field goal on October 1. The Minnesota linebacking corps was considered a problem area by head coach Norm Van Brocklin during the 1961 season, which led to Rubke's departure after the campaign's conclusion.

Dwayne Rudd

Seasons: 1997–98 Linebacker Height: 6'2"
Number: 57 Alabama Weight: 241

Scouts throughout the National Football League tell players how unpredictable the draft can be. The unexpected often occurs, leaving surprised high picks elated and projected top selections baffled.

Dwayne Rudd fell into that category in 1997. Thought to be among the first half-dozen players selected, the Alabama linebacker was still available when the Vikings' turn came with the 20th overall pick. Head coach Dennis Green and his staff did not hesitate to call Rudd's name, believing at the time they had the steal of the draft.

Those feelings still exist.

Dwayne Rudd

With Minnesota fielding an established linebacking corps in 1997, Rudd did not have an opportunity to show his talents on the gridiron during the early portions of his rookie season. Yet, by producing a handful of sacks in his limited opportunities, Rudd's playing time increased as the campaign progressed. He excelled on blitzes and did a laudable job in pass coverage. He started the final four games of the season and finished with 44 tackles and five sacks, the third-best total ever for a Vikings rookie.

An offseason of success in the weight room combined with a year's worth of experience enabled Rudd to step to the forefront in 1998 and earn second-team All-Pro recognition. He improved on all his weaknesses—namely, shedding blockers and playing under control—to dominate at the outside linebacker spot and run down opponents unlike any Viking since Matt Blair. A pure athlete, his lateral speed, quickness, range and strength make him equally effective against the pass and the run, resulting in 113 tackles, good for second on the team, and two sacks.

Rudd also tied the single-season NFL record by returning two fumbles for a touchdown during the 1998 season. He returned a Neil O'Donnell fumble 63 yards to paydirt in a 24–3 win over Cincinnati on November 15 for the sixth-longest fumble return in team annals. His 94-yard return in the 48–22 victory over the Bears represents the longest in Vikings' history. That feat was tainted, however, when Rudd taunted Chicago before slide-stepping into the end zone. The play drew a 15-yard penalty, and Rudd learned his lesson.

"It was part of the emotion of the game, when I got caught up in the moment," said Rudd, who apologized to the Bears after the contest. "It was a spur-of-the-moment thing that won't happen again."

If he were playing in a major media market, Dwayne Rudd would be a household name. In time, he will reach that distinction with Minnesota.

Mike Ruether

Season: 1994 Offensive Lineman Height: 6'4"
Number: 65 Texas Weight: 279

Released by Atlanta midway through the 1994 season, Mike Ruether signed with the Vikings, thanks in large part to his previous relationship with Minnesota offensive line coach Keith Rowen, formerly with the Falcons. Ruether replaced Frank Cornish as the Vikings' backup center but did not see any game action during the campaign's final seven contests.

Pat Russ

Season: 1963 Defensive Tackle Height: 6'3"
Number: 75 Purdue Weight: 250

A college teammate of fellow Viking Larry Bowie, Pat Russ spent the entire 1962 season on the Minnesota taxi squad after joining the team as a 14th-round draft pick. He re-signed with the Vikings in 1963 and played in all 14 games on special teams and as a reserve defensive lineman.

Reggie Rutland

Seasons: 1987–92 Cornerback Height: 6'1"
Number: 48 Georgia Tech Weight: 188

Born Reggie Rutland before changing his name to Najee Mustafaa while on the injured reserve list in his final year with the Vikings, the former Georgia Tech standout picked the perfect time to make a name for himself in the National Football League.

After playing in nickel coverages during seven regular-season games as a rookie while overcoming a knee injury, the fourth-round draft choice helped halt the heavily favored Saints in the playoffs with his first career interception in the Vikings' 44–10 victory. A week later, on January 9, 1988, in the 36–24 pounding of San Francisco, Rutland picked off a Joe Montana aerial and returned the football 45 yards to paydirt, increasing the Minnesota lead to 20–3 in the second quarter.

Rutland became the starter at right cornerback for the final seven games of the 1988 season after Issiac Holt was injured, and emerged as a fixture in the Viking secondary for the next four years. He was third on the team with three interceptions and 14 special teams tackles in 1988. Rutland paced the club with 12 passes defensed in 1989 while intercepting two passes in a 26–14 win over Green Bay on October 15. He also returned a fumble 27 yards for a touchdown during a 24–10 triumph at Tampa Bay on November 12.

Rutland intercepted two more passes in 1990 while defensing 12 tosses, and blocking an extra-point attempt against Philadelphia. He then set the Viking record for the longest defensive touchdown by returning an interception 97 yards against the Rams on December 15, 1991, to seal a 20–14 win. He finished that game with seven solo tackles and two defensed passes while picking off three tosses for the season.

Five years of productivity led to little for Mustafaa in 1992. The cornerback worked out in training camp for one week before spending the rest of the campaign on injured reserve with a back problem. Believing he could have played if he possessed the desire, the Minnesota front office provided no resistance when Mustafaa signed a three-year, $3.6 million deal with Cleveland the following spring.

S

Sean Salisbury

Seasons: 1990–94	Quarterback	Height: 6'5"
Number: 12	Southern Cal	Weight: 217

Baseball has pitchers known as swingmen, hurlers who can take the mound in a moment's notice as either a starter or reliever. Sean Salisbury filled that role during his five years with the Vikings, with the former standout in the Canadian Football League always ready to step in whenever needed.

Salisbury's biggest contributions came late in 1992. With Rich Gannon's performance erratic and ineffective, Salisbury made his first start in the National Football League and guided the Vikings to a 31–17 win over the Rams on November 29. He started three of the final four games that season, with his best outing coming in the finale. Salisbury completed 20 of 33 passes for 292 yards and two touchdowns in the 27–7 pounding of the Packers on December 27. For the year, the Vikings were 3–1 in games Salisbury started.

Signed out of the CFL in 1990 after leading Winnipeg to the Grey Cup two years earlier, Salisbury did not take a snap as Minnesota's third-string quarterback in his first year with the team, and was deactivated for all 16 games in 1991. After proving he could be a valuable reliever in 1992, Salisbury further proved his worth while filling in for the injury-prone Jim McMahon in 1993. After playing sparingly in the season's first half, he took over the starting duties for all four November games. His best showing occurred in the 26–23 upset win at Denver on November 14, when Salisbury threw for 366 yards and two touchdowns to lead the come-from-behind victory.

Salisbury did not use his best judgment in 1994. With McMahon gone, the Vikings offered Salisbury a lucrative contract, only to have the quarterback reject it. He signed with Houston as a free agent but lost the starting assignment and was released in training camp. Minnesota reacquired Salisbury the day before the season opener for a hair above the NFL minimum salary. He spent his final year with the Vikes backing up Warren Moon, leading Minnesota to a 21–14 win over the 49ers on December 26, 1994, in his only start and appearance of the year.

Ron Sams

Season: 1984	Center	Height: 6'4"
Number: 72	Pittsburgh	Weight: 265

Dennis Swilley's one-year retirement during the 1984 season opened the door for Ron Sams. Acquired off waivers from the Packers prior to the start of the regular season, Sams played in 12 games and made 10 starts in the middle of the offensive line, even though he had not played the center position since his high school days. While his performance was at least equal to the team's overall showing that year, Sams lost his job as well as a spot on the Vikings' roster when Swilley and head coach Bud Grant returned in 1985.

Ken Sanders

Seasons: 1980–81   Defensive End   Height: 6'5"
Number: 89   Howard Payne   Weight: 245

A former starter with the Lions who led Detroit with nine sacks in 1977, Ken Sanders played behind first-team defensive ends Randy Holloway and Mark Mullaney during his two seasons with the Vikings. Obtained off waivers from Detroit, Sanders played in six of the first seven games in 1980 prior to succumbing to an elbow injury. He then took the field for nine contests in 1981 to end his career in the National Football League by playing in an even 100 games.

Bob Sapp

Seasons: 1997–98   Guard   Height: 6'4"
Number: 78   Washington   Weight: 303

The Vikings plucked Bob Sapp off the waiver wire after the Bears released their third-round draft choice at the end of his rookie training camp. Sapp spent the entire 1997 season on the Minnesota roster, but was inactive for the first 13 games before playing on special teams in the regular-season finale and the two playoff contests.

Sapp was inactive for the first 10 games of the 1998 slate before he became only the second Viking to be suspended for violating the National Football League's policy on anabolic steroids. Minnesota released the offensive guard when his four-game suspension ended in December.

Mike Saxon

Seasons: 1994–95   Punter   Height: 6'3"
Number: 4   San Diego State   Weight: 205

After letting Harry Newsome depart in the offseason, the Vikings maintained their quality punting just prior to the 1994 season when they reunited special teams coach Gary Zauner with his former college pupil, veteran Mike Saxon. The former Aztec, who credited Zauner with his development as a punter, averaged 42.7 yards per punt in 1994, good for seventh in the league, with a team-record 28 downed inside the 20-yard line. His efforts were not fully appreciated in the numbers, for Saxon's boots had height, distance and direction, traits that consistently placed Minnesota opponents in poor field position.

Saxon continued to excel in 1995. He averaged 40.9 yards on 72 punts and had 21 efforts come to rest inside the 20. Saxon also did his job in a timely manner, for not one of his 153 punts in purple was blocked by the opponent.

Despite his success, Saxon was released after the final cutdowns in 1996. The Vikings opted to go with Mitch Berger, who was deemed a better long-term prospect with the ability to reach the end zone on kickoffs. Making the event more tearful was the change of heart by the Minnesota coaching staff. The Vikings had announced they would carry three kickers before deciding to release Saxon and sign rookie special teams performer Harold Morrow.

John Scardina

Season: 1987   Tackle   Height: 6'4"
Number: 78   Lincoln   Weight: 265

John Scardina's career in the National Football League consisted of his three starts at left tackle for the Vikings' replacement team in 1987.

Ed Schenk

Season: 1987   Tight End   Height: 6'4"
Number: 89   Central Florida   Weight: 230

Ed Schenk caught one pass for 10 yards during his three appearances with the Minnesota replacement team in 1987.

Roy Schmidt

Season: 1970   Guard   Height: 6'3"
Number: 68   Long Beach State   Weight: 248

A former Saint, Falcon and Redskin, Roy Schmidt played in four games for the Vikings in 1970. Most of his playing time came along the line on field goal and extra point attempts, although he did see some brief action at guard.

Bob Schmitz

Season: 1966   Linebacker   Height: 6'1"
Number: 54   Montana   Weight: 235

The Vikings picked up Bob Schmitz off waivers from Pittsburgh in November 1966. After five-and-a-half years with the Steelers, Schmitz played sparingly in two games with Minnesota during the final month of the campaign, which proved to be the end of his career in the National Football League.

Bob Schnelker

Season: 1961   End   Height: 6'3"
Number: 80   Bowling Green   Weight: 214

Bob Schnelker is the answer to the trivia question, Who is the first player to score a touchdown for the Vikings in franchise history? In Minnesota's first game, on September 17, 1961, Schnelker caught a 14-yard pass from quarterback Fran Tarkenton during the second quarter to give the purple a 10–0 lead on its way to a 37–13 upset of the Bears. The reception also was the first touchdown toss of Tarkenton's career, which ended with an NFL record-setting 342, a total that currently ranks second all-time.

Acquired from the Giants in a five-player trade before the 1961 season, Schnelker served as the Vikings' starting tight end during the first half of the team's maiden voyage. He caught six passes for 70 yards in six contests before he was traded to the the Steelers in exchange for safety Dean Derby. Schnelker returned to Minnesota in 1986 as the Vikings' offensive coordinator, a position he retained under head coach Jerry Burns through the 1990 season.

Adam Schreiber

Seasons: 1990–93   Center   Height: 6'4"
Number: 60   Texas   Weight: 288

After three years as a reserve center, guard and long snapper with the Vikings, Adam Schreiber spent the 1993 season as Minnesota's starter in the middle of the offensive line. With Kirk Lowdermilk having bolted to Indianapolis via free agency, Schreiber stepped in and did a solid job, particularly with his line calls and leadership, while working with quarterbacks Jim McMahon and Sean Salisbury. He and his linemates protected the signal-callers well, establishing a team record by not allowing a sack in three consecutive games.

Born on February 2, 1962, the day John Glenn entered space for the first time, Schreiber signed with Minnesota as a Plan B free agent prior to the 1990 season. In his first year with the Vikes, he served as the long snapper on punts and was used at left guard on short-yardage situations, with Randall McDaniel moving into the backfield. Special teams was his primary assignment in 1991. He maintained that job in 1992 and also saw time at right guard, including his first start, in the season-opening 23–20 win over Green Bay on September 6.

Despite his solid contributions in 1993, Schreiber was let go just prior to the 1994 training camp after refusing to accept a paycut. The Vikings instead signed free agent center Frank Cornish, a major disappointment, while Schreiber joined the Giants and spent the next three seasons in New York.

Jeff Schuh

Season: 1986   Linebacker   Height: 6'3"
Number: 53   Minnesota   Weight: 234

A defensive end for the University of Minnesota and an All-Big Ten performer in 1980, Jeff Schuh returned to the Twin Cities for the final two games of the 1986 regular season. Acquired after being released by the Packers, Schuh made four tackles on special teams in his two outings with the Vikings.

Randy Scott

Season: 1987   Linebacker   Height: 6'1"
Number: 50   Alabama   Weight: 223

A six-year veteran with Green Bay, Randy Scott played with the Vikings for two replacement games in 1987 and registered nine tackles versus Chicago on October 11.

Todd Scott

Seasons: 1991–94   Safety   Height: 5'10"
Number: 38   Southwestern Louisiana   Weight: 207

At his best, Todd Scott was regarded as one of only a handful of safeties in the National Football League who could cover like a cornerback. His timing was uncanny. Just ask Jim Harbaugh, who fell victim to one of the most meaningful interceptions in Viking lore.

Minnesota entered the Chicago game on October 4, 1992, with a surprising 3–1 record. Yet the Bears had silenced the Metrodome crowd for most of the afternoon, building a 20–0 lead heading into the fourth quarter. Thoughts of victory were virtually nonexistent in the minds of most Minnesota fans before lightning struck, wearing number 38.

On the third play of the quarter, Harbaugh called an audible when he noticed wide receiver Neal Anderson was matched one-on-one with Scott. Harbaugh took a short drop and threw across the field, to his left. Scott read the play perfectly. The safety stepped in front of Anderson, bobbled the ball for a brief second, then scampered 35 yards to paydirt.

"You hope for a play like that," said Scott, who ignited a Viking rally that concluded in a 21–20 victory and helped the team reach the playoffs for the first time since 1989. "It's the kind of thing you dream about and, when I bobbled it, I thought I'd blown it. But when I got a grip on it, I was gone."

While that play proved to be the beginning of the end for Harbaugh and Bears head coach Mike Ditka in Chicago, Scott went on to earn Pro Bowl recognition and a place on the All-Madden team while emerging as one of the inspirational leaders on the defense. Minnesota's sixth-round draft choice in 1991, he finished the 1992 regular season with five picks, including a team record-tying three in the 42–7 win over Cincinnati on September 27, and 73 tackles, good for third on the team.

But just as it looked as if Scott would become a fixture in the Minnesota secondary, his performance began to wane, starting late in 1993, when he started the first 11 games before succumbing to bruised ribs. After making 61 tackles and two interceptions that year, Scott had 57 total hits and no steals in 1994. He fell victim to several blown coverages and was no longer the hard hitter or excellent cover man he had been. For those reasons, the Vikings bid Scott adieu during the offseason.

Bucky Scribner

Seasons: 1987–89 Punter Height: 6'
Number: 13 Kansas Weight: 203

The replacement games in 1987 helped Bucky Scribner return to the National Football League for more than the brief mid-season charade. After two years with the Packers followed by two seasons out of the loop, the left-footed Scribner punted in the Vikings' final replacement game, on October 18. Released when the union returned to work, he was re-signed and released during the first week of November, then re-signed a final time on December 8. Scribner took over for the injured Greg Coleman and averaged 41.3 yards per punt for the remainder of the campaign, including the playoffs.

Scribner also handled the Vikings' punting chores for the next two years. The owner of the Big Eight Conference record for career punting average, Scribner was eighth in the NFC with an average of 40.3 yards per punt and had two blocked in 1988. His performance fell to 39.8 yards per pooch in 1989, good for ninth in the conference. That showing led the Vikings to sign Plan B free agent Harry Newsome for the 1990 campaign.

Ron Selesky

Season: 1987 Center Height: 6'1"
Number: 60 North Central College Weight: 266

Two games with the Vikings' replacement team in 1987 comprised Ron Selesky's career in the National Football League.

Robin Sendlein

Seasons: 1981–84 Linebacker Height: 6'3"
Number: 57 Texas Weight: 225

Many Minnesota fans are familiar with Robin Sendlein. He is known in Viking lore as the player sent to Miami (along with a second-round draft pick) just prior to the 1985 season for the signing rights to former United States Football League wide receiver Anthony Carter.

Yet, prior to his departure, Sendlein had a productive tenure in purple. A second-round draft choice in 1981, the All-Southwest Conference standout served as a special teams performer during his four seasons with the Vikes and emerged as a starter at outside linebacker when Matt Blair was injured during Sendlein's final campaign with the team.

Sendlein, who missed only one game in four years with the Vikings, had a knack for blocking punts. His first came as a rookie, when his punt rejection against Green Bay set up Minnesota's go-ahead field goal in the Vikings' 30–13 win on September 27, 1981. He victimized Detroit next on September 25, 1983, a block that was recovered in the end zone by Dave Huffman for a touchdown in Minnesota's 20–17 victory. Sendlein's third blocked punt rolled out of the end zone for a safety on November 6, 1983, against Tampa Bay.

In 1984, Sendlein started the season's first eight games and continued to see significant defensive action after Blair returned from a knee injury. He ranked 10th on the team with 97 tackles and tied for second with 17 special teams hits, performances that helped make his services desirable to the Dolphins the following summer. A head injury that led to concussion syndrome forced his retirement from the game at the end of the 1987 season.

Joe Senser

Seasons: 1979–84 Tight End Height: 6'4"
Number: 81 West Chester State Weight: 240

As a teenager, Joe Senser always envisioned playing professional basketball. After all, he did not take the gridiron until his senior year of high school, and as a four-year starter at West Chester State, he broke Lew Alcindor's NCAA record by shooting .699 from the field in his final season on the hardwood.

His basketball jones notwithstanding, Senser was an excellent tight end for the Vikings, with his accomplishments cut short only by a variety of injuries during his six seasons on the Minnesota roster. Even so, he fell just short of Stu Voigt's records for tight ends before everyone's stats were shattered by Steve Jordan in the late 1980s and 1990s.

Minnesota's sixth-round draft choice in 1979, Senser spent his rookie season on injured reserve with a back injury. He moved into the "messenger" rotation in 1980, splitting time with Voigt and catching 42 passes with a team-high seven touchdown receptions. With Voigt having retired, Senser took his game to a higher level in 1981. He earned Pro Bowl recognition after setting an NFC record for the most receptions by a tight end in a season with 79 grabs. Senser also led the team with 1,004 receiving yards, at the time the fourth-highest in Vikings history. He added eight touchdowns and had a single game-best 11 catches against Green Bay on November 29. Those 11 grabs represent the most receptions ever for a Viking tight end in one contest.

His performance against the Packers came with a price, however. As he crossed the goal line for the 16th time as a Viking, Senser was hit, seriously injuring his right knee. The ailment affected him for the rest of his career, resulting ultimately in Senser being fitted with an artificial knee.

In 1982, he aggravated the knee again, yet still started every game and caught at least one pass in each contest to finish with 29 receptions for 261 yards. Knee surgery kept him out of action for the entire 1983 campaign, while a foot ailment limited him to eight games and one start in 1984, when he caught 15 tosses for 110 yards.

Though willing to continue his football career in 1985, Senser's body would not respond to the punishment. Although forced to retire from football during training camp that year, Senser remains a Minnesota fixture by owning two restaurants in the Twin Cities bearing his name.

Ed Sharockman

Seasons: 1962–72 Defensive Back Height: 6'
Number: 45 Pittsburgh Weight: 195

Minnesota general manager Bert Rose surprised the National Football League when, in the fourth round of the 1961 draft, he selected Wyoming cornerback Chuck Lamson as a "future," a player with college eligibility remaining who could be drafted since his class was graduating. Rose then shocked the circuit by doing the same thing in the fifth round, tabbing Pitt

Ed Sharockman

quarterback/defensive back Ed Sharockman. While the Steelers' Buddy Parker exploded in anger, Rose announced that Sharockman would be with the Vikings later that year since the Pitt coaching staff no longer wanted the maverick on its club.

As it turned out, Sharockman did not debut in Minnesota until 1962. He reported to the College All-Star camp in Chicago in 1961, only to head north with a broken leg, forcing him to miss all of his rookie campaign. Nevertheless, it quickly became evident why the Steelers so wanted Sharockman's services, for the multi-talented athlete stepped into the Vikings' lineup and remained there for the next decade.

Despite struggling with pulled muscles in his legs during his first couple of training camps, Sharockman used his quickness to excel against the short passing game. While his lack of blazing speed could lead to problems on deep routes, his fierce competitiveness enabled him to succeed more often than not. No one was tougher in the secondary than Sharockman, who shrugged off countless injuries, including at least seven broken noses, to place third on the Vikings' all-time list with 40 interceptions and second with 804 interception return yards.

Sharockman made an impact immediately with Minnesota. Nicknamed "Psycho" by head coach Norm Van Brocklin and known as "Bozo" to his teammates, the right cornerback intercepted six passes in 1962 and ran 88 yards to paydirt with a fumble recovery at Detroit on December 12. That return currently ranks as the second-longest fumble recovery in team annals and marked the first time in Vikings history a player returned a fumble for a touchdown. He picked off five passes in 1963 and took one back 47 yards for a touchdown against Green Bay on October 13. He added six more picks in 1965, among them a 40-yard return for six points against Detroit on December 12, and had four steals in 1968.

A hard hitter and solid tackler, Sharockman enjoyed putting his helmet on opponents, which allowed him to overcome constant nagging injuries to make outstanding plays. Several of those performances occurred on special teams. Sharockman returned kicks and punts at various times during his first seven years with Minnesota, with his 76-yarder representing the longest effort by a Viking in 1966.

After sharing starting duties with Bobby Bryant in 1969, Sharockman rebounded with one of his best seasons in 1970. In addition to leading the team with seven interceptions, he had one of the best games ever by a Viking defensive player during a 54–13 thumping of Dallas on October 18. Sharockman scored two touchdowns, one on a 23-yard return of a blocked punt and another on a 34-yard interception. He also set up a third score when he returned his second pick 43 yards. Sharockman recovered another blocked punt in the end zone for a touchdown in a 26–0 victory over New Orleans on September 27.

Sharockman had six more interceptions in 1971, then played in half the games in 1972 before receiving his release midway through the campaign. A member of the Vikings' Silver Anniversary All-Time Team, he led Minnesota in interceptions on four occasions, a team record Sharockman shares with Bryant and Joey Browner.

George Shaw

Season: 1961 — Quarterback — Height: 6'
Number: 14 — Oregon — Weight: 185

George Shaw was a major part of the Vikings' initial master plan. General manager Bert Rose realized Minnesota's inaugural team would be comprised of misfits, outcasts and rookies. One way to help offset the impending inconsistency would be to employ a veteran quarterback who could lead the expansion team during its first couple of seasons while developing a prospect, such as Fran Tarkenton. Rose deemed that leader to be Shaw, for whom Minnesota surrendered its first-round draft pick in 1962 to the New York Giants.

The plan lasted less than one game. Fundamentally sound and knowledgeable, Shaw had been a steady backup to Charlie Conerly with the Giants in 1959 and 1960. Yet serious leg injuries suffered during an earlier stint with the Colts left the signalcaller somewhat tentative and gun-shy. Although he played with heart and had the tools to succeed, Shaw quickly proved to be what the young Vikings did not need under center.

Shaw was the starting quarterback in the Vikings' first game, against Chicago on September 17, 1961. After failing to score deep in Bears territory, Shaw was yanked by head coach Norm Van Brocklin in the second quarter in favor of Tarkenton, a rookie who proceeded to guide Minnesota to a shocking 37–13 upset. Shaw was given the starting assignment in the third game against a former employer—Baltimore—but the same scenario was replayed. Tarkenton remained the starter for the rest of the season, leaving Shaw in his familiar reserve role.

The situation did not improve the following summer. Van Brocklin berated Shaw in the quarterback's hometown of Portland, Oregon, where the Vikings lost a 33–24 pre-season game to the Rams. Released by Minnesota shortly thereafter, he played one year with Denver before retiring from professional football. In his only year in purple, Shaw completed 46 of 91 pass attempts for 530 yards, four touchdowns and four interceptions.

Jerry Shay

Seasons: 1966–67 — Defensive Tackle — Height: 6'3"
Number: 73 — Purdue — Weight: 250

An All-American during his senior season at Purdue, Jerry Shay was the Vikings' first-round draft choice in 1966. He played for the College All-Stars in August, causing him to miss most of his rookie training camp and limiting his playing time during the regular season. He saw action in 14 games, and started against Detroit and Chicago late in the campaign.

Shay played in just one game in 1967 prior to being traded to Atlanta in exchange for tight end Billy Martin the following offseason.

Ashley Sheppard

Seasons: 1993–95 — Linebacker — Height: 6'3"
Number: 59 — Clemson — Weight: 240

Minnesota's fifth-round draft choice in 1993, Ashley Sheppard spent two seasons as a member of the Vikings' special teams while seeing defensive action on goal-line and short-yardage situations. An All-Atlantic Coast Conference performer at Clemson, he made six hits on kick coverages as a rookie before missing the last six games with a sprained ankle. Sheppard added 11 special teams tackles in 1994 while playing in seven contests. Released during training camp in 1995, he returned briefly during the campaign in November but did not see any action before receiving his second and final release from the Vikes two weeks later.

Will Sherman

Season: 1961   Flanker   Height: 6'3"
Number: 43   St. Mary's   Weight: 197

An All-Pro cornerback while with the Rams in the 1950s, Will Sherman arrived in Minnesota prior to the team's first season in exchange for a future draft pick. Head coach Norm Van Brocklin envisioned Sherman contributing on offense as an end, then shifted him to flanker during the later stages of the preseason in order to employ a "three-end" system. Sherman wound up catching two passes—one for 32 yards and the other for eight—in eight games with the Vikings. That proved to be his final season in the National Football League.

Lebron Shields

Season: 1961   Defensive End   Height: 6'4"
Number: 77   Tennessee   Weight: 250

A reserve offensive tackle taken from Baltimore in the veterans pool, Lebron Shields was moved to defensive end by the Vikings. He responded with the best performance of any lineman in the Minnesota camp until a knee injury suffered against San Francisco in the third pre-season game hurt his progress. Shields wound up playing in just six games for the Vikings in 1961, which turned out to be the swan song of his two-year career in the National Football League.

Jeff Siemon

Seasons: 1972–82   Linebacker   Height: 6'3"
Number: 50   Stanford   Weight: 235

The headlines typically featured other members of the Viking defense, but the glue that held the unit together for most of the 1970s was middle linebacker Jeff Siemon. Though not particularly quick, the tough, relentless and intelligent hitter—"The Minister of Defense"—was among the game's elite at his position, always taking the field regardless of how many bumps and bruises his body might bear.

A native of Rochester, Minnesota, who attended college at Stanford, Siemon was deemed to possess the potential to become the next Dick Butkus. Though immensely more sane than the Chicago Bear, Siemon proved worthy of his first-round status, a pick the Vikings obtained from New England for Joe Kapp. He became a four-time Pro Bowl participant and a team catalyst with his disciplined approach and his extraordinary nose for the football.

Deemed the best linebacker in college football in 1971, Siemon suited up for the Vikes a year later and started eight games as a rookie after Lonnie Warwick was hurt. The youngster played so well against both the pass and the run that head coach Bud Grant made an unusual assessment by predicting Siemon "could become a star" in the National Football League.

He lived up to that billing in 1973 by earning his first trip to the Pro Bowl. Siemon started every game, equalled his 1972 output by intercepting a pair of passes, recovered three fumbles, and blocked a field goal attempt. More of the same followed in 1974, with Siemon playing penalty-free football throughout the campaign. He picked off two more enemy aerials, caused four fumbles, and was the leading tackler in Super Bowl VIII with 10 stops.

In 1975, Siemon overcame a sprained knee he suffered in the last pre-season game to lead the Vikings in tackles with 91 solo hits and pace the line-

Jeff Siemon

backers with three interceptions. He also caused one fumble and recovered another. A third Pro Bowl appearance came after the 1976 season, when the middle linebacker made 146 primary tackles, 42 assists, caused two fumbles, and blocked a field goal try, against the Giants. He again rose to the occasion in the Super Bowl, registering 15 tackles versus Oakland.

Siemon suffered a leg injury in 1977 but still garnered his fourth Pro Bowl invitation thanks to 107 tackles and 54 assists. He led the Vikings with 170 hits and 59 assists in 1978, yet failed to intercept a pass for the first time in his seven professional seasons. Recurring leg ailments caused Siemon to miss starts in the first four games of 1979, yet he answered the bell every week and made 115 unassisted hits.

A pre-season injury and the emergence of Scott Studwell forced Siemon to play a reserve role for all but three games in 1980. That same year, Siemon was named the Fellowship of Christian Athletes' "Professional Athlete of the Year," an annual award presented to the player "whose caliber of commitment and influence is the source of inspiration and strength both on and off the field." Siemon became the only person to win both the professional and collegiate versions of the honor.

Siemon moved back into the starting lineup in 1981, when the Vikings changed from a 4–3 to a 3–4 defense, and made 92 tackles. He was traded to the Chargers after the 1981 season and reclaimed by Minnesota on waivers from San Diego on September 7, 1982. Siemon played in all nine regular-season games as a backup in 1982 and registered seven primary hits.

With 1,012 solo tackles, 374 assists, seven quarterback sacks, 14 caused fumbles, 10 recovered fumbles and 11 interceptions, Siemon decided to end his football career by retiring shortly after the 1984 training camp commenced. A year later, he was named to the Vikings' Silver Anniversary All-Time Team.

Arnold Simkus

Season: 1967 Defensive End Height: 6'4"
Number: 69 Michigan Weight: 245

Arnold Simkus joined the Vikings as a free agent during training camp in 1967 and earned a job playing behind Carl Eller and Jim Marshall. A starter during a few pre-season games, Simkus gave the standout first-team an occasional breather in 11 contests during his only season in purple.

Howard Simpson

Season: 1964 Tackle Height: 6'5"
Number: 75 Auburn Weight: 230

The Vikings were impressed with the size Howard Simpson possessed upon signing him as a college free agent out of Auburn in 1964. He showed marginal progress in training camp and even played along the offensive line during three regular-season games late in his rookie campaign before it was determined his ceiling in the National Football League had been reached.

William Sims

Season: 1994 Linebacker Height: 6'3"
Number: 57 Southwestern Louisiana Weight: 260

William Sims made the Vikings' practice squad as a college free agent in 1994 before joining the roster shortly thereafter. He played exclusively on special teams in eight games, making 10 solo tackles and two assisted hits while missing six contests with a severe groin pull. His tenure as a Viking ended after his first season in purple when Carolina collected him in the expansion draft.

Scott Sisson

Season: 1996　　　　　　　Kicker　　　　　　　　Height: 6'
Number: 9　　　　　　　　Georgia Tech　　　　　Weight: 196

Possessing an accurate leg that lacked distance, Scott Sisson served as Minnesota's field goal kicker for the 1996 season and led the team in scoring with 96 points. Connecting on 22 of 29 field goal attempts and all 30 extra-point tries, Sisson was at his best late in games, when he converted 15 of 17 three-pointers during the fourth quarter and overtime, including game-winners against the Bears on September 15 and Oakland on November 17.

Despite his consistency, including 10 straight in September, Sisson made just three of seven tries from 40 yards or beyond, with 44 yards representing his longest successful attempt. A poor kickoff man, he was released the following August in training camp, losing his job to his best friend, Greg Davis. When Davis was let go after four games, Sisson was not contacted, with the Vikings opting for Eddie Murray instead.

Mike Slaton

Season: 1987　　　　　　　Safety　　　　　　　　Height: 6'2"
Number: 35　　　　　　　　South Dakota　　　　　Weight: 194

The Vikings' ninth-round draft pick in 1986 who was cut during his rookie training camp, Mike Slaton returned to play in one game for Minnesota's replacement team in 1987.

Larry Smiley

Season: 1973　　　　　　　Defensive End　　　　　Height: 6'4"
Number: 74　　　　　　　　Texas Southern　　　　Weight: 240

Minnesota's 16th-round draft choice in 1973, Larry Smiley was listed as the Vikings' third-string left defensive end, behind starter Carl Eller and reserve Bob Lurtsema, as a rookie but did not see action for a single play. He was released the following year during training camp after showing little progress.

Cedric Smith

Season: 1990　　　　　　　Running Back　　　　　Height: 5'10"
Number: 30　　　　　　　　Florida　　　　　　　　Weight: 223

Cedric Smith, whose claim to fame in college came as Emmitt Smith's (no relation) blocking back, played in 15 games for the Vikings in 1990 after joining the team as a fifth-round draft choice. Smith registered 19 yards on nine carries, returned one kickoff for 16 yards, and made three tackles on special teams as a rookie. After one year in the Upper Midwest, he toiled four more years in the National Football League, mainly as a special teams performer.

Daryl Smith

Season: 1989　　　　　　　Cornerback　　　　　　Height: 5'9"
Number: 25　　　　　　　　North Alabama　　　　Weight: 190

Signed as a Plan B free agent from Cincinnati in 1989, Daryl Smith played in five games with the Vikings that fall, with nearly all of his appearances involving special teams.

Fernando Smith

Seasons: 1994–97 Defensive End Height: 6'6"
Number: 95 Jackson State Weight: 277

The Vikings felt they found a replacement for the departed Chris Doleman when they drafted Fernando Smith in the second round in 1994. Although not nearly as dominant as Doleman, Smith did attempt to fill the void, but not before taking two full years to develop into a starter in the National Football League.

Primarily a special teams performer as a rookie, Smith opened the 1995 campaign as the starter at right end but quickly became a reserve at defensive end and tackle while leading the team with two blocked kicks. The departure of Roy Barker in 1996 gave Smith an opportunity to prove himself. He responded by ranking second on the team with 9.5 sacks, including two sacks in three separate games. His two-sack showing in the 24–22 win over Detroit on December 8 helped him earn NFC Defensive Player of the Week honors. He also paced the linemen with 79 tackles and six passes defensed.

Injuries to an ankle, groin and both big toes kept Smith from progressing to the next level in 1997. He gave a valiant effort by playing through the ailments in the first half, but was often ineffective in his pursuit from the left side. He wound up losing his starting job to rookie Stalin Colinet and finished the year with 57 total tackles, four sacks and a forced fumble.

With Smith coming off hernia surgery late in the offseason and slated to earn $1.6 million in 1998, he was released by Minnesota after failing to pass his physical. Smith was picked up by Jacksonville, where he served in a backup capacity.

Gordon Smith

Seasons: 1961–65 Tight End Height: 6'2"
Number: 87 Missouri Weight: 200

Having won the Orange Bowl in 1960, the University of Missouri coaching staff helped a couple of its players get a look in the National Football League. One Tiger coach mentioned Gordy Smith to Minnesota assistant Stan West. Smith received an invitation to training camp in 1961 and wound up as the only one of 40 free agents to survive the final cuts.

Despite being a rookie, Smith bumped veteran Bob Schnelker from the starting tight end job midway through the Vikings' maiden season. He wound up catching 12 passes for 320 yards and four touchdowns, including a season-long 71-yard scoring reception against the 49ers on November 26. Smith had 123 receiving yards during that contest, the second-highest total for a Minnesota tight end in team history.

A knee injury limited Smith to four games and seven catches for 138 yards and a touchdown in 1962. He shared the tight end job with Jerry Reichow in 1963, finishing with six receptions for 177 yards. One of his biggest grabs as a Viking occurred on December 1, when Smith caught a 54-yard touchdown toss from Ron VanderKelen in the 17–17 tie with Chicago.

Smith shared the tight end duties with Hal Bedsole for the next two years, catching 10 tosses in 1964 and a career-high 22 passes for 439 yards, an average of 19.6 yards per reception, and five touchdowns in 1965. His biggest catch may have come on the only play quarterback Fran Tarkenton ever admitted he called a scramble. On fourth down and a mile to go in the waning moments on October 4, Smith overcame a collision with Tom Hall to pull in a 44-yard pass and get out of bounds. That play set up Fred Cox's game-winning 27-yard field goal in the 24–23 triumph over Green Bay, marking the first time the Vikings defeated the Packers and head coach Vince Lombardi.

Yet, after his best year in the National Football League, Smith decided to retire from the game. His absence was felt the following fall when Bedsole went down with a trick knee, necessitating the move of wide receiver Red Phillips to tight end.

Greg Smith

Season: 1984
Number: 91
Defensive Tackle
Kansas
Height: 6'3"
Weight: 261

A free agent who made the Minnesota roster in 1984, Greg Smith played in all 16 games and started six times when either Mark Mullaney or Doug Martin was felled by injuries. Considered a pass rush specialist even though he never reached the quarterback, Smith was second among the Vikings' defensive linemen with 62 total tackles, including 22 primary hits. He also found the football on two kickoffs, returning the pigskin 26 yards, with a long run of 15 yards.

Jimmy Smith

Season: 1987
Number: 43
Running Back
Elon
Height: 6'
Weight: 205

Jimmy Smith played for the Redskins and Raiders in 1984 before reappearing in the National Football League three years later as a Vikings replacement player. In one game in purple, Smith rushed seven times for 13 yards and averaged 21 yards on two kickoff returns.

Lyman Smith

Season: 1978
Number: 79
Defensive Tackle
Duke
Height: 6'5"
Weight: 250

Miami's third-round draft choice in 1978, Lyman Smith joined the Vikings at the start of his rookie campaign after the Duke graduate was released by the Dolphins. Smith played in 11 games for Minnesota, with most of his action involving goal-line and short-yardage situations. Placed on injured reserve the following August, Smith's tenure in purple ended on October 17, 1979, when he was activated and subsequently waived.

Robert Smith

Seasons: 1993–98
Numbers: 26, 20
Running Back
Ohio State
Height: 6'2"
Weight: 212

Robert Smith's reputation preceded him to Minnesota. Labelled a prima donna and troublemaker while at Ohio State, Smith had moments that validated such claims. He held out of training camp three of his first four years with the Vikings and, as one of the more intelligent players ever to wear purple, often walked to the beat of a different drummer when around his teammates.

Yet those claims proved meaningless compared to the three main things Smith displayed. One, when healthy, he had as much talent as anyone who has ever carried the ball for the Vikings. Two, injuries seem to hit Smith more often than hurricanes form in the Atlantic. And three, while different, Smith is in no way a bad apple or a malcontent.

Nevertheless, as Minnesota's first first-round pick since 1988, Smith found himself under the microscope upon his arrival to the Twin Cities in 1993. He was deemed an oddball when, upon gaining 1,126 yards as a freshman with the Buckeyes, he left the team after assistant coach Elliott Uzelac demanded that Smith attend a morning practice instead of a chemistry class. He later returned for the 1992 season and gained 819 yards on 147 carries before entering the National Football League's draft as a junior. Still, some wondered if Smith had the desire to succeed at such a high level.

"Maybe there are some people with lingering doubts about my dedication," Smith said during his first mini-camp. "But if you look at my career, it shows pretty clearly that my dedication has always been there. All along, I've shown my love of the game. By coming out early, I've crystallized how I love this game and want to play it at its highest level."

Although the early days would not be the last time Smith's dedication was questioned, his greatest obstacle was not so much defenders in the National Football League, but injuries. As a rookie, he made his first start on November 28, 1993, against New Orleans and gained 94 yards on 24 carries. He finished third on the club with 399 yards rushing while missing games with the chicken pox, an inner ear infection and a season-ending knee injury.

A hip ailment cost him two games in 1994, when he gained 106 yards on 31 carries and caught 15 passes as a third-down back. In 1995, he replaced the departed Terry Allen as the starter and was on pace to set the team's single-season rushing record by gaining 632 yards, only to have a high ankle sprain steal his effectiveness at midseason. The same scenario played out in 1996, with Smith leading the NFL with 693 yards on the ground before he tore ligaments in his left knee against Chicago on October 28.

Robert Smith

Finally, in 1997, after many wondered if Smith would ever carry the pigskin for the Vikings again, he moved into the class of the NFL's elite running backs. While an ankle sprain kept him out of two games, Smith set the Minnesota marks for rushing yards in a season with 1,266, most 100-yard games in a season with six, season rushing average with 5.5 yards per carry, and consecutive carries without a fumble with 352. Even Smith knew he was considered among the best when he and the Vikings arrived in Green Bay in September and saw a dummy dressed in his uniform hanging with a noose around its neck.

"For the first time in my career I looked up and saw somebody had a number 26 doll that was hanging in the stands," Smith said. "That was it. Being hung in effigy is what every player wants. You know you've made it when they really hate you."

Smith became even more effective in 1998. He raced 74 yards to paydirt against St. Louis in a 38–31 win on September 13 for the second-longest scoring gallop in team history. He also gained 179 yards rushing during the contest, the second-highest total in Vikings lore. Two weeks later, versus Chicago, Smith's 67-yard touchdown reception represents the longest catch of his career and the fourth-longest in team history by a Vikings running back. He later earned NFC Player of the Week honors for his 134-yard performance against Detroit on October 25.

A sprained right knee suffered against Dallas on November 26 forced Smith to miss two games. He returned in time to gain 174 yards in the final two contests of the regular season to finish with 1,187 yards on 249 carries. That performance pushed Smith into fifth place on the Vikings' all-time list for rushing yards with 4,282.

Smith then played a significant role in the Vikings' post-season success in 1998. He set a Minnesota playoff record with 124 rushing yards during the 41–21 win over Arizona on January 10, 1999, breaking the previous mark of 118 yards, set by Chuck Foreman against the Rams on December 26, 1976. He also carried the offense against Atlanta by gaining 71 yards, with most of those yards coming in the fourth quarter of the NFC Championship Game.

True, his career may have featured a few bumps and bruises early on, but that is all in the past. In fact, by the time Smith decides he has given enough to professional football, he may be considered the greatest running back in Minnesota history.

Robert Smith

Season: 1985 Defensive Lineman Height: 6'5"
Number: 74 Grambling Weight: 255

Never to be confused with the Vikings' star running back by the same name a decade later, Minnesota's first Robert Smith was a reserve defensive end and tackle who made 10 stops on defense and seven more hits on special teams in 1985. Smith joined the Vikes after being the team's second-round selection in the 1984 supplemental draft and spending all of the previous campaign on the United States Football League's Arizona Wranglers' injured reserve list.

Rod Smith

Season: 1996 Cornerback Height: 5'11"
Number: 47 Notre Dame Weight: 187

Rod Smith proved how hard it is to come home and play. Signed as a free agent, the Roseville, Minnesota, native had difficulty recovering from a sprained ankle he suffered in the final pre-season game and was inactive for the first seven regular-season contests of 1996. His fate was sealed when he irritated the coaching staff by missing some team meetings while injured, with the Vikings releasing Smith in favor of newcomer Tomur Barnes.

Steve Smith

Seasons: 1968–70 Defensive End Height: 6'5"
Number: 74 Michigan Weight: 250

Acquired during training camp in 1968, Steve Smith spent three seasons on the Vikings' special teams and as a backup defensive end and offensive tackle. A tight end in college, Smith possessed excellent speed for a player his size, enabling him to serve on all of Minnesota's kicking units. Despite suffering a knee injury against the Colts in the 1968 playoffs, Smith answered the bell for every game while in purple. He was traded with second-, third- and sixth-round draft picks to Philadelphia for Norm Snead in 1971.

Wayne Smith

Season: 1987 Cornerback Height: 6'
Number: 40 Purdue Weight: 171

With the Viking secondary weakened by the injury to Reggie Rutland, Minnesota signed seven-year veteran Wayne Smith on November 11, 1987, after he had toiled for the club's replacement team in October. Smith took the field in six contests, made five solo tackles on defense, seven hits on special teams, and intercepted a pass that he returned 24 yards. Smith did not see action in the regular-season finale or in the playoffs due to the return of Rutland from injured reserve on December 25.

Norm Snead

Season: 1971	Quarterback	Height: 6'4"
Number: 16	Wake Forest	Weight: 215

Joe Kapp's departure in 1970 left the Vikings with Gary Cuozzo and Bob Lee to handle the quarterbacking chores. The duties were split three ways in 1971, when 32-year-old Norm Snead was added to the equation after being obtained just prior to the draft from Philadelphia in exchange for defensive end Steve Smith and picks in the second, third and sixth rounds.

A rough preseason resulted in Snead's ranking third on the depth chart to open the 1971 campaign. Cuozzo served as the Vikings' starter for most of the season's first half, and Lee handled the first-string duties down the stretch. Strong-armed with an even temperament, Snead started the third and fourth games of the campaign—shutout victories over the Bills and Eagles. He also relieved Cuozzo to lead Minnesota to a 17–10 victory over the Giants on October 31, with Snead's 55-yard touchdown toss to Bob Grim in the fourth quarter deciding the outcome. Snead could not find the magic a week later, however, when he failed to guide the Vikings to victory over the 49ers after Cuozzo opened the game by misfiring on his first 10 passes.

Snead took the field just briefly in the team's final six regular-season games. Packaged with Bob Grim, Vince Clements and first- and second-round draft picks to New York for Fran Tarkenton the following offseason, Snead's lone year in purple saw him complete 37 of 75 pass attempts for 470 yards, one touchdown and six interceptions.

Ariel Solomon

Season: 1996	Offensive Lineman	Height: 6'5"
Number: 69	Colorado	Weight: 290

Minnesota upgraded its depth along the offensive line by signing free agent Ariel Solomon for the 1996 season. Solomon could play any of the five line positions, but received nearly all of his action during 16 game appearances while serving on the Vikings' kick protection teams for field-goal and extra-point attempts. With the return of veteran Scott Dill and the injury recovery by Everett Lindsay, Solomon's services were not needed in 1997, when he signed with Detroit.

Jesse Solomon

Seasons: 1986–89	Linebacker	Height: 6'
Number: 54	Florida State	Weight: 236

The Vikings struck gold late in the 1986 draft by selecting Jesse Solomon in the 12th round. He developed into a two-year starter and three-year contributor before becoming one of the key ingredients of the Herschel Walker deal with Dallas in 1989.

Solomon started four games as a rookie, filling in for the injured Scott Studwell once and a hurt David Howard on three occasions. After making 96 total tackles and two interceptions in his first season, he became the defensive leader with 92 solo stops, three forced fumbles and one pick in 1987. A year later, Solomon again paced the defense with 96 primary hits while intercepting four passes before a knee injury in the season finale sidelined him for the playoffs.

His best game as a Viking took place on December 4, 1988. Solomon shared NFC Defensive Player of the Week accolades with teammate Carl Lee after recording 10 tackles, one sack and intercepting a pass and returning it 78 yards for a touchdown in the 45–3 win over New Orleans.

Solomon concluded his days in purple with four games in 1989 prior to joining the Cowboys after the October 13 trade for Walker. He played five more years in the National Football League with four different teams.

Willie Spencer

Season: 1976
Number: 31
Running Back
no college
Height: 6'
Weight: 230

A high school All-American from Massillon, Ohio, Willie Spencer did not play college football, opting instead to spend two years in the Canadian Football League's minor leagues before two standout seasons in the World Football League. A strong runner and sound blocker, Spencer made the Vikings' roster out of training camp in 1976 and played in three games, rushing for two yards on four carries with one fumble.

Tim Starks

Season: 1987
Number: 34
Defensive Back
Kent State
Height: 5'9"
Weight: 175

Tim Starks took the field for one game with Minnesota's replacement team in 1987.

Robert Steele

Season: 1979
Number.: 82
Wide Receiver
North Alabama
Height: 6'4"
Weight: 196

A backup wide receiver, Robert Steele played in all 16 games for the Vikings in 1979, with most of his action coming on special teams. His biggest contribution involved blocking a punt that led to a touchdown in the Vikings' 23–22 win at Tampa Bay on November 25. Steele also caught one pass for 10 yards during the season.

Bob Stein

Season: 1975
Number: 52
Linebacker
Minnesota
Height: 6'3"
Weight: 235

A former Golden Gopher who attended high school in Saint Louis Park, Minnesota, Bob Stein joined the Vikings during the 1975 season after opening the campaign with the Chargers. Seeing most of his activity on special teams, Stein played nine games in purple during his seventh and final season in the National Football League. He later emerged as the general manager of the NBA's Minnesota Timberwolves.

Jan Stenerud

Seasons: 1984–85
Number: 3
Kicker
Montana State
Height: 6'2"
Weight: 190

Acquired from Green Bay in 1984 for a seventh-round draft choice, Jan Stenerud spent the last two seasons of his 19-year, Hall-of-Fame career with the Vikings. Despite being 42 years old when he first donned purple, Stenerud was Minnesota's lone Pro Bowl representative following the 1984 season.

One of the game's first soccer-style kickers, the former Chief connected on 20 of 23 field-goal attempts, good for a league-leading 87 percent, and all but one of his 31 extra-point tries in 1984. His 54-yarder in the 27–20 win over Atlanta on September 16 represents the longest successful three-pointer in Vikings team history. He added a 53-yarder, tied for the second-longest field goal in Minnesota annals, with two seconds remaining to give the Vikes a 27–24 triumph over Tampa Bay on November 4.

As consistent as Stenerud was in 1984, he was equally erratic in 1985. He succeeded on just 15 of 26 tries from three-point territory. And while he missed only two PATs in 43 attempts, one miscue proved to be the difference in a 14–13 loss at Atlanta on December 15. With his production declining, Stenerud decided to call it a career at the end of the season.

Mike Stensrud

Season: 1986 Defensive Tackle Height: 6'5"
Number: 74 Iowa State Weight: 280

A starter for most of his seven years with the Oilers, Mike Stensrud joined the Vikings as a free agent following the fourth game of the 1986 campaign. The veteran defensive tackle played in purple for 11 games, starting four, and registered 19 total tackles. Stensrud's best showing with Minnesota came at Cincinnati on November 23, when the lineman posted two solo hits and his lone sack of the season.

Joe Stepanek

Season: 1987 Defensive End Height: 6'5"
Number: 73 Minnesota Weight: 268

Joe Stepanek played in one replacement game for the Vikings in 1987. The former Golden Gopher recorded a sack when he tackled Green Bay quarterback Alan Risher in the end zone in the fourth quarter on October 4.

Bill Stephanos

Seasons: 1981–82 Tackle Height: 6'4"
Number: 71 Boston College Weight: 262

Minnesota's 11th-round draft choice in 1981, Bill Stephanos spent all of his rookie year on injured reserve with a back problem. He made the active roster in 1982, but returned to the injured list on September 7 for the remainder of the campaign after suffering a concussion in the final pre-season contest, against New Orleans. Waived during the last cuts of 1983, Stephanos never played in a regular-season game for the Vikings.

Mac Stephens

Season: 1991 Linebacker Height: 6'3"
Number: 95 Minnesota Weight: 220

Mac Stephens, a former Golden Gopher, came and went during the 1991 campaign. He played in three games during his encore in the Metrodome, recording one primary hit and a solo tackle on defense.

Todd Steussie

Seasons: 1994–98 Tackle Height: 6'6"
Number: 73 California Weight: 321

When Gary Zimmerman decided he no longer wanted to be a Viking after the 1992 season, a major hole was created at the critical left tackle spot. Rookie Everett Lindsay provided a laudable effort before succumbing to injuries in 1993. The job was then handed to another rookie, first-round pick Todd Steussie, in 1994. Four years later, Steussie has made Zimmerman little more than a distant memory.

Teaming with Randall McDaniel, Steussie has given the Vikings one of their most effective left sides along the offensive line in Minnesota history. A smart, intense and dedicated player, Steussie is an excellent drive blocker who pulls and leads well. Though not the quickest player in the league, he

Todd Steussie

has learned how to handle speed rushers by maintaining blocks. Steussie has become equally adept in the running and passing game, and is a major reason such young players as Brad Johnson and Robert Smith were able to develop so rapidly.

"Todd is one of the better tackles in the league," said offensive line coach Mike Tice. "He's tough and smart, a great athlete. People who rate players have Todd rated as one of the top tackles in the league."

In 1994, Steussie joined fellow first-rounder Dewayne Washington as the first Vikings to start all 16 games as a rookie. He earned perennial all-rookie recognition before overcoming an injured shoulder that required off-season surgery in 1995. In fact, Steussie had not missed a start since his debut in the National Football League, a string that reached 75 games, before missing the Tampa Bay contest on November 1, 1998, with a left knee injury.

Well-deserved Pro Bowl honors came Steussie's way in 1997. He re-signed with Minnesota prior to the 1998 season and continued to prove he is one of the best left tackles in the business, earning second-team All-Pro and Pro Bowl recognition. The punishing run blocker continued to do an outstanding job of protecting the quarterback's blind side in pass protection, and was a significant, if unheralded, reason for Randall Cunningham's resurgence as one of the NFL's top quarterbacks.

James Stewart

Seasons: 1995–96 Running Back Height: 6'2"
Number: 28 Miami (Fla.) Weight: 246

James Stewart, Minnesota's fifth-round pick in 1995, looked to be the steal of the draft during his rookie campaign. After an impressive showing in the preseason, Stewart emerged briefly in November after Robert Smith was shelved with an ankle injury. He paced the Vikings with 63 yards on 13 carries in a 27-24 win over Green Bay on November 5. Two weeks later, during a 43-24 victory over New Orleans, Stewart gained 77 yards, including a 51-yard scamper, the second-longest run by a rookie in Viking annals.

Unfortunately for Stewart, the Saints game proved to be his finale in purple. He broke his left fibula during the contest and missed the remainder of the 1995 season. A year later, after leading the team with 107 rushing yards in the 1996 preseason, Stewart broke his left leg again, ironically, against New Orleans. He missed all of the 1996 slate, then was released during training camp in 1997.

Mark Stewart

Seasons: 1983–84 Linebacker Height: 6'2"
Number: 95 Washington Weight: 232

A consensus All-American as a college senior, Mark Stewart was unable to maintain that level of play in the professional ranks. Drafted by the Vikings in the fifth round in 1983, Stewart spent all of his rookie season on injured reserve after straining the Achilles tendon in his left leg during the first week of training camp. A year later, it became obvious that the ailment took away some of his outstanding speed. Stewart made the Minnesota roster in 1984, but was released after four games, on October 6.

Ken Stills

Season: 1990
Number: 27
Safety
Wisconsin
Height: 5'10"
Weight: 186

Ken Stills, a Plan B free agent signee from Green Bay, overcame an early-season torn calf muscle to play in 12 games for the Vikings in 1990. While most of his action came as a defensive back in nickel and dime packages, Stills started three games at safety in December and recorded five tackles against both the Buccaneers and Raiders. He finished the campaign with 20 total hits and one defensed pass.

Steve Stonebreaker

Seasons: 1962–63
Number: 82
Tight End-Linebacker
Detroit
Height: 6'3"
Weight: 222

Steve Stonebreaker saw action with the Vikings as a tight end in the early stages of the 1962 season after being drafted in the 12th round in 1961 as a "future." He managed to catch 12 passes for 227 yards, including a 19-yard touchdown toss from Fran Tarkenton against Green Bay on October 14. Yet, after dropping as many passes as he caught while running poor routes, Stonebreaker's aggressive approach was deemed more effective at covering tight ends than serving as one, resulting in spot duty at linebacker late in the campaign.

Stonebreaker played in all 14 games in 1963 as a reserve linebacker prior to being traded to Baltimore for guard Palmer Pyle in 1964.

Thomas Strauthers

Seasons: 1989–91
Number: 94
Defensive End
Jackson State
Height: 6'4"
Weight: 265

A Plan B free agent signee, Thomas Strauthers served as a backup defensive lineman who excelled in rushing the passer for three years. After registering a sack and four tackles during his first season in purple, Strauthers posted 13 hits in 1990 and placed third on the team with four quarterback dumps, including a two-sack effort at Philadelphia on October 15. In 1991, he recorded 25 total tackles, while his 2.5 sacks ranked fifth on the Vikings.

Fred Strickland

Season: 1993
Number: 53
Linebacker
Purdue
Height: 6'2"
Weight: 250

Fred Strickland joined Minnesota in 1993 after struggling with injuries for most of his five years with the Rams. Signed to provide more bulk and run-stuffing ability to a defense that was speed-oriented, Strickland replaced Mike Merriweather at the weak outside linebacker position and gave a yeoman's effort, placing second on the team with 81 solo tackles, 137 total hits and 5.5 tackles for loss. Though one of the more pleasant surprises of the 1993 campaign, Strickland was allowed to sign with Green Bay the following year while the Vikings went with a blossoming Ed McDaniel.

Korey Stringer

Seasons: 1995–98
Number: 77
Tackle
Ohio State
Height: 6'4"
Weight: 353

When the word "pancake" is mentioned in the same sentence as Korey Stringer's name, there can be two entirely different meanings. The more positive association centers on the right tackle's ability to dominate in

Korey Stringer

the running game by burying (or "pancaking") defenders when his stamina is at its peak. Conversely, the word also can relate to the lineman's massive diet, which caused Stringer to fight the battle of the bulge during the early stages of his career.

A first-round draft choice in 1995 and one of the two heaviest players ever to wear purple, Stringer became the Vikings' starter at right tackle in the second game of his rookie year after veteran Rick Cunningham succumbed to a knee injury in the season opener against Chicago. Stringer never relinquished the job after Cunningham returned, starting 15 games in 1995 (the third-highest total for a Minnesota rookie) before missing just one start in each of the next two seasons prior to sitting out two contests with a groin injury in 1998.

Though always productive during his first three seasons in the National Football League, Stringer emerged as an outstanding right tackle in 1998, and improved to the point where he may be the Vikings' best all-around offensive lineman. His success can be attributed to better physical conditioning. After repeated attempts to lose weight, including an unsuccessful stint at the Duke University weight clinic, Stringer dropped nearly 50 pounds from his highest mark and played at 340. The added quickness and agility was apparent, with Stringer dominating Reggie White at Green Bay on October 5 and allowing just one sack in the first half of the season.

A good athlete who is light on his feet for his size, Stringer excels at run-blocking, and is good in pass protection when his stamina is strong. He teams with 350-pound David Dixon on the right side, with no front wall offering more mass. More importantly, no line offers two players who have made more improvements in the recent past, which has had a direct correlation to the Vikings' improved offensive ways. It is for that reason Minnesota extended Stringer's contract by five years for $18 million toward the end of the 1998 slate.

Scott Studwell

Seasons: 1977–90   Linebacker   Height: 6'2"
Number: 55   Illinois   Weight: 228

The eyes. Look into a man's eyes and his soul will be revealed. In the case of Scott Studwell, one glance would render one of the game's most intense competitors who combined intelligence and strength to dominate opponents for more than a decade in the National Football League.

Despite having broken most of Dick Butkus' tackling records at Illinois, Studwell was still available when the Vikings selected in the ninth round of the 1977 draft. Many scouts worried about his speed, or lack thereof, but Studwell insisted that he was timed while he weighed 260 pounds after playing defensive tackle, and was in the midst of bringing his weight down in order to compete as a linebacker. His alibi proved correct. By the time his NFL playing days came to a close, he topped all of Minnesota's hits charts, retiring with 1,981 total tackles.

Studwell started three games as a rookie due to injuries suffered by veterans and responded with 42 tackles, including 10 stops during a 14–7 win over Atlanta on October 30, 1977. His role consisted primarily of special teams action in 1978 before Studwell started the first four games of the 1979 slate at middle linebacker when Jeff Siemon was injured. He finished his third season with 79 hits and another 14 tackles on special teams, good for second on the team.

Those efforts earned Studwell the starting job at middle linebacker in 1980. In his first year after taking over for Siemon, Studwell paced the

Vikings with 151 unassisted hits prior to making 13 tackles and four assists in the playoff contest against Philadelphia. He made a smooth transition from the 4–3 defense to the 3–4 in 1981 and again led the team in stops. The same story followed in 1982, although Studwell missed a game with a knee injury, as well as in 1983. He had an unbelievable game against Detroit on December 5, 1983, recording 14 tackles, three assists and one sack.

Studwell again led the team in tackles in 1984. He set a club record with 16 solo hits against San Francisco on December 8, 1984, and twice made 14 stops, versus Chicago on October 28 and Denver on November 18. A broken thumb that caused him to miss two games did not keep Studwell from leading the team in tackles for a sixth straight year in 1985. He added another page to the record book with 24 total tackles (16 solo, eight assists) against the Lions on November 17, surpassing his previous best of 20, which Studwell had done three times to that point.

In 1986, although his string of leading the team in hits was snapped while registering 82 primary stops, Studwell became the Vikings' all-time leading tackler, surpassing Matt Blair's total of 1,452. His first Pro Bowl appearance came in 1987, the same year Studwell surpassed Blair and Siemon to become Minnesota's career leader in unassisted tackles. He earned his second trip to Hawaii in 1988 by knocking ball carriers off their pins a team-high 131 times. Studwell then led the Vikings in tackles for the eighth time in 10 years and set a club mark with six seasons of more than 100 hits by registering 102 tackles and 71 assists in 1989, when he was a second-team All-NFC pick by UPI. His 21 stops against Pittsburgh on September 24 were the second-highest in team history.

Studwell had 61 stops in 1990 before deciding his knees had taken all the abuse they could withstand after 14 NFL seasons. A member of the Vikings' Silver Anniversary All-Time Team in 1985, he holds the team record for total tackles in a career (1,981), solo tackles in a career (1,308), most tackles in a season (230 in 1981), and most tackles in a game (24, versus Detroit in 1985). No other player in Vikings history has as many as 1,500 total tackles.

While his performance no longer comes on the field, Studwell continues to contribute to the Vikings' winning ways. Since 1992, the former linebacker has served as Minnesota's player personnel coordinator.

Scott Studwell

Charlie Sumner

Seasons: 1961–62
Number: 26
Defensive Back
William & Mary
Height: 6'1"
Weight: 195

A four-year starter with the Bears and one of the most prolific interceptors in Chicago annals, Charlie Sumner was taken from George Halas' team in the veterans pool in 1961. He started 13 games for the Vikings during the franchise's first season and picked off two passes. Sumner then played in all 14 contests in 1962 and ranked fifth on the team with three interceptions for 46 return yards. His final pickoff set up a first-quarter Minnesota touchdown against the Colts on December 16.

Sumner's playing days ended after the 1962 season, but he remained in the National Football League for several years as a coaching assistant.

Milt Sunde

Seasons: 1964–74   Guard   Height: 6'2"
Number: 64   Minnesota   Weight: 250

When Milt Sunde was drafted in the 20th and final round by the Vikings in 1964, the Minnesota management made the selection as a token of appreciation for Murray Warmath, one of the team's owners and a relative of Sunde's. Shortly thereafter, Sunde was anything but a kind gesture. He emerged as a fixture on the offensive line for 11 seasons and is considered one of the most consistent guards in Minnesota history. He also owns the distinction of being the lowest round draft choice to ever start for the Vikings.

A 185-pounder during his high school days in Bloomington, Sunde was a late bloomer on the gridiron. He was a two-way tackle at 215 pounds in college, yet earned Big Ten All-Academic recognition. He played defensive tackle beside Carl Eller in college, and was deemed by head coach Bud Grant as one of the smartest and hardest working players ever to wear a purple uniform.

By pumping iron in an old barn in back of his father's business in Bloomington, Sunde added 13 pounds between his final college game and his first day in training camp. After starting several games at left guard as a rookie, he reported to the team in 1965 at 250 pounds and emerged as one of the league's best young blockers in the middle of the offensive line. His dedication and desire enabled Sunde to maintain his starting job for nine years before sharing duties during his final two campaigns, in 1973 and 1974.

A Pro Bowl player in 1966 and a member of the Vikings' Silver Anniversary All-Time Team, Sunde's other most notable accomplishment came during training camp in 1967. Grant was in his first year as the Vikings' head coach, and he demanded that his players be disciplined in all phases of their lives. To exemplify that, Grant had Sunde, a member of the National Guard, instruct his teammates during the blazing August sun on the proper way to stand during the pre-game rendition of the National Anthem. The training lasted more than 30 minutes, and occurred more than once. Although some team members scoffed at the training, it later became the model and required procedure for the entire NFL.

Milt Sunde

Doug Sutherland

Seasons: 1971–80   Defensive Tackle   Height: 6'3"
Number: 69   Superior State   Weight: 253

The most unheralded member of the Purple People Eaters, Doug Sutherland replaced Gary Larsen at defensive tackle and did not miss a beat alongside Carl Eller, Jim Marshall and Alan Page. By the time Sutherland was ready to move on, he was the last remaining member of the fabled line, and did a laudable job of serving as the aging veteran who kept the team together during a time of transition.

Acquired from New Orleans in exchange for Bill Harris in 1971, Sutherland saw limited action on special teams during his first season in purple. He toiled briefly at guard, linebacker and along the defensive line in 1972 before settling at defensive tackle in 1973. A move to the starting lineup in place of Larsen followed in 1974, with Sutherland responding with eight quarterback sacks from the middle of the line.

He maintained his starting role for the remainder of the decade. Sutherland had eight sacks and two caused fumbles in both 1975 and 1976, and led the team with eight tackles for lost yardage in 1976. He dropped four signalcallers behind the line of scrimmage and made 60 tackles in 1977. He added five sacks and 54 hits in 1978. Sutherland extended his consecutive

Doug Sutherland

starts streak to 79 games, including the first 10 of 1979, before a shoulder injury he suffered during training camp resulted in a disappointing season. Sutherland regained his starting form in 1980 and led the Vikings with 5.5 sacks while making 48 unassisted hits.

With the Vikings having several first-round draft picks ready to start in 1981, Sutherland wound up spending his final year in the National Football League with Seattle.

Archie Sutton

Seasons: 1965–67	Tackle	Height: 6'4"
Number: 72	Illinois	Weight: 265

The Vikings were counting on Archie Sutton to shore up some of their problems along the offensive line upon drafting him in the second round in 1965. Instead, injuries marred the former All-Big Ten's professional career, limiting him to just 19 games in three seasons with Minnesota.

Most of Sutton's playing time came as a rookie in 1965, when he saw action in all 14 games on the line protection units for field goals and extra-point attempts. Expected to compete for starting honors at tackle when Errol Linden was taken by Atlanta during the expansion draft in 1966, Sutton missed training camp and most of the regular season with knee trouble and phlebitis. Doug Davis earned the job in Sutton's absence and maintained his hold on the job in 1967, limiting Sutton to two appearances in his last season in the National Football League.

Paul Sverchek

Season: 1984	Defensive Tackle	Height: 6'3"
Number: 94	Cal-Poly SLO	Weight: 252

The fact that Paul Sverchek played three games with the Vikings in 1984 is amazing when his background is taken into consideration. Minnesota's eighth-round draft pick in 1984 did not play football in high school and did not take up the sport until his junior year of college, after throwing the shot and discus at Cuesta Junior College. A natural athlete, he progressed rapidly enough to merit three games on the Vikings' special teams before being waived, re-signed and waived again in September of 1984.

Bill Swain

Season: 1964	Linebacker	Height: 6'2"
Number: 52	Oregon	Weight: 230

A journeyman who toiled for the Rams, Vikings, Giants and Lions during six seasons in the National Football League, Bill Swain wore purple in his second professional campaign, playing in all 14 games during the 1964 slate. A special teams performer who could handle all three linebacker slots, Swain provided depth behind Rip Hawkins, Roy Winston and Bill Jobko. He was traded in 1965 to the Giants for a sixth-round draft choice.

John Swain

Seasons: 1981–84	Cornerback	Height: 6'1"
Number: 29	Miami (Fla.)	Weight: 190

John Swain spent four seasons dogging receivers in the Vikings' secondary. Minnesota's fourth-round draft choice in 1981, Swain started the season opener in place of John Turner and saw action in 11 other games, intercepting two passes and making six tackles on special teams. He joined the starting lineup for the fifth contest of the 1982 slate, when Turner moved to safety in place of Kurt Knoff. After picking off two tosses in the strike-shortened season, Swain started seven contests around a sprained ankle in 1983 and tied for the team lead with six steals, including two in the 20–17 overtime win at Green Bay on October 23.

Swain divided his playing time at cornerback and safety in 1984 while suffering a concussion during the season's ninth game. He finished what proved to be his final year in purple with a career-high 43 solo stops while intercepting a pair of passes. He was released after angering head coach Bud Grant with a nonchalant effort in the final pre-season game in 1985.

Dennis Swilley

Seasons: 1977–83, 1985–87 Center Height: 6'3"
Number: 67 Texas A&M Weight: 266

The Vikings had plans for Dennis Swilley upon drafting him in the second round in 1977. Minnesota's outstanding offensive line was beginning to show its age, and the All-Southwest Conference performer at guard and tackle looked to be a perfect fit, regardless of where the need might be.

A backup guard and special teams performer who saw action in every game during his rookie year, Swilley was hampered by a leg injury in 1978, yet was tough enough to take the field for all 14 contests. He then had the unenviable task of replacing veteran Mick Tingelhoff at center in 1979, even though Swilley had never played the position until training camp. He did a solid job, however, and for the next five years started every game except one, when he stepped aside to let Jim Langer start the final contest of his Hall-of-Fame career, in 1981.

Considered by head coach Bud Grant to be one of the most underrated centers in the National Football League, Swilley decided to retire from the game for one year. He sat out the 1984 campaign, opting instead to attend classes and oversee the construction of the home he designed in Aubrey, Texas. Swilley returned to the Vikings and started 13 games in 1985 and all 16 contests in 1986. He gave way to Kirk Lowdermilk in 1987, and suffered a broken leg in the 10th game of the season.

Swilley retired from the professional ranks for a second and final time during the 1988 training camp, having started 101 games for the Vikings over his 10-year career.

Darryl Talley

Season: 1996	Linebacker	Height: 6'4"
Number: 55	West Virginia	Weight: 235

Ed McDaniel's blown knee extended Darryl Talley's career in the National Football League for one more campaign. Signed during training camp in 1996 after McDaniel was lost for the season, the 36-year-old Talley played in 12 games for the Vikings, recording 40 primary hits and 55 total stops with 1.5 tackles for loss. An impressively conditioned athlete, Talley's age had robbed him of his speed and Pro Bowl ability, and may have played a role in breaking his consecutive games streak of 221 straight contests, snapped in the season's second week, against his former team, Atlanta.

Fran Tarkenton

Seasons: 1961–66, 1972–78	Quarterback	Height: 6'
Number: 10	Georgia	Weight: 185

Minnesota general manager Bert Rose and scouting director Joe Thomas held their breath late in the second round of the 1961 draft. With running back Tommy Mason and middle linebacker Rip Hawkins already in tow, the two members of the Vikings' skeleton front office were hoping that the quarterback they had ranked second to Wake Forest's Norm Snead in the draft would slip to the third round. Georgia's Fran Tarkenton, a head-strong signalcaller with impressive command and presence whose only perceived weakness centered on his ability to throw deep, failed to go in the initial two phases, leaving him for Minnesota and further adding to one of the most impressive drafts in the history of the National Football League.

While the brief snub from the established league momentarily caused the quarterback to seriously consider overtures from the American Football League's Boston Patriots, who offered $3,500 more than Minnesota, Tarkenton signed with the Vikings, and wasted little time providing fans throughout the country with a harbinger that would last for nearly two decades.

Three minutes after replacing starter George Shaw in Minnesota's first game, Tarkenton had thrown a 14-yard touchdown pass to Bob Schnelker—the first in Vikings history—against the heavily favored Chicago Bears. In the third quarter, he fired scoring strikes to Hugh McElhenny and Jerry Reichow before connecting with Dave Middleton in the final period. If that wasn't enough, the man who would become known as "The Scrambler" ran to paydirt for the team's fifth touchdown. By the time the dust settled at Metropolitan Stadium on September 17, Tarkenton had beaten the Bears' blitz with audibles that produced short passes to guide the fledgling team to a 37–13 bashing of the Bears. Tarkenton completed 17 of 23 pass attempts for 250 yards and four touchdowns and added a three-yard rushing touchdown in the fourth quarter. His 259 combined yards accounted for all but 92 of Minnesota's offensive total of 351 yards.

Impressed with Tarkenton's leadership abilities and guile, head coach

Norm Van Brocklin had no problem turning the starting duties over to a rookie for good four games deep into the 1961 season. The Dutchman worked with Tarkenton and constantly referred to the rookie as "Cracker" or "Peach." Granted, Tarkenton's passes knuckled as much as they spiraled, but even at a young age the quarterback proved he had no equal in reading defenses. His confidence entered into the strata of necessary arrogance, always feeling that he could make any play a positive experience.

Tarkenton responded to his duties by throwing 18 touchdown passes, at the time the second-best mark by a rookie quarterback in league annals, and completed 56.1 percent of his attempts, which topped the NFL rookie mark. In addition to throwing four touchdown passes against the Bears, he matched the feat against the Rams and again versus Chicago in the season finale. By year's end, Tarkenton ranked second to the Bears' Mike Ditka in Rookie of the Year balloting.

The quarterback and head coach developed a mutual admiration society for the first couple of years before egos began to bump. Dutch loved Tarkenton's competitive fire. The quarterback thrived on challenges. When opponents threatened to blitz, Tark picked a defense apart with a perfectly called audible. He also possessed great instincts, which helped him become a successful scrambler when his make-shift offensive line failed.

Opponents tried to bear down on Tarkenton in 1962, and despite heavy pressure from the charging defenders, he tossed 22 touchdowns, passed for 2,595 yards and rushed for 361 more. The harder defensive players rushed, the more Tarkenton succeeded. Many of his passes were completed while dodging heavy traffic, with Tarkenton displaying an incredible ability to find open receivers, many of whom were his fourth and even fifth option on a particular play.

"We just didn't give Francis the protection he needed," said center Mick Tingelhoff. "If he had always had a good line, he never would have had to start scrambling."

"I never scrambled with any design," said Tarkenton, who rushed for a career-high 99 yards against the Rams on November 5, 1961. "I was trying to complete a pass, to move the team. But it's interesting. The old-timers have never accepted me as a good quarterback because I've run out of the pocket too often. All that does is amuse me."

A co-captain along with linebacker Rip Hawkins in 1963, Tarkenton improved his completion percentage to 57.2 while throwing 15 touchdown passes and rushing for 11 others. He then ranked second among NFL quarterbacks in 1964, thanks in part to his 22 touchdown tosses, and was named Most Valuable Player of the Pro Bowl by completing eight of 13 passes for 172 yards in the West's 34–14 win. He rushed for 356 yards in 1965 to rank 27th in the league while placing sixth in the league among passers.

Fran Tarkenton

Tarkenton was a master at improvising. A classic example came against the Packers on October 4, 1964. The Vikings trailed by two points and faced a fourth down-and-22 on their own 36. Tarkenton raised his head from the Minnesota huddle and saw the Green Bay defense spread across 40 yards. He told everyone eligible to go deep. Upon taking the snap, the quarterback immediately started to scramble in the backfield before seeing Tom Hall break free at the Green Bay 20. Tarkenton heaved the ball, only to have Gordon Smith step in front of the pass and pull it in, setting up Fred Cox's game-winning field goal to give the Vikings a 24–23 victory, their first triumph over the Packers in team history.

Despite his success improvising, Tarkenton and Van Brocklin started to have frequent disagreements, particularly about the quarterback remaining in the pocket longer on most plays. The love-hate relationship between the two reached a head late in the 1966 season. Tarkenton, who completed 53.6 percent of his passes that year with 17 touchdowns while gaining 376 yards with four scores on the ground, was looking forward to playing in front of numerous friends and family members in Atlanta on December 4. Yet, when the lineup was announced upon the Vikings' arrival in the Georgia capital, Bob Berry was tabbed the starting quarterback. Van Brocklin claimed he wanted to get a better look at the young Berry, but made the move to embarrass Tarkenton, who was considered self-serving by his head coach. Tarkenton returned to the lineup the following week, but the two's relationship would end shortly thereafter.

Tarkenton tired of Dutch's constant Jekyll-and-Hyde behavior as well as the head coach's suggestions that the quarterback was not a team player. When Van Brocklin started to suggest to the press that he might trade Tarkenton, the signalcaller beat Dutch to the punch by sending a letter to the Vikings' owners asking for a deal. Van Brocklin wound up resigning after the 1966 slate, and Tarkenton was traded a few weeks later to the New York Giants. In exchange for Tarkenton, Minnesota received first- and second-round draft picks in 1967, a first-rounder in 1968 and a second-round selection in 1969. Those choices produced Clint Jones, Bob Grim, Ron Yary and Ed White, making it one of the best trades in team history.

After five moderately successful seasons in the Big Apple that resulted in his being hung in effigy during the 1971 slate, Tarkenton returned to the Upper Midwest in 1972. "Going back to the Vikings is like slipping into an old shoe," said the Scrambler at the press conference announcing his return. General manager Jim Finks acquired Tarkenton for a bundle, including Grim, Snead, practice team member Vince Clements, a first-round pick in 1972 and a third-rounder in 1973. Tarkenton brought with him a new offensive concept that head coach Bud Grant and offensive coordinator Jerry Burns incorporated.

Used mostly in the "purple formation," a one-back set that employed Chuck Foreman beginning in 1973 more often than not, Tarkenton took the leadership reins and drove the Vikings to their greatest stretch in team history. After a disappointing 7–7 season his first year back (a campaign that saw Tarkenton set club passing records with 372 attempts, 215 completions and 115 consecutive attempts without an interception), he erased the label of being a ".500 quarterback" by guiding Minnesota to three of the next four Super Bowls. He also established himself as the most proficient passer the NFL had ever seen. Tarkenton was nothing short of a genius at penetrating zone defenses that became prevalent in the 1970s, constantly dissecting the linebackers with short tosses to the running backs before beating secondaries with a deep pass when they least expected it.

Tarkenton practically carried the offense on his back in 1972. He ranked third in the NFL in passing. When the Vikings gave up 41 points to the Rams on November 19, Tarkenton countered with 319 yards passing and four touchdowns, including a 76-yarder to Bill Brown, a 70-yarder to John Henderson and a 66-yarder to John Gilliam, to lead Minnesota to a 45–41 victory.

Tarkenton was often a philosopher, a trait that enabled him to serve as chairman of the board of Behavioral Systems Consultants, Inc., during his playing days. He preached that the quarterback was not necessarily the most important player on the field.

"The number one thing is not to beat your team," Tarkenton said. "You have to know what risks to take, what not. It's not a matter of conservative or wide open football. The long pass can be the most conservative in the book. The intermediate pass, 20 to 25 yards, the most dangerous. There are times and places for both. That's why the game is 80 percent mental, making the decisions that help the team the most or put it in the least jeopardy."

In 1973, Tarkenton threw for 2,113 yards and 15 touchdowns while surrendering a career-low seven interceptions to lead the Vikings to Super Bowl VIII. He was equally effective in 1974, despite experiencing a dead arm for much of the season after injuring it during the playoff game against Dallas at the end of the previous year. After the 1974 slate, Tarkenton went to see baseball relief pitcher and noted exercise physiologist Mike Marshall about the ailment. Marshall suggested a training schedule that included weight-lifting. Tarkenton's arm responded beautifully, and appeared as strong as ever for the next couple of seasons.

Tarkenton rebounded and was at his best in 1975, when he was named the NFL's Most Valuable Player. One of the best games of his career took place that season, with the quarterback completing 24 of 30 attempts for 285 yards and three touchdowns during a 28–17 victory over Green Bay on November 2. The Scrambler completed a career-high 64.2 percent of his passes, throwing for 2,994 yards and 25 touchdowns. He also set the Vikings' single-season records for pass attempts, completions, yardage and touchdowns.

"If one word could describe Francis, it's enthusiasm," Grant said. "He brings as much enthusiasm into football as any rookie we've ever had. He fits perfectly the adage that the longer you play quarterback in this league, the better you get."

He also moved atop the record books in several career categories. Tarkenton established the NFL record with his 2,931st completion, to Ed Marinaro during a 28–13 victory over San Diego on November 23. He then connected with Chuck Foreman during a 35–13 triumph at Buffalo on December 20 for the 290th and 291st touchdown passes of his career, bypassing Johnny Unitas' former mark.

When asked about setting the records, Tarkenton responded in typical fashion. "They matter, but only in the right context. They don't mean anything during the season. If I can reach them eventually, they will tell me some time in the offseason, when you can afford a glow and ego, that I have been able to achieve something in the game."

Tarkenton was nearly as effective in 1976. He set a club record by throwing 155 straight passes without an interception. He completed 84 percent of his tosses against Seattle on November 14, also a club record, and established another mark at the time when he threw 46 passes against the Bears on October 31. Despite his constant movement, he never missed a start until a rib injury kept him from starting against Pittsburgh, on October 4.

"You don't achieve greatness without durability," Grant said of Tarkenton. "That's the best ability you can have. Francis has great instincts and that keeps him from getting hurt."

Despite his death-defying approach, Tarkenton never suffered a serious injury until he broke his leg during the 42–10 win over Cincinnati on November 13, 1977, forcing him to miss the final six games as well as two playoff contests. He returned to chase the elusive Super Bowl victory in 1978, guiding Minnesota to its sixth straight playoff appearance with his best statistical season, completing 60.3 percent of his passes for 3,468 yards and 25 touchdowns. Yet, with Foreman missing extended time with a knee injury, Tarkenton had to throw the ball more often than not and established his career-high with 32 interceptions. At age 38, he decided to go out on top and pursue other ventures in life that offered more potential for success than another season or two under center.

"I love the whole time I spent in the NFL," Tarkenton said upon announcing his retirement from the game. "I didn't achieve everything I wanted, but who does? The fun is in the hunt. Now the hunt is over."

When he retired after the 1978 season, Tarkenton held league records with 6,647 passing attempts, 3,686 completions, 343 touchdown passes and 47,003 passing yards. Eight years later he became the first Vikings player to be inducted into the Pro Football Hall of Fame.

"A lot of people did say I wouldn't make it because of my size and my scrambling," said Tarkenton, who made 171 starts for Minnesota, leading the purple to a 92–73–6 record. "It went on and on and on. But I believed in what I could do. I never let it get to me."

Named to the Vikings' Silver Anniversary All-Time Team in 1985, Tarkenton passed for more than 2,000 yards over the course of 16 straight seasons, played in five Pro Bowls with Minnesota (1964–65, 1974–76), and earned All-Pro recognition on two occasions (1973 and 1976). He also completed 2,635 passes on 4,569 attempts for 33,098 yards and 239 touchdowns, all of which remain club records.

Robert Tate

Seasons: 1997–98 Wide Receiver Height: 5'10"
Number: 83 Cincinnati Weight: 187

Minnesota's sixth-round draft pick in 1997, Robert Tate looked to be the long-term answer to the Vikings' kickoff return woes during his first preseason. Beginning with the Hall of Fame Game against Seattle, Tate blazed through opposing defenders to give his team excellent field position throughout the exhibition season.

Yet, once the regular season began, Tate looked more tentative, a trait caused in part by a propensity to fumble. He wound up averaging 19.6 yards per return in the first four games of 1997 before injuring an ankle and being placed on injured reserve.

Tate returned to the Minnesota roster in 1998 and proved to be a good open-field runner with quick moves and excellent vision. Although most of his action came on special teams, where he returned two kickoffs for 43 yards and made 11 tackles on the coverage units, Tate played in some third-down passing situations. He caught his first pass as a professional, a 17-yard grab during the 28–14 victory over Green Bay on November 22.

Pete Tatman

Season: 1967 Running Back Height: 6'1"
Number: 33 Nebraska Weight: 225

Pete Tatman escaped from the Vikings' taxi squad to play in five games during the 1967 season. Minnesota's 10th-round draft pick in 1967 who had served as a linebacker during his first two years in college, Tatman played primarily on special teams and returned one kickoff for 14 yards.

Terry Tausch

Seasons: 1982–88 Guard Height: 6'5"
Number: 66 Texas Weight: 276

Terry Tausch, Minnesota's second-round draft choice in 1982 after earning consensus All-America recognition as a senior at Texas, developed into a consistent, aggressive right guard for the Vikings during the 1980s.

After suffering a knee injury on the first day of his first training camp that limited him to two games as a rookie, Tausch saw action in 10 contests as a reserve guard in 1983. He started 15 games at right guard and one on the left side in 1984, and made 29 straight starts before a sprained knee caused him to miss the Tampa Bay matchup late in 1985.

A national Punt, Pass and Kick champion at age 13, Tausch returned to his starting job for all of 1986. He also started the first five non-strike games in 1987 before an ankle injury suffered in practice landed him on injured reserve on November 13. He started every game again in 1988, then signed with San Francisco as an unrestricted free agent for the 1989 campaign.

Willie Teal

Seasons: 1980–86   Cornerback   Height: 5'10"
Number: 37   Louisiana State   Weight: 192

The Vikings needed assistance in the secondary in 1980 and targeted Willie Teal to help solve their problems. In fact, Minnesota wanted Teal so badly in the second round of the 1980 draft that the team traded its second- and third-round selections to San Francisco in order to nab the LSU Tiger.

Teal responded to the challenge with several solid seasons in the defensive backfield. After missing all but two games with a knee injury as a rookie, he moved into the starting lineup a year later and intercepted four passes to tie for the team lead. He matched that output in 1982, with three of his picks coming in the 35–7 victory over Chicago on November 28.

In 1983, Teal recorded a career-high 72 solo tackles and intercepted three tosses. A knee sprain hampered his production in 1984, yet he was the only Viking to return an interception for a touchdown during the campaign, taking a pick back 53 yards against Green Bay on December 16. He was back at right cornerback for all 16 games in 1985, with his best performance occurring in the 28–23 win at Philadelphia on December 1. Teal had three solo stops, one interception, one defensed pass and one recovered fumble, which he carried back 65 yards to paydirt on the play that turned the tide for the purple.

An injured left knee cost Teal his starting job in 1986. After playing in 11 games that year, he was waived in the final cutdowns the following August.

Mike Teeter

Season: 1991   Defensive Tackle   Height: 6'2"
Number: 67   Michigan   Weight: 263

Mike Teeter teeter-tottered on and off the Vikings' roster in 1991. Claimed off waivers on September 3, he was active but did not play against Atlanta five days later. Waived and re-signed the following week, Teeter served eight weeks on the Minnesota practice squad before seeing brief action against Detroit on November 24. That proved to be his lone regular-season appearance in purple.

Derek Tennell

Seasons: 1992–93   Tight End   Height: 6'5"
Number: 46   UCLA   Weight: 285

A former replacement player with Cleveland in 1987, Derek Tennell wound up as one of the league's more fortunate reserves. He played in nine playoff games with four different teams and picked up a Super Bowl ring after signing with Dallas late in the 1992 campaign.

Tennell joined the Vikings four games into the 1992 schedule after Mike Tice succumbed to a back injury. He used his size and athleticism to pull in two passes before being handed his walking papers in early November.

Re-signed by Minnesota in the offseason, he caught another 15 tosses for 122 yards in 1993, but was not consistent enough to last beyond the 1994 training camp with the Vikings.

Andre Thomas

Season: 1987 Running Back Height: 6'
Number: 35 Mississippi Weight: 205

In one game with the Vikings' replacement team in 1987, Andre Thomas gained four yards on six carries. He was more successful through the airways, catching two passes for 13 yards.

Broderick Thomas

Season: 1995 Linebacker Height: 6'4"
Number: 51 Nebraska Weight: 242

Broderick Thomas' tenure in Minnesota produced mixed results. Signed to a lucrative free-agent contract prior to the 1995 season, Thomas was expected to be a premier pass rusher from the linebacker position while stuffing the run any time the ball headed in his direction. He produced six sacks and six tackles for lost yardage while adding 64 primary hits, but was burned numerous times by tight ends on pass-receiving routes.

Charged with illegally carrying a hand gun in an airport on his way to training camp, Thomas concluded his lone season with the Vikes by being arrested for driving under the influence, and was released before his contract expired.

Henry Thomas

Seasons: 1987–94 Defensive Tackle Height: 6'2"
Number: 97 Louisiana State Weight: 267

He was far from the largest presence in the middle of the defensive line. But with his hard-nosed style and lightning-fast reflexes that arose from his cocked stance over the center, Henry Thomas was an outstanding tackle and run-stopper while serving as the leader of an undersized Minnesota defense in the early 1990s.

The Vikings' third-round draft choice in 1987, Thomas established himself in his first season, earning spots on the UPI and *Football Digest* all-rookie teams after leading Minnesota's linemen with 81 total tackles. He received honorable mention All-Pro recognition in 1988 while registering six sacks, four fumble recoveries, 80 total tackles and his first touchdown, a two-yard roll after picking up a loose ball in the 43–3 bashing of Dallas on November 13.

A fixture by the 1989 season, Thomas had nine sacks and 94 tackles, and was equally effective in stuffing the run and putting pressure on the quarterback. Always in the thick of things, Thomas visited the end zone again that year with his 27-yard fumble recovery for a touchdown against Pittsburgh on September 24.

Moved to tackle for 11 games in place of the injured Keith Millard in 1990, Thomas responded with a career-high 109 total tackles. His first Pro Bowl invitation followed in 1991, when Thomas had eight sacks and 100 total stops. The emergence of John Randle further helped Thomas' cause in 1992, when he earned his second Pro Bowl trip.

An ankle injury cost Thomas the final three regular-season games in 1993, yet he still was named a second-team All-Pro after recording nine sacks and combining with Randle to dump quarterbacks on 21.5 occasions, the most in NFL history for two interior linemen. Again the heart and soul of the

Henry Thomas

defense in 1994, Thomas had 65 total tackles, seven sacks and a team-high 8.5 tackles for loss. His leadership and superior all-around play were major reasons the Vikings' defense was ranked as the league's best for the second straight season.

Thomas' career in Minnesota ended when he decided to chase the dollar signs to Detroit as a free agent. His departure hurt the Vikings, for it is no coincidence the defense was no longer ranked among the league's best in the immediate three seasons after Thomas last filled the nose tackle slot.

Orlando Thomas

Seasons: 1995–98 Safety Height: 6'1"
Numbers: 42, 43 Southwest Louisiana Weight: 211

Not since Paul Krause in the 1970s have the Vikings had a safety with a better nose for the football than Orlando Thomas. Since taking over starting duties at free safety during the 1995 campaign, Thomas has picked off 17 passes and recovered seven fumbles despite requiring nearly a year to fully recover from a serious knee injury he suffered at the conclusion of his second season.

Thomas proved early on that interceptions would be his calling card. A second-round draft choice in 1995, he paced the National Football League in picks with nine and 13 total takeaways as a rookie. Thomas also led the team with 19 passes defensed and four fumble recoveries. He scored his first touchdown when he took a lateral from Jack Del Rio and raced 45 yards to paydirt in Minnesota's 44–24 win over Pittsburgh on September 24.

After earning spots on most all-rookie teams, Thomas continued to be a ballhawk in 1996. He led the Vikings with five interceptions, including a spectacular pass breakup/interception against Dallas. He sprained the anterior cruciate ligament in his left knee in the second quarter of the playoff loss to the Cowboys, but rebounded from surgery to return to the lineup by the season opener in 1997.

Despite his laudable return, Thomas struggled with several nagging hamstring injuries in 1997 and did not have an outstanding season. Completely healthy in 1998, Thomas was back to his previous form and solidified the secondary with his strong sideline-to-sideline coverage in center field. He registered 69 tackles, intercepted two passes, and served as a primary reason for Minnesota's improved defense during the Central Division championship season.

John Thornton

Season: 1993 Defensive Tackle Height: 6'3"
Number: 94 Cincinnati Weight: 303

With Henry Thomas hobbled by an ankle injury, the Vikings signed John Thornton to provide depth to the defensive line late in the 1993 season. Thornton was inactive during his two games with the team, then was released before the playoff game with the Giants in order to add kickoff specialist Richard Jones to the roster. Re-signed the following offseason, Thornton was waived a final time by Minnesota during the 1994 training camp.

Mike Tice

Seasons: 1992–93, 1995	Tight End	Height: 6'7"
Numbers: 83, 87	Maryland	Weight: 253

A former starting quarterback at the University of Maryland, Mike Tice served as Seattle's starting tight end for most of the 1980s. After signing with Minnesota as a Plan B free agent in 1992, he overcame a torn pectoral muscle during his first training camp with the Vikings and a broken bone in his lower back to become the dominating blocker the team needed at the position.

"I'm a role player and have no problem with blocking," said Tice, who was named winner of the Vikings' Terry Dillon Award after the 1992 slate. "I get the same satisfaction out of making a great block and seeing Terry (Allen) run 17 yards, or having great pass protection on a defensive end. That is satisfaction because it's a team game."

Tice also had excellent hands, allowing him to pull in five passes for 65 yards in 1992 and another six for 39 yards in 1993. He caught two touchdown tosses, among them a 34-yard aerial against Green Bay during a 27–7 victory on December 27, 1992, which proved to be the longest reception of Tice's career. He also contributed on special teams by blocking a Gary Anderson field goal attempt to help the Vikings beat the Steelers, 6–3, on December 20, 1992.

When Adrian Cooper went down for the second time in as many years in 1995, Dennis Green contacted Tice about filling in for the last three games of the season. Despite having not played in nearly two years, he returned to catch three passes for 22 yards, then remained in Minnesota as the Vikings' tight ends coach in 1996 before becoming coach of the offensive line in 1997.

Mike Tilleman

Season: 1966	Defensive Tackle	Height: 6'6"
Number: 74	Montana	Weight: 285

Minnesota's 12th-round draft pick in 1965, Mike Tilleman made the Vikings' roster in 1966 after spending the previous campaign on the team's taxi squad. A loss of 35 pounds from his 300-plus pound frame aided Tilleman's efforts, resulting in his playing 12 games as a reserve along with a couple starts in place of the injured Paul Dickson.

That proved to be his only season in purple, for Tilleman was nabbed by New Orleans during the expansion draft in 1967. The timber man from Montana went on to play 10 more years in the National Football League.

Mick Tingelhoff

Seasons: 1962–78	Center	Height: 6'2"
Number: 53	Nebraska	Weight: 240

Scouting during the early 1960s may not have been as sophisticated as it is today, yet with two professional leagues drafting 20 players per team, it is hard to believe that Mick Tingelhoff arrived in the Twin Cities as a college free agent prior to the 1962 campaign. The story becomes even more amazing when the center earned All-Pro recognition after his third season for the first of seven times during his 17-year career in the National Football League.

As a green pea out of Nebraska, Tingelhoff was courted by the Vikings and Cardinals, but chose Minnesota because he figured he would have a better shot at making the young team. He figured right. Signed by assistant coach Stan West at the recommendation of Tingelhoff's college coaches, the player known as "Country" became a starter before his initial training camp concluded. He excelled with his tremendous quickness, a trait that enabled him to pick up blitzes with consistency and perform the fine art of option blocking. He also possessed a leadership ability that encompassed the entire team and the durability to remain in the lineup for nearly two decades.

Donning his signature, black high-top cleats to protect his left ankle that had been dislocated in college, Tingelhoff took over the starting center duties in the second pre-season game of 1962, against the Rams, and never lost the job before leaving the game on his own terms after the 1978 slate. He was named the team's top rookie by the Viking Fan Club in 1962, and emerged as one of the game's best centers in 1963 before earning all-league honors from the Associated Press and United Press International in 1964. All-Pro recognition came again in 1965, with Tingelhoff mastering the ability to pick up the right man by employing his agility and toughness to bury linebackers on running plays and squash the progress of charging nose tackles on passing downs.

More All-Pro honors came in 1966, 1967 and 1968. In addition to his consistency, Tingelhoff's most impressive trait centered on his ability to excel in the game's most precious moments. The tougher the yards and the blocking came as the Vikings drove toward an opponent's goal line, the more aggressive and effective Tingelhoff became. Pound for pound, he may have been the toughest player ever to wear purple.

Said head coach Bud Grant, "Mick is a durable player and a proud player. He is not big but he has excellent speed and he excels at picking up the blitzer." In addition to All-Pro recognition in 1969, he was named the recipient of the 1,000 Yard Club's "Best Blocker in the NFL" award. His seventh All-Pro honors came in 1970.

A leg injury slowed Tingelhoff for much of 1971 and broke his All-Pro streak, but did not force him out of the lineup. Reunited with quarterback Fran Tarkenton in 1972, Tingelhoff remained one of the game's top centers for the next several years. He was named Minnesota's offensive captain after Grady Alderman retired in 1974, and worked with Tarkenton to make the Vikings perennial Super Bowl contenders. He led the offense in minutes played in 1974, and earned his sixth and final trip to the Pro Bowl after the 1976 campaign.

"Durability probably fits Mick best, as it does Jim Marshall," Grant said in 1975. "You have to give credit to those people that play each week. Mick is not the biggest, the strongest or the fastest, but he may be the most durabilest, if there is such a word. He loves being a Viking."

Tingelhoff succeeded despite playing at 240 pounds, a weight many considered to be too small for a center in the 1970s. Yet Tingelhoff made up for any lack of size with quickness, near-perfect technique and experience. Never was he intimidated by an opponent. Grant even went so far as to say, "I don't recall Mick ever having a bad game."

A six-time Pro Bowl performer, Tingelhoff holds the league record among offensive linemen for playing in 240 consecutive regular-season games. He actually started 328 straight games, counting pre-season, regular season and post-season contests, until a leg infection in the preseason of 1977 snapped the string. Otherwise, the only game he did not start was his first pre-season game, in 1962, and two pre-season games in 1974 when the veteran players were on strike.

Tingelhoff could have sat on more than one occasion due to various ailments and no one would have said a word. But the center says his desire to do the job to the best of his ability kept him taking the field every time the whistle blew.

"I learned the value of work when I grew up on our farm in Ne-

Mick Tingelhoff

braska," Tingelhoff said. "My father, who worked full days at 70 years old, taught me how to work hard."

Tingelhoff's responsibilities also included special teams, serving as the Vikings' long snapper throughout most of his career until Doug Dumler took over the job in 1976. Regardless of what roles he handled, Tingelhoff performed them as well and with as much consistency as anyone at his position in league annals.

"Mick certainly has to go down as one of the greatest centers in NFL history," Grant said. Added Tarkenton, "There aren't more than three or four guys in the history of this game who have had the kind of career at his position that Mick has."

Named to the Vikings' Silver Anniversary All-Time Team in 1985, Tingelhoff earned All-Pro honors on seven straight occasions, more than any other Minnesota player other than Randall McDaniel. He also played in 20 post-season games, including four Super Bowls, to round out one of the more amazing careers in the NFL.

Dave Tobey

Seasons: 1966–67　　Linebacker　　Height: 6'3"
Number: 51　　Oregon　　Weight: 233

Dave Tobey played in all 14 games as a rookie with Minnesota in 1966. Most of his action came on special teams, although he did see extended time at linebacker against Green Bay after Roy Winston had to leave the contest with an injury.

Acquired during the 1966 training camp from Pittsburgh for an eighth-round draft pick, the Portland, Oregon native played in two more games with the Vikings in 1967. His final professional experience was a seven-game stint with Denver in 1968.

Gino Torretta

Season: 1993　　Quarterback　　Height: 6'2"
Number: 13　　Miami (Fla.)　　Weight: 219

Gino Torretta developed a small cult following during his brief stint with the Vikings. The 1992 Heisman Trophy winner who was bypassed in the NFL draft until Minnesota plucked him in the seventh and final round, Torretta served as the third-string quarterback throughout the 1993 season. He saw action in the finale against Kansas City, but did not attempt a pass in his lone series.

"The Heisman means nothing up here," Torretta said. "This is like starting all over again as a college freshman. Everybody has to earn a position. I just have to wait for my turn the way we did at Miami."

Torretta's turn in Minnesota came to an end during his second training camp. He was released in favor of free agent Andre Ware, who was gone a few days later when the Vikings re-signed Sean Salisbury. Torretta later had third-string opportunities with Detroit, San Francisco and Seattle.

Mel Triplett

Seasons: 1961–62　　Running Back　　Height: 6'1"
Number: 33　　Toledo　　Weight: 215

Mel Triplett joined Hugh McElhenny to give the Vikings one of the game's most experienced rushing backfields during the 1961 season. When not blocking for the King or rookie Tommy Mason, Triplett rolled up 407 yards on 80 carries from the fullback position. He also caught 10 passes for 41 yards, but had a hard time maintaining possession of the pigskin, losing the football on four occasions. His top performance came on December 17, when he registered the second 100-yard rushing contest in Viking history, gaining 121 yards on 15 carries against the Bears.

Acquired from the Giants along with Bob Schnelker and Bob Schmidt for two draft choices and the rights to Zeke Smith and Dave Whitsell in the spring of 1961, Triplett played a similar role during the franchise's second season. While his rushing production fell to 160 yards on 52 carries, he found the end zone on three occasions—twice on short runs and the third on a three-yard toss from Fran Tarkenton. He was traded to Cleveland for wide receiver Leon Clarke before the 1963 season.

Tony Truelove

Season: 1987 — Running Back — Height: 5'11"
Number: 32 — Livingston — Weight: 205

Tony Truelove made several moves, but all involved roster changes. Signed as a free agent just prior to training camp in 1987, the running back was placed on injured reserve prior to the season opener, on September 5. Activated on October 20, Truelove did not play against Denver or Seattle before being waived on November 5.

Olanda Truitt

Season: 1993 — Wide Receiver — Height: 6'
Number: 89 — Mississippi State — Weight: 186

The Vikings felt as if they had added an extra draft choice upon claiming Olanda Truitt off waivers from the Raiders just prior to the 1993 season. Los Angeles' fifth-round selection, Truitt was inactive for half of the 16 games in 1993. Otherwise, he caught four passes late in the slate, including a season-best 13-yarder against New Orleans on November 28.

With Minnesota possessing a deep receiving corps and Truitt showing little progress in running better routes, he was released the following year in training camp.

Esera Tuaolo

Seasons: 1992–96 — Defensive Tackle — Height: 6'2"
Numbers: 98, 95 — Oregon State — Weight: 276

Every time Esera Tuaolo gained any momentum in his career, a road block arose and forced the defensive tackle to seek a detour.

Green Bay's second-round draft pick in 1991, Tuaolo had an outstanding rookie season before falling out of favor with new head coach Mike Holmgren for the lineman's inability to serve as a two-gap nose tackle. The Vikings quickly picked up Tuaolo in November 1992 and watched him do a workmanlike job behind Henry Thomas the following two seasons.

Once Thomas left Minnesota to sign with Detroit, the quick, yet undersized Tuaolo stepped in and played well throughout the 1995 campaign, leading the defensive linemen with six tackles for loss and two fumble recoveries while placing second with 59 stops. Yet, during the season finale against Cincinnati, Tuaolo ruptured his Achilles tendon and missed more than half of training camp in 1996.

With Tuaolo sidelined, second-year lineman Jason Fisk played well during training camp. Although Tuaolo regained his starting job by the second week of the 1996 season, Fisk emerged as the starter by midyear while Tuaolo experienced continued trouble with his Achilles tendon. As a result, Tuaolo finished the campaign with just 23 primary hits and 2.5 sacks.

The emergence of Fisk led to the Vikings' decision to allow Tuaolo to sign with Buffalo. In doing so, Minnesota lost not only a decent presence in the middle of the line, but a darn good singer of the National Anthem.

Bob Tucker

Seasons: 1977–80 Tight End Height: 6'3"
Number: 38 Bloomsburg State Weight: 230

Even though the Vikings already had one of the game's best tight ends in Stu Voigt, Minnesota acquired former All-Pro Bob Tucker from the Giants six games deep into the 1977 season in exchange for a fifth-round draft choice. Tucker, who was acquired based on the recommendation of former teammate Fran Tarkenton, spent the last three-and-a-half years of his career in purple and gave the team its best depth ever at the crucial position.

Tucker did not take long to fit into the Minnesota offense. In his debut with the team, the former high school teacher caught three passes, including a six-yard touchdown toss in the fourth quarter of the 14–7 win over Atlanta on October 30. He concluded the 1977 season with 15 receptions for 200 yards as a Viking before pulling in 47 catches for 540 yards in 1978.

His production fell in 1979, when Tucker and Voigt alternated taking plays to quarterback Tommy Kramer in the Viking huddle. Even so, he caught 24 passes for 223 yards and two touchdowns. His role was similar during his final NFL season, in 1980. Tucker hauled in 15 tosses for 173 yards, with his lone touchdown coming on a four-yard pass from Kramer in the season opener, a 24–23 win over Atlanta on September 7.

John Turner

Seasons: 1978–83, 1985, 1987 Defensive Back Height: 6'1"
Number: 27 Miami (Fla.) Weight: 195

A second-round draft pick in 1978, John Turner spent eight different seasons in the Minnesota secondary. Initially a left cornerback before shifting to safety for the fifth game of the 1982 campaign, Turner made life interesting on a defense that was feeling the effects of transition in the late 1970s and early 1980s.

Slowed during his rookie year with a broken foot, Turner intercepted one pass during the 1978 regular season before starting the playoff game against Los Angeles in place of the injured Nate Wright. He moved into the starting lineup a year later at left cornerback, where he had the unenviable task of covering the opponents' top receiver. With pigskins filling the air, Turner ranked fourth on the team with 82 solo tackles while picking off two passes. He added 107 primary hits in 1980 while leading the team with six interceptions, including a team-tying record three against the Bears in the 10–7 win on October 12.

A cracked bone above his right ankle limited Turner to 41 unassisted tackles in 10 starts in 1981. Despite the disappointment of missing part of the season, he intercepted three passes in a game for the second time in his career, this time against Tampa Bay. He replaced Kurt Knoff at safety early in the 1982 campaign and responded with 42 solo tackles, good for second on the team. His best games that year came when Turner intercepted a pass tipped by Mark Mullaney and returned the ball 33 yards for a touchdown in the 31–27 win over Dallas on January 3, 1983. He added two interceptions six days later in the 30–24 playoff victory over Atlanta.

After tying for the team lead with six interceptions in 1983, Turner was traded to San Diego the following year during training camp for a third-round draft choice. Head coach Bud Grant returned to the Vikings in 1985 and one of his first moves involved re-signing Turner. The defensive back intercepted a pass in his first game back with Minnesota and paced the squad with five picks during season. Waived during the final cutdowns in 1986, Turner came back for a final time when he played in two replacement games in 1987. He concluded his career with 28 interceptions.

Maurice Turner

Seasons: 1984–85　　　　Running Back　　　　Height: 5'11"
Number: 24　　　　　　　Utah State　　　　　Weight: 192

Maurice Turner and the Vikings had the quintessential on-again, off-again relationship. Minnesota's 12th-round draft pick in 1983, Turner was released during his first training camp. He returned to Mankato a year later and was waived again, only to be re-signed after the season's second game. He went on to play in 13 contests and rank fifth on the club in special teams tackles.

Back in purple in 1985, Turner registered 16 tackles on special teams and returned four kickoffs for 61 yards prior to being waived following the 10th game. He finished the season with Green Bay, but was re-signed by Minnesota the following offseason. Turner received his final release from the Vikings during training camp in 1986.

Mike Turner

Season: 1987　　　　　Guard　　　　　　Height: 6'3"
Number: 61　　　　　　Louisiana State　　Weight: 255

Mike Turner was on the Vikings' replacement team roster in 1987 but did not take the field during any of the three games.

U

Artie Ulmer

Season: 1997	Linebacker	Height: 6'2"
Numbers: 54, 53	Valdosta State	Weight: 243

Artie Ulmer's professional career got off to a careless start. Minnesota's seventh-round draft choice in 1997, Ulmer was suspended for the first four games of his rookie season after testing positive during training camp for steroid use. He showed enough potential as a special teams player and linebacker that the Vikings placed him on the 53–man roster one week after his suspension ended in October. Inactive for the last 11 games of the campaign, the former defensive lineman from Valdosta (Ga.) State performed well in NFL Europe during the spring of 1998, but was released by Minnesota the following August in training camp.

Ron VanderKelen

Seasons: 1963–67   Quarterback   Height: 6'1"
Number: 15   Wisconsin   Weight: 190

After making a handful of starts when head coach Norm Van Brocklin and starter Fran Tarkenton were feuding, Ron VanderKelen entered training camp in 1967 as the leading candidate to replace the traded superstar at quarterback. However, after a couple of unimpressive showings during the exhibition season, VanderKelen's below-average arm and apparent "reserve quarterback syndrome" caused him to lose favor with first-year head coach Bud Grant.

Joe Kapp was imported from Canada, placing pressure on VanderKelen to respond. He did just that in the season opener with San Francisco, putting together a three-touchdown rally in the fourth quarter before the Vikings dropped a 27–21 decision on September 17. Lopsided losses to the Rams and Bears the next two weeks found VanderKelen resuming his backup role for the remainder of what proved to be his final season in Minnesota.

VanderKelen arrived in the Land of 10,000 Lakes as a free agent in 1963 after the "Wisconsin Whiz Kid" led the Badgers to a Rose Bowl comeback over Southern Cal and guided the College All-Stars to a 20–17 win over the Green Bay Packers. He landed the backup job as a rookie, and was pressed into emergency service against the Bears on December 1. VanderKelen sailed the Viking ship smoothly enough to earn a 17–17 tie against Chicago. He also started in Minnesota's 34–13 victory over Philadelphia on December 15 to further strengthen his grasp on the backup job early in his career.

Yet, with his run-pass option talents better suited for college than the National Football League, VanderKelen played sparingly over the next three years. His greatest overall contribution to the team may have come in assisting Kapp with the Vikings' offense, a tutelage that cost VanderKelen his starting job. Nevertheless, he finished his career completing 107 of 252 attempts for 1,375 yards with six touchdowns and 11 interceptions. In 1967, he was 45 of 115 for three scores and seven pickoffs.

With his work done in Minnesota, VanderKelen was reunited with Van Brocklin when he was traded to Atlanta in 1968 for fifth- and seventh-round draft choices.

Sean Vanhorse

Season: 1996   Cornerback   Height: 5'10"
Number: 37   Howard   Weight: 180

The Vikings brought in free agent Sean Vanhorse to serve as an extra defensive back and play on the kick coverage units. He saw action in nine games during the 1996 slate and recorded four tackles on defense and five more hits on special teams. His season as well as his Minnesota career ended in late November when he was placed on injured reserve with a torn muscle in his right shoulder.

Larry Vargo

Seasons: 1964–65	Defensive Back	Height: 6'3"
Number: 25	Detroit	Weight: 215

Acquired with Mike Bundra from Detroit in exchange for two draft picks just prior to the 1964 season, Larry Vargo gained a starting berth in the Minnesota secondary at free safety, beginning with the 24–7 win over San Francisco on November 8. His presence upgraded the Vikings' defensive backfield and served as a contributing factor in the team's 4–1–1 finish to the campaign.

Vargo returned to the starting lineup in 1965 and played in all but one game while placing third on the team with three interceptions. His tenure in purple ended after two seasons when Vargo and Jim Prestel were traded to the Giants in exchange for Bill Briggs and a sixth-round draft choice.

Ruben Vaughan

Season: 1984	Defensive Tackle	Height: 6'2"
Number: 69	Colorado	Weight: 261

A former 49er and Raider who had four sacks with Los Angeles in 1982, Ruben Vaughan was waived by the Vikings at the end of training camp in 1984, re-signed on September 15, then waived again on October 16. During his month in purple, Vaughan saw limited action in five games.

John Vella

Season: 1980	Tackle	Height: 6'4"
Number: 71	Southern Cal	Weight: 258

John Vella's career in the National Football League began as a second-round draft pick of the Raiders in 1972. Four years later he started at right tackle against Minnesota in Super Bowl XI. His career concluded in 1980 when the bearded lineman was picked up by the Vikings on September 17. Active for 14 regular-season games, Vella made brief appearances in eight contests.

Jim Vellone

Seasons: 1966–70	Guard	Height: 6'2"
Number: 63	Southern Cal	Weight: 255

There may not have been a more popular player in purple than Jim Vellone during the late 1960s. The outgoing, uproarious and passionate offensive guard also was as fierce a competitor as there was in the National Football League, a trait Vellone needed in order to get the most mileage out of a body that often refused to keep up with his love for life.

Vellone put together a solid college career at Southern Cal, but four knee operations left him undrafted in 1966. The rookie free agent managed to stick with the Vikings when second-team guard Ken Byers suffered a knee injury during the final week of training camp. By midseason of his first year, Vellone had moved into the starting lineup and remained there for most the next five years, even as the pain in his legs increased with every play on the gridiron. In 1969, a doctor told Vellone he would have arthritis by age 45. Vellone said that was fine, for football was worth any rude results.

"Football is still a man's world, it's about the only damned thing left that isn't automated," Vellone said. "It's the camaraderie, too . . . the love of working with men and sharing with them. Hell, for me the check is the bonus. The satisfaction of playing means more than money."

Vellone continued to serve the Vikings well, particularly in passing situations, until he underwent a routine physical during the early stages of training camp in 1971. It was then the doctors discovered Vellone had leukemia. Although his football days ended at that time, he fought the illness for six more years. Vellone died on August 21, 1977, but his booming, baritone voice is still heard by his teammates who appreciated his desire to win and his love for life.

Stu Voigt

Seasons: 1970–80 Tight End Height: 6'1"
Number: 83 Wisconsin Weight: 225

Stu Voigt never set any speed records while running pass patterns, yet he got the job done by catching nearly every aerial thrown his way, making him one of Fran Tarkenton's favorite receivers. When the ball was not headed in his direction, "Chainsaw" was a tenacious blocker, displaying the same strength that helped him establish the University of Wisconsin records in the discus and shot put.

A running back and tight end for the Badgers, Voigt was selected in the 10th round of the 1970 draft by Minnesota. He saw the majority of his action as a rookie on special teams before displaying soft hands while filling in for an injured John Beasley in 1971. Voigt caught 15 passes for 214 yards and his first touchdown, a six-yard pass from Gary Cuozzo against Dallas on Christmas Day in the first round of the playoffs. He then caught six passes in a reserve role in 1972.

Voigt became a starter in 1973 and grabbed 23 passes for 318 yards and two touchdowns. He became Tarkenton's favorite third-down target, especially when opponents focused their pass coverage on John Gilliam, thereby leaving Voigt single-covered by a linebacker. He also emerged as one of the game's best blocking tight ends. Chainsaw was basically an extra offensive lineman, and posted consistent success against larger opponents. "We felt we improved tremendously at the position when we inserted Stu into the lineup," head coach Bud Grant said after the 1973 slate.

He emerged as a greater offensive threat and had the best year of his career in 1974. Voigt caught at least one pass in 12 of the 14 regular-season games and finished the campaign with 32 receptions for 268 yards and five touchdowns, marking the most catches for a Minnesota tight end since 1962.

Stu Voigt

Voigt caught a pass in every one of the 13 games he played in 1975, and set the team record at the position with 34 catches, including two touchdown receptions versus the Bears during a 28–3 win on October 5 and eight receptions for 74 yards against Washington on November 30. By 1976, most opposing coaches considered Voigt the league's most underrated tight end and made sure he was covered at all times. Although his production fell to 28 catches for 303 yards, Voigt helped lead the Vikings to their fourth Super Bowl appearance by catching touchdown tosses in two of the three playoff games. He pulled in an 18-yard touchdown toss from Tarkenton to open the scoring in a 35–20 victory over the Redskins in the first round, on December 18, and grabbed a 13-yard throw from Bob Lee to close out the scoring in Super Bowl XI.

Voigt started to share some of the tight end duties with Bob Tucker in 1977, yet still caught 20 passes for 212 yards, including one of the many highlights from his career. The Vikings lined up for the potential game-winning field goal in overtime against the Bears on October 16 when Grant surprised the masses. Paul Krause leaped from his position as holder and connected with Voigt for a wide-open touchdown from 11 yards out to give Minnesota the 22–16 victory.

Tucker took over the starting duties in 1978 and limited Voigt to short-yardage situations and four catches for 21 yards. Two of his 15 receptions in 1979 went for scores—a three-yarder from Tommy Kramer in a 30–27 win over Chicago on October 21, and a two-yard toss from Kramer against Tampa Bay on October 28. Voigt played in just three games in 1980 prior to being waived on September 23, when the Vikings signed tight end Bob Bruer.

Voigt did not play again in the National Football League and retired with 177 catches for 1,919 yards and 17 touchdowns in 131 games. He has remained a part of the Minnesota organization as a color commentator on the radio broadcasts, and was named to the Vikings' Silver Anniversary All-Time Team in 1985.

Bill Waddy

Season: 1984
Number: 88
Wide Receiver
Colorado
Height: 5'11"
Weight: 192

A former Ram who never lived up to high hopes in Los Angeles, Bill Waddy played in four games for the Vikings during the 1984 campaign. His contributions consisted of three rushes for 24 yards and three kickoff returns for a 21.3-yard average. He also gathered one punt return and lost three yards before fumbling. Not surprisingly, Waddy was gone faster than head coach Les Steckel.

Don Wagoner

Season: 1984
Number: 31
Defensive Back
Kansas
Height: 5'10"
Weight: 180

Don Wagoner, who attended the same high school—Wingate Andrews High in High Point, North Carolina—as Ted Brown, joined the running back in Minnesota on October 31, 1984. Active for seven games but playing in only four, Wagoner had two solo tackles and two assisted hits on special teams before missing the last three contests with a calf injury.

Van Waiters

Season: 1992
Number: 54
Linebacker
Indiana
Height: 6'4"
Weight: 240

The Vikings needed backup help at linebacker late in the 1992 training camp. Refusing to dip into the free agent market, Minnesota waited for other teams to make their final cuts, then jumped when Van Waiters showed up on the waiver wire after being released by Cleveland.

Viking fans were familiar with Waiters. In 1989, he scored the winning touchdown for the Browns on a pass from holder Mike Pagel during a fake field goal in overtime, giving Cleveland a 23–17 triumph on December 17.

In 1992, Waiters spelled starter Carlos Jenkins on the strong side and made one start while seeing most of his action in short yardage situations and on special teams. He made 19 tackles, with eight coming on kick coverage, prior to becoming expendable when the Vikings drafted Ashley Sheppard the following spring.

Bobby Walden

Seasons: 1964–67
Number: 39
Punter
Georgia
Height: 6'
Weight: 190

Having received his release after two injury-plagued seasons in the Canadian Football League, Bobby Walden decided to pass through the Twin Cities and visit an old college teammate prior to completing the drive to his farm in Georgia. The punter and Fran Tarkenton caught up on some old times as members of the Georgia Bulldogs until the quarterback convinced his employer as well as Walden to go through a tryout. The Vikings liked what they saw, and watched Walden lead the National Football League with an average of 46.4 yards per punt in 1964.

Minnesota had suffered through some mediocre punting efforts during its first three seasons, with Mike Mercer, John McCormick and Fred Cox driving the ball with less than satisfactory results. Walden, conversely, followed his NFL-best showing with a 42.1-yard average in 1965, a 41.1-yard norm in 1966, and a 41.6-yard average in 1967. Walden's 70-yard punt versus San Francisco was the NFL's longest in 1966. He also booted a 76-yarder in his final season with the Vikings.

A halfback in college, the extroverted Walden also earned a reputation for running with the football while in punt formation, even if no one on the Viking sideline was expecting such an event. His first such gallop came against Chicago in 1964, when he scampered 18 yards for a first down.

Traded to Pittsburgh in 1968 for a fifth-round draft pick, Walden went on to serve as the Steelers' punter during their championship seasons in the 1970s.

Adam Walker

Season: 1987 — Running Back — Height: 5'11"
Number: 49 — Carthage College — Weight: 220

Adam Walker's career in the National Football League consists of two games with the Vikings' replacement team. He rushed five times for 24 yards and caught two passes for three yards.

Herschel Walker

Seasons: 1989–91 — Running Back — Height: 6'1"
Number: 34 — Georgia — Weight: 225

No name in Viking lore represents more negative association than that of Herschel Walker. It's not that the former Heisman Trophy winner did anything wrong during his three years in Minnesota. His efforts were laudable and even impressive when he was given the opportunity to succeed. But the running back's role was never defined, for he served as a divisive force between head coach Jerry Burns and general manager Mike Lynn.

Walker's name lives in infamy due to the cost of bringing his services to the Twin Cities. In the most lopsided deal in the history of the National Football League, Walker came to Minnesota along with third-, fifth- and 10th-round draft choices in 1990 and a third-rounder in 1991 from Dallas. In exchange, the Vikings sent the Cowboys Darrin Nelson, Issiac Holt, David Howard, Jesse Solomon and Alex Stewart along with eight draft picks, including a first, second and sixth in 1990, a first and second in 1991, and a first, second and third in 1992. Lynn said the deal would bring the Vikings a Super Bowl victory, and nothing short of that would be considered success. Unfortunately, the trade benefited only the Cowboys, who began building toward their dominance in the first half of the 1990s while Minnesota was crippled by a lack of depth.

The early returns looked favorable, however. Minnesota had been among the bottom five teams in rushing since the start of the 1988 season and desperately needed someone to carry the pigskin. Walker looked to be the answer in his first game with the Vikings, a 26–14 win on October 15, 1989, in front of 62,075 fans, at that point the largest crowd ever to see the Vikings play at the Metrodome. Walker slaughtered the Green Bay defense for 148 yards to become the first Viking to rush for more than 100 yards in his purple

Herschel Walker

debut. His first gallop from scrimmage was a 47-yarder, most of which was accomplished without one shoe.

A month later, against Philadelphia on November 19, Walker became the first Minnesota player ever to return the opening kickoff for a touchdown when he raced 93 yards to paydirt. By the end of the season, he led the team in rushing attempts (169), yards (669) and touchdowns (five), and was sixth in receptions (22) despite playing only the last 11 games of the season with the Vikings.

In 1990, Walker led the NFL in combined net yards with 2,051 upon leading the Vikings with 184 carries for 770 yards and nine touchdowns. He also finished fourth on the team with 35 catches for 315 yards, and ranked fifth in the NFC by averaging 22.5 yards on kickoff returns. Yet, Walker did not emerge as the go-to player on the offense. His best rushing game that season was his 99-yard effort in the 24–21 win over Seattle on November 18, a total that was aided by a 58-yard touchdown run.

Walker again led the team in 1991 with 198 carries, 825 yards and 10 touchdowns on the ground. He added 33 catches for 204 yards, and five kickoff returns for a 16.6-yard norm. Though solid, Walker's production did not match what Lynn surrendered to the Cowboys on October 13, 1989, a date that just happened to be Friday the 13th. Walker simply never felt comfortable in any formation Burns and offensive coordinator Bob Schnelker concocted.

With Lynn out of the picture by the 1991 season and Dennis Green replacing Burns as head coach in 1992, Walker was released by Minnesota and signed with the Giants. In 1997, he was back with Dallas, continuing to serve as one of the league's best special teams players and an excellent reserve running back.

Jay Walker

Seasons: 1996–97
Number: 6
Quarterback
Howard
Height: 6'3"
Weight: 229

A free agent who played minor league baseball with the California Angels for two years out of high school and toiled briefly with the Patriots immediately after college, Jay Walker beat out incumbent Chad May for the third-string quarterback job in 1996. His lone experience came during a 41–17 win over Arizona on December 1, when he completed both of his pass attempts for 31 yards.

Walker also received one snap in 1997 while Randall Cunningham had to leave the field temporarily. With Todd Bouman showing signs of developing into a strong signalcaller, Walker was not re-signed as a free agent after the season.

Jimmy Walker

Season: 1987
Number: 93
Defensive Tackle
Arkansas
Height: 6'2"
Weight: 265

Jimmy Walker, a seven-year veteran of the Canadian Football League and a corrections officer in charge of outdoor recreation for inmates in the Atlanta prison system upon signing with Minnesota, played in two replacement games for the Vikings in 1987 and registered a sack.

Jackie Wallace

Seasons: 1973–74   Cornerback   Height: 6'3"
Number: 25   Arizona   Weight: 197

The Vikings' second-round draft choice in 1973, Jackie Wallace overcame a disappointing rookie season to emerge as a starter during his second campaign in purple. The defensive back reported late to training camp in 1973 and spent the entire slate on the inactive list prior to contributing to Minnesota's winning ways a year later.

With Bobby Bryant shelved due to a broken arm, Wallace stepped in and started 13 regular-season games. He intercepted one aerial, and used his good speed to help shut down opponents' passing games. Wallace improved as the season progressed, with head coach Bud Grant saying the cornerback's play in Super Bowl IX represented the benchmark of the player's career. His most important play came in the NFC Championship Game during the 14–10 win over Los Angeles on December 29. Wallace deflected a pass that resulted in an end-zone interception, ending the Rams' scoring threat.

Wallace also contributed to the Vikings' cause as a punt returner. He paced the team in 1974 by averaging 7.6 yards on 25 efforts.

Chris Walsh

Seasons: 1994–98   Wide Receiver   Height: 6'1"
Number: 81   Stanford   Weight: 198

If a role player can be a team leader, it's Chris Walsh. For the past five seasons, Walsh has been the heart-and-soul of the special teams. He led the unit with 16 tackles in 1996, and placed second on the squad with 24 hits in 1995 and 16 stops in 1998. His all-out hustle causes many returners to see stars, and is a major reason the Vikings have upgraded their kick coverage since 1994.

While making the most of his opportunities on special teams, Walsh has contributed on occasion at wide receiver. The team's leading pass catcher during his first three preseasons in Minnesota, he became a part of the regular offense during the final six games of 1996, a period that coincided with the emergence of his road roommate, quarterback Brad Johnson. Walsh caught four passes for 39 yards, including his first career touchdown, a seven-yarder against Denver on November 24.

In 1997, Walsh became the team's third-down possession receiver. He caught a career-high 11 passes for 114 yards, with seven of his receptions going for a first-down conversion on third down. Walsh pulled in the game-winning touchdown pass in the 27–24 win over Chicago on September 7. He also did an excellent job of blocking, with Arizona safety Tommy Bennett on the receiving end of two blind-side hits that left the Cardinal defensive back unconscious.

John Ward

Seasons: 1970–75   Guard-Center   Height: 6'4"
Number: 72   Oklahoma State   Weight: 250

Minnesota's first-round draft choice in 1970, John Henry Ward was an aggressive, hard-working cowboy from Oklahoma who was hindered by injuries during his six seasons with the Vikings.

An All-American offensive tackle in college and a two-time Big Eight Conference heavyweight wrestling champion, Ward was moved to defensive tackle as a rookie and saw limited action in two years backing up the Purple People Eaters. His inactivity led to a shift back to offense, with head coach

Bud Grant saying, "He's too good a player not to be playing, and with our front four, his chance of playing (defense) are not that good."

Ward saw significant action at guard in 1972 and took over the starting duties at right guard for the first eight games a year later before suffering a broken leg. He missed the last five contests of 1973 as well as the entire 1974 slate. Ward was back in action for all 14 games and returned to the starting lineup during the 1975 campaign. The Vikings even envisioned Ward replacing Mick Tingelhoff at center before Tampa Bay nabbed him in the Buccaneers' expansion draft.

Lonnie Warwick

Seasons: 1965–72 Linebacker Height: 6'3"
Number: 59 Tennessee Tech Weight: 238

Lonnie Warwick

An ex-Golden Gloves boxer, Lonnie Warwick's most notorious event as a Viking occurred after a loss to Green Bay in 1967. Joe Kapp was adamant during a post-game party that the quarterback's fumble had cost the team a victory. Warwick believed otherwise, focusing the blame on his defensive performance. The two took the disagreement outside. Kapp suffered a pair of shiners, while Warwick came away with a reconfigured nose. They also emerged the best of friends.

That tough-as-nails attitude is what made Warwick and Kapp successful. In Warwick's case, the player described once by an out-of-town newspaper reporter as "downright hostile" combined with Wally Hilgenberg and Roy Winston to form one of the top linebacking corps in pro football. Warwick took the game personally, for it had served as his ticket out of the coal mines from his native West Virginia. Succeeding against him was akin to taking food off his family's table. Such occurrences were rare, however, for Warwick also had the athletic ability and uncanny instincts on the field that almost always left the linebacker on the winning side.

The hell-raising Warwick signed as a free agent with Minnesota in 1964 at the behest of his college coach, even though the player still had eligibility remaining at Tennessee Tech. He spent the 1964 season on the Vikings' taxi squad, was tabbed the team's top rookie in 1965 when he replaced the injured Bill Jobko, then moved inside and earned the starting job at middle linebacker in 1966 after Rip Hawkins retired unexpectedly. Warwick contributed nearly every time he took the field, even on special teams. In fact, he scored the franchise's first touchdown via a blocked punt when he fell on the pigskin in the end zone during a 38–35 victory at Los Angeles on October 3, 1965.

A savage tackler against the run who also defended well against the pass, Warwick struggled with injuries during his first two years as a starter. After saying he was "disgusted" with his performance in 1968, he fine-tuned his game prior to the 1969 season. Warwick dropped 25 pounds in order to improve his quickness and agility, which helped him play at a greater depth against the passing game, particularly when he was matched up with a tight end or running back.

After leading all linebackers with four interceptions in 1969, Warwick had three more picks in 1970 before playing in only 10 games due to knee injuries in 1971 and 1972. He lost his starting job at middle linebacker to Jeff Siemon during the 1972 campaign, and was traded shortly thereafter to Atlanta with Bob Lee in exchange for Bob Berry and a first-round draft choice.

Dewayne Washington

| Seasons: 1994–97 | Cornerback | Height: 5'11" |
| Number: 20 | North Carolina State | Weight: 186 |

First impressions were nothing short of spectacular for Dewayne Washington. The first cornerback ever selected in the first round by the Vikings, Washington joined Lem Barney and Ronnie Lott as the only rookies in the history of the National Football League to score three defensive touchdowns when he accomplished the feat in 1994. He also earned Defensive Rookie of the Year accolades from *College and Pro Football Weekly*, and joined fellow first-rounder Todd Steussie as the first rookies in Minnesota annals to start every game.

Washington's rise to prominence began when he picked off his first pass. In the 42–14 win over Chicago on September 18, 1994, he recorded the longest interception by a Viking rookie by taking an Eric Kramer aerial 81 yards for a touchdown. Washington added a spectacular 54-yard interception return for a score in the 33–27 overtime win against the Bears on December 1, then scooped up a fumble and trotted 17 yards to paydirt in the 21–14 victory over San Francisco on December 26. For the year, Washington had 71 total tackles, three picks and 12 passes defensed.

Those first impressions, however, were not followed with consistent success. Washington suffered an injured shoulder in the third game of the 1995 slate and finished the year second on the team with 11 passes defensed and 65 tackles. After undergoing shoulder surgery during the offseason, he bounced back to lead the Vikings with 19 passes defensed, good for third-best in Minnesota history, and ranked fifth on the team with 83 tackles in 1996. He also reacquainted himself with the end zone, taking a Jeff Brady lateral 27 yards for the team's first touchdown in the season-opening 17–13 win over Detroit on September 1.

Yet inconsistency continued to be the defining trait of Washington. He had his most disappointing season in 1997, intercepting four passes, defensing another 11 tosses, and making 88 tackles. Though fluid and possessing great speed, Washington frustrated the Viking coaches with the large cushions he gave receivers along with countless blown coverages. His inability to defend receivers one-on-one led to his signing a free-agent deal with Pittsburgh with no reaction from Minnesota prior to the 1998 season.

Gene Washington

| Seasons: 1967–72 | Wide Receiver | Height: 6'3" |
| Number: 84 | Michigan State | Weight: 208 |

Joe Kapp's eyes sparkled the first time he took the practice field with rookie Gene Washington. The quarterback described Washington as "The Thoroughbred," and was most impressed with the receiver's outstanding speed, jumping ability, and tight pass patterns.

"As a pass receiver, Gene Washington is a quarterback's dream," Kapp said in 1967. His hands may not have been the softest, but Washington got off the line faster than anyone in the National Football League. He served as a deep threat, something that Kapp and other quarterbacks love to have packed in their offensive arsenal.

The seventh overall selection in the 1967 draft after an All-America career at Michigan State, Washington caused the blood pressure among defensive backs to sky-rocket. Defenders knew six points could be on the scoreboard in a heartbeat. Such was the case in the receiver's fourth professional game, when Washington pulled in an 85-yard touchdown pass against St. Louis on October 8. Despite sharing time with veteran Paul Flatley, Washington went on to catch 13 passes for 384 yards—an amazing 29.5-yard average—tops in the NFL in 1967.

His development continued in 1968, with head coach Bud Grant saying, "Gene has the potential to be one of the best. He responded very well to the challenge of being a starter." Those words came on the heels of Washington's 46 receptions for 756 yards and six touchdowns. His biggest catch was a fourth-quarter scoring grab from Kapp at Franklin Field that led the Vikings to a 24–17 win over Philadelphia on December 15 and their first division crown. Another crucial performance occurred against the Redskins at The Met, where Washington pulled in two first-half touchdown passes from Kapp—one a 61-yarder—in Minnesota's 27–14 victory on November 3.

He followed that effort with 39 grabs for 821 yards and nine scores in 1969, numbers that are more impressive considering the fact he was double-teamed throughout the season. Washington opened the campaign with a 48-yard touchdown bomb from Gary Cuozzo against the New York Giants on September 21. A week later, he pulled in two of Kapp's NFL-record seven touchdown tosses and concluded the 52–14 victory over the Colts with six catches for 172 yards. Washington also was on the receiving end of a 75-yard touchdown throw from Kapp in the 27–7 NFL Championship Game victory against Cleveland on January 4, 1970. He then took over the Vikings' career touchdown leadership and earned a trip to the Pro Bowl by catching 44 passes for 702 yards and four touchdowns in 1970.

But just as it looked as if he was headed for a Hall-of-Fame career, Washington was hampered by a bone spur in his foot that arose during training camp in 1971. The injury affected his speed and leaping ability, limiting him to 12 receptions for 165 yards. Surgery that fused a bone from his hip to his foot followed after the 1972 slate, when he pulled in 18 passes for 259 yards.

The pain from the ailment, originally obtained during his days as a hurdler, brought a premature end to his playing days. Traded to Denver before the 1973 season in exchange for wide receiver Rod Sherman and a fifth-round draft choice, Washington retired from football after one year as a Bronco. He currently ranks first in Vikings' annals with 13 receiving plays of more than 50 yards during his career, including five in 1969. He also is second in team history with four consecutive seasons of leading the team in receptions.

Harry Washington

Season: 1978 — Wide Receiver — Height: 6'
Number: 80 — Colorado State — Weight: 180

A rookie free agent who made the Vikings' roster out of training camp in 1978, Harry Washington caught one pass in 10 regular-season games after placing third on the team in receptions during the preseason. The former college track star also returned four kickoffs for a 17.8-yard average.

Keith Washington

Season: 1995 — Defensive End — Height: 6'4"
Number: 96 — Nevada-Las Vegas — Weight: 270

One of three rookie free agents to make the Vikings' roster in 1995, Keith Washington showed tremendous promise as a defensive end during his first training camp. He opened the season on the practice squad, but was activated on October 15 when Detroit tried to sign the lineman. After being inactive for four games, Washington was placed on injured reserve on November 15 with an ankle injury. The following summer, he recorded 11 tackles, one sack and one forced fumble during the preseason, but was released due to the emergence of Fernando Smith and Derrick Alexander.

Kevin Webster

Season: 1987　　　　　　　Center　　　　　　　Height: 6′2″
Number: 68　　　　　　　Northern Iowa　　　　Weight: 260

Kevin Webster reminded no one of former Steelers center Mike Webster during his three-game stint as the starting center for Minnesota's replacement team in 1987.

Tripp Welborne

Season: 1992　　　　　　　Safety　　　　　　　Height: 6′
Number: 32　　　　　　　Michigan　　　　　　Weight: 205

Tripp Welborne probably wondered what curse he was under during the early 1990s. Forced to sit out his senior senior at Michigan after suffering a serious knee injury, the Vikings' seventh-round draft choice in 1992 recovered in time to compete in Minnesota's training camp the following August. Yet, in his second professional game, Welborne tore up his other knee while running downfield on kickoff coverage late in a 31–14 victory over Detroit on October 15, 1992. The joint required reconstructive surgery, which effectively ended his career in the National Football League.

Mike Wells

Seasons: 1973–74　　　　　Quarterback　　　　　Height: 6′5″
Number: 15　　　　　　　Illinois　　　　　　　Weight: 225

The Maytag repairman had nothing on Mike Wells, Minnesota's fourth-round draft pick in 1973. Wells saw no regular-season action as the Vikings' third-string quarterback during his two seasons with the club. On the inactive list throughout the 1973 slate, Wells was on injured reserve for all of the following campaign. His lone experience in the National Football League came in 1977, when he served as the Bengals' holder on field goals and extra points for seven games.

Charlie West

Seasons: 1968–73　　　　　Defensive Back　　　　Height: 6′1″
Number: 40　　　　　　　Texas-El Paso　　　　　Weight: 197

Part Apache Indian and 100 percent athlete, Charlie West was a significant component in one of the more important drafts in Vikings lore. With Minnesota accumulating substantial talent after a stellar draft that included Clint Jones, Gene Washington, Alan Page, Bob Grim, Bobby Bryant and John Beasley in 1967, the team added such standouts as West, Ron Yary, Oscar Reed and Bob Lee a year later. All four were quick contributors, with West enjoying the greatest amount of early success among the quartet.

In fact, West, the Vikings' second-round draft choice, went to the head of the class by earning team rookie-of-the-year honors in 1968. He ranked among the leaders in the National Football League with a 26.1-yard average on 22 kickoff returns and a 10.0-yard norm on 20 punt returns. West also tied the NFL record for the longest punt return with a 98-yarder in the 27–14 win over Washington on November 3, just the third punt return for a touchdown in Minnesota history. While that spectacular effort remains the longest punt return in team annals, West received a stern warning from head coach Bud Grant, who told the player, "If you ever field a punt at the 2-yard line again, you're out of here."

Drafted in the second round out of Texas-El Paso in 1968, West signed a professional baseball contract as an outfielder with the Cincinnati Reds before opting to join the Vikings after hitting .183 during a 19-game stint in the Florida State League. A reserve cornerback and strong safety during his first two seasons, he was sixth in the NFL with 39 returns for 245 yards and 19 fair catches in 1969, and also carried back nine kickoffs for 240 yards. His long kickoff return against the Rams set the tone for the game and helped guide Minnesota to its 11th straight victory of the season.

West started three games in 1970 while again serving as the team's top kick returner. Switched from cornerback to strong safety in 1971, he responded to the change by leading the Vikings with seven interceptions. Said Grant, "We were pleased as punch with Charlie's play at corner, but when he went to safety, it was a case of going from a very good corner to an outstanding safety."

The following year, West joined Gene Washington and Clint Jones and approached management by negotiating their contracts together. While the tactic did little to enhance the players' values, West found himself on the move again. He wound up as the starting left cornerback and intercepted three passes before a knee injury that required surgery brought his season to a premature end. Another knee surgery just prior to training camp led to a poor season in 1973. West's tenure in Minnesota ended in 1974 when he was traded to Detroit for a third-round draft pick.

Ronnie West

Season: 1992 Wide Receiver-Running Back Height: 6'1"
Number: 35 Pittsburgh State Weight: 215

Ronnie West's outstanding athletic ability may have kept him from making more of an impact with the Vikings. Minnesota's ninth-round draft pick in 1992 opened his rookie season on the practice squad before being activated when a rash of injuries afflicted the receiving and rushing units. West flip-flopped between the two positions during practice, based on the team's needs. Otherwise, he played in 12 regular-season games on special teams, and ran back two kickoffs for 27 yards. West underwent knee surgery in training camp the following year and missed the entire 1993 season.

David Westbrooks

Season: 1990 Defensive End Height: 6'4"
Number: 92 Howard Weight: 252

Signed as a free agent on November 7, 1990, David Westbrooks participated on the Vikings' practice squad for six weeks prior to being activated for the season's final two games. He did not play in either contest, and was released the following year during training camp.

Leonard Wheeler

Season: 1997 Cornerback Height: 6'
Number: 37 Troy State Weight: 190

A former Bengal who was signed as a free agent two days into training camp in 1997, Leonard Wheeler emerged as a valuable fifth defensive back and special teams player during his one season in purple. A backup at both cornerback and safety, Wheeler saw extensive action as a nickel back before relieving the disappointing Dewayne Washington down the stretch. He recorded 29 tackles, two sacks and three defensed passes on the year. Wheeler was even more effective on special teams, making 14 hits on kick coverages and posting six tackles and a fumble recovery at Green Bay on September 21.

Wheeler's performance created demand on the free-agent front. He wound up signing a lucrative deal with the Carolina Panthers.

Danta Whitaker

Season: 1992 Tight End Height: 6'4"
Number: 82 Mississippi Valley State Weight: 252

One of four tight ends on the Minnesota roster in 1992, Dante Whitaker played behind starter Steve Jordan and served primarily as a blocker and on special teams. He toiled in six games and caught one pass before being placed on injured reserve with a groin ailment on October 21. He was released by the Vikings six weeks later.

Brad White

Season: 1987 Defensive Tackle Height: 6'2"
Number: 62 Tennessee Weight: 261

A five-year veteran of the National Football League with Tampa Bay and Indianapolis, Brad White played one game for the Vikings' replacement team in 1987.

Ed White

Seasons: 1969–77 Guard Height: 6'2"
Number: 62 California Weight: 270

Ed White joined a veteran Viking team in 1969, when he was the only rookie to make the regular-season roster. The first-round selection arrived in the Upper Midwest as one of the game's strongest players with an aggressiveness that caused defenders to wilt under the punishment the guard delivered over the course of a game. A powerful pass-blocker, White battled as if he were involved in a heavyweight fight. Had that actually been the case, he would have been deemed an undefeated champion.

The Minnesota coaching staff believed that White could have been a Pro Bowl-caliber defensive tackle, the position at which he earned All-American honors at Cal. He instead became a student of the offensive game and served as a reserve guard during his rookie campaign before making a handful starts in his sophomore season. He then moved into the starting left guard spot in 1971 after Jim Vellone was diagnosed with leukemia.

It did not take White long to emerge as one of the league's best guards. While pass-blocking was considered his forte, he possessed enough quickness and speed to lead the charge on sweeps and quarterback roll-outs. He blossomed into a premier lineman in 1973 and started to receive the recognition on a national basis a year later, despite shifting from left guard to right guard due to the arrival of Andy Maurer. White garnered All-Pro recognition in 1974 and 1975, and played in his first Pro Bowl during the latter campaign. A second Pro Bowl appearance came in his sixth year as a starter, in 1976.

White also developed a reputation for his incredible feats off the field during his days in purple. He possessed an enormous appetite, and consumed more food than anyone on the team. He also could beat any teammate in arm-wrestling, including most who used two hands against White's right arm.

White's career in Minnesota began to sag in 1977. He held out that season due to contract differences with general manager Mike Lynn, missed the first game, and did not regain his starting job until the season's seventh contest. Nevertheless, White earned a third straight trip to the Pro Bowl, then demanded to be traded the following offseason. He wound up getting what he asked for when the team sent the guard to the Chargers for running back Rickey Young. Lynn later said he regretted the deal more than any other he made. By the time he retired, White, who was named to the Vikings' Silver Anniversary All-Time Team in 1985, had played in 241 games, the most for a guard in the history of the National Football League.

James White

Seasons: 1976–83 Defensive Tackle Height: 6'3"
Number: 72 Oklahoma State Weight: 270

Following in the footsteps of a legend is never easy for a young player. And when that youngster has the added pressure of being a first-round draft choice, the obstacles can be even more difficult to overcome.

Just ask James "Duck" White. The Vikings' first pick of the 1976 draft entered the starting lineup for the seventh game of the 1978 campaign, replacing Alan Page at right tackle. White went on to experience solid success over the next four years while making 74 consecutive starts in the middle of the Minnesota defense.

An All-American at Oklahoma State whose 4.8 speed in the 40 was considered his strength, White possessed impressive physical tools for a defensive lineman. As a rookie in 1976, he had two quarterback sacks and a recovered fumble as a reserve defensive tackle. He added two more sacks as a backup in 1977 before taking over for Page a year later, when White had 44 primary tackles and four quarterback dumps.

White established himself in 1979, starting every game at right tackle. He led the defensive line with 63 unassisted hits and placed second among his teammates with five sacks. Moved to left tackle in 1981, he was again the line's leading tackler with 58 solo stops while posting 3.5 sacks. He also paced the team in tackles for lost yardage in 1980 and 1981, registering four and seven hits, respectively.

In 1982, White again answered the call for every game, although he started just two. He shared the nose tackle duties with Charlie Johnson when the Vikings went from the 4–3 defense to the 3–4 alignment. Playing mostly in passing situations, White used his speed to record four sacks in the regular season and two more in the playoffs. He added 45 total tackles, a sack and his only career interception as a reserve in 1983 before being among the final cuts of training camp in 1984.

Jose White

Season: 1995 Defensive Tackle Height: 6'3"
Number: 97 Howard Weight: 274

Jose White, Minnesota's seventh-round draft choice in 1995, was inactive during the first three games of his rookie season prior to being transferred to the practice squad for the remainder of the campaign. He was released the following August after failing to make the necessary adjustments to play for the Vikings, but wound up catching on as a reserve with Jacksonville.

Sammy White

Seasons: 1976–86 Wide Receiver Height: 5'11"
Number: 85 Grambling Weight: 190

The heat in Mankato had yet to subside when Fran Tarkenton approached a nervous rookie wide receiver who was fretting about making the Vikings' veteran roster. The future Hall of Famer looked straight into the second-round draft choice's eyes and said, "Sammy White, we're going to make you a superstar."

Many scouts wondered if White had the ability to play at the game's top level. But within his first season in purple, a year in which he replaced the departed John Gilliam and emerged as one of the league's premier deep threats, White silenced any skeptics and proved Tarkenton a prophet. He became the third Viking to win Rookie of the Year honors after making 51 catches. He also earned an invitation to the Pro Bowl, and served as a key component in Minnesota's fourth Super Bowl trip by leading all NFC receivers with 906 yards and 10 touchdown catches.

"I never expected to have that type of season," White said. "There were so many great moments. To get 51 catches and 10 touchdowns in the pros was a great thrill. It was just a great feeling for me, a rookie, to be playing on a championship team and contributing."

The outgoing and personable White had a much tougher critic than the scouts. After all, under head coach Bud Grant, the Land of 10,000 Lakes was anything but the Land of Opportunity for young players. White, however, was impressive enough to become the first rookie to start an entire season under the legendary head coach. White even emerged as Tarkenton's go-to receiver, beginning with the first game of the 1976 season.

White had struggled with his confidence during training camp, wondering if he possessed the necessary skills to beat the game's best defensive backs. His self-esteem started to rise when he caught a touchdown pass in the final pre-season game, against Cincinnati. Two weeks later, there was no question he could perform against the best the National Football League had to offer.

In the lidlifter against New Orleans, White discovered just how good Tarkenton can make his receivers. With time running out in the first half, the quarterback scrambled in the backfield for 28 seconds, a period so long that right tackle Ron Yary had to knock his man down on three separate occasions. While Tarkenton worked his magic, White continued to move. When the receiver finally got open, Tarkenton hit White with a 47-yard strike for a touchdown in Minnesota's 40–9 victory.

A week later, White pulled in nine passes for 139 yards and a touchdown during a 10–10 tie with Los Angeles. He went on to become the first Minnesota rookie to catch three scoring passes in one game, accomplishing the feat at Miami in a 29–7 win over the Dolphins on December 11. He added two more touchdown tosses during the 35–20 playoff victory over Washington on December 18. On one of his scoring passes against the Redskins, White proved his athleticism by tipping an apparent interception away from Ken Houston before making a diving grab. White then scrambled to his feet and took the pigskin the final two yards to paydirt.

Sammy White

White also entered the record books during his rookie season. He posted a club-record 210 receiving yards against Detroit on November 7, yet learned a valuable lesson in the process. White was on the receiving end of a 52-yard pass from Tarkenton. Just prior to reaching the end zone, he raised the pigskin above his head to celebrate, but lost the football when Lem Barney made a diving, shoe-string tackle. Detroit's Levi Johnson recovered the loose ball in the end zone, negating a sure six points for the Vikings.

"I thought Barney was completely out of the play," White said after the game. "I raised the ball in the air to show a little emotion and Barney managed to trip me up. I wasn't showboating. I've never been that type."

Spiking was a capital offense in Grant's book. That fact combined with the mental error was enough to send shivers down White's spine. Grant, however, gave the rookie another chance on the next series and watched

White catch a touchdown toss from Tarkenton before carrying the pigskin through the end zone. He also never erred in such a manner again.

"That last touchdown sure felt good," White said. "But I learned a lesson that day."

In fact, it was not long before Grant became one of White's biggest fans. Less than two years later, the head coach said, "What more can you say about Sammy White? He's smart, he's coachable, he has fine athletic skills and he had a great year last season. He will have another one next year and the year after that and the year after that. We've just come to expect that from Sammy, and we get it."

In addition to being a deep threat, White's best attribute was his ability to hang on to passes in traffic. Although he did not possess world-class speed, he was faster against defenders than against the clock, as evidenced by his great acceleration after catching the football. His hands were consistent, his route-running improved from his first day in camp and became a strength, and his durability was outstanding, leading to an 11-year stint on the Minnesota roster.

Avoiding the sophomore jinx, White played in the Pro Bowl for the second straight year in 1977 after catching 41 passes, including nine for touchdowns. He set another club record by pulling in touchdown tosses in four consecutive contests, and had the longest reception of the season when he grabbed a 69-yard heave from Tommy Kramer in the final two minutes to beat San Francisco, 28–27, on December 4.

White was always available for the unexpected. Against Detroit in 1977, Ahmad Rashad looked to be hemmed in near the sideline on a short pass play, only to hand the pigskin to White, who dashed diagonally across the gridiron for 50 yards to paydirt in Minnesota's 14–7 win on October 9.

By the end of White's third season, following his NFC-high nine scoring grabs in 1978, he held the Viking record for most touchdown receptions. He also scored in four straight games to equal the mark he set the year before, while catching 53 passes for 741 yards.

Facing more double-teaming and a variety of zone defenses, White's production fell to 42 catches for four touchdowns in 1979. Another steady performance followed in 1980, when he pulled in 53 passes for 887 yards and five touchdowns. Aside from his rookie season, White had his best year in 1981, becoming just the fourth Viking to surpass the 1,000-yard mark by catching a career-high 66 tosses for 1,001 yards and three scores.

After six of the most productive seasons of anyone ever to wear purple, White battled injuries during his last five years. He was tied for second in the conference in receptions entering the sixth game of the 1982 slate before hurting his knee against Baltimore and missing the rest of the campaign, finishing with 29 catches for 503 yards and five touchdowns. A pulled muscle in his lower back suffered in the 11th game, against Green Bay, forced White to sit out the last five contests of the 1983 season, but not before he finished second on the team with 412 yards while catching 29 passes with four touchdowns. A pulled hamstring and a split tongue cost White a couple of games in 1984, when he caught 21 passes for 399 yards and paced the team with a 19-yard average. Named to the Vikings' Silver Anniversary All-Time Team in 1985, White missed the first 10 games that season with a groin pull before playing in the final six and catching eight passes for 76 yards.

The ailments kept White from taking the field in 1986 and led to his retirement on December 21. His 60 points in 1976 rank second to Randy Moss on the Vikings' rookie scoring list, while his 51 receptions tie Paul Flatley for second among first-year players. His 6,400 yards during his career are third in Minnesota history, and his 210 yards against Detroit in 1976 represent the most productive day ever for a Viking receiver. White's average gain of 16.3 yards per catch ranks second in Minnesota annals, his 50 touchdown catches rank third, and his three touchdown grabs in one game, achieved against Miami on December 11, 1976, and Chicago on November 28, 1982, are tied for second.

Without a doubt, Tarkenton and the Vikings helped make Sammy White a superstar.

Solomon Wilcots

Season: 1991　　　　　　　Safety　　　　　　　Height: 5'11"
Number: 41　　　　　　　　Colorado　　　　　　Weight: 200

Solomon Wilcots played in all 16 games for the Vikings in 1991 after arriving from Cincinnati as a Plan B free agent. He started one contest at strong safety, recording two solo tackles and four assists during Minnesota's 35–21 win over Green Bay on November 17. A week earlier, against Chicago, Wilcots forced a fumble on special teams. For the year, the reserve defensive back had 14 defensive tackles and another eight hits on kick coverages.

A.D. Williams

Season: 1961　　　　　　　End　　　　　　　　Height: 6'2"
Number: 82　　　　　　　　Pacific　　　　　　　Weight: 210

Acquired off waivers during the Vikings' first training camp, A.D. Williams was considered one of the Minnesota's initial "finds." The end paced the purple in receptions during the preseason before he suffered a separated shoulder in the exhibition game with the 49ers on August 26.

Williams returned in time to play in 13 games during the maiden voyage, ranking sixth on the team with 13 receptions for 174 yards. He caught a season-long 49-yard pass from Fran Tarkenton to set up Minnesota's only score against Dallas on September 24. A week later, Williams hauled in a seven-yard toss from George Shaw for the Vikings' first touchdown versus Baltimore.

Ben Williams

Season: 1998　　　　　　　Defensive Tackle　　　Height: 6'2"
Number: 98　　　　　　　　Minnesota　　　　　　Weight: 282

A member of the Vikings' practice squad for most of the 1998 season, Ben Williams joined the 53–man roster after he turned down a chance to sign with the Eagles in December. Comfortable with his role and the familiar surroundings, the former Golden Gopher played in his first game in the National Football League on December 26 and recorded a tackle during the 26–16 win over Tennessee.

Jeff Williams

Season: 1966　　　　　　　Running Back　　　　Height: 6'1"
Number: 23　　　　　　　　Oklahoma State　　　Weight: 210

The Vikings purchased Jeff Williams' contract from Joliet of the Professional Football League of America during the 1966 season. A calcified leg muscle kept Williams from playing at full speed, yet he managed to average 20.3 yards on three kickoff returns. Williams also rushed once for two yards and lost two yards on four punt returns.

Jimmy Williams

Seasons: 1990–91	Linebacker	Height: 6'3"
Number: 58	Nebraska	Weight: 225

A nine-year veteran with the Lions, Jimmy Williams joined the Vikings on December 4, 1990, and played in the season's final four games, recording three tackles. Williams then took over a starting role at linebacker in 1991 after Mark Dusbabek was lost for the season with a knee injury. Williams was ninth on the team with 39 primary tackles while adding 34 assists.

Williams' worth reaped rewards for the Vikings several years later. He was traded to Tampa Bay in 1992 for a ninth-round draft choice that Minnesota used to select quarterback Brad Johnson.

Moe Williams

Seasons: 1996–98	Running Back	Height: 6'1"
Number: 21	Kentucky	Weight: 196

With his slashing running style, Moe Williams has attracted favorable comparisons to Terry Allen. His opportunities have been limited to infrequent appearances at running back and on special teams, yet the Minnesota coaching staff believes Williams has the talent to be a big contributor to the explosive offense.

The Vikings' third-round draft choice in 1996, Williams missed nearly half of his rookie season with an ankle injury after a strong showing in training camp. He recorded nine tackles on special teams in his first year, then saw his role increase the following season after injuries shelved kick returner Robert Tate and running backs Robert Smith and Leroy Hoard. He finished the campaign with 59 yards on 22 carries, 14 yards on four receptions, and 388 yards on 16 kickoff returns. Williams also made 17 tackles on special teams, and another three hits during the playoffs.

Williams' best game came against New England on November 2, when he gained 43 yards rushing and scored his first touchdown in the 23–18 win over the Patriots. More important, he had his first career 100-yard game on kickoff returns with 137 yards. Williams set the tone by taking the opening boot up the middle of the field then down the right sideline for 74 yards, the 12th-longest in team history and the longest since Herschel Walker's 93-yarder in 1989.

"He might not be the big-play guy, but he seems to be able to find the holes and break certain tackles," said special teams coach Gary Zauner. "Moe has been very fundamentally sound."

Despite his success, bad luck struck Williams in 1998. After making four tackles on special teams and returning two kickoffs for 19 yards, Williams replaced an injured Smith against Chicago on December 1. On his first play from scrimmage of the year, Williams caught a screen pass and raced 64 yards before suffering a season-ending foot injury at the conclusion of the run.

Tony Williams

Seasons: 1997–98	Defensive Tackle	Height: 6'1"
Number: 94	Memphis	Weight: 291

The promise shown by Tony Williams, Minnesota's fifth-round draft choice in 1997, was one reason the Vikings released 1996 second-rounder James Manley. Though inactive for most of his rookie season before starting the final two games when John Randle moved to defensive end, Williams impressed with his ability to clog the middle and halt running plays by getting in the opponent's backfield. He concluded the campaign with 19 total tackles, plus another dozen hits in the playoffs.

Williams possesses excellent quickness and an explosive first step that has drawn comparisons to Randle. In fact, Williams' improvement in 1998 allowed Randle to move along the defensive line, thereby causing havoc for all five offensive linemen. Williams responded to the increased playing time by registering 36 total hits as well as his first sack in the National Football League, dumping Tampa Bay's Trent Dilfer in the 31–7 win over Tampa Bay on September 6.

Walt Williams

Seasons: 1981–82   Cornerback   Height: 6'1"
Number: 44   New Mexico State   Weight: 185

Signed in the preseason by Minnesota after being released by Detroit, Walt Williams played in all 16 games for the Vikings in 1981, making five starts. He responded with 28 solo tackles, six assists and one forced fumble. Williams also was credited with the safety against Atlanta on November 23. He returned to the Vikings in 1982 and played in one game before being waived on September 15.

Leonard Willis

Season: 1976   Wide Receiver   Height: 5'10"
Number: 80   Ohio State   Weight: 180

Minnesota's fourth-round draft choice in 1976, Leonard Willis was used exclusively as the team's kick returner during his rookie campaign. The former JUCO All-American averaged 23 yards on 24 kickoff returns and a team-high 6.9 yards on 30 punt returns in 1976. His best outing came during his professional debut, when he ran back four punts for a 15-yard norm in a 40–9 win over New Orleans on September 12.

Brett Wilson

Season: 1987   Running Back   Height: 6'
Number: 27   Illinois   Weight: 220

The Vikings' starting fullback for the 1987 replacement team, Brett Wilson gained 16 yards on five carries and 14 yards on two receptions.

David Wilson

Season: 1992   Safety   Height: 5'11"
Number: 24   California   Weight: 201

Few players have been involved in more transactions in one year than David Wilson was as a rookie. The Vikings' seventh-round draft pick in 1992, Wilson was waived during training camp before joining Minnesota's practice squad at the start of the season. Released again by the Vikings, he signed with New England, only to wind up back in purple at midseason. He moved to the active roster for the final three games of the campaign and saw action on special teams during wins against Pittsburgh and Green Bay.

Tom Wilson

Season: 1963   Running Back   Height: 6'
Number: 24   no college   Weight: 214

A former professional baseball player who toiled three years in the Air Force, Tom Wilson was acquired by the Vikings from Cleveland before the 1963 season in exchange for a 10th-round draft choice. A seven-year veteran of the National Football League at the time he was obtained by Minnesota, Wilson played in purple for eight games in 1963. He carried the ball 73 times for 282 yards and caught seven passes for 48 yards. He also scored four touchdowns, with three coming on short-yardage plunges in the final four games. His other score was a 30-yard gallop up the middle against the Colts on November 17.

Wade Wilson

Seasons: 1981–91   Quarterback   Height: 6'3"
Number: 11   East Texas State   Weight: 203

Football, much like life, is not always fair. Wade Wilson can relate. Although he was the first quarterback to take the Vikings to the NFC Championship Game in a decade, Wilson had difficulty receiving his due. The fans and media never deemed him the answer, considering him instead as the replacement for Tommy Kramer, only without the cheers and accolades that accompanied T.K.

Yet, when he was at the top of his game, Wilson was one of the most effective Viking quarterbacks in team history. He threw the long pass as well as anyone in Minnesota annals, and scrambled better than any signalcaller this side of Fran Tarkenton. He was productive even when he was not threading every pass through defenders' arms and into the hands of Anthony Carter, Steve Jordan or another purple receiver. But when he was not at the top of his game, Wilson could cause the Viking offense to stop with a resounding thud, and the signalcaller's critics responded.

Drafted in the eighth round as a punter and an NAIA All-American quarterback out of East Texas State in 1981, Wilson saw limited action as a rookie, most of which came against the Raiders at The Met after Steve Dils succumbed to a separated shoulder during the game. He completed six of 13 passes for 46 yards and two interceptions.

Wilson did not take the field for a regular-season game in 1982 and played in just one contest in 1983. He started the season finale against Cincinnati on December 17 and completed 16 of 28 passes for 124 yards, one touchdown and two interceptions in the 20–14 Vikings victory. Wilson started five games and played in a total of eight during the 1984 slate, completing 102 of 195 attempts for 1,019 yards, five touchdowns and 11 interceptions.

Wade Wilson

His lone start in 1985, on December 1, provided an excellent example of Wilson's hot-and-cold streaks. His performance in the first half was deemed poor enough by head coach Bud Grant that Wilson was replaced by little-used backup Steve Bono. Bono was even less effective, forcing Grant to reinsert Wilson with 11:42 remaining in the fourth quarter. Initially angered by the move, Wilson guided Minnesota to three of its four fourth-quarter touchdowns to lead the Vikings to a 28–23 triumph after trailing 23–0 early in the period. Wilson connected with Allen Rice on a seven-yard touchdown strike to begin the rally, hit Anthony Carter for a 36-yarder with 3:58 to play, then completed a 42-yarder to Carter with 1:11 remaining.

Wilson earned a larger role in 1986. He played in nine games and started three that year. In the season finale against New Orleans, the quarterback was named NFC Offensive Player of the Week for completing 24 of 39 passes for 361 yards and three touchdowns in Minnesota's 33–17 win over the Saints on December 21.

With Kramer suffering nerve damage in his neck during an August exhibition game against New England, Wilson received his first extended playing time in 1987 after starting just 10 games in his first seven years. He started seven of the 12 regular-season contests and paced the Vikings in nearly every passing category. He won NFC Offensive Player of the Week honors for the second time in his career for completing 17 of 38 passes for 285 yards and three touchdowns, including a game-winning 41-yarder to Hassan Jones with less than a minute to play against the Rams on September 20. Wilson then guided the Vikings to stunning upsets over the Saints and 49ers in the postseason before narrowly dropping a decision to Washington in the NFC Championship Game. In the process, Wilson established eight club playoffs records, including 298 passing yards against San Francisco on January 9, 1988.

Based on that showing, Minnesota fans expected Wilson to become one of the league's elite passers. It never happened, and Wilson became the target of the fans' wrath. Yet, behind the scenes, the quarterback and offensive coordinator Bob Schnelker bickered over the play-calling, which left much to be desired.

Even so, Wilson earned his first Pro Bowl invitation in 1988 after taking starting honors from Kramer during the second half of the season and leading the NFC with a 91.5 quarterback rating. He was the NFC Player of the Week upon passing for 335 yards on October 23 during a 49–20 win over Tampa Bay, and was named NFC Offensive Player of the Month in November for leading the Vikings to a 4–0 record while completing 65.1 percent of his passes. Never was he hotter than during a 44–17 victory over Detroit on November 6, when Wilson succeeded on 28 of 35 pass attempts for 391 yards and two touchdowns, including 14 of 15 in the first half.

An injured ring finger caused Wilson to miss nearly four full games in 1989, yet he still led the team in all passing categories. He also posted two 300-yard games, against Green Bay on November 26 (308 yards on 23 of 38 attempts) and versus Cincinnati on December 25 (303 yards and two touchdowns on 19 completions). An injured right thumb and separated right shoulder sandwiched Wilson's 1990 season, which consisted of six games. The highlight of his campaign was the seventh 300-yard passing day of his career, a feat he achieved in one half against Tampa Bay on December 16, when he completed 24 of 39 tosses for 374 yards.

Wilson started the first five games of the 1991 season and completed 72 of 122 passes for 825 yards and three touchdowns, two of which went to Cris Carter in a 20–19 victory over Atlanta on September 8. But after Minnesota won just two of those five contests, head coach Jerry Burns decided to go with Rich Gannon under center for the rest of the way.

Though still a productive quarterback, Wilson was released by Minnesota prior to the 1992 season and spent the next seven years in the National Football League as a part-time starter and excellent reserve for the Falcons, Cowboys and Raiders. His 1,665 attempts, 12,135 career yards, 66 touchdown tosses and 929 completions rank third in team annals, while his 14 straight pass completions against Detroit in 1988 is the franchise's second-longest streak, just two short of the record.

Wayne Wilson

Season: 1986 Running Back Height: 6'3"
Number: 45 Shepherd Weight: 215

Acquired on September 3, 1986, from New Orleans in a trade that sent wide receive Mike Jones to the Saints, Wayne Wilson looked like a worn-out used car during his brief stint with the Vikings. In seven games with Minnesota, Wilson gained 14 yards on eight rushing attempts and 33 yards on two catches. Unimpressed with the results, head coach Jerry Burns released the running back on October 29. Wilson returned to the Saints to play in the season's final five games.

Carl Winfrey

Season: 1971 Linebacker Height: 6'
Number: 36 Wisconsin Weight: 230

Carl Winfrey made the Minnesota roster as a college free agent in 1971 and earned the nickname "Mr. Sock" for his hard-hitting ways on special teams. He played in all 14 regular-season games and saw virtually no action at linebacker until the playoff loss to Dallas on Christmas Day, when Winfrey stepped in for the injured Roy Winston and played well against the run.

Roy Winston

Seasons: 1962–76 Linebacker Height: 5'11"
Number: 60 Louisiana State Weight: 228

What kind of punishment did Roy Winston apply while serving as the Vikings' starting left outside linebacker? Miami's Larry Csonka once said Winston hit him so hard with his helmet that the running back went to the sidelines in tears.

That was the type of player "Moonie" was, so gritty that his pre-game regimen included throwing up in the locker room. He said the vomiting got the adrenaline flowing properly through his body. Based on his on-field performances, Winston may have been on to something. Few players have combined more quickness, strength and intuition than Winston, who led the Vikings with 11 tackles for lost yardage in 1963 and eight such hits in 1972.

The spirited Winston also succeeded with his physical and mental attributes. His upper body was among the strongest of his generation. He also knew his opponents' tendencies. Rarely out of position to unleash his fury, Winston possessed a knack for smelling out a play before it unfolded. His strength, as Csonka could attest, was stopping the running game, while Winston's football intelligence foiled more than a few opponents' attempts at success.

Dubbed too short by many pro scouts, Winston and his hell-raising ways off the field initially clashed with Bud Grant when he replaced Norm Van Brocklin as head coach in 1967. The moody Winston hated the cold weather, so much so that he headed for his native Louisiana as soon as the curtain fell on the football season. He also cared little for Grant's disciplined approach, particularly the absence of heaters on the sidelines. Yet, a brief encounter between the two after Winston had partied excessively during training camp turned the tables. The linebacker ran with the new system and eventually became an even better football player.

He joined the Vikings as the team's second pick in 1962, drafted out of LSU in the fourth round. With his outstanding strength and 6.0 speed in the 50-yard dash, Winston could have played cornerback as well as linebacker, and even saw limited time at guard on the offensive line. After playing spar-

Roy Winston

ingly as a rookie, he began to make significant strides during training camp in 1963 and earned a starting job with his hard hits and outstanding range. He showed his ability to make the big play by picking up a Earl Gross fumble and racing 26 yards to paydirt against Green Bay on October 13. Winston also received little attention for one of his best performances. He picked off three passes against the 49ers on October 25, 1964, at Kezar Stadium, but most observers talked only about Jim Marshall's wrong-way run after the 27–22 Minnesota win.

Winston emerged as one of the National Football League's top linebackers with his best season in 1966. He moved from outside linebacker to the middle upon the surprising retirement of Rip Hawkins and took his game to higher level. Though undersized for his new position, Winston quickly proved he was one of the loop's most underrated defensive players, a label he held for the remainder of his career.

"You watch the game, you look at the films and you can't find 'Moonie' making a mistake," Grant said. "I don't know of many more underrated players than Roy. He's one of the finest linebackers in the game."

A foot injury caused Winston to get off to a slow start in 1967, yet the savvy defender rebounded to have an outstanding season. His performance played a key role in the Vikings' first division title in 1968 before he intercepted three aerials in 1969. He also picked off a toss in 1970, and scored the second touchdown of his career when he took a lateral from Marshall after a fumble recovery and reached the end zone during a 27–10 victory over Kansas City on September 20. Winston set the tone for the 1971 division crown versus Detroit in the second-to-last game of the season. Winston picked off quarterback Greg Landry's sideline pass on the Lions' first possession and scampered 29 yards to paydirt in Minnesota's 29–10 triumph.

Winston won a trip to coach Jocko Nelson's lodge on the Gunflint Trail for his three interceptions in 1972, a season that Grant later described as Winston's best in the NFL. A couple of nagging injuries slowed Winston's efforts in 1973, yet he managed to register the lone safety of his career. Winston nailed John Brockington in the Packer end zone during an 11–3 victory over Green Bay on September 30.

A hand injury caused him to miss three games in 1974. Even so, he caused two fumbles, recovered one loose ball, and sacked the quarterback twice on blitzes. Winston started nine games and made 46 tackles in 1975 but missed five contests with a chronic shoulder problem that required surgery after the season. He saw action in seven games in 1976 before calling it a career.

"He's probably one of our most intelligent players; knows as much about the game of football as anybody we have," Grant said of Winston in 1975. "Roy is a perfect example of a guy who is not big enough, not fast enough, not tall enough to play, but does, and well. A player who doesn't get the recognition he deserves."

Named to the Vikings' Silver Anniversary All-Time Team in 1985, Winston is currently tied for third on the Minnesota charts with 15 years of service.

Phil Wise

Seasons: 1977–79	Safety	Height: 6'
Number: 29	Nebraska-Omaha	Weight: 193

The Vikings added a veteran defensive back prior to the 1977 season when they acquired Phil Wise from the Jets for eighth- and 10th-round draft choices. A special teams player who also took the field in nickel- and dime-packages, the former college running back played in 15 games during his first year in purple. His lone interception of the campaign snuffed out Detroit's last scoring opportunity in Minnesota's 30–21 win on December 17.

His role increased in 1978, when Wise became the starting strong safety after Jeff Wright succumbed to a knee injury. He started every game and led the defensive backs with 118 tackles, good for third on the team. Wise also picked off two passes in helping Minnesota make its sixth straight playoff appearance.

In 1979, Wise opened the season on the exempt list. Restored to the roster on September 15, he was released six days later after playing in one game.

Craig Wolfley

Seasons: 1990–91	Guard	Height: 6'1"
Number: 73	Syracuse	Weight: 277

A 10-year veteran with the Steelers, Craig Wolfley signed with Minnesota as a Plan B free agent and served as a backup right guard in 1990. Wolfley started two games and played in six others during his first year in purple. He also saw a couple of plays at tight end in short yardage and goal-line situations.

In 1991, Wolfley served strictly in a reserve capacity while playing in all 16 games on the protection teams for field goal and point-after-touchdown attempts.

Jeff Womack

Season: 1987	Running Back	Height: 5'9"
Number: 33	Memphis State	Weight: 188

Jeff Womack served in purple for three replacement games in 1987, gaining 20 yards on nine carries and returning five kickoffs for a 15.4-yard average. Womack's best showing came against Tampa Bay on October 18, when he had 46 yards on five receptions, including a 23-yard touchdown grab.

Kailee Wong

Season: 1998	Linebacker	Height: 6'2"
Number: 52	Stanford	Weight: 260

Minnesota had visions of Chris Doleman when the team selected Kailee Wong with its second-round pick in the 1998 draft. An All-American defensive end under former Vikings assistant coach Tyrone Willingham at Stanford, Wong showed the speed, strength and agility to cover the tight end in pass coverage, stuff the run, and serve as a pass rusher as an outside linebacker.

After contributing on special teams during the first half of his rookie season, Wong began to push Dixon Edwards for starting honors during the last half of the 1998 slate. He saw increased action as a nickel pass rusher and made 19 tackles with 1.5 sacks before a sprained right ankle forced him to go on the injured reserve list for the playoffs.

Mike Wood

Season: 1978   Punter   Height: 5'11"
Number: 5   Southeast Missouri State   Weight: 199

Minnesota's eighth-round draft pick in 1978, Mike Wood's claim to fame in college was his place-kicking abilities. A soccer-style kicker, Wood did not impress Bud Grant. The head coach opted to go with Rick Danmeier, whose straight-ahead approach replaced the retired Fred Cox.

Wood did get the nod for the Vikings' punting chores, at least for the first seven games of the 1978 regular season. But after averaging just 35.5 yards on 31 punts, Wood was headed to St. Louis, while the Vikings began their long relationship with Greg Coleman.

Barry Word

Season: 1993   Running Back   Height: 6'2"
Number: 23   Virginia   Weight: 242

When Terry Allen went down with a ruptured knee ligament during training camp in 1993, head coach Dennis Green made a move to strengthen his depleted running corps. The Vikings acquired Barry Word from Kansas City for a fifth-round draft choice, hoping that the powerful former Chief could return to his Pro Bowl form.

Word looked like a good fit early on. In his first start with the Vikings, he rambled for 94 yards on 24 carries and caught a career-high five passes for 54 yards in the 10–7 victory over Chicago on September 12. A 65-yard effort on 19 attempts followed in the 15–13 win against Green Bay a week later. He then had performances of 46, 53 and 78 yards in the next three contests, but also had trouble maintaining possession of the football, losing three fumbles. Rookie Robert Smith started to see more action as Green lost confidence in Word's ability to hang on to the pigskin.

When Smith was lost for the season with a knee injury on December 5, Word, who had been sulking as a reserve, did not respond. As a result, Scottie Graham took over in the backfield and led the Vikings to the playoffs while Word ended his one year in purple with 458 yards on 142 carries.

Felix Wright

Seasons: 1991–92   Safety   Height: 6'2"
Number: 22   Drake   Weight: 196

Felix Wright, an instinctive player who possessed a knack for being around the football, signed as a Plan B free agent with the Vikings in 1991. He combined with Joey Browner to give Minnesota two of the most active and hardest-hitting safeties in the game. Wright started all 16 contests during his first year in purple and ranked third on the team with 135 total tackles. He also forced two fumbles, and picked off passes in wins over Atlanta and Tampa Bay.

Injuries hampered Wright for much of 1992 before forcing him to miss the final three games of the regular season. While losing some playing time to Vencie Glenn, Wright contributed 28 total tackles and intercepted one pass that he returned 20 yards. Unsigned after the season, his final appearance in the National Football League came with the Chiefs when he was picked up for the 1993 playoffs.

Jeff Wright

Seasons: 1971–77	Defensive Back	Height: 5'11"
Number: 23	Minnesota	Weight: 190

A local product from Edina who captained head coach Murray Warmath's Golden Gopher team as a senior and established school records for interceptions, Jeff Wright was a fixture in the Vikings' secondary during the franchise's winningest era. He was a sure tackler and a dependable, versatile defensive back who used his great instincts on the gridiron to play all four positions in the defensive backfield with equal assurance.

One of Wright's biggest plays came in the NFC Championship Game against the Rams on December 29, 1974. Los Angeles quarterback James Harris scrambled over nearly every blade of the Metropolitan Stadium grass before finding Harold Jackson in the clear with a cross-field pass. Jackson looked to have an easy stroll into the end zone before Wright made the play from the far sidelines, knocking Jackson out of bounds at the 2-yard line. The Vikings' defense responded with a patented goal-line stand, culminating with Wally Hilgenberg's interception in the end zone, to secure a 14–10 victory and another Super Bowl appearance.

Selected in the 15th round, Wright joined first-round selection Leo Hayden as the lone rookies to make the Vikings' veteran roster in 1971. He saw some action as a reserve safety and on special teams before making his first start at strong safety and intercepting two passes against Green Bay during a 27–13 win on October 29. He picked off three aerials in both 1972 and 1973, and upgraded his tackling ability significantly during the latter campaign upon taking over starting honors after Karl Kassulke suffered his near-fatal motorcycle accident one day prior to training camp.

Wright played strong safety, free safety and cornerback in 1974 and recorded an interception at all three positions. He also intercepted a pass against St. Louis in the playoffs to set up Fred Cox's stay-ahead field goal during the Vikings' 30–14 win on December 21.

Injuries started to take their toll in 1975. Wright suffered a pre-season knee injury but came back to see action for three games before hurting the joint again. He recovered to become the Vikings' starter at strong safety in 1976 and played all four secondary positions. Wright registered 83 tackles and a quarterback sack, and deflected a punt during the season-opening 40–9 win over New Orleans on September 12. He paced the backfield with 73 solo hits and 39 assists in 1977. Wright also caused two fumbles, recovered two and intercepted a pair of passes, including one pick in the playoffs against Los Angeles that halted the Rams' final threat in the waning minutes of Minnesota's 14–7 triumph on December 26.

That proved to be Wright's swan song, however. He had knee surgery two weeks prior to the 1978 training camp and tried diligently to return to action, but to no avail. A sixth knee operation in 1979 brought to an end one of the most productive careers of any Minnesota defensive back.

Nate Wright

Seasons: 1971–80	Cornerback	Height: 5'11"
Number: 43	San Diego State	Weight: 180

Through no fault of his own, Nate Wright was the victim of the most controversial play in Vikings history.

The 1975 Vikings are considered by many to be the franchise's best team ever. The club had gone 12–2 during the regular season, and had pulled off a stellar fourth-quarter drive in the first round of the playoffs to lead Dallas by a 14–10 margin. With nothing but total desperation left in the waning seconds, Cowboys quarterback Roger Staubach heaved the pigskin downfield to receiver Drew Pearson. Wright's coverage was near-perfect. Yet, with one of the more athletic moves ever seen, Pearson leaped and pushed Wright to the ground before making the grab for the game-winning touchdown. No flag was thrown by the officials, giving Dallas the win and Minnesota an early off-season.

Signed as a rookie free agent by Atlanta in 1969 before being sold to the Cardinals that same year, Wright was considered the extra man when he and tight end Bob Brown were acquired by Minnesota from St. Louis before the 1971 season in exchange for Dale Hackbart, Mike McGill and a fourth-round draft pick. Wright quickly proved that he could add speed and quickness to the Minnesota defensive backfield along with a strong tackling ability at cornerback.

Wright took advantage of being an emergency starter in 1973 and kept the job. He intercepted three tosses, plus one more in the playoffs, during his first season in the lineup. After two full years with the Vikings, head coach Bud Grant believed Wright had become one of the most improved players on the team.

"I can't say I was more pleased with anybody's performance than I have been with Nate's," Grant said following the 1973 season.

Wright proceeded to lead the Vikings with six interceptions in 1974, a total he accumulated in the team's first five games. Wright had two picks during a 32–17 win over Green Bay on September 15 and in Minnesota's 23–21 triumph at Dallas on October 6. He also scored the decisive touchdown by returning a fumble 20 yards to paydirt in the 30–14 playoff victory over St. Louis on December 21. Such success caused teams to avoid the steady and dependable Wright throughout the 1975 slate, when he failed to intercept a pass.

Teams started to throw Wright's way again in 1976 and the cornerback made them pay by pacing the team with seven interceptions. His best outings included back-to-back two-pick performances, against Seattle during a 27–21 win on November 14 and a 17–10 triumph over Green Bay a week later.

In 1977, Wright scored a touchdown on 27-yard fumble recovery against Oakland on December 11. He also intercepted three passes in the regular season and one in the NFC title game, against Dallas. Five more enemy aerials landed in Wright's hands in 1978 along with his first quarterback sack before he suffered a broken arm in the regular-season finale and missed the playoffs.

More injury problems followed in 1979, including additional surgery on the broken wrist he suffered in 1978 that did not heal properly. The ailment forced Wright into a reserve role for the first 11 games, yet he still tied for the team lead with four interceptions. He then broke a bone in his wrist during the 11th game and missed the rest of the slate on injured reserve.

Wright overcame the ailments to play in all 16 games in 1980, when he picked off the final two passes of his career. He currently ranks fifth in Minnesota history with 31 interceptions for 272 return yards.

Nate Wright

Ray Yakavonis

Seasons: 1980–83	Defensive Tackle	Height: 6'4"
Number: 91	East Stroudsburg State	Weight: 250

Injuries in the National Football League prevented Ray Yakavonis from reliving his Division II All-American days at East Stroudsburg State, when the team's defense was known as the "Big Yak Attack," named after its leader.

Minnesota's sixth-round draft choice in 1980, Yakavonis spent all of his rookie season on injured reserve after hurting his knee during his first training camp. Moved from defensive end to nose tackle when the Vikings shifted to a 3–4 defense in 1981, he played a reserve role and contributed six tackles and a fumble recovery in 15 games.

Yakavonis missed the first seven games of the 1982 slate by residing on injured reserve, and played in only the last two regular-season games and both playoff contests. A repeat occurred in 1983, Yakavonis' last year in purple, when he opened the season on the injured list. Activated on October 7, he played in two games prior to being waived by Minnesota on December 5 and joining Kansas City for the campaign's duration.

Ron Yary

Seasons: 1968–81	Tackle	Height: 6'5"
Number: 73	Southern Cal	Weight: 255

Ask most scouts and coaches around the National Football League in the 1970s to name the prototype tackle and Ron Yary would head the list. Though at 255 pounds he would be considered severely undersized by today's standards, the right tackle dominated larger defenders with his outstanding agility and incredible ability to move an opponent where Yary wanted. He was powerful and determined with a Polish temper that led to his becoming one of the best offensive linemen in league history.

Yary joined the Vikings under the heat of an intense spotlight. The 1968 draft was the first of the NFL-AFL merger, and thanks to the Fran Tarkenton deal with the New York Giants, Minnesota owned the first overall pick. To no one's surprise, the purple went with Yary, a consensus All-American and winner of the Outland Trophy and Knute Rockne Award at USC who proceeded to put together a career worthy of Hall of Fame enshrinement.

A special teams performer and reserve as a rookie in 1968, Yary showed head coach Bud Grant enough to say, "Yary is just a growing boy. But when he grows up, he's going to be a superstar." The lineman lived up to those words. After missing the first part of the 1969 slate while in active military duty with a reserve unit, he replaced the injured Doug Davis at right tackle during the campaign. His strength and unmatched desire were immediately apparent. Yary also impressed the masses by handling Rams end Deacon Jones with relative ease and leading the charge on the ground in Minnesota's 20–13 win over Los Angeles on December 7.

Ron Yary

A starter throughout the 1970 season, Yary overcame a plethora of holding penalties and a tendency to relax against weaker opponents to earn Pro Bowl and All-Pro recognition in 1971. Practically every time the Vikings needed a yard or two for a first down or six points, the team ran behind Yary, who was a great straight-ahead run blocker with amazing balance and an ability to recover quickly. Opposing teams knew the play was coming, yet Yary's drive led to success nearly every time.

Yary earned Pro Bowl and All-Pro recognition for six straight seasons, from 1971–76, with his Pro Bowl string reaching seven in 1977. After starting every game in 1978 and 1979, Yary managed to start 14 games as well as the playoff contest in 1980 despite playing with a broken foot and a broken ankle. The ailments, however, did force him to miss his first two starts since 1969.

A classic example of Yary's dogged persistence appeared center stage during the season opener in 1976. With time running out in the first half, the Vikings were trying to dent the scoreboard once more from midfield. Quarterback Fran Tarkenton took the snap and began to scramble for 28 seconds, a lifetime for most offensive linemen. Yary, however, did his part by knocking his man off his pins not once, but on three occasions. That protection allowed Tarkenton to find Sammy White open for a 47–touchdown toss and help send the Vikings to a 40–9 victory over the Saints.

Yary started every game in 1981 before being traded prior to the following season to the Rams for a 10th-round draft pick. The team's offensive captain at the time of the deal, Yary played in 202 contests, starting 182, including all four Super Bowls with Minnesota. He also was named to the Vikings' Silver Anniversary All-Time Team in 1985.

Jim Young

Seasons: 1965–66   Running Back-End   Height: 6'
Number: 34   Queens Ontario   Weight: 205

One of the few Canadians in the National Football League during the 1960s, Jim Young signed with Minnesota as a free agent in 1965 after he was the Canadian Football League's first overall draft pick a year earlier. He emerged from the Vikings' taxi squad when Tommy Mason went down with a knee injury and played a role in the team's strong finish, returning four punts for seven yards and four kickoffs for a 19.5-yard norm.

With the Vikings stocked at running back, Young moved to end during training camp in 1966. Possessing excellent hands and above-average speed, he did not have a chance to live up to his potential after suffering a shoulder separation against the Bears. Young wound up playing in just four games, averaging 21 yards on five kickoff returns.

Rickey Young

Seasons: 1978–83   Running Back   Height: 6'2"
Number: 34   Jackson State   Weight: 195

Rickey Young may have been listed as a running back, but his greatest contributions to the Vikings came in catching the football. Immediately upon arriving in the Upper Midwest after being acquired from San Diego in exchange for guard Ed White, Young became a favorite target of Fran Tarkenton, who would dump swing passes to the running back in order to offset blitzes and other defensive schemes. This, in effect, was the true beginning of the so-called West Coast offense, although Bill Walsh is credited with its creation.

After leading the Chargers in rushing for three years, Young proved to have all the tools necessary to be a solid team player and significant force

Rickey Young

on the Minnesota offense. He debuted in purple by pacing the National Football League with 88 catches in 1978, setting a league record for passes caught by a running back and a total that currently ranks fourth in team history. He was also part of an NFL mark when he was one of four Viking players with at least 50 receptions. Five times he carried a pass into the end zone. Young added another score while placing second on the team with 417 yards rushing on 134 carries.

The backfield teammate of Walter Payton at Jackson State, Young continued to excel in the short passing game with Tommy Kramer under center. The Kramer-to-Young tandem resulted in 72 receptions and four touchdowns in 1979, including a team-record 15 catches at New England on December 16. Young also led the team in rushing with 708 yards on 188 carries.

In 1980, he was second on the team in rushing with 351 yards and 64 catches, marking the first time in his career he did not lead in his team in at least one of the two categories. With Ted Brown in the swing of things by 1981, Young had 129 yards on the ground and 43 catches out of the backfield. While his production fell to 49 yards rushing and four catches in 1982, his three-yard plunge in the 17–10 win over Tampa Bay on September 12 was the first touchdown ever scored in the Metrodome. He also registered the last touchdown of the regular season by catching a 14-yard pass in the 31–27 triumph over Dallas on January 3, 1983.

Young's production increased in 1983, to 21 catches, good for sixth on the team. At the time he was waived during the final cutdowns in the 1984 training camp, he ranked fourth in Vikings history with 292 receptions, eighth with 2,255 yards receiving, and ninth with 1,744 rushing yards.

Frank Youso

Seasons: 1961–62   Tackle   Height: 6′4″
Number: 72   Minnesota   Weight: 260

It's doubtful Frank Youso ever used Norm Van Brocklin as a reference for future employment. The reverse can be said as well. Acquired from the New York Giants in the veterans pool, Youso never saw eye-to-eye with the Minnesota head coach. Though immensely strong, smart and talented, Youso did not emerge as an outstanding tackle with the Vikings, partly because the Dutchman always believed the lineman was not providing a full effort. The two bickered constantly, leaving ill will in its path.

A native of International Falls, Minnesota, who earned All-Big Ten honors as a Golden Gopher, Youso played in all 14 games in 1961 as the starting right tackle. Youso then saw action in 13 contests in 1962, when the Viking offensive line featured more leaks than a worn-out hose. After he was replaced by Errol Linden in the starting lineup, Youso wound up spending his final three professional seasons with Oakland.

Z

Godfrey Zaunbrecher

Seasons: 1971–73   Center   Height: 6'1"
Number: 51   Louisiana State   Weight: 240

Head coach Bud Grant was honest when asked to evaluate Godfrey Zaunbrecher's performance during the reserve center's four years in purple. "He has done everything but play," Grant said. "It's a matter if he can play up to the standards set by Mick Tingelhoff at that position."

The answer, of course, was "no." That should not be embarrassing to Zaunbrecher, for few centers in the history of the National Football League have ever played to Tingelhoff's standards. As a result, Zaunbrecher, the Vikings' 11th-round draft choice in 1970, was limited to giving Tingelhoff an occasional breather during blowouts after spending his first season on the Minnesota taxi squad. Zaunbrecher appeared in four games in 1971, seven contests in 1972 and five games in 1973. Grant said several times that he thought Zaunbrecher had the talent to start in the NFL, yet that opportunity never presented itself with the Vikings.

Gary Zimmerman

Seasons: 1986–92   Tackle   Height: 6'6"
Number: 65   Oregon   Weight: 283

The past two decades have witnessed a change in offensive strategy throughout the National Football League. Teams throughout the 1980s and 1990s have employed attacks more dependent on passing, thereby requiring different skills among the offensive linemen, who ultimately determine how successful any scheme will be.

When pro football's history of the last two decades of the 20th century is written, Gary Zimmerman will be deemed one of the game's premier technicians at left tackle. Throughout his first seven years in the NFL, Zimmerman excelled in pass protection, particularly with his ability to guard the quarterback's blind side. He accomplished the feat by blocking on the move better than anyone who has worn pads at the game's highest level.

"Gary is probably the best technician I've ever coached," said John Michels, Minnesota's offensive line coach from 1967–93. "He had most of it when he got here. He's like a fine watch; you don't fix it if it's not broken. In our stats he made a mistake once every 32 plays. That's incredible considering the nearest person to him on our team made one every 17."

Zimmerman joined the Vikings after playing two seasons in the up-start United States Football League as a tackle and long snapper with the Los Angeles Express. Minnesota had to work a complicated deal to acquire his rights from the New York Giants. On draft day, April 29, 1986, the Vikes sent their first- and third-round picks to San Diego for the Chargers' first- and second-round selections. The Vikings then traded two second-round selections to the Giants in exchange for Zimmerman.

He immediately solidified the Vikings' offensive line by gaining start-

Gary Zimmerman

ing honors at left tackle during his first visit to Mankato. Zimmerman received All-Pro recognition from *Sports Illustrated* during his initial season with Minnesota, then earned a starting assignment in the Pro Bowl following his superb performance in 1987, the same year he was named "Miller Lite Lineman of the Year."

In 1988, Zimmerman showed why he earned a reputation for being one of the toughest tackles in the league, a player always willing to play with pain. Among the more durable players in purple, he started every game during his days in Minnesota, a string that extended to 108 regular-season games and seven more in the playoffs.

He overcame a bruised sternum suffered against Miami on October 2 to start every game during the 1988 season and become a unanimous All-Pro selection. He extended his starting string to 60 games in 1989, when he received All-Pro and Pro Bowl honors again. At the end of the slate, despite playing in just four seasons during the decade, Zimmerman was voted to the second-team All-NFL team of the 1980s.

Zimmerman provided another classic example of how tough he was during the 1990 campaign. Various ailments that led to surgery on his ankle and elbow as soon as the season ended hampered Zimmerman throughout the fall, yet he started all 16 games once again. He returned in better shape a year later and helped the Vikings lead the NFC in rushing for the first time in franchise history by piling up 2,201 yards on the ground. Zimmerman then earned his fourth and final trip to the Pro Bowl with Minnesota by excelling in new head coach Dennis Green's more varied scheme in 1992, when the Vikings returned to the playoffs after a two-year hiatus.

Always a man of principle, Zimmerman's career with the Vikings ended because of his unhappiness regarding his contract. He was the lone no-show at the 1993 mini-camp after seeing other less-talented offensive linemen around the league sign for deals larger than his $950,000 annual salary. Refusing to play for that amount, Zimmerman said he would retire if not traded. The Vikings had no interest in restructuring the tackle's contract, and shipped him to Denver for the Broncos' first- and sixth-round picks in 1994 and a second rounder in 1995. Minnesota used those picks to draft cornerback Dewayne Washington and tight end Andrew Jordan, respectively, in 1994 and safety Orlando Thomas in 1995. Zimmerman, meanwhile, remained with Denver through the 1997 season.

THREE

• • •

THE COACHES
THE NUMBERS

Head Coaches

Norm Van Brocklin

Norm Van Brocklin concluded his Hall-of-Fame playing days on top. The quarterback led Philadelphia to the NFL Championship in 1960 before surprising many observers by retiring and accepting the head coaching job of the expansion Minnesota Vikings. The fiery leader made sure the purple was nothing less than competitive during the franchise's first half-dozen seasons, and even guided the team to the brink of the playoffs in 1964.

A native of Parade, South Dakota, Van Brocklin's Minnesota teams mirrored his playing style. As a quarterback for the Rams and Eagles, Dutch had a keen sense of how to shred an opponent's defense. He passed that knowledge on to Fran Tarkenton, whose scrambling style could not have been more different than Van Brocklin's pocket approach. Nevertheless, the two legendary offensive minds helped make the Vikings one of the most successful expansion teams in NFL history.

Van Brocklin expected perfection, which often created tension on the team. The head coach became so frustrated at one point in 1965 that he announced his resignation during the season before retuning a day later. He had trouble communicating with his players after that episode. In fact, Van Brocklin and Tarkenton rarely spoke during their last year together. Feeling it was time to move on after six years at the Viking helm, Van Brocklin resigned for the second and final time in February 1967.

Year	Won	Lost	Tied	Place
1961	3	11	0	Seventh
1962	2	11	1	Sixth
1963	5	8	1	Fourth (tied)
1964	8	5	1	Second (tied)
1965	7	7	0	Fifth (tied)
1966	4	9	1	Sixth (tied)
Totals	29	51	4	

Bud Grant

Six years after he was initially considered for the Vikings' head coaching helm, Bud Grant accepted the job for the first time on March 10, 1967. A native of Superior, Wisconsin, who had been a multi-sport athlete at the University of Minnesota, Grant was a relative unknown in the NFL, yet had led the Winnipeg Blue Bombers to four Grey Cup Championships in 10 years as head coach of the Canadian Football League club.

Grant quickly turned the Vikings into winners. He succeeded by employing discipline and dedication to his job, and expected nothing less from his players. One of his first acts as head coach was to make sure his team stood at attention for the National Anthem. On the sidelines during games, Grant appeared stoic and unemotional. He also turned the cold Minnesota weather into an advantage late in the season and during the playoffs, refusing to allow his team to employ heaters on the bench or wear gloves on the field. The tactics worked, resulting in 11 Central Division titles, 10 playoff victories and four trips to the Super Bowl.

Off the field, Grant is known for his practical jokes and love of the outdoors. Yet, no matter what endeavors he has chosen in his life, Grant has al-

Bud Grant

ways enjoyed success. His Vikings defenses dominated. With the help of offensive coordinator Jerry Burns, he tailored his offense to the personnel. Grant also won at least a game or two every season by employing the league's best special teams. No one in the history of the game has used a better team concept, which is one major reason he was inducted into the Pro Football Hall of Fame in 1994.

Grant initially retired from the coaching ranks after the 1983 season, saying he wanted to experience other avenues in life. After the Vikings had a turbulent 1984 slate, he returned for one season to get the team back on track before unpacking his fishing and hunting gear a final time.

Year	Won	Lost	Tied	Playoffs	Place
1967	3	8	3		Fourth
1968	8	6	0	0–1	First
1969	12	2	0	2–1	First
1970	12	2	0	0–1	First
1971	11	3	0	0–1	First
1972	7	7	0		Third
1973	12	2	0	2–1	First
1974	10	4	0	2–1	First
1975	12	2	0	0–1	First
1976	11	2	1	2–1	First
1977	9	5	0	1–1	First
1978	8	7	1	0–1	First
1979	7	9	0		Third
1980	9	7	0	0–1	First
1981	7	9	0		Fourth
1982	5	4	0	1–1	Fourth (tied)
1983	8	8	0		Fourth
1985	7	9	0		Third
Totals	**158**	**96**	**5**	**10–12**	

Les Steckel

After five seasons as the Vikings' receivers coach, Les Steckel was promoted to head coach on January 29, 1984, following Bud Grant's first retirement. At age 38, Steckel was the youngest head coach in the league, and his inexperience showed. He overhauled the coaching staff and employed a regimen similar to his military background. Those moves and questionable coaching decisions created some disgruntled troops. That led to another change at the end of the season, when Grant replaced Steckel and returned to the Vikings' helm.

Year	Won	Lost	Tied	Place
1984	3	13	0	Fifth
Totals	**3**	**13**	**0**	

Jerry Burns

Jerry Burns received his just reward after serving as the Vikings' offensive coordinator since 1968 when he was named Minnesota's fourth head coach in team annals on January 7, 1986. The transition from Bud Grant to

Burns was smooth, for the two men offered similar approaches to the game. Burns, in fact, may have been a little more loveable than his predecessor, although he also displayed his emotions much more often than Grant.

Burns continued to employ his innovative approach to the offense, particularly during the early stages of his head coaching career. He also did a fine job of molding the Vikings into a competitive team, taking the purple to the NFC Championship Game during his second season before posting an 11–5 mark in 1988, Minnesota's best regular-season record since 1976.

That success, combined with some dealings by general manager Mike Lynn, created some unrealistic expectations in the Upper Midwest, which proved to be an albatross for Burns. The Vikings were expected to reach the Super Bowl in 1989 and 1990, particularly after Lynn risked the team's future by acquiring running back Herschel Walker. Yet, without adequate depth, Minnesota failed to advance deep in the playoffs after winning the Central Division in 1989 before posting back-to-back disappointing records the next two years.

Having guided the Vikings to three playoff appearances, Burns announced his retirement on December 3, 1991, effective at the end of the season.

Year	Won	Lost	Tied	Playoffs	Place
1986	9	7	0		Second
1987	8	7	0	2–1	Second
1988	11	5	0	1–1	Second
1989	10	6	0	0–1	First
1990	6	10	0		Fifth
1991	8	8	0		Third
Totals	**55**	**46**	**0**	**3–3**	

Dennis Green

The Vikings proved they were committed to change when they hired Dennis Green as the franchise's fifth head coach on January 10, 1992. Green had no previous connections to Minnesota, but possessed an impressive resume. In addition to working under Bill Walsh with the San Francisco 49ers, Green had placed the Northwestern football program on solid ground before turning around a struggling Stanford team as the Cardinal head coach from 1989–91.

Green brought a new attitude to the Twin Cities that produced immediate results. He became the most successful first-year head coach in Vikings history by winning 11 games as well as the Central Division in 1992. He went on to win two more division crowns in his first seven seasons, including a franchise-record 15 victories in 1998. He also owned the best overall winning percentage, .634, of any Viking head coach.

Green succeeded by recognizing talent. Under his direction, the Vikings built the league's deepest team with consistently productive drafts. As the scout team coach during practice, Green developed raw players into Pro Bowl performers, including such projects as center Jeff Christy and linebacker Ed McDaniel. The head coach also generated enthusiasm and loyalty from his players, who realized Green's determination to make Minnesota the best team it possibly could be.

Through the 1998 campaign, the Vikings had reached the playoffs six times in seven seasons under Green and had never posted a losing record.

Dennis Green

Tough Enough To Be Vikings

During that time, Green joined Pittsburgh's Bill Cowher as the NFL head coaches with the most longevity with the same team. Before Green's tenure in Minnesota comes to a close, his records may be the ones that set the standard in Viking lore.

Year	Won	Lost	Tied	Playoffs	Place
1992	11	5	0	0–1	First
1993	9	7	0	0–1	Second
1994	10	6	0	0–1	First
1995	8	8	0		Fourth
1996	9	7	0	0–1	Second
1997	9	7	0	1–1	Fourth
1998	15	1	0	1–1	First
Totals	**71**	**41**	**0**	**2–6**	

Assistant Coaches

Hubbard Alexander
  Wide Receivers 1998
Neill Armstrong
  Defensive Backs 1969
  Defensive Coordinator 1970–77
Dave Atkins
  Tight Ends 1997–98
Mark Asanovich
  Assistant Strength and Conditioning 1995
Tom Batta
  Defensive Line 1984
  Defensive Assistant/Kicking Teams 1985
  Tight Ends/Special Teams 1986–91
  Special Teams 1992–93
Maxie Baughan
  Linebackers 1990–91
Raymond Berry
  Receivers 1984
Brian Billick
  Tight Ends 1992
  Offensive Coordinator 1993–98
Bud Bjornaraa
  Strength 1984
Darrel Brewster
  Offensive Ends 1961–63
Dean Brittenham
  Conditioning 1984
Jerry Brown
  Offensive Assistant 1988
  Wide Receivers 1989
  Defensive Backs 1990–91
John Brunner
  Running Backs 1987–91
Jerry Burns
  Offensive Coordinator 1968–85
Jack Burns
  Offensive Coordinator 1992–93
Marion Campbell
  Defensive Line 1964–66
Lew Carpenter
  Offensive Ends 1964–66

Jim Carr
   Defensive Backfield 1966–68, 1978–81
Pete Carroll
   Defensive Backs 1985–89
Tom Cecchini
   Defensive Line 1980–83
Rollie Dotsch
   Running Backs 1987
Tony Dungy
   Defensive Coordinator 1992–95
Jack Faulkner
   Defensive Backfield 1965
Foge Fazio
   Inside Linebackers 1995
   Defensive Coordinator 1996–98
Ross Fichtner
   Defensive Backs 1984
Chris Foerster
   Assistant Offensive Line 1993–94
   Tight Ends 1995
Jeff Friday
   Assistant Strength and Conditioning 1996–98
Harry Gilmer
   Defensive Backs 1961–64
Carl Hargrave
   Offensive Assistant 1994
   Running Backs 1995–98
Wade Harman
   Coaching Assistant 1997–98
Bob Hollway
   Defensive Line 1967–68
   Defensive Coordinator 1969–70, 1978–83, 1985
   Research and Development 1984
   Special Assistant/Football Operations 1986
Jed Hughes
   Defensive Backs 1982–83
Monte Kiffin
   Linebackers 1986–89
   Defensive Coordinator 1991
   Inside Linebackers 1992–94
Bob Leahy
   Offensive Assistant 1984
John Levra
   Defensive Line 1995–97

Tom McCormick
  Offensive Backfield 1963–66
Buster Mertes
  Offensive Backfield 1967–83
  Quality Control 1984
John Michels
  Offensive Line 1967–83, 1985–93
  Offensive Backs 1984
Tom Moore
  Assistant Head Coach/Offense 1990
  Offensive Coordinator 1991
  Wide Receivers 1992–93
Chip Myers
  Wide Receivers 1995–97
  Quarterbacks 1998
Jocko Nelson
  Linebackers 1971–78
Tom Olivadotti
  Inside Linebackers 1996–98
Jack Patera
  Defensive Line 1969–75
Andre Patterson
  Defensive Line 1998
Floyd Peters
  Defensive Coordinator 1986–90
Dan Radakovich
  Offensive Line 1984
Floyd Reese
  Linebackers 1979–83, 1985
  Defensive Coordinator 1984
Dick Rehbein
  Wide Receivers 1984–88
  Assistant Offensive Coordinator 1989
  Wide Receivers 1990–91
Jerry Rhome
  Wide Receivers 1994
Keith Rowen
  Offensive Line 1994–96
Buddy Ryan
  Defensive Line 1976–77
Bob Schnelker
  Offensive Coordinator 1986–90
Willie Shaw
  Defensive Backs 1992–93

Ray Sherman
  Quarterbacks 1995–97
Richard Solomon
  Outside Linebackers 1992–93
  Defensive Backs 1994–98
Les Steckel
  Receivers 1979–83
Mike Sweatman
  Linebackers/Special Teams 1984
John Teerlinck
  Defensive Line 1992–94
Mike Tice
  Tight Ends 1996
  Offensive Line 1997–98
Marc Trestman
  Running Backs 1985–86
  Administrative Assistant to Head Coach 1990
  Quarterbacks 1991
Trent Walters
  Outside Linebackers 1994–98
Murray Warmath
  Defensive Line 1978–79
Stan West
  Defensive Line 1961–63
Steve Wetzel
  Strength and Conditioning 1992–98
Paul Wiggin
  Defensive Line 1985–91
Tyrone Willingham
  Running Backs 1992–94
Mike Wolf
  Assistant Strength and Conditioning 1992–94
Walt Yowarsky
  Offensive Line 1961–66
Gary Zauner
  Special Teams 1994–98

Uniform Numbers in Viking Lore

1
Benny Ricardo (1983), Chuck Nelson (1986–88), Warren Moon (1994–96), Gary Anderson (1998).

2
Teddy Garcia (1989).

3
Jan Stenerud (1984–85), Rich Karlis (1989), Richard Jones (1993), Eddie Murray (1997).

4
Archie Manning (1983–84), Dale Dawson (1987*), Donald Igwebuike (1990), Mike Saxon (1994–95).

5
Mike Wood (1978), Larry Miller (1987*), Todd Krueger (1987*), Chad May (1995), Greg Davis (1997).

6
Jim Gallery (1990), Jay Walker (1996–97).

7
Rick Danmeier (1977–83), Tony Adams (1987*), Fuad Reveiz (1990–95), Randall Cunningham (1997–98).

8
Greg Coleman (1978–87), Todd Bouman (1997–98).

9
Tommy Kramer (1977–89), Jim McMahon (1993), Scott Sisson (1996).

10
Fran Tarkenton (1961–66, 1972–78), King Hill (1968).

11
Joe Kapp (1967–69), Mike Eischied (1972–74), John Reaves (1979), Wade Wilson (1981–91), Jay Fiedler (1998).

12
Tom McNeil (1970), Neil Clabo (1975–77), Steve Dils (1979–83), Keith Bishop (1987*), Sean Salisbury (1990–94).

13
Mike Livingston (1980), Steve Bono (1985–86), David Bruno (1987*), Bucky Scribner (1987–89), Gino Torretta (1993).

14
George Shaw (1961), Fred Cox (1963–77), Gilbert Renfroe (1990), Brad Johnson (1992–98).

15
John McCormick (1962), Ron VanderKelen (1963–67), Gary Cuozzo (1968–71), Mike Wells (1973–74).

16
Norm Snead (1971), Rich Gannon (1987–92).

17
Charley Britt (1964), Bob Berry (1965–67, 1973–76), Bill Cappleman (1970), Mitch Berger (1996–98).

18
Mike Mercer (1961–62), Harry Newsome (1990–93), Tony Bland (1998).

19
Lance Rentzel (1965–66), Bob Lee (1968–72, 1975–78).

20
Tommy Mason (1961–66), Bobby Bryant (1967–80), Darrin Nelson (1982–89, 1991–92), Robert Smith (1993), Dewayne Washington (1994–97), Kerry Cooks (1998).

21
Chuck Lamson (1962–63), Tom Michel (1964), Jim Lindsey (1966–72), Joe Blahak (1974–75, 1977), Rufus Bess (1982–87), Terry Allen (1990–94), Charles Mincy (1995), Moe Williams (1996–98).

22
Dick Pesonen (1961), Billy Butler (1962–64), Jeff Jordan (1965–67), Paul Krause (1968–79), Jarvis Redwine (1981–83), Steve Freeman (1987), Ken Johnson (1989–90), Felix Wright (1991–92), Ivory Lee Brown (1993), David Palmer (1994–98).

23
Jamie Caleb (1961), Lee Calland (1963–65), Jeff Williams (1966), Jeff Wright (1971–77), Ted Brown (1979–86), Terry Love (1987*), Mike Mayes (1991), Barry Word (1993), Shelly Ham-

monds (1995), Tomur Barnes (1996), Steven Hall (1996), Torrian Gray (1997–98).

24
Rich Mostardi (1961), Tom Wilson (1963), Ted Dean (1964), Phil King (1965–66), Art Powell (1968), Terry Brown (1972–75), Larry Brune (1980), Bryan Howard (1982), Maurice Turner (1984–85), Wymon Henderson (1987–88), Pat Eilers (1990–91), David Wilson (1992), Jayice Pearson (1993), Robert Griffith (1994–98).

25
Dean Derby (1961–62), Terry Dillon (1963), Larry Vargo (1964–65), John Charles (1970), Jackie Wallace (1973–74), Nate Allen (1976–79), Kurt Knoff (1979–82), Marcellus Greene (1984), Daryl Smith (1989), Alonzo Hampton (1990), Vencie Glenn (1992–94), Alfred Jackson (1995–96), Tony Darden (1998).

26
Charlie Sumner (1961–62), Terry Kosens (1963), Clint Jones (1967–72), Bob Grim (1976–77), Marvin Cobb (1980), David Evans (1986–87), Audray McMillian (1989–93), Robert Smith (1994–98).

27
Bobby Reed (1962–63), Bob Grim (1967–71), Calvin Demery (1972), Autry Beamon (1975–76), John Turner (1978–83, 1985, 1987*), Mike Lush (1986), Brett Wilson (1987*), Brad Edwards (1988–89), Ken Stills (1990), Anthony Parker (1992–94), Corey Fuller (1995–98).

28
Dick Haley (1961), Tom Hall (1964–66), Earl Denny (1967–68), Ted Provost (1970), Ahmad Rashad (1976–82), Ted Rosnagle (1985, 1987*), Izel Jenkins (1993), James Stewart (1995–96), Anthony Phillips (1998).

29
Karl Kassulke (1963–72), Randy Poltl (1974), Phil Wise (1977–79), John Swain (1981–84), Jamie Fitzgerald (1987*), Darrell Fullington (1988–90), Charles Evans (1992–98).

30
Bill Brown (1962–74), Issiac Holt (1985–89), Cedric Smith (1990), Keith Henderson (1992), Bobby Phillips (1995), Antonio Banks (1997, 1998).

31

Clancy Osborne (1961–62), Darrell Lester (1964), Willie Spencer (1976), Nelson Munsey (1978), Eddie Payton (1980–82), Dan Wagoner (1984), Rick Fenney (1987–91), Eric Everett (1992), Scottie Graham (1993–96), Duane Butler (1997–98).

32

Raymond Hayes (1961), Bill McWatters (1964), Oscar Reed (1968–74), Jimmy Edwards (1979), Tony Galbreath (1981–83), Tony Truelove (1987), Steve Harris (1987*), Darryl Harris (1988), Rick Bayless (1989), Tripp Welborne (1992), Shawn Jones (1993), Amp Lee (1994–96), Robert Green (1997).

33

Mel Triplett (1961–62), Bill Barnes (1965–66), Pete Tatman (1967), Brent McClanahan (1973–80), Rick Bell (1983), Jeff Womack (1987), Jessie Clark (1989–90), Roger Craig (1992–93), Harold Morrow (1996–98).

34

Jim Young (1965–66), Al Randolph (1973), Rickey Young (1978–83), Tim Starks (1987*), Herschel Walker (1989–91), Brian Davis (1994), Ramos McDonald (1998).

35

Doug Mayberry (1961–62), Bob Ferguson (1963), Bill Harris (1969–70), Robert Miller (1975–80), Kyle Morrell (1985–86), Andre Thomas (1987*), Mike Slaton (1987*), Ronnie West (1992), Chris Johnson (1996).

36

Jim Christopherson (1962), John Kirby (1964–69), Carl Winfrey (1971), Manfred Moore (1977), Sam Harrell (1980–82, 1987*), Allen Rice (1984–90), Ron Carpenter (1993), Malik Boyd (1994).

37

Mike Fitzgerald (1966–67), Al Coleman (1967), Willie Teal (1980–86), Phil Frye (1987*), Randy Baldwin (1991), Lamar McGriggs (1993–94), Donald Frank (1995), Sean Vanhorse (1996), Leonard Wheeler (1997), Jimmy Hitchcock (1998).

38

Bob Tucker (1977–80), Fletcher Louallen (1987*), Todd Scott (1991–94), Anthony Bass (1998).

39
Hugh McElhenny (1961–62), Billy Walden (1964–67), Mark Kellar (1976–78), Carl Lee (1983–93).

40
Jack Morris (1961), Tom Franckhauser (1962–63), Preston Carpenter (1966), Charlie West (1968–73), Windlan Hall (1976–77), Doug Paschal (1980–81), Wayne Smith (1987), Anthony Prior (1996–97).

41
Gene Johnson (1961), Dave Osborn (1965–75), Neal Guggemos (1986–87), Solomon Wilcots (1991).

42
John Gilliam (1972–75), D.J. Dozier (1987–90), Harlon Barnett (1995–96), Orlando Thomas (1997–98).

43
Will Sherman (1961), Gary Hill (1965), Brady Keys (1967), Nate Wright (1971–80), Jeff Colter (1984), Jimmy Smith (1987*), Orlando Thomas (1995–96), Greg Briggs (1997, 1998).

44
Billy Gault (1961), George Rose (1964–66), Leo Hayden (1971), Chuck Foreman (1973–79), Walt Williams (1981–82), Dave Casper (1983), Keith Kidd (1984–85, 1987*), John Harris (1986–88), Michael Brim (1989–90), Leroy Hoard (1996–98).

45
Ed Sharockman (1962–72), Pete Athas (1975), Tom Hannon (1977–84), Wayne Wilson (1986), Leonard Moore (1987*).

46
Earsell Mackbee (1965–69), Alfred Anderson (1984–91), Derek Tennell (1992–93), John Gerak (1995).

47
Justin Rowland (1961), Dick James (1965), Ron Groce (1976), Tim Baylor (1979–80), Joey Browner (1983–91), Rod Smith (1996), Charles Emanuel (1997).

48
Larry Marshall (1974), Sammy Johnson (1976–78), Reggie Rutland (1987–92), Todd Harrison (1993).

49

Dale Hackbart (1966–70), Ed Marinaro (1972–75), Keith Nord (1979–85), Dave Lewis (1987*), Adam Walker (1987*), Travis Curtis (1989), Obafemi Ayanbadejo (1998).

50

Dick Grecni (1961), Jim Hargrove (1967–70), Jeff Siemon (1972–82), Dennis Fowlkes (1983–85), Ray Berry (1987–92), Randy Scott (1987*), Bobby Abrams (1993–94), Jeff Brady (1995–97).

51

Dave Tobey (1966–67), Hap Farber (1970), Godfrey Zaunbrecher (1971–73), Jim Hough (1978–86), Pete Najarian (1987*), David Howard (1988–89), Carlos Jenkins (1991–94), Broderick Thomas (1995), Ben Hanks (1996).

52

Bill Lapham (1961), Bill Swain (1964), Noel Jenke (1971), Ron Porter (1973), Bob Stein (1975), Joe Harris (1979), Dennis Johnson (1980–85), Randy Rasmussen (1987–89), Jim Dick (1987*), William Kirksey (1990), David Bavaro (1992), Richard Brown (1994–96), Kailee Wong (1998).

53

Mick Tingelhoff (1962–78), Henry Johnson (1980–82), Tim Meamber (1985), Jeff Schuh (1986), Sam Anno (1987–88); Steve Ache (1987*); David Braxton (1989–90), Richard Newbill (1990), Ivan Caesar (1991), Fred Strickland (1993), Tuineau Alipate (1995), Artie Ulmer (1997), Kivuusama Mays (1998).

54

Karl Rubke (1961), Bob Schmitz (1966), Paul Faust (1967), Fred McNeill (1974–85), Jesse Solomon (1986–89), Van Waiters (1992), Bruce Holmes (1993), David Garnett (1993–94, 1996), Greg Briggs (1997), Artie Ulmer (1997).

55

Cliff Livingston (1962), John Campbell (1963–64), Don Hansen (1966–67), Mike McGill (1968–70), Amos Martin (1972–76), Scott Studwell (1977–90), Jack Del Rio (1992–95), Darryl Talley (1996), Ron George (1997), Bobby Houston (1998).

56

Mike Reilly (1969), Wayne Meylan (1970), Carl Gersbach (1971–72), Scott Anderson (1974, 1976), David Huffman

(1979–83), Bill Dugan (1984), Chris Martin (1984), Chris Doleman (1985–93), Phil Micech (1987*), Pete Bercich (1995–98).

57
Bill Jobko (1963–65), Doug Dumler (1976–77), Paul Harris (1978), Derrel Luce (1979–80), Robin Sendlein (1981–84), Chris Martin (1987–88), Mike Merriweather (1989–92), William Sims (1994), Dwayne Rudd (1997–98).

58
Rip Hawkins (1961–65), Wally Hilgenberg (1968–79), Jim Langer (1980–81), Walker Lee Ashley (1983–88, 1990), Jimmy Williams (1990–91), Ed McDaniel (1992–98).

59
Jim Leo (1961–62), Bob Lacey (1964), Lonnie Warwick (1965–72), Matt Blair (1974–85), Fabray Collins (1987*), Pete Najarian (1987), Mark Dusbabek (1989–92), Ashley Sheppard (1993–95), Dixon Edwards (1996–98).

60
Roy Winston (1962–76), Matt Hernandez (1984), Ron Selesky (1987*), Dan McQuaid (1988), Bubba Baker (1988), Mark Rodenhauser (1989), Adam Schreiber (1990–93), Reggie McElroy (1994).

61
Larry Bowie (1962–68), Wes Hamilton (1976–85), Don Bramlett (1987*), Mike Turner (1987*), Everett Lindsay (1993–98).

62
Bob Denton (1961–64), Ed White (1969–77), Brent Boyd (1980–86), Chris Foote (1987–91), Brad White (1987*), Jeff Christy (1993–98).

63
Jim Battle (1963), Jim Vellone (1966–70), Nick Bebout (1980), Kirk Lowdermilk (1985–92), Kurt Ploeger (1987*), Frank Cornish (1994), Keith Alex (1995), Isaac Davis (1998).

64
Mike Rabold (1961–62), Milt Sunde (1964–74), Grant Feasel (1984–86), Mark Hanson (1987*), Ted Million (1987*), Randall McDaniel (1988–98).

65

Gerry Huth (1961–63), Steve Lawson (1973–75), Neil Elshire (1981), Charlie Johnson (1982–84), Gary Zimmerman (1986–92), Mike Ruether (1994).

66

Ken Peterson (1961), Ken Byers (1964–66), John Pentecost (1967), Bookie Bolin (1968–69), Frank Gallagher (1973), Andy Maurer (1974–75), Terry Tausch (1982–88), John Gerak (1993–96).

67

Grady Alderman (1961–74), Dennis Swilley (1977–83, 1985–87), Mike Teeter (1991), Rick Cunningham (1995).

68

Roy Schmidt (1970), Pete Perreault (1971), Charles Goodrum (1972–78), Mel Mitchell (1980), Curtis Rouse (1982–86), Greg Koch (1987), Kevin Webster (1987*), John Adickes (1989), Paul Blair (1990), Mike Morris (1991–98).

69

Palmer Pyle (1964), Arnold Simkus (1967), Doug Sutherland (1971–80), Ruben Vaughan (1984), Hasson Arbubakrr (1984), Wayne Jones (1987), Frank Ori (1987*), Todd Kalis (1988–93), Ariel Solomon (1996), LeShun Daniels (1997).

70

Jim Marshall (1961–79).

71

Ed Culpepper (1961), Doug Davis (1966–72), David Boone (1974), Steve Niehaus (1979), John Vella (1980), Bill Stephanos (1981–82), Mark MacDonald (1985–88), Derek Burton (1987*), Ken Clarke (1989–91), Bernard Dafney (1992), David Dixon (1994–98).

72

Frank Youso (1961–62), Archie Sutton (1965–67), John Ward (1970–75), James White (1976–83), Ron Sams (1984), David Huffman (1985–90), Scott Adams (1991–93), Jason Fisk (1995–98).

73

Bill Bishop (1961), Errol Linden (1962–65), Jerry Shay (1966–67), Ron Yary (1968–81), Neil Elshire (1982–86), Stafford

The Coaches—The Numbers

Mays (1987–88), Joe Stepanek (1987*), Craig Wolfley (1990–91), Rory Graves (1993), Todd Steussie (1995–98).

74
Dave O'Brien (1963–64), Mike Tilleman (1966), Steve Smith (1968–70), Larry Smiley (1973), Bart Buetow (1976), Frank Myers (1978–80), Robert Smith (1985), Mike Stensrud (1986), Mike McCurry (1987*), Brian Habib (1989–92), Orlando Bobo (1997–98).

75
Pat Russ (1963), Mike Bundra (1964), Howard Simpson (1964), Bob Breitenstein (1967), Bob Lurtsema (1971–76), Randy Holloway (1978–84), Keith Millard (1985–91), Bernard Dafney (1993–94), Chris Hinton (1994), James Manley (1996–97), Matt Birk (1998).

76
Paul Dickson (1961–70), Joe Jackson (1977), Bob Lingenfelter (1978), Dave Roller (1979–80), Tim Irwin (1981–93), Scott Dill (1996–97), Chris Liwienski (1998).

77
Lebron Shields (1961), Gary Larsen (1965–74), Mark Mullaney (1975–87), Bubba Baker (1988), Brad Culpepper (1992–93), Korey Stringer (1995–98).

78
Steve Riley (1974–84), Mike Hartenstine (1987), John Scardina (1987*), William Gay (1988), Barry Bennett (1988), Chris Hinton (1996), Bob Sapp (1997–98).

79
Jim Prestel (1961–65), Chuck Arrobio (1966), Jerry Patton (1971), Lyman Smith (1978), Doug Martin (1980–89), Roosevelt Nix (1994), Eric Moss (1997–98).

80
Bob Schnelker (1961), Jim Boylan (1963), John Henderson (1968–72), Sam McCullum (1974–75), Leonard Willis (1976), Harry Washington (1978), Terry LeCount (1979–84, 1987*), Larry Brown (1987*), Jim Gustafson (1985–90), Cris Carter (1990–98).

81
Leon Clarke (1963), Carl Eller (1964–78), Joe Senser (1979–84), Anthony Carter (1985–93), Rickey Parks (1987*), Chris Walsh (1994–98).

82

A.D. Williams (1961), Steve Stonebreaker (1962–63), Jim Phillips (1965–67), Bob Goodridge (1968), Jim Lash (1973–76), Robert Steele (1979), Bob Bruer (1980–84), Carl Hilton (1986–89), Ron Daugherty (1987*), Dante Whitaker (1992), Qadry Ismail (1993–96), Andrew Glover (1997–98).

83

Don Joyce (1961), Don Hultz (1963), John Powers (1966), Stu Voigt (1970–80), Steve Jordan (1982–94), Andrew Jordan (1994), Mike Tice (1995), David Frisch (1996), Robert Tate (1997–98).

84

Dave Middleton (1961), Oscar Donahue (1962), Gene Washington (1967–72), Carroll Dale (1973), Steve Craig (1974–78), Sam McCullum (1982–83), Dwight Collins (1984), Jay Carroll (1985), Hassan Jones (1986–92), James Brim (1987*), Eric Guliford (1993–94), Tony Bland (1996–97), Randy Moss (1998).

85

Tom Adams (1962), Paul Flatley (1963–67), John Hilton (1970), Gary Ballman (1973), John Holland (1974), Sammy White (1976–86), Steve Finch (1987*), Ryan Bethea (1988), Brent Novoselsky (1989–94), Greg DeLong (1995–98).

86

Ray Poage (1963), Hal Bedsole (1964–66), Marlin McKeever (1967), Tom Hall (1968–69), Al Denson (1971), Rhett Dawson (1973), Mike Mularkey (1983–88), Willie Gillespie (1987*), Darryl Ingram (1989), Pat Newman (1990), Jake Reed (1991–98).

87

Gordon Smith (1961–65), John Beasley (1967–73), Clint Haslerig (1975), Kevin Miller (1978–80), Leo Lewis (1981–91), Clifton Eley (1987*), Mike Tice (1992–93), Adrian Cooper (1994–95), Hunter Goodwin (1996–98).

88

Fred Murphy (1961), Charley Ferguson (1962), Alan Page (1967–78), Mardye McDole (1981–83), Bill Waddy (1984), Don Hasselbeck (1984), Buster Rhymes (1985–87), Marc May (1987*).

89

Jerry Reichow (1961–64), Billy Martin (1968), Kent Kramer (1969–70), Robert Brown (1971), Doug Kingsriter (1973–75), Doug Cunningham (1979), Ken Sanders (1980–81), Harold Jackson (1982), Mike Anthony Jones (1983–85), Greg Richardson

(1987–88), Ed Schenk (1987*), Paul Coffman (1988), Jarrod Delaney (1989), Mike Alonzo Jones (1990–91), Joe Johnson (1992), Olando Truitt (1993), Ray Rowe (1994), Andrew Jordan (1994–97), Matthew Hatchette (1997–98).

90
Ray Yakavonis (1980–83), John Haines (1984), Fred Molden (1987*), John Galvin (1989), Ira Hillary (1990), Robert Harris (1992–94), Derrick Alexander (1995–98).

91
Greg Smith (1984), Joe Phillips (1986), Dan Coleman (1987*), Brian Habib (1988), Willie Fears (1990), Greg Manusky (1991–93), Martin Harrison (1994–96).

92
Kelly Quinn (1987*), David Westbrooks (1990), Roy Barker (1992–95), Duane Clemons (1996–98).

93
Jimmy Walker (1987*), John Randle (1990–98).

94
Paul Sverchek (1984), Chris Martin (1984), Tim Bryant (1987*), Thomas Strauthers (1989–91), John Thornton (1993), Robert Goff (1996), Tony Williams (1997–98).

95
Mark Stewart (1983–84), Gerald Robinson (1986–87), Mac Stephens (1991), Esera Tuaolo (1992), Fernando Smith (1994–97).

96
Tim Newton (1985–89), Skip McClendon (1992), Keith Washington (1995), Jerry Ball (1997–98).

97
Tony Norman (1979, 1987*), Henry Thomas (1987–94), Jose White (1995).

98
Chris Martin (1985–86), George Hinkle (1992), Esera Tuaolo (1993–96), Ben Williams (1998).

99
David Howard (1985–87), Al Noga (1988–92), James Harris (1993–95), Stalin Colinet (1997–98).

* indicates replacement player in 1987.

PASSING STATISTICS

Pass Completions–Career
1. Fran Tarkenton (1961–66, 1972–78)   2,635
2. Tommy Kramer (1977–89)   2,011
3. Wade Wilson (1981–91)   929
4. Warren Moon (1994–96)   882
5. Brad Johnson (1992–98)   618
6. Rich Gannon (1987–92)   561
7. Joe Kapp (1967–69)   351
8. Steve Dils (1979–84)   336
9. Randall Cunningham (1997–98)   303
10. Gary Cuozzo (1968–71)   276

Passing Yards–Career
1. Fran Tarkenton (1961–66, 1972–78)   33,098
2. Tommy Kramer (1977–89)   24,775
3. Wade Wilson (1981–91)   12,135
4. Warren Moon (1994–96)   10,102
5. Brad Johnson (1992–98)   6,463
6. Rich Gannon (1987–92)   6,457
7. Joe Kapp (1967–69)   4,807
8. Randall Cunningham (1997–98)   4,205
9. Steve Dils (1979–84)   3,867
10. Gary Cuozzo (1968–71)   3,552

Touchdown Passes–Career
1. Fran Tarkenton (1961–66, 1972–78)   239
2. Tommy Kramer (1977–89)   159
3. Wade Wilson (1981–91)   66
4. Warren Moon (1994–96)   58
5. Brad Johnson (1992–98)   44
6t. Rich Gannon (1987–92)   40
6t. Randall Cunningham (1997–98)   40
8. Joe Kapp (1967–69)   37
9. Gary Cuozzo (1968–71)   18
10t. Steve Dils (1979–84)   15
10t. Bob Lee (1969–72, '75–78)   15

Pass Completions–Season
1. Warren Moon, 1995   377
2. Warren Moon, 1994   371
3. Fran Tarkenton, 1978   345

4.	Tommy Kramer, 1981	322
5.	Tommy Kramer, 1979	315
6.	Tommy Kramer, 1980	299
7.	Tommy Kramer, 1985	277
8.	Brad Johnson, 1997	275
9.	Fran Tarkenton, 1975	273
10.	Randall Cunningham, 1998	259

Passing Yards–Season

1.	Warren Moon, 1994	4,264
2.	Warren Moon, 1995	4,228
3.	Tommy Kramer, 1981	3,912
4.	Randall Cunningham, 1998	3,704
5.	Tommy Kramer, 1980	3,582
6.	Tommy Kramer, 1985	3,522
7.	Fran Tarkenton, 1978	3,468
8.	Tommy Kramer, 1979	3,397
9.	Brad Johnson, 1997	3,036
10.	Tommy Kramer, 1986	3,000

Touchdown Passes–Season

1.	Randall Cunningham, 1998	34
2.	Warren Moon, 1995	33
3.	Tommy Kramer, 1981	26
4t.	Fran Tarkenton, 1975	25
4t.	Fran Tarkenton, 1978	25
6.	Tommy Kramer, 1986	24
7.	Tommy Kramer, 1979	23
8t.	Fran Tarkenton, 1964	22
8t.	Fran Tarkenton, 1962	22
10.	Brad Johnson, 1997	20

Passing Yards–Game

1.	490	Tommy Kramer @ Washington, Nov. 2, 1986
2.	456	Tommy Kramer vs. Cleveland, Dec. 14, 1980
3.	449	Joe Kapp vs. Baltimore, Sept. 28, 1969
4.	444	Tommy Kramer @ San Diego, Oct. 11, 1981
5.	442	Randall Cunningham @ Green Bay, Oct. 5, 1998
6.	420	Warren Moon vs. New Orleans, Nov. 6, 1994
7.	411	Tommy Kramer vs. Chicago, Sept. 19, 1985
8.	407	Fran Tarkenton @ San Francisco, Oct. 24, 1965
9.	400	Warren Moon vs. New York Jets, Nov. 20, 1994
10.	395	Tommy Kramer vs. Atlanta, Sept. 7, 1980

RUSHING STATISTICS

Rushing Yards–Career
1. Chuck Foreman (1973–79) — 5,879
2. Bill Brown (1962–74) — 5,757
3. Ted Brown (1979–86) — 4,546
4. Dave Osborn (1965–75) — 4,320
5. Robert Smith (1993–98) — 4,282
6. Darrin Nelson (1982–89, 1991–92) — 4,231
7. Tommy Mason (1961–66) — 3,252
8. Terry Allen (1991–94) — 2,795
9. Fran Tarkenton (1961–66, 1972–78) — 2,543
10. Alfred Anderson (1984–91) — 2,374

Rushing Yards–Season
1. Robert Smith, 1997 — 1,266
2. Terry Allen, 1992 — 1,201
3. Robert Smith, 1998 — 1,187
4. Chuck Foreman, 1976 — 1,155
5. Chuck Foreman, 1977 — 1,112
6. Chuck Foreman, 1975 — 1,070
7. Ted Brown, 1981 — 1,063
8. Terry Allen, 1994 — 1,031
9. Dave Osborn, 1967 — 972
10. Ted Brown, 1980 — 912

Rushing Yards–Game
1. 200 — Chuck Foreman @ Philadelphia, Oct. 24, 1976
2. 179 — Robert Smith @ St. Louis, Sept. 13, 1998
3. 179 — Ted Brown @ Green Bay, Oct. 23, 1983
4. 172 — Terry Allen @ Pittsburgh, Dec. 20, 1992
5. 169 — Robert Smith @ Buffalo, Aug. 31, 1997
6. 166 — Scottie Graham vs. Kansas City, Dec. 26, 1993
7. 160 — Robert Smith vs. Indianapolis, Dec. 21, 1997
8. 159 — Terry Allen @ Chicago, Sept. 18, 1994
9. 156 — Chuck Foreman @ Detroit, Dec. 17, 1977
10t. 155 — Clinton Jones vs. Atlanta, Nov. 28, 1971
10t. 155 — Dave Osborn vs. Green Bay, Dec. 3, 1967

Longest Runs
80 yards — Clinton Jones vs. Chicago, Nov. 2, 1969 (touchdown)
78 yards — Robert Smith at Buffalo, Aug. 31, 1997 (touchdown)
76 yards — Robert Smith vs. Indianapolis, Dec. 21, 1997

74 yards Robert Smith vs. St. Louis, Sept. 13, 1998 (touchdown)
73 yards Dave Osborn vs. San Francisco, Sept. 17, 1967
73 yards Clinton Jones vs. Atlanta, Nov. 28, 1971 (touchdown)
72 yards Darrin Nelson vs. Denver, Oct. 26, 1987
71 yards Tommy Mason at Detroit, Dec. 9, 1962
71 yards Herschel Walker at Tampa Bay, Dec. 8, 1989 (touchdown)
70 yards Tommy Mason vs. Baltimore, Nov. 17, 1963 (touchdown)

Receiving Statistics

Receptions–Career
1. Cris Carter (1990–98)   745
2. Steve Jordan (1982–94)   498
3. Anthony Carter (1985–93)   478
4. Ahmad Rashad (1976–82)   400
5. Sammy White (1976–86)   393
6. Jake Reed (1991–98)   342
7. Ted Brown (1979–86)   339
8. Chuck Foreman (1973–79)   336
9. Rickey Young (1978–83)   292
10. Bill Brown (1962–74)   284

Receiving Yards–Career
1. Cris Carter (1990–98)   8,997
2. Anthony Carter (1985–93)   7,636
3. Sammy White (1976–86)   6,400
4. Steve Jordan (1982–94)   6,307
5. Ahmad Rashad (1976–82)   5,489
6. Jake Reed (1991–98)   5,481
7. John Gilliam (1972–75)   3,297
8. Bill Brown (1962–74)   3,177
9. Gene Washington (1967–72)   3,087
10. Chuck Foreman (1973–79)   3,057

Receptions–Season
1t. Cris Carter, 1995   122
1t. Cris Carter, 1994   122
3. Cris Carter, 1996   96
4. Cris Carter, 1997   89
5. Rickey Young, 1978   88

6.	Cris Carter, 1993	86
7.	Jake Reed, 1994	85
8.	Ted Brown, 1981	83
9.	Ahmad Rashad, 1979	80
10.	Cris Carter, 1998	78

Receiving Yards–Season
1.	Cris Carter, 1995	1,371
2.	Jake Reed, 1996	1,320
3.	Randy Moss, 1998	1,313
4.	Cris Carter, 1994	1,256
5.	Anthony Carter, 1988	1,225
6.	Jake Reed, 1994	1,175
7.	Jake Reed, 1995	1,167
8.	Cris Carter, 1996	1,163
9.	Ahmad Rashad, 1979	1,156
10.	Jake Reed, 1997	1,138

Receptions–Game
1.	15	Rickey Young @ New England, Dec. 16, 1979
2.	14	Cris Carter @ Arizona, Oct. 2, 1994
3t.	12	Jake Reed @ Chicago, Sept. 7, 1997
3t.	12	Cris Carter @ San Francisco, Dec. 18, 1995
3t.	12	Cris Carter vs. New Orleans, Nov. 19, 1995
3t.	12	Cris Carter @ Arizona, Nov. 12, 1995
3t.	12	Cris Carter vs. Houston, Oct. 8, 1995
3t.	12	Cris Carter vs. New Orleans, Nov. 6, 1994
3t.	12	Darrin Nelson vs. San Diego, Oct. 20, 1985
3t.	12	Ted Brown @ Tampa Bay, Sept. 5, 1981
3t.	12	Rickey Young @ New Orleans, Sept. 3, 1978
3t.	12	Bob Grim @ New York Giants, Oct. 31, 1971

Receiving Yards–Game
1.	210	Sammy White vs. Detroit, Nov. 17, 1976
2.	202	Paul Flatley @ San Francisco, Oct. 24, 1965
3.	190	Randy Moss @ Green Bay, Oct. 5, 1998
4.	188	Anthony Carter vs. Detroit, Nov. 6, 1988
5.	184	Anthony Carter @ Dallas, Nov. 26, 1987
6.	179	Steve Jordan @ Washington, Nov. 2, 1986
7.	177	Sammy White vs. Chicago, Nov. 28, 1982
8.	174	Paul Flatley vs. Detroit, Nov. 24, 1963
9.	172	Gene Washington vs. Baltimore, Sept. 28, 1969
10.	167	Cris Carter @ Arizona, Oct. 2, 1994

Longest Receptions
1.   89   Charley Ferguson at Chicago, Nov. 11, 1962
2.   85   Qadry Ismail vs. Detroit, Sept. 10, 1995
3.   85   Gene Washington vs. St. Louis, Oct. 8, 1967
4.   83   Gene Washington vs. Baltimore, Sept. 28, 1969
5.   82   Jake Reed at Oakland, Nov. 17, 1996
6.   78   Cris Carter at Philadelphia, Oct. 15, 1990
7.   77   Qadry Ismail vs. New Orleans, Nov. 19, 1995
8.   76   Bill Brown at Los Angeles Rams, Nov. 19, 1972
9.   76   Ahmad Rashad at Chicago, Sept. 21, 1980
10. 76   Leo Lewis at Washington, Nov. 2, 1986

Scoring Statistics

Career Scoring
1.   Fred Cox (1963–77)   1,365
2.   Fuad Reveiz (1990–95)   598
3.   Cris Carter (1990–98)   466
4.   Bill Brown (1962–74)   456
5.   Chuck Foreman (1973–79)   450
6.   Rick Danmeier (1977–83)   364
7.   Anthony Carter (1985–93)   324
8.   Ted Brown (1979–86)   318
9.   Sammy White (1976–86)   300
10. Chuck Nelson (1986–88)   293

Career Touchdowns
1.   Cris Carter (1990–98)   82
2.   Bill Brown (1962–74)   76
3.   Chuck Foreman (1973–79)   75
4.   Anthony Carter (1985–93)   54
5.   Ted Brown (1979–86)   53
6.   Sammy White (1976–86)   50
7.   Tommy Mason (1961–66)   39
8.   Dave Osborn (1965–75)   36
9.   Ahmad Rashad (1976–82)   34
10. Jake Reed (1991–98)   30

KICKING STATISTICS

Field Goals–Career
1. Fred Cox (1963–77) — 282
2. Fuad Reveiz (1990–95) — 133
3. Rick Danmeier (1978–83) — 70
4. Chuck Nelson (1986–88) — 55
5t. Jan Stenerud (1984–85) — 35
5t. Gary Anderson (1998) — 35
7. Rich Karlis (1989) — 31
8. Benny Ricardo (1983) — 25
9. Scott Sisson (1996) — 22
10. Donald Igwebuike (1990) — 14

Field Goals–Season
1. Gary Anderson, 1998 — 35
2. Fuad Reveiz, 1994 — 34
3. Rich Karlis, 1989 — 31
4. Fred Cox, 1970 — 30
5t. Fuad Reveiz, 1995 — 26
5t. Fuad Reveiz, 1993 — 26
5t. Fred Cox, 1969 — 26
8. Benny Ricardo, 1983 — 25
9. Fred Cox, 1965 — 23
10t. Scott Sisson, 1996 — 22
10t. Chuck Nelson, 1986 — 22
10t. Fred Cox, 1971 — 22

DEFENSIVE STATISTICS

Sacks–Career
1. Carl Eller (1964–78) — 130
2. Jim Marshall (1961–79) — 127
3. Alan Page (1967–78) — 108
4. John Randle (1990–98) — 96
5. Chris Doleman (1985–93) — 84.5
6. Doug Martin (1980–89) — 60.5
7. Henry Thomas (1987–94) — 56
8. Keith Millard (1985–91) — 53
9. Mark Mullaney (1975–87) — 41.5
10. Gary Larsen (1965–74) — 37

Sacks–Season
1.	Chris Doleman, 1989	21
2t.	Keith Millard, 1989	18
2t.	Alan Page, 1976	18
4.	John Randle, 1997	15.5
5t.	Carl Eller, 1977	15
5t.	Carl Eller, 1969	15
7.	Chris Doleman, 1992	14.5
8.	John Randle, 1994	13.5
9t.	Alan Page, 1975	13
9t.	Carl Eller, 1970	13
9t.	Jim Marshall, 1969	13

Interceptions–Career
1.	Paul Krause (1968–79)	53
2.	Bobby Bryant (1967–80)	51
3.	Ed Sharockman (1962–72)	40
4.	Joey Browner (1983–91)	37
5.	Nate Wright (1971–80)	31
6.	Carl Lee (1983–93)	29
7.	John Turner (1978–83, 1985, 1987)	22
8t.	Audray McMillian (1989–93)	19
8t.	Karl Kassaulke (1963–72)	19
10.	Orlando Thomas (1994–98)	18

Interceptions–Season
1.	Paul Krause, 1975	10
2.	Orlando Thomas, 1995	9
3t.	Audray McMillian, 1992	8
3t.	Carl Lee, 1988	8
3t.	Issiac Holt, 1986	8
3t.	Bobby Bryant, 1969	8
7t.	Jimmy Hitchcock, 1998	7
7t.	Joey Browner, 1990	7
7t.	Bobby Bryant, 1978	7
7t.	Nate Wright, 1976	7
7t.	Bobby Bryant, 1973	7
7t.	Charlie West, 1971	7
7t.	Ed Sharockman, 1970	7
7t.	Paul Krause, 1968	7

SOURCES

Bud: The Other Side of the Glacier by Bill McGrane
The Football Encyclopedia by David Neft and Richard Cohen
Kassulke by Karl Kassulke and Ron Pitkin
Minneapolis Star-Tribune
Pro Football Weekly
The Sporting News
Sports Illustrated
St. Paul Pioneer-Press
Tarkenton by Jim Klobuchar and Fran Tarkenton
Total Football edited by Bob Carroll, Michael Gershman, David Neft and John Thorn
True Hearts and Purple Heads by Jim Klobuchar
Viking Update
Vikings media guides
Vikings prospectus
Vikings yearbooks